MICHELIN

TOURIST *and* MOTORING ATLAS
ATLAS ROUTIER *et* TOURISTIQUE
STRASSEN- *und* REISEATLAS
TOERISTISCHE WEGENATLAS
ATLANTE STRADALE *e* TURISTICO
ATLAS DE CARRETERAS *y* TURÍSTICO

Great Britain & Ireland

Contents

Inside front cover
Key to map pages

IV **Route planning** - 1/1 000 000
XX **Unitary Authorities**
XXI **Shipping Services**
XXII **Distances**

1 **Key to maps**
2 **Great Britain**- 1/300 000
76 **Ireland** - 1/300 000
104 **Greater London** -1/200 000

106 **Key: Welsh and Irish**
107 **Key to town plan symbols**
108 **Index Great Britain**
Index Ireland

Inside back cover
Key

Sommaire

Intérieur de couverture
Tableau d'assemblage

IV **Grands itinéraires** - 1/1 000 000
XX **Unitary Authorities**
XXI **Liaisons maritimes**
XXII **Tableau de distances**

1 **Légende**
2 **Grande-Bretagne** - 1/300 000
76 **Irlande** - 1/300 000
104 **Greater London** - 1/200 000

106 **Légende : Gallois et gaélique**
107 **Légende des plans de ville**
108 **Index Grande-Bretagne**
Index Irlande

Intérieur de couverture
Légende complète

Inhaltsübersicht

Umschlaginnenseite
Übersicht

IV **Reiseplanung** - 1/1 000 000
XX **Unitary Authorities**
XXI **Schiffsverbindungen**
XXII **Entfernungstabelle**

1 **Zeichenerklärung**
2 **Großbritannien** - 1/300 000
76 **Irland** - 1/300 000
104 **Greater London** - 1/200 000

106 **Zeichenerklärung: walisisch und irisch**
107 **Zeichenerklärung für Stadtpläne**
108 **Register Großbritannien**
Register Irland

Umschlaginnenseite
Zeichenerklärung

Inhoud

Binnenzijde van het omslag
Overzichtskaart

IV **Grote verbindingswegen** - 1/1 000 000
XX **Unitary Authorities**
XXI **Scheepvaartverbindingen**
XXII **Afstandstabel**

1 **Verklaring van tekens**
2 **Groot-Brittannië** - 1/300 000
76 **Ierland** - 1/300 000
104 **Greater London** - 1/200 000

106 **Verklaring van de tekens: Welsh en Iers**
107 **Verklaring van de tekens: stadsplattegronden**
108 **Register Groot-Brittannië**
Register Ierland

Binnenzijde van het omslag
Verklaring van alle tekens

Sommario

Copertina interna
Quadro d'insieme

IV **Grandi itinerari** - 1/1 000 000
XX **Unitary Authorities**
XXI **Collegamenti marittimi**
XXII **Tabella distanze**

1 **Legenda**
2 **Gran Bretagna** - 1/300 000
76 **Irlanda** - 1/300 000
104 **Greater London** - 1/200 000

106 **Legenda: Gallese e Gaelica**
107 **Legenda piante di città**
108 **Indice Gran Bretagna**
Indice Irlanda

Copertina interna
Legenda completa

Sumario

Portada interior
Mapa índice

IV **Información general** - 1/1 000 000
XX **Unitary Authorities**
XXI **Enlaces marítimos**
XXII **Cuadro de distancias**

1 **Signos convencionales**
2 **Gran Bretaña** - 1/300 000
76 **Irlanda** - 1/300 000
104 **Greater London** - 1/200 000

106 **Signos convencionales: Galés y Gaélico**
107 **Signos convencionales de los planos de ciudades**
108 **Índice Gran Bretaña**
Índice Irlanda

Contraportada interior
Signos convencionales

Town plans / Plans de villes / Stadtpläne / Stadsplattegronden / Piante di Città / Planos de ciudades

Great Britain

108 Aberdeen
109 Bath
109 Birmingham
110 Birmingham area
111 Blackpool
111 Bournemouth
111 Bradford
112 Brighton
112 Bristol
113 Cambridge
113 Canterbury
113 Cardiff/Caerdydd
113 Carlisle
114 Chester
114 Coventry
115 Derby
115 Dover
116 Dundee
116 Durham
116 Edinburgh area
117 Edinburgh
117 Exeter
120 Glasgow area
121 Glasgow
121 Gloucester
122 Ipswich
122 Kingston upon Hull
122 Leeds
123 Leeds area
124 London
126 Leicester
126 Lincoln
126 Liverpool area
127 Liverpool
128 Manchester area
129 Manchester
130 Newcastle upon Tyne
130 Newport
130 Norwich
131 Nottingham
131 Oxford
132 Perth
133 Plymouth
133 Portsmouth
134 Reading
134 Sheffield
135 Southampton
136 Stirling
136 Stoke on Trent area
136 Stoke on Trent
137 Stratford upon Avon
137 Sunderland
137 Swansea/Abertawe
138 Swindon
138 Warwick
138 Winchester
139 Windsor
139 Wolverhampton
139 York

Channel Tunnel / Tunnel sous la Manche

118 Folkestone Terminal
119 Terminal de Calais (F)

Ireland

141 Belfast area
142 Belfast
143 Cork/Corcaigh
144 Dublin area
145 Dublin/Baile Átha Cliath
146 Galway/Gaillimh
146 Killarney/Cill Airne
147 Limerick/Luimneach
147 Londonderry

Route planning

Grands itinéraires

Reiseplanung

Afstanstabel

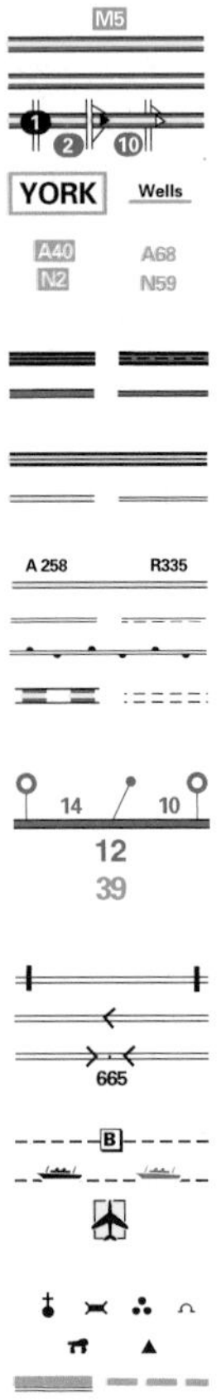

Road classification

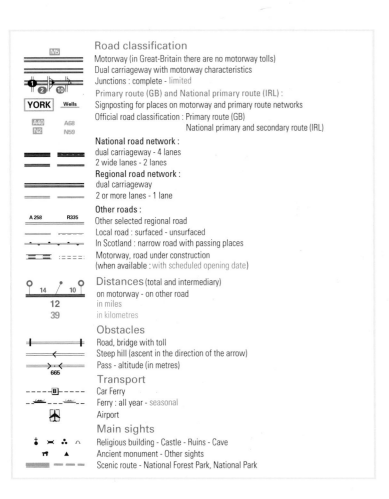

Motorway (in Great-Britain there are no motorway tolls)
Dual carriageway with motorway characteristics
Junctions : complete - limited
Primary route (GB) and National primary route (IRL) :
Signposting for places on motorway and primary route networks
Official road classification : Primary route (GB)
National primary and secondary route (IRL)

National road network :
dual carriageway - 4 lanes
2 wide lanes - 2 lanes

Regional road network :
dual carriageway
2 or more lanes - 1 lane

Other roads :
Other selected regional road
Local road : surfaced - unsurfaced
In Scotland : narrow road with passing places
Motorway, road under construction
(when available : with scheduled opening date)

Distances (total and intermediary)

on motorway - on other road
in miles
in kilometres

Obstacles

Road, bridge with toll
Steep hill (ascent in the direction of the arrow)
Pass - altitude (in metres)

Transport

Car Ferry
Ferry : all year - seasonal
Airport

Main sights

Religious building - Castle - Ruins - Cave
Ancient monument - Other sights
Scenic route - National Forest Park, National Park

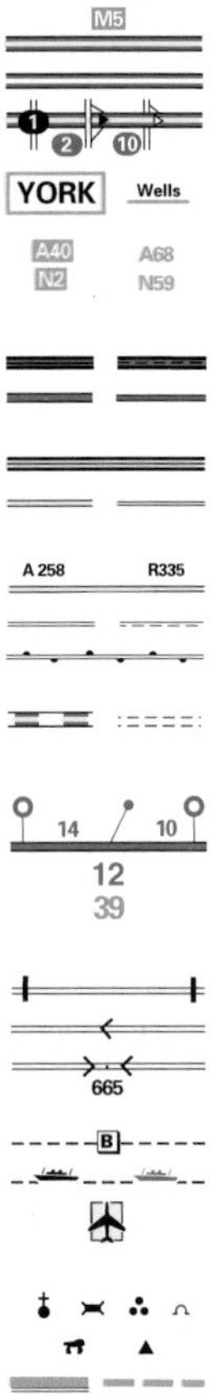

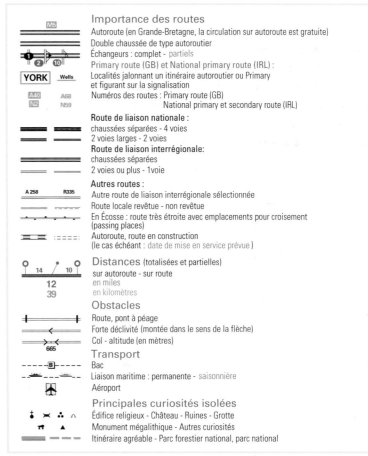

Importance des routes

Autoroute (en Grande-Bretagne, la circulation sur autoroute est gratuite)
Double chaussée de type autoroutier
Échangeurs : complet - partiels
Primary route (GB) et National primary route (IRL) :
Localités jalonnant un itinéraire autoroutier ou Primary et figurant sur la signalisation
Numéros des routes : Primary route (GB)
National primary et secondary route (IRL)

Route de liaison nationale :
chaussées séparées - 4 voies
2 voies larges - 2 voies

Route de liaison interrégionale:
chaussées séparées
2 voies ou plus - 1voie

Autres routes :
Autre route de liaison interrégionale sélectionnée
Route locale revêtue - non revêtue
En Écosse : route très étroite avec emplacements pour croisement (passing places)
Autoroute, route en construction
(le cas échéant : date de mise en service prévue)

Distances (totalisées et partielles)

sur autoroute - sur route
en miles
en kilomètres

Obstacles

Route, pont à péage
Forte déclivité (montée dans le sens de la flèche)
Col - altitude (en mètres)

Transport

Bac
Liaison maritime : permanente - saisonnière
Aéroport

Principales curiosités isolées

Édifice religieux - Château - Ruines - Grotte
Monument mégalithique - Autres curiosités
Itinéraire agréable - Parc forestier national, parc national

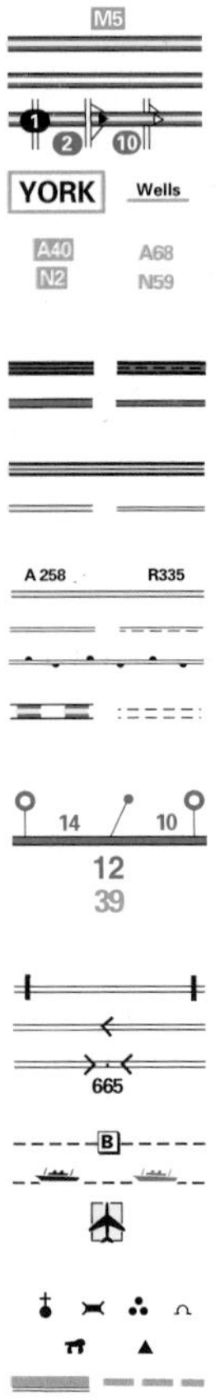

Verkehrsbedeutung der Straßen

Autobahn (Benutzung in Großbritannien kostenlos)
Schnellstraße mit getrennten Fahrbahnen
Anschlußstellen : Autobahnein- und/oder -ausfahrt
Primary route (GB) und National primary route (IRL) :
Orte, die sich an einer Autobahnstrecke oder Primary route befinden und als Richtungshinweise angegeben sind
Straßennummern : Primary route (GB)
National primary und secondary route (IRL)

Nationale Hauptverbindungsstraße :
getrennte Fahrbahnen - 4 Fahrspuren
2 breite Fahrspuren - 2 Fahrspuren

Überregionale Verbindungsstraße :
getrennte Fahrbahnen
2 oder mehr Fahrspuren - 1 Fahrspur

Andere Straßen :
Andere überregionale Verbindungsstraße
Regionale Straße mit Belag - ohne Belag
In Schottland : sehr schmale Straße mit Ausweichstellen (passing places)
Autobahn, Straße im Bau
(ggf. voraussichttliches Datum der Verkehrsfreigabe)

Entfernungen (Gesamt- und Teilentfernung)

auf der Autobahn - auf anderen Straßen
in Meilen
in Kilometern

Verkehrsbehinderungen

Gebührenpflichtige Straße oder Brücke
Starkes Gefälle (Steigung in Pfeilrichtung)
Paß und Höhenangabe (in Metern)

Transport

Fähre
Schiffsverbindung : ganzjährig - während der Saison
Flughafen

Abgelegene, wichtige Sehenswürdigkeiten

Kirchliches Gebäude - Schloß, Burg - Ruine - Höhle
Steidenkmal - Sonstige Sehenswürdigkeiten
Reizvolle Strecke - Waldschutzgebiet, Nationalpark

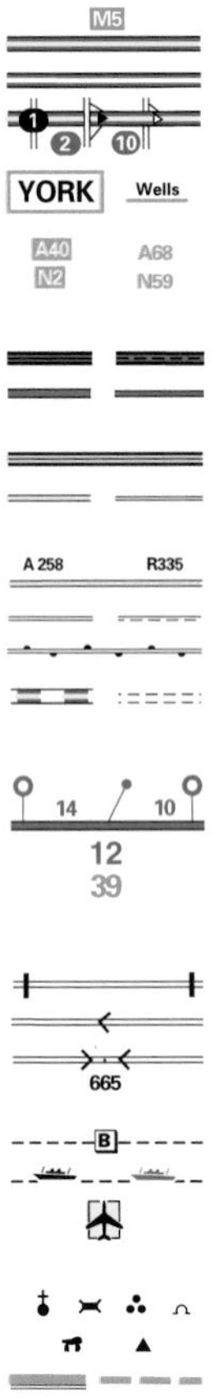

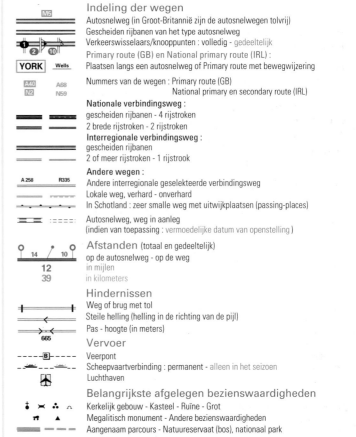

Indeling der wegen

Autosnelweg (in Groot-Britannië zijn de autosnelwegen tolvrij)
Gescheiden rijbanen van het type autosnelweg
Verkeerswisselaars/knooppunten : volledig - gedeeltelijk
Primary route (GB) en National primary route (IRL) :
Plaatsen langs een autosnelweg of Primary route met bewegwijzering
Nummers van de wegen : Primary route (GB)
National primary en secondary route (IRL)

Nationale verbindingsweg :
gescheiden rijbanen - 4 rijstroken
2 brede rijstroken - 2 rijstroken

Interregionale verbindingsweg :
gescheiden rijbanen
2 of meer rijstroken - 1 rijstrook

Andere wegen :
Andere interregionale geselekteerde verbindingsweg
Lokale weg, verhard - onverhard
In Schotland : zeer smalle weg met uitwijkplaatsen (passing-places)
Autosnelweg, weg in aanleg
(indien van toepassing : vermoedelijke datum van openstelling)

Afstanden (totaal en gedeeltelijk)

op de autosnelweg - op de weg
in mijlen
in kilometers

Hindernissen

Weg of brug met tol
Steile helling (helling in de richting van de pijl)
Pas - hoogte (in meters)

Vervoer

Veerpont
Scheepvaartverbinding : permanent - alleen in het seizoen
Luchthaven

Belangrijkste afgelegen bezienswaardigheden

Kerkelijk gebouw - Kasteel - Ruïne - Grot
Megalitisch monument - Andere bezienswaardigheden
Aangenaam parcours - Natuureservaat (bos), nationaal park

Grandi itineri

Información general

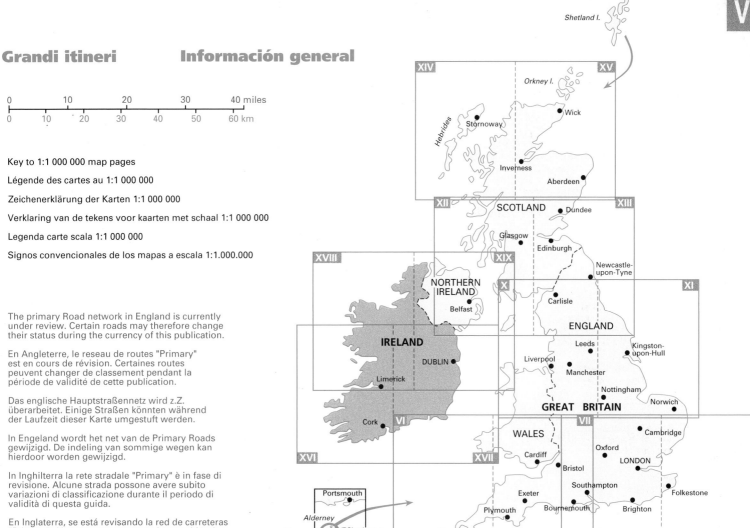

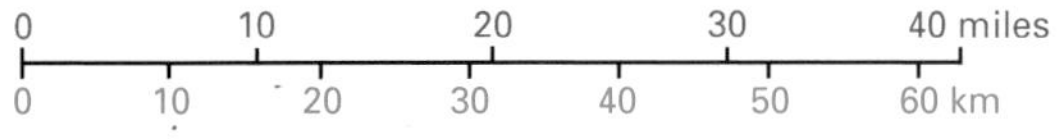

Key to 1:1 000 000 map pages

Légende des cartes au 1:1 000 000

Zeichenerklärung der Karten 1:1 000 000

Verklaring van de tekens voor kaarten met schaal 1:1 000 000

Legenda carte scala 1:1 000 000

Signos convencionales de los mapas a escala 1:1.000.000

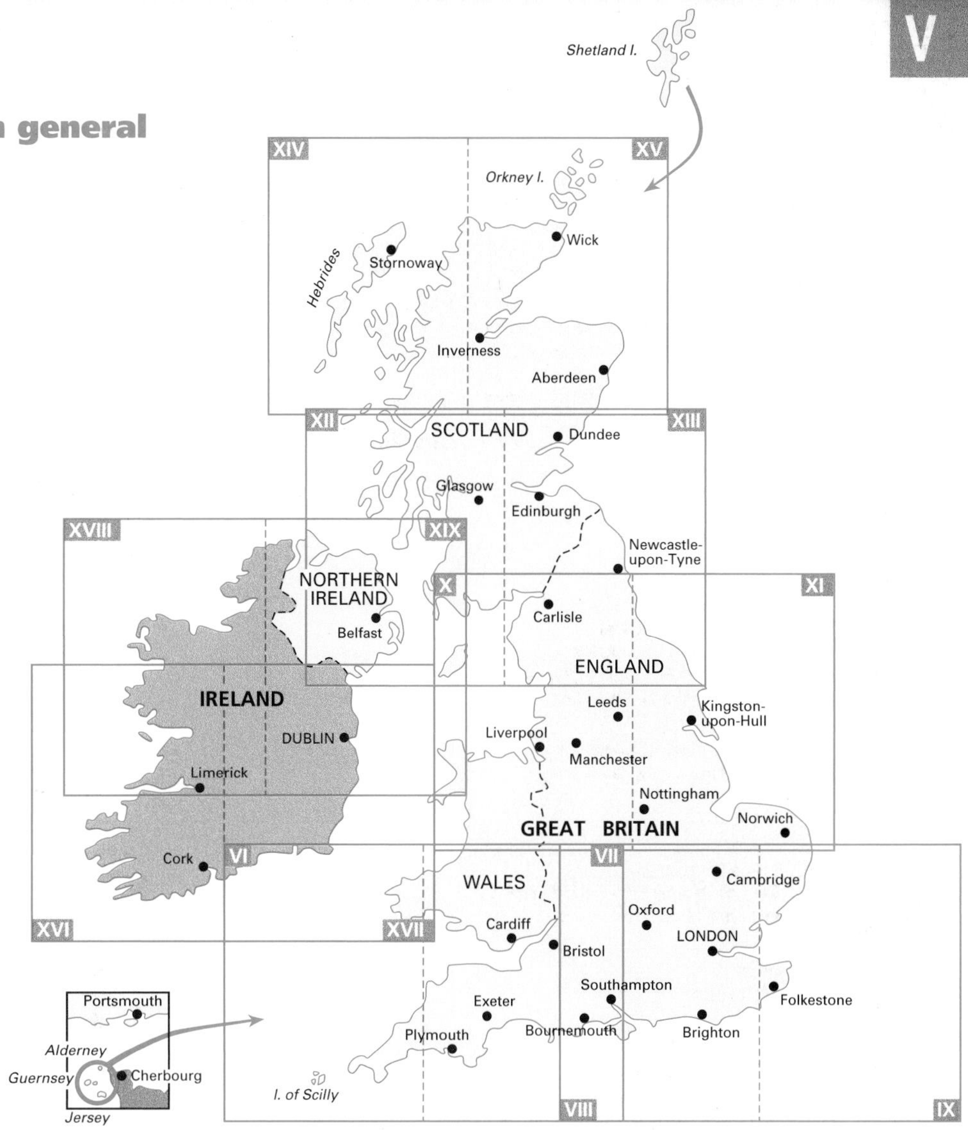

The primary Road network in England is currently under review. Certain roads may therefore change their status during the currency of this publication.

En Angleterre, le reseau de routes "Primary" est en cours de révision. Certaines routes peuvent changer de classement pendant la période de validité de cette publication.

Das englische Hauptstraßennetz wird z.Z. überarbeitet. Einige Straßen könnten während der Laufzeit dieser Karte umgestuft werden.

In Engeland wordt het net van de Primary Roads gewijzigd. De indeling van sommige wegen kan hierdoor worden gewijzigd.

In Inghilterra la rete stradale "Primary" è in fase di revisione. Alcune strada possone avere subito variazioni di classificazione durante il periodo di validità di questa guida.

En Inglaterra, se está revisando la red de carreteras "Primary". Algunas carreteras pueden cambiar de clasificación durante el periodo de validez de esta publicación.

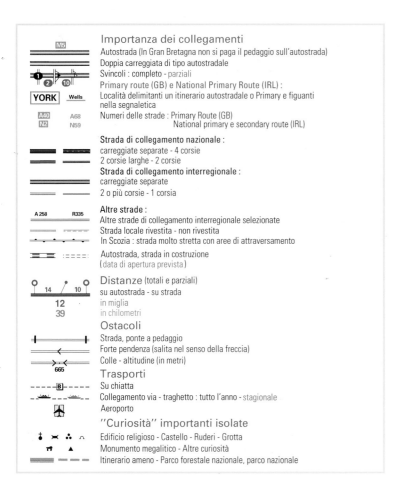

Importanza dei collegamenti

M5
Autostrada (In Gran Bretagna non si paga il pedaggio sull'autostrada)
Doppia carreggiata di tipo autostradale
1 2 10 Svincoli : completo - parziali
Primary route (GB) e National Primary Route (IRL) :
YORK Wells Località delimitanti un itinerario autostradale o Primary e figuanti nella segnaletica
A40 A68 N2 N59 Numeri delle strade : Primary Route (GB)
National primary e secondary route (IRL)

Strada di collegamento nazionale :
carreggiate separate - 4 corsie
2 corsie larghe - 2 corsie
Strada di collegamento interregionale :
carreggiate separate
2 o più corsie - 1 corsia

Altre strade :
A 258 R335 Altre strade di collegamento interregionale selezionate
Strada locale rivestita - non rivestita
In Scozia : strada molto stretta con aree di attraversamento
Autostrada, strada in costruzione
(data di apertura prevista)

Distanze (totali e parziali)

14 10 su autostrada - su strada
12 in miglia
39 in chilometri

Ostacoli

Strada, ponte a pedaggio
Forte pendenza (salita nel senso della freccia)
665 Colle - altitudine (in metri)

Trasporti

B Su chiatta
Collegamento via - traghetto : tutto l'anno - stagionale
Aeroporto

"Curiosità" importanti isolate

Edificio religioso - Castello - Ruderi - Grotta
Monumento megalitico - Altre curiosità
Itinerario ameno - Parco forestale nazionale, parco nazionale

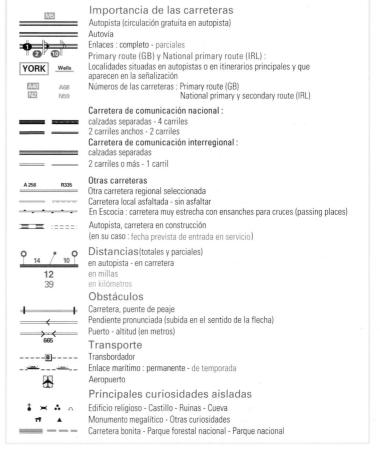

Importancia de las carreteras

M5
Autopista (circulación gratuita en autopista)
Autovía
1 2 10 Enlaces : completo - parciales
Primary route (GB) y National primary route (IRL) :
YORK Wells Localidades situadas en autopistas o en itinerarios principales y que aparecen en la señalización
A40 A68 N2 N59 Números de las carreteras : Primary route (GB)
National primary y secondary route (IRL)

Carretera de comunicación nacional :
calzadas separadas - 4 carriles
2 carriles anchos - 2 carriles
Carretera de comunicación interregional :
calzadas separadas
2 carriles o más - 1 carril

Otras carreteras
A 258 R335 Otra carretera regional seleccionada
Carretera local asfaltada - sin asfaltar
En Escocia : carretera muy estrecha con ensanches para cruces (passing places)
Autopista, carretera en construcción
(en su caso : fecha prevista de entrada en servicio)

Distancias (totales y parciales)

14 10 en autopista - en carretera
12 en millas
39 en kilómetros

Obstáculos

Carretera, puente de peaje
Pendiente pronunciada (subida en el sentido de la flecha)
665 Puerto - altitud (en metros)

Transporte

B Transbordador
Enlace marítimo : permanente - de temporada
Aeropuerto

Principales curiosidades aisladas

Edificio religioso - Castillo - Ruinas - Cueva
Monumento megalítico - Otras curiosidades
Carretera bonita - Parque forestal nacional - Parque nacional

VI
Bunmahon
Tramore
Dunmore East
Dungarvan
Dún Garbhán
Dungarvan Harbour
Helvick Head
Waterford Harbour
Hook Head
Kilmore Quay
Saltee Islands
Harbour / Calafort Ros Láir
Carnsore Point
Youghal
Eochaill
Ardmore
Youghal Bay
Ballycotton
Pembroke
Roscoff
Cherbourg
ST. GEORGE'S CHANNEL
Strumble Head
Pembrokeshire Coast National Park
St. David's Head
St. David's
PEMBROKESHIRE
Fishguard
Abergwaun
St. Bride's Bay
Haverfordwest/
Hwlffordd
Milford Haven/
Aberdaugleddau
Neyland
Pembroke Dock/
Doc Penfro
Pembroke
Rosslare
St. Govan's Head
Rosslare
Poole
Portsmouth
Alderney
Cap de la Hague
Nez de Jobourg
Cherbourg
Cap Lévy
Beaumont
Weymouth
Poole
Guernsey
St. Peter Port
Sark
les Pieux
Valognes
Bricquebec
Barneville-Carteret
Carteret
St. Sauveur-le-V.
Portbail
la Haye-du-Puits
Jersey
Gorey
St-Hélier
Lessay
Portsmouth
Weymouth
St. Malo-de-la-Lande
Agon-Coutainville
Montmartin
Bréhal
I. Chausey
Granville
St. Pair
la Haye-Pesnel
Jullouville
Carolles
Sartilly
Avranches
Cap Fréhel
St. Malo
Paramé
Rothéneuf
Pnte du Grouin
Cancale
Dinard
St. Lunaire
Sables-d'Or
St. Cast
St. Briac
Erquy
St. Jacut
le Mont-St. Michel
Matignon
le Vivier
André
Pléneuf
St. Servan
Châteauneuf
Ploubalay
Tresco
St. Martin's
Isles of Scilly
St. Mary's
Tintagel
Padstow
Wadebridge
CORNWALL
Bodmin
Newquay
Fraddon
St. Austell
St. Ives
Hayle
Truro
Tregony
Mevagissey
Camborne
Redruth
Penryn
St. Just
Penzance
St. Michael's Mount
St. Mawes
Sennen
Land's End
Helston
Falmouth
Mount's Bay
St. Keverne
Lizard
Lizard Point

BIRMINGHAM
Stourbridge
Halesowen
Kidderminster
Bewdley
Stourport
Bromsgrove
Redditch
Droitwich
Worcester
Henley
Alcester
Stratford-upon-Avon
Evesham
Pershore
Chipping Campden
Broadway
Tewkesbury
Winchcombe
Stow-on-the-Wold
Cheltenham
Gloucester
Northleach
Burford
Bibury
Cirencester
Lechlade
Fairford
Cricklade
Swindon
Marlborough
Hungerford
Devizes
Pewsey
Upavon
Calne
Chippenham
Malmesbury
Tetbury
Nailsworth
Stroud
Painswick
Dursley
Chipping Sodbury
Wroughton
Avebury
Melksham
Trowbridge
Bradford-on-Avon
Westbury
Warminster
Frome
Bath
Keynsham
Corsham
WILTSHIRE
Shrewton
Stonehenge
Amesbury
Lopcombe Corner
Wilton
Salisbury
Fordingbridge
Ringwood
Cranborne
Wimborne Minster
Blandford Forum
Shaftesbury
Gillingham
Mere
Wincanton
Bruton
Shepton Mallet
Longleat House
Wells
Glastonbury
Street
Cheddar gorge
Radstock
Beckington
BRISTOL
Avonmouth
Portishead
Clevedon
Congresbury
Weston-Super-Mare
Burnham
Bridgwater
Taunton
Wellington
Langport
Othery
Ilchester
Yeovil
Sherborne
Henstridge
Sturminster Newton
Bere Regis
Wareham
Corfe Castle
Swanage
Poole
BOURNEMOUTH
Christchurch
Lymington
The Needles
ISLE OF W
Dorchester
Weymouth
Isle of Portland
Fortuneswell
Bill of Portland
St. Alban's Head
Abbotsbury
Bridport
Lyme Regis
Beaminster
Crewkerne
Chard
Ilminster
Axminster
Seaton
Honiton
Ottery St. Mary
Sidmouth
Budleigh Salterton
Exmouth
Dawlish
Teignmouth
Torquay
Torbay
Paignton
Brixham
Kingswear
Dartmouth
Totnes
Kingsbridge
Salcombe
Start Point
Newton Abbot
Bovey Tracey
Ashburton
Buckfastleigh
Modbury
Newton Ferrers
Plymstock
PLYMOUTH
Plympton
Saltash
Torpoint
Liskeard
Looe
Polperro
Callington
Tavistock
Princetown
Dartmoor
National Park
High Willhays
Moretonhampstead
Okehampton
EXETER
Crediton
Cullompton
Tiverton
Bampton
South Molton
Launceston
Camelford
Holsworthy
Hatherleigh
Winkleigh
Stratton
Bude
Kilkhampton
Great Torrington
Bideford
Clovelly
Northam
Barnstaple
Braunton
Croyde
Ilfracombe
Combe Martin
Lynton
Lynmouth
Porlock
Minehead
Dunster
Watchet
Williton
Exmoor
Simonsbath
DEVON
SOMERSET
DORSET
Lyme Bay
BRISTOL CHANNEL
Carmarthen Bay
Worms Head
Rhossili
Port-Eynon
The Mumbles
Swansea / Abertawe
Port Talbot
Neath / Castell-nedd
Llanelli
Burry Port
Kidwelly
Pembrey
Tenby / Dinbych-y-pysgod
Saundersfoot
Pendine
St. Clears / Sanclêr
Whitland
Carmarthen / Caerfyrddin
CARMARTHENSHIRE
Cardigan / Aberteifi
Newcastle Emlyn
Llandysul
Lampeter
Aberporth
New Quay
Aberaeron
Llanrhystud
CEREDIGION
Tregaron
Synod Inn
Devil's Bridge
Llangurig
Rhayader / Rhaeadr
POWYS
Llandrindod Wells
Builth Wells / Llanfair-ym-Muallt
Llanwrtyd Wells
Llandovery / Llanymddyfri
Llangadog
Llandeilo
Ammanford
Cross Hands
Pontarddulais
Pontardawe
Black Mountain
Brecon Beacons National Park
Brecon / Aberhonddu
Sennybridge
Talgarth
Hay-on-Wye
Black Mountains
Crickhowell
Abergavenny / Y Fenni
Merthyr Tydfil
Hirwaun
Aberdare / Aberdar
Mountain Ash / Aberpennar
Rhondda
Maesteg
Bridgend / Pen-y-bont
Porthcawl
Cowbridge
Pontypridd
Caerphilly
Bargoed
Tredegar
Ebbw Vale / Glyn Ebwy
Brynmawr
Blaenavon
Abertillery
Pontypool
Cwmbran
Risca
Bedwas
NEWPORT / CASNEWYDD
CARDIFF / CAERDYDD
Penarth
Barry / Barri
Usk
Raglan
Monmouth / Trefynwy
Chepstow / Cas-gwent
Severn Bridge
Lydney
Coleford
Newnham
Ross-on-Wye
Pontrilas
Hereford
HEREFORD
Ledbury
Great Malvern
Upton
Bromyard
Leominster
Kington
Presteigne
Knighton
Ludlow
Clun
Craven Arms
Tenbury Wells
WORCESTER
GLOUCESTER
WALES
CAMBRIA
Severn Estuary
Cork
Santander
Roscoff
St. Malo
Jersey
Guernsey
Cherbourg

ENGLAND
COVENTRY
Rugby
Kettering
Corby
Market Harborough
WARWICK
NORTHAMPTON
CAMBRIDGE
Huntingdon
Ely
Thetford
Bury St. Edmunds
Newmarket
Cambridge
Wellingborough
Royal Leamington Spa
Warwick
Stratford-upon-Avon
BEDFORD
Bedford
Milton Keynes
Banbury
Cheltenham
OXFORD
Buckingham
Luton
Stevenage
HERTFORD
Hertford
Bishop's Stortford
Harlow
Chelmsford
Colchester
IPSWICH
Sudbury
ESSEX
Aylesbury
BUCKINGHAM
Oxford
Swindon
Cirencester
High Wycombe
St. Albans
Watford
Hemel Hempstead
LONDON
Reading
Windsor
Maidenhead
Slough
Heathrow
Richmond
Kingston
Croydon
Dartford
Basildon
Southend-on-Sea
Brentwood
Rochester
Chatham
Maidstone
KENT
Ashford
Tonbridge
Royal Tunbridge Wells
Sevenoaks
Guildford
SURREY
Reigate
Crawley
Gatwick
Basingstoke
Newbury
Andover
HAMPSHIRE
Winchester
Salisbury
Stonehenge
SOUTHAMPTON
PORTSMOUTH
Fareham
Gosport
Chichester
W. SUSSEX
BRIGHTON
Worthing
Hove
Lewes
Eastbourne
Hastings
Bexhill
E. SUSSEX
BOURNEMOUTH
Bognor Regis
ISLE OF WIGHT
Newport
Cowes
Ryde
Ventnor
St. Catherine's Point
The Needles
Swanage
Beachy Head
Newhaven
Cherbourg
Jersey
Guernsey
St Malo
Caen
le Havre
Dieppe
MANCHE
PAS DE
St. Valery-en-Caux
Veules-les-Roses
Varengeville
Veulettes
Offranville

Attleborough
Bungay
Lowestoft
Harleston
Beccles
Diss
Scole
Halesworth
Southwold
Dennington
Yoxford
Saxmundham
Leiston
Aldeburgh
Woodbridge
Felixstowe
Harwich
Esbjerg
Göteborg
Hoek van Holland
Hamburg
The Naze
Walton-on-the-Naze
Frinton-on-Sea
Clacton-on-Sea
Schevening
DEN HAAG
('S-GRAVENHAGE)
Kingston upon Hull
Hoek van Holland
Harwich
Europoort
Maassluis
Brielle
Vlaarding
Haringvlietdam
Goeree
Hellevoetsluis
Ouddorp
Overflakkee
Schouwen
Duiveland
Haamstede
Zierikzee
Nd Beveland
Stavenisse
Tholen
Domburg
Veere
Walcheren
ZEELAND
Middelburg
Goes
Zd Beveland
Kruiningen
Vlissingen
Hoedekenskerke
Breskens
Terneuzen
Kingston upon Hull
Dover
Birchington
Margate
Herne Bay
North Foreland
Broadstairs
Ramsgate
Canterbury
Sandwich
Deal
South Foreland
Dover
Oostende
Tunnel
sous la Manche
Folkestone
Heist
Knokke-Heist
Zeebrugge
Blankenberge
Sluis
Oostburg
IJzendijke
De Haan
Oostende
(BRUGES)
BRUGGE
Maldegem
Zelzate
Hulst
ANTW
Middelkerke-Bad
Nieuwpoort
Jabbeke
Oostkamp
Eeklo
Stekene
St-Niklaas
Gistel
Lokeren
Koksijde-Bad
De Panne
Aalter
Evergem
GENT
(GAND)
Bray-Dunes
Malo-les-Bains
Dunkerque
Veurne
Diksmuide
Tornhout
Tielt
Deinze
Zele
Wetteren
(Alost)
Aalst
Gravelines
Bergues
Hondschoote
WEST-
VLAANDEREN
Roeselare
(Roulers)
Ingelmunster
OOST-
VLAANDEREN
Calais
Cap Blanc Nez
Wissant
Terminal
Guines
Audruicq
Bourbourg
Wormhout
Poperinge
Harelbeke
Kortrijk
(Courtrai)
Waregem
Oudenaarde
Ninove
Cap Gris Nez
Marquise
Ardres
Steenvoorde
Ieper
(Ypres)
Menen
Wervik
(Renaix)
Ronse
Geraardsbergen
BRUS
Wimereux
PAS-
St Omer
Cassel
Arques
Bailleul
Comines
Tourcoing
Mouscron
Lessines
Enghien
Boulogne
le Portel
Lumbres
Hazebrouck
Armentières
Roubaix
(Doornik)
Tournai
Desvres
Aire
Merville
Estaires
LILLE
V. d'Ascq
Hardelot-Plage
Samer
Fauquembergues
Thérouanne
Haubourdin
Braine-le-Comte
Soignies
Le Touquet-Paris-Plage
Hucqueliers
DE-
Norrent-Fontes
Lillers
la Bassée
Seclin
Cysoing
Leuze
Beloeil
Etaples
Fruges
Heuchin
Béthune
Bruay
la-Buissière
Carvin
Pont-à-Marcq
Péruwelz
HAINAUT
Montreuil
Noeux
Bully
Hénin-Beaumont
Orchies
St Amand-les-Eaux
Condé
Mons
(Bergen)
Berck-Plage
Campagne-les-H.
Hesdin
Houdain
Liévin
Lens
Douai
NORD
Marchiennes
Bruay-s-l'E.
Quiévrain
Valenciennes
Fort-Mahon-Plage
CALAIS
St Pol-s-
Aubigny
Denain
Maubeuge
Rue
Crécy-en-P.
Frévent
Avesnes-le-Cte
Vitry-en-A.
Aniche
Bavay
Hautmont
le Crotoy
Auxi-le-Château
Arras
Beaumetz-lès-L.
Bouchain
le Quesnoy
Berlaimont
Aulnoye-Aymeries
Nouvion
Marquion
Cambrai
Cayeux
St Valery
Pas-en-Artois
Solesmes
Sars-Poteries
Ault
Mers
Abbeville
St Riquier
Bernaville
Doullens
Caudry
Landrecies
Avesnes
le Tréport
Criel
Eu
Moyenneville
Ailly-le-H. Clocher
Domart-en-P.
Bapaume
le Cateau
le Nouvion-en-T.
Acheux
Wassigny
la Capelle
Hallencourt
SOMME
Villers-Bocage
Albert
le Catelet
Gamaches
Airaines
Flixecourt
Picquigny
Roisel
Bohain-en-V.
Envermeu
Blangy
Oisemont
Corbie
Bray
Péronne
Hirson
Molliens-Dreuil
St Nicolas-d'A.
Villers-Bretonneux
Vermand
St Quentin
Origny-Ste Benoite
Guise
Tunnel sous la Manche

X
Dumfries
Newton Stewart
Castle Douglas
Gatehouse of Fleet
Dalbeattie
Kirkcudbright
Wigtown
Whithorn
Isle of Whithorn
Burrow Head
Solway Firth
Carlisle
Brampton
Longtown
Hexham
NEWCASTLE-UPON-TYNE
Gateshead
Jarrow
Blyth
Morpeth
Washington
Durham
Consett
CUMBRIA
Maryport
Workington
Whitehaven
St. Bees Head
Cockermouth
Keswick
Penrith
Cross Fell
Alston
DURHAM
Bishop Auckland
Barnard Castle
Darlington
Stockton-on-Tees
Appleby
Brough
Kirkby Stephen
Lake District National Park
Cumbrian Mountains
Ambleside
Windermere
Kendal
Coniston
Bowness
Ulverston
Barrow-in-Furness
Grange-Over-Sands
Morecambe
Heysham
Lancaster
Carnforth
Sedbergh
Kirkby Lonsdale
Richmond
Leyburn
Hawes
Bedale
Northallerton
Thirsk
Scotch Corner
Yorkshire Dales National Park
PENNINES
NORTH YORK
Ripon
Harrogate
Knaresborough
Skipton
Settle
Point of Ayre
Ramsey
Snaefell
Douglas
Ronaldsway
Belfast
Dublin
Fleetwood
Cleveleys
BLACKPOOL
LANCASHIRE
Clitheroe
Lytham St. Anne's
Preston
Blackburn
Burnley
Nelson
Colne
Keighley
BRADFORD
LEEDS
Halifax
Huddersfield
Wakefield
Barnsley
Rotherham
SHEFFIELD
Southport
Ormskirk
Formby
Chorley
Bolton
Bury
Rochdale
Oldham
Wigan
St. Helens
LIVERPOOL
Liverpool Bay
Wallasey
Birkenhead
Warrington
Widnes
Runcorn
MANCHESTER
Stockport
Glossop
Peak District National Park
Macclesfield
Buxton
Chesterfield
CHESHIRE
Northwich
Knutsford
Wilmslow
Chester
Crewe
Congleton
Leek
Nantwich
STOKE-ON-TRENT
Newcastle-under-Lyme
DERBY
Derby
Matlock
Ashbourne
Uttoxeter
Stafford
Burton-upon-Trent
Amlwch
Great Ormes Head
Llandudno
Colwyn Bay
Rhyl
Conwy
Bangor
ANGLESEY
Menai Bridge
Caernarfon
Llanberis
Snowdon
Snowdonia
Betws-y-Coed
Denbigh / Dinbych
Mold / Yr Wyddgrug
Flint / Fflint
Wrexham / Wrecsam
Llangollen
Oswestry
Whitchurch
Market Drayton
GWYNEDD
Snowdonia National Park
Bala
Harlech
Porthmadog
Criccieth
Ffestiniog
Dolgellau
Cader Idris
Barmouth
Tywyn
Aberdovey
Machynlleth
Aberystwyth
Llanidloes
Newtown / Drenewydd
Welshpool / Y Trallwng
Montgomery
Shrewsbury
SHROPSHIRE
Telford
WREKIN
Ironbridge
Much Wenlock
Church Stretton
Bridgnorth
STAFFORD
Cannock
Lichfield
Rugeley
Walsall
WOLVERHAMPTON
Dudley
BIRMINGHAM
Sutton Coldfield
Tamworth
Nuneaton
Hinckley
Coalville
Ashby de la Zouch
LEICESTER

Göteborg
Amsterdam
Hartlepool
Redcar
Marske-by-the-Sea
Saltburn-by-the-Sea
Brotton
Guisborough
Loftus
Whitby
Cleveland Hills
North York Moors
National Park
Scalby
Scarborough
Helmsley
Pickering
Filey
Easingwold
Malton
Norton
Flamborough Head
Bridlington
E. RIDING
OF
YORKSHIRE
Wetwang
Gt. Driffield
Beeford
Market Weighton
Leven
Hornsea
Beverley
Selby
Barlby
Howden
KINGSTON-UPON-HULL
Hedon
Withernsea
Patrington
Kilnsea
Snaith
Goole
Humber Bridge
Barton-upon-Humber
River Humber
Immingham Dock
Immingham
N. LINCS
N.E. LINCS
Thorne
Crowle
Scunthorpe
Great Grimsby
Spurn Head
Cleethorpes
Rotterdam
Zeebrugge
Doncaster
Brigg
Humberside
Caistor
Epworth
Bawtry
Gainsborough
Market Rasen
Louth
East Retford
Mablethorpe
Sutton-on-Sea
Wragby
Tuxford
Lincoln
Alford
Ollerton
Horncastle
Partney
Woodhall Spa
Spilsby
Skegness
Newark-on-Trent
Southwell
Leadenham
LINCOLN
NOTTINGHAM
Sleaford
Boston
Bingham
Grantham
West Bridgford
Donington
Sutterton
The Wash
Hunstanton
Wells-next-the-Sea
Sheringham
Cromer
Blakeney
Holt
Mundesley
Sandringham House
Fakenham
North Walsham
Guist
Aylsham
Holbeach
Long Sutton
Melton Mowbray
Bourne
Spalding
King's Lynn
Low Street
RUTLAND
NORFOLK
Oakham
Stamford
Crowland
Wisbech
East Dereham
LEICESTER
Swaffham
Acle
Great Yarmouth
Oadby
Uppingham
Eye
Guyhirn
Outwell
Stradsett
NORWICH
Peterborough
Downham Market
Watton
Wymondham
Gorleston-on-Sea
Market
Corby
Whittlesey
March

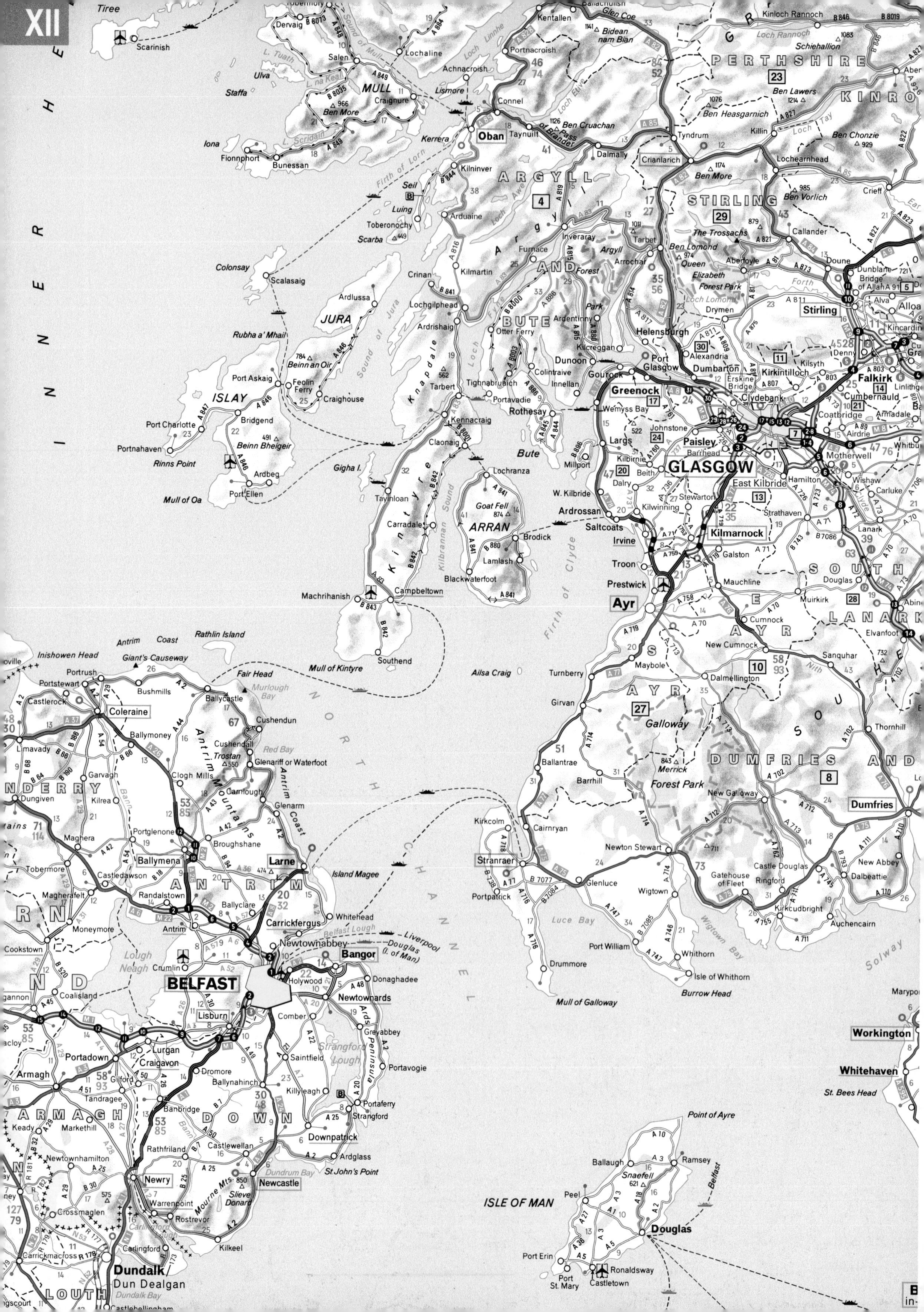
Tiree
Scarinish
INNER HEBRIDES
Dervaig
Lochaline
Salen
Ulva
Staffa
MULL
Craignure
Ben More
Iona
Fionnphort
Bunessan
Lismore
Achnacroish
Oban
Kerrera
Connel
Taynuilt
Kentallen
Glen Coe
Bidean nam Bian
Portnacroish
Ben Cruachan
Pass of Brander
Dalmally
Tyndrum
Crianlarich
Kinloch Rannoch
Loch Rannoch
Schiehallion
PERTHSHIRE
Aberfeldy
Ben Lawers
Ben Heasgarnich
Killin
Loch Tay
Ben Chonzie
Lochearnhead
Ben More
Ben Vorlich
Crieff
STIRLING
Callander
The Trossachs
Ben Lomond
Queen Elizabeth Forest Park
Aberfoyle
Doune
Dunblane
Bridge of Allan
Stirling
Alloa
Kilninver
Seil
Luing
Arduaine
Toberonochy
Scarba
Firth of Lorn
ARGYLL
Inveraray
Furnace
Argyll Forest Park
Arrochar
Tarbet
Kilmartin
Crinan
Lochgilphead
Ardrishaig
Otter Ferry
Ardentinny
Kilcreggan
Dunoon
Helensburgh
Alexandria
Dumbarton
Drymen
Port Glasgow
Gourock
Greenock
Colintraive
Innellan
Tighnabruaich
Portavadie
Rothesay
Bute
Wemyss Bay
Largs
Millport
Colonsay
Scalasaig
JURA
Ardlussa
Rubha a' Mhail
Port Askaig
Feolin Ferry
Craighouse
ISLAY
Port Charlotte
Bridgend
Portnahaven
Rinns Point
Beinn Bheigeir
Ardbeg
Port Ellen
Mull of Oa
Gigha I.
Tarbert
Kennacraig
Claonaig
Knapdale
Kintyre
Tayinloan
Carradale
Kilbrannan Sound
Lochranza
Goat Fell
ARRAN
Brodick
Lamlash
Blackwaterfoot
Machrihanish
Campbeltown
Southend
Mull of Kintyre
Kirkintilloch
Kilsyth
Falkirk
Cumbernauld
Clydebank
Coatbridge
Airdrie
GLASGOW
Paisley
Johnstone
Barrhead
Kilbirnie
Beith
Dalry
W. Kilbride
Ardrossan
Saltcoats
Kilwinning
Stewarton
East Kilbride
Hamilton
Motherwell
Wishaw
Carluke
Lanark
Strathaven
Kilmarnock
Irvine
Troon
Galston
Prestwick
Ayr
Mauchline
Douglas
Muirkirk
Cumnock
Elvanfoot
New Cumnock
Sanquhar
Firth of Clyde
Ailsa Craig
Turnberry
Maybole
Dalmellington
Girvan
Ballantrae
Barrhill
Galloway Forest Park
Merrick
DUMFRIES AND GALLOWAY
New Galloway
Thornhill
Dumfries
Kirkcolm
Cairnryan
Stranraer
Portpatrick
Newton Stewart
Glenluce
Wigtown
Castle Douglas
Gatehouse of Fleet
Ringford
Kirkcudbright
Auchencairn
New Abbey
Dalbeattie
Luce Bay
Port William
Whithorn
Isle of Whithorn
Drummore
Mull of Galloway
Burrow Head
Solway Firth
Maryport
Workington
Whitehaven
St. Bees Head
Rathlin Island
Antrim Coast
Giant's Causeway
Inishowen Head
Portrush
Portstewart
Bushmills
Ballycastle
Fair Head
Murlough Bay
Castlerock
Coleraine
Cushendun
Cushendall
Red Bay
Trostan
Glenariff or Waterfoot
Limavady
Ballymoney
Garvagh
Cloghmills
Antrim Mountains
Carnlough
Dungiven
Kilrea
Glenarm
Portglenone
Broughshane
Maghera
Ballymena
Larne
Island Magee
Tobermore
Castledawson
Magherafelt
Randalstown
Ballyclare
Antrim
Whitehead
Carrickfergus
Moneymore
Belfast Lough
Newtownabbey
Liverpool
Douglas (I. of Man)
Bangor
Cookstown
Lough Neagh
Crumlin
BELFAST
Holywood
Donaghadee
Coalisland
Newtownards
Lisburn
Comber
Greyabbey
Ards Peninsula
Portadown
Lurgan
Craigavon
Saintfield
Strangford Lough
Portavogie
Armagh
Gilford
Dromore
Ballynahinch
Tandragee
Killyleagh
Portaferry
Strangford
Banbridge
ARMAGH
DOWN
Keady
Markethill
Downpatrick
Rathfriland
Castlewellan
Ardglass
St John's Point
Newtownhamilton
Dundrum Bay
Newry
Mourne Mts.
Slieve Donard
Newcastle
Warrenpoint
Crossmaglen
Rostrevor
Kilkeel
Carlingford
Carlingford Lough
Carrickmacross
Dundalk
Dun Dealgan
Dundalk Bay
LOUTH
Castlebellingham
NORTH CHANNEL
Point of Ayre
Ballaugh
Ramsey
Snaefell
Peel
ISLE OF MAN
Douglas
Port Erin
Port St. Mary
Castletown
Ronaldsway

ANGUS
Pitlochry
Brechin
Montrose
Kirriemuir
Alyth
Glamis Castle
Forfar
Rattray
Blairgowrie
Dunkeld
Meigle
Coupar Angus
Sidlaw Hills
Arbroath
Dundee
Monifieth
Carnoustie
Buddon Ness
Perth
Tay
Newport-on-Tay
Tayport
Leuchars
St. Andrews
Newburgh
Auchtermuchty
Auchterarder
Cupar
FIFE
Fife Ness
Falkland
Crail
Anstruther
Pittenweem
St. Monans
Kinross
Glenrothes
Leven
Methil
Buckhaven
Elie
Lochgelly
Cowdenbeath
Dunfermline
Kirkcaldy
Firth of Forth
Burntisland
Inverkeithing
Hopetoun House
Bo-Ness
Forth Bridge
S. Queensferry
Leith
North Berwick
Aberlady
East Linton
Dunbar
Prestonpans
Musselburgh
Tranent
Haddington
Livingston
EDINBURGH
Dalkeith
Loanhead
Cockburnspath
St. Abb's Head
Lammermuir Hills
Eyemouth
Penicuik
Pentland Hills
West Linton
Carnwath
Moorfoot Hills
SCOTTISH UPLANDS
Berwick-upon-Tweed
Duns
Greenlaw
Lauder
Peebles
Innerleithen
Galashiels
Earlston
Melrose
Mellerstain
Dryburgh
Kelso
Coldstream
Biggar
Tweed
Holy Island
Belford
Bamburgh
Newtown St. Boswells
Selkirk
Broad Law
BORDERS
Wooler
The Cheviot
Jedburgh
Hawick
Moffat
Teviot
Alnwick
Northumberland
National Park
Carter Bar
The Cheviot Hills
Warkworth
Amble
Rothbury
Felton
GALLOWAY
NORTHUMBERLAND
The Border
Kielder Resr.
Otterburn
Forest
Park
North Tyne
Langholm
Lockerbie
Annan
Ashington
Newbiggin-by-the-Sea
Morpeth
Blyth
Bedlington
Belsay
Seaton Delaval
Whitley Bay
Canonbie
Longtown
Bowness-on-Solway
Hadrian's Wall
Chollerford
NEWCASTLE UPON-TYNE
Tynemouth
South Shields
Jarrow
Bergen
Stavanger
Hamburg
Göteborg
Amsterdam
Greenhead
Brampton
Hexham
Corbridge
Prudhoe
Gateshead
S. Tyne
Carlisle
Silloth
Abbey Town
Wigton
Thursby
Aspatria
Bothel
Alston
Consett
Stanley
Washington
Chester-le-Street
Lanchester
SUNDERLAND
Seaham
Houghton-le-Spring
Derwent
Durham
Horden
CUMBRIA
Cross Fell
Wolsingham
Peterlee
Cockermouth
Skiddaw
Penrith
Wear
Crook
Spennymoor
Hartlepool
Keswick
Derwent water
Buttermere
Frizington
Egremont
Lake District National Park
Cumbrian Mountains
Ullswater
Rosthwaite
Patterdale
Shap
Appleby
Middleton-in-Teesdale
DURHAM
W. Auckland
Bishop Auckland
Sedgefield
Newton Aycliffe
Billingham
Redcar
Marske-by-the-Sea
Saltburn-by-the-Sea
Brotton
Stockton-on-Tees
Middlesbrough
Guisborough
Loftus
Barnard Castle
Brough
Bowes
Darlington
Tees-side
Eaglescliffe
Whitby
Scafell Pikes
Gosforth
Grasmere
Ambleside
Orton
Tebay
Kirkby Stephen
Scotch Corner
Coniston
Windermere
Bowness
Reeth
Richmond
Swale
Cleveland Hills
North York Moors National Park
Broughton-in-Furness
Kendal
Sedbergh
Hawes
Leyburn
Bedale
Northallerton
Millom
Ulverston
Greenodd
Whernside
Yorkshire Dales
Thirsk
Helmsley
Pickering
Scalby
Scarborough
Dalton
Grange-Over-Sands
Kirkby Lonsdale
PENNINE
NORTH YORKSHIRE
Barrow-in-Furness
Morecambe
Carnforth
Ingleton
Clapham
National
Ripon
Filey
NORTH SEA

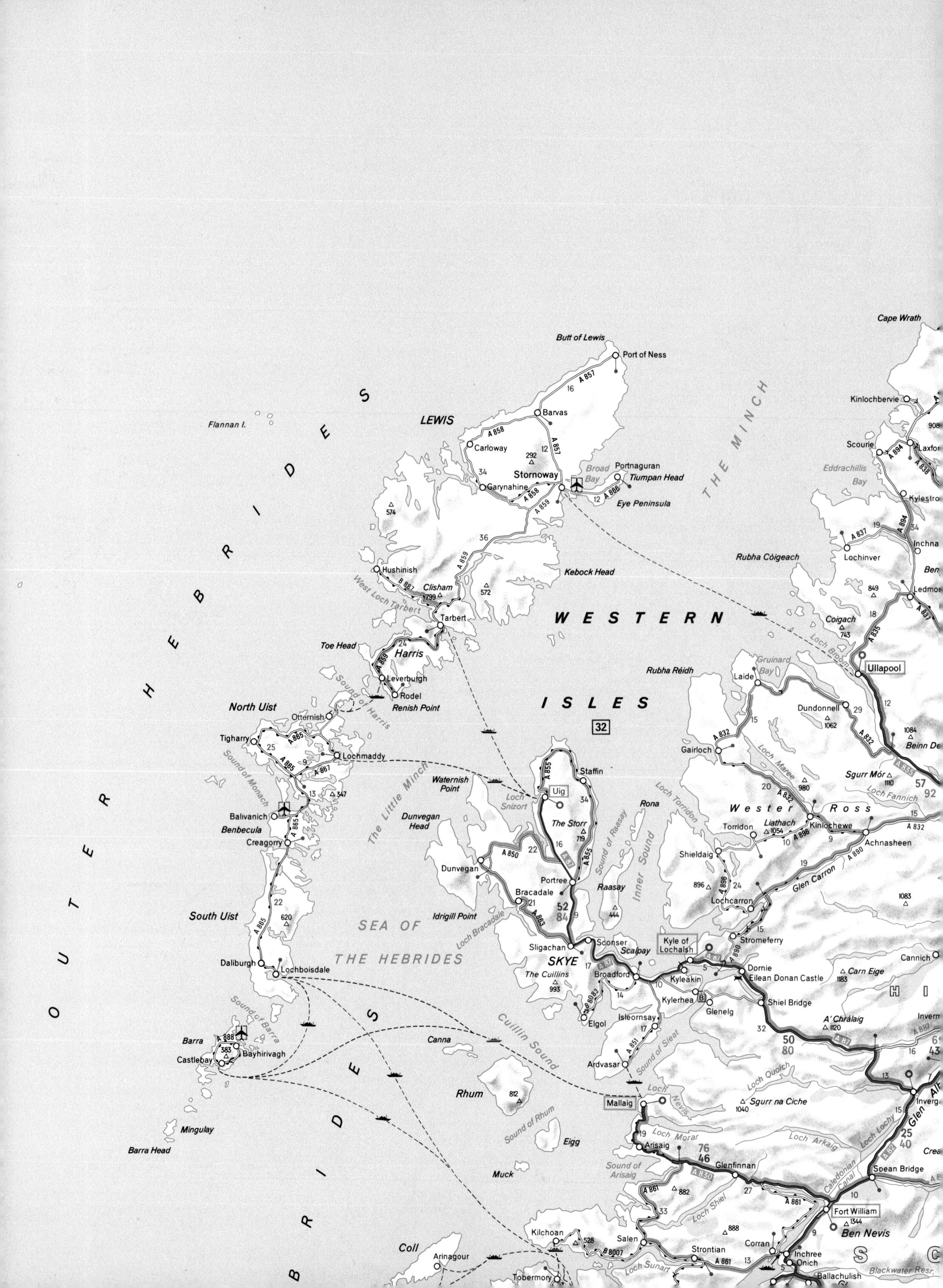
OUTER HEBRIDES
Flannan I.
LEWIS
Butt of Lewis
Port of Ness
Barvas
Carloway
Stornoway
Garynahine
Broad Bay
Portnaguran
Tiumpan Head
Eye Peninsula
THE MINCH
Hushinish
Clisham
799
West Loch Tarbert
Tarbert
Kebock Head
Toe Head
Harris
Leverburgh
Rodel
Renish Point
Sound of Harris
North Uist
Otternish
Tigharry
Lochmaddy
Sound of Monach
Balivanich
Benbecula
Creagorry
South Uist
Daliburgh
Lochboisdale
Sound of Barra
Barra
Castlebay
Bayhirivagh
Mingulay
Barra Head
WESTERN
ISLES
32
Waternish Point
The Little Minch
Dunvegan Head
Loch Snizort
Uig
Staffin
The Storr
Rona
Sound of Raasay
Inner Sound
Raasay
Dunvegan
Portree
Bracadale
Idrigill Point
Loch Bracadale
SEA OF
THE HEBRIDES
Sligachan
SKYE
The Cuillins
Sconser
Scalpay
Broadford
Elgol
Isleornsay
Ardvasar
Sound of Sleat
Cuillin Sound
Canna
Rhum
Sound of Rhum
Eigg
Muck
Coll
Arinagour
Kilchoan
Tobermory
Salen
Loch Sunart
Strontian
Kyle of Lochalsh
Kyleakin
Kylerhea
Glenelg
Dornie
Eilean Donan Castle
Shiel Bridge
Stromeferry
Lochcarron
Glen Carron
Shieldaig
Torridon
Liathach
Loch Torridon
Kinlochewe
Achnasheen
Wester Ross
Loch Maree
Gairloch
Laide
Gruinard Bay
Rubha Réidh
Dundonnell
Ullapool
Loch Broom
Coigach
Rubha Còigeach
Lochinver
Ledmore
Inchna
Kylestrome
Eddrachillis Bay
Scourie
Laxford
Kinlochbervie
Cape Wrath
Beinn De
Sgurr Mór
Loch Fannich
Carn Eige
Cannich
A' Chràlaig
Loch Quoich
Sgurr na Ciche
Mallaig
Loch Nevis
Loch Morar
Arisaig
Sound of Arisaig
Loch Arkaig
Loch Lochy
Glenfinnan
Loch Shiel
Caledonian Canal
Spean Bridge
Fort William
Ben Nevis
Corran
Inchree
Onich
Ballachulish
Blackwater Resr.

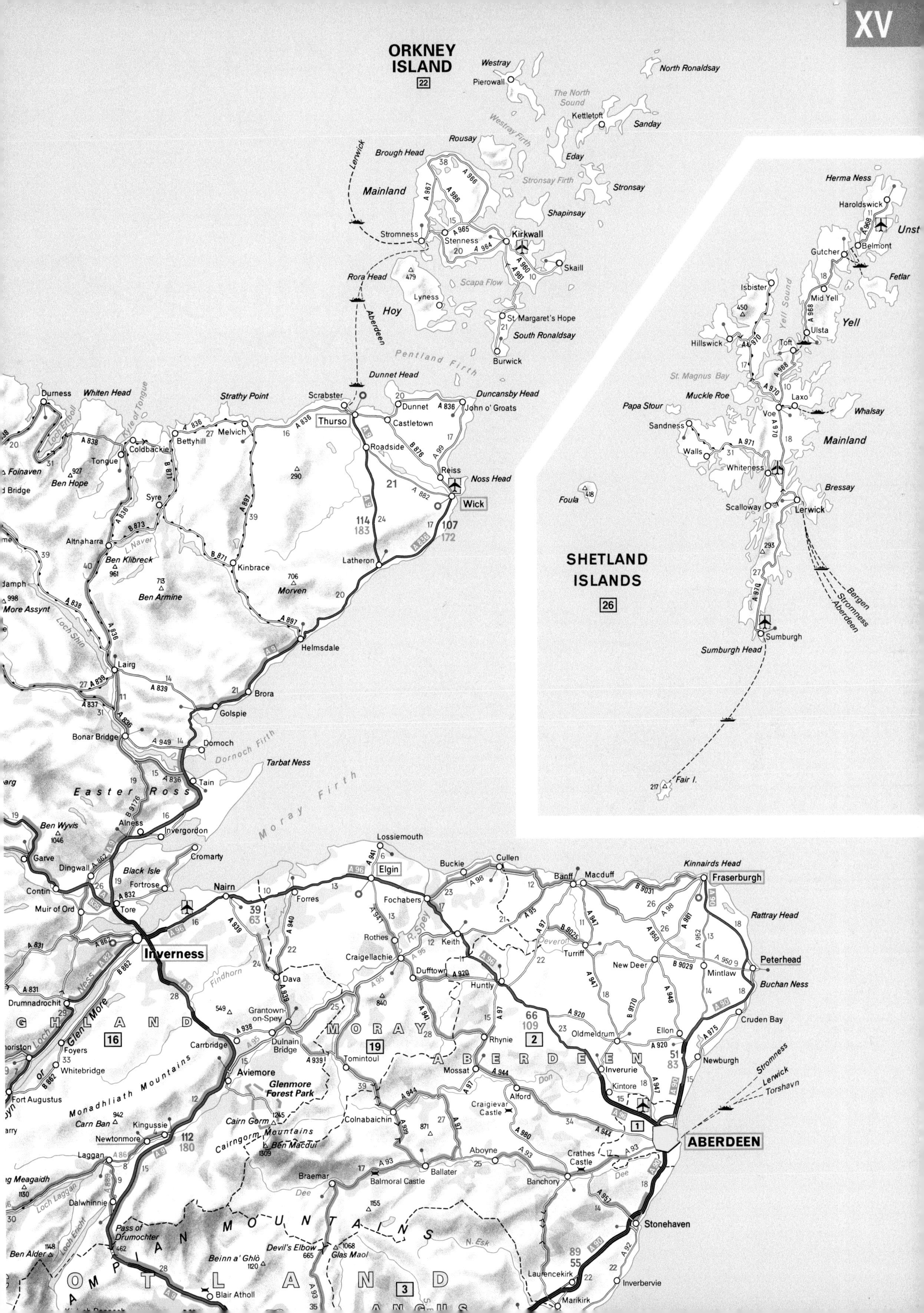
ORKNEY ISLAND
22
Westray
Pierowall
North Ronaldsay
The North Sound
Westray Firth
Kettletoft
Sanday
Rousay
Eday
Brough Head
Lerwick
Mainland
Stronsay Firth
Stronsay
Shapinsay
Stromness
Stenness
Kirkwall
Skaill
Rora Head
Scapa Flow
Hoy
Lyness
Aberdeen
St Margaret's Hope
South Ronaldsay
Burwick
Pentland Firth
Dunnet Head
Durness
Whiten Head
Kyle of Tongue
Loch Eriboll
Strathy Point
Scrabster
Duncansby Head
Dunnet
John o' Groats
Thurso
Castletown
Coldbackie
Bettyhill
Melvich
Tongue
Foinaven
Ben Hope
Roadside
Reiss
Noss Head
Wick
Syre
Altnaharra
L. Naver
Ben Klibreck
Kinbrace
Latheron
Ben Armine
Morven
More Assynt
Loch Shin
Helmsdale
Lairg
Brora
Golspie
Bonar Bridge
Dornoch
Dornoch Firth
Tarbat Ness
Tain
Easter Ross
Moray Firth
Ben Wyvis
Alness
Invergordon
Cromarty
Garve
Dingwall
Black Isle
Fortrose
Contin
Muir of Ord
Tore
Nairn
Inverness
Forres
Lossiemouth
Elgin
Buckie
Cullen
Banff
Macduff
Kinnairds Head
Fraserburgh
Rattray Head
Fochabers
R. Spey
Rothes
Keith
Craigellachie
Turriff
New Deer
Peterhead
Mintlaw
Buchan Ness
Findhorn
Dava
Dufftown
Huntly
Drumnadrochit
Loch Ness
Glen More
Grantown-on-Spey
Dulnain Bridge
Carrbridge
Cruden Bay
HIGHLAND
16
MORAY
19
ABERDEEN
2
Rhynie
Oldmeldrum
Ellon
Newburgh
Foyers
Whitebridge
Tomintoul
Mossat
Inverurie
Kintore
Aviemore
Glenmore Forest Park
Fort Augustus
Monadhliath Mountains
Alford
Craigievar Castle
Don
Stromness
Lerwick
Torshavn
Carn Ban
Cairn Gorm
Cairngorm Mountains
Ben Macdui
Colnabaichin
Kingussie
Newtonmore
1
ABERDEEN
Laggan
Aboyne
Crathes Castle
Braemar
Balmoral Castle
Ballater
Banchory
Dee
Meagaidh
Loch Laggan
Dalwhinnie
Stonehaven
Loch Ericht
Pass of Drumochter
GRAMPIAN MOUNTAINS
N. Esk
Ben Alder
Devil's Elbow
Glas Maol
Beinn a' Ghlò
Laurencekirk
Inverbervie
HIGHLAND
Blair Atholl
3
Marikirk
SHETLAND ISLANDS
26
Herma Ness
Haroldswick
Unst
Belmont
Gutcher
Fetlar
Isbister
Yell Sound
Mid Yell
Yell
Ulsta
Hillswick
Toft
St. Magnus Bay
Muckle Roe
Papa Stour
Laxo
Whalsay
Voe
Sandness
Mainland
Walls
Whiteness
Bressay
Foula
Scalloway
Lerwick
Bergen
Stromness
Aberdeen
Sumburgh
Sumburgh Head
Fair I.

Inishturk
Louisburgh
Croagh Patrick
Westport / Cathair na Mart
Kiltamagh
Ballaghaderreen
Frenchpark
Elphin
Inishbofin
Inishshark
Murrisk
Mweelrea Mts.
Ballintober
Claremorris
Ballyhaunis
ROSCOMMON
Castlerea
Tulsk
Strokestown
Rinvyle Pt.
Killary Harbour
Partry Mountains
Letterfrack
Leenane
Lough Mask
Ballinrobe
Ballymoe
The Twelve Pins
Maumturk Mts
Kilmaine
Dunmore
Lanesborough
Clifden / An Clochán
Connemara
Clonbur
Cong
Glennamaddy
Roscommon / Ros Comáin
Slyne Head
Roundstone
Maam Cross
Lough Corrib
Tuam / Tuaim
Headford
IRELAND
Gortmore
Oughterard
Mount Bellew
Ballyforan
Lough Ree
Carna
Kilkieran Bay
GALWAY
Athlone / Baile Átha Luain
Lettermullan
Gorumna Island
Spiddal
Galway / Gaillimh
Barna
Oranmore
Athenry
Ballinasloe / Béal Átha na Sluaighe
Aran Islands
Inishmore
Kilronan
Galway Bay
Craughwell
Loughrea
Clonmacnoise
Ferbane
Black Head
Ardrahan
Clonfert
Inishmaan
Kinvarra
Ballyvaughan
Banagher
Cloghan
Kilcormac
Inisheer
Lisdoonvarna
Gort
Portumna
Kilfenora
Birr
Kinnitty
Cliffs of Moher
Lahinch
Ennistimon
Corrofin
Slieve Bloom
Milltown Malbay
CLARE
Borrisokane
Spanish Point
Ennis / Inis
Tulla
Scarriff
Roscrea
Lough Derg
Nenagh / An tAonach
Moneygall
Knappogue
Broadford
Creegh
Kilmurry
Killaloe
Kilkee
Newmarket on Fergus
Dolla
Templemore
Killadysert
Shannon
Bunratty
Kilrush
Killimer
Labasheeda
River Shannon
Newport
TIPPERARY
Loop Head
Kilbaha
LIMERICK / LUIMNEACH
Milestone
Thurles / Durlas
Mouth of the Shannon
Ballybunnion
Tarbert
Askeaton
Adare
Holy Cross
Ballyduff
Listowel
Rathkeale
Croom
Kerry Head
Rock of Cashel
Ballyheige
LIMERICK
Newcastle West
Abbeyfeale
Hospital
Cashel / Caiseal
Killenaule
Brandon Head
Tralee Bay
Tipperary / Tiobraid Árann
Fethard
Sybil Head
Brandon Mountain
Tralee / Trá Lí
Dromcolliher
Kilmallock
Rath Luirc (Charleville)
Slievenamon
Clogher Head
Dingle
Anascaul
Slieve Mish Mts.
Castleisland
Galty Mountains
Caher
Great Blasket I.
Slea Head
Castlemaine
Newmarket
Buttevant
Kildorrery
Clogheen
Clonmel / Cluain Meala
Dingle Bay
Killorglin
KERRY
Boberbue
Kanturk
Mitchelstown
Knockmealdown Mts.
Comeragh Mts.
Glenbeigh
Killarney / Cill Airne
Ring of Kerry
Muckross House
Mallow / Mala
Doulus Head
Knight's Town
Carrantuohill
Rathmore
Fermoy
Lismore
Cappoquin
Valencia Island
Cahersiveen
Iveragh
Macgillycuddy's Reeks
Millstreet
CORK
Mangerton Mountain
Derrynasaggart Mts.
Tallow
Dungarvan / Dún Garbhán
Waterville
L. Currane
Kilgarvan
St. Finan's Bay
Sneem
Kenmare
CORK / CORCAIGH
Bolus Head
Macroom
Coachford
Blarney
Dungarvan Bay
Helvick Head
Skellig
Kenmare River
Lauragh
Midleton
Youghal / Eochaill
Ardmore
Beara
Glengarriff
Pass of Keimaneigh
Caha Mts
Cobh / An Cóbh
Youghal Bay
Castletownbere
Bantry / Beanntraí
Dunmanway
Bandon
Ringaskiddy
Crosshaven
Ballycotton
Dursey Island
Bere I.
Bantry Bay
Kinsale
Sheep's Head
Timoleague
Dunmanus Bay
Rosscarbery
Clonakilty
Swansea
Skull
Skibbereen
Old Head of Kinsale
Roscoff
Mizen Head
Roaringwater Bay
Galley Head
Toe Head
Clear Island

Cavan/ An Cabhán
CAVAN
Shercock
Bailieborough
Ballyjamesduff
Virginia
Kingscourt
Carrickmacross
LOUTH
Dundalk/
Dun Dealgan
Dundalk Bay
Carlingford
Carlingford Lough
Kilkeel
Castlebellingham
Ardee
Clogherhead
Monasterboice
Old Mellifont
Slane
Newgrange
Drogheda/
Droichead Átha
Duleek
Balbriggan
Naul
Skerries
Lusk
Rush
FINGAL
Ashbourne
Swords
Malahide
Portmarnock
Howth
DUBLIN/BAILE ÁTHA CLIATH
Dún Laoghaire
Dalkey
S. DUBLIN
Bray
Enniskerry
Kippure
Powerscourt
Greystones
IRISH SEA
Douglas (I. of Man)
Liverpool
Holyhead/
Caergybi
Holy Island
Llanerchymedd
Rhosneigr
Isle of Anglesey
Newborough
Caernarfon
Caernarfon Bay
Nefyn
Lleyn Peninsula
Pwllheli
Abersoch
Aberdaron
Port Erin
Port St. Mary
Castletown
LONGFORD
Longford/
An Longfort
Granard
Sheelin
L. Ramor
Oldcastle
Kells
Castlepollard
L. Derravaragh
WESTMEATH
Mullingar/
An Muileann gCearr
L. Owel
L. Ennell
Royal Canal
Delvin
Athboy
Navan/
An Uaimh
MEATH
Trim
Dunshaughlin
Kinnegad
Innfield
Kilcock
Maynooth
Lucan
Clondalkin
Kilbeggan
Tullamore/
Tulach Mhór
Edenderry
OFFALY
KILDARE
Grand Canal
Liffey
Newbridge
(An Droichead Nua)
Portarlington
Kildare
Naas
Russborough
Monasterevin
Mountmellick
Kilcullen
Poulaphouca Resr.
Hollywood
Portlaoise
Athy
WICKLOW
Wicklow Mountains
Glendalough
Laragh
Rathnew
Wicklow/Cill Mhantáin
Wicklow Head
Lugnaquillia Mountain
Baltinglass
Rathdrum
Aughrim
Tinahely
Arklow/
An tInbhear Mór
LAOIS
Abbeyleix
Durrow
Castlecomer
Castledermot
Carlow/
Ceatharlach
Tullow
CARLOW
Freshford
KILKENNY
Kilkenny/
Cill Chainnigh
Bagenalstown
(Muine Bheag)
Carnew
Gorey
Bunclody
Courtown
Callan
Thomastown
Jerpoint
Graiguenamanagh
Borris
Blackstairs Mts.
Kiltealy
Enniscorthy/
Inis Córthaidh
Cahore Point
WEXFORD
Carrick-on-Suir/
Carraig na Siúire
New Ross
Blackwater
Waterford/
Port Láirge
Wexford/
Loch Garman
Rosslare
Rosslare Harbour/
Calafort
Ros Láir
Arthurstown
Wellington Bridge
WATERFORD
Bunmahon
Tramore
Dunmore East
Waterford Harbour
Hook Head
Kilmore Quay
Saltee Islands
Carnsore Point
Pembroke
Roscoff
Cherbourg
ST. GEORGE'S CHANNEL
Cardigan Bay
Llanrhystud
Aberaeron
New Quay
Synod Inn
Aberporth
Cardigan/
Aberteifi
Strumble Head
Newport
Pembrokeshire Coast National Park
Newcastle Emlyn
Fishguard/
Abergwaun
Crymych
St. David's Head
St. David's
PEMBROKESHIRE
CARMARTHEN
Carmarthen
Caerfyrddin
St. Bride's Bay
Haverfordwest/
Hwlffordd
Whitland
St. Clears/
Sanclêr
Narberth
Milford Haven/
Aberdaugleddau
Neyland
Cross Hands
Pendine
Kidwelly
Pembroke Dock/
Doc Penfro
Saundersfoot
Burry Port
Pembroke
Tenby/
Dinbych-y-pysgod
Llanelli
Carmarthen Bay
St. Govan's Head
Swansea
Rhossili
Worms Head
Port-Eynon

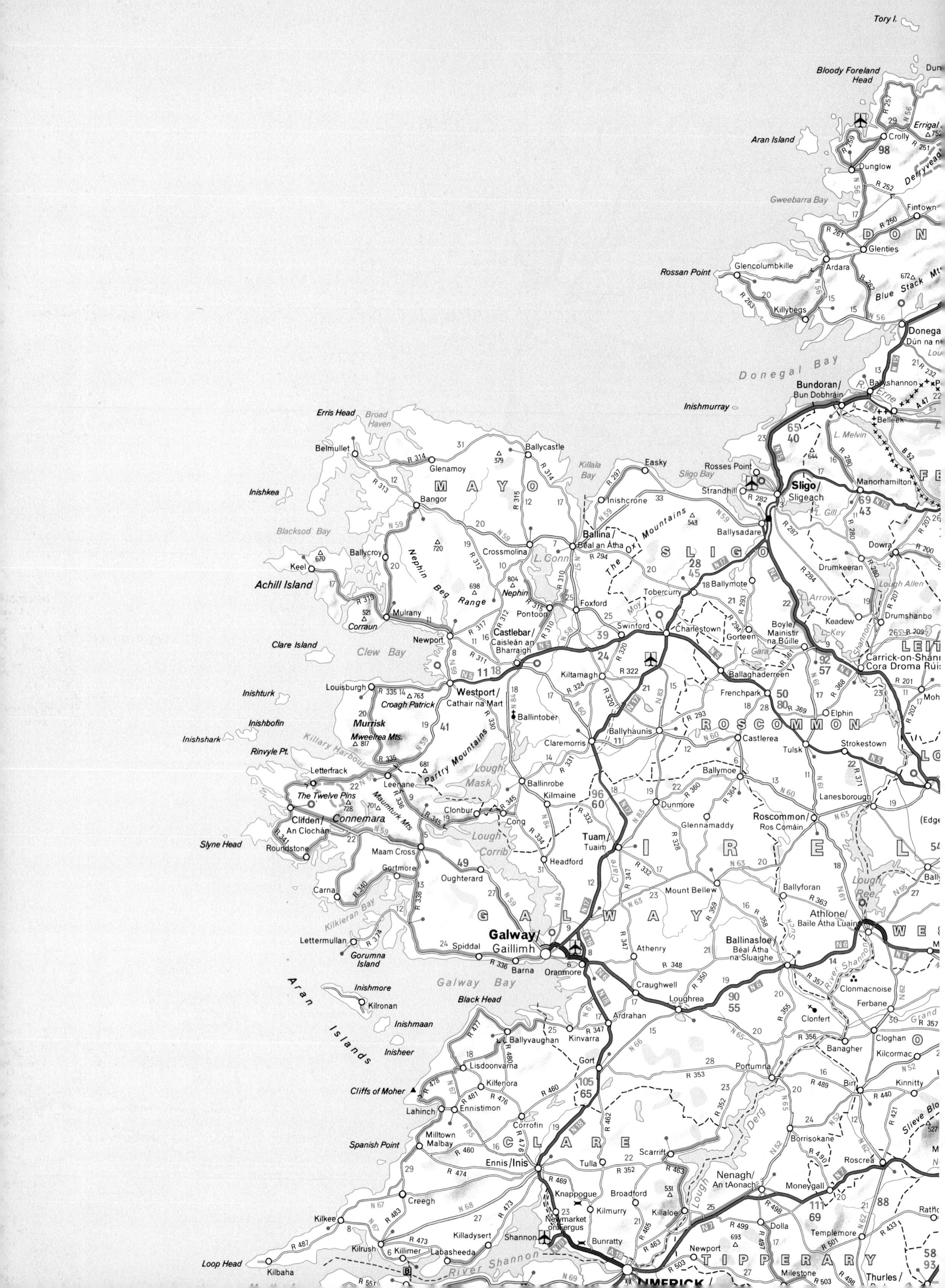
Tory I.
Bloody Foreland Head
Aran Island
Crolly
Errigal
Dunglow
Gweebarra Bay
Fintown
Glenties
Rossan Point
Glencolumbkille
Ardara
Blue Stack Mts
Killybegs
Donegal
Dún na nGall
Donegal Bay
Bundoran/
Bun Dobhráin
Ballyshannon
Belleek
Inishmurray
L. Melvin
Manorhamilton
Rosses Point
Sligo Bay
Strandhill
Sligo/
Sligeach
L. Gill
Ballysadare
Dowra
Drumkeeran
Lough Allen
Erris Head
Broad Haven
Belmullet
Glenamoy
Ballycastle
Killala Bay
Easky
Inishkea
MAYO
Bangor
Inishcrone
Blacksod Bay
Ballina/
Béal an Átha
The Ox Mountains
SLIGO
Ballycroy
Crossmolina
L. Conn
Keel
Achill Island
Nephin Beg Range
Nephin
Ballymote
Tobercurry
Corraun
Mulrany
Pontoon
Foxford
Boyle/
Mainistir na Búille
Keadew
Drumshanbo
Clare Island
Clew Bay
Newport
Castlebar/
Caisleán an Bharraigh
Swinford
Charlestown
Gorteen
L. Gara
L. Key
Carrick-on-Shannon
Cora Droma Rúisc
Westport/
Cathair na Mart
Kiltamagh
Ballaghaderreen
Frenchpark
Elphin
Inishturk
Louisburgh
Croagh Patrick
Ballintober
Inishbofin
Murrisk
Mweelrea Mts.
Ballyhaunis
ROSCOMMON
Inishshark
Killary Harbour
Partry Mountains
Claremorris
Castlerea
Tulsk
Strokestown
Rinvyle Pt.
Letterfrack
Leenane
Lough Mask
Ballinrobe
Ballymoe
The Twelve Pins
Maumturk Mts
Kilmaine
Lanesborough
Clifden/
An Clochán
Connemara
Clonbur
Cong
Dunmore
Glennamaddy
Roscommon/
Ros Comáin
Slyne Head
Roundstone
Maam Cross
Lough Corrib
Tuam/
Tuaim
Headford
IRELAND
Gortmore
Oughterard
Mount Bellew
Ballyforan
Lough Ree
Carna
Kilkieran Bay
GALWAY
Athlone/
Baile Átha Luain
Lettermullan
Gorumna Island
Galway/
Gaillimh
Spiddal
Barna
Oranmore
Athenry
Ballinasloe/
Béal Átha na Sluaighe
Galway Bay
Aran Islands
Inishmore
Kilronan
Black Head
Craughwell
Loughrea
River Shannon
Clonmacnoise
Ferbane
Inishmaan
Ardrahan
Clonfert
Inisheer
Ballyvaughan
Kinvarra
Banagher
Cloghan
Kilcormac
Lisdoonvarna
Gort
Portumna
Cliffs of Moher
Kilfenora
Birr
Kinnitty
Lahinch
Ennistimon
Corrofin
Borrisokane
Slieve Bloom
Spanish Point
Milltown Malbay
CLARE
Scarriff
Lough Derg
Ennis/Inis
Tulla
Roscrea
Nenagh/
An tAonach
Moneygall
Creegh
Knappogue
Broadford
Kilmurry
Killaloe
Kilkee
Newmarket on Fergus
Dolla
Templemore
Killadysert
Shannon
Bunratty
Kilrush
Killimer
Labasheeda
Loop Head
Kilbaha
Newport
TIPPERARY
Milestone
Thurles
LIMERICK

Inishtrahull
Malin Head
Fanad Head
Inishowen
Slieve Snaght
Lough Swilly
Culdaff
Carndonagh
Portsalon
Carrigart
Moville
Buncrana
Quigley's Point
Lough Foyle
Rathmullan
Millford
Muff
Rathmelton
Letterkenny/
Leitir Ceanainn
Grianan of Aileach
Eglinton
Londonderry
LONDONDERRY
Limavady
Castlerock
Portstewart
Portrush
Coleraine
Bushmills
Giant's Causeway
Antrim Coast
Rathlin Island
Inishowen Head
Fair Head
Ballycastle
Murlough Bay
Cushendun
Cushendall
Red Bay
Trostan
Glenariff or Waterfoot
Antrim Mountains
Carnlough
Glenarm
Antrim Coast
Ballymoney
Clogh Mills
Garvagh
Kilrea
Dungiven
Claudy
Dunnamanagh
Sperrin Mountains
Sawel Mountain
Maghera
Portglenone
Ballymena
Broughshane
Larne
Island Magee
Strabane
Lifford
Stranorlar
Ballybofey
Plumbridge
Castlederg
Newtownstewart
Gortin
Tobermore
Castledawson
Magherafelt
Randalstown
ANTRIM
Ballyclare
Antrim
Carrickfergus
Whitehead
Belfast Lough
Newtownabbey
Bangor
Holywood
Donaghadee
Newtownards
BELFAST
Crumlin
Lough Neagh
NORTHERN IRELAND
Omagh
TYRONE
Cookstown
Moneymore
Kesh
Dromore
Lower Lough Erne
Irvinestown
Fintona
Dungannon
Coalisland
Ballygawley
Aughnacloy
Lisburn
Comber
Greyabbey
Ards Peninsula
Strangford Lough
Portavogie
FERMANAGH
Enniskillen
Belcoo
Fivemiletown
Portadown
Lurgan
Craigavon
Dromore
Ballynahinch
Saintfield
Killyleagh
Portaferry
Strangford
Armagh
Gilford
Tandragee
Banbridge
DOWN
Downpatrick
Ardglass
St. John's Point
Lisnaskea
Upper Lough Erne
Rossiea
Monaghan/
Muineachán
ARMAGH
Keady
Markethill
Castlewellan
Rathfriland
Dundrum Bay
Newcastle
Slieve Donard
Mourne Mts
Kilkeel
Newtownbutler
Clones
MONAGHAN
Newtownhamilton
Newry
Warrenpoint
Rostrevor
Carlingford Lough
Carlingford
Belturbet
Ballyconnell
Swanlinbar
Ballybay
Castleblayney
Cootehill
Crossmaglen
Killashandra
Cavan/ An Cabhán
CAVAN
Shercock
Carrickmacross
Dundalk/
Dun Dealgan
Dundalk Bay
LOUTH
Bailieborough
Kingscourt
Castlebellingham
Ballyjamesduff
Virginia
Lough Sheelin
Lough Ramor
Oldcastle
LONGFORD
Longford/
An Longfort
Granard
Ardee
Monasterboice
Clogherhead
Kells
Old Mellifont
Slane
Drogheda/
Droichead Átha
Castlepollard
L. Derravaragh
Royal Canal
Navan/
An Uaimh
Newgrange
Duleek
Boyne
MEATH
Athboy
Delvin
Trim
Mullingar/
An Muileann gCearr
Ballymore
L. Owel
L. Ennell
WESTMEATH
Naul
Balbriggan
FINGAL
Skerries
Lusk
Rush
Dunshaughlin
Ashbourne
Swords
Malahide
Portmarnock
Howth
Kinnegad
Kilbeggan
Clara
Tullamore/
Tulach Mhór
Innfield
Maynooth
Kilcock
Edenderry
Lucan
Liffey
DUBLIN/BAILE ÁTHA CLIATH
Dún Laoghaire
Dalkey
Clondalkin
S. DUBLIN
KILDARE
OFFALY
Grand Canal
Newbridge
(An Droichead Nua)
Portarlington
Kildare
Monasterevin
Naas
Russborough
Kippure
Enniskerry
Bray
Greystones
Powerscourt
Poulaphouca Resr.
Hollywood
Mountmellick
Kilcullen
Portlaoise
Mountrath
LAOIS
Athy
WICKLOW
Wicklow Mountains
Glendalough
Laragh
Rathnew
Wicklow/ Cill Mhantáin
Wicklow Head
Lugnaquillia Mountain
Baltinglass
Abbeyleix
Castledermot
Rathdrum
Durrow
Castlecomer
Carlow/
Ceatharlach
Barrow
Aughrim
Tullow
Tinahely
Freshford
CARLOW
Arklow
NORTH CHANNEL
IRISH SEA
ISLE OF MAN
Liverpool
Douglas (I. of Man)
Brodick
Lamlash
Blackwaterfoot
Machrihanish
Campbeltown
Southend
Mull of Kintyre
Ailsa Craig
Prestwick
Ayr
Firth of Clyde
Turnberry
Girvan
Ballantrae
Barrhill
Kirkcolm
Cairnryan
Stranraer
Portpatrick
Glenluce
Newton Stewart
Luce Bay
Port William
Drummore
Mull of Galloway
Ballaugh
Snaefell
Peel
Port Erin
Port St. Mary
Castletown
Ronaldsway
Holyhead/
Caergybi
Holy Island
Llanerchymedd
Rhosneigr
Isle of Anglesey
Newborough
Caernarfon
Caernarfon Bay
Nefyn
1-1999

Local government areas in England have been subject to revision since April 1996.

En Angleterre, les limites administratives sont en cours de modification depuis Avril 1996.

Seit April 1996 werden die englischen Verwaltungsgrenzen neu geordnet.

Sinds april 1996 worden de administratieve grensen in Engeland gewijzigd.

Dall'aprile 1996 in Inghilterra i confini amministrativi sono in fase di cambiamento.

En Inglaterra, se están modificando los límites administrativos desde Abril de 1996.

UNITARY AUTHORITIES

WALES

1. Anglesey/Sir Fôn
2. Blaenau Gwent
3. Bridgend/ Pen-y-bont ar Ogwr
4. Caerphilly/Caerffili
5. Cardiff/Caerdydd
6. Carmarthenshire/ Sir Gaerfyrddin
7. Ceredigion
8. Conwy
9. Denbighshire/Sir Ddinbych
10. Flintshire/Sir y Fflint
11. Gwynedd
12. Merthyr Tydfil/ Merthyr Tudful
13. Monmouthshire/Sir Fynwy
14. Neath Port Talbot/ Castell-nedd Phort Talbot
15. Newport/Casnewydd
16. Pembrokeshire/Sir Benfro
17. Powys
18. Rhondda Cynon Taff/ Rhondda Cynon Taf
19. Swansea/Abertawe
20. Torfaen/Tor-faen
21. Vale of Glamorgan/ Bro Morgannwg
22. Wrexham/Wrecsam

SCOTLAND

1. Aberdeen City
2. Aberdeenshire
3. Angus
4. Argyll and Bute
5. Clackmannanshire
6. City of Edinburgh
7. City of Glasgow
8. Dumfries and Galloway
9. Dundee City
10. East Ayrshire
11. East Dunbartonshire
12. East Lothian
13. East Renfrewshire
14. Falkirk
15. Fife
16. Highland
17. Inverclyde
18. Midlothian
19. Moray
20. North Ayrshire
21. North Lanarkshire
22. Orkney Islands
23. Perthshire and Kinross
24. Renfrewshire
25. Scottish Borders
26. Shetland Islands
27. South Ayrshire
28. South Lanarkshire
29. Stirling
30. West Dunbartonshire
31. West Lothian
32. Western Isles

SHIPPING SERVICES
Car ferries

All the year round

At least 6 sailings daily

One or more sailings daily

One or more sailings weekly

* Infrequent service

Hovercraft service

Seasonal

One or more sailings daily

One or more sailings weekly

* Infrequent service

The service is liable to interruption during the Christmas and New Year holidays or at other periods (eg Sundays or for maintenance) ☐

**Full details from companies*

LIAISONS MARITIMES
Transport des autos

Permanentes

Au moins 6 liaisons par jour

Une ou plusieurs liaisons par jour

Une ou plusieurs liaisons par semaine

* Liaison à faible fréquence

Liaison assurée par aéroglisseur

Saisonnières

Une ou plusieurs liaisons par jour

Une ou plusieurs liaisons par semaine

* Liaison à faible fréquence

Interruption possible des services lors des fêtes de Noël et de fin d' année, ou à certaines autres périodes. ☐

**S'adresser aux compagnies*

SCHIFFSVERBINDUNGEN
Autotransport

Ganzjährig

Mindestens 6 Fahrten täglich

Eine oder mehrere Fahrten täglich

Eine oder mehrere Fahrten pro Woche

*Nur wenige Fahrten

Mit Luftkissenboot

Während der Saison

Eine oder mehrere Fahrten täglich

Eine oder mehrere Fahrten pro Woche

* Nur wenige Fahrten

Um Weihnachten und Neujahr sowie gelegentlich während des Jahres kann der Fährbetrieb unterbrochen sein. ☐

**Auskunft erteilen die jeweiligen Gesellschaften*

SCHEEPVAARTVERBINDINGEN
Vervoer van auto's

Permanente diensten

Minstens 6 diensten per dag

Eén of meer diensten per dag

Eén of meer diensten per week

* Slechts enkele diensten

Per hovercraft

Diensten in het zomerseizoen

Eén of meer diensten per dag

Eén of meer diensten per week

* Slechts enkele diensten

De diesten worden mogelijk onderbroken op de Kerstdagen, Nieuwjaarsdag, of gedurende bepaalde andere periodes. ☐

**Zich wenden tot de ondernemingen*

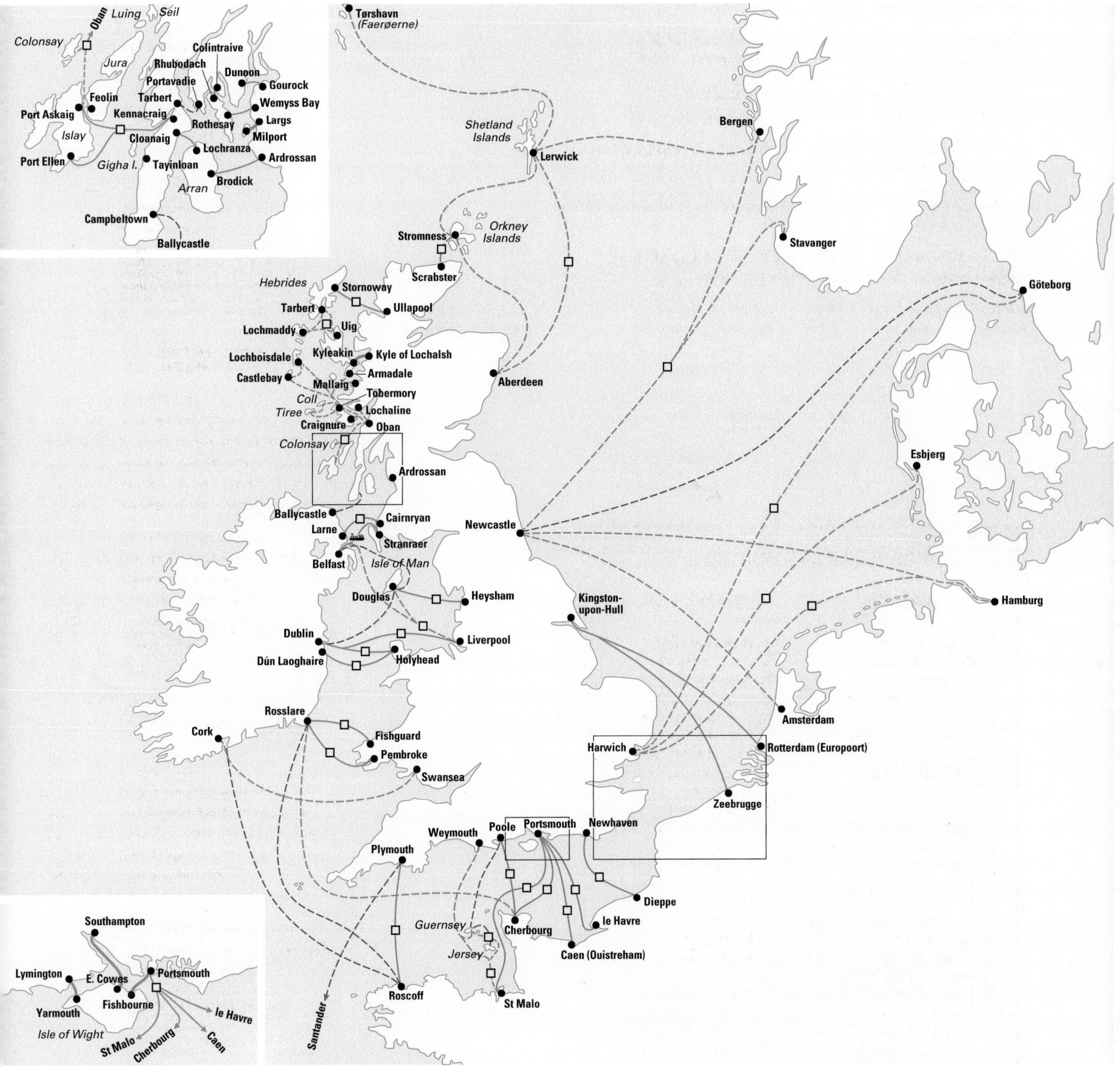
Colonsay
Oban
Luing
Seil
Jura
Colintraive
Rhubodach
Portavadie
Dunoon
Gourock
Port Askaig
Feolin
Tarbert
Kennacraig
Wemyss Bay
Largs
Islay
Cloanaig
Rothesay
Milport
Lochranza
Port Ellen
Gigha I.
Tayinloan
Ardrossan
Brodick
Arran
Campbeltown
Ballycastle
Tørshavn
(Faerøerne)
Shetland
Islands
Lerwick
Bergen
Stromness
Orkney
Islands
Scrabster
Stavanger
Hebrides
Stornoway
Ullapool
Tarbert
Lochmaddy
Uig
Göteborg
Kyleakin
Kyle of Lochalsh
Lochboisdale
Armadale
Castlebay
Mallaig
Aberdeen
Tobermory
Coll
Tiree
Lochaline
Craignure
Oban
Colonsay
Esbjerg
Ardrossan
Ballycastle
Cairnryan
Larne
Newcastle
Stranraer
Belfast
Isle of Man
Douglas
Heysham
Kingston-
upon-Hull
Hamburg
Dublin
Liverpool
Dún Laoghaire
Holyhead
Amsterdam
Rosslare
Cork
Fishguard
Harwich
Rotterdam (Europoort)
Pembroke
Swansea
Zeebrugge
Weymouth
Poole
Portsmouth
Newhaven
Plymouth
Dieppe
Guernsey
Cherbourg
le Havre
Jersey
Caen (Ouistreham)
Southampton
Lymington
E. Cowes
Portsmouth
Fishbourne
Yarmouth
le Havre
Isle of Wight
St Malo
Cherbourg
Caen
Roscoff
St Malo
Santander

COLLEGAMENTI MARITTIMI Trasporto di auto		ENLACES MARITIMOS Transporte de vehiculos
Permanente		**Permanentes**
Almeno 6 collegamenti quotidiani	———	Al menos 6 enlaces diarios
Uno o più collegamenti quotidiani	———	Uno o más enlaces diarios
Uno o più collegamenti settimanali	– – – – –	Uno o más enlaces semanales
* Collegamento poco frequente	....	Enlaces poco frecuentes*
Collegamento assicurato da aliscafo	(overcraft)	Enlace por overcraft
Stagionale		**De temporada**
Uno più collegamenti quotidiani	———	Uno o varios enlaces diarios
Uno più collegamenio settimanali	– – – – –	Uno o varios enlaces semanales
* Collegamento poco frequente	....	Enlaces poco frecuentes *
Possibile sospensione dei servizi in occasione delle feste natalizie, Capodanno o in particolari altri periodi **Rivolgersi alle companie*	□	*Posible interrupción de los servicios en Navidades y Fin de Año, o en otros periodos* **Dirigirse a las compañías*

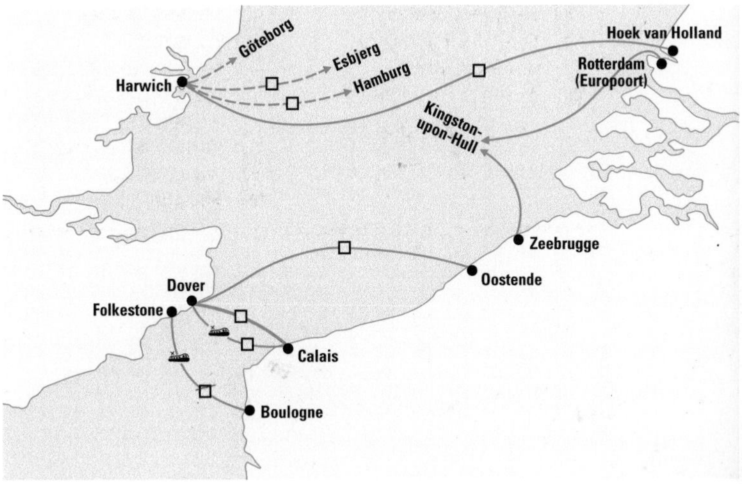
Göteborg
Hoek van Holland
Esbjerg
Harwich
Hamburg
Rotterdam
(Europoort)
Kingston-
upon-Hull
Zeebrugge
Oostende
Dover
Folkestone
Calais
Boulogne

Distances Entfernungen Afstandstabel Distanze Distancias

All distances are quoted in miles and kilometres.

miles in red

kilometres in blue

The distances quoted are not necessarily the shortest but have been based on the roads which afford the best driving conditions and are therefore the most practical.

Example:

Oxford – Killarney:

Oxford – Fishguard 214 m. or 344 km.
Rosslare – Killarney 163 m. or 261 km.
377 m. or 605 km.

Les distances sont indiquées en miles et en kilomètres

miles en rouge

kilomètres en bleu

Les distances sont comptées à partir du centre-ville et par la route la plus pratique, c'est-à-dire celle qui offre les meilleures conditions de roulage, mais qui n'est pas nécessairement la plus courte.

Exemple :

Oxford – Killarney:

Oxford – Fishguard 214 m. ou 344 km.
Rosslare – Killarney 163 m. ou 261 km.
377 m. ou 605 km.

Die Entfernungen sind in Meilen und in Kilometern angegeben.

in Rot: Meilen

in Blau: Kilometer

Die Entfernungen gelten ab Stadtmitte unter Berücksichtigung der günstigsten (nicht immer kürzesten) Strecke.

Beispiel:

Oxford – Killarney:

Oxford – Fishguard 214 m. oder 344 km.
Rosslare – Killarney 163 m. oder 261 km.
377 m. oder 605 km.

De afstanden zijn vermeld in mijl en in kilometer

mijl in het rood

kilometer in het blauw

De afstanden zijn berekend van centrum tot centrum langs de meest geschikte, maar niet noodzakelijkerwijze kortste route.

Voorbeeld:

Oxford – Killarney:

Oxford – Fishguard 214 m. of 344 km.
Rosslare – Killarney 163 m. of 261 km.
377 m. of 605 km.

Le distanze sono indicate in miglia e in chilometri.

miglia in rosso

chilometri in blu

Le distanze sono calcolate a partire dal centro delle città e seguendo la strada che, pur non essendo necessariamente la più breve, offre le migliori condizioni di viaggio.

Esempio:

Oxford – Killarney:

Oxford – Fishguard 214 m. o 344 km.
Rosslare – Killarney 163 m. o 261 km.
377 m. o 605 km.

Las distancias se indican en millas y en kilómetros.

millas en rojo

kilómetros en azul

El kilometraje está calculado desde el centro de la ciudad y por la carretera más práctica para el automovilista, que no tiene porqué ser la más corta.

Ejemplo:

Oxford – Killarney:

Oxford – Fishguard 214 m. o 344 km.
Rosslare – Killarney 163 m. o 261 km.
377 m. o 605 km.

Ireland

Kilometres

	Belfast	Cork	Drogheda	Dublin	Dundalk	Galway	Killarney	Larne	Limerick	Londonderry	Omagh	Rosslare	Sligo	Tullamore	Waterford
Belfast		422	120	167	86	314	467	36	366	116	109	311	200	227	330
Cork	263		302	256	337	195	89	456	92	479	426	193	326	205	117
Drogheda	75	188		48	35	223	348	154	246	188	135	191	204	109	210
Dublin	104	159	30		82	218	301	201	199	229	175	144	219	105	164
Dundalk	53	210	22	51		247	382	120	281	163	110	226	171	134	245
Galway	195	121	139	136	154		215	342	104	275	250	265	144	132	228
Killarney	291	55	216	187	238	134		501	112	476	412	261	346	227	189
Larne	23	284	96	125	75	213	312		400	122	120	345	225	261	364
Limerick	228	57	153	124	175	65	70	249		365	301	197	235	116	125
Londonderry	72	298	117	142	102	171	296	76	227		54	373	132	258	387
Omagh	68	265	84	109	69	155	256	75	187	34		319	106	205	334
Rosslare	193	120	119	90	140	165	163	215	123	232	199		323	164	76
Sligo	124	203	127	137	106	90	215	140	146	82	66	201		160	295
Tullamore	141	127	68	65	83	82	141	162	72	161	127	102	99		136
Waterford	205	73	131	102	152	142	118	226	78	241	208	48	183	84	

Miles

Great Britain

Kilometres

	Aberdeen	Birmingham	Brighton	Bristol	Cambridge	Cardiff	Carlisle	Dover	Dundee	Edinburgh	Exeter	Fishguard	Glasgow	Harwich	Holyhead	Hull	Inverness	Kyle of Lochalsh	Leeds	Liverpool	London	Manchester	Middlesbrough	Newcastle	Northampton	Norwich	Nottingham	Oban	Oxford	Penzance	Plymouth	Portsmouth	Southampton	Stranraer	Swansea	Thurso
Aberdeen		693	964	827	751	858	368	946	108	197	949	852	238	872	741	581	176	302	523	574	879	565	440	368	776	789	635	287	804	1129	1016	938	909	378	831	361
Birmingham	431		269	143	158	175	328	328	585	488	265	298	483	279	278	233	742	768	196	165	194	145	290	344	92	265	86	628	109	445	332	242	214	500	234	927
Brighton	600	167		259	195	310	600	170	858	760	278	483	755	208	550	426	1014	1041	427	437	89	417	521	575	208	274	317	901	173	458	345	78	99	772	369	1200
Bristol	514	89	161		246	72	461	321	719	621	123	246	617	337	412	381	876	902	344	299	200	279	438	492	184	353	234	762	119	303	190	154	122	634	131	1061
Cambridge	467	99	121	153		296	426	198	643	551	370	470	581	107	428	235	812	866	247	315	91	268	330	384	87	108	144	726	133	550	437	212	214	598	356	997
Cardiff	534	109	193	45	184		493	372	751	653	182	180	648	388	365	412	908	934	376	274	251	310	469	524	235	403	265	794	170	362	249	245	216	665	65	1093
Carlisle	229	204	372	287	265	307		647	260	163	583	487	158	546	376	255	417	443	198	208	513	200	154	96	411	464	309	303	439	764	651	572	544	175	466	602
Dover	588	204	106	200	123	231	402		838	746	401	545	802	212	598	429	1006	1088	441	485	124	464	524	579	242	278	351	948	235	582	469	229	232	819	431	1192
Dundee	67	364	532	447	400	467	162	521		89	841	744	124	764	633	473	211	284	415	466	771	458	333	260	669	681	527	190	696	1021	908	830	801	264	723	396
Edinburgh	123	303	472	386	343	406	101	464	56		743	647	73	672	536	381	258	331	323	368	639	360	241	168	540	589	435	199	599	924	811	732	704	213	626	443
Exeter	590	165	173	76	230	113	363	250	523	462		356	739	432	534	503	998	1024	466	421	295	401	560	614	316	474	356	884	251	180	73	213	179	755	241	1183
Fishguard	530	186	301	153	292	112	303	339	463	402	221		642	562	266	465	901	927	377	267	424	310	490	544	409	577	365	787	344	536	423	419	390	320	118	1086
Glasgow	148	300	469	383	361	403	98	499	77	46	459	399		702	531	410	281	289	353	363	668	355	309	247	566	619	465	149	594	919	806	727	699	139	621	466
Harwich	542	174	130	210	67	242	340	132	475	418	269	349	436		549	315	933	987	368	436	129	389	451	505	211	110	265	847	223	613	500	267	276	719	447	1118
Holyhead	461	173	342	256	266	227	234	372	394	333	332	166	330	341		354	790	817	266	156	464	200	379	433	362	490	289	676	389	714	601	523	494	186	298	975
Hull	361	145	265	237	146	256	159	267	294	237	313	289	255	196	220		641	696	98	212	322	158	143	214	232	247	157	556	286	683	570	420	392	427	471	827
Inverness	110	461	630	545	505	564	259	626	131	160	620	560	175	580	491	399		129	584	623	928	614	501	429	825	850	696	186	853	1178	1065	987	958	421	880	188
Kyle of Lochalsh	188	478	646	561	539	581	276	676	177	206	637	577	180	614	508	433	80		639	649	954	641	575	502	852	904	750	203	879	1204	1091	1013	985	425	906	281
Leeds	325	122	266	214	154	234	123	275	258	201	290	234	220	229	166	61	363	397		123	327	70	102	156	225	285	120	498	279	646	533	413	384	370	435	769
Liverpool	357	103	271	186	196	170	130	301	290	229	262	166	226	271	97	132	387	404	77		351	57	236	290	248	363	176	509	276	601	488	410	381	380	280	808
London	546	121	55	124	57	156	319	77	479	397	183	264	416	80	288	201	577	593	204	218		331	418	472	108	185	217	814	95	475	362	128	139	685	310	1113
Manchester	352	90	259	173	167	193	125	289	285	224	249	193	221	242	124	98	382	398	44	36	206		182	237	228	306	117	501	256	581	468	390	361	372	289	800
Middlesbrough	274	180	324	272	205	292	96	326	207	150	348	305	192	280	236	89	312	357	64	147	260	114		73	319	368	214	437	373	740	627	506	478	326	528	687
Newcastle	229	214	357	306	239	326	60	360	162	105	382	338	153	314	269	133	267	312	97	181	293	147	46		373	422	268	364	427	794	681	561	532	264	583	614
Northampton	483	57	130	115	54	146	256	151	416	336	196	254	352	132	225	144	513	530	140	155	68	142	198	232		194	115	712	72	496	383	205	177	583	294	1011
Norwich	490	165	171	219	67	251	288	173	423	366	295	359	385	69	305	154	528	562	177	226	115	190	229	262	121		195	764	240	654	541	316	318	636	462	1035
Nottingham	395	53	197	145	90	165	193	218	328	271	221	227	289	165	180	98	433	466	75	110	135	73	133	167	71	122		610	169	536	423	302	274	482	324	881
Oban	178	391	559	474	452	493	189	589	118	124	550	489	93	527	421	346	116	126	310	316	506	311	272	227	442	475	379		739	1064	951	873	844	284	766	374
Oxford	501	68	108	74	83	106	274	146	434	373	156	214	370	139	243	178	531	548	174	173	59	160	232	266	45	149	105	460		431	318	137	109	612	229	1040
Penzance	702	277	285	188	342	225	475	362	635	574	112	333	571	381	444	425	732	749	402	374	295	361	460	494	308	407	333	662	268		127	394	359	936	421	1363
Plymouth	632	207	215	118	272	155	405	291	565	504	46	263	501	311	374	354	662	679	332	304	225	291	390	423	238	336	263	591	198	79		281	246	823	308	1250
Portsmouth	584	151	49	96	132	152	357	142	517	456	133	260	453	166	326	261	614	631	257	256	80	243	315	349	128	197	188	543	85	245	175		34	745	304	1173
Southampton	566	133	62	76	133	135	339	144	499	438	111	243	435	172	308	244	596	613	239	238	86	225	297	331	110	198	170	526	68	223	153	22		717	276	1145
Stranraer	235	311	479	394	372	414	109	509	164	133	470	199	86	447	116	266	262	264	230	237	426	231	203	164	363	395	299	177	380	582	511	463	445		638	606
Swansea	517	146	229	82	221	41	290	268	450	389	150	73	386	278	186	293	547	564	271	174	193	180	329	362	183	288	202	476	143	262	192	189	171	396		1065
Thurso	225	577	745	660	620	679	374	741	246	276	735	675	290	695	606	514	117	175	478	502	692	497	427	382	628	643	548	232	646	847	777	729	711	377	662	

Miles

Key

A full key to symbols appears inside the front cover

Roads

CHIEVELEY Motorway - Service areas

Junctions : complete, limited

❶ ❷ ❸ Numbered junctions

Dual carriageway with motorway characteristics

Major road :
dual carriageway
4 lanes - 2 wide lanes
2 lanes - 2 narrow lanes

Regional road network :
dual carriageway - 2 wide lanes
2 lanes - 2 narrow lanes
Other roads : surfaced - unsurfaced

Motorway, road under construction
(with scheduled opening date)

14 10 24 39 Distances on motorway and road :
in miles - in kilometres

Transportation

Railway - Passenger station

Car ferries
(seasonal services : in red)
boat - hovercraft
15 ferry (maximum load : in metric tons)

Airport - Airfield

Towns

Towns having a plan in the
Michelin Guides
Red Hotel and Restaurant Guides
Green Tourist Guide

Légende

Voir la légende complète à l'intérieur de la couverture

Routes

CHIEVELEY Autoroute - Aires de service
(sur autoroute, la circulation est gratuite)

Échangeurs : complet, partiels

❶ ❷ ❸ Numéros d'échangeurs

Double chaussée de type autoroutier

Route de liaison principale :
à chaussées séparées
à 4 voies - à 2 voies larges
à 2 voies - à 2 voies étroites

Route de liaison régionale :
à chaussées séparées - à 2 voies larges
à 2 voies - à 2 voies étroites
Autre route : revêtue - non revêtue

Autoroute, route en construction
(le cas échéant : date de mise en service prévue)

14 10 24 39 Distances sur autoroute et route :
en miles - en kilomètres

Transports

Voie ferrée - Station voyageurs

Transport des autos
(liaisons saisonnières : signe rouge)
par bateau - par aéroglisseur
15 par bac (charge maximum en tonnes)

Aéroport - Aérodrome

Localités

Localités possédant un plan dans les
Guides Michelin
Rouges "Hôtels et Restaurants"
Verts "Touristiques"

Zeichenerklärung

Vollständige Zeichenerklärung siehe Umschlaginnenseite

Straßen

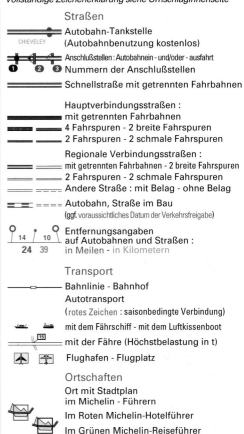

CHIEVELEY Autobahn-Tankstelle
(Autobahnbenutzung kostenlos)

Anschlußstellen : Autobahnein - und/oder - ausfahrt

❶ ❷ ❸ Nummern der Anschlußstellen

Schnellstraße mit getrennten Fahrbahnen

Hauptverbindungsstraßen :
mit getrennten Fahrbahnen
4 Fahrspuren - 2 breite Fahrspuren
2 Fahrspuren - 2 schmale Fahrspuren

Regionale Verbindungsstraßen :
mit getrennten Fahrbahnen - 2 breite Fahrspuren
2 Fahrspuren - 2 schmale Fahrspuren
Andere Straße : mit Belag - ohne Belag

Autobahn, Straße im Bau
(ggf. voraussichtliches Datum der Verkehrsfreigabe)

14 10 24 39 Entfernungsangaben
auf Autobahnen und Straßen :
in Meilen - in Kilometern

Transport

Bahnlinie - Bahnhof

Autotransport
(rotes Zeichen : saisonbedingte Verbindung)
mit dem Fährschiff - mit dem Luftkissenboot
15 mit der Fähre (Höchstbelastung in t)

Flughafen - Flugplatz

Ortschaften

Ort mit Stadtplan
im Michelin - Führern
Im Roten Michelin-Hotelführer
Im Grünen Michelin-Reiseführer

Verklaring van de tekens

Zie binnenkant kaft voor volledige verklaring van de tekens

Wegen

CHIEVELEY Autosnelweg - Service plaatsen
(geen tol op autosnelwegen)

Verkeerswisselaars/Aansluitingen : volledig - gedeeltelijk

❶ ❷ ❸ Nummers knooppunten

Gescheiden rijbanen van het type autosnelweg

Hoofdverbindingsweg :
met gescheiden rijbanen
met 4 rijstroken - met 2 brede rijstroken
met 2 rijstroken - met 2 smalle rijstroken

Secundaire verbindingswegen :
met gescheiden rijbanen - met 2 brede rijstroken
met 2 rijstroken - met 2 smalle rijstroken
Andere weg : verhard - onverhard

Autosnelweg, weg in aanleg
(indien van toepassing : vermoedelijke datum
van openstelling)

14 10 24 39 Afstanden op autosnelweg en wegen :
in mijlen - in kilometers

Vervoer

Spoorweg - Station

Vervoer van auto's
(dienst in het seizoen : rood teken)
per boot - per hovercraft
15 per veerpont (maximum draagvermogen in t.)

Luchthaven - Vliegveld

Plaatsen

Plaatsen met een plattegrond in de
Michelingidsen :
de Rode met Hotels en Restaurants
de Groene met toeristishe bezienswaardigheden

Legenda

Vedere la legenda completa all'interno della copertina

Strade

CHIEVELEY Autostrada - Area di servizio
(non si paga il pedaggio sull'autostrada)

Svincoli : completo, parziali

❶ ❷ ❸ Svincoli numerati

Doppia carreggiata di tipo autostradale

Strada principale :
a carreggiate separate
a 4 corsie - a 2 corsie larghe
a 2 corsie - a 2 corsie strette

Strada regionale :
a carreggiate separate
a 2 corsie o più - a 2 corsie strette
Altra strada : con rivestimento - senza rivestimento

Autostrada, strada in costruzione
(data di apertura prevista)

14 10 24 39 Distanze su autostrada e strada :
in miglia - in chilometri

Trasporti

Ferrovia - Stazione viaggiatori

Trasporto auto
(collegamenti stagionali : segno rosso)
per nave - per aliscafo
15 per chiatta (carico massimo in tonnellate)

Aeroporto - Aerodromo

Località

Località con pianta nelle
Guide Michelin
Rosse "Hotels e Ristoranti"
Verdi "Turistiche"

Signos convencionales

Para más información ver en el interior de la contraportada

Carreteras

CHIEVELEY Autopista - Áreas de servicio
(circulación gratuita en autopista)

Accesos : completo - parciales

❶ ❷ ❸ Números de los accesos

Autovía

Carretera general :
con calzadas separadas
con 4 carriles - con 2 carriles anchos
con 2 carriles - con 2 carriles estrechos

Carretera regional :
con calzadas separadas - con 2 carriles anchos
con 2 carriles - con 2 carriles estrechos
Otra carretera : asfaltada - sin asfaltar

Autopista, carretera en construcción
(en su caso : fecha prevista de entrada en servicio)

14 10 24 39 Distancias en autopista y en carretera :
en millas - en kilómetros

Transportes

Línea férrea - Estación de viajeros

Transporte de coches
(enlaces de temporada : signo rojo)
por barco - por overcraft
15 por barcaza (carga máxima en toneladas)

Aeropuerto - Aeródromo

Localidades

Localidad con plano en la Guía Michelin
Rojas "Hoteles y Restaurantes"
Verdes "Turistica"

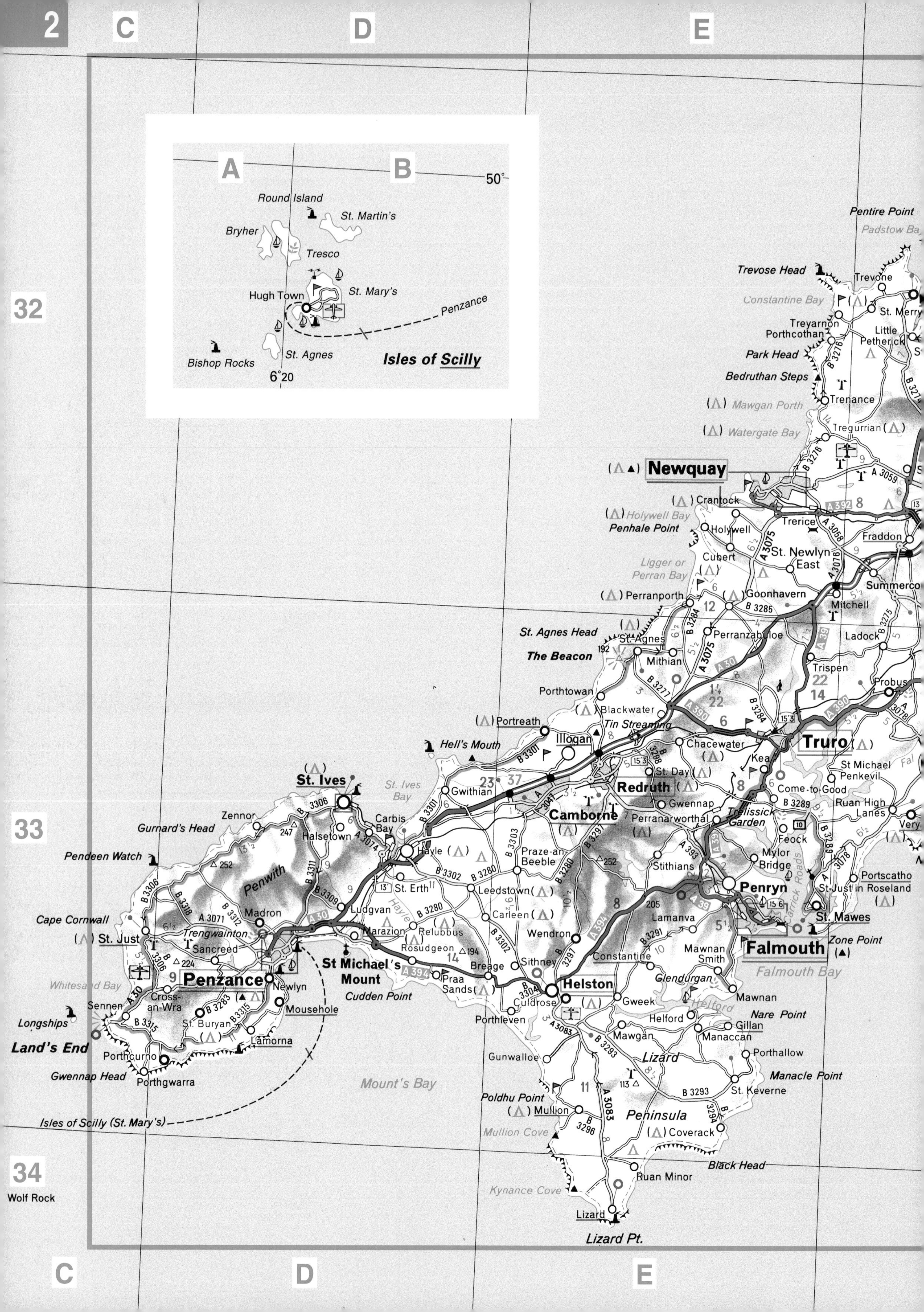
C
D
E
32
33
34
Wolf Rock
A
B
50°
Round Island
St. Martin's
Bryher
Tresco
St. Mary's
Hugh Town
Penzance
Bishop Rocks
St. Agnes
Isles of Scilly
6°20
Pentire Point
Padstow Ba
Trevose Head
Trevone
Constantine Bay
St. Merry
Treyarnon
Porthcothan
Little Petherick
Park Head
Bedruthan Steps
Trenance
Mawgan Porth
Watergate Bay
Tregurrian
Newquay
Crantock
Holywell Bay
Penhale Point
Holywell
Trerice
Fraddon
St. Newlyn East
Cubert
Ligger or Perran Bay
Perranporth
Goonhavern
Summerco
Mitchell
St. Agnes Head
St. Agnes
Perranzabuloe
Ladock
The Beacon
Mithian
Trispen
Porthtowan
Probus
Blackwater
Tin Streaming
Portreath
Illogan
Chacewater
Truro
Hell's Mouth
Kea
St Michael Penkevil
St. Ives
St. Ives Bay
St. Day
Redruth
Come-to-Good
Gwithian
Gwennap
Ruan High Lanes
Zennor
Carbis Bay
Camborne
Perranarworthal
Trelissick Garden
Feock
Gurnard's Head
Halsetown
Very
Hayle
Praze-an-Beeble
Stithians
Mylor Bridge
Pendeen Watch
Penwith
St. Erth
Portscatho
St. Just in Roseland
Leedstown
Penryn
Ludgvan
Cape Cornwall
Madron
Carleen
Lamanva
St. Mawes
St. Just
Trengwainton
Marazion
Relubbus
Wendron
Falmouth
Zone Point
Sancreed
Rosudgeon
Mawnan Smith
St Michael's Mount
Sithney
Constantine
Falmouth Bay
Breage
Whitesand Bay
Penzance
Newlyn
Praa Sands
Helston
Glendurgan
Cudden Point
Cross-an-Wra
Culdrose
Helford
Mawnan
Sennen
Mousehole
Porthleven
Gweek
Nare Point
Longships
St. Buryan
Helford
Gillan
Land's End
Lamorna
Mawgan
Manaccan
Porthcurno
Lizard
Porthallow
Gunwalloe
Gwennap Head
Porthgwarra
Mount's Bay
Manacle Point
St. Keverne
Poldhu Point
Mullion
Peninsula
Isles of Scilly (St. Mary's)
Mullion Cove
Coverack
Black Head
Ruan Minor
Kynance Cove
Lizard
Lizard Pt.

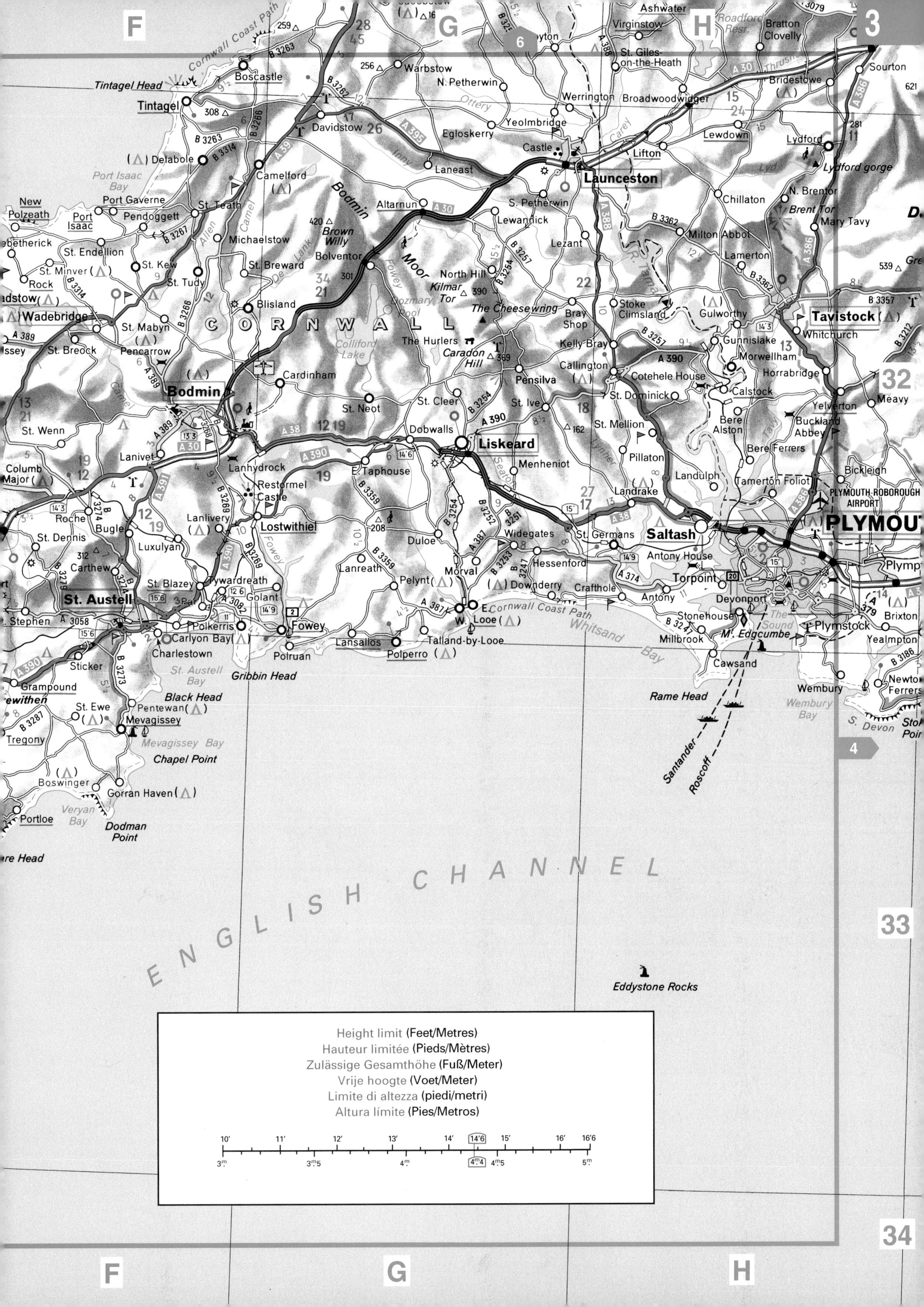

F
G
H
3
6
32
33
34
4
Cornwall Coast Path
Tintagel Head
Tintagel
Boscastle
Warbstow
N. Petherwin
Ashwater
Virginstow
St. Giles-on-the-Heath
Bratton Clovelly
Roadford Resr.
Sourton
Bridestowe
Broadwoodwidger
Werrington
Yeolmbridge
Egloskerry
Davidstow
Camelford
Delabole
Port Isaac Bay
Port Gaverne
New Polzeath
Port Isaac
Pendoggett
St. Teath
Michaelstow
St. Endellion
St. Minver
Rock
St. Kew
St. Tudy
St. Breward
Wadebridge
St. Mabyn
St. Breock
Pencarrow
Blisland
Bodmin Moor
Brown Willy
Altarnun
Bolventor
Laneast
Launceston
Castle
Lifton
Lewdown
Lydford
Lydford gorge
S. Petherwin
Lewannick
Lezant
Chillaton
N. Brentor
Brent Tor
Mary Tavy
Milton Abbot
Lamerton
Tavistock
Whitchurch
Gulworthy
Stoke Climsland
North Hill
Kilmar Tor
The Cheesewring
Bray Shop
Kelly Bray
Dozmary Pool
Colliford Lake
CORNWALL
The Hurlers
Caradon Hill
Pensilva
Callington
Gunnislake
Morwellham
Horrabridge
Cotehele House
Calstock
St. Dominick
Yelverton
Meavy
Buckland Abbey
Bere Alston
Bere Ferrers
Cardinham
Bodmin
St. Neot
St. Cleer
St. Ive
St. Mellion
Pillaton
Landulph
Tamerton Foliot
Bickleigh
PLYMOUTH-ROBOROUGH AIRPORT
PLYMOUTH
St. Wenn
Lanivet
Columb Major
Lanhydrock
Restormel Castle
Dobwalls
Liskeard
Menheniot
E. Taphouse
Roche
Bugle
St. Dennis
Luxulyan
Lanlivery
Lostwithiel
Duloe
Widegates
St. Germans
Landrake
Saltash
Carthew
St. Blazey
Tywardreath
Golant
Lanreath
Pelynt
Morval
Hessenford
Downderry
Crafthole
Antony House
Antony
Torpoint
Devonport
Stonehouse
Plymstock
Plymp
Brixton
Yealmpton
St. Austell
St. Stephen
Polkerris
Carlyon Bay
Charlestown
Fowey
Polruan
Lansallos
Polperro
Talland-by-Looe
E. Looe
W. Looe
Whitsand Bay
Millbrook
Mt. Edgcumbe
The Sound
Cawsand
Wembury
Wembury Bay
Newton Ferrers
S. Devon
Rame Head
Santander
Roscoff
Sticker
St. Austell Bay
Gribbin Head
Grampound
St. Ewe
Pentewan
Black Head
Mevagissey
Mevagissey Bay
Tregony
Chapel Point
Boswinger
Gorran Haven
Veryan Bay
Portloe
Dodman Point
ENGLISH CHANNEL
Eddystone Rocks
Height limit (Feet/Metres)
Hauteur limitée (Pieds/Mètres)
Zulässige Gesamthöhe (Fuß/Meter)
Vrije hoogte (Voet/Meter)
Limite di altezza (piedi/metri)
Altura límite (Pies/Metros)
10′ 11′ 12′ 13′ 14′ 14′6 15′ 16′ 16′6
3m 3m5 4m 4m4 4m5 5m

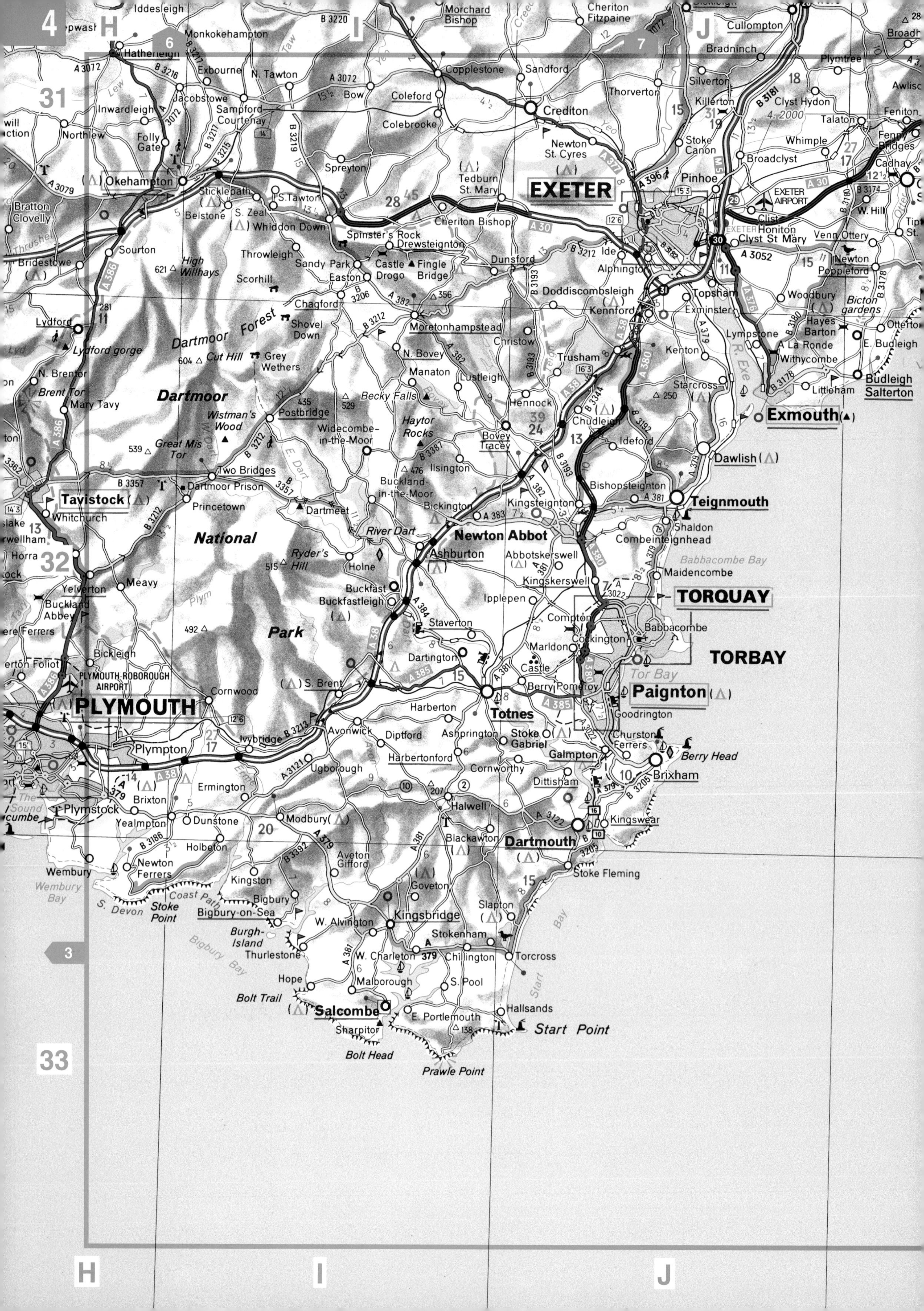
Hatherleigh
Monkokehampton
Iddesleigh
Morchard Bishop
Cheriton Fitzpaine
Cullompton
Bradninch
Exbourne
N. Tawton
Copplestone
Sandford
Plymtree
Jacobstowe
Inwardleigh
Sampford Courtenay
Bow
Coleford
Crediton
Thorverton
Silverton
Killerton
Clyst Hydon
Feniton
Talaton
Northlew
Folly Gate
Colebrooke
Newton St. Cyres
Stoke Canon
Whimple
Fenny Bridges
Broadclyst
Cadhay
Okehampton
Spreyton
Tedburn St. Mary
EXETER
Pinhoe
Honiton
EXETER AIRPORT
Bratton Clovelly
Sticklepath
Belstone
S. Zeal
S.Tawton
Whiddon Down
Cheriton Bishop
Clyst St Mary
Venn Ottery
W. Hill
Sourton
Spinster's Rock
Drewsteignton
Ide
Alphington
Newton Poppleford
Bridestowe
High Willhays
Throwleigh
Sandy Park
Castle Drogo
Fingle Bridge
Dunsford
Easton
Scorhill
Doddiscombsleigh
Topsham
Woodbury
Bicton gardens
Kennford
Exminster
Chagford
Shovel Down
Moretonhampstead
Christow
Lympstone
Hayes Barton
Otterton
Lydford
Lydford gorge
Dartmoor Forest
Cut Hill
Grey Wethers
N. Bovey
Trusham
Kenton
A La Ronde
E. Budleigh
Withycombe
N. Brentor
Brent Tor
Dartmoor
Manaton
Lustleigh
Starcross
Budleigh Salterton
Littleham
Mary Tavy
Postbridge
Becky Falls
Hennock
Exmouth
Wistman's Wood
Haytor Rocks
Widecombe-in-the-Moor
Bovey Tracey
Chudleigh
Ideford
Great Mis Tor
Dawlish
Ilsington
Two Bridges
Dartmoor Prison
Buckland-in-the-Moor
Bishopsteignton
Tavistock
Princetown
Dartmeet
Bickington
Kingsteignton
Teignmouth
Whitchurch
Shaldon
National
River Dart
Newton Abbot
Combeinteignhead
Ryder's Hill
Ashburton
Abbotskerswell
Babbacombe Bay
Maidencombe
Yelverton
Meavy
Holne
Kingskerswell
TORQUAY
Buckland Abbey
Buckfast
Buckfastleigh
Ipplepen
Compton
Babbacombe
Park
Staverton
Cockington
TORBAY
Bickleigh
Dartington
Marldon
Castle
Tor Bay
PLYMOUTH-ROBOROUGH AIRPORT
S. Brent
Berry Pomeroy
Paignton
PLYMOUTH
Cornwood
Harberton
Totnes
Goodrington
Avonwick
Diptford
Ashprington
Stoke Gabriel
Churston Ferrers
Plympton
Ivybridge
Harbertonford
Cornworthy
Galmpton
Berry Head
Brixham
Ugborough
Dittisham
Ermington
Brixton
Plymstock
Halwell
Kingswear
Yealmpton
Dunstone
Modbury
Blackawton
Dartmouth
Holbeton
Aveton Gifford
Wembury
Newton Ferrers
Stoke Fleming
Wembury Bay
Kingston
Goveton
Bigbury
Coast Path
S. Devon
Stoke Point
Slapton
Bigbury-on-Sea
Kingsbridge
W. Alvington
Stokenham
Burgh Island
Thurlestone
Bigbury Bay
W. Charleton
Chillington
Torcross
Hope
Malborough
S. Pool
Bolt Trail
Salcombe
E. Portlemouth
Hallsands
Sharpitor
Start Point
Bolt Head
Prawle Point
H
I
J
31
32
33

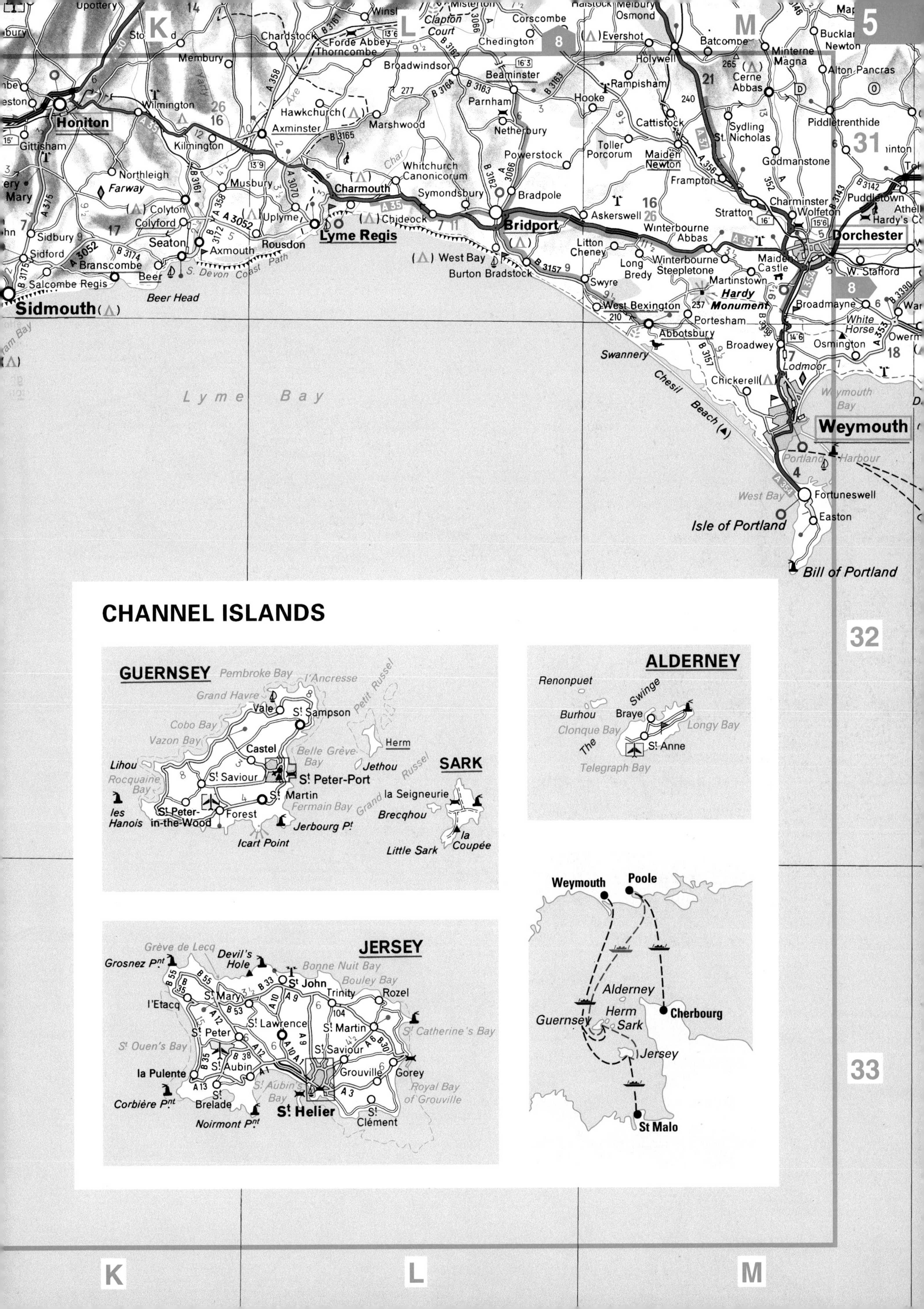
K
L
M
5
Honiton
Sidmouth
Axminster
Seaton
Beer
Beer Head
Branscombe
Salcombe Regis
Sidford
Sidbury
Colyton
Colyford
Axmouth
Rousdon
Uplyme
Lyme Regis
Charmouth
Chideock
Bridport
West Bay
Burton Bradstock
Beaminster
Broadwindsor
Thorncombe
Forde Abbey
Chardstock
Membury
Wilmington
Kilmington
Gittisham
Northleigh
Farway
Musbury
Hawkchurch
Marshwood
Whitchurch Canonicorum
Symondsbury
Bradpole
Netherbury
Parnham
Powerstock
Corscombe
Chedington
Evershot
Hooke
Rampisham
Cattistock
Toller Porcorum
Maiden Newton
Frampton
Askerswell
Litton Cheney
Long Bredy
Winterbourne Abbas
Winterbourne Steepleton
Martinstown
Hardy Monument
Swyre
West Bexington
Abbotsbury
Portesham
Swannery
Chesil Beach
Chickerell
Broadwey
Weymouth
Weymouth Bay
Portland Harbour
West Bay
Fortuneswell
Easton
Isle of Portland
Bill of Portland
Dorchester
Maiden Castle
Charminster
Wolfeton
Stratton
Cerne Abbas
Minterne Magna
Sydling St. Nicholas
Godmanstone
Piddletrenthide
Alton Pancras
Puddletown
Hardy's Cottage
W. Stafford
Broadmayne
White Horse
Osmington
Lodmoor
Batcombe
Holywell
Osmond
Lyme Bay
S. Devon Coast Path
CHANNEL ISLANDS
GUERNSEY
Pembroke Bay
L'Ancresse
Grand Havre
Vale
St Sampson
Cobo Bay
Vazon Bay
Castel
Lihou
Rocquaine Bay
St Saviour
St Peter-Port
St Martin
les Hanois
St Peter-in-the-Wood
Forest
Fermain Bay
Jerbourg Pt
Icart Point
Petit Russel
Belle Grève Bay
Herm
Jethou
Grand Russel
SARK
la Seigneurie
Brecqhou
Little Sark
la Coupée
ALDERNEY
Renonpuet
Swinge
Burhou
Braye
Clonque Bay
Longy Bay
The
St Anne
Telegraph Bay
JERSEY
Grève de Lecq
Grosnez Pnt
Devil's Hole
Bonne Nuit Bay
Bouley Bay
St John
St Mary
Trinity
Rozel
l'Etacq
St Lawrence
St Martin
St Catherine's Bay
St Peter
St Ouen's Bay
St Saviour
St Aubin
la Pulente
Grouville
Gorey
Royal Bay of Grouville
St Aubin's Bay
Corbière Pnt
St Brelade
Noirmont Pnt
St Helier
St Clément
Weymouth
Poole
Alderney
Herm
Guernsey
Sark
Cherbourg
Jersey
St Malo
31
32
33

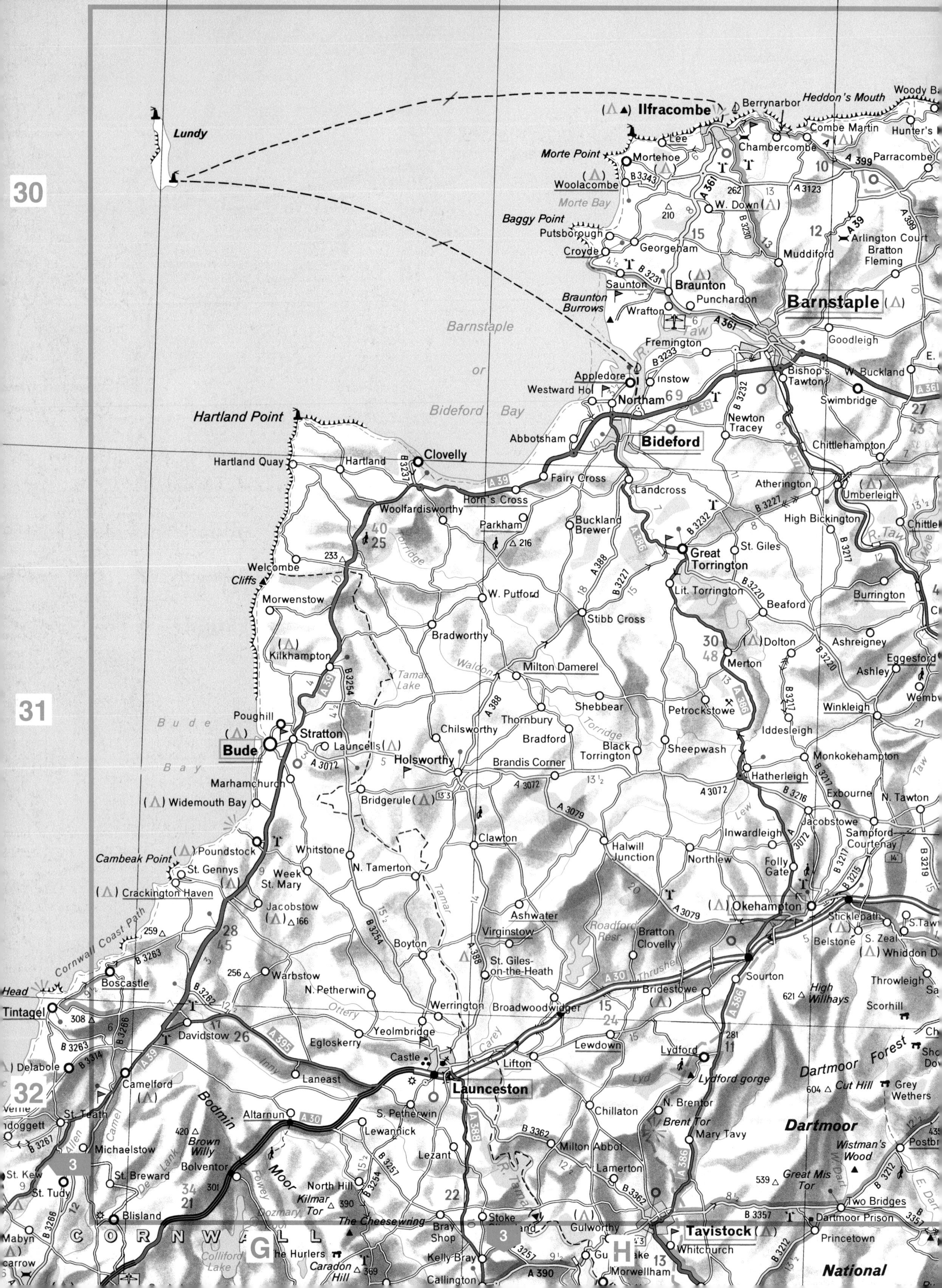
Lundy
Ilfracombe
Berrynarbor
Heddon's Mouth
Woody Bay
Combe Martin
Hunter's Inn
Lee
Chambercombe
Parracombe
Morte Point
Mortehoe
Woolacombe
Morte Bay
W. Down
Baggy Point
Putsborough
Croyde
Georgeham
Muddiford
Arlington Court
Bratton Fleming
Saunton
Braunton
Braunton Burrows
Wrafton
Puncharden
Barnstaple
Goodleigh
Fremington
Barnstaple or Bideford Bay
Appledore
Instow
Bishop's Tawton
W. Buckland
Westward Ho!
Northam
Swimbridge
Hartland Point
Newton Tracey
Abbotsham
Bideford
Chittlehampton
Hartland Quay
Hartland
Clovelly
Fairy Cross
Landcross
Atherington
Umberleigh
Horn's Cross
Woolfardisworthy
Parkham
Buckland Brewer
High Bickington
Great Torrington
St. Giles
Welcombe
Cliffs
Lit. Torrington
Beaford
Burrington
Morwenstow
W. Putford
Stibb Cross
Bradworthy
Dolton
Ashreigney
Kilkhampton
Merton
Eggesford
Ashley
Milton Damerel
Tamar Lake
Shebbear
Winkleigh
Poughill
Bude Bay
Thornbury
Petrockstowe
Iddesleigh
Stratton
Launcells
Chilsworthy
Bradford
Bude
Black Torrington
Sheepwash
Holsworthy
Brandis Corner
Monkokehampton
Marhamchurch
Hatherleigh
Widemouth Bay
Bridgerule
Exbourne
N. Tawton
Jacobstowe
Sampford Courtenay
Inwardleigh
Poundstock
Whitstone
Clawton
Halwill Junction
Northlew
Folly Gate
Cambeak Point
St. Gennys
Week St. Mary
N. Tamerton
Crackington Haven
Jacobstow
Okehampton
Sticklepath
Ashwater
Roadford Resr.
Belstone
S. Zeal
Whiddon Down
Cornwall Coast Path
Virginstow
Bratton Clovelly
St. Giles-on-the-Heath
Boyton
Boscastle
Warbstow
Sourton
Bridestowe
Throwleigh
Tintagel
N. Petherwin
High Willhays
Scorhill
Werrington
Broadwoodwidger
Davidstow
Yeolmbridge
Egloskerry
Lewdown
Lydford
Delabole
Castle
Lifton
Laneast
Lydford gorge
Dartmoor Forest
Camelford
Launceston
Cut Hill
Grey Wethers
Bodmin Moor
Altarnun
S. Petherwin
Chillaton
N. Brentor
Brent Tor
Mary Tavy
Dartmoor
St. Teath
Lewannick
Milton Abbot
Michaelstow
Brown Willy
Lezant
Wistman's Wood
Bolventor
Lamerton
St. Kew
St. Breward
Great Mis Tor
St. Tudy
North Hill
Kilmar Tor
Two Bridges
Blisland
Dozmary Pool
Stoke Climsland
Dartmoor Prison
The Cheesewring
Bray Shop
Gulworthy
Tavistock
Princetown
Mabyn
The Hurlers
Kelly Bray
Whitchurch
Colliford Lake
Caradon Hill
Morwellham
Callington
National
CORNWALL
R. Taw
R. Tamar
Torridge
Waldon
Tamar
Ottery
Inny
Carey
Lyd
Thrushel
Lew
Camel
Allen
De Lank
Fowey
W. Dart
E. Dart
Mole
A 39
A 361
A 399
A 377
A 386
A 388
A 3072
A 3079
A 30
A 395
A 390
B 3343
B 3231
B 3230
B 3233
B 3232
B 3227
B 3237
B 3217
B 3220
B 3211
B 3216
B 3215
B 3219
B 3254
B 3263
B 3262
B 3266
B 3314
B 3267
B 3257
B 3362
B 3357
B 3212
B 3351
B 3123
A 3123
216
233
210
262
259
256
308
420
301
390
369
281
621
604
539
166
G
H
30
31
32

7
I
J
K
16
Foreland Point
Lynton
Lynmouth
Valley of the Rocks
Somerset and N. Devon Coast Path
Watersmeet
Culbone
Oare
Porlock Weir
Porlock
Allerford
Selworthy
Minehead
Bridgwater Bay
Berrow Flats
Berrow
Brent Knoll
Burnham-on-Sea
Stert Flats
Highbridge
Steart
Huntspill
R. Parrett
Doone Valley
Exmoor Forest
Exmoor National Park
Challacombe
Simonsbath
Exford
Luccombe
Wootton Courtenay
Dunkery Beacon
Dunster
Carhampton
Timberscombe
Watchet
Washford
Cleeve Abbey
Williton
Bilbrook
W. Quantoxhead
Kilve
Stogursey
Stockland Bristol
Holford
Combwich
Nether Stowey
Cannington
Wheddon Cross
Luxborough
Monksilver
Stogumber
Combe Sydenham
Crowcombe
Quantock Hills
Spaxton
Wembdon
Barford
Brayford
Withypool
Winsford
Brendon Hills
Exton
Brompton Regis
Brompton Ralph
Lydeard St Lawrence
W. Bagborough
N. Petherton
Tarr Steps
Barle
Hawkridge
Dane's Brook
Gaulden
Combe Florey
Bishops Lydeard
Broomfield
Kingston St. Mary
Monkton
Cheddon Fitzpaine
SOMERSET
N. Molton
Molland
Dulverton
Upton
Skilgate
Huish Champflower
Wiveliscombe
Halse
Taunton Deane
South Molton
Brushford
Exebridge
Morebath
Milverton
Norton Fitzwarren
TAUNTON
Creech St Michael
Ash Mill
Bishop's Nympton
Alswear
Shillingford
Langford Budville
Bradford
Trull
Stoke St. Mary
Bampton
Oakford
Wellington
W. Buckland
Poundisford Park
Hatch
Meshaw
Holcombe Rogus
Pitminster
Staple Fitzpaine
King's Nympton
Rackenford
Knightshayes Court
Sampford Peverell
Wellington Mon.
Blackdown Hills
Ashill
Little Dart
Witheridge
Bolham
Culmstock
Buckland St. Mary
Horton
Thelbridge
Tiverton
Halberton
Uffculme
Hemyock
Churchingford
Chawleigh
Willand
Combe St. Nicholas
DEVON
Lapford
Kentisbeare
Dunkeswell
Upottery
Yarcombe
Bickleigh
Cheriton Fitzpaine
Morchard Bishop
Cullompton
Broadhembury
Stockland
Chardstock
Bradninch
Plymtree
Membury
Copplestone
Sandford
Silverton
Awliscombe
Weston
Honiton
Wilmington
Thorverton
Killerton
Clyst Hydon
Talaton
Feniton
Axminster
Bow
Coleford
Crediton
Colebrooke
Newton St. Cyres
Stoke Canon
Whimple
Fenny Bridges
Gittisham
Kilmington
Spreyton
Tedburn St. Mary
EXETER
Pinhoe
Broadclyst
Cadhay
Ottery St. Mary
Northleigh
Farway
Musbury
Exeter Airport
Clyst Honiton
W. Hill
Colyton
Colyford
Uplyme
Cheriton Bishop
Spinster's Rock
Drewsteignton
Castle Drogo
Fingle Bridge
Clyst St Mary
Venn Ottery
Tipton St. John
Sidbury
Seaton
Axmouth
Rousdon
Dunsford
Ide
Alphington
Newton Poppleford
Sidford
Branscombe
Beer
S. Devon Coast Path
Easton
Doddiscombsleigh
Topsham
Woodbury
Salcombe Regis
Beer Head
Kennford
Exminster
Bicton gardens
Sidmouth
Moretonhampstead
Christow
Lympstone
Hayes Barton
Otterton
Ladram Bay
N. Bovey
Trusham
Kenton
A La Ronde
E. Budleigh
Manaton
Lustleigh
Withycombe
Becky Falls
Hennock
Starcross
Littleham
Budleigh Salterton
Haytor Rocks
Chudleigh
Exmouth
Widecombe-in-the-Moor
Bovey Tracey
Ideford
Dawlish
Ilsington
Buckland-in-the-Moor
Bishopsteignton
Bickington
Kingsteignton
Teignmouth
Shaldon
River Dart
Newton Abbot
Combeinteignhead
31
32
8
5
4

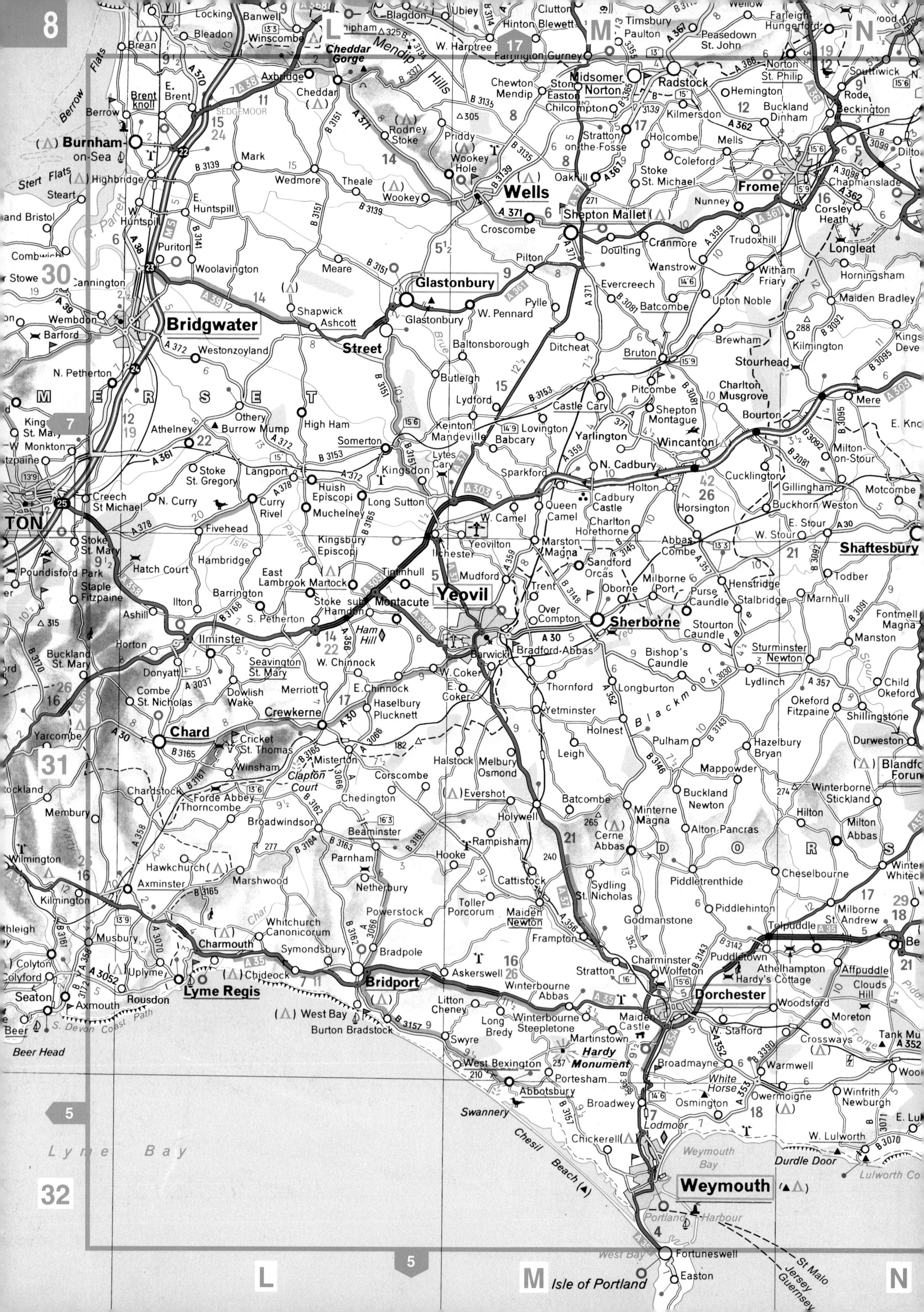

Locking
Banwell
Blagdon
Ubley
Clutton
Timsbury
Farleigh Hungerford
Bleadon
Winscombe
Hinton Blewett
Paulton
Peasedown St. John
Brean
Cheddar Gorge
Mendip
W. Harptree
Farrington Gurney
Midsomer Norton
Radstock
Norton St. Philip
Southwick
Berrow Flats
Axbridge
Chewton Mendip
Ston Easton
Hemington
Rode
Brent Knoll
E. Brent
Cheddar
Hills
Chilcompton
Kilmersdon
Buckland Dinham
Beckington
Berrow
SEDGEMOOR
Rodney Stoke
Priddy
Stratton on-the-Fosse
Holcombe
Mells
Burnham-on-Sea
Wookey Hole
Coleford
Dilton
Stert Flats
Highbridge
Mark
Wedmore
Theale
Stoke St. Michael
Wells
Oakhill
Frome
Chapmanslade
Steart
Wookey
Nunney
Corsley Heath
E. Huntspill
Shepton Mallet
and Bristol
W. Huntspill
R. Parrett
Croscombe
Cranmore
Trudoxhill
Combwich
Puriton
Doulting
Longleat
Woolavington
Meare
Pilton
Wanstrow
Witham Friary
Horningsham
Stowe
Cannington
Glastonbury
Evercreech
Upton Noble
Maiden Bradley
Wembdon
Bridgwater
Shapwick
Ashcott
W. Pennard
Pylle
Batcombe
Barford
Street
Brue
Baltonsborough
Ditcheat
Brewham
Kilmington
Kings Deve
Westonzoyland
Bruton
Stourhead
N. Petherton
Butleigh
Charlton Musgrove
Mere
M E R S E T
Pitcombe
Lydford
Castle Cary
Shepton Montague
Bourton
Othery
Burrow Mump
Athelney
High Ham
Keinton Mandeville
Lovington
Babcary
Yarlington
Wincanton
E. Knoyle
King St. Mary
W. Monkton
Somerton
Lytes Cary
Milton-on-Stour
Stoke St. Gregory
Langport
Kingsdon
Sparkford
N. Cadbury
Cucklington
Huish Episcopi
Holton
Gillingham
Motcombe
Creech St Michael
N. Curry
Curry Rivel
Long Sutton
Cadbury Castle
Horsington
Buckhorn Weston
TON
Muchelney
Queen Camel
W. Camel
Charlton Horethorne
E. Stour
Fivehead
W. Stour
Stoke St. Mary
Isle
Kingsbury Episcopi
Ilchester
Yeovilton
Marston Magna
Abbas Combe
Shaftesbury
Hatch Court
Hambridge
Parrett
Sandford Orcas
Poundisford Park
Staple Fitzpaine
East Lambrook
Martock
Tintinhull
Mudford
Yeovil
Trent
Milborne Port
Henstridge
Todber
Ashill
Ilton
Barrington
Stoke sub Hamdon
Montacute
Oborne
Purse Caundle
Stalbridge
Marnhull
S. Petherton
Over Compton
Sherborne
Fontmell Magna
Horton
Ilminster
Ham Hill
Barwick
Bradford Abbas
Stourton Caundle
Manston
Buckland St. Mary
Seavington St. Mary
W. Chinnock
Bishop's Caundle
Sturminster Newton
Donyatt
W. Coker
E. Coker
Lydlinch
Child Okeford
Combe St. Nicholas
Dowlish Wake
Merriott
E. Chinnock
Thornford
Longburton
Okeford Fitzpaine
Crewkerne
Haselbury Plucknett
Yetminster
Blackmoor
Vale
Shillingstone
Yarcombe
Chard
Cricket St. Thomas
Holnest
Pulham
Hazelbury Bryan
Durweston
Winsham
Misterton
Leigh
Halstock
Melbury Osmond
Blandford Forum
Clapton Court
Corscombe
Mappowder
Chardstock
Forde Abbey
Thorncombe
Evershot
Batcombe
Buckland Newton
Winterborne Stickland
Membury
Chedington
Holywell
Minterne Magna
Hilton
Broadwindsor
Beaminster
Cerne Abbas
Alton Pancras
Milton Abbas
Wilmington
Rampisham
Hawkchurch
Parnham
Hooke
Piddletrenthide
Axminster
Marshwood
Netherbury
Cattistock
Sydling St. Nicholas
Cheselbourne
Kilmington
Powerstock
Toller Porcorum
Maiden Newton
Piddlehinton
Milborne St. Andrew
Whitchurch Canonicorum
Godmanstone
Musbury
Char
Frampton
Tolpuddle
Charmouth
Symondsbury
Bradpole
Colyton
Uplyme
Chideock
Askerswell
Stratton
Charminster
Wolfeton
Puddletown
Athelhampton
Affpuddle
Lyme Regis
Bridport
Winterborne Abbas
Hardy's Cottage
Clouds Hill
Seaton
Axmouth
Rousdon
Dorchester
Woodsford
Litton Cheney
Winterbourne Steepleton
Maiden Castle
Moreton
Beer
S. Devon Coast Path
West Bay
Burton Bradstock
Long Bredy
W. Stafford
Swyre
Martinstown
Crossways
Tank Mu
Beer Head
Hardy Monument
Warmwell
West Bexington
Portesham
Broadmayne
Frome
Abbotsbury
White Horse
Owermoigne
Winfrith Newburgh
Swannery
Broadwey
Osmington
Lodmoor
E. Lu
Chesil
Chickerell
W. Lulworth
Weymouth Bay
Durdle Door
Lulworth Co
Lyme Bay
Beach
Weymouth
Portland Harbour
West Bay
Fortuneswell
St Malo
Jersey
Guernsey
Easton
Isle of Portland
L
M
N

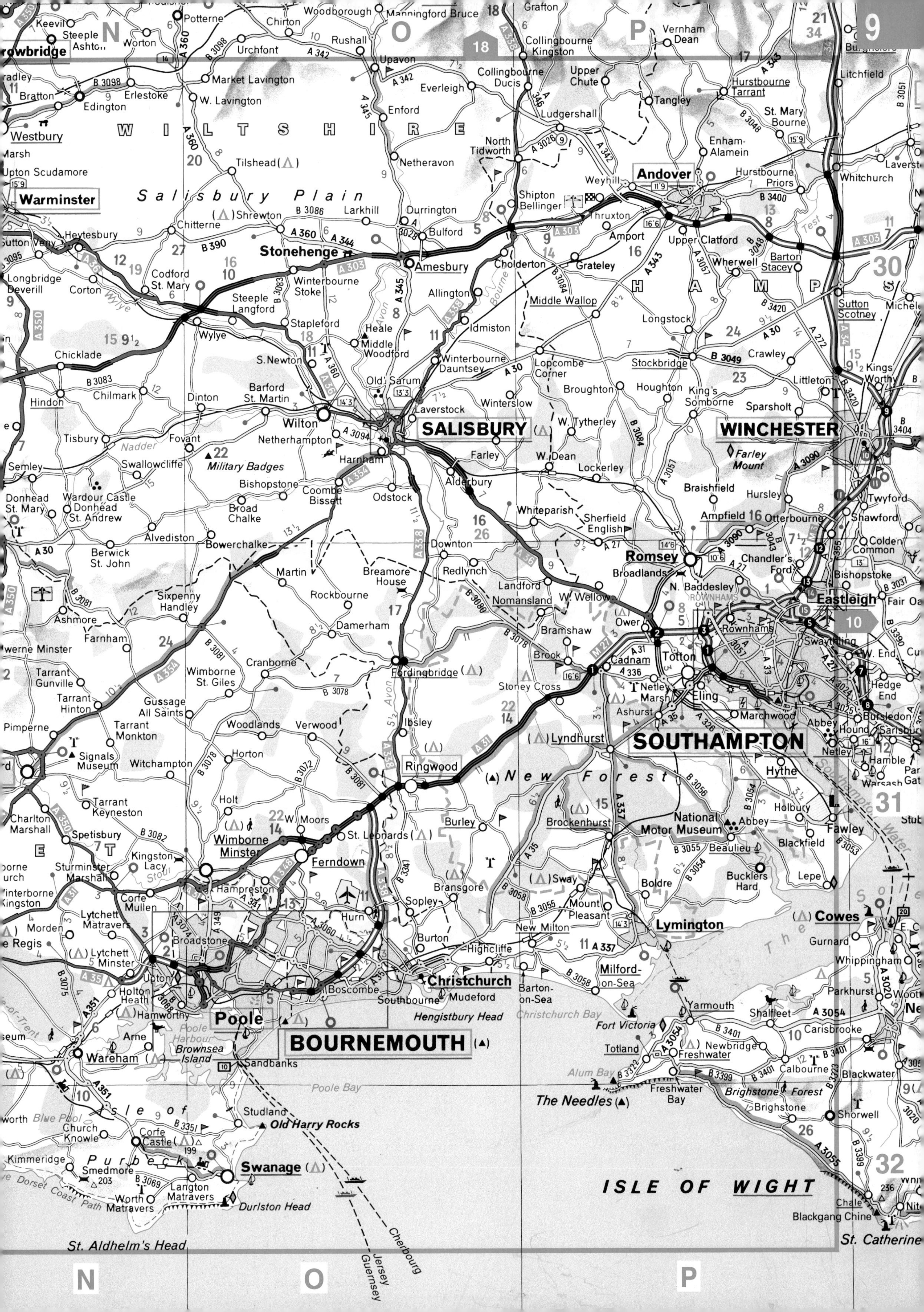

9
18
N
O
P
WILTSHIRE
Salisbury Plain
Trowbridge
Keevil
Steeple Ashton
Worton
Potterne
Chirton
Woodborough
Manningford Bruce
Grafton
Collingbourne Kingston
Vernham Dean
Urchfont
Rushall
Upavon
Market Lavington
Bratton
Edington
Erlestoke
W. Lavington
Everleigh
Collingbourne Ducis
Upper Chute
Hurstbourne Tarrant
Litchfield
Tangley
Ludgershall
St. Mary Bourne
Westbury
Enford
North Tidworth
Enham-Alamein
Netheravon
Tilshead
Andover
Hurstbourne Priors
Whitchurch
Laverstoke
Upton Scudamore
Warminster
Weyhill
Shipton Bellinger
Thruxton
Shrewton
Larkhill
Durrington
Bulford
Amport
Upper Clatford
Chitterne
Heytesbury
Sutton Veny
Stonehenge
Amesbury
Cholderton
Grateley
Wherwell
Barton Stacey
Longbridge Deverill
Codford St. Mary
Corton
Winterbourne Stoke
Steeple Langford
Allington
Middle Wallop
Longstock
Sutton Scotney
Micheldever
Stapleford
Wylye
Heale
Middle Woodford
Idmiston
Chicklade
S. Newton
Winterbourne Dauntsey
Lopcombe Corner
Stockbridge
Crawley
Kings Worthy
Littleton
Hindon
Chilmark
Barford St. Martin
Dinton
Old Sarum
Broughton
Houghton
King's Somborne
Sparsholt
Wilton
Laverstock
Winterslow
W. Tytherley
SALISBURY
WINCHESTER
Tisbury
Nadder
Fovant
Netherhampton
Harnham
Farley
W. Dean
Farley Mount
Semley
Swallowcliffe
Military Badges
Lockerley
Alderbury
Braishfield
Hursley
Twyford
Donhead St. Mary
Wardour Castle
Donhead St. Andrew
Bishopstone
Coombe Bissett
Broad Chalke
Odstock
Whiteparish
Sherfield English
Ampfield
Otterbourne
Shawford
Alvediston
Berwick St. John
Bowerchalke
Downton
Romsey
Colden Common
Chandler's Ford
Broadlands
Bishopstoke
Martin
Breamore House
Redlynch
Landford
Nomansland
N. Baddesley
Rownhams
Eastleigh
Fair Oak
Sixpenny Handley
Ashmore
Rockbourne
W. Wellow
Ower
Farnham
Damerham
Bramshaw
Rownhams
Swaythling
Iwerne Minster
Cranborne
Brook
Cadnam
Totton
W. End
Tarrant Gunville
Wimborne St. Giles
Fordingbridge
Stoney Cross
Netley Marsh
Eling
Hedge End
Tarrant Hinton
Gussage All Saints
Ashurst
Marchwood
Bursledon
Pimperne
Tarrant Monkton
Woodlands
Verwood
Ibsley
Lyndhurst
SOUTHAMPTON
Abbey
Hound
Sarisbury
Netley
Hamble
Signals Museum
Witchampton
Horton
Ringwood
New Forest
Hythe
Warsash
Tarrant Keynestone
Holt
Burley
Brockenhurst
National Motor Museum
Holbury
Charlton Marshall
Spetisbury
W. Moors
Fawley
Wimborne Minster
St. Leonards
Beaulieu
Blackfield
Sturminster Marshall
Kingston Lacy
Stour
Ferndown
Bransgore
Bucklers Hard
Lepe
Hampreston
Boldre
Sway
Corfe Mullen
Lytchett Matravers
Hurn
Sopley
Mount Pleasant
Cowes
Morden
Broadstone
Burton
New Milton
Lymington
Gurnard
Bere Regis
Lytchett Minster
Highcliffe
Whippingham
Upton
Christchurch
Barton-on-Sea
Milford-on-Sea
Holton Heath
Boscombe
Southbourne
Mudeford
Parkhurst
Hamworthy
Poole
Hengistbury Head
Christchurch Bay
Yarmouth
Shalfleet
Poole Harbour
Fort Victoria
Arne
Brownsea Island
BOURNEMOUTH
Totland
Newbridge
Carisbrooke
Wareham
Sandbanks
Freshwater
Calbourne
Blackwater
Alum Bay
Poole Bay
Freshwater Bay
The Needles
Brighstone Forest
Blue Pool
Isle of Purbeck
Studland
Old Harry Rocks
Brighstone
Shorwell
Church Knowle
Corfe Castle
Kimmeridge
Smedmore
Swanage
Dorset Coast Path
Langton Matravers
Worth Matravers
Durlston Head
ISLE OF WIGHT
Chale
Blackgang Chine
St. Catherine's
St. Aldhelm's Head
Cherbourg
Jersey
Guernsey
The Solent
Southampton Water
10
30
31
32

Kingsclere
Old Burghclere
Pamber End
Sherfield on Loddon
Sherborne St. John
Mattingley
Hartley Wintney
Hawley
Frimley
Bisley
Knaphill
Horsell
Woking
Deepcut
Mayford
Ripley
Litchfield
Basingstoke
Basing
Hook
Fleet
Winchfield
Mytchett
Pirbright
Farnborough
Worplesdon
Church Crookham
Crookham Village
N. Warnborough
Odiham
Aldershot
Upper Hale
Ash
Tongham
Normandy
Stoughton
Onslow Village
Burpham
Clandon
Guildford
Shalford
St. Mary Bourne
Oakley
Overton
Laverstoke
Whitchurch
Hurstbourne Priors
N. Waltham
Upton Grey
Herriard
S. Warnborough
Crondall
Farnham
Seale
Compton
Wonersh
Barton Stacey
Preston Candover
Bentley
Birdworld
Frensham
Elstead
Bramley
Godalming
Milford
Witley
Hambledon
Holybourne
Alton
Binsted
Bentworth
Sutton Scotney
Micheldever
Medstead
Kingsley
Bordon
Churt
Devil's Punch Bowl
Hindhead
Grayshott
Headley
Whitehill
Dunsfold
Chiddingfold
Grayswood
Haslemere
Alfold
Crawley
Kings Worthy
Littleton
Old Alresford
New Alresford
Four Marks
Selborne
Ropley
E. Tisted
Greatham
Shottermill
Liphook
Linchmere
Plaistow
Northchapel
Harestock
Winchester
Cheriton
Bramdean
Liss
Rake
Milland
Fernhurst
Kirdford
Lurgashall
Wisborough Green
Twyford
Shawford
Otterbourne
W. Meon
Warnford
Steep
Langrish
Rogate
Easebourne
Lodsworth
Tillington
Petworth
Owslebury
Colden Common
Marwell Zoological Park
East Meon
Petersfield
Stedham
Midhurst
Cowdray House
Bishopstoke
Eastleigh
Lower Upham
Fair Oak
Droxford
Corhampton
Meonstoke
Elsted
Harting
Queen Elizabeth
Fittleworth
Bishop's Waltham
Clanfield
Cocking
Heyshott
Duncton
Swaythling
W. End
Curdridge
Shedfield
Hambledon
South Downs
Roman Villa
Bignor
Bury
Compton
Chilgrove
Singleton
Charlton
Hedge End
Botley
Wickham
Denmead
Cowplain
Forest of Bere
Waterlooville
Rowland's Castle
Stoughton
Lavant
Goodwood House
Earetham
Slindon
Bursledon
Abbey
Hound
Netley
Sarisbury
Fareham
Southwick
Widley
Purbrook
Havant
Funtington
Hamble
Warsash
Park Gate
Titchfield
Portchester
Castle
Cosham
Westbourne
Emsworth
Fontwell
Arundel
Southbourne
Bosham
W. Thorney
Fishbourne
Tangmere
Eastergate
Aldingbourne
Yapton
Chichester
Ford
Climping
Littlehampton
Hythe
Holbury
Fawley
Blackfield
Lepe
Stubbington
Bridgemary
Lee on-the-Solent
Portsmouth Harbour
Langstone Harbour
Chichester Harbour
Birdham
N. Mundham
Middleton-on-Sea
Hayling Island
S. Hayling
W. Wittering
Sidlesham
Felpham
Bognor Regis
Aldwick
Pagham
E. Wittering
Gosport
Southsea
PORTSMOUTH
Cowes
E. Cowes
Osborne House
Gurnard
Whippingham
Fishbourne
Quarr
Spithead
Ryde
Seaview
Selsey
Selsey Bill
Parkhurst
Wootton Bridge
Havenstreet
Newport
St. Helens
Shalfleet
Carisbrooke
Robin Hill
Bembridge
Brading
Foreland
Calbourne
Arreton
Alverstone
Blackwater
Forest
Newchurch
Brighstone
Sandown
Shorwell
Godshill
Shanklin
le Havre
Caen
Wroxall
Whitwell
Bonchurch
Chale
Niton
Ventnor
Blackgang Chine
St Lawrence
St. Catherine's Point
St. Malo
Cherbourg
The Solent
Southampton Water
Q
R
30
31
32

11
20
30
31
32
12
S
T
U
SURREY
SUSSEX
EAST SUSSEX
WEST SUSSEX
Cobham
Leatherhead
Ockham
Wisley
Ashtead
Tadworth
Banstead
Chipstead
Kingswood
Woldingham
Caterham
Sevenoaks
Ightham
Borough Green
W. Malling
Wateringbury
Mereworth
Fetcham
Great Bookham
East Horsley
Polesden Lacey
Box Hill
Redhill
Godstone
Oxted
Limpsfield
Westerham
Sundridge
Chartwell
Knole
Ightham Mote
Shipbourne
Crockham Hill
Four Elms
Hildenborough
Hadlow
E. Peckham
R. Medway
Tonbridge
Paddock Wood
Dorking
Reigate
Gomshall
Westcott
Shere
Sutton
Abinger Common
Leith Hill
North Holmwood
Leigh
Salfords
South Nutfield
Blindley Heath
Horley
Smallfield
Edenbridge
Chiddingstone
Penshurst
Hever
Smart's Hill
Speldhurst
Southborough
Brenchley
Pembury
Lingfield
Dormans Land
Newdigate
Charlwood
Capel
Ockley
Ewhurst
Cranleigh
Gatwick Airport
Crawley
Copthorne
Felbridge
East Grinstead
Crawley Down
Turners Hill
Groombridge
Royal Tunbridge Wells
Lamberhurst
Scotney
Rusper
Rudgwick
Warnham
Horsham
Broadbridge Heath
St. Leonard's Forest
Wakehurst Place
Standen
W. Hoathly
Forest Row
Hartfield
Eridge Green
Frant
Wadhurst
Bewl Water
Mannings Heath
Balcombe
Handcross
Nymans
Wych Cross
Chelwood Gate
Ashdown Forest
Crowborough
Rotherfield
Ticehurst
Itchingfield
Lr. Beeding
Ardingly
Horsted Keynes
Nutley
Danehill
Mayfield
Burwash
Billingshurst
Southwater
Cuckfield
Lindfield
Fletching
Maresfield
Buxted
Sheffield Park
Uckfield
Heathfield
Coolham
Cowfold
Bolney
Haywards Heath
Newick
Blackboys
Framfield
Waldron
Brightling
Dallington
W. Grinstead
Burgess Hill
Wivelsfield
Chailey
Ditchling Common
Pulborough
W. Chiltington
Dial Post
Partridge Green
Thakeham
Ashington
Albourne
Hurstpierpoint
Keymer
Barcombe Cross
Halland
E. Hoathly
Horam
Rushlake Green
Storrington
Henfield
Hassocks
Ditchling
Westmeston
Clayton
Plumpton
Chiddingly
Hellingly
Herstmonceux
Boreham Street
Washington
Steyning
Small Dole
Pyecombe
Ditchling Beacon
Lewes
Ringmer
Laughton
Glyndebourne
Upr. Dicker
Amberstone
Wartling
Upr. Beeding
Fulking
Poynings
Stanmer Park
Castle
South Downs Way
Findon
Shoreham
Southwick
Falmer
Beddingham
Glynde
Ripe
Selmeston
Michelham Priory
Hailsham
Westham
Rodmell
Firle
Pevensey
Angmering
Sompting
Lancing
Portslade
Hove
BRIGHTON
Woodingdean
Rottingdean
Wilmington
Polegate
Willingdon
Preston
Rustington
Littlehampton
WORTHING
Peacehaven
Alfriston
S. Heighton
The Long Man
Jevington
Charleston Manor
Langney Point
Newhaven
Seaford
Eastdean
Seven Sisters
Birling Gap
Beachy Head
EASTBOURNE
Dieppe
SOUTH DOWNS
M 25
M 26
M 23
A 25
A 22
A 23
A 24
A 26
A 27
A 29
A 264
A 272
A 275
A 281
A 283
A 259
A 267
A 21

12
U
V
W
20
21
29
30
31
11
Erith
Dartford Tunnel
Grays Thurrock
Tilbury
Cliffe
St. Mary's Hoo
Isle of Grain
Grain
Sheerness
Dartford
Swanscombe
Northfleet
Gravesend
High Halstow
Stoke
Wallend
Minster
Warden Point
Leysdown-on-Sea
Eastchurch
Isle of Sheppey
Higham
Shorne
Hoo St. Werburgh
Rochester
Queenborough
Wilmington
Darenth
Istead Rise
Cobham
Swanley
Longfield
Hartley
Cuxton
Brompton
Gillingham
Upchurch
Iwade
Lower Halstow
The Swale
Farningham
Meopham
Luddesdown
Chatham
Rainham
Newington
Sittingbourne
Orpington
Eynsford
Ash
Halling
Wigmore
Walderslade
West Kingsdown
Burham
Oare
Faversham
Bapchild
Teynham
Snodland
Otford
Kemsing
Wrotham
New Hythe
Aylesford
Boxley
Detling
Thurnham
Bredgar
Boughton
Biggin Hill
Ightham
W. Malling
Larkfield
Bearsted
Doddington
Newnham
Sheldwich
Selling
Shottenden
Sevenoaks
Sundridge
Borough Green
E. Malling
Barming
Westerham
Knole
Mereworth
Wateringbury
MAIDSTONE
Hollingbourne
Lenham
Warren St.
Stalisfield
Chartwell
Ightham Mote
Shipbourne
W. Farleigh
Loose
Leeds
Harrietsham
Crockham Hill
Hadlow
Yalding
Coxheath
Sutton Valence
Ulcombe
Charing
Challock
Four Elms
Hildenborough
E. Peckham
R. Medway
N. Downs Way
Wye
Chiddingstone
Leigh
Tonbridge
Egerton
Pluckley
Kennington
Hever
Penshurst
Paddock Wood
Marden
Staplehurst
Headcorn
Hothfield
Brenchley
Smarden
Ashford
Smart's Hill
Speldhurst
Southborough
Pembury
Horsmonden
Bethersden
Kingsnorth
Royal Tunbridge Wells
Goudhurst
Frittenden
Biddenden
Shadoxhurst
High Halden
Groombridge
Lamberhurst
Sissinghurst
Tenterden
Woodchurch
Hartfield
Scotney
Bedgebury Pinetum
Cranbrook
Bilsington
Frant
Eridge Green
Wadhurst
Bewl Water
Iden Green
Benenden
Rolvenden
Hamstreet
Newchurch
Ashdown Forest
Crowborough
Hawkhurst
Small Hythe
Isle of Oxney
Romney Marsh
St. Mary in-the-Marsh
Rotherfield
Ticehurst
Sandhurst
Appledore
Ivychurch
Brenzett
Mayfield
Hurst Green
Bodiam Castle
Wittersham
Brookland
Burwash
Etchingham
Salehurst
Northiam
Beckley
Iden
New Romney
Buxted
Maresfield
Robertsbridge
Peasmarsh
Walland Marsh
Uckfield
Heathfield
Brightling
Lydd
Blackboys
Framfield
Broad Oak
Udimore
Rye
Camber
Waldron
Rushlake Green
Dallington
Sedlescombe
Brede
Horam
Whatlington
Icklesham
Winchelsea
Rye Bay
Halland
E. Hoathly
Battle
Westfield
Pett
Chiddingly
Herstmonceux
Boreham Street
Ninfield
Crowhurst
Guestling
Fairlight
Ringmer
Laughton
Hellingly
Upr. Dicker
Amberstone
Ripe
Wartling
Cooden Beach
Castle
Michelham Priory
Hailsham
St. Leonards
HASTINGS
Selmeston
W. Firle
South Downs Way
Westham
Bexhill
Polegate
Wilmington
Pevensey
Alfriston
The Long Man
Willingdon
S. Heighton
Jevington
Langney Point
Charleston Manor
Seaford
EASTBOURNE
Eastdean
Birling Gap
Seven Sisters
Beachy Head
Dieppe
KENT
SUSSEX
NORTH DOWNS
EAST SUSSEX
M 25
M 26
M 20
M 2
A 2
A 20
A 21
A 22
A 26
A 28
A 229
A 249
A 259
A 264
A 268
A 27

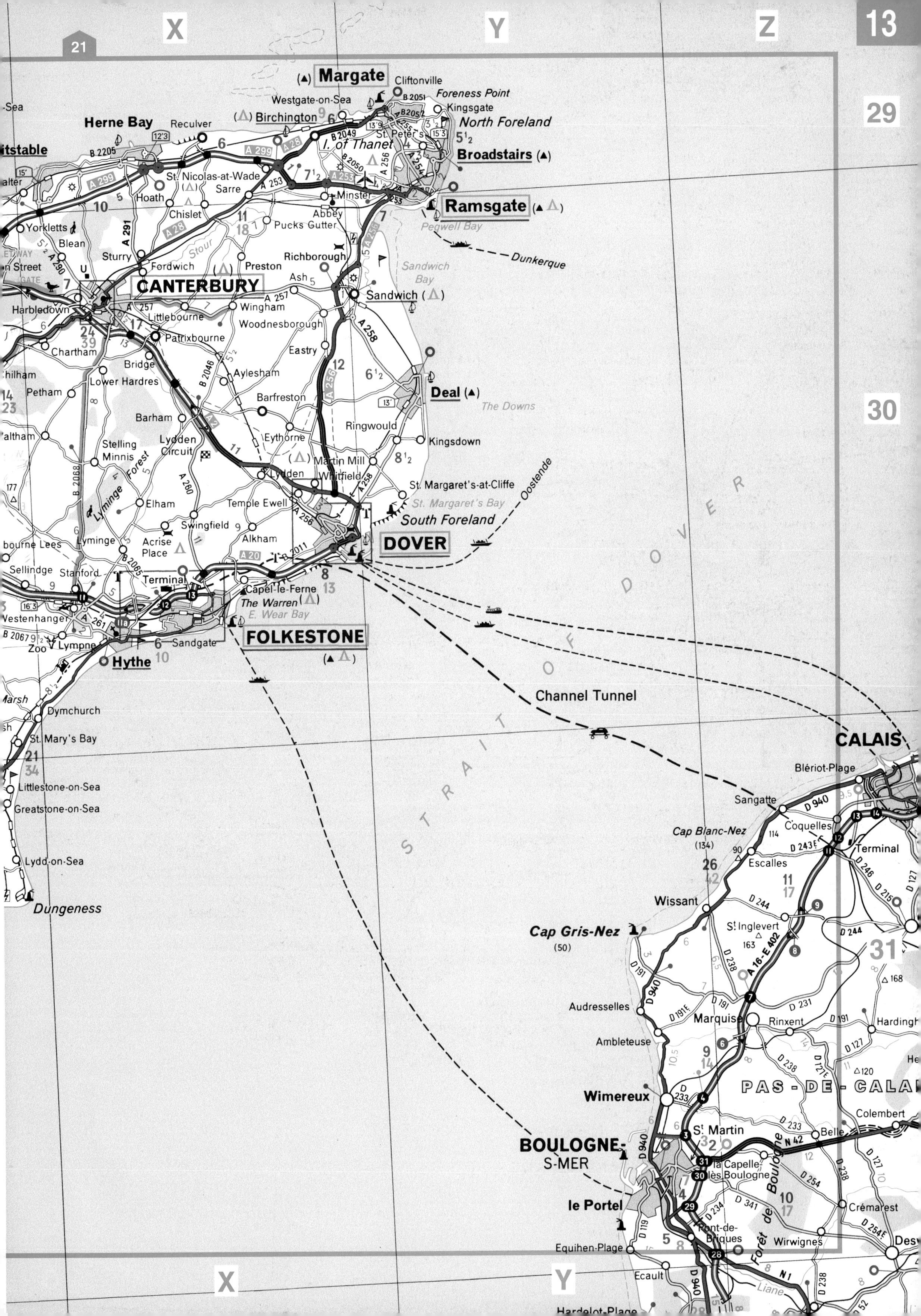
X
Y
Z
21
29
30
31
Margate
Cliftonville
Foreness Point
Westgate-on-Sea
Kingsgate
Birchington
North Foreland
Herne Bay
Reculver
I. of Thanet
St. Peter's
Broadstairs
Whitstable
St. Nicolas-at-Wade
Sarre
Minster
Ramsgate
Hoath
Chislet
Abbey
Pegwell Bay
Yorkletts
Pucks Gutter
Dunkerque
Blean
Stour
Richborough
Sturry
Fordwich
Preston
Sandwich Bay
Ash
CANTERBURY
Sandwich
Harbledown
Wingham
Littlebourne
Woodnesborough
Patrixbourne
Chartham
Eastry
Bridge
Aylesham
Chilham
Lower Hardres
Deal
Petham
Barfreston
The Downs
Barham
Ringwould
Eythorne
Waltham
Lydden Circuit
Kingsdown
Stelling Minnis
Martin Mill
Lyminge Forest
Lydden
Whitfield
St. Margaret's-at-Cliffe
Oostende
Elham
Temple Ewell
St. Margaret's Bay
South Foreland
Swingfield
Acrise Place
Alkham
DOVER
Lyminge
Brabourne Lees
Sellindge
Stanford
Terminal
Capel-le-Ferne
Westenhanger
The Warren
E. Wear Bay
FOLKESTONE
Zoo
Lympne
Sandgate
Hythe
Channel Tunnel
STRAIT OF DOVER
Marsh
Dymchurch
St. Mary's Bay
CALAIS
Littlestone-on-Sea
Blériot-Plage
Greatstone-on-Sea
Sangatte
Cap Blanc-Nez
Coquelles
Terminal
Lydd-on-Sea
Escalles
Dungeness
Wissant
St. Inglevert
Cap Gris-Nez
Audresselles
Marquise
Rinxent
Hardinghen
Ambleteuse
Wimereux
PAS-DE-CALAIS
St. Martin
Colembert
BOULOGNE-S-MER
Belle
la Capelle-lès-Boulogne
Forêt de Boulogne
le Portel
Crémarest
Pont-de-Briques
Wirwignes
Equihen-Plage
Desvres
Ecault
Liane
Hardelot-Plage
A 299
A 28
A 253
A 256
A 254
A 255
A 291
A 290
A 257
A 258
B 2046
B 2068
A 260
B 2065
A 20
B 2011
A 261
B 2067
B 2205
B 2049
B 2050
B 2051
B 2052
D 940
D 243E
D 246
D 215
D 127
D 244
D 238
A 16-E 402
D 191
D 191E
D 231
D 233
N 42
D 254
D 341
D 234
D 119
N 1
D 254E

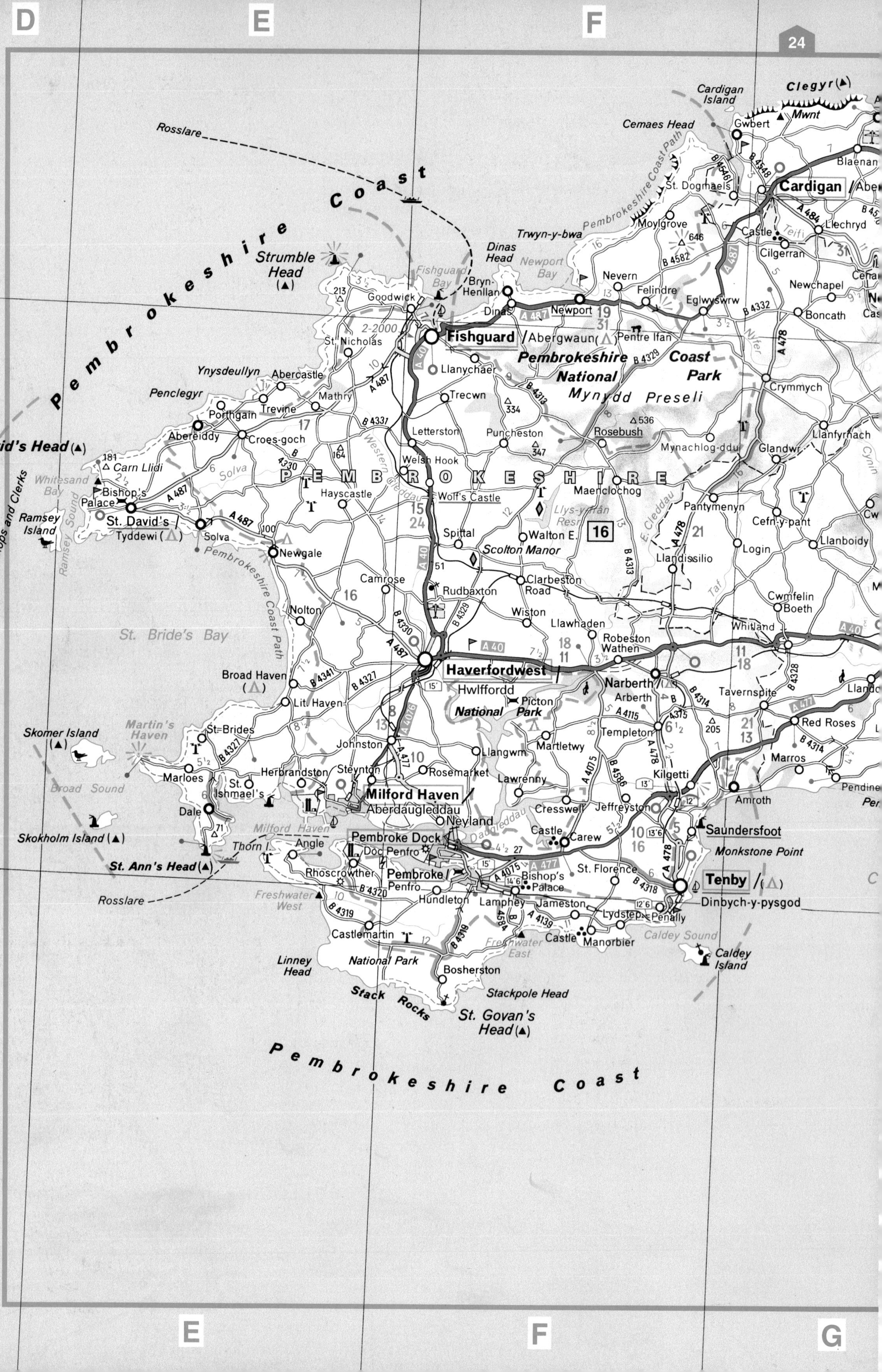

D
E
F
24
27
28
29
E
F
G
Rosslare
Pembrokeshire Coast
Strumble Head (▲)
Cardigan Island
Clegyr (▲)
Mwnt
Cemaes Head
Gwbert
Blaenan
Pembrokeshire Coast Path
St. Dogmaels
Cardigan
B 4546
B 4548
Moylgrove
646
Trwyn-y-bwa
Castle
Llechryd
Teifi
Cilgerran
A 484
Dinas Head
Newport Bay
Nevern
B 4582
Felindre
Newchapel
A 487
Fishguard Bay
Bryn-Henllan
Dinas
Newport
19
31
Eglwyswrw
B 4332
Boncath
213
Goodwick
2-2000
St. Nicholas
Fishguard
Abergwaun (Δ)
Pentre Ifan
Nyfer
A 478
Pembrokeshire National
Coast Park
Mynydd Preseli
Crymmych
Ynysdeullyn
Abercastle
Llanychaer
B 4313
B 4329
Penclegyr
Mathry
Trecwn
334
Porthgain
Trevine
A 40
St. David's Head (▲)
Abereiddy
17
Croes-goch
B 4331
Letterston
Puncheston
536
Rosebush
Mynachlog-ddu
Llanfyrnach
Glandwr
181
Carn Llidi
B 4330
164
347
Western Cleddau
Solva
PEMBROKESHIRE
Whitesand Bay
Bishop's Palace
A 487
Welsh Hook
Maenclochog
Pantymenyn
Cefn-y-pant
Bishops and Clerks
Ramsey Sound
Ramsey Island
St. David's
Tyddewi (Δ)
Solva
100
Hayscastle
Wolf's Castle
15
24
Llys-y-frân Resr.
E. Cleddau
Spittal
Walton E.
16
21
Login
Llanboidy
Newgale
Pembrokeshire Coast Path
Scolton Manor
B 4313
Llandissilio
51
Camrose
Clarbeston Road
Rudbaxton
Taf
16
Cwmfelin Boeth
Nolton
B 4329
Wiston
Llawhaden
B 4330
Whitland
St. Bride's Bay
18
11
Robeston Wathen
A 40
Haverfordwest
Hwlffordd
Broad Haven (Δ)
B 4341
B 4327
15'
Narberth
Arberth
11
18
B 4328
Tavernspite
Llanddo
Picton
National Park
B 4314
A 4115
B 4315
205
A 477
Red Roses
Skomer Island (▲)
Martin's Haven
St. Brides
Lit. Haven
Templeton
21
13
B 4314
Johnston
A 4076
A 477
10
Llangwm
Martletwy
Marros
B 4327
Marloes
Herbrandston
Steynton
Rosemarket
A 4075
B 4586
Lawrenny
Kilgetti
Broad Sound
St. Ishmael's
Milford Haven
Aberdaugleddau
Cresswell
Jeffreyston
Amroth
Pendine
Dale
71
Neyland
Daugleddau
Castle
Carew
Saundersfoot
Skokholm Island (▲)
Milford Haven
Pembroke Dock
Doc Penfro
Monkstone Point
Thorn I.
Angle
St. Ann's Head (▲)
15'
A 4075
27
10
16
A 478
Rosslare
Rhoscrowther
Pembroke
Penfro
Bishop's Palace
St. Florence
Tenby
(Δ)
Freshwater West
B 4320
Hundleton
Lamphey
Jameston
B 4318
Dinbych-y-pysgod
B 4319
B 4584
A 4139
Lydstep
Penally
Castlemartin
Castle
Manorbier
Caldey Sound
Freshwater East
Linney Head
National Park
B 4319
Caldey Island
Bosherston
Stack Rocks
Stackpole Head
St. Govan's Head (▲)
Pembrokeshire Coast

G
H
I
CEREDIGION
CARMARTHENSHIRE
NEATH PORT TALBOT
SWANSEA
Ynys-Lochtyn
Llangrannog
Llwyndafydd
Llanarth
Synod Inn
Mydroilyn
Ystrad Aeron
Bwlchllan
Llanddewi Brefi
Llangybi
Talgarreg
Brynhoffnant
Cribyn
Lampeter/ Llanbedr Pont Steffan
Bettws Evan
Rhydlewis
Ffostrasol
Cwrt-newydd
Llanwnen
Beulah
Penrhiwpal
Pontshaen
Rhydowen
Llanwenog
Farmers
Cwmcoy
Aber-Banc
Horeb
Llandysul
Llanybydder
Mynydd Pencarreg
Llanfihangel ar-Arth
Newcastle Emlyn/ Castell Newydd Emlyn
Drefach
Llangeler
Pumsaint
Dolaucothi Gold Mines
Rhydcymerau
Crug-y-bar
Cilycwn
Cynghordy
Moelfre
Cilrhedyn
Pencader
Gwyddgrug
Llansawel
Forest of Brechfa
Abergorlech
Talley
Llandovery
Llanymddyfri
Trelech
Cwmduad
Llanpumsaint
Brechfa
Llanwrda
Myddfai
Llangadog
Trelech a'r Betws
Cynwyl Elfed
Pontarsais
Llanfynydd
Twynllanan
Newchurch
Carmarthen/ Caerfyrddin
Abergwili
Nantgaredig
Pont-ar-Gothi
Llangathen
Rhosmaen
Llandeilo
Llangunnor
Llanarthney
Gelli Aur
Trapp
Castle
Black Mountain
Bancyfelin
St. Clears
Sanclêr
Llangynog
Llangain
Llanddarog
Porthyrhyd
Llangyndeyrn
Drefach
Castell-y-Rhingyll
Llandybie
Glanaman
Brynamman
Cwmllynfell
Llan-y-bri
Llansteffan
Laugharne
Castle
Cross Hands
Tumble
Ammanford/ Rhydaman
Gwaun-Cae-Gurwen
Ystradgynlais
Llandyfaelog
Pontyberem
Ferryside
Pontyates
Llan-non
Gurnos
Ystalyfera
Seven Sisters
Onllwyn
Kidwelly/ Cydweli
Trimsaran
Swansea Valley
Crynant
Glyn-neath
Pendine Sands
Pontarddulais
Pontardawe
Cilybebyll
Rhos
Vale of Neath
Burry Port/ Porth Tywyn
Hendy
Llangennech
Felindre
Clydach
Resolven
Blaengwrach
Carmarthen Bay
Pembrey
Llanelli
Gorseinon
Sgiwen
Tonna
Glyncorrwg
Whitford Point
Gowerton
Morriston
Neath / Castell-nedd
Penrhyn Gŵyr
Crofty
Penclawdd
Briton Ferry
Cymmer
Abergwynfi
Llanmadoc
Three Crosses
Cwmafan
Afan Argoed
Caerau
Burry Holms
Weobley
Llanrhidian
Killay
Nantyffyllon
Blaengarw
Llangenith
Arthur's Stone
Ilston
Cefn Bryn
Bishopston
SWANSEA/ ABERTAWE
Port Talbot
Maesteg
Gower
Rhossili Bay
Reynoldston
Taibach
Pontycymer
Llangynwyd
Rhossili
Penmaen
Oxwich
Nicholaston
Oxwich Bay
The Mumbles
Margam
Margam Park
Worms Head
Mumbles Head
Swansea Bay
Port-Eynon
Horton
Tondu
Port-Eynon-Point
Aberkenfig
Cork
Kenfig
Pyle
Laleston
Nottage
Tythegston
Porthcawl
Ogmore-by-Sea
Tusker Rock
St. Brides Major
Abergwesyn
Towy Forest
Pen y Gurnos
Llyn Brianne
Bryn Brawd
Cambrian Woollen Mill
Llanwrtyd Wells
Rhandirmwyn
Mynydd Mallaen
Tirabad
Crychan Forest
Mynydd Bwlch-y-Groes
Llywel
Trecastle
Usk Resr.
Glas Fynydd Forest
Crai
Fforest Fawr
Dan-yr-Ogof
Craig-y-nos
Abercraf
Ystradfellte
Pontneddfechan

Dolaucothi Gold Mines
Crug-y-bar
Cilycwn
Cynghordy
Crychan
Upper Chapel
Merthyr Cynog
Glasbury
Three Cocks
Llyswen
Bronllys
Talgarth
Rhos Dirion
Capel-y-ffin
Llandovery
Llanymddyfri
Mynydd Bwlch-y-Groes
Llanfihangel Nant Bran
Felinfach
Llanfilo
Talley
Llanwrda
Myddfai
Llywel
Brecon
Aberhonddu
Castell Dinas
Waun Fâch
Llangadog
Usk Resr.
Trecastle
Sennybridge
Llangorse
Llangorse Lake
Twynllanan
Glas Fynydd Forest
Crai
Llanfrynach
Rhosmaen
Llandeilo
Heol Senni
Brecon Beacons
Talybont-on-Usk
Bwlch
Tretower
Black Mountain
Brecon Beacons
Neuadd Resrs.
Talybont Resr.
Crickhowell
Trapp
Castle
Forest Fawr
Llangynidr
Llandybie
Dan-yr-Ogof
Craig-y-nos
National Park
Cwm Taf
Mynydd Llangynidr
Pontsticill Resr.
Gilwern
Glanaman
Brynamman
Ystradfellte
Trefil
Brynmawr
Ammanford
Rhydaman
Gwaun-Cae-Gurwen
Cwmllynfell
Abercraf
Garwnant Forestry Commission Visitor Centre
Pontsticill
Merthyr Tydfil
Beaufort
Nantyglo
Clydach Gorge
Gurnos
Ystradgynlais
Onllwyn
Penderyn
Cefn-Coed-y-cymmer
Tredegar
Ebbw Vale
Glyn Ebwy
Blaina
NEATH
Ystalyfera
Seven Sisters
Pontneddfechan
Glyn-neath
RHONDDA
Hirwaun
Rhymney
Rhymni
Abertillery
Swansea Valley
PORT TALBOT
Pontlottyn
New Tredegar
Cwm
SWANSEA
Pontardawe
Crynant
Vale of Neath
Blaengwrach
Rhigos
Aberdare
Aberdâr
Troedyrhiw
Felindre
Cilybebyll
Rhos
Resolven
CYNON
Cwmbach
Deri
Bedlinog
Llanhilleth
Clydach
Aberaman
Merthyr Vale
Bargoed
Oakdale
Sgiwen
Tonna
Glyncorrwg
Tynewydd
Cwmaman
Griffith
Morriston
Treherbert
Maerdy
Mountain Ash
Aberpennar
Treharris
Gelligaer
Blackwood
Newbridge
Neath
Castell-nedd
Cymmer
Abergwynfi
Treorchy
Rhondda
Abercynon
Hengoed
Abercarn
Briton Ferry
Afan Argoed
Caerau
Nant-y-moel
Tylorstown
Ynysybwl
Nelson
CAERPHILLY
Cwmcarn
Henllys
Cwmafan
Nantyffyllon
Blaengarw
Clydach Vale
Tonypandy
TAFF
Porth
Cilfynydd
Ynysddu
Crosskeys
Cymer Forest
Pontycymer
Ogmore Vale
Gilfach Goch
Llanbradach
Risca
SWANSEA
ABERTAWE
Port Talbot
Taibach
Maesteg
Fawr
Cymmer
Senghenydd
Bedwas
Machen
BRIDGEND
Tonyrefail
Rogerstone
Margam
Llangynwyd
Llangeinor
Pontypridd
Caerphilly
Caerffili
Mumbles Head
Swansea Bay
Margam Park
Beddau
Thornhill
Parc Cefn Onn
Tondu
Bryncethin
Llanharan
Aberkenfig
Pencoed
Llantrisant
Pentyrch
Tongwynlais
Lisvane
Kenfig
Pyle
Bridgend
Pen-y-bont
Pontyclun
Llanharry
Miskin
Llanishen
Laleston
Coychurch
Radyr
Whitchurch
St. Mellons
Nottage
Tythegston
Ystradowen
St. Fagans
Rumney
Porthcawl
Ewenny
Colwinston
VALE
St. Brides Super Ely
Pendoylan
St. Nicholas
Ely
CARDIFF
CAERDYDD
Ogmore-by-Sea
Llysworney
Cowbridge
Bont-faen
Bonvilston
Beaupre Castle
Dinas Powys
Tusker Rock
St. Brides Major
Llandow
OF
Wenvoe
Wick
GLAMORGAN
Eglwys Brewis
Penarth
Nash Point
St. Donats
Llantwit Major
St. Athan
Penmark
Sully
East Aberthaw
Rhoose
Porthkerry
Swanbridge
Barry
Barri
Breaksea Point
Flat Holm
Steep Holm
Weston-super
Foreland Point

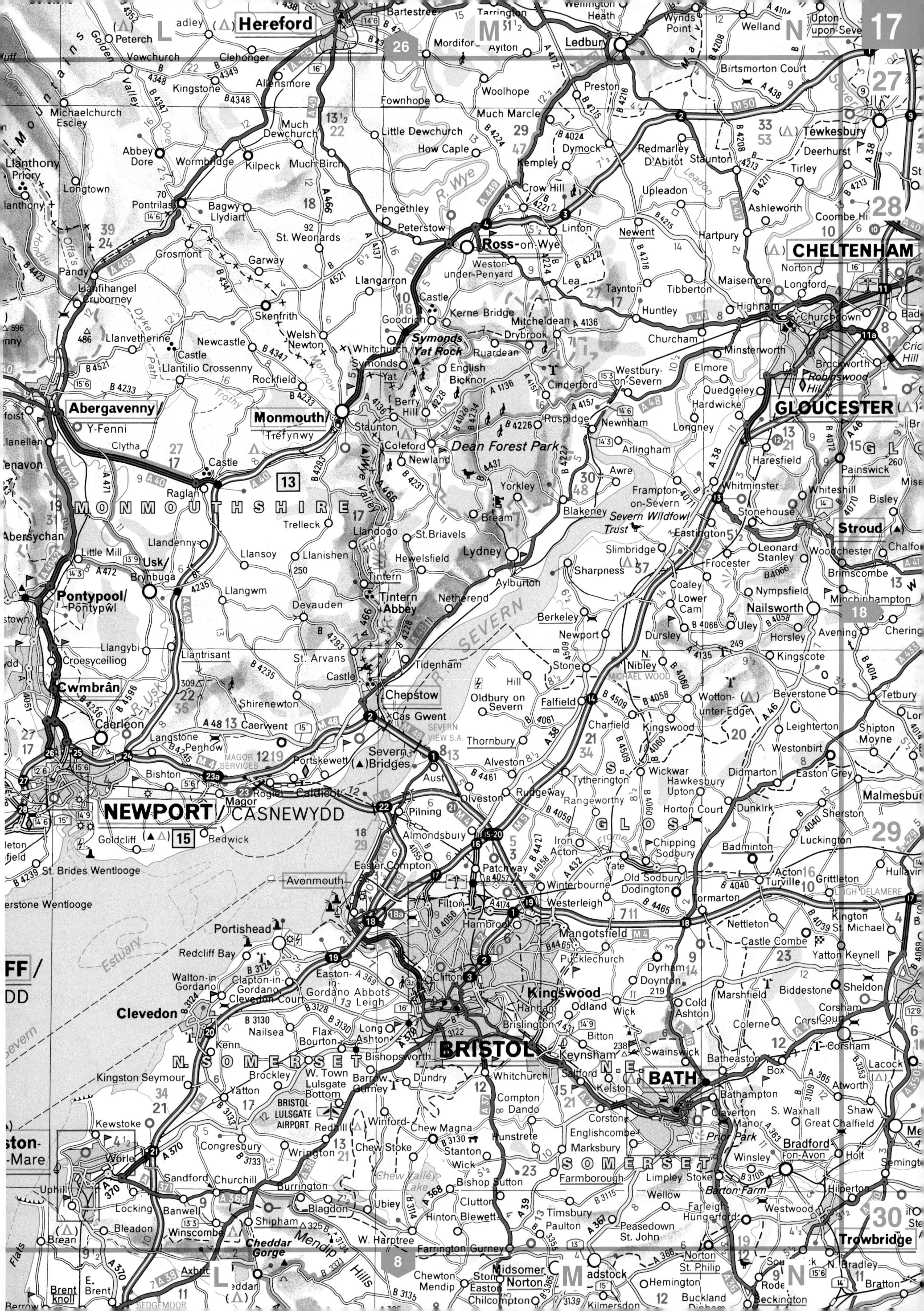

17
Hereford
Peterchurch
Vowchurch
Clehonger
Kingstone
Allensmore
Michaelchurch Escley
Abbey Dore
Wormbridge
Kilpeck
Much Dewchurch
Much Birch
Little Dewchurch
How Caple
Fownhope
Mordiford
Bartestree
Tarrington
Ledbury
Wellington Heath
Wynds Point
Welland
Upton-upon-Severn
Birtsmorton Court
Woolhope
Much Marcle
Preston
Dymock
Redmarley D'Abitot
Staunton
Tewkesbury
Deerhurst
Tirley
Kempley
Crow Hill
Upleadon
Ashleworth
Coombe Hill
Longtown
Llanthony Priory
Pontrilas
Bagwy Llydiart
St. Weonards
Pengethley
Peterstow
Ross-on-Wye
Linton
Newent
Hartpury
CHELTENHAM
Norton
Longford
Grosmont
Garway
Pandy
Llanfihangel Crucorney
Skenfrith
Llangarron
Weston-under-Penyard
Lea
Taynton
Tibberton
Maisemore
Goodrich
Castle
Kerne Bridge
Mitcheldean
Huntley
Highnam
Churchdown
Llanvetherine
Newcastle
Welsh Newton
Whitchurch
Symonds Yat Rock
Drybrook
Ruardean
Churcham
Minsterworth
Llantilio Crossenny
Rockfield
Symonds Yat
English Bicknor
Cinderford
Westbury-on-Severn
Elmore
Brockworth
Robinswood Hill
Abergavenny
Y-Fenni
Monmouth
Trefynwy
Staunton
Berry Hill
Coleford
Newland
Dean Forest Park
Ruspidge
Newnham
Quedgeley
Hardwicke
Longney
GLOUCESTER
Clytha
Castle
Raglan
Arlingham
Awre
Frampton-on-Severn
Haresfield
Painswick
MONMOUTHSHIRE
Yorkley
Bream
Blakeney
Severn Wildfowl Trust
Whitminster
Stonehouse
Whiteshill
Bisley
Llandenny
Trelleck
Llandogo
St. Briavels
Eastington
Stroud
Little Mill
Usk/Brynbuga
Llansoy
Llanishen
Hewelsfield
Lydney
Slimbridge
Frocester
Leonard Stanley
Woodchester
Pontypool/Pontypŵl
Llangwm
Devauden
Tintern
Tintern Abbey
Netherend
Aylburton
Sharpness
Coaley
Lower Cam
Nympsfield
Nailsworth
Minchinhampton
Brimscombe
Berkeley
Dursley
Uley
Horsley
Avening
Newport
Llangybi
Croesyceiliog
Llantrisant
St. Arvans
Tidenham
Stone
N. Nibley
Kingscote
Cwmbrân
Shirenewton
Hill
Chepstow
Oldbury on Severn
Falfield
Wotton-under-Edge
Beverstone
Tetbury
Caerleon
Caerwent
Cas Gwent
Charfield
Kingswood
Leighterton
Shipton Moyne
Langstone
Penhow
Thornbury
Westonbirt
Portskewett
Severn Bridges
Alveston
Tytherington
Wickwar
Hawkesbury Upton
Didmarton
Easton Grey
Bishton
Magor
Rogiet
Caldicot
Aust
Olveston
Rudgeway
Rangeworthy
Horton Court
Dunkirk
Sherston
Malmesbury
NEWPORT/CASNEWYDD
Pilning
Almondsbury
Iron Acton
Chipping Sodbury
Badminton
Luckington
Goldcliff
Redwick
Easter Compton
Patchway
Yate
Old Sodbury
Acton Turville
Grittleton
St. Brides Wentlooge
Avonmouth
Winterbourne
Dodington
Tormarton
Filton
Westerleigh
Nettleton
Kington St. Michael
Hambrook
Mangotsfield
Castle Combe
Yatton Keynell
Portishead
Redcliff Bay
Pucklechurch
Dyrham
Doynton
Biddestone
Sheldon
Walton-in-Gordano
Clapton-in-Gordano
Easton-in-Gordano
Gordano Abbots Leigh
Clifton
Kingswood
Marshfield
Corsham
Clevedon
Clevedon Court
Nailsea
Flax Bourton
Long Ashton
Bishopsworth
Hanham
Brislington
Wick
Cold Ashton
Colerne
Bitton
BRISTOL
Keynsham
Swainswick
Batheaston
Box
Lacock
Kenn
N. SOMERSET
Brockley
W. Town
Lulsgate Bottom
BRISTOL LULSGATE AIRPORT
Barrow Gurney
Dundry
Whitchurch
Saltford
Kelston
N.E. BATH
Bathampton
Atworth
Kingston Seymour
Yatton
Compton Dando
Corston
Claverton
S. Wraxall
Shaw
Great Chalfield
Kewstoke
Redhill
Winford
Chew Magna
Stanton Wick
Englishcombe
Marksbury
Prior Park
Bradford-on-Avon
Holt
Weston-super-Mare
Worle
Congresbury
Wrington
Chew Stoke
Hunstrete
SOMERSET
Farmborough
Winsley
Limpley Stoke
Uphill
Sandford
Churchill
Banwell
Burrington
Blagdon
Chew Valley Lake
Ubley
Bishop Sutton
Clutton
Hinton Blewett
Timsbury
Paulton
Wellow
Barton Farm
Farleigh Hungerford
Westwood
Hilperton
Locking
Bleadon
Winscombe
Shipham
Cheddar Gorge
Mendip Hills
W. Harptree
Farrington Gurney
Peasedown St. John
Trowbridge
Brean
Axbridge
Cheddar
Chewton Mendip
Midsomer Norton
Radstock
Norton St. Philip
Rode
N. Bradley
Bratton
Brent Knoll
E. Brent
Chilcompton
Kilmersdon
Hemington
Buckland Dinham
Beckington
SEDGEMOOR

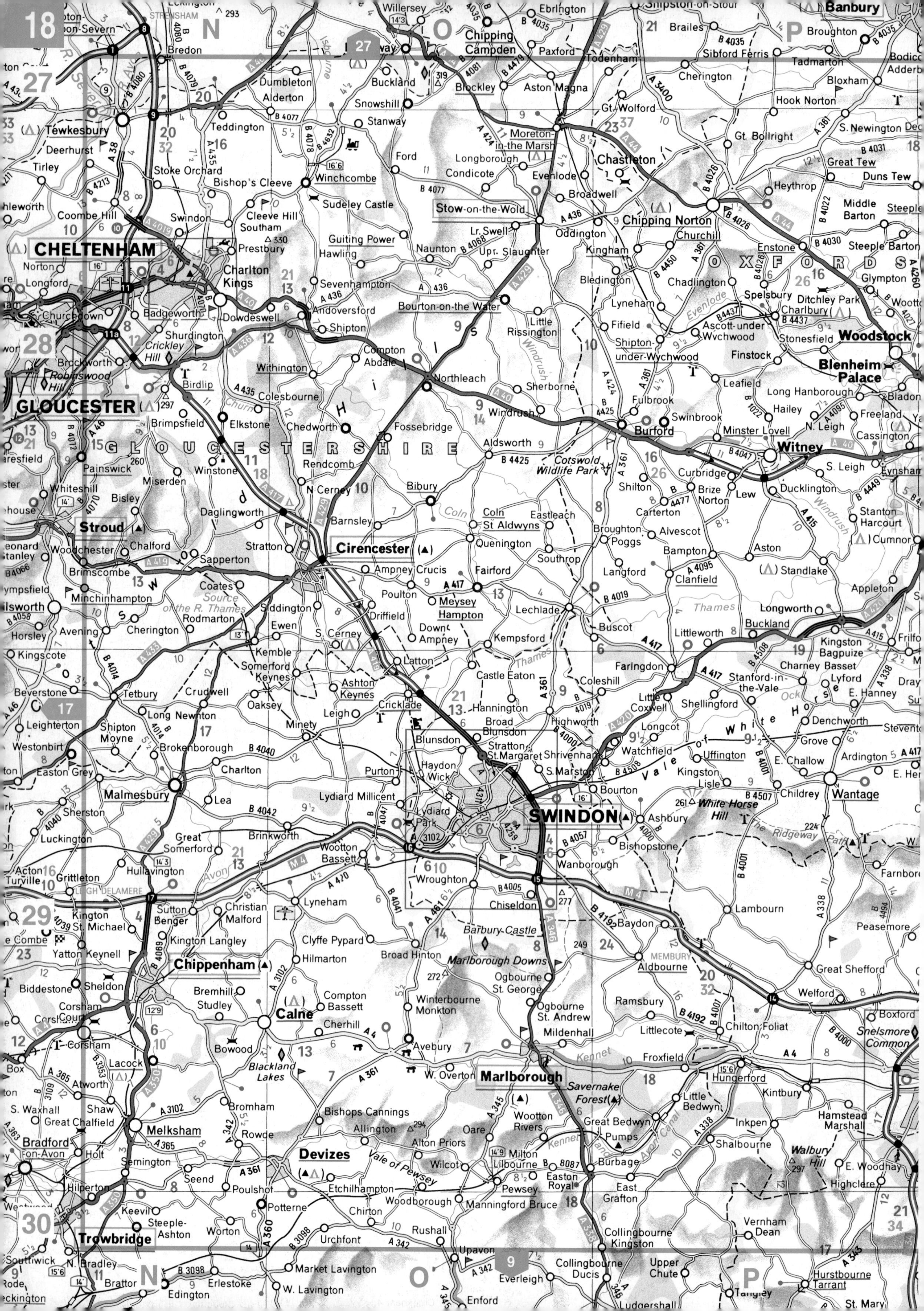
18
N
O
P
27
28
29
30
17
9
Willersey
Ebrington
Shipston-on-Stour
Banbury
Strensham
Bredon
Tewkesbury
Deerhurst
Tirley
Dumbleton
Alderton
Teddington
Buckland
Snowshill
Stanway
Chipping Campden
Paxford
Todenham
Brailes
Broughton
Sibford Ferris
Tadmarton
Cherington
Bloxham
Hook Norton
Blockley
Aston Magna
Gt. Wolford
Moreton-in-the-Marsh
Longborough
Condicote
Evenlode
Chastleton
Gt. Rollright
S. Newington
Great Tew
Duns Tew
Heythrop
Middle Barton
Steeple Barton
Enstone
Stoke Orchard
Bishop's Cleeve
Winchcombe
Ford
Sudeley Castle
Cleeve Hill
Southam
Prestbury
Swindon
Coombe Hill
CHELTENHAM
Norton
Longford
Churchdown
Charlton Kings
Badgeworth
Dowdeswell
Andoversford
Shurdington
Crickley Hill
Shipton
Brockworth
Robinswood Hill
GLOUCESTER
Birdlip
Brimpsfield
Elkstone
Colesbourne
Withington
Compton Abdale
Chedworth
Fossebridge
Northleach
Guiting Power
Hawling
Naunton
Sevenhampton
Stow-on-the-Wold
Lr. Swell
Upr. Slaughter
Bourton-on-the Water
Little Rissington
Broadwell
Oddington
Kingham
Bledington
Chipping Norton
Churchill
Chadlington
Lyneham
Fifield
Shipton-under-Wychwood
Ascott-under-Wychwood
Spelsbury
Charlbury
Ditchley Park
Glympton
Woodstock
Blenheim Palace
Stonesfield
Finstock
Leafield
Long Hanborough
Hailey
Freeland
N. Leigh
Cassington
Witney
Minster Lovell
Swinbrook
Fulbrook
Burford
Sherborne
Windrush
Aldsworth
Cotswold Wildlife Park
Shilton
Curbridge
Brize Norton
Lew
Ducklington
S. Leigh
Eynsham
Stanton Harcourt
Cumnor
Carterton
Alvescot
Broughton Poggs
Bampton
Aston
Standlake
Clanfield
Langford
Eastleach
Southrop
Coln St Aldwyns
Quenington
Bibury
Fairford
Lechlade
Buscot
Kempsford
Appleton
Longworth
Buckland
Littleworth
Kingston Bagpuize
Faringdon
Charney Basset
Lyford
E. Hanney
Stanford-in-the-Vale
Shellingford
Denchworth
Grove
Wantage
Ardington
Childrey
E. Challow
Uffington
Kingston Lisle
Longcot
Watchfield
Shrivenham
Little Coxwell
Coleshill
Highworth
Hannington
Castle Eaton
Broad Blunsdon
Blunsdon
Stratton St.Margaret
S.Marston
Bourton
SWINDON
Ashbury
White Horse Hill
Bishopstone
Wanborough
Lambourn
Farnborough
Peasemore
Great Shefford
Baydon
Aldbourne
Ramsbury
Welford
Boxford
Chilton Foliat
Littlecote
Froxfield
Hungerford
Kintbury
Snelsmore Common
Hamstead Marshall
Inkpen
Shalbourne
Walbury Hill
E. Woodhay
Highclere
Little Bedwyn
Great Bedwyn
Savernake Forest
Marlborough
Mildenhall
Ogbourne St. Andrew
Ogbourne St. George
Marlborough Downs
Barbury Castle
Chiseldon
Wroughton
Wootton Bassett
Lydiard Park
Lydiard Millicent
Purton
Haydon Wick
Cricklade
Latton
Ashton Keynes
Leigh
Minety
Oaksey
Somerford Keynes
Kemble
Ewen
Siddington
S. Cerney
Driffield
Down Ampney
Meysey Hampton
Poulton
Ampney Crucis
Cirencester
Barnsley
Stratton
N Cerney
Rendcomb
Daglingworth
Sapperton
Coates
Source of the R. Thames
Rodmarton
Cherington
Avening
Horsley
Nailsworth
Minchinhampton
Brimscombe
Chalford
Woodchester
Stroud
Bisley
Miserden
Winstone
Whiteshill
Painswick
GLOUCESTERSHIRE
COTSWOLD HILLS
OXFORDS
Kingscote
Beverstone
Tetbury
Crudwell
Long Newnton
Shipton Moyne
Leighterton
Westonbirt
Easton Grey
Brokenborough
Charlton
Malmesbury
Lea
Sherston
Luckington
Great Somerford
Brinkworth
Hullavington
Grittleton
Acton Turville
Leigh Delamere
Kington St. Michael
Sutton Benger
Christian Malford
Lyneham
Kington Langley
Yatton Keynell
Castle Combe
Biddestone
Sheldon
Chippenham
Corsham Court
Corsham
Box
Lacock
Atworth
S. Wraxhall
Shaw
Great Chalfield
Melksham
Bradford-on-Avon
Holt
Semington
Hilperton
Trowbridge
Keevil
Steeple Ashton
Southwick
N. Bradley
Brattor
Edington
Erlestoke
Seend
Poulshot
Worton
Potterne
Devizes
Rowde
Bromham
Bowood
Calne
Bremhill
Studley
Hilmarton
Compton Bassett
Cherhill
Clyffe Pypard
Broad Hinton
Winterbourne Monkton
Avebury
W. Overton
Blackland Lakes
Bishops Cannings
Allington
Alton Priors
Wilcot
Oare
Wootton Rivers
Milton Lilbourne
Pewsey
Easton Royal
Burbage
Pumps
East Grafton
Manningford Bruce
Woodborough
Etchilhampton
Chirton
Vale of Pewsey
Urchfont
Rushall
Upavon
Market Lavington
W. Lavington
Enford
Everleigh
Collingbourne Ducis
Collingbourne Kingston
Upper Chute
Tangley
Vernham Dean
Hurstbourne Tarrant
St. Mary
Ludgershall
Vale of White Horse
The Ridgeway Path
Windrush
Evenlode
Thames
Coln
Churn
Kennet
Kennet and Avon Canal
Ock
Avon
Isbourne
R. Severn
R. Avon
M 4
M 5
A 40
A 44
A 417
A 419
A 420
A 429
A 436
A 361
A 338
A 4
A 346
A 345
A 342
A 350
A 365
A 3102
A 424
A 4095
A 415
A 433
A 46
A 3400
MEMBURY

Brackley
Hatch
Stowe
School
Stony Stratford
Deanshanger
Wicken
Milton
Keynes
Conquest
Hough
Whitfield
Brackley
Buckingham
Maids
Moreton
Beachampton
Shenley
Church End
Aspley Guise
Ampthill
Steppingley
Flitton
King's Sutton
Aynho
Croughton
Finmere
Great Ouse
Whaddon
Bletchley
Woburn
Sands
Husborne
Crawley
Flitwick
Shillington
Thornborough
Tingewick
Woburn Abbey
Wild Animal
Kingdom
Barton-in-
the-Clay
Cottisford
Padbury
Gt.
Horwood
Newton
Longville
Gt. Brickhill
Stockgrove
Milton
Bryan
Harlington
Fritwell
Stoke Lyne
Mursley
Stoke
Hammond
Leighton
Buzzard
Toddington
Somerton
Fringford
Winslow
Ardley
Cherwell Valley
Steeple Claydon
Hockliffe
Upr. Heyford
Stratton Audley
Stewkley
Linslade
Stanbridge
Caversfield
Claydon House
Leagrave
Lr. Heyford
Middleton
Stoney
Marsh Gibbon
BUCKINGHAMSHIRE
Dunstable
Bicester
Launton
Grendon
Underwood
Wing
Ascott
House
Totternhoe
Tackley
Chesterton
Blackthorn
Eaton Bray
Kirtlington
Weston-
on-the-Green
Quainton
Whitchurch
Mentmore
Edlesborough
Caddington
Wendlebury
Ambrosden
Ludgershall
Wingrave
Cheddington
Whipsnade
Merton
Arncott
Waddesdon
Markyate
Bletchingdon
Ivinghoe
Charlton-
on-Otmoor
Bierton
Grand Union
Flamstead
Begbroke
Islip
Horton-
cum-Studley
Brill
Aylesbury
Kidlington
Oakley
Thame
Stone
Weston
Turville
Aston Clinton
Tring
Aldbury
Hartwell
Wolvercote
Marston
Stanton
St. John
Cuddington
Stoke Mandeville
Halton
Potten End
Hemel
Hempstead
Worminghall
Haddenham
Long
Crendon
Wendover
Northchurch
Berkhamsted
Owlswick
Headington
Wheatley
Tiddington
Cholesbury
OXFORD
Towersey
Kimble
N. Hinksey
Thame
Longwick
Ashley Green
Bourne
End
Great
Milton
Rycote
Princes
Risborough
Chartridge
Kennington
Garsington
Tetsworth
Sydenham
Chinnor
Great
Missenden
Chesham
Kings Langley
Abbots
Langley
Radley
Nuneham
Courtenay
Little
Milton
Saunderton
Prestwood
Speen
Stoke
Talmage
Lacey Green
Little
Missenden
Chesham
Bois
Little
Chalfont
Chenies
Abingdon
Chislehampton
Stadhampton
Easington
Aston Rowant
Penn
Street
Watford
Clifton
Hampden
Chalgrove
Lewknor
Stokenchurch
Hughenden
Holmer
Green
Amersham
Chorleywood
Croxley
Green
Drayton
St. Leonard
Cuxham
Watlington
W. Wycombe
Hazlemere
Rickmansworth
Appleford
Dorchester
Brittwell
Salome
Ibstone
High
Wycombe
Penn
Beaconsfield
Chalfont
St. Giles
Long
Wittenham
Shillingford
The Ridgeway Path
Fingest
Loudwater
Harefield
Didcot
Benson
Ewelme
Lane End
Chalfont
St. Peter
Brightwell
Wallingford
Pishill
Harwell
S. Moreton
Stonor
Flackwell
Heath
Gerrards Cross
Denham
E. Hagbourne
Crowmarsh
Gifford
Cholsey
Nettlebed
Fawley
Marlow
Bourne End
Wooburn
Aston
Tirrold
Nuffield
Hambleden
Cookham
Cliveden
House
Stoke Poges
Blewbury
Highmoor Cross
Bix
Greys Court
Bisham
Moulsford
S. Stoke
Medmenham
Maidenhead
Farnham
Royal
Wexham
Street
E. Ilsley
Streatley
Woodcote
Checkendon
Henley-
on-Thames
Hurley
Taplow
Burnham
Slough
Iver
Compton
Goring
Knowl
Hill
Langley
Sonning
Common
Shiplake
Wargrave
Bray
Eton
Basildon
Whitchurch
Mapledurham
Hampstead
Norris
White
Waltham
Datchet
Windsor
Heathrow
Airport
Pangbourne
Purley
Caversham
Sonning
Twyford
Yattendon
Chieveley
READING
Woodley
Winkfield
Old Windsor
Staines
Hermitage
Bradfield
Bucklebury
Theale
Earley
Binfield
Windsor
Great
Park
Egham
Stanwell
Feltham
Ashford
Donnington
Cold Ash
Whitley
Winnersh
Ascot
Englefield
Green
Sunbury
Shaw
Thatcham
Sulhamstead
Burghfield
Shinfield
Arborfield
Wokingham
Bracknell
Sunninghill
Virginia
Water
Laleham
Newbury
Woolhampton
Aldermaston
Padworth
Mortimer
Swallowfield
Sunningdale
Chertsey
Shepperton
Addlestone
Brimpton
Finchampstead
Crowthorne
Windlesham
Bagshot
Silchester
Sandhurst
Royal Military
Academy
Weybridge
Heath End
Tadley
Stratfield
Saye
Stratfield
Turgis
Wellington
Eversley
Chobham
Burghclere
Ecchinswell
Bramley
Heckfield
Yateley
Blackwater
Camberley
Lightwater
Byfleet
Kingsclere
Pamber End
Sherfield
on Loddon
Hawley
Frimley
Bisley
Knaphill
Woking
Wisley
Old
Burghclere
Mattingley
Hartley
Wintney
W. Heath
Deepcut
Ripley
Sherborne
St. John
Mayford
Litchfield
Hook
Fleet
Mytchett
Pirbright
Worplesdon
Basingstoke
Basing
Winchfield
Crookham
Village
Church
Crookham
Farnborough
Stoughton
Burpham
Clandon Park
East Horsley

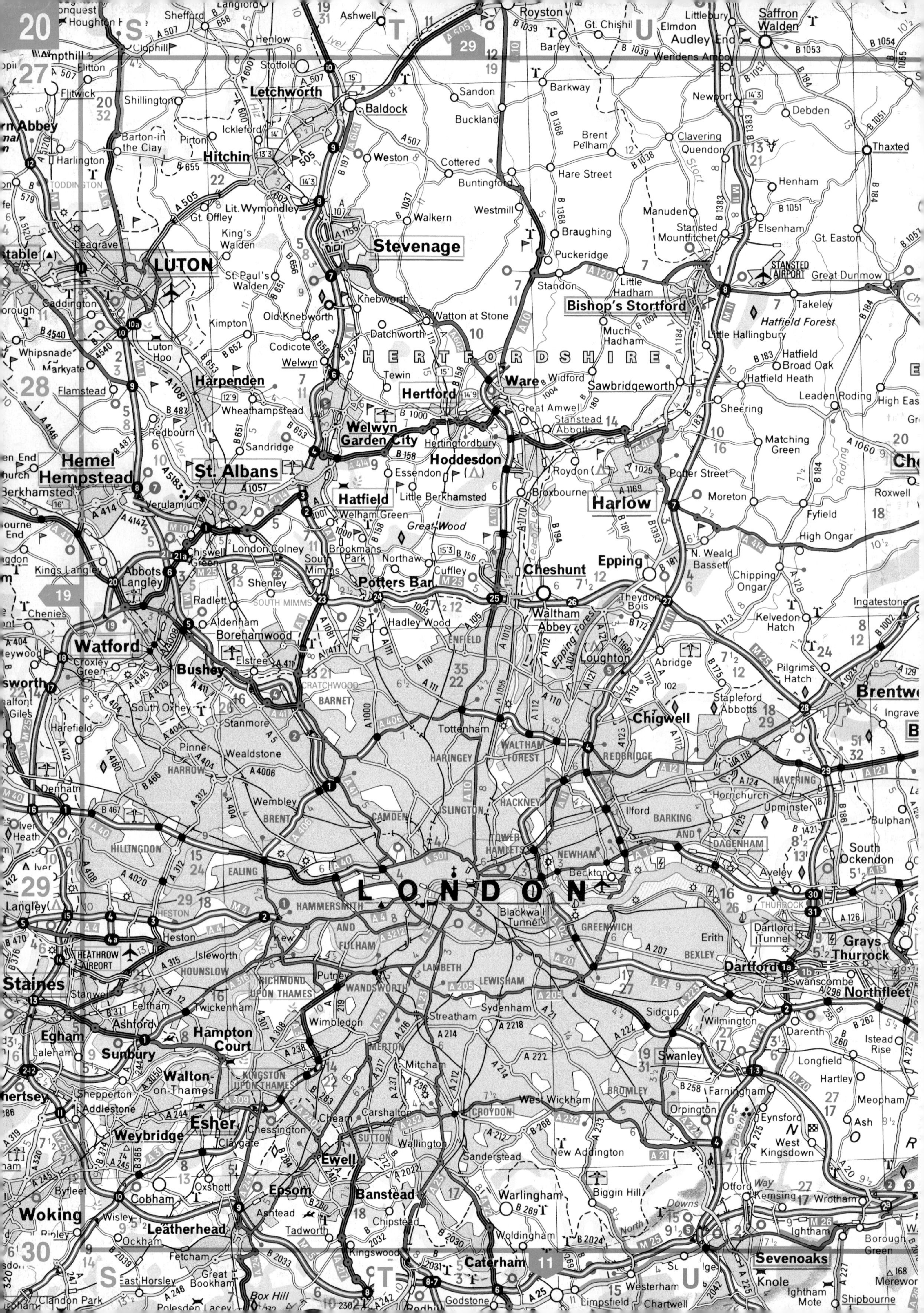
LONDON
HERTFORDSHIRE
LUTON
Stevenage
Letchworth
Baldock
Hitchin
Royston
Saffron Walden
Bishop's Stortford
Harpenden
Hertford
Ware
Welwyn Garden City
Hatfield
Hoddesdon
St. Albans
Hemel Hempstead
Harlow
Epping
Cheshunt
Waltham Abbey
Potters Bar
Watford
Bushey
Borehamwood
Loughton
Chigwell
Brentwood
Staines
Egham
Sunbury
Hampton Court
Esher
Weybridge
Woking
Cobham
Leatherhead
Epsom
Ewell
Banstead
Caterham
Sevenoaks
Swanley
Dartford
Grays Thurrock
Northfleet
Stansted Airport
Heathrow Airport
Great Dunmow
Thaxted
Takeley
Hatfield Forest
Dunstable
Berkhamsted
Elstree
Barnet
Enfield
Harrow
Hillingdon
Ealing
Hounslow
Richmond upon Thames
Kingston upon Thames
Croydon
Bromley
Bexley
Greenwich
Lewisham
Lambeth
Wandsworth
Hammersmith and Fulham
Camden
Islington
Hackney
Tower Hamlets
Newham
Barking and Dagenham
Redbridge
Havering
Waltham Forest
Haringey
Brent
Sutton
Merton
Thurrock
Warlingham
Biggin Hill
North Downs
Box Hill
Chartwell
Knole
Shipbourne

Bumpstead
Great Yeldham
Gestingthorpe
Castle Hedingham
Castle
Sible Hedingham
Finchingfield
Wethersfield
Great Bardfield
Gosfield
Halstead
Pebmarsh
Bures
Great Cornard
Stoke-by-Nayland
Nayland
Wormingford
Higham
Stratford St. Mary
E. Bergholt
Flatford Mill
Dedham
Capel St. Mary
Belstead
Nacton
Woolverstone
Trimley Heath
Holbrook
Shotley Gate
Mistley
R. Stour
Parkeston
Harwich
Dovercourt
Manningtree
Lawford
Ramsey
Ardleigh
Great Horkesley
Wakes Colne
W. Bergholt
Earls Colne
Bocking Churchstreet
Braintree
Stebbing
Rayne
Felsted
Black Notley
Coggeshall
Blackwater
Feering
Kelvedon
Silver End
Eight Ash Green
Colne
Mile End
Marks Tey
Copford
Beacon End
COLCHESTER
Elmstead Market
Great Bromley
Wix
Great Oakley
Tendring
Weeley
Thorpe-le-Soken
Walton-on-the-Naze
Frinton-on-Sea
Kirby Cross
Little Clacton
Great Bentley
Thorrington
Alresford
Wivenhoe
Layer-de-la-Haye
Messing
Layer Marney
Abberton Resr.
Langenhoe
R. Colne
Brightlingsea
St. Osyth
Clacton-on-Sea
Jaywick
Colne Point
Witham
Terling
Rivenhall End
Tiptree
Peldon
Mersea Island
Cudmore Grove
W. Mersea
Tolleshunt D'Arcy
Tollesbury
Great Totham
Little Waltham
Broomfield
Chelmsford
Hatfield Peverel
Boreham
Heybridge
Goldhanger
Little Baddow
Maldon
Danbury
R. Blackwater
Bradwell-on-Sea
Sales Point
Great Baddow
E. Hanningfield
Purleigh
Lower Mayland
Steeple
Margaretting
W. Hanningfield
Woodham Ferrers
Cold Norton
Latchingdon
Southminster
Althorne
Hanningfield Resr.
Stock
Rettendon
Hyde Hall
S. Woodham Ferrers
S. Hanningfield
Burnham-on-Crouch
Billericay
Runwell
Hullbridge
Canewdon
R. Crouch
Foulness Point
Wickford
Battlesbridge
Hockley
Ashingdon
Rochford
Foulness Island
Basildon
Hawkwell
Rayleigh
Laindon
Pitsea
Thundersley
Benfleet
Hadleigh
Leigh-on-Sea
Westcliff
Great Wakering
Thorpe
Shoeburyness
Shoebury Ness
Pitsea Hall
Horndon-on-the-Hill
Corringham
Canvey Island
SOUTHEND-ON-SEA
Stanford-le-Hope
R. THAMES
Vlissingen
Tilbury
Cliffe
St. Mary's Hoo
Allhallows
Isle of Grain
Grain
Stoke
Wallend
Sheerness
Gravesend
High Halstow
R. Medway
Minster
Warden Point
Higham
Shorne
Hoo St. Werburgh
Queenborough
Eastchurch
Leysdown-on-Sea
Rochester
Isle of Sheppey
Cobham
Brompton
Upchurch
Iwade
Lower Halstow
Whitstable
Herne Bay
Reculver
Birchington
Westgate-
Cuxton
Gillingham
Chatham
Newington
Rainham
Wigmore
Sittingbourne
The Swale
Seasalter
St. Nicolas-at-Wade
Sarre
Luddesdown
Halling
Walderslade
Oare
Faversham
Yorkletts
Hoath
Chislet
Burham
Snodland
Bapchild
Teynham
Blean
Sturry
Fordwich
Preston
New Hythe
Aylesford
Boxley
Detling
Bredgar
Boughton Street
CANTERBURY
Ash
Wingham
Larkfield
Thurnham
Newnham
Harbledown
Littlebourne
Malling
E. Malling
Barming
Bearsted
Doddington
Sheldwich
Selling
Woodnesborough
Wateringbury
MAIDSTONE
Hollingbourne
Warren St.
Stalisfield
Shottenden
Chartham
Patrixbourne
Bridge
Eastry
Lower Hardres
Aylesham
W. Farleigh
Loose
Leeds
Lenham
Chilham
ESSEX
DOWNS
22
23
28
29
30
12
13

U
V
W
Soham
Freckenham
Barton Mills
Icklingham
West Stow
Stanton
Fordham
Wicken
Tuddenham
Ingham
Gt. Livermere
Ixworth
Walsham le Willows
Chippenham
Fornham All Saints
Risby
SUFF
Bacton
Cottenham
Burwell
Kentford
Higham
Moulton
Waterbeach
Histon
Milton
Girton
Newmarket
Barrow
Bury St. Edmunds
Elmswell
Beyton
Woolpit
Anglesey Abbey
Lode
Swaffham Bulbeck
Dalham
Ashley
Horringer
Ickworth House
Hargrave Green
Chesterton
Bottisham
Dullingham
Lidgate
Whepstead
Rattlesden
Great Finborough
Stowmarket
Felsham
Fulbourn
Burrough Green
Brinkley
Wickhambrook
Hawkedon
Lawshall
Cockfield
Trumpington
Gt. Shelford
Stradishall
Hartest
Alpheton
Ringshall
Hitcham
Bildeston
Sawston
Abington
Balsham
Thurlow
Lavenham
Chelsworth
Whittlesford
Linton
Horseheath
Glemsford
Cavendish
Kedington
Haverhill
Clare
Long Melford
Monks Eleigh
Duxford
Imperial War Museum
Gt. Chesterford
Clare Castle
Ashdon
Sudbury
Kersey
Hadleigh
Steeple Bumpstead
Newton
Boxford
Great Cornard
Chishill
Elmdon
Littlebury
Saffron Walden
Audley End
Wendens Ambo
Great Yeldham
Gestingthorpe
Castle Hedingham
Stoke-by-Nayland
Higham
Capel St.
Great Sampford
Sible Hedingham
Bures
Nayland
Stratford St. Mary
Newport
Debden
Finchingfield
Pebmarsh
Wormingford
Clavering
Quendon
Thaxted
Wethersfield
Great Bardfield
Halstead
Great Horkesley
Henham
Gosfield
Earls Colne
Wakes Colne
W. Bergholt
Mile End
Manuden
Stansted Mountfitchet
Elsenham
Gt. Easton
Bocking Churchstreet
Eight Ash Green
Elmstead Market
Stebbing
Braintree
Beacon End
Marks Tey
Copford
COLCHESTER
Wivenhoe
Little Hadham
Stansted Airport
Great Dunmow
Rayne
Coggeshall
Feering
Layer-de-la-Haye
Bishop's Stortford
Takeley
Felsted
Hatfield Forest
Black Notley
Kelvedon
Messing
Thorrington
Much Hadham
Little Hallingbury
Silver End
Layer Marney
Abberton Resr.
Langenhoe
Hatfield Broad Oak
Hatfield Heath
ESSEX
Witham
Rivenhall End
Tiptree
Peldon
Sawbridgeworth
Leaden Roding
High Easter
Terling
Mersea Island
Sheering
Great Waltham
Little Waltham
Tolleshunt D'Arcy
Matching Green
Broomfield
Hatfield Peverel
Great Totham
W. Mersea
Chelmsford
Boreham
Goldhanger
Tollesbury
Potter Street
Heybridge
Sales Point
Harlow
Moreton
Roxwell
Little Baddow
Maldon
R. Blackwater
Bradwell-on-Sea
Fyfield
Writtle
Danbury
High Ongar
Great Baddow
N. Weald Bassett
E. Hanningfield
Purleigh
Epping
Chipping Ongar
Margaretting
Woodham Ferrers
Lower Mayland
Steeple
Theydon Bois
Ingatestone
W. Hanningfield
Latchingdon
Southminster
Cold Norton
Althorne
Kelvedon Hatch
Hanningfield Resr.
Stock
Rettendon
Hyde Hall
Burnham-on-Crouch
Abridge
S. Hanningfield
S. Woodham Ferrers
Billericay
Pilgrims Hatch
Runwell
Hullbridge
Canewdon
R. Crouch
Foulness
Stapleford Abbotts
Brentwood
Wickford
Battlesbridge
Hockley
Ashingdon
Chigwell
Ingrave
Hawkwell
Rochford
Foulness Island
Basildon
Rayleigh
REDBRIDGE
Laindon
Pitsea
Thundersley
HAVERING
Hornchurch
Upminster
Benfleet
Hadleigh
Great Wakering
Langdon Hills
Leigh-on-Sea
Ilford
BARKING
Bulphan
Pitsea Hall
Westcliff
Thorpe
Shoeburyness
Cam
Granta
Stour
Lark
Brett
Colne
Blackwater
Chelmer
Pant
Brain
Stort
Roding
A 11
A 14
A 45
A 134
A 143
A 1307
A 1092
A 1017
A 120
A 131
A 12
A 130
A 414
A 128
A 127
A 13
A 129
A 132
M 11
M 25
B 1102
B 1061
B 1053
B 1054
B 1057
B 1051
B 184
B 1383
B 1018
B 1022
B 1026
B 1010
B 1012
B 1013
B 1014
B 1021
B 1020
29
27
20
28
30
21

X
Y
Z
31
27
28
29
Laxfield
Bramfield
Heveninghan
Dunwich
Occold
Stoke Ash
Peasenhall
Darsham
Westleton
Yoxford
Badingham
Middleton
Dennington
Wetheringsett
Lonely Farm Leisure Park
Kelsale
Theberton
Saxtead Green
Castle
Rendham
Debenham
Earl Soham
Framlingham
Saxmundham
Leiston
Aldringham
Thorpeness
Pettaugh
Earl Stonham
Deben
Marlesford
Snape
Aldeburgh
Charsfield
Tunstall
Wickham Market
Otley
Ufford
Sudbourne
Grundisburgh
Melton
Butley
Claydon
Tuddenham
Woodbridge
Orford
R. Alde
Orford Ness
Somersham
Whitton
Martlesham
Bramford
Kesgrave
Waldringfield
Shottisham
Hollesley
Sproughton
Hollesley Bay
IPSWICH
Copdock
Sandlings
Belstead
Nacton
R. Deben
Bawdsey
Kirton
St. Mary
R. Orwell
Woolverstone
Trimley Heath
Holbrook
E. Bergholt
Felixstowe
Shotley Gate
Flatford Mill
R. Stour
Mistley
Parkeston
Göteborg
Hoek van Holland
Hamburg
Esbjerg
Manningtree
Ramsey
Harwich
Dovercourt
Wix
Great Bromley
Great Oakley
Tendring
The Naze
Weeley
Thorpe-le-Soken
Walton-on-the Naze
Great Bentley
Kirby Cross
Frinton-on-Sea
Little Clacton
Brightlingsea
St. Osyth
Clacton-on-Sea
Grove
Jaywick
Colne Point
s Point

F
G
H
32
25
26
27
Bardsey Island (▲)
Tal-y-Bont
Bontddu
Llanaber
A 496
Barmouth/
Abermaw
A 493
Arthog
Barmouth Bay
Fairbourne
622
Llwyngwril
Castell y Bere
A 493
Llanegryn
Bryncrug
Dolgoch
Falls
Tywyn
406
Aberdovey/
Aberdyfi
Aberdovey Bar
Dovey
Dyfi
Ynyslas
B 4353
18
29
Borth
Tal-y-bont
B 4353
A 487
B 4572
Bow Street
Llangorwen
Penrhyncoch
(▲) Aberystwyth
Llanbadarn Fawr
12
B 4340
Chancery
Ystwyth
A 485
Llanfihangel
y-Creuddyn
Llanilar
B 4575
A 487
Llanddeiniol
B 4576
Llangwyryfon
Lledrod
Llanrhystud
361
B 4337
Mynydd Bach
Llansantffraid
Llanon
37
23
A 485
Aberaeron
B 4577
Cross Inn
236
174
B 4571
B 4578
A 485
Cilcennin
B 4576
Llangeitho
B 4342
New Quay/
Ceinewydd
A 482
B 4337
B 4342
Bwlchllan
Llanarth
C E R E D I G I O N
Ynys-Lochtyn
Llwyndafydd
A 486
Mydroilyn
Aeron
B 43425
Ystrad
Aeron
7
Llangrannog
26
16
A 487
Synod Inn
217
Llangybi
Teifi
Cardigan
Island
Clegyr (▲)
Aberporth
B 4334
B 4321
B 4338
Talgarreg
A 482
A 485
Cemaes Head
Gwbert
Mwnt
Brynhoffnant
A 486
B 4338
324
Cribyn
B 4333
Bettws
Evan
Pembrokeshire Coast Path
Blaenannerch
Rhydlewis
B 4459
Cwrt-
newydd
Llanwnen
Lampeter/
Llanbedr
Pont Steffan
B 4548
B 4546
St. Dogmaels
Cardigan
/Aberteifi
Beulah
B 4571
Ffostrasol
Pontshaen
A 475
Valley
A 475
A 485
Farmers
Moylgrove
A 484
B 4570
B 4333
Ceri
Penrhiwpal
27
Rhydowen
Llanwenog
B 4338
A 482
646
Castle
Llechryd
Teifi
Llanybydder
415
Mynydd Pencarreg
Cilgerran
A 487
31
Cwmcoy
Aber-Banc
Horeb
B 4476
Teifi
B 4582
Nevern
Newport Bay
Cenarth
A 475
Llandysul
Llanfihangel
ar-Arth
Pumsaint
Felindre
Newchapel
Newcastle Emlyn/
Castell Newydd Emlyn
A 484
Drefach
Llangeler
B 4336
Rhydcymerau
Newport
19
31
Eglwyswrw
B 4332
Boncath
B 4459
Crug
Bergwaun
Pentre Ifan
14
A 478
Moelfre
335
169
Pencader
15
Llansawel
Pembrokeshire
Coast
National
Park
G
Cilrhedyn
A 484
Gwyddgrug
A 485
Brechfa
B 4310
B 4337
B 4302
Crymmych
B 4299
314
355
Abergorlech
Talley
C A R D I G A N   B A Y

WALES
POWYS
CAMBRIAN
Dolgellau
Cader Idris
Cross Foxes Hotel
Maesglasau
Minffordd
Tal-y-llyn
Corris
Aberangell
Mallwyd
Dinas-Mawddwy
Dovey Forest
Aran Fawddwy
Llanymawddwy
Bwlch Oerddrws
Cemmaes
Cemmaes Road
Llanwrin
Alternative Technology Centre
Machynlleth
Glaspwll
Eglwysfach
Dyfnant Valley
Darowen
Talywern
Llan
Llanbrynmair
Pandy
Moelfre
Pennant
Dylife
Staylittle
Glaslyn
Ffrwd Fawr
Nant-y-moch Resr.
Bontgoch Elerch
Hafren Forest
Plynlimon (Pumlumon Fawr)
Clywedog Resr.
Pant Mawr
Llangurig
Ponterwyd
Devil's Bridge / Pontarfynach
Mynach Falls
Rheidol
Cwmystwyth
Pontrhydygroes
Ysbyty Ystwyth
Trawsallt
Pontrhydfendigaid
Strata Florida Abbey
Tregaron
Craig Coch Resr.
Garreg-ddu Resr.
Claerwen Resr.
Caban Coch Resr.
Elan Village
Elan Valley
Rhayader
Rhaeadr
Bryn Till Wind Farm
St. Harmon
Llanidloes (Δ)
Llandinam
Trefeglwys
Caersws
Llanwnog
Carno
Bryn Amlwg
Llanwnog
Dyfnant Forest
Llanwddyn
Llangadfan
Llanerfyl
Nant yr Eira
Llanfair-Caereinion
Llanfihangel-yng-Ngwynfa
Dolanog
Meifod
Pentrebeirdd
Guilsfield
Llanfyllin
Llansantffraid-ym-Mechain
Four Crosses
Llandrinio
Llanymynech
Middletown
Buttington
Welshpool / Y Trallwng
Powis
Forden
Kingswood
Chirbury
Montgomery
Trefaldwyn
Abermule
Priestweston
Church Stoke
Berriew
Llanwyddelan
Adfa
New Mills
Tregynon
Bettws Cedewain
Bwlch-y-ffridd
Newtown / Drenewydd
Llanllwchaiarn
Kerry
Dolfor
Cilfaesty Hill
Mainstone
Bishop's Castle
Lydham
Anchor
Newcastle
Clun
Felindre
Beguildy
Beacon Hill
Offa's Dyke Path
Knighton / Trefyclawdd
Llangunllo
Llanbister
Bwlch-y-Sarnau
Rhyddhywel
Llanddewi Ystradenni
Llanfihangel Rhydithon
Whitton
Presteigne
Radnor Forest
Penybont
Crossgates
Llandegley
Llandrindod-Wells (Δ)
New Radnor
Old Radnor
Walton
Kington
Llanfihangel-Nant-Melan
Gwaunceste Hill
Hundred House
Gladestry
Glascwm
Disserth
Newbridge on Wye
Cwmbach
Cilmery
Builth Wells / Llanfair-ym-Muallt
Gorllwyn
Drygarn Fawr
Bryn Crwn
Abergwesyn
Towy Forest
Pen y Gurnos
Llyn Brianne
Beulah
Garth
Cambrian Wollen Mill
Llangammarch Wells (Δ)
Llanwrtyd Wells
Rhandirmwyn
Mynydd Mallaen
Cilycwn
Cynghordy
Crychan Forest
Tirabad
Mynydd Eppynt
Upper Chapel
Merthyr Cynog
Aberedw
Erwood
Crickadarn
Painscastle
Bryngwyn
Newchurch
Clyro
Llowes
Glasbury
Hay-on-Wye (Δ)
Llanigon
Three Cocks
Llyswen
Bronllys
Talgarth
Felinfach
Hay Bluff
Dorstone
Bredwardine
Winforton
Whitney-on-Wye
Eardisley
Llandovery
Llanfihangel Nant Bran
Mynydd Bwlch-y-Groes

SHREWSBURY
Telford
WOLVERHAM
Kidderminster
Ludlow
Leominster
Hereford
Great Malvern
Stour
Bridgnorth
Much Wenlock
Wellington
Oakengates
Shifnal
Dawley
Iron Bridge
Madeley
Broseley
Newport
Church Stretton
Bishop's Castle
Knighton/ Trefyclawdd
Presteigne
Kington
Hay-on-Wye
Bromyard
Ledbury
Tenbury Wells
Bewdley
Stourport-on-Severn
Cleobury Mortimer
Craven Arms
Clun
Weobley
S H R O P S H I R E
H E R E F O R D S H I R E
W R E K I N
W O R C E
Four Crosses
Llandrinio
Guilsfield
Buttington
Powis
Kingswood
Chirbury
Church Stoke
Lydham
Mainstone
Newcastle
Clunbury
Hopton Castle
Bucknell
Brampton Bryan
Whitton
Walton
Pembridge
Lyonshall
Eardisley
Kinnersley
Whitney-on-Wye
Willersley
Winforton
Bredwardine
Dorstone
Llanigon
Hay Bluff
Peterchurch
Vowchurch
Michaelchurch
Madley
Clehonger
Allensmore
Maesbrook
Kinnerley
Nesscliff
Baschurch
Walford
Bomere Heath
Albrighton
Hadnall
Astley
Shawbury
Waters Upton
High Ercall
Crudgington
Edgmond
Forton
Gnosall
Lilleshall
Donnington
Sheriffhales
Wheaton Aston
Weston-under-Lizard
Albrighton
Tettenhall
Pattingham
Shipley
Claverley
Halfpenny Green
Highgate Common
Enville
Kinver
Quatt
Bildsgreen
Highley
Kingsford
Upper Arley
Wolverley
Stone
Bicton
Alberbury
Ford
Middletown
Westbury
Yockleton
Great Hanwood
Bayston Hill
Atcham
Upton Magna
Condover
Pontesbury
Minsterley
Worthen
Hope
Shelve
Pennerley
Stiperstones
Ratlinghope
Wentnor
Picklescott
Dorrington
Longnor
Leebotwood
Woolstaston
All Stretton
Cardington
Lit. Stretton
Hope Bowdler
Acton Scott
Acton Burnell
Cressage
Buildwas Abbey
Harley
Little Wenlock
The Wrekin
Hughley
Bourton
Morville
Monkhopton
Shipton
Stanton Long
Ditton Priors
Wenlock Edge
Corve Dale
Munslow
Tugford
Diddlebury
Cleobury North
Brown Clee Hill
Burwarton
Billingsley
Stottesdon
Stoke St. Milborough
Titterstone Clee Hill
Farlow
Kinlet
Hopton Wafers
Cleehill
Wyre Forest
Callow Hill
Mamble
Culmington
Wistanstow
Lydbury N.
Edgton
Stokesay
Clungunford
Bromfield
Leintwardine
Caynham
Ludford
Richards Castle
Wigmore
Lingen
Orleton
Brimfield
Aymestrey
Croft
Luston
Berrington Hall
Kingsland
Shobdon
Monkland
Dilwyn
Hope under Dinmore
Queenswood
Bodenham
Canon-Pyon
Wellington
Wormsley
Moreton-on-Lugg
Sutton St. Nicholas
Burghill
Credenhill
Byford
Felton
Burley Gate
Ullingswick
Stoke Lacy
Pencombe
Withington
Newtown
Bartestree
Mordiford
Tarrington
Aylton
Ashperton
Woolhope
Fownhope
Much Marcle
Preston
Newnham Bridge
Stockton-on-Teme
Kyre Park
Hatfield
Thornbury
Collington
Clifton-upon-Teme
Bredenbury
Knightwick
Alfrick
Acton Green
Leigh Sinton
Ridgeway Cross
Castle Frome
Bosbury
Colwall Stone
Wellington Heath
Wynds Point
Wyche
Malvern Wells
Hanley Swan
Welland
Rhydd
Powick
Birtsmorton Court
Abberley
Dunley
Gt Witley
Shrawley
Ombersley
Shelsley Beauchamp
Holt Heath
Martley
Grimley
Hallow
Lower Broadheath
Broadwas
R. Severn

Rugeley
Cannock Chase Forest
Cannock
Lichfield
Brownhills
Tamworth
Aldridge
WALSALL
Sutton Coldfield
West Bromwich
DUDLEY
SANDWELL
Oldbury
BIRMINGHAM
Halesowen
Solihull
Bromsgrove
Redditch
Swadlincote
Ashby de la Zouch
Coalville
Hinckley
Nuneaton
Bedworth
COVENTRY
Kenilworth
Warwick
Royal Leamington Spa
STRATFORD UPON-AVON
WORCESTER
Evesham
Banbury
Shipston-on-Stour
Chipping Campden
Broadway
Alcester
Atherstone
Market Bosworth
Coleshill
Meriden
Henley
Studley
Pershore
Droitwich
Walton-upon-Trent
Barton
Yoxall
Alrewas
Hednesford
Chasetown
Wednesfield
Willenhall
Bilston
Sedgley
Darlaston
Wednesbury
Tipton
Brierley Hill
Rowley Regis
Warley
Edgbaston
King's Heath
Hall Green
Castle Bromwich
Hagley
Romsley
Rubery
Hockley Heath
Knowle
Dorridge
Hampton
Berkswell
Balsall Common
Kingsbury
Polesworth
Fazeley
Shenstone
Wall
Elford
Clifton Campville
Whittington
Measham
Ibstock
Shepshed
Earl Shilton
Burbage
Bulkington
Keresley
Allesley
Longford
Binley
Baginton
Stoneleigh
Ryton-on-Dunsmore
Wolston
Brandon
Bretford
Southam
Harbury
Whitnash
Bishop's Tachbrook
Barford
Wellesbourne
Kineton
Gaydon
Ettington
Halford
Tredington
Ilmington
Mickleton
Ebrington
Hidcote Manor
Blockley
Snowshill
Willersey
Bretforton
Welford
Bidford
Pebworth
Cleeve Prior
Temple Grafton
Wilmcote
Mary Arden's House
A. Hathaway's Cottage
Charlecote Park
Snitterfield
Claverdon
Wootton Wawen
Aston Cantlow
Feckenham
Inkberrow
Himbleton
Flyford Flavell
Upton Snodsbury
Pinvin
Fladbury
Elmley Castle
Eckington
Bredon
Defford
Hanbury
Astwood Bank
Headless Cross
Tanworth
Alvechurch
Cofton Hackett
Wythall
Catshill
Chaddesley Corbett
Belbroughton
Blakedown
Clent
Cutnall Green
Avoncroft Museum
WARWICKSHIRE
WORCESTERSHIRE

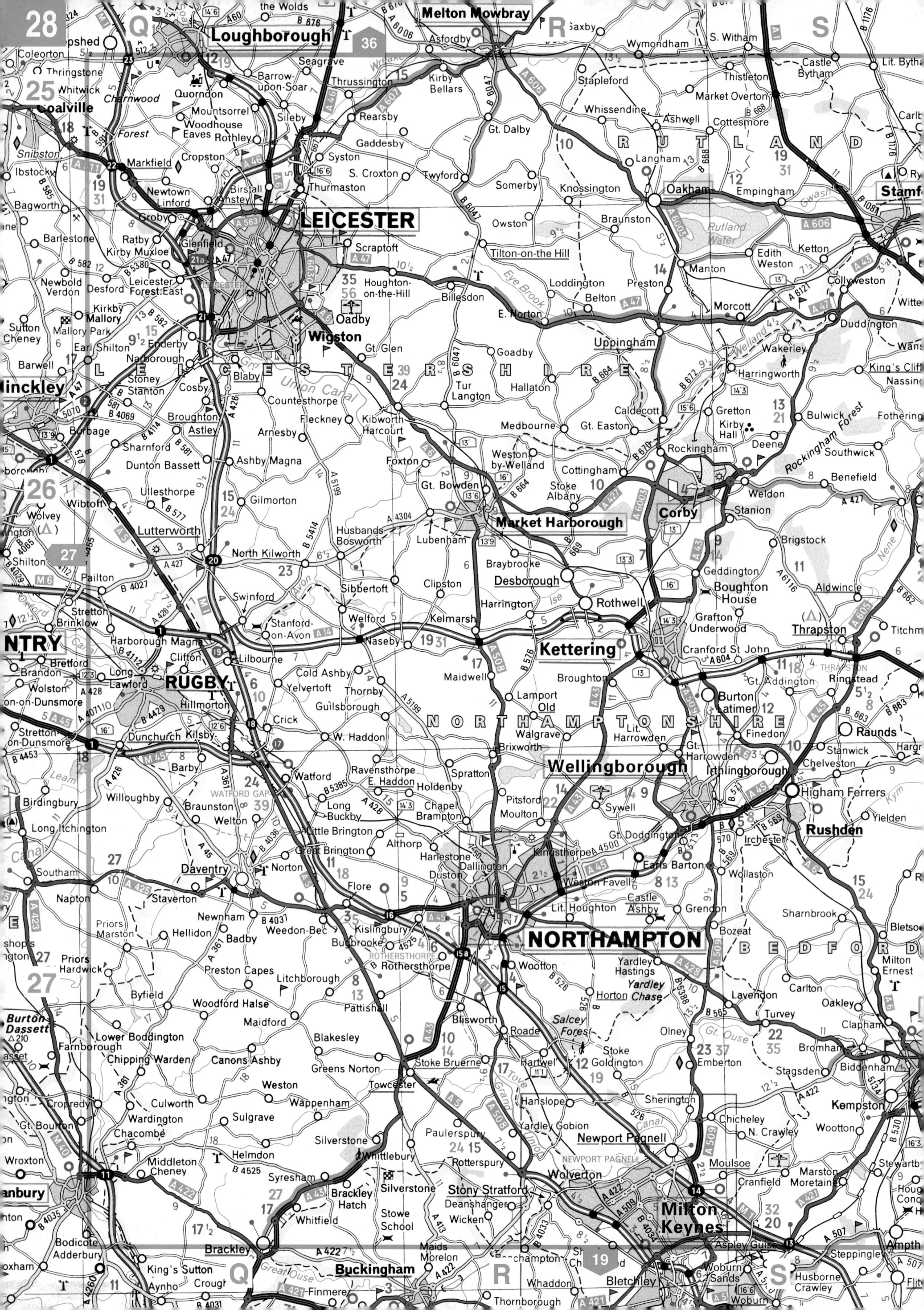
Loughborough
Melton Mowbray
LEICESTER
Coalville
Hinckley
Oadby
Wigston
Oakham
RUTLAND
LEICESTERSHIRE
Uppingham
Market Harborough
Corby
Desborough
Rothwell
Kettering
Thrapston
Lutterworth
RUGBY
Daventry
NORTHAMPTONSHIRE
Wellingborough
Higham Ferrers
Rushden
NORTHAMPTON
BEDFORD
Towcester
Newport Pagnell
Milton Keynes
Stony Stratford
Wolverton
Brackley
Buckingham
Bletchley
Banbury
Kempston
Rutland Water
Rockingham Forest
Salcey Forest
Yardley Chase
Charnwood Forest
Grand Union Canal
Stamford
Q
R
S
25
26
27
36
19

Spalding
Bourne
Thurlby
Baston
Market Deeping
Deeping St. James
Deeping St. Nicholas
Cowbit
Moulton Chapel
Holbeach St. Johns
Whaplode Drove
Sutton St. James
Tydd St. Mary
Tydd St. Giles
Sutton St. Edmund
Gedney Hill
Leverington
Crowland
Parson Drove
Wisbech St. Mary
Wisbech
Terrington St. Clement
Clenchwarton
Walpole St. Andrew
Walpole St. Peter
W. Walton
Tilney St. Lawrence
Wiggenhall St. Mary Magdalen
Emneth
Stow Bridge
Outwell
Upwell
Downham Market
Nordelph
Denver
Crimplesham
Stradsett
W. Dereham
Wereham
Stoke Ferry
Hilgay
Southery
Marham
Shouldham
E. Winch
W. Winch
Glinton
Burghley House
Helpston
Marholm
Eye
Thorney
PETERBOROUGH
Castor
Alwalton
Elton
Old Fletton
Whittlesey
Guyhirn
Friday Bridge
March
Christchurch
Welney
Yaxley
Norman Cross
Warmington
Pondersbridge
Wimblington
Doddington
Benwick
Manea
Ramsey St. Mary's
Stilton
Holme
Polebrook
Barnwell
Conington
Sawtry
Ramsey
Upwood
Chatteris
Littleport
Downham
CAMBRIDGESHIRE
Mepal
Sutton
Ely
Prickwillow
Lakenheath
Clopton
Winwick
Lit. Raveley
Warboys
Abbots Ripton
Somersham
Witchford
Haddenham
Alconbury
Lit. Stukeley
Old Hurst
Earith
Stretham
Soham
Isleham
Mildenhall
Spaldwick
Huntingdon
St. Ives
Needingworth
Over
Hinchingbrooke House
Brampton
Hemingford Grey
Fenstanton
Willingham
Wicken
Fordham
Freckenham
Chippenham
Kimbolton
Grafham Water
Buckden
Godmanchester
Swavesey
Cottenham
Offord Cluny
Hilton
Longstanton
Burwell
Staughton Highway
Pertenhall
Graveley
Oakington
Waterbeach
Papworth Everard
Boxworth
Bar Hill
Histon
Milton
Girton
Anglesey Abbey
Lode
Swaffham Bulbeck
Newmarket
Bottisham
Madingley
Chesterton
St. Neots
Eltisley
Bolnhurst
Eaton Socon
Coton
CAMBRIDGE
Caxton
Gt. Gransden
Bourn
Comberton
Kingston
Grantchester
Trumpington
Fulbourn
Dullingham
Burrough Green
Brinkley
BEDFORD
Tempsford
Gamlingay
Haslingfield
Gt. Shelford
Gt. Barford
Sandy
Potton
Harston
Sawston
Balsham
Willington
Orwell
Abington
Thurlow
Shepreth
Whittlesford
Linton
Horseheath
Haverhill
Elstow
Wrestlingworth
Aeroplane Museum
Fowlmere
Duxford
Biggleswade
Kneesworth
Melbourn
Imperial War Museum
Gt. Chesterford
Ashdon
Wilstead
Old Warden
Steeple Morden
Southill
Langford
Royston
Gt. Chishill
Elmdon
Littlebury
Saffron Walden
Steeple Bumpstead
Shefford
Ashwell
Henlow
Clophill
Barley
Audley End
Stotfold
Wendens Ambo
Great Sampford
Letchworth
Baldock
Sandon
Barkway
Newport
Debden
Shillington
Buckland
Finchingfield
R. Nene
Old Nene
R. Gt. Ouse
New Bedford
Old Bedford
Little Ouse
Bedford Levels
Cam
Ivel

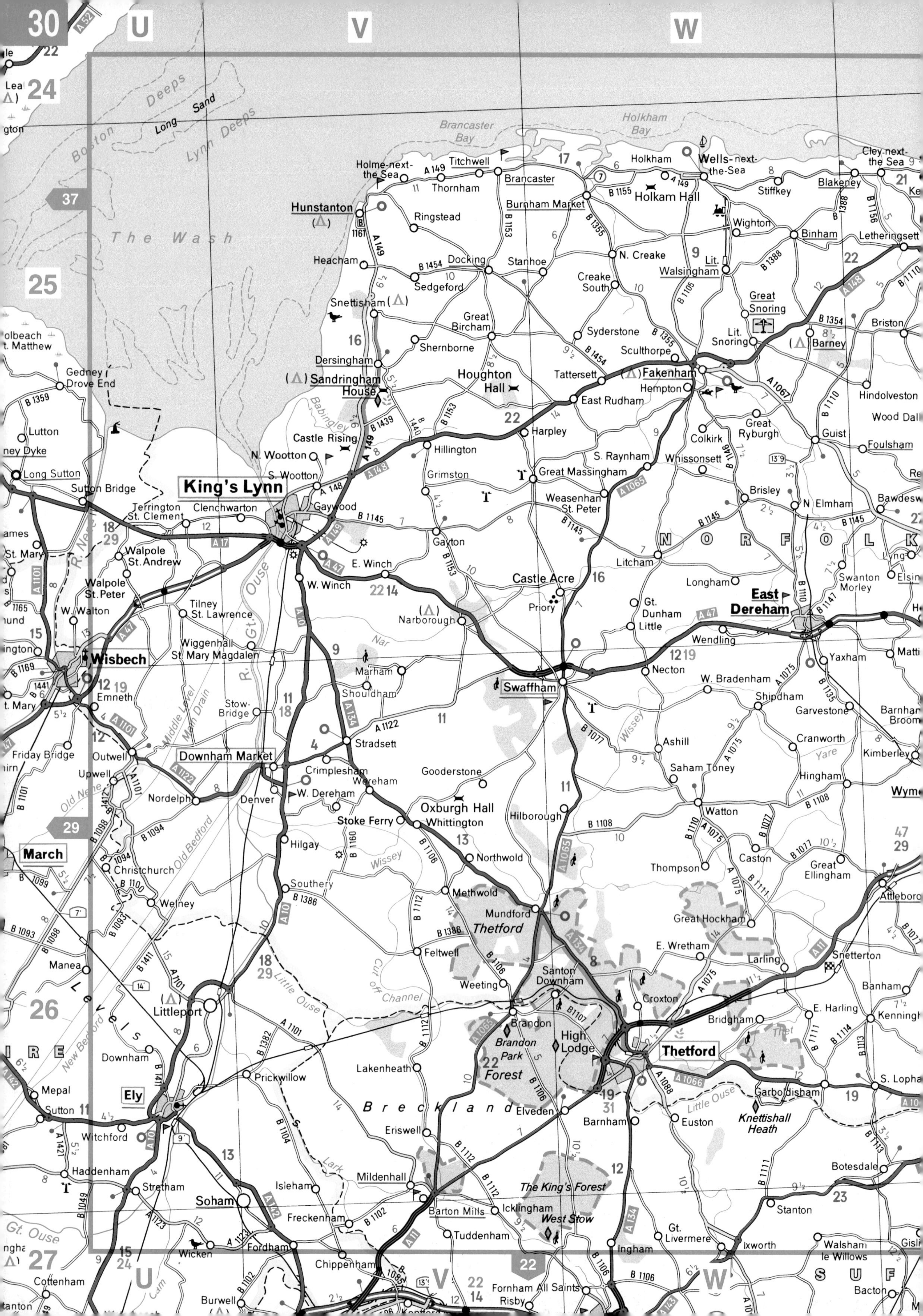
U
V
W
Boston Deeps
Long Sand
Lynn Deeps
The Wash
Brancaster Bay
Holkham Bay
Holme-next-the Sea
Titchwell
Brancaster
Thornham
Hunstanton
Ringstead
Burnham Market
Holkham
Holkham Hall
Wells-next-the-Sea
Stiffkey
Blakeney
Cley-next-the Sea
Wighton
Binham
Letheringsett
Heacham
Docking
Stanhoe
N. Creake
Lit. Walsingham
Sedgeford
Creake South
Snettisham
Great Bircham
Great Snoring
Syderstone
Sculthorpe
Lit. Snoring
Barney
Briston
Shernborne
Dersingham
Sandringham House
Houghton Hall
Tattersett
Fakenham
Hempton
Hindolveston
East Rudham
Great Ryburgh
Wood Dal
Harpley
Castle Rising
N. Wootton
S. Wootton
Hillington
Colkirk
Guist
Foulsham
S. Raynham
Whissonsett
Grimston
Great Massingham
King's Lynn
Gaywood
Brisley
N Elmham
Bawdeswell
Weasenham St. Peter
Sutton Bridge
Long Sutton
Terrington St. Clement
Clenchwarton
Gayton
NORFOLK
Litcham
Lyng
Swanton Morley
Walpole St. Andrew
Walpole St. Peter
E. Winch
W. Winch
Castle Acre
Priory
Longham
East Dereham
Gt. Dunham
Little Dunham
Tilney St. Lawrence
W. Walton
Narborough
Wendling
Wiggenhall St. Mary Magdalen
Wisbech
Marham
Swaffham
Necton
Yaxham
Emneth
Shouldham
W. Bradenham
Shipdham
Garvestone
Stow Bridge
Middle Level Main Drain
R. Gt. Ouse
Stradsett
Ashill
Cranworth
Kimberley
Friday Bridge
Outwell
Upwell
Downham Market
Crimplesham
Wereham
Gooderstone
Saham Toney
Hingham
Nordelph
Denver
W. Dereham
Oxburgh Hall
Hilborough
Watton
Stoke Ferry
Whittington
March
Hilgay
Northwold
Thompson
Caston
Great Ellingham
Christchurch
Southery
Methwold
Welney
Mundford
Thetford
Great Hockham
Attleborough
Feltwell
E. Wretham
Larling
Snetterton
Manea
Weeting
Santon Downham
Croxton
Banham
Littleport
Brandon
High Lodge
Bridgham
E. Harling
Kenninghall
Downham
Brandon Park
Thetford Forest
Mepal
Ely
Prickwillow
Lakenheath
Sutton
Breckland
Elveden
Barnham
Euston
Knettishall Heath
Garboldisham
S. Lopham
Witchford
Eriswell
Little Ouse
Cut off Channel
Haddenham
Stretham
Soham
Isleham
Mildenhall
Barton Mills
The King's Forest
Botesdale
Stanton
Freckenham
Icklingham
West Stow
Tuddenham
Wicken
Fordham
Ingham
Gt. Livermere
Ixworth
Walsham le Willows
Chippenham
Cottenham
Burwell
Fornham All Saints
Risby
Bacton
SUFFOLK
Gt. Ouse
The Levels
New Bedford
Old Bedford
Old Nene
Lark
Wissey
Nar
Yare
Thet
Gedney Drove End
Lutton
Holbeach St. Matthew
Terrington
Leal
Gt. Ouse
Snetterton

X Y Z

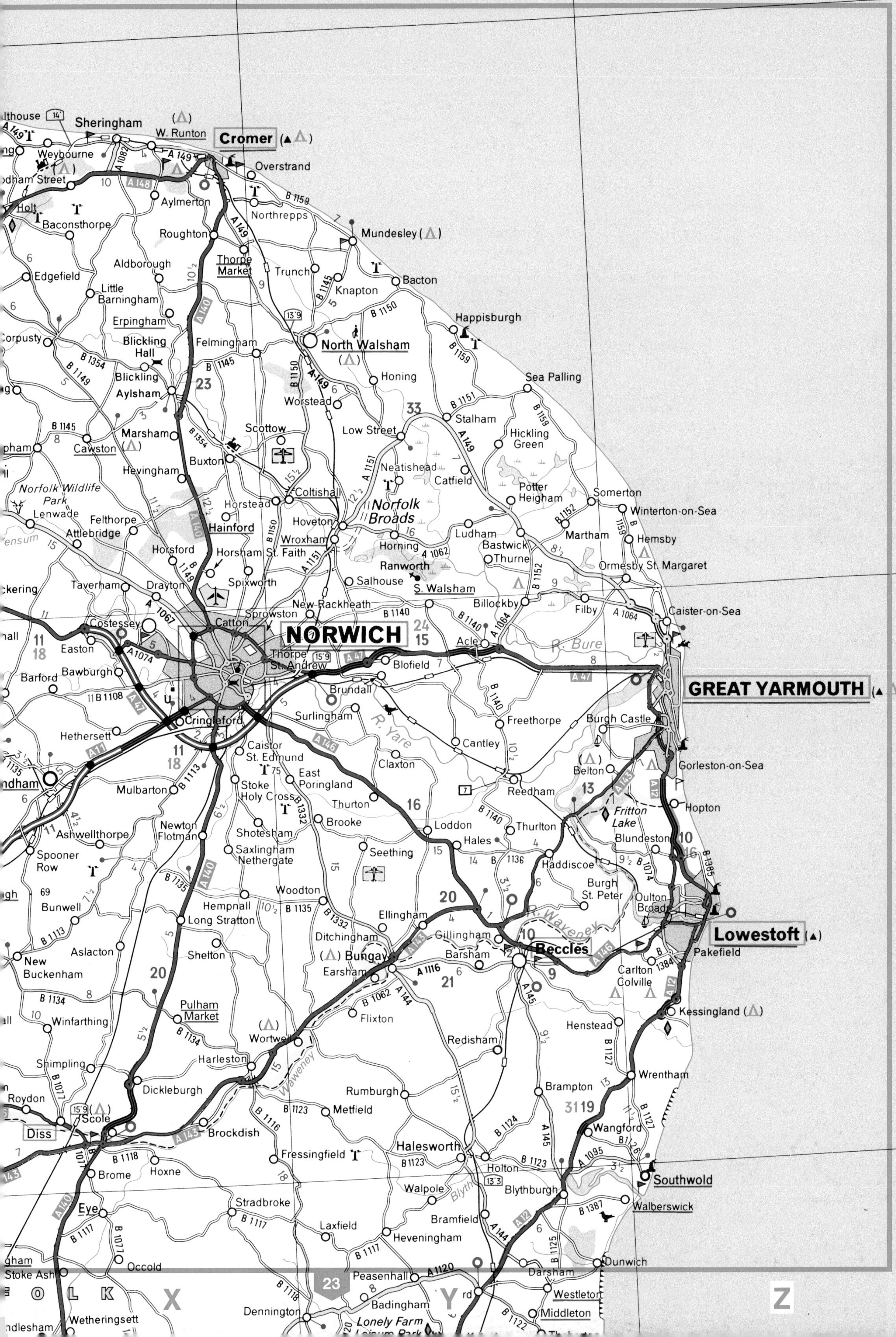

25

26

27

X Y Z

F G H

23

24

25

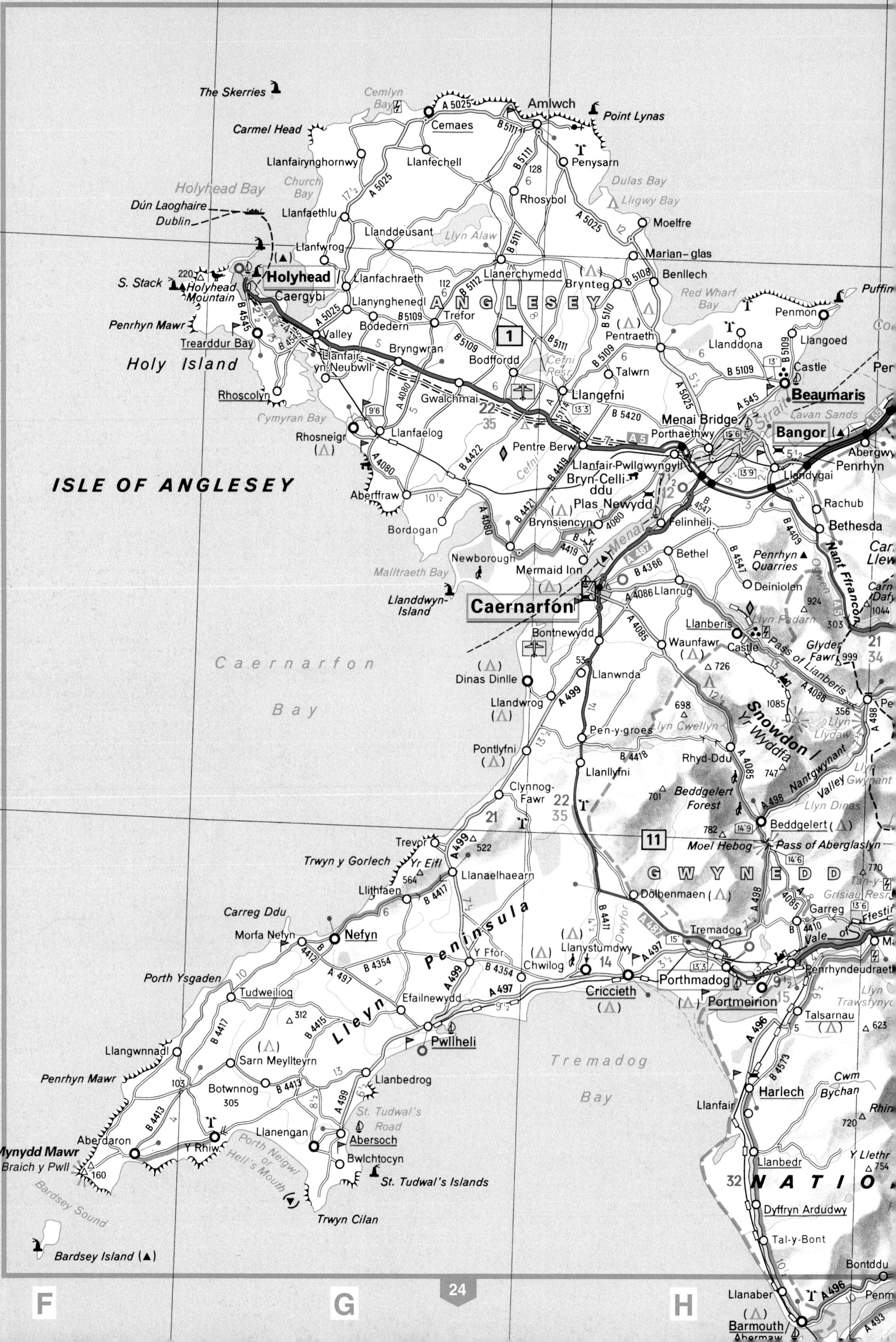

F G H

24

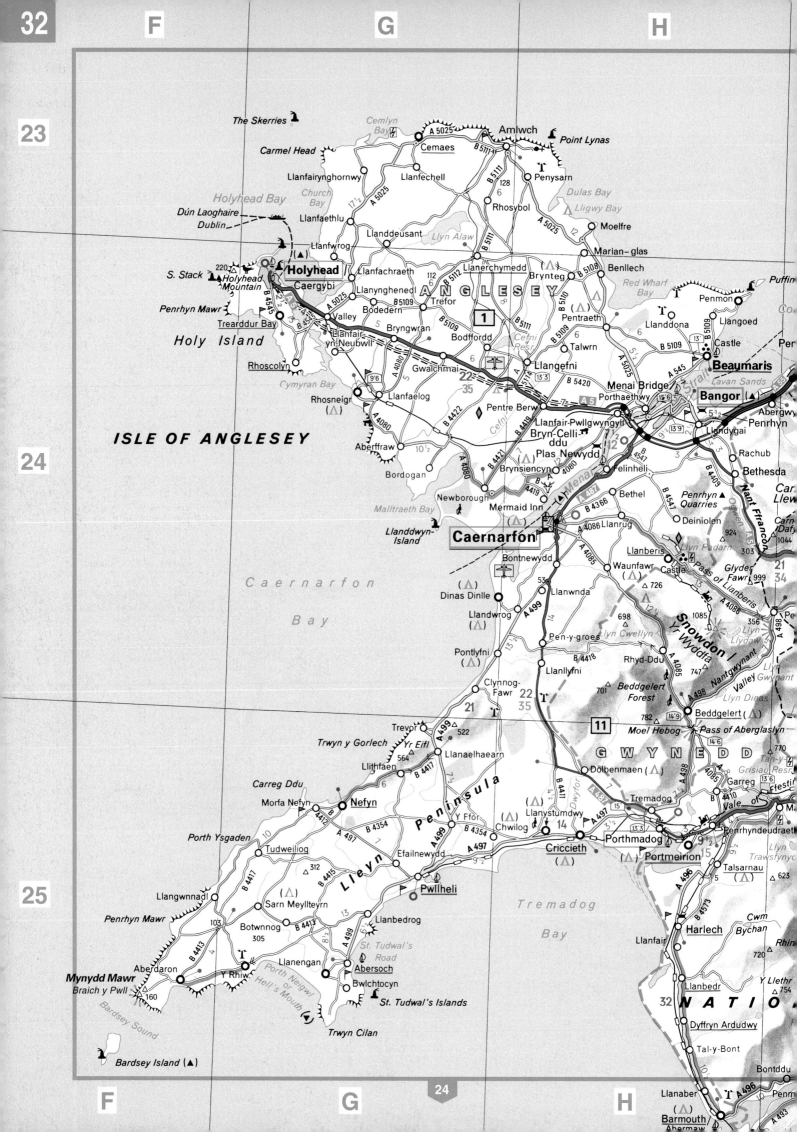

I
J
K
38
Dublin
Douglas (Isle of Man)
Belfast
Blundellsands
Crosby
23
Bootle
Liverpool Bay
New Brighton
Wallasey
Hoylake
Moreton
BIRKENHEAD
West Kirby
Irby
Thurstaston
Pensby
Heswall
Thornton Hough
Parkgate
Neston
Willaston
Welsh Channel
Talacre
Point of Ayr
River Dee
Afon Dyfrdwy
Great Orme's Head
Llandudno
Lit. Ormes Head
Penrhyn Bay
Rhos-on-Sea
Colwyn Bay / Bae Colwyn
Rhyl
Prestatyn
Deganwy
Llandudno Junction
Mochdre
Old Colwyn
Llanddulas
Abergele
Kinmel Bay
Pensarn
Rhuddlan
Dyserth
Castle
Trelawnyd
Llanasa
Mostyn
Holywell / Treffynnon
Greenfield
Bagillt
Flint / Fflint
Connah's Quay
Queensferry
Ewloe
Northop
Northop Hall
Buckley / Bwcle
Mold / Yr Wyddgrug
Halkyn
Babell
Caerwys
Afon-wen
Tremeirchion
Bodfari
Nannerch
Cilcain
Loggerheads
Moel Fammau
FLINTS
Conwy
Llanfairfechan
Penmaenmawr
Llansanffraid Glan Conwy
Bodnant Garden
Tal-y-Cafn
Tal-y-Bont
Foel-Fras
Dolgarrog
Llyn Eigiau Resr.
Llyn Cowlyd Resr.
Trefriw
Llanrwst
Gwydir Castle
Swallow Falls
Capel Curig
Betws-y-Coed
Moel-siabod
Carnedd
Dolwyddelan
Penmachno
Capel Garmon
Nebo
SNOWDONIA
Llechwedd Slate Caverns
Blaenau Ffestiniog
Ffestiniog
Vale of Conwy
CONWY
Betws-yn-Rhos
Llanfair Talhaiarn
Llannefydd
Llangernyw
Llansannan
Gwytherin
Bodelwyddan
St. Asaph
Trefnant
Henllan
Denbigh / Dinbych
Bylchau
Llanrhaeadr
Llandyrnog
DENBIGHSHIRE
Ruthin / Rhuthun
Brenig Resr.
Cyffylliog
Clocaenog
Clocaenog Forest
Clawdd-newydd
Llanfihangel Glyn Myfyr
Pentrefoelas
Ysbyty Ifan
Cerrigydrudion
Betws Gwerfil Goch
Maerdy
Llanelidan
Bryneglwys
Gwyddelwern
Rug
Corwen
Llangwm
Carnedd y Filiast
Llantysilio Mountain
Horseshoe Pass
Valle Crucis
Llangollen
Glyndyfrdwy
Plas Newydd
Offa's Dyke
Llanferres
Nercwys
Leeswood
Treuddyn
Llanfynydd
Llanarmon yn-Ial
Pentre Celyn
Llandegla
Bwlchgwyn
Caergwrle
Brymbo
Coedpoeth
Rhostyllen
Rhosllanerchrugog
Cefn-mawr
Pont Cysyllte
Chirk
Chirk Castle
Penyffordd
Waun y Llyn
Trawsfynydd
Moel Llyfnant
Llyn Celyn
Fron-Goch
Bala
Llyn Tegid or Bala Lake
Llandderfel
Llandrillo
Cynwyd
Moel Fferna
Glyn Ceiriog
Vale of Ceiriog
Llwynmawr
Weston Rhyn
Selattyn
Foel Wen
Moel Sych
Berwyn
Llanarmon Dyffryn Ceiriog
Oswestry
Llangywer
Aberhirnant Forest
Llanuwchllyn
Coed y Brenin Forest
Rhobell Fawr
Pistyll Rhaeadr
Tan-y-pistyll
Llangynog
Llansilin
Llanrhaeadr-ym Mochnant
Trefonen
Llangedwyn
Pen-y-bont-fawr
Lake Vyrnwy
Llanwddyn
Llanfyllin
Llansantffraid-ym-Mechain
Pant
Llynclys
Llanymynech
Maesbrook
Four Crosses
Llandrinio
Ganllwyd
Llanfachreth
Aran Fawddwy
Llanymawddwy
Llanelltyd
Dolgellau
Bwlch Oerddrws
Cross Foxes Hotel
Dinas Mawddwy
Dyfnant Forest
Llanfihangel-yng-Ngwynfa
Pentrebeirdd
25
24
34
22
10
9
8

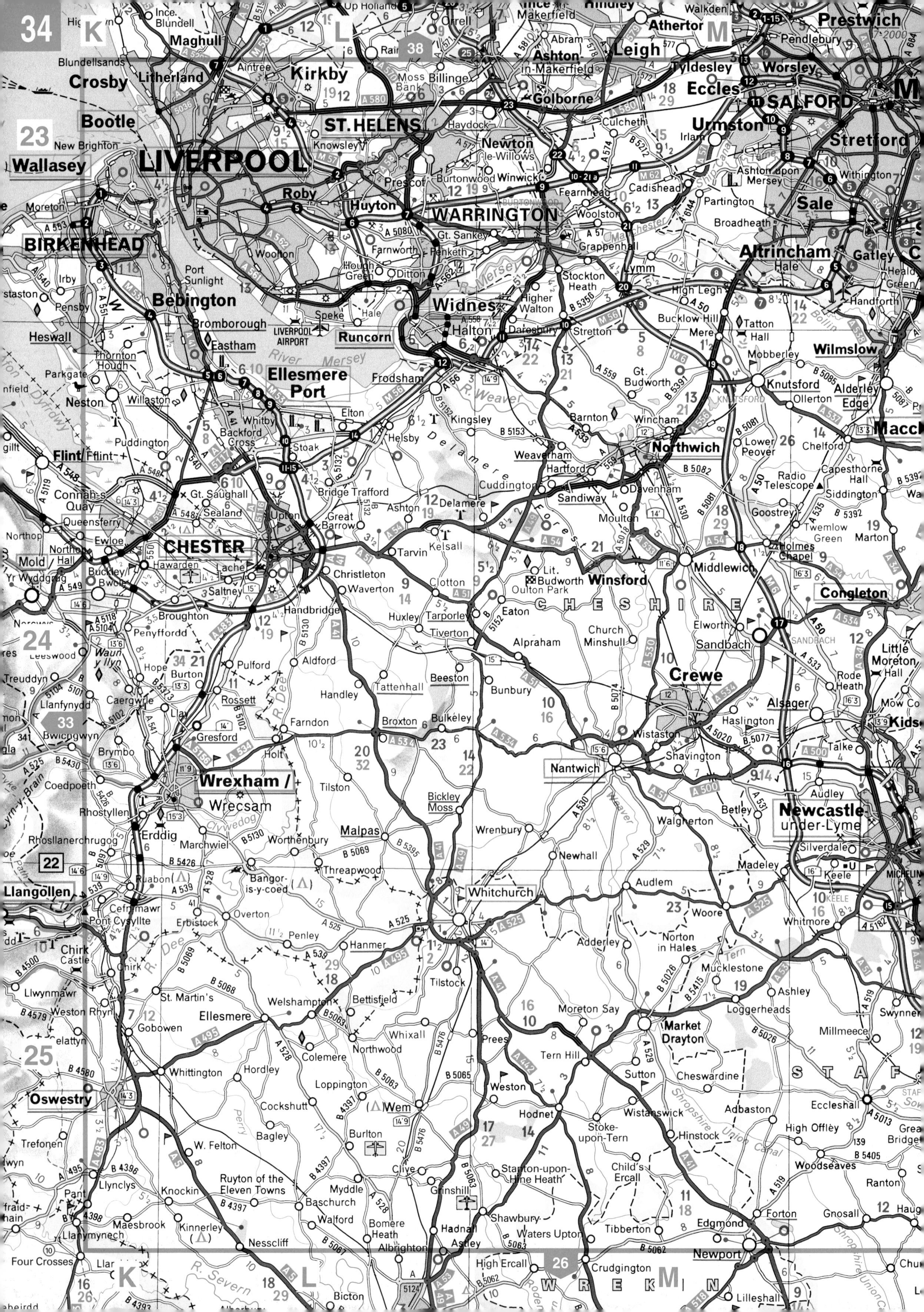

LIVERPOOL
Crosby
Litherland
Maghull
Kirkby
Bootle
Wallasey
New Brighton
BIRKENHEAD
ST. HELENS
Knowsley
Prescot
Huyton
Roby
WARRINGTON
Newton le-Willows
Haydock
Golborne
Ashton in-Makerfield
Leigh
Atherton
Tyldesley
Eccles
SALFORD
Prestwich
Pendlebury
Worsley
Urmston
Stretford
Sale
Altrincham
Hale
Gatley
Partington
Cadishead
Lymm
Widnes
Runcorn
Halton
LIVERPOOL AIRPORT
Speke
Hale
River Mersey
Ellesmere Port
Frodsham
Helsby
Bebington
Bromborough
Eastham
Heswall
Neston
Parkgate
Willaston
Irby
Pensby
Moreton
Port Sunlight
Wilmslow
Knutsford
Mobberley
Tatton Hall
Northwich
Barnton
Wincham
Weaverham
Hartford
Sandiway
Cuddington
Davenham
Moulton
Winsford
Middlewich
Holmes Chapel
Congleton
Sandbach
Alsager
Crewe
Nantwich
Wistaston
Shavington
Haslington
Flint / Fflint
Connah's Quay
Queensferry
Ewloe
Mold / Yr Wyddgrug
Buckley / Bwcle
Hawarden
Saltney
CHESTER
Christleton
Waverton
Tarvin
Kelsall
Delamere
Tarporley
Tattenhall
Beeston
Bunbury
Broxton
Farndon
Holt
Rossett
Gresford
Wrexham / Wrecsam
Erddig
Ruabon
Llangollen
Chirk
Chirk Castle
Malpas
Whitchurch
Bangor-is-y-coed
Overton
Hanmer
Ellesmere
Oswestry
Whittington
Wem
Prees
Hodnet
Market Drayton
Audlem
Woore
Betley
Madeley
Keele
Newcastle-under-Lyme
Audley
Talke
Kidsgrove
Loggerheads
Eccleshall
Newport
Shawbury
High Ercall
Nesscliff
Baschurch
Ruyton of the Eleven Towns
Knockin
Llanymynech
Four Crosses
Lilleshall
CHESHIRE
STAFF
WREKIN

MANCHESTER
Ashton-under-Lyne
Stalybridge
Mossley
Dukinfield
Audenshaw
Denton
Hyde
Bredbury
Romiley
STOCKPORT
Marple
Hazel Grove
Bramhall
Disley
Poynton
Lyme Park
Adlington Hall
Kettleshulme
Bollington
Macclesfield Forest
Gawsworth Hall
Wincle
Bosley
Hightown
Biddulph
Leek
Endon
Tunstall
Cheddleton
Hanley
Cellarhead
STOKE-ON-TRENT
Fenton
Longton
Dilhorne
Blythe Bridge
Trentham
Barlaston
Draycott-in-the-Moors
Stone
Hilderstone
Milwich
Sandon
Gayton
Weston
Stowe-by-Chartley
Stafford
Weeping Cross
Blithfield Hall
Blithfield Resr
Rugeley
Cannock Chase Forest
Brereton
Armitage
King's Bromley
Yoxall
Barton
Abbots Bromley
Newborough
Needwood Forest
Draycott-in-the-Clay
Marchington
Uttoxeter
Church Leigh
Upper Tean
Cheadle
Kingsley
Oakamoor
Alton Towers
Alton
Ellastone
Rocester
Doveridge
Sudbury Hall
Sudbury
Tutbury
Hatton
Hilton
Rolleston
Stretton
Horninglow
Burton-upon-Trent
Walton-upon-Trent
Rosliston
Linton
Overseal
Moira
Ashby de la Zouch
Swadlincote
Winshill
Newton Solney
Repton
Willington
Etwall
Sutton-on-the-Hill
Great Cubley
Longford
Shirley
Mayfield
Ashbourne
Hulland
Brailsford
Kedleston Hall
Allestree
Duffield
Turnditch
Belper
Kirk Ireton
Kniveton
Carsington Reservoir
Wirksworth
Brassington
Parwich
Fenny Bentley
Thorpe
Ilam
Dovedale
Waterhouses
Cauldon
Ipstones
Grindon
Onecote
Alstonefield
Warslow
Hartington
Longnor
Flash
Buxton
Dove Holes
Whaley Bridge
Chapel-en-le-Frith
Chinley
New Mills
Newtown
Hayfield
Kinder Scout
Edale
Mam Tor
Blue John Cavern
Castleton
Hope
Bradwell
Hathersage
Bamford
Ladybower Resr
Glossop
Hadfield
Hollingworth
Tintwistle
Woodhead
Bleaklow Hill
Pennine Way
Peak District
National Park
High Peak
Hope Forest
Derwent Dale
Howden Resr
Derwent Resr
Langsett
Stocksbridge
Thurgoland
Wortley
Penistone
Crane Moor
Pilley
Birdwell
Wombwell
Darfield
Hoyland Nether
Wath-upon-Dearne
Swinton
Conisbrough
Rawmarsh
Wentworth
Greasbrough
Chapeltown
Grenoside
Bradfield
Ecclesfield
ROTHERHAM
Walkley
SHEFFIELD
Handsworth
Woodhouse
Gleadless
Abbeydale
Dore
Beauchief
Totley
Mosborough
Killamarsh
Eckington
Dronfield
Renishaw
Barlborough
Holmesfield
Whittington
Staveley
Brimington
Calow
Chesterfield
Hasland
Bolsover
Clowne
Creswell
Harthill
Kiveton
Beighton
Aston
Wickersley
Bramley
Thrybergh
Grindleford
Eyam
Froggatt
Calver
Baslow
Tideswell
Gt. Longstone
Chatsworth House
Barlow
Taddington
Ashford
Bakewell
Flagg
Monyash
Haddon Hall
Rowsley
Stone Edge
Wingerworth
Youlgreave
Arbor Low
Nine Ladies
Two Dales
DERBYSHIRE
Ashover
Clay Cross
Wingfield
Hardwick Hall
Pleasley
Mansfield
Tibshelf
Morton
South Normanton
Higham
Alfreton
Winster
Matlock
Matlock Bath
Riber Castle
Cromford
S. Wingfield
Crich
Whatstandwell
Somercotes
Pinxton
Selston
Swanwick
Ripley
Codnor
Heanor
Eastwood
Kilburn
Smalley
Kimberley
Ilkeston
NOTTING
Chaddesden
Ockbrook
Spondon
Stapleford
DERBY
Mickleover
Littleover
Borrowash
Alvaston
Breaston
Draycott
Long Eaton
Shardlow
Chellaston
Shelton Lock
Swarkestone
Weston-on-Trent
Castle Donington
EAST MIDLANDS AIRPORT
Kegworth
Melbourne
Ticknall
Calke Abbey
Staunton Harold Reservoir
Foremark Reservoir
Donington Park
Shepshed
Coleorton
Thringstone
Whitwick
Charnwood
Coalville
Toton
Beeston
Wollaton Hall
Bramcote
Annesley Woodhouse
Kirkby-in-Ashfield
Penkridge
Cannock
Gnosall
Eccleshall
Chadderton
Failsworth
Lees
Droylsden

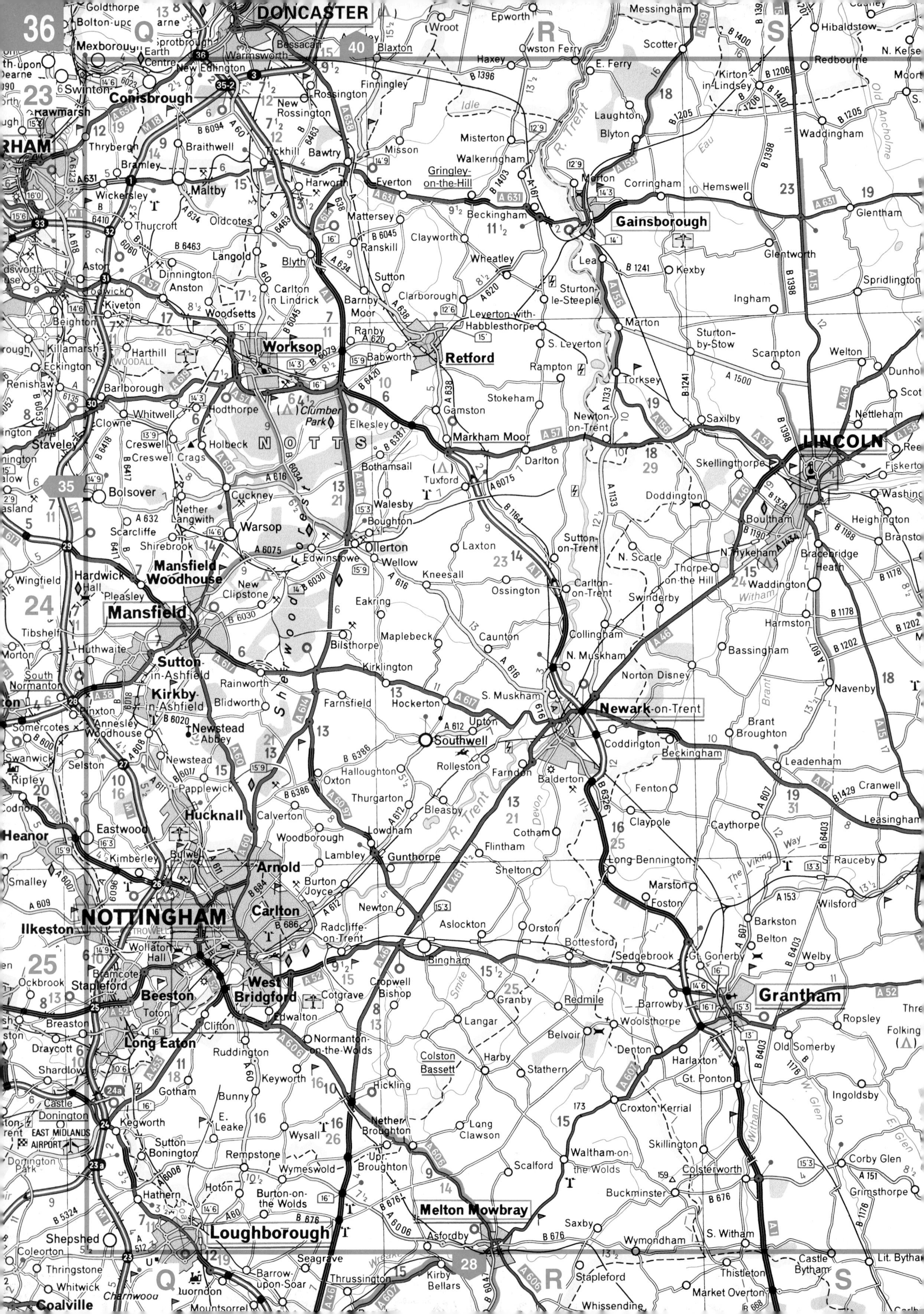
DONCASTER
Mexborough
Conisbrough
Rawmarsh
Swinton
Maltby
Bawtry
Tickhill
Harworth
Blyth
Worksop
Retford
Gainsborough
LINCOLN
NOTTS
Clumber Park
Markham Moor
Tuxford
Ollerton
Edwinstowe
Bolsover
Warsop
Mansfield Woodhouse
Mansfield
Sutton-in-Ashfield
Kirkby-in-Ashfield
Newstead Abbey
Hucknall
Arnold
Carlton
NOTTINGHAM
West Bridgford
Beeston
Long Eaton
Ilkeston
Eastwood
Heanor
Ripley
Southwell
Newark-on-Trent
Bingham
Grantham
Melton Mowbray
Loughborough
Shepshed
Coalville
Kegworth
EAST MIDLANDS AIRPORT
Castle Donington
Staveley
Clowne
Whitwell
Creswell Crags
Saxilby
Torksey
Misterton
Gringley-on-the-Hill
Everton
Beckingham
Sturton-le-Steeple
Collingham
Waddington
Navenby
Leadenham
Caythorpe
Long Bennington
Bottesford
Sedgebrook
Belvoir
Harlaxton
Colsterworth
Corby Glen
Castle Bytham
Barrow-upon-Soar
Kirby Bellars
Asfordby
Keyworth
Ruddington
Cotgrave
Gunthorpe
Lowdham
Calverton
Bleasby
Rolleston
Farndon
Balderton
Coddington
Claypole
Welbourn
R. Trent
Sherwood Forest

LINCS.
LINCOLNSHIRE
Lincolnshire Wolds
Rotterdam
Zeebrugge
Holton-le-Clay
Tetney
Caistor
Swallow
Nettleton
Kelsey
Marshchapel
N. Thoresby
Fulstow
Grainthorpe
N. Somercotes
Thoresway
Wold Newton
Ludborough
Conisholme
Stainton-le-Vale
Binbrook
Saltfleet
Osgodby
Tealby
Alvingham
Market Rasen
Rase
Middle Rasen
Ludford
Welton-le-Wold
Louth
Theddlethorpe St.Helen
Willingham Forest
Grimoldby
Linwood
Hainton
Legbourne
Mablethorpe
Faldingworth
Donington-on-Bain
Trusthorpe
East Barkwith
Tathwell
Withern
Maltby-le-Marsh
Sutton-on-Sea
Wickenby
Holton
Cadwell Park
Burwell
Scamblesby
Wragby
Bain
S. Thoresby
Huttoft
Belchford
Alford
Mumby
Tetford
Minting
Baumber
Ulceby
Hogsthorpe
Chapel St.Leonards
Willoughby
Bardney
Bucknall
Horncastle
Hagworthingham
Horsington
Ingoldmells
Partney
Spilsby
Candlesby
Burgh-le-Marsh
Potterhanworth
Old Bolingbroke
Nocton
The Viking Way
Irby
Skegness
Woodhall Spa
Haltham
Keal
Dunston
Steeping
Mareham-le-Fen
Martin
Scopwick
Tattershall
Coningsby
Wainfleet All Saints
Walcott
Eastville
Stickney
Friskney
Billinghay
East Fen
West Fen
Digby
N. Kyme
Wrangle
Ruskington
Frithville
Sibsey
R. Witham
Old Leake
S. Kyme
Deeps
Long Sand
Langrick
Hobhole Drain
Benington
Boston Deeps
Lynn Deeps
Kirkby-la-Thorpe
Boston
Holland Fen
Sleaford
Heckington
Freiston
Holme-next the Sea
Wyberton
Fishtoft
Hunstanton
Helpringham
Kirton End
Scredington
Swineshead
The Wash
Heacham
Bicker
Kirton
Donington
Sutterton
Snettisham
Fosdyke
Billingborough
South Forty Foot Drain
Gosberton
Holbeach St. Matthew
Dersingham
Dowsby
Risegate
Holbeach Marsh
Gedney Drove End
Sandringham House
Rippingale
Surfleet
R. Welland
Saracen's Head
Kirby Underwood
Pinchbeck
Weston
Whaplode
Fleet Hargate
Lutton
Castle Rising
Pinchbeck W
Gedney Dyke
N. Wootton
Morton
Moulton
Holbeach
Long Sutton
S. Wootton
Spalding
Sutton Bridge
King's Lynn
Terrington St. Clement
Clenchwarton
Gaywood
Bourne
Moulton Chapel
Sutton St. James
R. Nene
Thurlby
Tydd St. Mary
Walpole St. Andrew
Deeping St. Nicholas
Glen
St. Johns
Tydd St. Giles
Walpole St.Peter
Ouse
E. Winch
W. Winch
T
U
V
23
24
25
41
29
30
A 16
A 18
A 631
A 46
A 157
A 153
A 1104
A 1031
A 1028
A 158
A 52
A 155
A 17
A 1121
A 151
A 15
A 149
A 148
A 47
A 1101
A 1111
B 1205
B 1434
B 1225
B 1203
B 1201
B 1200
B 1202
B 1399
B 1373
B 1449
B 1190
B 1191
B 1195
B 1183
B 1192
B 1189
B 1188
B 1184
B 1209
B 1395
B 1394
B 1391
B 1181
B 1117
B 1397
B 1357
B 1359
B 1165
B 1168
B 1390
B 1439
B 1145
B 1161

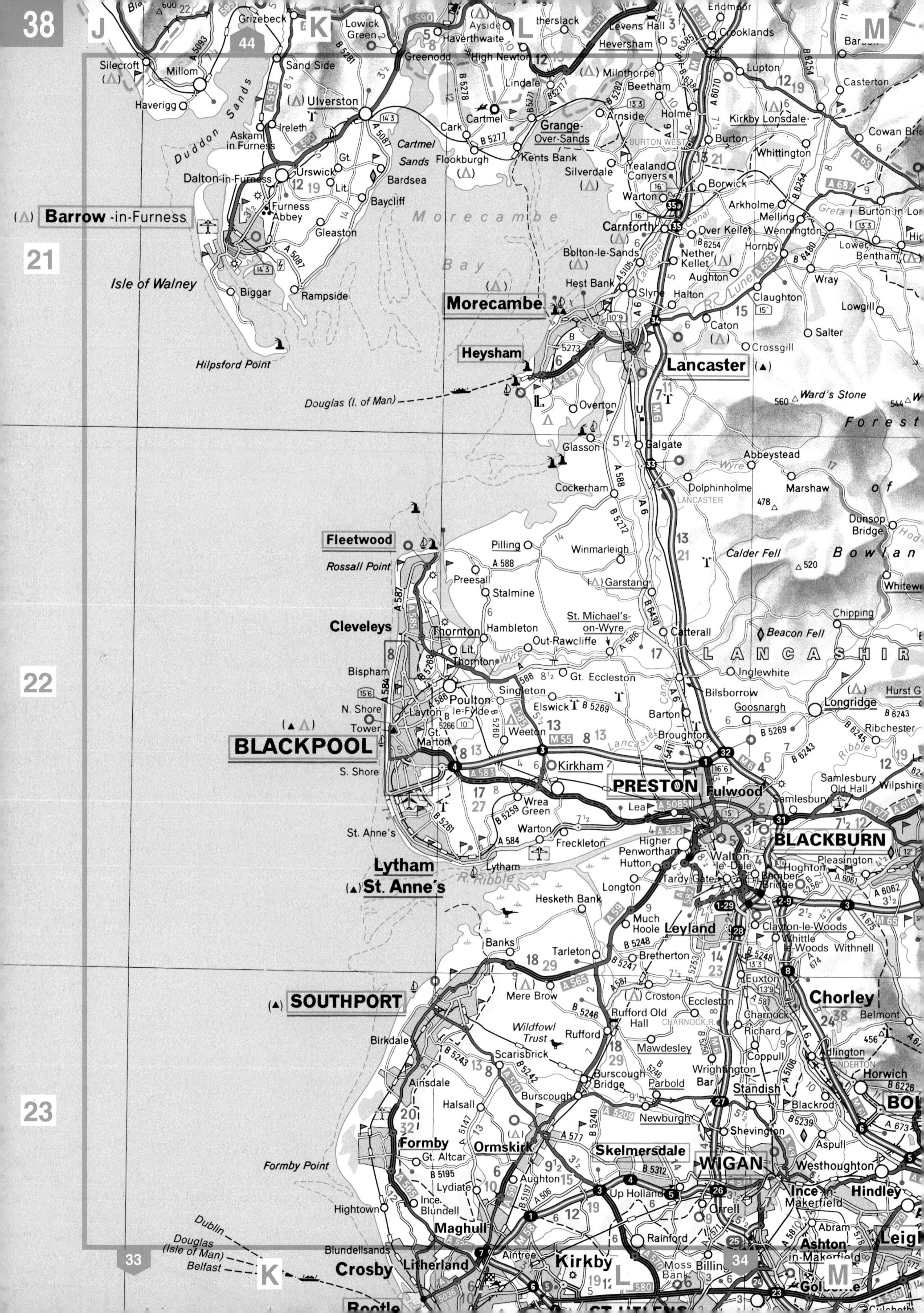

J
K
L
M
44
Grizebeck
Lowick Green
Ayside
Levens Hall
Crooklands
Haverthwaite
Greenodd
High Newton
Heversham
Silecroft
Millom
Sand Side
Lindale
Milnthorpe
Lupton
Duddon Sands
Ulverston
Beetham
Casterton
Haverigg
Askam in Furness
Ireleth
Cartmel
Arnside
Holme
Kirkby Lonsdale
Cark
Grange-Over-Sands
Burton
Cowan Bridge
Cartmel Sands
Flookburgh
Kents Bank
Whittington
Dalton-in-Furness
Urswick
Bardsea
Silverdale
Yealand Conyers
Borwick
Furness Abbey
Baycliff
Warton
Arkholme
Barrow-in-Furness
Gleaston
Morecambe Bay
Carnforth
Over Kellet
Melling
Wennington
Bolton-le-Sands
Nether Kellet
Hornby
Bentham
Isle of Walney
Biggar
Rampside
Hest Bank
Aughton
Wray
Morecambe
Slyne
Halton
Claughton
Caton
Lowgill
Salter
Crossgill
Heysham
Lancaster
Hilpsford Point
Ward's Stone
Douglas (I. of Man)
Overton
Forest of Bowland
Glasson
Galgate
Abbeystead
Cockerham
Dolphinholme
Marshaw
Dunsop Bridge
Fleetwood
Pilling
Winmarleigh
Calder Fell
Rossall Point
Preesall
Garstang
Stalmine
Cleveleys
Hambleton
St. Michael's-on-Wyre
Chipping
Thornton
Out-Rawcliffe
Catterall
Beacon Fell
Bispham
LANCASHIRE
Inglewhite
Gt. Eccleston
Singleton
Bilsborrow
Longridge
Hurst Green
N. Shore
Poulton-le-Fylde
Elswick
Goosnargh
Tower
Layton
Barton
Ribchester
BLACKPOOL
Weeton
Broughton
Gt. Marton
Kirkham
S. Shore
PRESTON
Fulwood
Samlesbury Old Hall
Wrea Green
Lea
St. Anne's
Warton
Freckleton
Higher Penwortham
BLACKBURN
Hutton
Walton-le-Dale
Pleasington
Lytham St. Anne's
Lytham
R. Ribble
Tardy Gate
Hoghton
Bamber Bridge
Longton
Hesketh Bank
Much Hoole
Leyland
Clayton-le-Woods
Whittle-le-Woods
Withnell
Banks
Tarleton
Bretherton
Euxton
Mere Brow
Croston
Eccleston
SOUTHPORT
Chorley
Rufford Old Hall
Charnock Richard
Belmont
Wildfowl Trust
Rufford
Birkdale
Mawdesley
Coppull
Adlington
Scarisbrick
Wrightington Bar
Horwich
Burscough Bridge
Parbold
Ainsdale
Standish
Burscough
Blackrod
Halsall
Newburgh
Shevington
Aspull
Formby
Ormskirk
Skelmersdale
WIGAN
Westhoughton
Gt. Altcar
Formby Point
Lydiate
Aughton
Up Holland
Ince-in-Makerfield
Hindley
Hightown
Ince Blundell
Orrell
Maghull
Rainford
Abram
Ashton-in-Makerfield
Leigh
Dublin
Douglas (Isle of Man)
Belfast
Blundellsands
Crosby
Litherland
Aintree
Kirkby
Moss Bank
Billinge
Golborne
Bootle
33
34
21
22
23

N
O
P
45
46
Yorkshire Dales National Park
Deepdale
Whernside
Kidstones
Carlton-in-Coverdale
E. Witton
Burnes
Carlton
Horsehouse
Walden Head
Middle Tongue
Langstrothdale
Chase
Buckden Pike
Masham Moor
Fearby
Masham
Healey
Well
Kirklington
W. Tanfield
Chapel le Dale
Ribblehead Station
Yockenthwaite
High Birkwith
Halton Gill
Buckden
Foxup
Pen-y-ghent
White Scar Caves
Ingleborough
Littondale
Arncliffe
Kettlewell
Great Whernside
NORTH
Nidderdale
Lofthouse
Ramsgill-in-Nidderdale
Kirkby Malzeard
North Stainley
Wath
21
Winksley
Studley Royal Gardens
Risplith
Fountains Abbey
Ingleton
Horton in Ribblesdale
Clapham
Austwick
Keasden
Stainforth
Malham Tarn
Kilnsey
Burn Moor
Langcliffe
Settle
Kirkby Fell
Malham
Threshfield
Grassington
Linton
Greenhow Hill
Pateley Bridge
Glasshouses
Brimham Rocks
Markington
Burnt Yates
Bishop Thornton
Summer Bridge
Dacre
Ripley
Kirkby Malham
Burnsall
Appletreewick
Washburn
Rathmell
Long Preston
Airton
Hetton
Rylstone
Brown Bank Head
Hampsthwaite
Forest Moor
Killinghall
Wigglesworth
Hellifield
Ribblesdale
The Strid
Blubberhouses
HARROGATE
Stocks Resr.
Gargrave
Embsay
Bolton Abbey
Priory
Round Hill
Fewston
Beckwithshaw
Slaidburn
Skipton
Draughton
Beamsley
Leeds and Liverpool Canal
Newton
Bolton-by-Bowland
Low Bradley
Addingham
Middleton
Askwith
N. Rigton
40
Gisburn
Thornton-in-Craven
Carleton
Farnley
Leathley
Sawley
Barnoldswick
Earby
Lothersdale
Silsden
Ilkley
Otley
Pool-in-Wharfedale
Harewood House
Grindleton
Rimington
Kildwick
Rombalds Moor
Burley in Wharfedale
Waddington
Chatburn
Cowling
Glusburn
Steeton
Menston
Guiseley
Bramhope
Bashall Eaves
Clitheroe
Pendle Hill
Blacko
Foulridge
Keighley
Morton
Yeadon
LEEDS AND BRADFORD AIRPORT
22
Barley
Colne
Wycoller
Keighley Moor
Oakworth
Baildon
Bingley
Gt. Milton
Barrowford
Sabden
Fence
Trawden
Haworth
Cullingworth
Horsforth
Whalley
Nelson
Boulsworth Hill
Shipley
LEEDS
Billington
Higham
Brierfield
Penistone Hill
Denholme
Calverley
Farsley
Read
Padiham
BURNLEY
Walshaw Dean Resrs.
Oxenhope
Gt. Harwood
MICHELIN
Worsthorne
Widdop Resr.
Thornton
Pudsey
Clayton-le-Moors
Altham
Towneley Hall
BRADFORD
Rishton
Hapton
Gorple Resrs.
Hebden Bridge
Queensbury
Shelf
Drighlington
Gildersome
Wainstalls
Illingworth
Birkenshaw
Church
Accrington
Heptonstall
Northowram
Morley
Oswaldtwistle
Dunnockshaw
Forest of Rossendale
Mytholmroyd
Luddenden
Wyke
Lofthouse
Cleckheaton
Gomersal
Tingley
Haslingden
Rawtenstall
Todmorden
Sowerby Bridge
Brighouse
Heckmondwike
Batley
HARTSHEAD MOOR
Liversedge
Bacup
Walsden
Dewsbury
Darwen
CALDERDALE
HALIFAX
Ossett
Mirfield
Elland
Horbury
Whitworth
Ripponden
Thornhill
Edgworth
Wardle
Littleborough
HUDDERSFIELD
Kirkheaton
Middlestown
Ramsbottom
ROCHDALE
Netherton
WOOLLEY EDGE
Criggle
Bromley Cross
BURY
Bamford
Milnrow
Slaithwaite
KIRKLEES
Flockton
Tottington
Farnley Tyas
Kirkburton
Meltham
Honley
Clayton West
Darton
Heywood
BIRCH
Shaw
Denshaw
Marsden
Netherthong
Shelley
Shepley
Skelmanthorpe
Little Lever
Radcliffe
Royton
Denby Dale
Kexbrough
Farnworth
Middleton
OLDHAM
Delph
Uppermill
Holmfirth
Silkstone
Kearsley
Whitefield
Holmbridge
Ingbirchworth
Walkden
Chadderton
Lees
Penistone
Dodworth
Atherton
Prestwich
Fallsworth
23
Pendlebury
Ashton-under-Lyne
Mossley
Crane Moor
Tyldesley
Worsley
Stalybridge
Woodhead
Thurgoland
Wortley
Pilley
Eccles
MANCHESTER
35
Langsett
Tintwistle
Stocksbridge
SALFORD
Audenshaw
Dukinfield
Hadfield
Bleaklow Hill

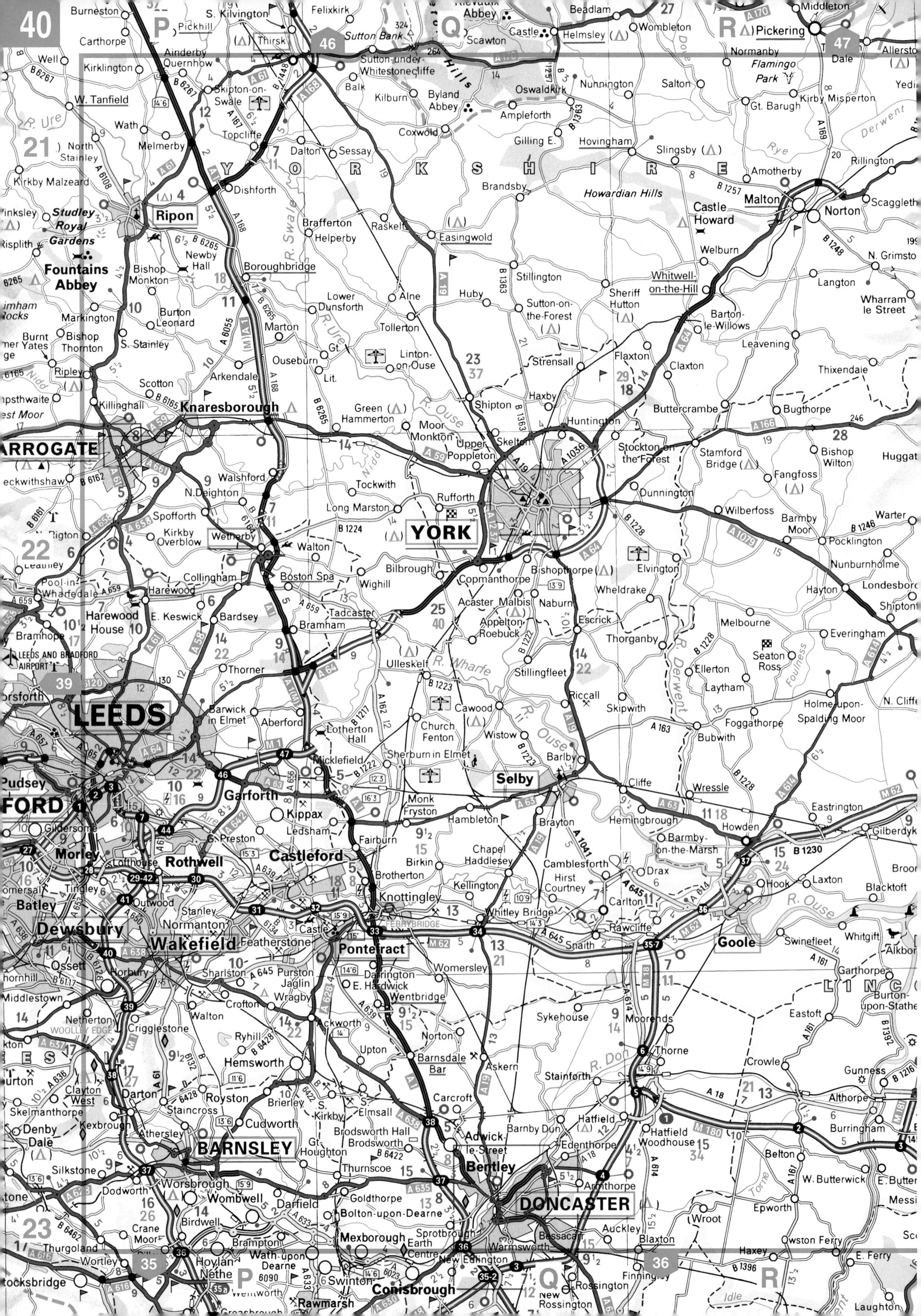
P
Q
R
46
47
21
22
23
39
35
36
Y O R K S H I R E
Burneston
Carthorpe
S. Kilvington
Pickhill
Thirsk
Felixkirk
Sutton Bank
Rievaulx Abbey
Beadlam
Helmsley
Wombleton
Middleton
Pickering
Kirklington
Ainderby Quernhow
Sutton-under-Whitestonecliffe
Scawton
Normanby
Flamingo Park
Allerston
Dale
W. Tanfield
Skipton-on-Swale
Balk
Kilburn
Byland Abbey
Oswaldkirk
Nunnington
Salton
Kirby Misperton
Gt. Barugh
Wath
Topcliffe
Coxwold
Ampleforth
R. Ure
Derwent
North Stainley
Melmerby
Dalton
Sessay
Gilling E.
Hovingham
Slingsby
Rye
Rillington
Amotherby
Kirkby Malzeard
Dishforth
Brandsby
Howardian Hills
Malton
Norton
Castle Howard
Scagglethorpe
Studley Royal Gardens
Ripon
Brafferton
Helperby
Raskelf
Easingwold
Fountains Abbey
Bishop Monkton
Newby Hall
Boroughbridge
Stillington
Welburn
Whitwell-on-the-Hill
Sheriff Hutton
Langton
N. Grimston
Wharram le Street
Markington
Burton Leonard
Lower Dunsforth
Alne
Huby
Sutton-on-the-Forest
Barton-le-Willows
Bishop Thornton
S. Stainley
Marton
Tollerton
Linton-on-Ouse
Strensall
Flaxton
Leavening
Claxton
Ripley
Nidd
Ouseburn
Gt.
Lit.
Arkendale
Scotton
Thixendale
Knaresborough
Green Hammerton
R. Ouse
Shipton
Haxby
Huntington
Buttercrambe
Bugthorpe
Killinghall
HARROGATE
Moor Monkton
Upper Poppleton
Skelton
Stockton on the Forest
Stamford Bridge
Bishop Wilton
Huggate
Walshford
N. Deighton
Tockwith
Long Marston
Rufforth
YORK
Dunnington
Fangfoss
Spofforth
Kirkby Overblow
Wetherby
Walton
Wilberfoss
Barmby Moor
Warter
Pocklington
Bilbrough
Bishopthorpe
Elvington
Nunburnholme
Collingham
Boston Spa
Wighill
Copmanthorpe
Wheldrake
Hayton
Londesborough
Harewood
Pool-in-Wharfedale
Acaster Malbis
Naburn
Appleton Roebuck
Escrick
Shipton
Harewood House
E. Keswick
Bardsey
Tadcaster
Bramham
Melbourne
Everingham
Thorganby
Bramhope
Leeds and Bradford Airport
Thorner
Ulleskelf
R. Wharfe
Stillingfleet
Seaton Ross
Ellerton
Laytham
R. Derwent
Foulness
LEEDS
Barwick in Elmet
Aberford
Lotherton Hall
Church Fenton
Cawood
Riccall
Skipwith
Holme-upon-Spalding Moor
N. Cliffe
Wistow
Bubwith
Foggathorpe
Sherburn in Elmet
Micklefield
Barlby
Selby
Cliffe
Wressle
Pudsey
Garforth
Kippax
Monk Fryston
Hambleton
Brayton
Hemingbrough
Eastrington
Gilberdyke
Gildersome
Ledsham
Fairburn
Barmby-on-the-Marsh
Howden
Morley
Lofthouse
Rothwell
G. Preston
Castleford
Birkin
Chapel Haddlesey
Camblesforth
Drax
Hook
Laxton
Blacktoft
Tingley
Batley
Outwood
Stanley
Brotherton
Knottingley
Kellington
Hirst Courtney
Carlton
R. Ouse
Dewsbury
Normanton
Wakefield
Featherstone
Castle
Ferrybridge
Pontefract
Whitley Bridge
Snaith
Rawcliffe
Goole
Swinefleet
Whitgift
Alkborough
Ossett
Horbury
Sharlston
Purston Jaglin
Darrington
E. Hardwick
Wentbridge
Womersley
Garthorpe
Hornhill
Middlestown
Crofton
Wragby
Netherton
Woolley Edge
Crigglestone
Walton
Ryhill
Ackworth
Sykehouse
Moorends
Eastoft
Burton-upon-Stather
Hemsworth
Upton
Norton
Barnsdale Bar
Askern
Stainforth
Thorne
R. Don
Crowle
Gunness
Clayton West
Darton
Royston
Brierley
S. Kirkby
Elmsall
Carcroft
Hatfield
Althorpe
Skelmanthorpe
Denby Dale
Kexbrough
Staincross
Cudworth
Athersley
BARNSLEY
Gt. Houghton
Brodsworth Hall
Brodsworth
Adwick-le-Street
Barnby Dun
Hatfield Woodhouse
Edenthorpe
Burringham
Belton
Silkstone
Worsbrough
Wombwell
Darfield
Thurnscoe
Goldthorpe
Bolton-upon-Dearne
Bentley
Armthorpe
DONCASTER
W. Butterwick
E. Butterwick
Messingham
Dodworth
Epworth
Wroot
Birdwell
Crane Moor
Thurgoland
Brampton
Mexborough
Sprotbrough
Earth Centre
Warmsworth
Bessacarr
Auckley
Blaxton
Haxey
Owston Ferry
Wortley
Hoyland Nether
Wath-upon-Dearne
Swinton
Conisbrough
New Edlington
Rossington
New Rossington
Finningley
E. Ferry
Stocksbridge
Wentworth
Rawmarsh
Idle
Laughton

T
U
21
22
23
S
Ayton
Eastfield
Ebberston
Wykeham
Seamer
Cayton
Lebberston
Brompton by Sawdon
The Carrs
Hertford
Gristhorpe
Filey
Filey Bay
Staxton
Muston
Sherburn
Ganton
Hunmanby
W. Heslerton
Reighton
Speeton
Bempton
Flamborough Head
Flamborough
Wintringham
Foxholes
Burton Fleming
Weaverthorpe
W. Lutton
Langtoft
Rudston
Carnaby
Bridlington
Bridlington Bay
Duggleby
Wolds
Kilham
Sledmere
Burton Agnes
Monument
Garton-on-the-Wolds
Nafferton
Wetwang
Barmston
Fridaythorpe
Gt. Driffield
Lissett
Kelk Beck
Old Howe
Yorkshire
Kirkburn
Wansford
Foston-on-the-Wolds
Skipsea
EAST RIDING OF YORKSHIRE
Beeford
N. Dalton
Bainton
Hutton Cranswick
N. Frodingham
Hull
Atwick
Middleton-on-the-Wolds
Watton
Bewholme
Lund
Lockington
Burshill
Brandesburton
Hornsea
Leven
Sigglesthorne
Mappleton
Market Weighton
Cherry Burton
Leconfield
Arram
Routh
Beverley
Withernwick
Sancton
Bishop Burton
R. Hull
Skirlaugh
Aldbrough
N. Newbald
Walkington
Wawne
Burton Constable Hall
Lit. Weighton
Cottingham
Sutton-on-Hull
Sproatley
Humbleton
N. Cave
Skidby
Riplingham
Bilton
Burton Pidsea
Tunstall
Willerby
Preston
Roos
S. Cave
Hedon
Withernsea
Elloughton
Swanland
Kirk Ella
Burstwick
Brough
Paull
KINGSTON-UPON-HULL
Hessle
N. Ferriby
Keyingham
Winestead
Hollym
Ottringham
Humber Bridge
Barton-upon-Humber
Whitton
Winteringham
New Holland
Patrington
Holmpton
Goxhill
Read's I.
NORTH LINCOLNSHIRE
Barrow-upon-Humber
Thornton Abbey
E. Halton
S. Ferriby
Winterton
Sunk Island
Easington
Immingham Dock
Normanby Hall
Thornton Curtis
S. Killingholme
R. HUMBER
Kilnsea
Old Ancholme
Ancholme
Appleby
Bonby
Ulceby
Immingham
GREAT GRIMSBY
Elsham
Kirmington
Stallingborough
SCUNTHORPE
Keelby
HUMBERSIDE AIRPORT
Spurn Head
Mouth of the Humber
Healing
Cleethorpes
Broughton
Barnetby-le-Wold
Gt. Limber
Gt. Coates
Bottesford
Wrawby
Laceby
Brigg
Humberston
Scawby
Grasby
N.E. LINCS
Cadney
Waltham
New Waltham
Hibaldstow
Swallow
Holton-le-Clay
Rotterdam
Zeebrugge
N. Kelsey
Caistor
Tetney
Redbourne
Kirton in Lindsey
Moortown
Nettleton
N. Thoresby
Marshchapel
S. Kelsey
Fulstow
Grainthorpe
Wold Newton
N. Somercotes

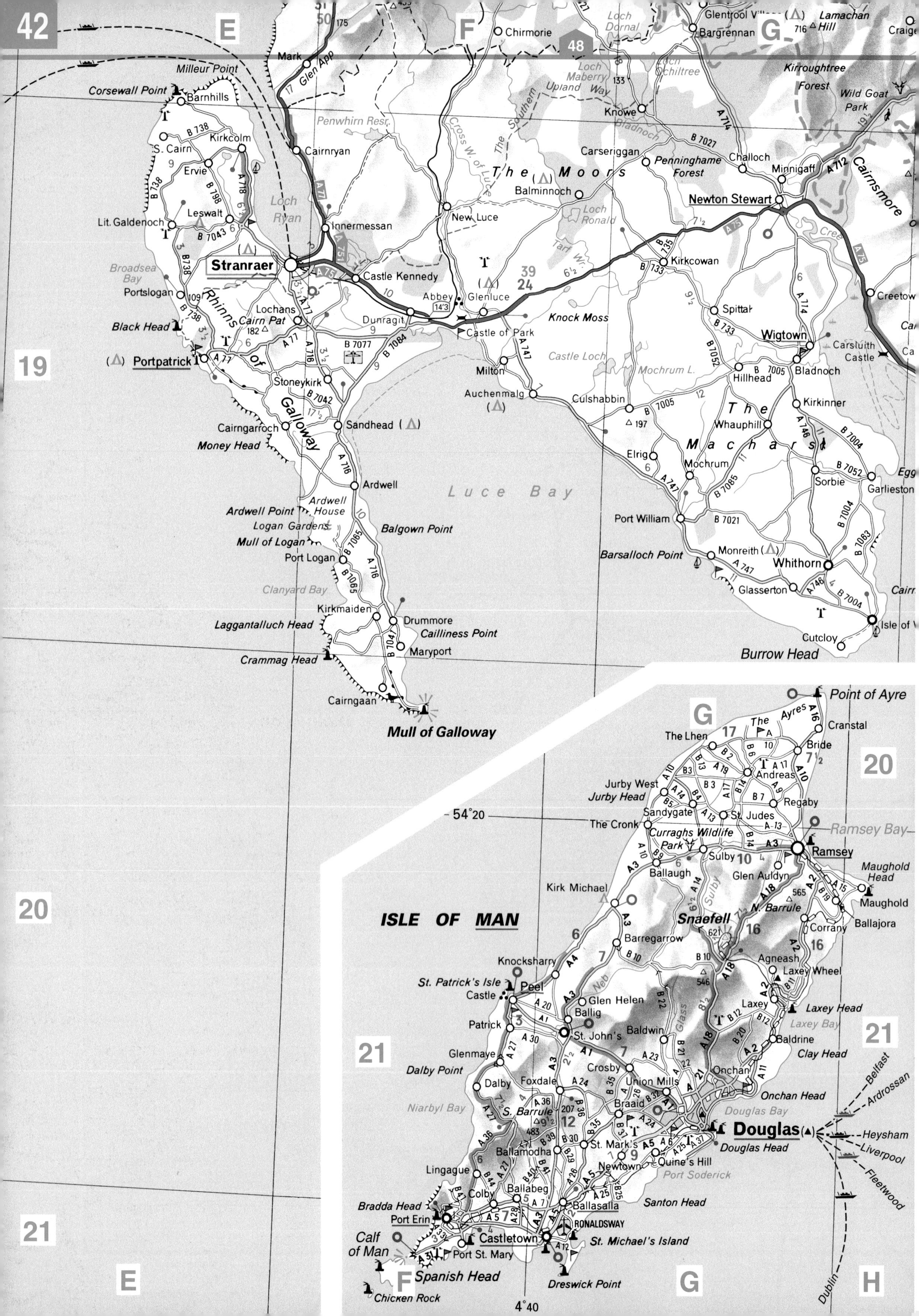
E
F
G
48
19
20
21
H
Chirmorie
Mark
Glen App
Loch Dornal
Bargrennan
Glentrool Village
Lamachan Hill
Loch Maberry
Loch Ryan
Southern Upland Way
Kirroughtree Forest
Wild Goat Park
Milleur Point
Corsewall Point
Barnhills
Knowe
Penwhirn Resr.
Cross W. of Luce
Bladnoch
Kirkcolm
S. Cairn
Cairnryan
Carseriggan
Penninghame Forest
Challoch
Minnigaff
Cairnsmore
Ervie
The Moors
Balminnoch
Newton Stewart
Leswalt
Lit. Galdenoch
Innermessan
New Luce
Loch Ronald
Tarf W.
Broadsea Bay
Stranraer
Castle Kennedy
Kirkcowan
Portslogan
Rhinns of Galloway
Abbey
Glenluce
Creetown
Lochans
Cairn Pat
Dunragit
Knock Moss
Spittal
Black Head
Castle of Park
Wigtown
Carsluith Castle
Portpatrick
Castle Loch
Mochrum L.
Milton
Hillhead
Bladnoch
Stoneykirk
Auchenmalg
Culshabbin
Kirkinner
Galloway
The Machars
Cairngarroch
Sandhead
Whauphill
Money Head
Elrig
Mochrum
Sorbie
Garlieston
Ardwell
Luce Bay
Ardwell House
Ardwell Point
Logan Gardens
Balgown Point
Port William
Mull of Logan
Port Logan
Barsalloch Point
Monreith
Whithorn
Clanyard Bay
Glasserton
Kirkmaiden
Drummore
Laggantalluch Head
Cailliness Point
Isle of Whithorn
Maryport
Cutcloy
Crammag Head
Burrow Head
Cairngaan
Mull of Galloway
Point of Ayre
The Ayres
Cranstal
The Lhen
Bride
Andreas
Jurby West
Jurby Head
Regaby
Sandygate
St. Judes
54°20
The Cronk
Curraghs Wildlife Park
Ramsey Bay
Ramsey
Sulby
Ballaugh
Glen Auldyn
Maughold Head
Kirk Michael
Maughold
N. Barrule
ISLE OF MAN
Snaefell
Ballajora
Corrany
Barregarrow
Agneash
Knocksharry
Laxey Wheel
St. Patrick's Isle
Peel
Castle
Glen Helen
Ballig
Laxey
Laxey Head
Patrick
Laxey Bay
St. John's
Baldwin
Baldrine
Glenmaye
Clay Head
Dalby Point
Crosby
Onchan
Dalby
Foxdale
Union Mills
Onchan Head
Belfast
Ardrossan
Niarbyl Bay
S. Barrule
Braaid
Douglas Bay
Douglas
Heysham
St. Mark's
Douglas Head
Liverpool
Ballamodha
Quine's Hill
Fleetwood
Newtown
Lingague
Port Soderick
Ballabeg
Colby
Santon Head
Bradda Head
Port Erin
Ballasalla
RONALDSWAY
Calf of Man
Castletown
St. Michael's Island
Port St. Mary
Spanish Head
Dreswick Point
Dublin
Chicken Rock
4°40

H
I
J
Galloway
Dumfries
Torthorwald
Collin
Dalton
Mouswald
Lochar Moss
Glencaple
Bankend
Ruthwell
Cummertrees
Caerlaverock Castle
Sweetheart Abbey
New Abbey
R. Nith
Mabie
Beeswing
Lochfoot
Shawhead
Glenkiln
Sculptures
Corsock
Crocketford
Knockvennie Smithy
Kirkpatrick Durham
Milton
Springholm
Parton
Mossdale
Raider's Road
Cairn Edward Forest
Loch Grannoch
Fell of Fleet
Woodhall Loch
L. Ken
Crossmichael
Townhead of Greenlaw
Haugh of Urr
Kirkgunzeon
Laurieston
Laurieston Forest
Castle Douglas
Dalbeattie
Criffel
Carsethorn
Kirkbean
Arbigland
Southerness
Southerness Point
Threave Garden
Bridge of Dee
Gelston
Palnackie
Dalbeattie Forest
Caulkerbush
Sandyhills
Kippford
Rockcliffe
Castlehill Point
Orchardton Tower
Rough I.
Auchencairn
Auchencairn Bay
Hestan I.
Balcary Point
Fleet
Big Water of Fleet
Glengap Forest
Miefield
Ringford
Gatehouse of Fleet
Cardoness Castle
Girthon
Twynholm
Tongland
Kirkcudbright
Sandgreen
Knockbrex
Islands of Fleet
Borgue
Borness
Borness Point
Ross
Lit. Ross
St. Mary's Isle
Kirkcudbright Bay
Townhead
Dundrennan
Abbey Head
Wigtown Bay
Head
Whithorn
SOLWAY FIRTH
Skinburness
Silloth
Beckfoot
Mawbray
Westnewton
Allonby
Allonby Bay
Aspatria
Crosby
Maryport
Dearham
Gilcrux
Plumbland
Flimby
Broughton Moor
Broughton
Cockermouth
Seaton
Workington
St. Clifton
Brigham
Greysouthen
Harrington
Dean
Distington
Ullock
Lowca
Parton
Moresby
Lamplugh
Whitehaven
Frizington
Ennerdale Bridge
Ennerdale Water
Cleator Moor
St. Bees Head
St. Bees
Egremont
Copeland Forest
Beckermet
Calder Bridge
Gosforth
Strands
Santon Bridge
Seascale
Eskdale Green
Holmrook
Drigg
Ravenglass
Muncaster
Whitfell
A 75
A 709
A 712
A 713
A 762
A 711
A 745
A 710
A 755
A 596
A 66
A 595
A 597
A 5086
A 594
B 794
B 795
B 736
B 727
B 793
B 796
B 725
B 724
B 7020
B 5300
B 5301
B 5302
B 5294
B 5295
B 5345
B 5344
B 5292
49
44
18
19
20

I
J
K
49
19
20
21
43
25
16
38
Haugh of Urr
Kirkgunzeon
New Abbey
Sweetheart Ab
Caerlaverock Castle
Ruthwell
Cummertrees
Powfoot
Annan
Eastriggs
Dornock
Rigg
Gretna
R. Eden
Castle Douglas
Dalbeattie
Threave Garden
Gelston
Palnackie
Dalbeattie Forest
Orchardton Tower
Kippford
Sandyhills
Caulkerbush
Criffel
569
Carsethorn
Kirkbean
Arbigland
Southerness
Southerness Point
Rockcliffe
Rough I.
Castlehill Point
Auchencairn
Auchencairn Bay
Hestan I.
Balcary Point
Dundrennan
Abbey Head
391
SOLWAY FIRTH
Bowness-on-Solway
Port Carlisle
Rockcliffe
Beaumont
Hadrian's Wall
Anthorn
Drumburgh
Cardurnock
Burgh-by-Sands
Thurstonfield
Moricambe Bay
Skinburness
Kirkbride
Kirkbampton
CARLISLE
Newton Arlosh
Silloth
Aikton
Gt. Orton
Cummersdale
Wampool
Waver
Beckfoot
Abbey Town
Thursby
Wigton
Waverton
Mawbray
Westward
Rosley
Caldew
Westnewton
Welton
Allonby
Aspatria
Mealsgate
Sebergh
Allonby Bay
Plumbland
Caldbeck
Ellen
Ireby
Crosby
Bothel
Uldale
Hesket Newmarket
Gilcrux
Binsey
447
Maryport
Dearham
Bewaldeth
Flimby
Broughton Moor
Derwent
Broughton
Cockermouth
Bassenthwaite
Knott
710
CUMB
Seaton
Bassenthwaite Lake
Mungrisdale
Workington
Brigham
Embleton
Skiddaw Forest
Saddleback or Blencathra
St. Clifton
Greysouthen
Thornthwaite Forest
931
Skiddaw
868
Harrington
High Lorton
Thornthwaite
Keswick
Threlkeld
Troutbeck
Whinlatter Pass
318
Greta
Dean
Distington
Ullock
Braithwaite
Castlerigg
Lowca
Brackenthwaite
Derwentwater
Dockray
Parton
Moresby
247
Lamplugh
Loweswater
Stair
Whitehaven
Crummock Water
Grange
851
Thirlspot
Frizington
Ennerdale Bridge
Buttermere
608
Glenridding
Buttermere
754
Thirlmere
949
Cleator Moor
Ennerdale Water
358
Rosthwaite
Helvellyn
Ehen
Honister Pass
St. Bees Head
St. Bees
Seathwaite
722
873
Egremont
Great Gable
899
Lake District National Park
Copeland Forest
Wasdale Head
692
Beckermet
Calder Bridge
977
Grasmere
Dove Cottage
Scafell Pikes
902
Rydal
Wast Water
Langdale Valley
Chapel Stile
Gosforth
Strands
CUMBRIAN MOUNTAINS
Lit. Langdale
390
Skelwith Bridge
Seascale
Santon Bridge
Eskdale Green
Boot
Hard Knott Pass
Wrynose Pass
393
The Tarn
Irt
Furness Fells
Windermere
Drigg
Holmrook
Eskdale
Esk
The Old Man
801
Hawkshead
Ravenglass
Muncaster
Coniston
Brantwood
Seathwaite
Duddon
Hill Top
Sawrey
Torver
Ulpha
Whitfell
572
Grizedale
Coniston Water
Grizedale Forest
Satterthwaite
Broughton Mills
Bootle
Selker Bay
Blawith
Broughton-in-Furness
Rusland
Windermere
Black Combe
600
Lowick Bridge
Oxen Park
Newby
Grizebeck
Lowick Green
Ayside
Haverthwaite
Greenodd
High Newton
Silecroft
Millom
Sand Side
Haverigg
Sands
Ulverston
A 711
A 745
B 736
B 794
B 793
A 710
B 727
B 724
A 74
B 5307
B 5302
A 596
B 5303
B 5304
B 5305
A 595
B 5301
B 5300
B 5299
A 594
A 591
A 66
B 5291
B 5086
B 5292
B 5289
A 597
A 5086
B 5294
B 5295
B 5345
B 5322
B 5343
A 593
B 5344
B 5285
A 5084
A 5092
A 5093
B 5281
A 590
B 5278

Gilsland
Once Brewed
Acomb
Corstopitum
Greenhead
Vindolanda
Haltwhistle
Henshaw
Haydon Bridge
Hexham
Smithfield
Walton
Lanercost
Scaleby
Brampton
Low Row
Plenmeller
Blackford
Irthington
Milton
Low Crosby
Farlam
Talkin
Midgeholme
Lambley
Whitfield
Catton
Whitley Chapel
Slaley
Broomhaugh
Warwick Bridge
Scotby
Wetheral
Castle Carrock
Cold Fell
King's Forest of Geltsdale
Knarsdale
Slaggyford
Whitfield Moor
Ninebanks
Allendale Town
Broadwell Ho
Derwent Res.
Blanchland
Pow Hill
Edmundbyers
Cumwhitton
Cotehill
Newbiggin
Wreay
Croglin
Ainstable
Armathwaite
Southwaite
High Hesket
Renwick
Gilderdale Forest
Alston
Carr Shield
Allenheads
Nenthead
Leadgate
Garrigill
Muggleswick Common
Rookhope
Cowshill
Stanhope
Inglewood Forest
Calthwaite
Kirkoswald
Lazonby
Gamblesby
Glassonby
Hartside Cross
Melmerby Fell
Melmerby
Gt. Salkeld
Plumpton
Burnhope Seat
Weardale
St. John's Chapel
Westgate
Eastgate
Skelton
Langwathby
Skirwith
Cross Fell
Kirkland
Milburn Forest
Tees
Langdon Common
Langdon Beck
Bollihope Common
Pawlaw
Newton Reigny
Penrith
Greystoke
Stainton
Culgaith
Milburn
Cow Green Resr.
Dufton Fell
Penruddock
Dacre
Clifton
Temple Sowerby
Kirkby Thore
Pennine Way
The High Force
Newbiggin
Middleton-in-Teesdale
Holwick
Hamsterley Forest
Pooley Bridge
Askham
Cliburn
Long Marton
Dufton
Brampton
High Cup Nick
Mickle Fell
Mickleton
Eggleston
Watermillock
Lowther Wildlife Park
Gt. Strickland
Helton
Morland
Murton
Hilton
Romaldkirk
Ullswater
King's Meaburn
Colby
Appleby
Sleagill
Selset Resr.
Hury
Cotherstone
Sandwick
Martindale
Bampton
Balderhead Resr.
Clove Lodge
Startforth
Dale Head
Rosgill
Sandford
Warcop
Brough
N. Stainmore
Shap
Crosby Ravensworth
Gt. Musgrave
Castle
Bowes
Haweswater Resr.
Gt. Asby
Shap Summit
Soulby
Winton
High Street
Harter Fell
Stainmore Forest
Kirkstone Pass
Shap Fells
Orton
Kirkby Stephen
Nateby
Tan Hill
Ambleside
Sadgill
Kelleth
Tebay
Ravenstonedale
Whaw
Kentmere
Troutbeck
Rogan's Seat
Langthwaite
Outhgill
Keld
Arkengarthdale
Langdale Fell
Ings
Staveley
Watchgate
The Calf
Thwaite
Muker
Gunnerside
Feetham
Swale Dale
Low Row
Bowness
Burneside
Grayrigg
Gt. Shunner Fell
Winster
Crook
Meal Bank
Cautley
East Bolton Moor
Underbarrow
Kendal
Castle Bolton
Crosthwaite
Sedbergh
Garsdale Head
Askrigg
Bainbridge
Killington Resr.
Garsdale
Hawes
Wensleydale
Old Hutton
Rise Hill
Aysgarth
Cartmel Fell
Levens
Dentdale
Dent
Lea Yeat
Marsett
Thoralby
W. Burton
Endmoor
Stalling Busk
Witherslack
Levens Hall
Crooklands
Deepdale
Yorkshire Dales National Park
Heversham
Barbon
Kidstones
Horsehouse
Lupton
Whernside
Middle Tongue
Walden Head
Beetham
Casterton
Langstrothdale Chase
Buckden Pike
Ribblehead
Yockenthwaite
Chapel le Dale

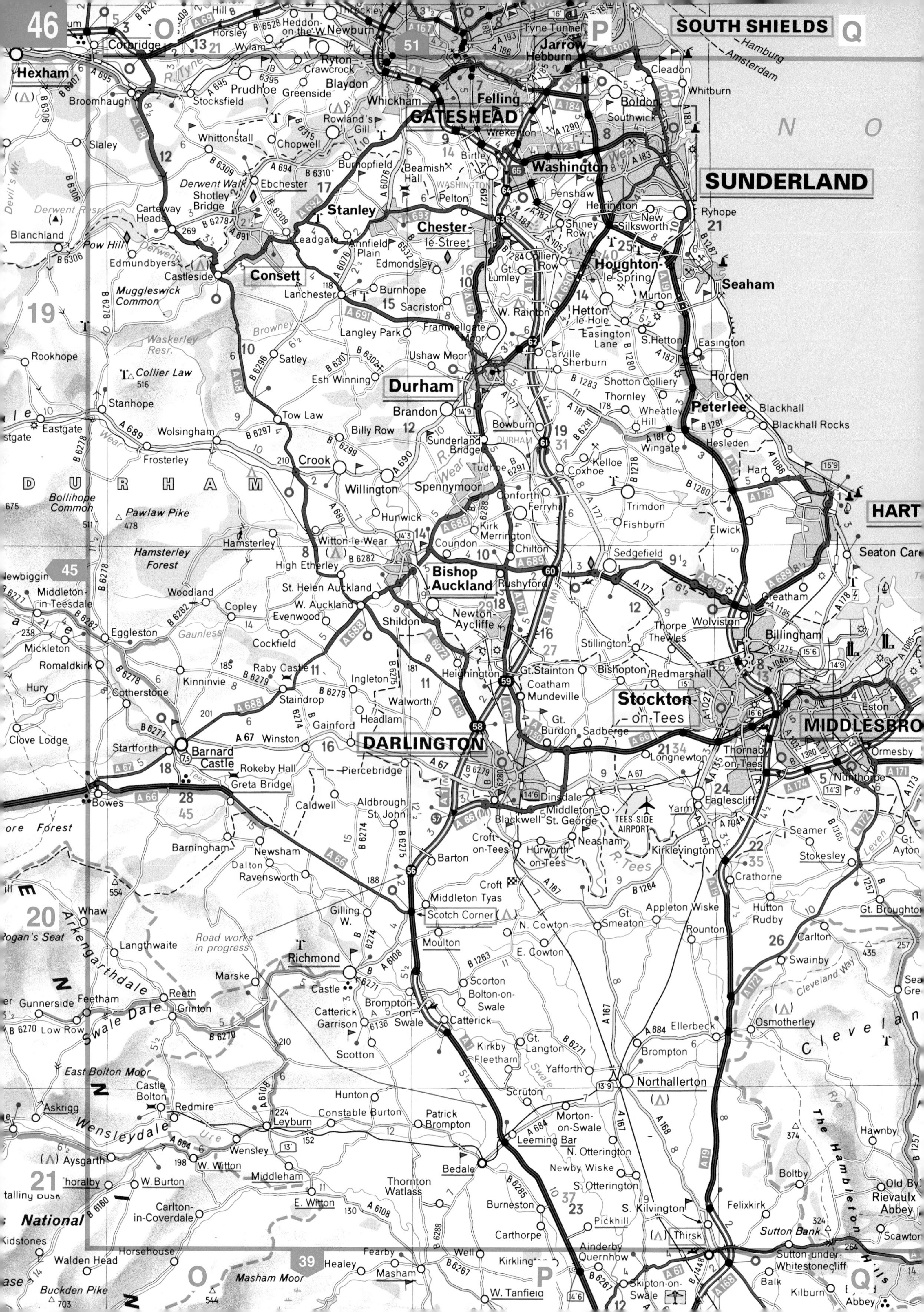

SOUTH SHIELDS
Hexham
Corbridge
Horsley
Heddon-on-the-W.
Newburn
Throckley
Wylam
Ryton
Crawcrock
Blaydon
Prudhoe
Greenside
Stocksfield
Broomhaugh
Whickham
GATESHEAD
Felling
Jarrow
Hebburn
Tyne Tunnel
Cleadon
Whitburn
Boldon
Southwick
Hamburg
Amsterdam
Slaley
Whittonstall
Chopwell
Rowland's Gill
Wrekenton
Birtley
Washington
SUNDERLAND
Ryhope
Derwent Walk
Ebchester
Shotley Bridge
Carterway Heads
Derwent Resr.
Blanchland
Pow Hill
Edmundbyers
Castleside
Consett
Leadgate
Annfield Plain
Stanley
Burnopfield
Beamish Hall
Pelton
Chester-le-Street
Penshaw
Herrington
New Silksworth
Shiney Row
Colliery Row
Houghton-le-Spring
Seaham
Gt. Lumley
Edmondsley
Lanchester
Burnhope
Sacriston
W. Rainton
Hetton-le-Hole
Murton
Easington Lane
S.Hetton
Easington
Muggleswick Common
Waskerley Resr.
Browney
Langley Park
Framwellgate Moor
Carville
Sherburn
Shotton Colliery
Horden
Rookhope
Collier Law
Satley
Esh Winning
Ushaw Moor
Durham
Stanhope
Tow Law
Brandon
Bowburn
Thornley
Wheatley Hill
Peterlee
Blackhall
Blackhall Rocks
Eastgate
Wolsingham
Frosterley
Billy Row
Sunderland Bridge
Wingate
Hesleden
Crook
Willington
Spennymoor
Tudhoe
Coxhoe
Kelloe
Hart
DURHAM
Bollihope Common
Pawlaw Pike
Hunwick
Ferryhill
Cornforth
Trimdon
Fishburn
Elwick
HART
Hamsterley
Hamsterley Forest
Witton-le-Wear
Coundon
Kirk Merrington
Chilton
Sedgefield
Seaton Carew
High Etherley
Bishop Auckland
Rushyford
Newbiggin
Middleton-in-Teesdale
Woodland
St. Helen Auckland
W. Auckland
Copley
Evenwood
Shildon
Newton Aycliffe
Thorpe Thewles
Wolviston
Greatham
Billingham
Eggleston
Mickleton
Gaunless
Cockfield
Stillington
Romaldkirk
Kinninvie
Raby Castle
Ingleton
Heighington
Gt. Stainton
Bishopton
Redmarshall
Hury
Cotherstone
Staindrop
Walworth
Coatham Mundeville
Stockton-on-Tees
Eston
MIDDLESBRO
Clove Lodge
Headlam
Gainford
Gt. Burdon
Sadberge
Startforth
Barnard Castle
Winston
DARLINGTON
Longnewton
Thornaby-on-Tees
Ormesby
Rokeby Hall
Greta Bridge
Piercebridge
Nunthorpe
Bowes
Caldwell
Aldbrough St. John
Dinsdale
Middleton-St. George
TEES-SIDE AIRPORT
Yarm
Eaglescliff
Blackwell
Croft-on-Tees
Hurworth-on-Tees
Neasham
Seamer
Gt. Ayton
Barningham
Newsham
Dalton
Ravensworth
Barton
Kirklevington
R. Tees
Stokesley
Crathorne
Whaw
Croft
Middleton Tyas
Scotch Corner
Gilling W.
N. Cowton
Gt. Smeaton
Appleton Wiske
Hutton Rudby
Gt. Broughton
Arkengarthdale
Langthwaite
Road works in progress
Moulton
E. Cowton
Rounton
Carlton
Richmond
Swainby
Marske
Castle
Scorton
Bolton-on-Swale
Cleveland Way
Gunnerside
Feetham
Reeth
Grinton
Swale Dale
Brompton-on-Swale
Catterick Garrison
Catterick
Osmotherley
Low Row
Scotton
Kirkby Fleetham
Gt. Langton
Ellerbeck
Brompton
Cleveland
East Bolton Moor
Castle Bolton
Yafforth
Scruton
Northallerton
Askrigg
Redmire
Hunton
Constable Burton
Patrick Brompton
Morton-on-Swale
Wensleydale
Leyburn
Leeming Bar
Hawnby
Aysgarth
W. Witton
Wensley
N. Otterington
Newby Wiske
Bedale
Boltby
Old Byland
Rievaulx Abbey
Thoralby
W. Burton
Middleham
Thornton Watlass
S. Otterington
E. Witton
Burneston
S. Kilvington
Felixkirk
National
Carlton-in-Coverdale
Pickhill
Sutton Bank
Scawton
Kidstones
Carthorpe
Thirsk
Horsehouse
Walden Head
Fearby
Well
Ainderby Quernhow
Kirklington
Sutton-under-Whitestonecliff
Healey
Masham
Masham Moor
Skipton-on-Swale
Balk
Buckden Pike
W. Tanfield
Kilburn
Byland Abbey
The Hambleton Hills
Rye

R
S
T
19
20
21
R T H S E A
POOL
UGH
Redcar (▲)
Marske-by-the-Sea
Saltburn-by-the-Sea
Brotton
Loftus
Staithes
Easington
Hinderwell
New Marske
Skelton
Boosbeck
Kettleness
REDCAR AND CLEVELAND
Liverton
Guisborough
Stanghow
CLEVELAND
B 1266
A 174
Lythe
Whitby (Δ)
Abbey
Scaling Reservoir
Sandsend
Ugthorpe (Δ)
22
329
236
Danby
299
Kildale
454
Castleton
Lealholm
Egton
Sleights
Ruswarp
Esk
Hawsker
(Δ)
B 1447
Robin Hood's Bay
Ingleby Greenhow
Westerdale
Glaisdale
Grosmont
B 1416
206
Hills
North York Moors
Egton High Moor
288
A 169
433
Westerdale Moor
432
Glaisdale Moor
Goathland
21
Cleveland Way
Ravenscar
454
Wheeldale Moor
Fylingdales Moor
Cockayne
National Park
299
A 171
Staintondale
201
Bransdale
Dove
Rosedale
355
Rosedale Abbey (Δ)
Harwood Dale
Cropton Forest
Langdale Forest
Derwent
Cloughton
Spaunton Moor
280
Hodge Beck
Hartoft End
Burniston
Helmsley Moor
Hutton-le-Hole
Langdale End
Scalby
Newton-on-Rawcliffe
Levisham
Hackness
Gillamoor
Lastingham
Seven
(Δ) Cropton
A 169
Dalby Forest
Appleton-le-Moors
SCARBOROUGH (▲Δ)
Kirkbymoorside
Sinnington
(Δ) Wrelton
Wykeham Forest
Beadlam
27
Middleton
A 170
Ayton
Eastfield
7½
Castle
Helmsley (Δ)
Wombleton
(Δ) Pickering
Ebberston
(Δ)
Wykeham
B 1261
Seamer
Snainton
Cayton
Normanby
Thornton Dale
Allerston
17
Brompton
Lebberston
A 1039
Flamingo Park
B 1415
B 1258
A 170
40
41
Oswaldkirk
Nunnington
Salton
Yedingham
The Carrs
Hertford
Gristhorpe
Filey (Δ)
Filey Bay
Gt. Barugh
Kirby Misperton
Staxton
A 1039
6 Muston

FIRTH OF CLYDE
SOUTH AYRSHIRE
EAST AYRSHIRE
DUMFRIES AND GALLOWAY
Farland Head
Seamill
Sannox Bay
Corrie
Horse I.
Ardrossan
Saltcoats
Stevenston
Kilwinning
Auchentiber
Stewarton
Lochgoin Resr.
Corse Hill
Waterside
Fenwick
Cunninghamhead
Kilmaurs
Crosshouse
Dreghorn
Kilmarnock
Whitelee Forest
Caldermill
Drumclog
Darvel
Newmilns
Greenholm
Galston
Hurlford
Riccarton
Irvine
Irvine Bay
Gatehead
Dundonald
Craigie
Symington
Loans
Troon
Lady I.
Brodick Bay
Clauchlands Point
Margnaheglish
Lamlash Bay
Holy Island
Kingscross Point
Whiting Bay
Dippin Head
Kildonan
Pladda
Monkton
PRESTWICK SCOTLAND AIRPORT
Prestwick
Tarbolton
Mauchline
Sorn
Limmerhaugh
Blackside
Middlefield
Catrine
Annbank Station
Stair
Annbank
AYR
Heads of Ayr
Alloway
Coylton
Ochiltree
Auchinleck
Holmhead
Cumnock
Dalblair
Drongan
Skares
Sinclairston
Hollybush
Rankinston
Dunure
Brown Carrick Hill
Dalrymple
Culzean Bay
Culzean Castle
Maybole
Kirkmichael
Patna
Waterside
New Cumnock
Connel Park
Kyle Forest
Dalleagles
Maidens
Crossraguel Abbey
Kirkoswald
Turnberry
Roan of Graigoch
Crosshill
Straiton
Dalmellington
Blackcraig Hill
Craigdarroch
Afton Resr.
Water of Girvan
Dailly
Old Dailly
Ailsa Craig
Girvan
Tallaminnock
Loch Finlas
Loch Doon
Carsphairn Forest
Cairnsmore of Carsphairn
S. Balloch
Loch Bradan Resr.
Craigmalloch
Barr
Changue Forest
Loch Riecawr
Carrick Forest
Carsphairn
Stinchar
Polmaddie Hill
Loch Macaterick
Meaul
Dundeugh Forest
Knowehead
Lendalfoot
Pinmore Mains
Galloway Forest Park
Bennane Head
Pinwherry
Colmonell
Merrick
Corserine
Forrest Lodge
Ballantrae Bay
Ballantrae
Loch Moan
Loch Enoch
Rhinns of Kells
The Glenkens
Barrhill
Glentrool Forest
Glen Trool Lodge
Loch Dee
Auchencrosh
Lochton
Loch Trool
Clatteringshaws Loch
Dalry
Bogue
New Galloway
Glentrool Village
Lamachan Hill
Chirmorie
Loch Dornal
Bargrennan
Craigencallie
Raider's Road
Mark
Glen App
Loch Maberry
Southern Upland Way
Loch Chiltree
Kirroughtree Forest
Wild Goat Park
Cairn Edward Forest
Knowe
Penwhirn Resr.
Cross W. of Luce
Bladnoch
Loch Grannoch
Fell of Fleet
Cairnryan
Carseriggan
Challoch
Penninghame Forest
The Moors
Minnigaff
Cairnsmore of Fleet
Woodhall Loch
Balminnoch
Newton Stewart
Loch Ryan
Innermessan
New Luce
Loch Ronald
Tarf Wr.
Big Water of Fleet
Laurieston Forest
Stranraer
Castle Kennedy
Kirkcowan
Glengap

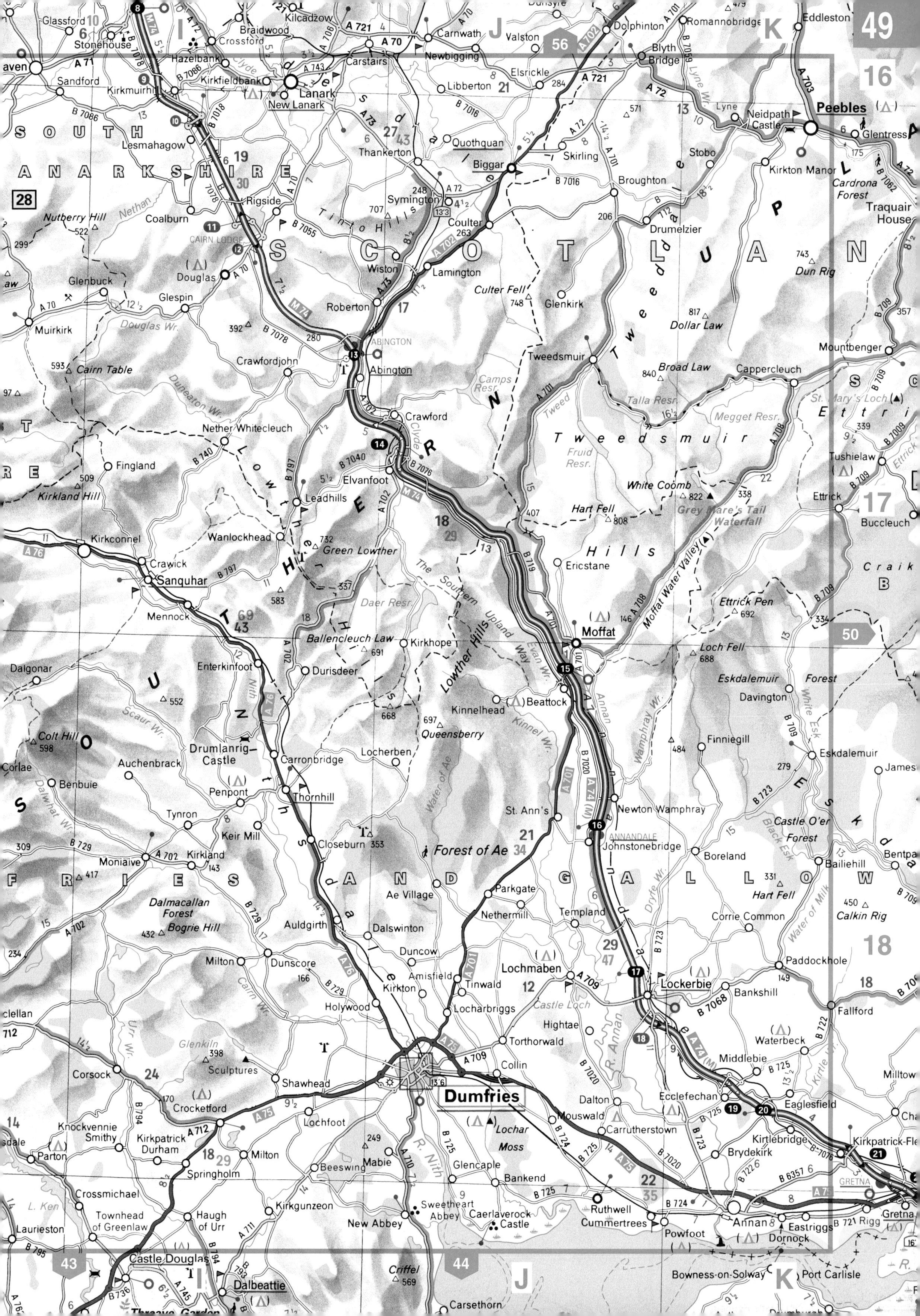
Glassford
Stonehouse
Braidwood
Crossford
Kilcadzow
Carnwath
Dolphinton
Romannobridge
Eddleston
Valston
Newbigging
Blyth Bridge
Hazelbank
Carstairs
Sandford
Kirkfieldbank
Lanark
New Lanark
Libberton
Elsrickle
Kirkmuirhill
Peebles
Neidpath Castle
Lyne
Glentress
SOUTH LANARKSHIRE
Lesmahagow
Thankerton
Quothquan
Biggar
Skirling
Stobo
Kirkton Manor
Cardrona Forest
Traquair House
Rigside
Symington
Broughton
Nutberry Hill
Coalburn
Tinto Hills
Coulter
Drumelzier
CAIRN LODGE
SCOTLAND
Douglas
Wiston
Lamington
Dun Rig
Glenbuck
Glespin
Culter Fell
Glenkirk
Muirkirk
Douglas Wr.
Roberton
Dollar Law
ABINGTON
Abington
Mountbenger
Cairn Table
Crawfordjohn
Tweedsmuir
Broad Law
Cappercleuch
Camps Resr.
Talla Resr.
St. Mary's Loch
Duneaton Wr.
Crawford
Megget Resr.
Nether Whitecleuch
Tweedsmuir
Fingland
Elvanfoot
Fruid Resr.
Tushielaw
Kirkland Hill
Leadhills
White Coomb
Grey Mare's Tail Waterfall
Ettrick
Buccleuch
Hart Fell
Kirkconnel
Wanlockhead
Green Lowther
Hills
Crawick
Sanquhar
Ericstane
Craik
The Southern Upland Way
Daer Resr.
Moffat Water Valley
Ettrick Pen
Mennock
Moffat
Ballencleuch Law
Kirkhope
Loch Fell
Dalgonar
Enterkinfoot
Durisdeer
Lowther Hills
Eskdalemuir
Forest
Davington
Beattock
Kinnelhead
Scaur Wr.
Queensberry
Colt Hill
Drumlanrig Castle
Carronbridge
Locherben
Finniegill
Eskdalemuir
Corlae
Auchenbrack
Benbuie
Penpont
Thornhill
Newton Wamphray
St. Ann's
Tynron
Keir Mill
Castle O'er Forest
Closeburn
ANNANDALE
Johnstonebridge
Forest of Ae
Moniaive
Kirkland
Boreland
Bailiehill
Bentpath
Parkgate
Ae Village
Hart Fell
Dalmacallan Forest
Nethermill
Templand
Corrie Common
Calkin Rig
Bogrie Hill
Auldgirth
Dalswinton
Duncow
Milton
Dunscore
Lochmaben
Paddockhole
Amisfield
Tinwald
Lockerbie
Bankshill
Kirkton
Holywood
Locharbriggs
Castle Loch
Fallford
Hightae
Torthorwald
Waterbeck
Glenkiln
Sculptures
Middlebie
Corsock
Shawhead
Collin
Milltown
Dumfries
Crocketford
Dalton
Ecclefechan
Eaglesfield
Lochfoot
Mouswald
Lochar Moss
Carrutherstown
Knockvennie Smithy
Kirkpatrick Durham
Kirtlebridge
Kirkpatrick-Fleming
Parton
Milton
Mabie
Beeswing
Glencaple
Brydekirk
Springholm
Bankend
GRETNA
Crossmichael
Sweetheart Abbey
Caerlaverock Castle
Ruthwell
Gretna
L. Ken
Townhead of Greenlaw
Haugh of Urr
Kirkgunzeon
New Abbey
Cummertrees
Annan
Eastriggs
Rigg
Laurieston
Powfoot
Dornock
Castle Douglas
Dalbeattie
Criffel
Bowness-on-Solway
Port Carlisle
Threave Garden
Carsethorn

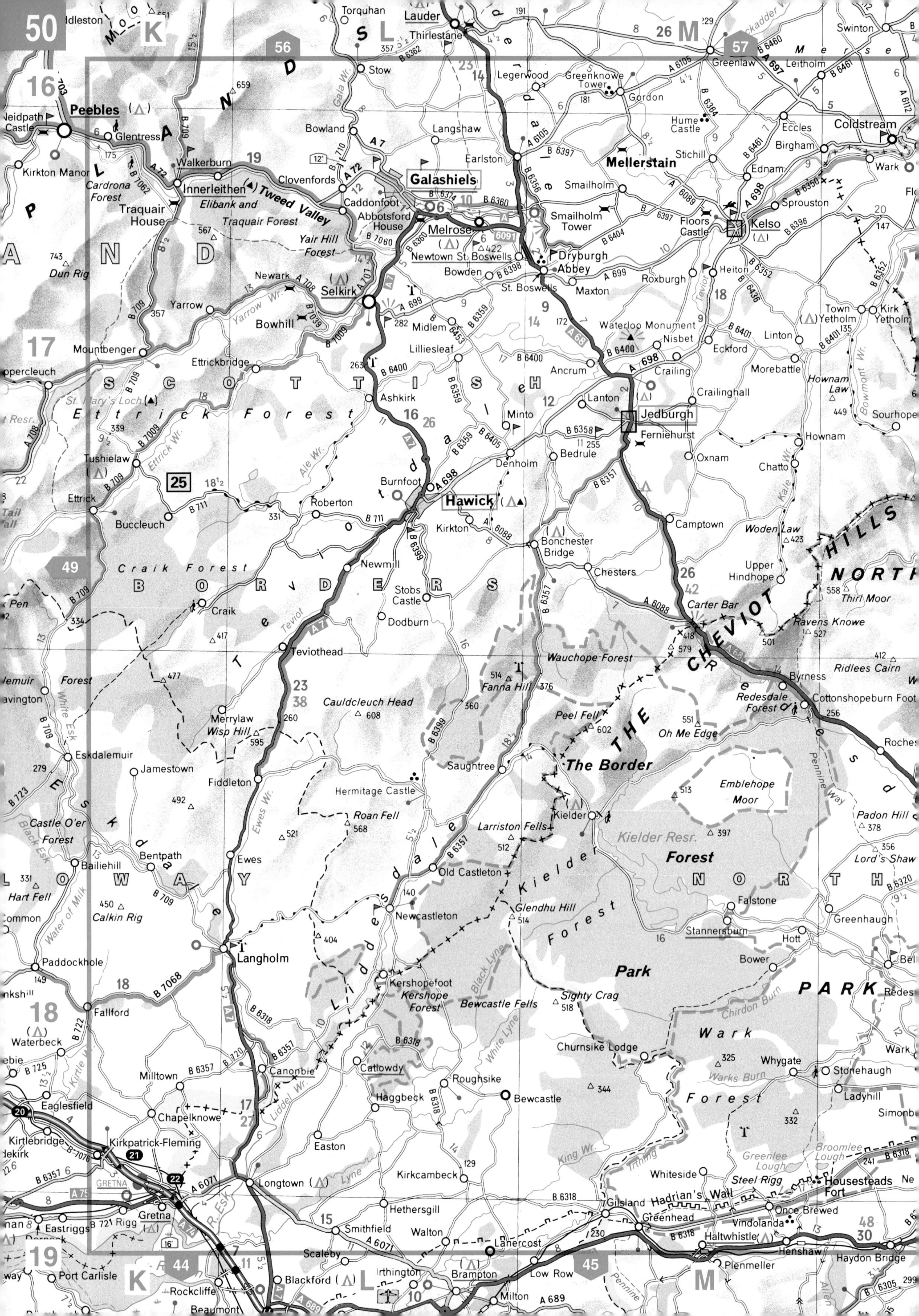
Peebles
Neidpath Castle
Glentress
Kirkton Manor
Cardrona Forest
Walkerburn
Innerleithen
Traquair House
Elibank and Traquair Forest
Tweed Valley
Clovenfords
Caddonfoot
Abbotsford House
Galashiels
Melrose
Newtown St. Boswells
Dryburgh Abbey
St. Boswells
Yair Hill Forest
Selkirk
Newark
Yarrow
Bowhill
Mountbenger
Ettrickbridge
St. Mary's Loch
Ettrick Forest
Tushielaw
Ettrick
Buccleuch
Dun Rig
Torquhan
Lauder
Thirlestane
Stow
Bowland
Langshaw
Earlston
Legerwood
Greenknowe Tower
Gordon
Hume Castle
Mellerstain
Stichill
Smailholm
Smailholm Tower
Floors Castle
Kelso
Ednam
Eccles
Coldstream
Birgham
Wark
Sprouston
Leitholm
Greenlaw
Swinton
Heiton
Roxburgh
Maxton
Bowden
Midlem
Lilliesleaf
Ashkirk
Ancrum
Waterloo Monument
Nisbet
Eckford
Crailing
Crailinghall
Linton
Town Yetholm
Kirk Yetholm
Morebattle
Hownam Law
Sourhope
Hownam
Chatto
Jedburgh
Ferniehurst
Oxnam
Lanton
Minto
Denholm
Bedrule
Hawick
Burnfoot
Roberton
Kirkton
Bonchester Bridge
Camptown
Chesters
Woden Law
Upper Hindhope
Carter Bar
Craik Forest
Craik
Newmill
Stobs Castle
Dodburn
Teviothead
Cauldcleuch Head
Fanna Hill
Wauchope Forest
Peel Fell
Oh Me Edge
Merrylaw
Wisp Hill
Eskdalemuir
Jamestown
Fiddleton
Hermitage Castle
Saughtree
The Border
Kielder
Kielder Resr.
Emblehope Moor
Roan Fell
Larriston Fells
Castle O'er Forest
Bailiehill
Bentpath
Ewes
Old Castleton
Newcastleton
Glendhu Hill
Kielder Forest Park
Hart Fell
Calkin Rig
Paddockhole
Langholm
Kershopefoot
Kershope Forest
Bewcastle Fells
Sighty Crag
Fallford
Waterbeck
Milltown
Canonbie
Catlowdy
Roughsike
Bewcastle
Haggbeck
Churnsike Lodge
Wark Forest
Whygate
Stonehaugh
Ladyhill
Eaglesfield
Chapelknowe
Kirtlebridge
Kirkpatrick-Fleming
Gretna
Eastriggs
Rigg
Longtown
Easton
Kirkcambeck
Hethersgill
Smithfield
Walton
Lanercost
Scaleby
Irthington
Brampton
Low Row
Milton
Blackford
Rockcliffe
Port Carlisle
Beaumont
Gilsland
Greenhead
Hadrian's Wall
Steel Rigg
Whiteside
Housesteads Fort
Once Brewed
Vindolanda
Haltwhistle
Henshaw
Haydon Bridge
Plenmeller
Byrness
Cottonshopeburn Foot
Redesdale Forest
Ridlees Cairn
Ravens Knowe
Thirl Moor
Rochester
Padon Hill
Lord's Shaw
Falstone
Stannersburn
Greenhaugh
Hott
Bower
Chirdon Burn
Greenlee Lough
Broomlee Lough
THE CHEVIOT HILLS
NORTHUMBERLAND NATIONAL PARK
SCOTTISH BORDERS
DUMFRIES AND GALLOWAY
Teviotdale
Eskdale
Liddesdale
Lauderdale
Redesdale

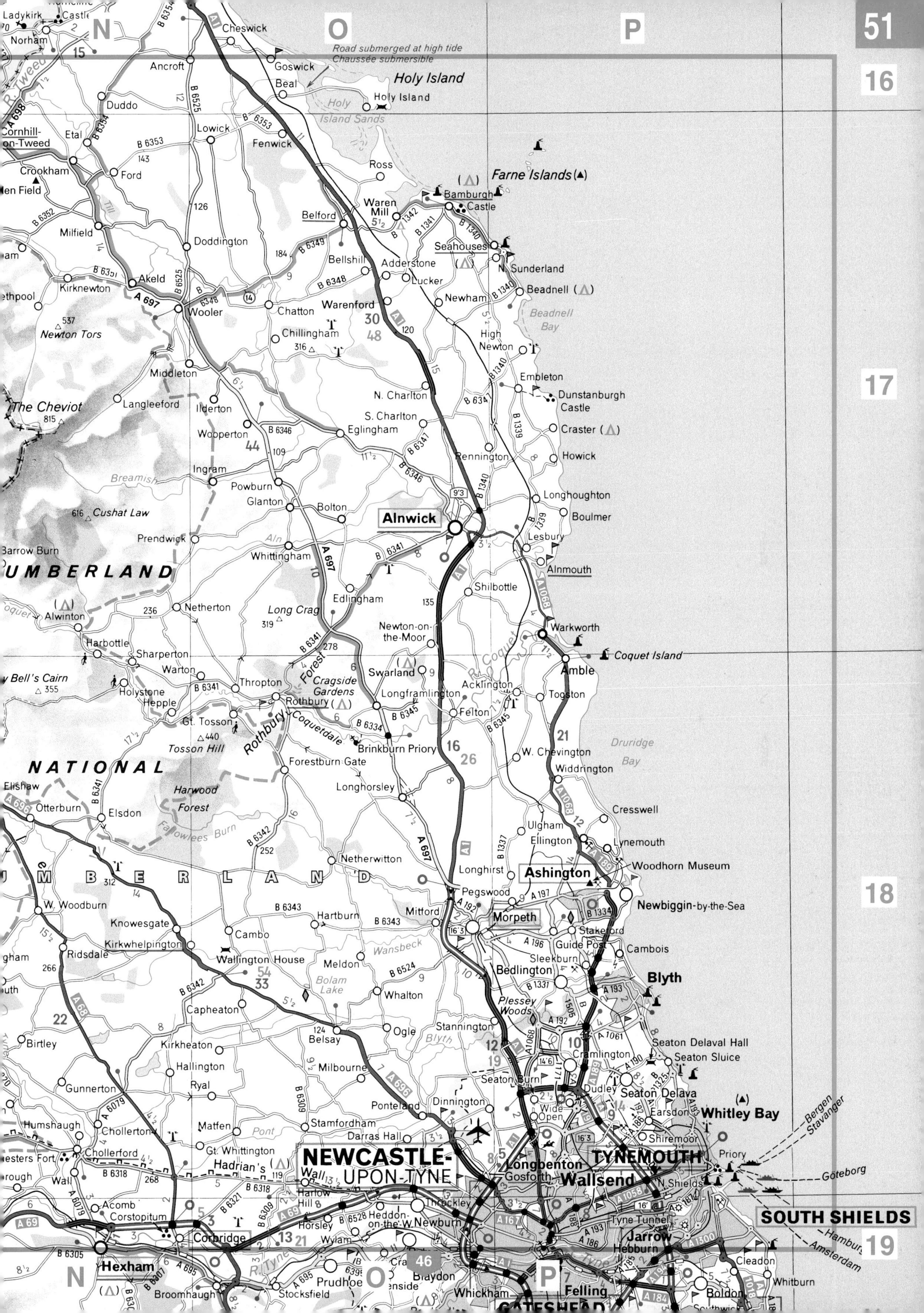
N
O
P
16
17
18
19
Ladykirk
Norham
Cheswick
Ancroft
Goswick
Road submerged at high tide
Chaussée submersible
Holy Island
Beal
Holy Island
Holy Island Sands
Duddo
Cornhill-on-Tweed
Etal
Lowick
Fenwick
Crookham
Ford
Ross
Farne Islands
Bamburgh
Castle
Waren Mill
Belford
Milfield
Doddington
Seahouses
Bellshill
Adderstone
Lucker
N. Sunderland
Akeld
Kirknewton
Wooler
Chatton
Warenford
Newham
Beadnell
Beadnell Bay
Newton Tors
Chillingham
High Newton
Middleton
Embleton
Dunstanburgh Castle
The Cheviot
Langleeford
Ilderton
N. Charlton
S. Charlton
Eglingham
Craster
Wooperton
Rennington
Howick
Ingram
Breamish
Powburn
Glanton
Longhoughton
Bolton
Boulmer
Alnwick
Cushat Law
Prendwick
Lesbury
Barrow Burn
Whittingham
Alnmouth
UMBERLAND
Shilbottle
Edlingham
Alwinton
Netherton
Long Crag
Newton-on-the-Moor
Warkworth
Harbottle
Sharperton
Coquet Island
Warton
Swarland
Amble
Bell's Cairn
Holystone
Thropton
Cragside Gardens
Acklington
Hepple
Rothbury
Longframlington
Togston
Gt. Tosson
Felton
Rothbury Forest
Coquetdale
Tosson Hill
Brinkburn Priory
W. Chevington
Druridge Bay
NATIONAL
Forestburn Gate
Widdrington
Elishaw
Longhorsley
Harwood Forest
Otterburn
Elsdon
Cresswell
Ulgham
Ellington
Lynemouth
Woodhorn Museum
Netherwitton
Longhirst
Ashington
Pegswood
Newbiggin-by-the-Sea
W. Woodburn
Hartburn
Mitford
Morpeth
Knowesgate
Stakeford
Kirkwhelpington
Cambo
Guide Post
Cambois
Ridsdale
Wallington House
Meldon
Wansbeck
Sleekburn
Bedlington
Blyth
Bolam Lake
Whalton
Capheaton
Plessey Woods
Stannington
Birtley
Ogle
Belsay
Kirkheaton
Cramlington
Seaton Delaval Hall
Seaton Sluice
Hallington
Milbourne
Seaton Burn
Gunnerton
Ryal
Dudley
Seaton Delaval
Ponteland
Dinnington
Wide Open
Whitley Bay
Humshaugh
Chollerton
Matfen
Stamfordham
Earsdon
Shiremoor
Bergen
Stavanger
Darras Hall
Chollerford
Gt. Whittington
Hadrian's Wall
NEWCASTLE-UPON-TYNE
Longbenton
Gosforth
TYNEMOUTH
Wallsend
Priory
N. Shields
Göteborg
Harlow Hill
Throckley
Acomb
Corstopitum
Heddon-on-the-Wall
Newburn
Horsley
Tyne Tunnel
SOUTH SHIELDS
Corbridge
Wylam
Jarrow
Hebburn
Hamburg
Amsterdam
Hexham
Cleadon
Prudhoe
Blaydon
Stocksfield
Broomhaugh
Whickham
Felling
Whitburn
Boldon
GATESHEAD

A
B
C
Iona
Baile Mór
Fionnphort
Bunessan
L. Assapol
A 849
376
Brolass
59
Carsaig
Carsaig Bay
Loch Buie
Rubha na Faoilinn
Ross of Mull
Erraid
Soa I.
Eilean a' Chalmain
Ardchiavaig
Ardalanish Bay
Rubh' Ardalanish
Malcolm's Point
Frank Lockwood's Island
Insh Island
Firth of Lorn
Easdale
W. Reef
Torran Rocks
Dubh-Fhèith
Garvellachs
Belnahua
Eilean Dubh Mór
Lunga
15
54
Scarba
449
Gulf of Corryvreckan
Dubh Artach
Rubh' a' Geodha
Kiloran Bay
143
139
Kiloran
B 8086
B 8087
An Rubha
Scalasaig
Colonsay
Staosnaig
Garvard
B 8085
Rubha Dubh
93
Dubh Eilean
Oronsay
Eilean nan Ron
Eilean Ghaoideamal
Glengarrisdale Bay
296
Glendebadel Bay
365
Beinn Bhreac
467
477
Lealt
Ardlussa
Shian Bay
Loch Righ Mór
Lussa Point
Eilean Dubh
JURA
A 846
Rubh' an t-Sàilein
Loch Tarbert
Rubha nan Crann
Keillmore
Island of Danna
Lagg
Rubha a' Mhail
Sgarbh Breac
364
Nave Island
Ardnave Point
Ardnave
Beinn an Oir
784
Paps of Jura
Jura Forest
Lowlandman's Bay
Kilmory
Eilean Mór
Point of Knap
An Clachan
Sanaigmore
Gortantaoid
Bunnahabhainn
Sound of Islay
16
Loch Gruinart
Leargybreck
561
Skervuile Lighthouse
B 8018
B 8017
Port Askaig
Feolin Ferry
Loch Finlaggan
Craighouse
Small Isles
Saligo Bay
Loch Gorm
Gruinart
Craigens
Ballygrant
A 846
Coul Point
Kilchoman
Machir Bay
A 847
Bridgend
Sorn
Am Fraoch Eilean
Jura Ho
Na Cùiltean
Kilberry Head
Rubha na Tràille
Brosdale Island
Kilchiaran
Bruichladdich
Kilchiaran Bay
Islay
Loch Indaal
Bowmore
ISLAY
Mc Arthur's Head
53
Ardpatrick Point
Port Charlotte
Rinns of Islay
232
Lossit Point
Laggan
Beinn Bheigeir
491
Ardtalla
Port Mór
Laggan Point
Laggan Bay
Nereabolls
Duich
B 8016
Rubbha na Faing
Portnahaven
Claggain Bay
West Tarbert Bay
East Tarbert Bay
Tarbert
Orsay
Rinns Point
ISLAY-PORT ELLEN AIRPORT
Glenegedale
Ardmore Point
Gigha Island
Sound of Gigha
347
Beinn Sholum
Eilean a' Chùirn
Ardminish
A 83
32
Rubha Mór
Kintra
Ardbeg
Craro Island
Leim
Gigalum Island
Tayinloan
17
Port Ellen
Eilean Imersay
Killean
The Oa
Cairraig Fhada
Cara Island
Lr. Killeyan
Risabus
Texa
Mull of Cara
Mull of Oa
Inerval
Muasdale
Rubha nan Leacan
53
Glenacardoch Point
Arnicle
Glenbarr

C
D
E
F
52
54
16
17
18
48
103
Rubha nan Crann
Keillmore
Island of Danna
Castle Sween
Lagg
Achahoish
Kilmory
Eilean Mór
Sliabh Gaoil
562
Knapdale
Lowlandman's Bay
Skervuile Lighthouse
Point of Knap
Loch Caolisport
Dubh Chreag
480
Small Isles
Loch nan Torran
Barmore Island
Tarbert
E. Loch Tarbert
W. Tarbert
Portavadie
Na Cùilean
Kilberry Head
Kilberry
B 8024
Kennacraig
Whitehouse
Ardpatrick
Ardpatrick Point
West Loch Tarbert
422
127
B 8001
Skipness Castle
Skipness Point
Claonaig
Clachan
Port Mór
West Tarbert Bay
East Tarbert Bay
Tarbert
Loch Ciaran
Ballochroy
Loch Garasdale
Crossaig
Gigha Island
Sound of Gigha
Ardminish
Craro Island
A 83
32
Tayinloan
322
Leim
Gigalum Island
Cara Island
Killean
Grogport
Mull of Cara
364
Carradale Water
KINTYRE
B 842
Muasdale
Barr W.
Carradale
Kilbrannan Sound
Glenacardoch Point
Arnicle
Dippen
B 879
Carradale Point
Glenbarr
454
Beinn an Tuirc
Carradale Bay
Bellochantuy
Saddell
Saddell Bay
Lussa Loch
Sgreadan Hill
397
Ugadale Bay
Skeroblingarry
Black Bay
Kilchenzie
Peninver
Ardnacross Bay
Machrihanish Bay
Machrihanish
Campbeltown
Campbeltown Loch
Island Davaar
B 843
Drumlemble
A 83
Stewarton
352
Knocknaha
Beinn Ghuilean
Cnoc Moy
446
Rubha Dùin Bhàin
Feochaig
Conie Glen
Johnston's Point
S. Carrine
Macharioch
Southend
Mull of Kintyre
Sanda Sound
Sheep Island
Sanda Island
Loch Sween
A 846
A 83
B 8024
Cruach nan Caorach
458
Aucnenbreck
Kilfinan
Craig Lodge
454
B 8000
Melldalloch
164
Tighnabruaich
Port Driseach
Kames
Millhouse
Kyles of Bute
207
Colintraive
Rhubodach
Coustonn
Loch Striven
506
Glenstriven
Cruach nan Capull
578
Clachaig
Sandbank
Dunoon
A 815
Corlarach Forest
322
Port Lamont
Innellan
Toward Point
Island of Bute
Windy Hill
278
Glecknabae
A 886
Strone Point
Castle
Port Bannatyne
Kildavanan
Ettrick Bay
Rothesay
Bogany Point
Ascog
Ardlamont Point
Straad
B 878
L. Fad
A 845
Bute
Inchmarnock
Great Cumbrae Island
Kingarth
Ardscalpsie Point
A 844
Kilchattan
Stravanan Bay
148
Little Cumbrae Island
Sound of Bute
Cock of Arran
Garroch Head
Lochranza
Catacol
Catacol Bay
A 841
199
570
Mid Sannox
Sannox Bay
Pirnmill
859
L. Tanna
Corrie
721
Beinn Bharrain
Goat Fell
874
ISLE OF ARRAN
Dougarie
Glen Iorsa
Glen Rosa
Brodick Castle
Brodick Bay
Brodick
Machrie Bay
512
B 880
Clauchlands Point
Marganheglish
Machrie
Lamlash
Lamlash Bay
Holy Island
Drumadoon Point
Blackwaterfoot
Drumadoon Bay
458
Kingscross Point
Whiting Bay
Brown Head
Lagg
Kilmory
140
Dippin Head
Kildonan
Bennan Head
Sound of Pladda
Pladda
338
Ailsa Craig

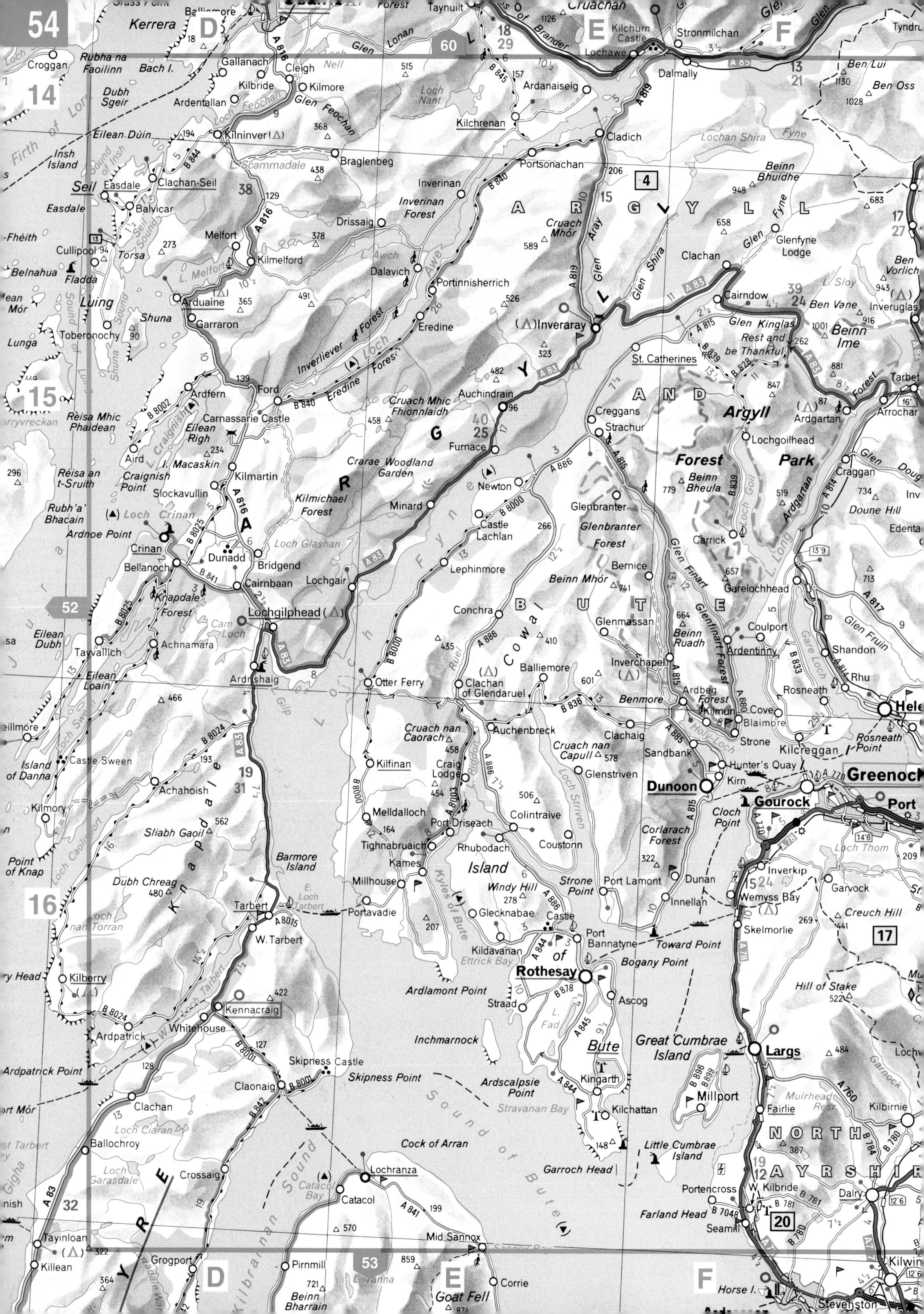
Kerrera
Croggan
Rubha na Faoilinn
Bach I.
Gallanach
Cleigh
Kilmore
Kilbride
Ardentallan
Glen Lonan
Glen Feochan
Loch Nant
Taynuilt
Pass of Brander
Cruachan
Kilchurn Castle
Lochawe
Stronmilchan
Dalmally
Ardanaiseig
Kilchrenan
Cladich
Ben Lui
Ben Oss
Dubh Sgeir
Firth of Lorn
Eilean Dùin
Kilninver
Insh Island
Seil
Easdale
Clachan-Seil
Balvicar
Braglenbeg
L. Scammadale
Portsonachan
Lochan Shira
Beinn Bhuidhe
Inverinan
Inverinan Forest
Drissaig
Cruach Mhór
Glen Aray
Glen Shira
Glen Fyne
Glenfyne Lodge
Clachan
Melfort
Kilmelford
Cullipool
Torsa
Belnahua
Fladda
Luing
L. Avich
Dalavich
Portinnisherrich
Cairndow
Ben Vane
Inveruglas
Ben Vorlich
L. Sloy
Arduaine
Garraron
Shuna
Toberonochy
Lunga
Eredine
Inverliever Forest
Loch Awe
Eredine Forest
Inveraray
Glen Kinglas
Rest and be Thankful
Beinn Ime
St. Catherines
Ford
Ardfern
Carnassarie Castle
Cruach Mhic Fhionnlaidh
Auchindrain
Argyll
Ardgartan
Tarbet
Arrochar
Creggans
Strachur
Lochgoilhead
Argyll Forest Park
Rèisa Mhic Phaidean
Eilean Righ
L. Craignish
Aird
I. Macaskin
Kilmartin
Crarae Woodland Garden
Furnace
Newton
Glen Douglas
Craggan
Rèisa an t-Sruith
Craignish Point
Slockavullin
Kilmichael Forest
Minard
Castle Lachlan
Glenbranter
Glenbranter Forest
Beinn Bheula
Loch Goil
Doune Hill
Rubh'a' Bhacain
Loch Crinan
Ardnoe Point
Crinan
Bellanoch
Dunadd
Bridgend
Loch Glashan
Carrick
Lephinmore
Bernice
Cairnbaan
Lochgair
Beinn Mhór
Garelochhead
Knapdale Forest
Lochgilphead
Conchra
Glenmassan
Beinn Ruadh
Coulport
Glen Fruin
Eilean Dubh
Tayvallich
Achnamara
Cowal
Glenfinart Forest
Ardentinny
Shandon
Ardrishaig
Otter Ferry
Clachan of Glendaruel
Balliemore
Inverchapel
Rhu
Rosneath
Eilean Loain
Ardbeg Forest
Benmore
Kilmun
Cove
Blairmore
Helensburgh
Auchenbreck
Clachaig
Holy Loch
Strone
Kilcreggan
Rosneath Point
Cruach nan Caorach
Cruach nan Capull
Sandbank
Hunter's Quay
Greenock
Castle Sween
Island of Danna
Kilfinan
Craig Lodge
Glenstriven
Dunoon
Kirn
Gourock
Port Glasgow
Achahoish
Loch Striven
Kilmory
Melldalloch
Port Driseach
Colintraive
Cloch Point
Sliabh Gaoil
Knapdale
Tighnabruaich
Rhubodach
Coustonn
Corlarach Forest
Loch Thom
Point of Knap
Barmore Island
Kames
Island
Inverkip
Millhouse
Strone Point
Port Lamont
Dunan
Garvock
Dubh Chreag
Windy Hill
Wemyss Bay
Creuch Hill
Tarbert
East Loch Tarbert
Portavadie
Kyles of Bute
Glecknabae
Innellan
Skelmorlie
W. Tarbert
Port Bannatyne
Toward Point
Kildavanan
Ettrick Bay
Bogany Point
Kilberry
Rothesay
Hill of Stake
Ardlamont Point
Ascog
Kennacraig
Straad
L. Fad
West Loch Tarbert
Whitehouse
Inchmarnock
Bute
Great Cumbrae Island
Largs
Ardpatrick
Skipness Castle
Skipness Point
Kingarth
Ardscalpsie Point
Ardpatrick Point
Claonaig
Millport
Stravanan Bay
Kilchattan
Fairlie
Muirhead Resr.
Kilbirnie
Clachan
Loch Ciaran
Sound of Bute
North Ayrshire
Ballochroy
Cock of Arran
Little Cumbrae Island
Garroch Head
Loch Garasdale
Crossaig
Lochranza
Catacol Bay
Catacol
Portencross
W. Kilbride
Dalry
Farland Head
Seamill
Kintyre
Kilbrannan Sound
Tayinloan
Killean
Grogport
Pirnmill
Mid Sannox
Sannox Bay
Corrie
Beinn Bharrain
Goat Fell
Horse I.
Stevenston
Kilwinning

G
H
I
61
48
49
56
14
15
16
Crianlarich
Ben More
Auchlyne
Glen Dochart
Ardchyle
Luib
Benmore
Meall an t-Seallaidh
Lochearnhead
Loch Earn
St. Fillans
Ardvorlich
Comrie
Crieff
Gilmerton
Monzie
Madderty
Invergeldie
Glen Lednock
Meall Tarsuinn
Glen Almond
Fowlis Wester
Balquhidder
Braes of Balquhidder
Inverlochlarig
Loch Voil
Kingshouse
Strathyre Forest
Strathyre
Ben Vorlich
Ben Halton
Culloch
Drummond Castle
Muthill
Dalchruin
Glen Artney
Water of Ruchill
Innerpeffray
Kinkell Bridge
Tullibardine
Stob a' Choin
29
STIRLING
Benvane
Meall Odhar
Uamh Bheag
Ben Ledi
Callander
Pass of Leny
Strath Gartney
Loch Katrine
Glen Finglas Resr.
Stronachlachar
Inversnaid Hotel
L. Arklet Resr.
The Trossachs
Brig o' Turk
L. Venachar
Ben Venue
Duke's Pass
Achray Forest
Menteith Hills
Kinlochard
Aberfoyle
Port of Menteith
Inchmahome
L. of Menteith
Ben Lomond
Queen Elizabeth Forest Park
Loch Ard Forest
Duchray Wr.
Rowardennan Lodge
Gartmore
Gualann
Conic Hill
Balmaha
Inchcailloch
Loch Lomond
Inchmurrin
Luss
West Highland Way
Braco
Ardoch
Greenloaning
Strathallan
Blackford
Steele's Knowe
Glen Eagles
Ogle Glen
Kinbuck
Dunblane
Doune
Deanston
Thornhill
Blair Drummond
Bridge of Allan
Ben Cleuch
Castle Campbell
Tillicoultry
Dollar
Menstrie
Alva
Wallace Mon.
Tullibody
Cambuskenneth
New Sauchie
Alloa
Clackmannan
Fallin
Bannockburn
Stirling
Cambusbarron
Gargunnock
Gargunnock Hills
Kippen
Arnprior
Buchlyvie
Balfron
Stronend
Fintry Hills
Fintry
Endrick Wr.
Carron Valley Resr.
Carron Valley Forest
Meikle Bin
Tomtain
Carron Bridge
Auchenbowie
Plean
Airth
Kincardine
Devilla Forest
Grangemouth
Stenhousemuir
Larbert
Dunipace
Denny
Bonnybridge
Falkirk
Redding
Polmont
Maddiston
Shieldhill
Avonbridge
Westfield
Drymen
Killearn
Gartocharn
Arden
Balloch
Alexandria
Jamestown
Bonhill
Renton
Cardross
Earl's Seat
Campsie Fells
Blanefield
Strathblane
Clachan of Campsie
Lennoxtown
Milton of Campsie
Kilsyth
Kilsyth Hills
Kilpatrick Hills
30
11
Dumbarton
Erskine Bridge
Duntocher
Old Kilpatrick
Milngavie
Torrance
Kirkintilloch
Lenzie
Condorrat
Cumbernauld
Slamannan
Longriggend
Riggend
Caldercruix
Blackridge
Armadale
Bearsden
Clydebank
Renfrew
Langbank
Bishopton
Kilmacolm
Houston
Bridge of Weir
Linwood
Ranfurly
Kilbarchan
Johnstone
PAISLEY
Barrhead
Howwood
GLASGOW
Rutherglen
Coatbridge
Airdrie
Muirhead
Stepps
Stand
Chapelhall
Salsburgh
Harthill
Longridge
Whitburn
Fauldhouse
Shotts
Stane
Holytown
Newarthill
Carfin
Mossend
Bellshill
Uddingston
Bothwell
Cambuslang
Blantyre
Carmunnock
Busby
Newton Mearns
East Kilbride
Hamilton
Motherwell
Wishaw
Cleland
Allanton
Newmains
Overtown
Law
Carluke
Dalserf
Larkhall
Braidwood
Kilcadzow
Crossford
Hazelbank
Lanark
New Lanark
Carstairs
Rootpark
Hare Hill
Forth
Braehead
Neilston
Uplawmoor
Hall
Beith
Barcraigs Resr.
Barrmill
Lugton
Dunlop
Eaglesham
Ballageich Hill
Lochgoin Resr.
Corse Hill
Auldhouse
Chapelton
Glassford
Stonehouse
Strathaven
Sandford
Kirkmuirhill
Caldermill
Stewarton
Fenwick
Cunninghamhead
Whitelee Forest
13
21
24
7
12
32
27

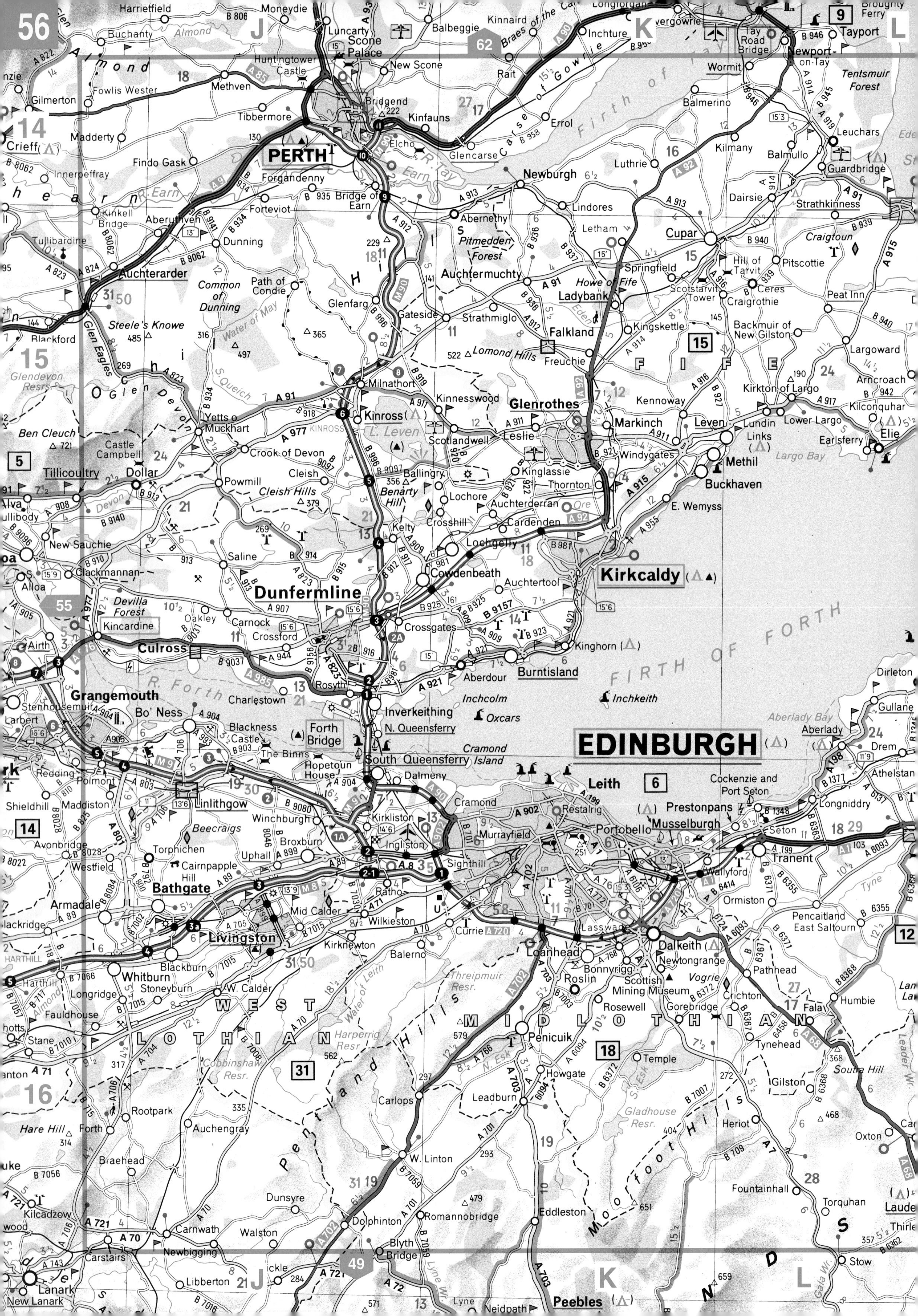
PERTH
Scone Palace
Luncarty
Balbeggie
Kinnaird
Inchture
Longforgan
Invergowrie
Tay Road Bridge
Tayport
Newport-on-Tay
Wormit
Tentsmuir Forest
Huntingtower Castle
New Scone
Bridgend
Kinfauns
Methven
Tibbermore
Almond
Gilmerton
Fowlis Wester
Madderty
Crieff
Findo Gask
Innerpeffray
Forgandenny
Bridge of Earn
Forteviot
Glencarse
Errol
Rait
Carse of Gowrie
Firth of Tay
Balmerino
Leuchars
Guardbridge
Balmullo
Kilmany
Luthrie
Newburgh
Lindores
Abernethy
Letham
Cupar
Dairsie
Strathkinness
Craigtoun
Pitscottie
Hill of Tarvit
Ceres
Craigrothie
Scotstarvit Tower
Springfield
Pitmedden Forest
Auchtermuchty
Howe of Fife
Ladybank
Strathmiglo
Falkland
Freuchie
Lomond Hills
Kingskettle
Backmuir of New Gilston
Peat Inn
Largoward
Arncroach
Kilconquhar
Kirkton of Largo
Lower Largo
Lundin Links
Elie
Earlsferry
Largo Bay
Leven
Methil
Buckhaven
E. Wemyss
Kennoway
Glenrothes
Markinch
Leslie
Windygates
Kinglassie
Thornton
Auchterderran
Cardenden
Lochgelly
Kirkcaldy
Auchtertool
Kinghorn
Burntisland
Aberdour
Kinross
L. Leven
Kinnesswood
Scotlandwell
Milnathort
Glenfarg
Gateside
Path of Condie
Common of Dunning
Dunning
Aberuthven
Auchterarder
Tullibardine
Kinkell Bridge
Steele's Knowe
Blackford
Glen Eagles
Glen Devon
Glendevon Resrs.
Ben Cleuch
Castle Campbell
Yetts o' Muckhart
Crook of Devon
Powmill
Cleish
Cleish Hills
Ballingry
Benarty Hill
Lochore
Crosshill
Kelty
Cowdenbeath
Dunfermline
Crossgates
Saline
Tillicoultry
Dollar
Alva
New Sauchie
Clackmannan
Alloa
Kincardine
Devilla Forest
Oakley
Carnock
Crossford
Culross
Rosyth
Charlestown
Inverkeithing
N. Queensferry
Forth Bridge
South Queensferry
Dalmeny
Inchcolm
Oxcars
Inchkeith
Cramond Island
FIRTH OF FORTH
R. Forth
Grangemouth
Bo' Ness
Blackness Castle
The Binns
Hopetoun House
Stenhousemuir
Larbert
Airth
Redding
Polmont
Shieldhill
Maddiston
Linlithgow
Beecraigs
Avonbridge
Westfield
Torphichen
Cairnpapple Hill
Bathgate
Armadale
Blackridge
Livingston
Whitburn
Blackburn
Harthill
Longridge
Stoneyburn
Fauldhouse
Stane
W. Calder
Mid Calder
Uphall
Broxburn
Winchburgh
Kirkliston
Ingliston
Ratho
Wilkieston
Kirknewton
Balerno
Currie
EDINBURGH
Leith
Cramond
Restalrig
Murrayfield
Portobello
Sighthill
Lasswade
Loanhead
Dalkeith
Newtongrange
Bonnyrigg
Roslin
Scottish Mining Museum
Vogrie
Rosewell
Gorebridge
Crichton
Pathhead
Musselburgh
Prestonpans
Cockenzie and Port Seton
Seton
Longniddry
Aberlady
Aberlady Bay
Gullane
Dirleton
Drem
Athelstaneford
Tranent
Wallyford
Ormiston
Pencaitland
East Saltoun
Humbie
Fala
Tynehead
Soutra Hill
Gilston
Heriot
Oxton
Fountainhall
Torquhan
Stow
Lauder
Temple
Gladhouse Resr.
Moorfoot Hills
Penicuik
Howgate
Leadburn
Threipmuir Resr.
Pentland Hills
Harperrig Resr.
Cobbinshaw Resr.
Carlops
W. Linton
Eddleston
Romannobridge
Dolphinton
Blyth Bridge
Dunsyre
Auchengray
Rootpark
Forth
Hare Hill
Braehead
Kilcadzow
Carnwath
Newbigging
Walston
Carstairs
Lanark
New Lanark
Libberton
Peebles
Neidpath
Lyne
WEST LOTHIAN
MIDLOTHIAN
FIFE
Water of Leith
R. Earn
R. Tay
S. Queich
Water of May
Devon
Tyne
Gala Wr.
Leader Wr.
Lyne Wr.
J
K
L
9
62
55
49
14
15
16
5
6
12
18
31

M
N
O
14
15
16
Buddon Ness
Inchcape or Bell Rock
63
St. Andrews Bay
St. Andrews
Boarhills
Kingsbarns
Carr Brigs
Fife Ness
Craighead
Crail
Kellie Castle
Kilrenny
Pittenweem
Anstruther
St. Monans
The East Neuk
Isle of May
A 917
B 9131
B 940
B 9171
Fidra
Craigleith
Bass Rock
North Berwick
Tantallon Castle
Kingston
Whitekirk
Tyne Mouth
Tyninghame
John Muir
W. Barns
Dunbar
Museum of Flight
Barns Ness
East Linton
Hailes Castle
Spott
Thorntonloch
Traprain Law
Stenton
Innerwick
Haddington
Cockburnspath
Pease Bay
Fast Castle
St. Abb's Head
Garvald
Oldhamstocks
Dunbar Common
Gifford
Clints Dod
Hills
Heart Law
St. Abbs
Grantshouse
Coldingham
Eyemouth
Lammermuir
Meikle Says Law
Whiteadder Resr.
Cranshaws
Eye Wr.
Auchencrow
Reston
Ayton
Burnmouth
Preston
Chirnside
Foulden
Longformacus
Whiteadder Wr.
Berwick-upon-Tweed
The Southern Upland Way
Manderston
Allanton
Hutton
Paxton
Duns
Tweedmouth
Spittal
Westruther
Polwarth
Whitsome
Horncliffe Castle
Lauder
Blackadder Wr.
Ladykirk
Swinton
Norham
Cheswick
Merse
Greenlaw
Leitholm
Ancroft
Goswick
Legerwood
Greenknowe Tower
Gordon
R. Tweed
Duddo
Beal
Holy Island
Road submerged at h
Chaussée submersibl
A 1
A 198
A 1087
A 1107
A 6112
A 6105
A 698
A 697
B 6355
B 6370
B 6438
B 6437
B 6461
B 6460
B 6456
B 6365
B 6354
B 6470
B 6525
B 6364
50
51

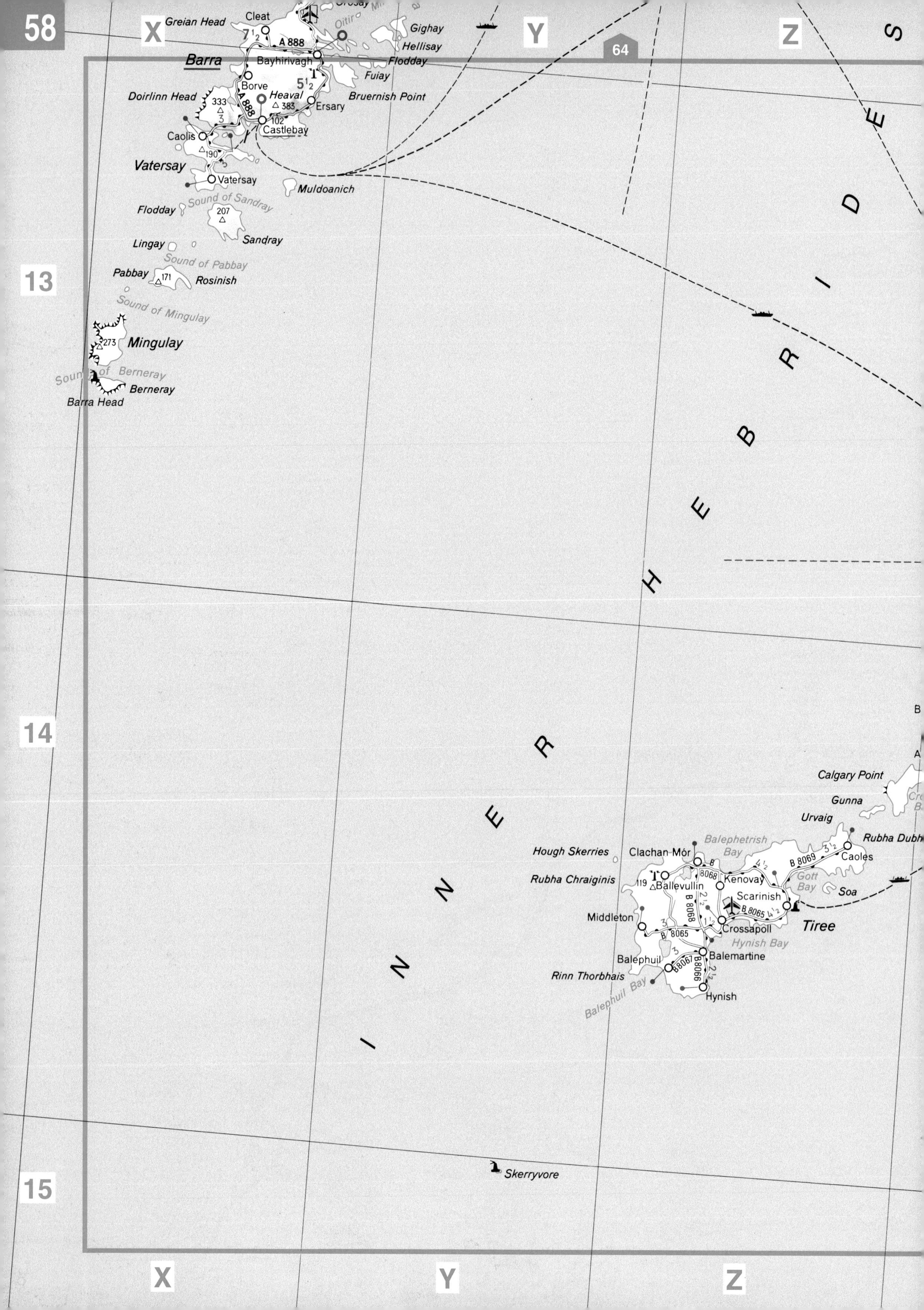
X
Y
Z
64
13
14
15
Greian Head
Cleat
A 888
Barra
Bayhirivagh
Gighay
Hellisay
Flodday
Fuiay
Borve
Doirlinn Head
Heaval
383
333
Bruernish Point
Ersary
102
Castlebay
Caolis
190
Vatersay
Vatersay
Muldoanich
Flodday
Sound of Sandray
207
Sandray
Lingay
Sound of Pabbay
Pabbay
171
Rosinish
Sound of Mingulay
273
Mingulay
Sound of Berneray
Berneray
Barra Head
HEBRIDES
INNER
Calgary Point
Gunna
Urvaig
Rubha Dubh
Balephetrish Bay
Caoles
Hough Skerries
Clachan Mór
B 8069
Kenovay
Gott Bay
Soa
Rubha Chraiginis
119
Ballevullin
B 8068
Scarinish
B 8065
Middleton
Crossapoll
Tiree
Hynish Bay
Balephuil
Balemartine
Rinn Thorbhais
B8067
B8066
Balephuil Bay
Hynish
Skerryvore

A
B
C
65
Garrisdale Point
A' Chill
210
Sanday
Rubha Shamhnan Insir
Kilmory
Sound of Canna
Humla
A' Bhrideanach
Orval
571
Kinloch
Loch Scresort
Harris
Askival
812
RHUM
Rubha nam Meirleach
Sound of Rhum
Clan Donald Centre
Armadale Bay
Ardvasar
280
Aird of Sleat
Point of Sleat
SOUND
Sound of Sleat
Mallaig
Rubha Raonuill
Airor
Knoyd
Inverie
Inverie Bay
12
548
Stoul
Bracora
Morar
North Morar
Loch Morar
Loch Nevis
A 830
Eilean Ighe
Luinga Bheag
Luinga Mhór
Arisaig
L. nan Ceall
South Arisaig
599
Rubh' Arisaig
Druimindarroch
L. nan Uamh
Eilean an t- Sidhe
Sound of Arisaig
Ardnish
Locha
Eilean nan Gobhar
L. Ailort
13
Rubha na Faing Móire
Roshven
Rois-Bheinn
882
Glenuig
Bay of Laig
Cleadale
Rubha an Fhasaidh
Eigg
An Sgurr
393
Galmisdale
Eilean Chathastail
Sound of Eigg
Eilean nan Each
137
Port Mór
Muck
igh-sgeir
Rubha Aird Druimnich
Eilean Shona
Farquhar's Point
L. Moidart
Moidart
Kinlochmoidart
Doirlinn
Ardtoe
A 861
103
Dalnabreck
Kentra Bay
B 8044
Acharacle
Ardshealach
Sanna
Kilmory
Ockle
357
Portuairk
Point of Ardnamurchan
Meall nan Con
Achosnich
437
Ardnamurchan
L. Mudle
133
B 8007
Kilchoan
528
Ben Hiant
490
Salen
Resipole
845
Beinn Resipole
Sunart
Ardery
Ardnas
Loch Sunart
Glenmore
Glenborrodale
Ardslignish
Oronsay
Sròn Bheag
Ardmore Point
Auliston Point
Carna
169
60
Cairns of Coll
Sùil Ghorm
Rubha Mór
Eilan Mór
Sorisdale
B 8072
Arnabost
B 8071
104
Coll
Arinagour
Loch Eatharna
B 8070
Eilean Ornsay
lyhaugh
leod
ssapol
Glengorm
Quinish Point
Quinish
Rubha nan Gall
Tobermory
Mishnish
Loch Teacuis
582
225
571
Morvern
Gleann Dubh
Caliach Point
Croig
Mornish
Calgary
Dervaig
B 8073
134
A 848
Calve Island
Drimnin
451
Sound of Mull
550
Loch Arienas
19
Calgary Bay
Ensay
342
Aros
10
Ardnacross
444
Killundine
B 849
Claggan
Gleann Geal
Larachbeg
Achranich
Loch Aline
Fiunary Forest
Fiunary
Treshnish Point
Haunn
176
Bellart
Loch Frisa
Salen Forest
A 884
Lochaline
14
513
Cairn na Burgh Beg
Achleck
Fladda
Loch Tuath
424
Salen
Fishnish Bay
A 849
11
Ardtornish Point
Treshnish Isles
Lunga
Gometra
313
Lagganulva
108
Sound of Ulva
Killiechronan
B 8035
Garmony
Forsa
Scallastle Bay
Ulva
Eorsa
Knock
Loch na Keal
L. Bà
Salen Forest
Rubha an Ridire
Bac Mór or Dutchman's Cap
Lit. Colonsay
Staffa
591
Tomsléibhe
766
Craignure
Duart Point
Torosay Castle
Duart Castle
Rubha Fiart
Bernera Island
Lynn of Lorn
Fingal's Cave
Inch Kenneth
Dun da Ghaoithe
761
Balnahard
Ben More
966
Lochdonhead
17
149
Glen More
Strathcoil
Grass Point
Kerrera
ISLE OF MULL
519
Balevulin
Ardmeanach
Rubha na h-Uamha
Tiroran
Ben Buie
698
Loch Spelve
Croggan
Rubha na Faoilinn
Bach I
Eilean Annraidh
L. Fuaron
717
503
Lochbuie
L. Uisg
Loch Scridain
Pennyghael
18
Dubh Sgeir
L. na Làthaich
100
Baile Mór
Iona
Sound of Iona
Fionnphort
A 849
376
Brolass
Loch Buie
405
Carsaig
Eilean Dùin
Firth of Lorn
Bunessan
L. Assapol
Ross of Mull
52
Carsaig Bay
Rubha nà Faoilinn
Insh Island
Sound of Insh
Erraid
Soa I.
Eilean a' Chalmain
Ardchiavaig
Ardalanish Bay
Malcolm's Point
Frank Lockwood's Island
Seil
Easdale

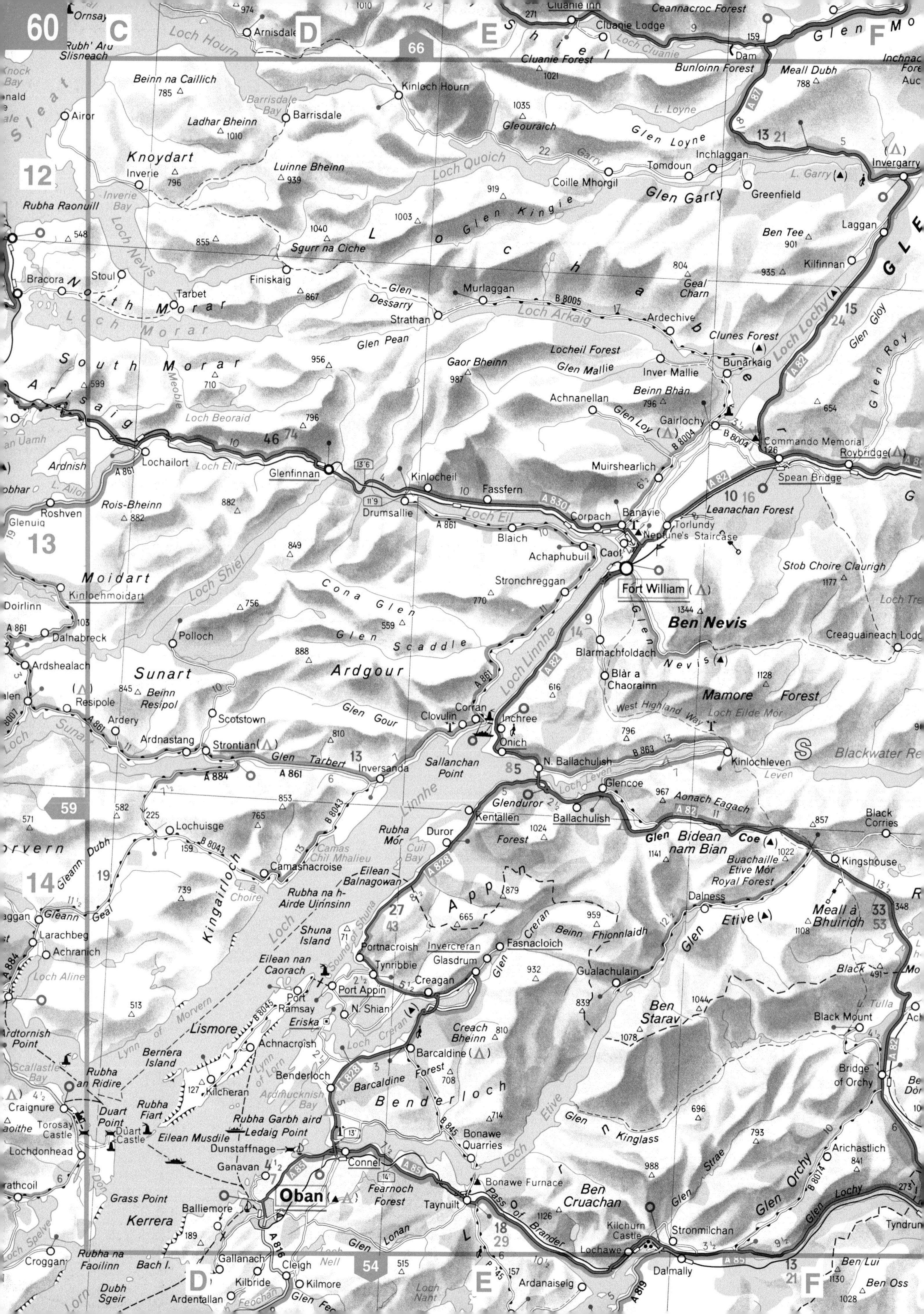

C
D
E
F
66
12
13
14
59
54
Ornsay
Rubh' Ard Slisneach
Arnisdale
Loch Hourn
Cluanie Inn
Ceannacroc Forest
Cluanie Lodge
Loch Cluanie
Cluanie Forest
Dam
Glen Moriston
Bunloinn Forest
Meall Dubh
Beinn na Caillich
Kinloch Hourn
Barrisdale Bay
Barrisdale
Airor
Ladhar Bheinn
Gleouraich
Glen Loyne
L. Loyne
Knoydart
Inverie
Inverie Bay
Luinne Bheinn
Loch Quoich
Garry
Tomdoun
Inchlaggan
Coille Mhorgil
Greenfield
Glen Garry
L. Garry
Invergarry
Rubha Raonuill
Loch Nevis
Sgurr na Ciche
Loch Arkaig
Ben Tee
Laggan
Kilfinnan
Stoul
Finiskaig
Bracora
North Morar
Tarbet
Loch Morar
Glen Dessarry
Strathan
Murlaggan
B 8005
Geal Charn
Ardechive
Clunes Forest
Loch Lochy
Glen Gloy
Glen Pean
Locheil Forest
Glen Mallie
Inver Mallie
Bunarkaig
Glen Roy
South Morar
Arisaig
Gaor Bheinn
Achnanellan
Beinn Bhàn
Glen Loy
Gairlochy
Meoble
Loch Beoraid
B 8004
Commando Memorial
Roybridge
Ardnish
Lochailort
Loch Eilt
Glenfinnan
Kinlocheil
Muirshearlich
Spean Bridge
A 861
A 830
A 82
A 87
Fassfern
Drumsallie
Loch Eil
Corpach
Banavie
Torlundy
Leanachan Forest
Rois-Bheinn
Roshven
Glenuig
Blaich
Neptune's Staircase
Achaphubuil
Caol
Fort William
Stob Choire Claurigh
Moidart
Kinlochmoidart
Loch Shiel
Cona Glen
Stronchreggan
Doirlinn
Dalnabreck
Polloch
Glen Scaddle
Ben Nevis
Creaguaineach Lodge
Loch Linnhe
Blarmachfoldach
Ardshealach
Sunart
Ardgour
Glen Nevis
Blàr a Chaorainn
Mamore Forest
Resipole
Beinn Resipol
Scotstown
Glen Gour
Corran
Clovulin
Inchree
West Highland Way
Loch Eilde Mòr
Ardery
Ardnastang
Strontian
Loch Sunart
Onich
Blackwater Reservoir
Glen Tarbert
Inversanda
Sallanchan Point
N. Ballachulish
B 863
Kinlochleven
A 884
Loch Leven
Glencoe
Aonach Eagach
Glenduror
Ballachulish
Kentallen
Lochuisge
B 8043
Duror
Forest
Glen Coe
Bidean nam Bian
Black Corries
Morvern
Gleann Dubh
Rubha Mór
Camas Chil Mhalieu
Cuil Bay
Buachaille Etive Mór
Royal Forest
Kingshouse
Camasnacroise
Eilean Balnagowan
A 828
Appin
Rubha na h-Airde Uinnsinn
Dalness
Kingairloch
Gleann Geal
Larachbeg
Achranich
Loch a' Choire
Shuna Island
Sound of Shuna
Beinn Fhionnlaidh
Glen Creran
Glen Etive
Meall à Bhuiridh
Loch Aline
Portnacroish
Invercreran
Glasdrum
Fasnacloich
Tynribbie
Eilean nan Caorach
Gualachulain
Black Mount
Port Appin
Creagan
Port Ramsay
N. Shian
Eriska
Lismore
Ben Starav
Ardtornish Point
Lynn of Morvern
B 8045
Achnacroish
Loch Creran
Creach Bheinn
Barcaldine
Bernera Island
Lynn of Lorn
Scallastle Bay
Rubha an Ridire
Benderloch
Barcaldine Forest
Bridge of Orchy
Kilcheran
Ardmucknish Bay
Craignure
Torosay Castle
Duart Point
Duart Castle
Rubha Fiart
Rubha Garbh aird
Ledaig Point
Eilean Musdile
B 845
Bonawe Quarries
Loch Etive
Glen Kinglass
Lochdonhead
Dunstaffnage
Connel
A 85
Ganavan
Arichastlich
Bonawe Furnace
Glen Strae
Glen Orchy
B 8074
Glen Lochy
Oban
Fearnoch Forest
Taynuilt
Ben Cruachan
Grass Point
Kerrera
Balliemore
Pass of Brander
Kilchurn Castle
Stronmilchan
Tyndrum
Loch Spelve
A 816
Glen Lonan
Lochawe
Dalmally
A 819
Croggan
Rubha na Faoilinn
Bach I.
Gallanach
Cleigh
Loch Nell
Ben Lui
Ben Oss
Kilbride
Kilmore
Loch Nant
Ardanaiseig
Dubh Sgeir
Ardentallan
Glen Feochan

Garragie Lodge
Coignafearn Forest
Inverdruie
Coylum
Fort Augustus
Glendoebeg
Sronlairig Lodge
Monadhliath Mountains
Alvie
Loch Morlich
Glen Brein
Carn Easgann Bàna
Highland Wildlife Park
Kincraig
Feshiebridge
Cairn Gorm
Newtown
Glendoe Forest
Glen Tarff
Carn Ban
Kingussie
Insh
Braeriach
Newtonmore
Ruthven Barracks
Loch Einich
Achlean
Cairn Toul
Corrieyairack Forest
Melgarve
Garvamore
Spey
Laggan
Catlodge
Glen Tromie
Glen Feshie
Glenfeshie Lodge
Glenfeshie Forest
Beinn Bhrotain
Strathmashie
Cromra
Brae Roy Lodge
Creag Meagaidh
Loch Laggan
Badenoch
Truim
Dalwhinnie
Lochan t-Seilich
Gaick Forest
Gaick Lodge
An Sgarsoch
Roughburn
Lochan na h-Earba
Ardverikie Forest
Pattack
Glen Spean
Fersit
Ben Alder Lodge
Glen Truim
Sronphadruig Lodge
Beinn Dearg
Bruar Lodge
Forest Lodge
Chno Dearg
Ben Alder Forest
Loch Ericht
Beinn Udlamain
Pass of Drumochter
Dalnaspidal Lodge
Forest of Atholl
Ben Alder
Loch Garry
Glen Garry
Glen Tilt
Beinn a' Ghlò
L. Ossian
Corrour Shooting Lodge
Corrour Forest
Sgor Gaibhre
Corrour Station
Rannoch Forest
Beinn Mholach
Loch Errochty
Bruar Falls
Blair Castle
Calvine
Dalchalloch
Blair Atholl
Glen Errochty
Beinn a' Chuallaich
Ben Vrackie
Killiecrankie
Queen's View
Pass of Killiecrankie
Moulin
Tressait
Kinloch Rannoch
Bridge of Ericht
Rannoch Sta
Loch Rannoch
Tummel Bridge
Foss
Loch Tummel
Linn of Tummel
Faskally
Pitlochry
L. Eigheach
Gaur
Bridge of Gaur
Carie
Schiehallion
Meall Tairneachan
A' Chruach
Loch Laidon
Grampian
Allt Camghouran
Perthshire and Kinross
Grandtully
Rannoch Moor
Glengoulandie
Carn Mairg
Balnaguard
Loch Bà
Meall Buidhe
Castle Menzies
Weem
St. Mary's
Tulla
Glen Lyon
Keltneyburn
Appin of Dull
Aberfeldy
Invervar
Fortingall
Loch an Daimh
Bridge of Balgie
Lyon
Kenmore
Stuchd an Lochain
Fearnan
Craigvinean Forest
Meall Buidhe
Cashlie
Acharn
Loch Lyon
Glen Cochill
Ben Lawers
Meall Dearg
Beinn Heasgarnich
Meall Ghaordie
Lawers
Ardtalnaig
Trochry
Loch Tay
Quaich
Garrow
Lochan na Lairige
L. Freuchie
Amulree
Kenknock
Glen Lochay
Strath Braan
Breadalbane
Meall nam Fuaran
Ardeonaig
Auchnafree
Meall nan Caorach
Killin
Beinn Cheathaich
Dochart
Almond
Creag Uchdag
Ben Chonzie
L. Lednock Resr.
Glen Lednock
Logiealmond
Harrietfield
Strath Fillan
Auchlyne
Glen Dochart
Ardchyle
Meall Tarsuinn
Sma' Glen
Glen Almond
Buchanty
Luib
Invergeldie
L. Turret
Lubhair
Crianlarich
Benmore
Ben More
Meall an t-Seallaidh
Lochearnhead
Loch Earn
St. Fillans
Monzie
Gilmerton
Fowlis Wester

Coylumbridge
The Queen's Forest
Alvie
Loch Morlich
Glenmore Forest Park
Cairn Gorm
Cairngorm Mountains
Braeriach
Ben Macdui
Cairn Toul
Loch Einich
Loch Avon
Glen Avon
Forest of Glenavon
Ben Avon
Beinn a' Bhuird
Glen Loin
Delnadamph Lodge
Corgarff Castle
Cock Bridge
Colnabaichin
Don
Brown Cow Hill
Morven
Migvie
Logie Coldstone
Tarland
Cromar
Ordie
Loch Davan
Dinnet
Glen Gairn
Bridge of Gairn
Crathie
Balmoral Castle
Ballater
Dee
Glen Tanar
Forest of Glen Tanar
Ballochan
Beinn Bhrotain
Forest of Mar
Glen Lui
Allanaquoich
Invercauld House
Braemar
Linn of Dee
Inverey
Glen Ey
Glen Clunie
Glen Callater
Glen Gelder
Glen Muick
Aucholzie
Balmoral Forest
Lochnagar
Loch Muick
Glas-allt Shiel
Cock Cairn
Mount Keen
MOUNTAINS
An Sgarsoch
An Socach
The Cairnwell
Devil's Elbow
Glas Maol
Broad Cairn
Glen Lee
Loch Lee
Auchronie
Inchgrundle
Tarfside
Glen Lochsie
Forest Lodge
Beinn a' Ghlo
Glen Tilt
Gleann Fearnach
Braedownie
Glen Clova
Mayar
Clova
Ben Tirran
White Hill
West Knock
Waterhead
Spittal of Glenshee
Auchavan
Runtaleave
Glen Prosen
Glenprosen Village
Glen Isla
Glen Shee
Glenisla Forest
Blair Atholl
Ben Vrackie
Straloch
Killiecrankie
Pass of Killiecrankie
Dalnavaid
Creag Dhubh
Kirkmichael
Clackavoid
Forter
Mount Blair
Brewlands Bridge
Kirkton of Glenisla
Backwater Resr.
Cat Law
Dykehead
Ogil
Fern
Moulin
Pitlochry
Linn of Tummel
Faskally
Blacklunans
Strathardle
Balintore
Pearsie
Dykends
Tannadice
L. of Lintrathen
Kirkton of Kingoldrum
Oathlaw
Forest of Alyth
Bridgend of Lintrathen
Kirriemuir
Grandtully
Ballinluig
Creag-nam-Mial
Tullymurdoch
Bridge of Craigisla
Reekie Linn
Lunanhead
Balnaguard
St. Mary's
Aberfeldy
Forest of Clunie
Bridge-of-Cally
Craigton
Forfar
Kingsmuir
Alyth
Ruthven
Dean Wr.
Glamis Castle
Douglastown
Dowally
Craigvinean Forest
Butterstone
Blairgowrie
Rattray
L. of Lowes
Clunie
Meigle
Eassie and Nevay
Glamis
Inverarity
Kirkbuddo
Strath Tay
Dunkeld
Inver
Birnam
Caputh
Meikleour
Newtyle
Lumley Den
Trochry
Strathbraan
Glen Cochill
Amulree
Kinclaven
R. Tay
Coupar Angus
Long L.
Balgray
Burrelton
Pitcur
Lundie
Sidlaw Hills
Auchterhouse
Newbigging
Cargill
Bankfoot
Meall nan Caorach
Little Glenshee
Stanley
King's Seat
Muirhead
Kirkton of Strathmartine
Kellas
DUNDEE
MICHELIN
Guildtown
Kinrossie
Abernyte
Longforgan
Broughty Ferry
Logiealmond
Harrietfield
Moneydie
Luncarty
Balbeggie
Kinnaird
Braes of the Carse
Invergowrie
Inchture
Tay Road Bridge
Tayport
Sma' Glen
Buchanty
Almond
Scone Palace
Newport-on-Tay
Huntingtower Castle
New Scone
Rait
Wormit
Fowlis Wester
Methven
Gilmerton
Carse of Gowrie
Firth of Tay
Balmerino
Bridgend
Tibbermore
Kinfauns
Tentsmuir Forest

ABERDEEN
Bridge of Don
Stoneywood
Bucksburn
Bankhead
Northfield
Mastrick
Kirkton of Skene
Elrick
Westhill
Skene
Dunecht
Fraser
Sauchen
Muir of Fowlis
Craigievar Castle
Tornaveen
Lumphanan
Loch of Skene
Echt
Garlogie
Girdle Ness
Nigg Bay
Cults
Bieldside
Loirston
Cove Bay
Hill of Fare
Torphins
Peterculter
Drum Castle
Maryculter
Kincardine O'Neil
Birsemore
Crathes Castle
Banchory
R. Dee
Marywell
Kirkton of Durris
Portlethen
Downies
Netherley
Cammachmore
Newtonhill
Muchalls
Lochton
Strachan
Water of Feugh
Glen Dye
Peter Hill
Kerloch
Mowtie
Rickarton
Hill of Trusta
Fetteresso Forest
Bridge of Dye
Stonehaven
Dunnottar Castle
Thornyhive Bay
Mount Battock
Water of Dye
Goyle Hill
Cairn o' Mount
Drumtochty Forest
Drumlithie
Bruxie Hill
Auchenblae
Catterline
Roadside of Kinneff
Fordoun
Fasque
Hill of Wirren
Howe of the Mearns
Arbuthnott
Kinneff
Fettercairn
Inverbervie
Bervie Bay
Gourdon
Doolie Ness
Laurencekirk
Castle
Luthermuir
Edzell
Johnshaven
Inchbare
N. Water Bridge
Marykirk
Milton Ness
St. Cyrus
R. N. Esk
Hillside
Brechin
R. South Esk
Bridge of Dun
Montrose
Montrose Basin
Scurdie Ness
Ferryden
Stones
Aberlemno
Farnell
Boddin Point
Guthrie
Friockheim
Lunan
Lunan Bay
Lunan Wr.
Inverkeilor
Lang Craig
Redford
Marywell
St. Vigeans
Carmyllie
Cliffs
Arbroath
Arbirlot
Muirdrum
E. Haven
Barry
Carnoustie
Buddon Ness
Inchcape or Bell Rock
A 90
A 92
A 93
A 94
A 96
A 944
A 956
A 957
A 980
A 933
A 934
A 935
A 937
A 930
B 9119
B 993
B 977
B 979
B 9125
B 9077
B 974
B 976
B 966
B 967
B 9120
B 9113
B 9134
B 961
B 965
B 9127
B 9128
M
N
O
12
13
14
69
57
1

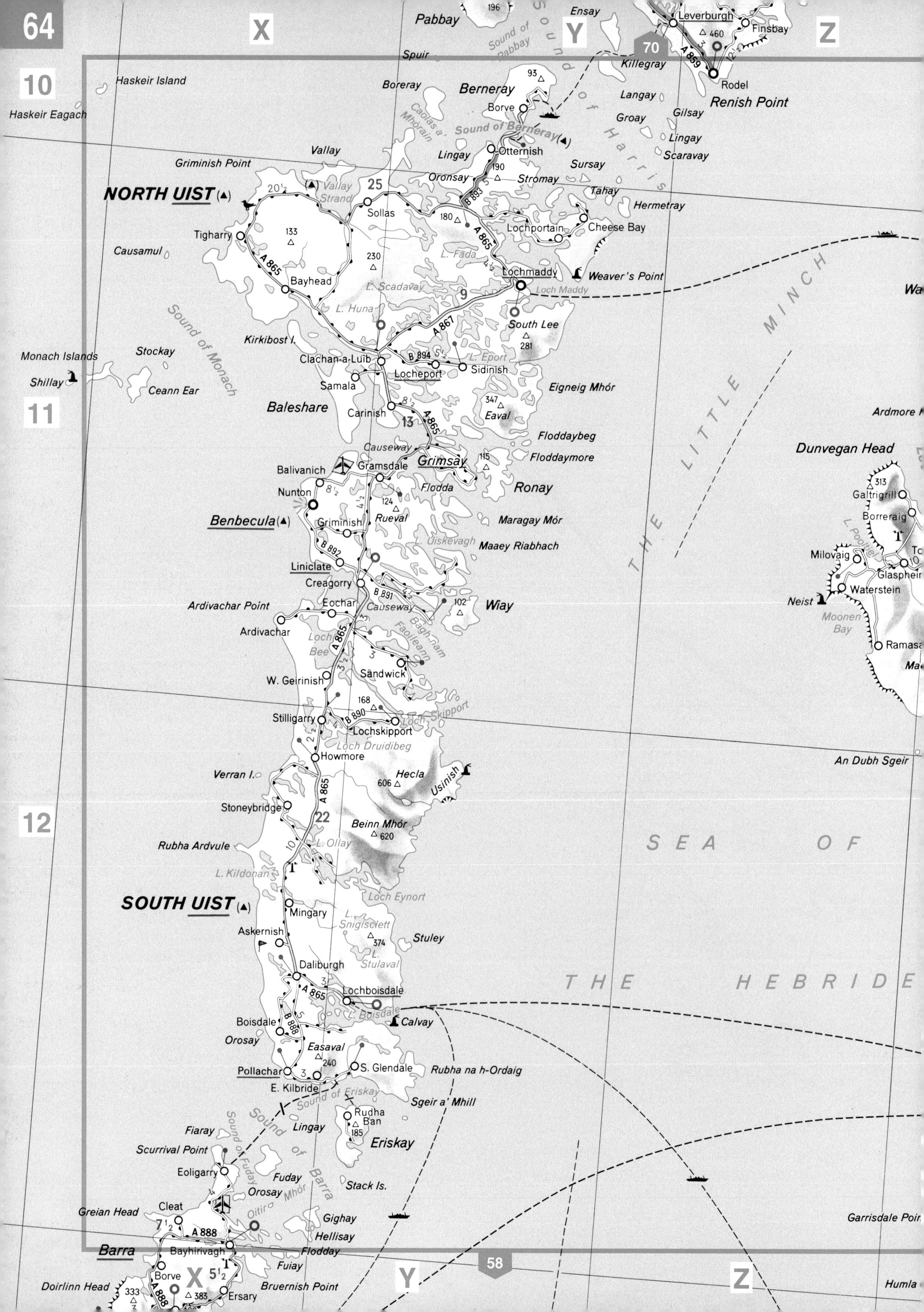
X
Y
Z
10
11
12
70
58
Haskeir Island
Haskeir Eagach
Pabbay
Spuir
Boreray
Berneray
Borve
Sound of Berneray
Sound of Pabbay
Sound of Harris
Ensay
Leverburgh
Finsbay
Killegray
Rodel
Renish Point
Langay
Gilsay
Groay
Lingay
Scaravay
Vallay
Griminish Point
Otternish
Sursay
Stromay
Oronsay
Tahay
Hermetray
NORTH UIST
Valley Strand
Sollas
Tigharry
Causamul
Lochportain
Cheese Bay
L. Fada
Lochmaddy
Weaver's Point
Loch Maddy
Bayhead
L. Scadavay
L. Huna
South Lee
Kirkibost I.
Stockay
Sound of Monach
Monach Islands
Shillay
Ceann Ear
Clachan-a-Luib
Locheport
Sidinish
L. Eport
Samala
Baleshare
Carinish
Eigneig Mhór
Eaval
Floddaybeg
Floddaymore
Causeway
Grimsay
Balivanich
Gramsdale
Flodda
Ronay
Nunton
Benbecula
Griminish
Rueval
Maragay Mór
L. Uiskevagh
Maaey Riabhach
Liniclate
Creagorry
Ardivachar Point
Eochar
Wiay
Ardivachar
Loch Bee
Bagh nam Faoileann
Sandwick
W. Geirinish
Stilligarry
Lochskipport
Loch Skipport
Loch Druidibeg
Howmore
Verran I.
Hecla
Usinish
Stoneybridge
Beinn Mhór
Rubha Ardvule
L. Ollay
L. Kildonan
Loch Eynort
SOUTH UIST
Mingary
L. Snigisclett
Askernish
Stuley
L. Stulaval
Daliburgh
Lochboisdale
L. Boisdale
Calvay
Boisdale
Orosay
Easaval
Pollachar
S. Glendale
Rubha na h-Ordaig
E. Kilbride
Sound of Eriskay
Sgeir a' Mhill
Rudha Ban
Eriskay
Lingay
Fiaray
Sound of Fuday
Sound of Barra
Scurrival Point
Eoligarry
Fuday
Orosay
Stack Is.
Oitir Mhór
Cleat
Greian Head
Gighay
Hellisay
Barra
Bayhirivagh
Flodday
Fuiay
Borve
Doirlinn Head
Bruernish Point
Ersary
THE LITTLE MINCH
SEA OF THE HEBRIDES
Dunvegan Head
Ardmore
Galtrigrill
Borreraig
L. Pooltiel
Milovaig
Glaspheir
Waterstein
Neist
Moonen Bay
Ramasa
An Dubh Sgeir
Garrisdale Point
Humla
A 865
A 867
A 859
B 893
B 894
B 892
B 891
B 890
B 888
A 888

A
B
C
D
71
59
66
Sgeir nam Maol
Fladda-chùain
Eilean Trodday
Rubha Hunish
Kilmaluag
Duntulm Castle
Lùb Score
Skye Croft Museum
Kilmuir
Flodigarry
Eilean Flodigarry
Kilvaxter
Quiraing
Staffin Bay
Staffin I.
Staffin
Kilt Rock
Totscore
Ascrib Islands
Trotternish Point
Uig
Balnaknock
Marishader
Garros
Beinn Edra
Culnaknock
Rubha nam Brathairean
Uig Bay
Loch Snizort
Earlish
Glenuachdarach
Rigg
Kingsburgh
The Storr
Old Man of Storr
Treaslane
Trotternish
Kensaleyre
Loch Leathan
L. Fada
Skeabost
Carbost
Achtalean
Glengrasco
Portree
Penifiler
Camastianavaig
Mugeary
L. Duagrich
Ollach
Pèinchorran
Glen Varragill
ISLE OF SKYE
Waternish
Geary
Halistra
Greshornish Point
Isay
Lusta
Beinn Bhreac
Claigan
Greshornish
Flashader
Edinbane
Bernisdale
Blackhill
Dunvegan Castle
Dunvegan
Colbost
Lonmore
Roskhill
Vatten
Roag
Caroy
Harlosh
Harlosh I.
Osdale
Bracadale
Tarner I.
Wiay
Ullinish
Idrigill Point
Oronsay
Loch Bracadale
Portnalong
Fiskavaig
Carbost
Talisker
Drynoch
L. Harport
Sligachan
L. Sligachan
Sconser
Glamaig
Loch Ainort
Luib
Glen Brittle Forest
Eynort
L. Eynort
Minginish
The Cuillins
Sgurr a' Ghreadaidh
Sgurr Alasdair
Glenbrittle House
Bualintur
L. Coruisk
L. na Creitheach
Bla Bheinn
Strathaird
L. Slapin
Torrin
Kilmarie
Elgol
Rubha na h-Easgainne
Tarskavaig Point
Rubh'an Dùnain
L. Brittle
Soay Sound
Mol-Chlach
Soay
Loch Scavaig
CUILLIN SOUND
Canna
A' Chill
Sanday
Sound of Canna
Rubha Shamhnan Insir
Kilmory
A' Bhrideanach
Orval
Kinloch
Loch Scresort
Sound of Raasay
Eilean Tigh
Eilean Fladday
Manish Point
Arnish
Brochel
I. of Raasay
Dùn Caan
Oskaig
Raasay Ho.
N. Fearns
Eyre Point
Caol Mór
Island of Rona
INNER SOUND
Scalpay
Mullach na Càrn
Longay
Pabay
Guillamon I.
Corry
Broadford Bay
Broadford
Red Hills
Skulamus
Breakish
Kyleakin
Kyle of Lochalsh
Erbusaig
Balmacara
Auchtertyre
Loch Alsh
Kylerhea
Glenelg Bay
Glenelg
Galltair
Heast
L. Eishort
Rubha Suisnish
Drumfearn
Ord
Isleornsay
Loch na Dal
Ornsay
Sandaig Is.
Upr. Sandaig
Tokavaig
Tarskavaig
Teangue
Knock Bay
Kilmore
Clan Donald Centre
Armadale Bay
Ardvasar
Aird of Sleat
Sleat
Sound of Sleat
Airor
Rubh' Ard Slisneach
Loch Hourn
Beinn na Caillich
Ladhar Bheinn
Knoydart
Inverie
Melvaig
N. Erradale
Inverewe Gardens
Poolewe
Longa Island
Gairloch
Loch Gairloch
Charlestown
Port Henderson
Opinan
Badachro
Shieldaig
L. Bad an Sgalaig
Redpoint
Red Point
Rubha na Fearn
Loch Torridon
Fearnmore
Lr. Diabaig
Arinacrinachd
Cuaig
Kenmore
Alligin Shuas
Kalnakill
Shieldaig
Loch Lundie
Applecross
Beinn Bhán
Bealach-na Bo
Meal Gorm
Toscaig
Eilean na Bà
Eilean Beag
Caolas Mór
Loch Kishorn
Achintraid
Eilean Mòr
Crowlin Is.
Loch Carron
Plockton
Duirinish
A 855
A 850
A 87
A 863
A 851
B 885
B 886
B 884
B 8036
B 883
B 8009
B 8083
B 8021

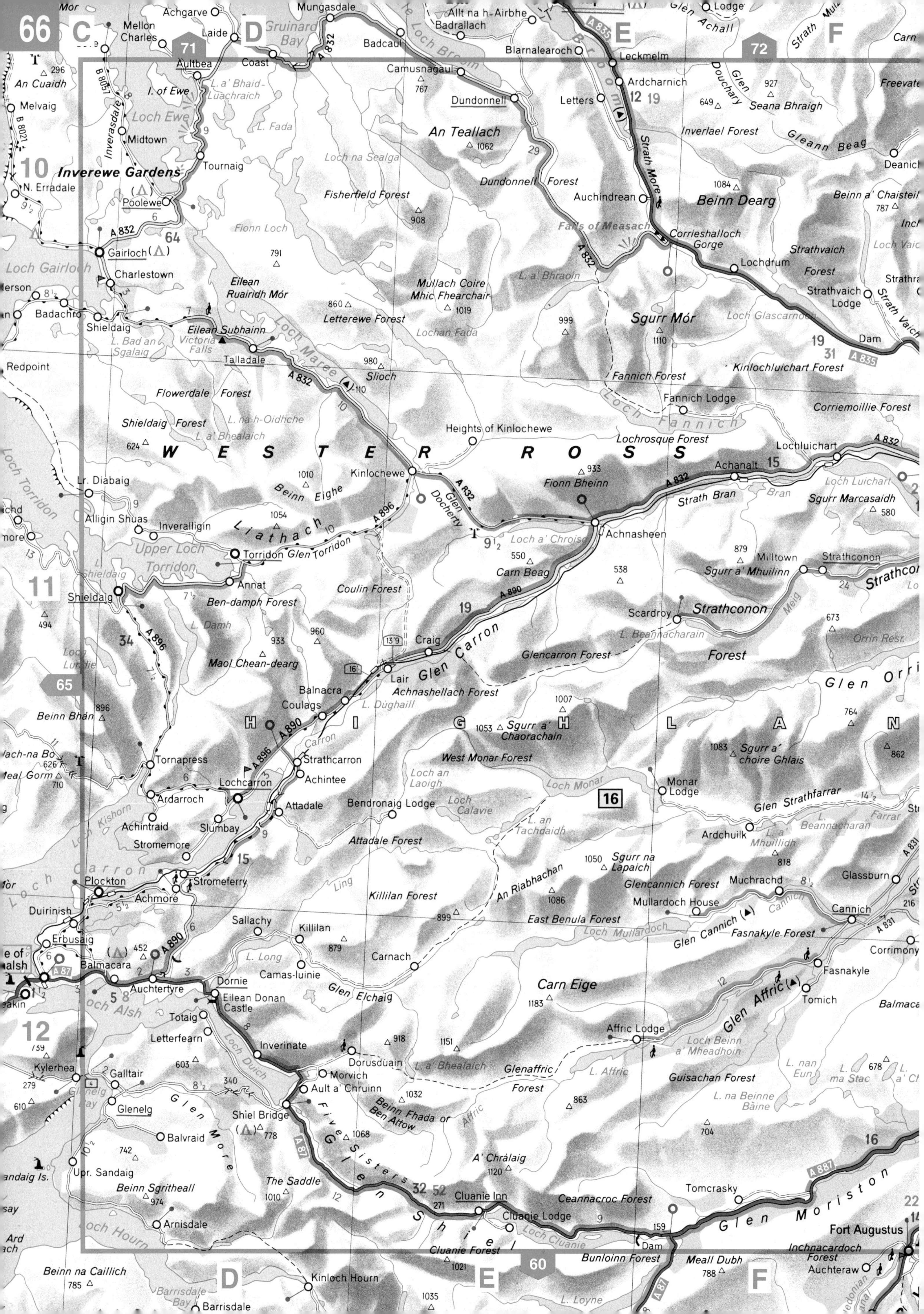
C
D
E
F
71
72
65
60
10
11
12
16
Mellon Charles
Achgarve
Laide
Gruinard Bay
Mungasdale
Allt na h-Airbhe
Badrallach
Badcaul
Loch Broom
Blarnalearoch
Leckmelm
Ardcharnich
Glen Achall
Lodge
Strath Mulzie
Carn
Aultbea
Coast
Camusnagaul
Dundonnell
Letters
Glen Douchary
Seana Bhraigh
Freevater
An Cuaidh
I. of Ewe
L. a' Bhaid-Luachraich
Melvaig
Loch Ewe
L. Fada
An Teallach
Strath More
Inverlael Forest
Gleann Beag
Inverasdale
Midtown
Tournaig
Loch na Sealga
Deanich
N. Erradale
Inverewe Gardens
Poolewe
Dundonnell Forest
Auchindrean
Beinn Dearg
Beinn a' Chaisteil
Fisherfield Forest
Fionn Loch
Falls of Measach
Corrieshalloch Gorge
Gairloch
Loch Gairloch
Charlestown
L. a' Bhraoin
Strathvaich Forest
Lochdrum
Loch Vaich
Eilean Ruairidh Mór
Mullach Coire Mhic Fhearchair
Strathvaich Lodge
Strath Vaich
Badachro
Shieldaig
Eilean Subhainn
Loch Maree
Letterewe Forest
Lochan Fada
Sgurr Mór
Loch Glascarnoch
Dam
L. Bad an Sgalaig
Victoria Falls
Talladale
Slioch
Redpoint
Fannich Forest
Kinlochluichart Forest
Flowerdale Forest
Loch Fannich
Fannich Lodge
Corriemoillie Forest
Shieldaig Forest
L. na h-Oidhche
L. a' Bhealaich
Heights of Kinlochewe
Lochrosque Forest
Lochluichart
W E S T E R R O S S
Kinlochewe
Fionn Bheinn
Achanalt
Loch Luichart
Lr. Diabaig
Beinn Eighe
Glen Docherty
Strath Bran
Sgurr Marcasaidh
Loch Torridon
Alligin Shuas
Inveralligin
Liathach
Achnasheen
Loch a' Chroisg
Upper Loch Torridon
Torridon
Glen Torridon
Carn Beag
Milltown
Strathconon
Sgurr a' Mhuilinn
Annat
Coulin Forest
Shieldaig
Ben-damph Forest
L. Damh
Scardroy
Strathconon
Meig
L. Beannacharain
Forest
Orrin Resr.
Maol Chean-dearg
Craig
Glen Carron
Glencarron Forest
Loch Lundie
Lair
Achnashellach Forest
Glen Orrin
Beinn Bhán
Balnacra
Coulags
L. Dùghaill
H I G H L A N
Sgurr a' Chaorachain
Sgurr a' choire Ghlais
Strathcarron
Achintee
West Monar Forest
Loch an Laoigh
Loch Monar
Tornapress
Lochcarron
Ardarroch
Monar Lodge
Glen Strathfarrar
Loch Kishorn
Achintraid
Slumbay
Attadale
Bendronaig Lodge
Loch Calavie
L. an Tachdaidh
Ardchuilk
L. a' Mhuillidh
L. Beannacharan
Farrar
Stromemore
Attadale Forest
Sgurr na Lapaich
Loch Carron
Plockton
Stromeferry
Achmore
Ling
Killilan Forest
An Riabhachan
Glencannich Forest
Muchrachd
Glassburn
Duirinish
Mullardoch House
Cannich
Sallachy
Killilan
East Benula Forest
Loch Mullardoch
Glen Cannich
Fasnakyle Forest
Erbusaig
Carnach
L. Long
Corrimony
Balmacara
Camas-luinie
Dornie
Glen Elchaig
Carn Eige
Fasnakyle
Glen Affric
Tomich
Balmacara
Auchtertyre
Eilean Donan Castle
Loch Alsh
Totaig
Letterfearn
Loch Duich
Affric Lodge
Loch Beinn a' Mheadhoin
Inverinate
Kylerhea
Dorusduain
L. a' Bhealaich
Glenaffric Forest
L. Affric
L. nan Eun
L. ma Stac
Galltair
Morvich
Ault a' Chruinn
Guisachan Forest
Glenelg Bay
Glenelg
Glen More
Shiel Bridge
Beinn Fhada or Ben Attow
Affric
L. na Beinne Bàine
Balvraid
Five Sisters
A' Chràlaig
Upr. Sandaig
Sandaig Is.
The Saddle
Glen Shiel
Beinn Sgritheall
Cluanie Inn
Tomcrasky
Ceannacroc Forest
Cluanie Lodge
Loch Cluanie
Glen Moriston
Fort Augustus
Arnisdale
Loch Hourn
Cluanie Forest
Bunloinn Forest
Meall Dubh
Inchnacardoch Forest
Auchteraw
Dam
Beinn na Caillich
Kinloch Hourn
Barrisdale Bay
Barrisdale
L. Loyne
A 832
A 835
A 896
A 890
A 87
A 831
A 887
B 8057
B 8021

EASTER ROSS
INVERNESS
Black Isle
MORAY FIRTH
Dornoch Firth
Cromarty Firth
Beauly Firth
Moray Firth
LOCH NESS
GLEN MOR
Strathdearn
Monadhliath Mountains
Drummossie Muir
Strathnairn
Stratherrick
The Aird
Bonar Bridge
Ardgay
Kincardine
Spinningdale
Clashmore
Dornoch
Embo
Evelix
Edderton
Fearn Lodge
Tain
Inver
Portmahomack
Wilkhaven
Tarbat Ness
Hill of Fearn
Hilton of Cadboll
Balintore
Kildary
Milton
Barbaraville
Nigg
Saltburn
Balnapaling
Invergordon
Alness
Dalnavie
Boathvic
Wyvis Lodge
Braeantra
Kildermorie Lodge
Eileanach Lodge
Ben Wyvis
Evanton
Balblair
Cromarty
Sutors Stacks
Cullicudden
Jemimaville
Millbuie Forest
Mount Eagle
Killen
Rosemarkie
Fortrose
Chanonry Point
Avoch
Munlochy
Tore
Dingwall
Strathpeffer
Maryburgh
Conon Bridge
Contin
Garve
Culbokie
Alcaig
Marybank
Muir of Ord
Redcastle
N. Kessock
Windhill
Beauly
Kirkhill
Kilmorack
Drumchardine
Cemetery
Culloden Battlefield
Clava Cairns
Kiltarlity
Dochgarroch
Glackossian
Scaniport
Essich
Abriachan
Dores
Balnafoich
Tombreck
Farr
Daviot
Moy
Ruthven
Tomatin
Slochd Summit
Slochd
Carrbridge
Landmark Visitor Centre
Duthil
Dulnain Bridge
Grantown on-Spey
Cottartown
Boat of Garten
Abernethy Forest
Nethy Bridge
Aviemore
Inverdruie
Coylumbridge
The Queen's Forest
Glenmore Forest Park
Alvie
Kincraig
Highland Wildlife Park
Dalmigavie
Eil
Coignafearn
Dalbeg
Coignafearn Forest
Croachy
Torness
Dunmaglass Lodge
Errogie
Inverfarigaig
Foyers
Lochgarthside
Whitebridge
Garragie Lodge
Glendoebeg
Sronlairig Lodge
Invermoriston
Knockie Lodge
Drumnadrochit
Lewiston
Urquhart Castle
Milton
Glen Urquhart
Glen Convinth
Fort George
Ardersier
Whiteness Head
Nairn
Tradespark
Auldearn
Brodie Castle
Dyke
Kintessack
Culbin Forest
Whitemire
Darnaway Forest
Littlemill
Cawdor
Clephanton
Croy
Stuart
INVERNESS DALCROSS AIRPORT
Ferness
Aitnoch
Dava
Findhorn
Croick
Strathcarron
Kyle of Sutherland
Loch Migdale
Diebidale Forest
Carn Bhrain
Carn Chuinneag
Kildermorie Forest
Beinn Tharsuinn
Morangie Forest
Ardross Forest
Loch Morie
Loch Glass
Meall Mór
Beinn nan Eun
Glen Glass
Clach Liath
Strathgarve Forest
Loch Garve
Falls of Rogie
Black Water
Loch Achilty
Loch Ussie
Findon Forest
Culbokie
Erchless Forest
Loch Bruicheach
Loch Ashie
Loch Duntelchaig
Loch Ruthven
Loch Mhór
Loch Moy
Carn nan tri-tighearnan
Beinn Bhuidhe Mhór
Carn Glas-choire
Glen Kyllachy
Carn na Saobhaidhe
Carn Coire na h-Easgainn
Geal-charn Mór
Meall Fuar-mhonoidh
Carn Easgann Bàna
Glen Brein
Loch Garten
Loch Morlich
Whiteness Sands
Innis Mhór
Loch Eye
Hill of Nigg
Nigg Bay
Cromarty Bay
Munlochy Bay
The Bar
A 9
A 836
A 949
A 862
A 832
A 835
A 96
A 82
A 831
A 833
A 939
A 940
A 938
A 95
B 9176
B 817
B 9163
B 9169
B 9160
B 9161
B 9006
B 9091
B 9090
B 9101
B 9092
B 9039
B 9165
B 9166
B 9168
B 9164
B 862
B 861
B 851
B 852
B 9154
B 9007
B 9153
B 970
73
68
61
G
H
I
10
11
12

I
J
K
L
10
11
12
67
62
Halliman Skerries
Covesea Skerries
Branderburgh
Hopeman
Lossiemouth
Burghead
Duffus
B 9040
Duffus Castle
Spynie Palace
Lossie Forest
Roseisle Forest
Burghead Bay
Spey Bay
Findhorn
Findhorn Bay
Newton
Elgin
Kingston
Garmouth
Portgordon
Buckie
Findochty
Portknockie
Cullen Bay
Cullen
Portessie
Lintmill
Fordyce
Sandend
Culbin Forest
Kintessack
Alves
Kinloss
Sueno's Stone
Miltonduff
Urquhart
Lhanbryde
A 96
Dyke
Brodie Castle
Forres
Monaughty Forest
Pluscarden Abbey
Thornhill
Mosstodloch
Fochabers
Speymouth Forest
Kirktown of Deskford
Aultmore
Gordonstown
Knoch Hill
Rafford
Whitewreath
Teindland Forest
R. Spey
Whitemire
Kellas
B 9010
Altyre Woods
Darnaway Forest
R. Findhorn
Dallas
19
M O R A Y
Rothes
Mulben
Newmill
Keith
Farmtown
Knock
Carn na Cailliche
Ben Aigan
Rosarie Forest
The Bin Forest
Ruthven
Milltown
Elchies Forest
Archiestown
Craigellachie
Strath Isla
Cairnie
Ferness
Lossie
Carn Kitty
Upr. Knockando
Carron
Aberlour
Cairnborrow
Huntly
Dufftown
Deveron
Aitnoch
Milltown of Edinvillie
A 920
Dava
Marypark
Strathbogie
Dava Moor
Carn na Lòine
Ballindalloch
Lochindorb
Auchnagallin
Advie
Ben Rinnes
Bridgend
Tillathrowie
Glen Rinnes
Glen Fiddich
Clashindarroch Forest
Clashindarroch
Hill of Foudland
Dellefure
Cottartown
Glenfiddich Lodge
Strath Spey
Glenlivet
Shenval
Corryhabbie Hill
Tap O' Noth
Kennethmont
Grantown-on-Spey
Cromdale
Hills of Cromdale
Minmore
Tomnavoulin
Blackwater Forest
Aldunie
Cabrach
Rhynie
Clatt
Dulnain Bridge
Duthil
Carrbridge
Strath Avon
Glen Livet
Knockandhu
The Buck
Correen Hills
Bridge of Brown
Ladder Hills
Lumsden
Nethy Bridge
Chapeltown
Badenyon
Mossat
Boat of Garten
Abernethy Forest
Loch Garten
Tomintoul
Carn Mòr
Kildrummy
Bridge of Alford
Dorback Lodge
Belnacraig
Kildrummy Castle
Glenbuchat Castle
Glenkindie
Howe of Alford
Lecht
Geal Charn
Lecht Road
Bellabeg
Bridge of Buchat
Towie
Coylumbridge
The Queen's Forest
Muir of Fowlis
Milton of Cushnie
Craigievar Castle
Loch Morlich
Glenmore Forest Park
Glen Loin
Cock Bridge
Colnabaichin
Don
Glen Avon
Delnadamph Lodge
Corgarff Castle
Migvie
Cairn Gorm
Forest of Glenavon
Brown Cow Hill
Morven
Tarland
Lumphanan
Cairngorm Mountains
Loch Avon
Ben Avon
Glen Gairn
Logie Coldstone
Cromar
Ordie
L. Davan
Beinn a' Bhuird
Ben Macdui
Cairn Toul
Dinnet
Aboyne
Kincardine O'Neil
Bridge of Gairn
Ballater
Birsemore
Dee
Crathie
Balmoral Castle
Braemar
Invercauld House
Glen Tanar
Marywell
Beinn Bhrotain
Allanaquoich

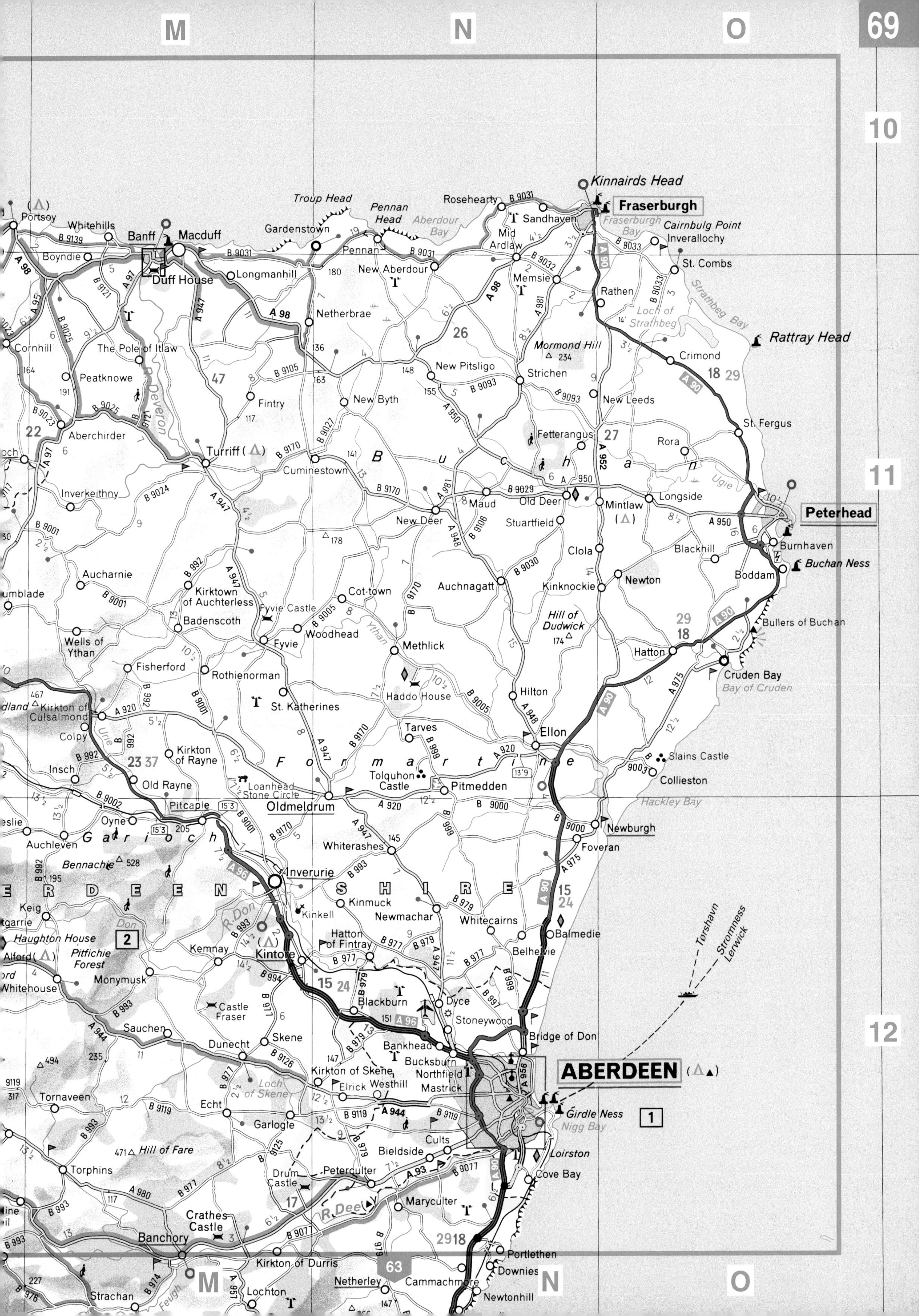
M
N
O
10
11
12
Kinnairds Head
Fraserburgh
Fraserburgh Bay
Cairnbulg Point
Inverallochy
St. Combs
Rosehearty
Sandhaven
Mid Ardlaw
Troup Head
Pennan Head
Aberdour Bay
Gardenstown
Pennan
New Aberdour
Portsoy
Whitehills
Banff
Macduff
Boyndie
Duff House
Longmanhill
Memsie
Rathen
Strathbeg Bay
Loch of Strathbeg
Rattray Head
Crimond
Netherbrae
Cornhill
The Pole of Itlaw
Peatknowe
Fintry
New Pitsligo
Mormond Hill
Strichen
New Leeds
New Byth
Aberchirder
R. Deveron
Turriff
Cuminestown
Fetterangus
St. Fergus
Rora
Buchan
Maud
Old Deer
Mintlaw
Longside
Peterhead
Inverkeithny
New Deer
Stuartfield
Blackhill
Burnhaven
Buchan Ness
Boddam
Clola
Newton
Auchnagatt
Kinknockie
Aucharnie
Kirktown of Auchterless
Cot-town
Fyvie Castle
Badenscoth
Woodhead
Fyvie
Wells of Ythan
Methlick
Hill of Dudwick
Bullers of Buchan
Hatton
Cruden Bay
Bay of Cruden
Fisherford
Rothienorman
St. Katherines
Haddo House
Hilton
Kirkton of Culsalmond
Colpy
Tarves
Ellon
Kirkton of Rayne
Formartine
Slains Castle
Collieston
Insch
Old Rayne
Loanhead Stone Circle
Tolquhon Castle
Pitmedden
Oldmeldrum
Hackley Bay
Pitcaple
Oyne
Newburgh
Foveran
Auchleven
Garioch
Whiterashes
Bennachie
Inverurie
ABERDEEN
SHIRE
Keig
Kinkell
Kinmuck
Newmachar
Whitecairns
Haughton House
Hatton of Fintray
Balmedie
Alford
Pitfichie Forest
Kemnay
Kintore
Belhelvie
Torshavn
Stromness
Lerwick
Monymusk
Whitehouse
Blackburn
Dyce
Castle Fraser
Stoneywood
Sauchen
Bridge of Don
Dunecht
Skene
Bankhead
Bucksburn
Northfield
Kirkton of Skene
Elrick
Westhill
Mastrick
ABERDEEN
Loch of Skene
Tornaveen
Echt
Girdle Ness
Nigg Bay
Garlogie
Cults
Hill of Fare
Bieldside
Loirston
Torphins
Peterculter
Drum Castle
Cove Bay
Maryculter
R. Dee
Crathes Castle
Banchory
Portlethen
Kirkton of Durris
Downies
Netherley
Cammachmore
Lochton
Strachan
Newtonhill
Feugh
A 98
A 90
A 950
A 952
A 947
A 948
A 981
A 920
A 96
A 975
A 956
A 944
A 93
A 980
A 97
63

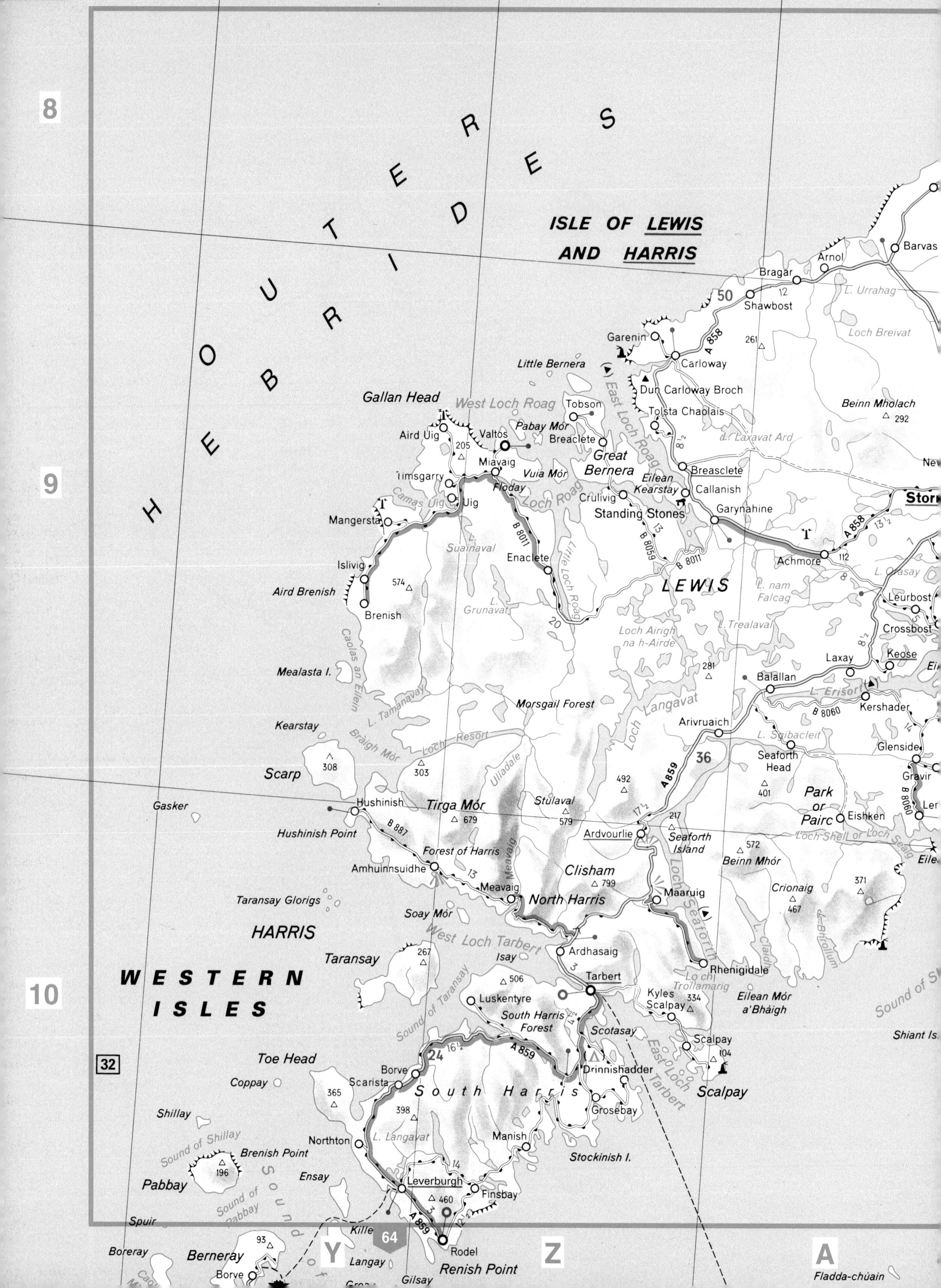
X
Y
Z
A
8
9
10
HEBRIDES
OUTER
ISLE OF LEWIS AND HARRIS
WESTERN ISLES
Barvas
Arnol
Bragar
Shawbost
L. Urrahag
Loch Breivat
Garenin
Carloway
Dun Carloway Broch
Little Bernera
East Loch Roag
Tobson
Tolsta Chaolais
Beinn Mholach
292
Gallan Head
West Loch Roag
Pabay Mór
Aird Uig
Valtos
Breaclete
L. Laxavat Ard
Great Bernera
Miavaig
Vuia Mór
Eilean Kearstay
Breasclete
Callanish
Timsgarry
Floday
Loch Roag
Crulivig
Standing Stones
Garynahine
Camas Uig
Uig
Mangersta
Suainaval
B 8011
B 8059
Achmore
A 858
Islivig
Enaclete
Little Loch Roag
LEWIS
L. nam Falcag
Aird Brenish
574
Brenish
L. Grunavat
Leurbost
Crossbost
L. Trealaval
Loch Airigh na h-Airde
Laxay
Keose
Mealasta I.
Caolas an Eilein
281
Balallan
L. Erisort
Kershader
B 8060
L. Tamanavay
Morsgail Forest
Loch Langavat
Arivruaich
Kearstay
Bràigh Mór
Loch Resort
L. Sgibacleit
Glenside
Seaforth Head
308
303
Scarp
A 859
36
Gravir
492
401
Park or Pairc
Gasker
Hushinish
Tirga Mór
679
Stulaval
579
217
Eishken
Hushinish Point
B 887
Ardvourlie
Seaforth Island
Loch Shell
572
Beinn Mhór
Forest of Harris
Amhuinnsuidhe
Clisham
799
Crionaig
467
371
Meavaig
Maaruig
Loch Seaforth
Taransay Glorigs
North Harris
Soay Mór
HARRIS
West Loch Tarbert
Isay
267
Taransay
Ardhasaig
Rhenigidale
506
Tarbert
Loch Trollamarig
Eilean Mór a'Bhàigh
Sound of Shiant
Luskentyre
Kyles Scalpay
334
South Harris Forest
Sound of Taransay
Scotasay
Scalpay
104
Shiant Is.
Toe Head
A 859
24
Borve
Drinnishadder
East Loch Tarbert
Coppay
Scarista
South Harris
Scalpay
365
Grosebay
398
Shillay
Sound of Shillay
L. Langavat
Manish
Northton
Brenish Point
Stockinish I.
196
Ensay
Pabbay
Leverburgh
Sound of Pabbay
460
Finsbay
Spuir
Kille
64
93
Boreray
Berneray
Rodel
Langay
Renish Point
Borve
Gilsay
Fladda-chùain

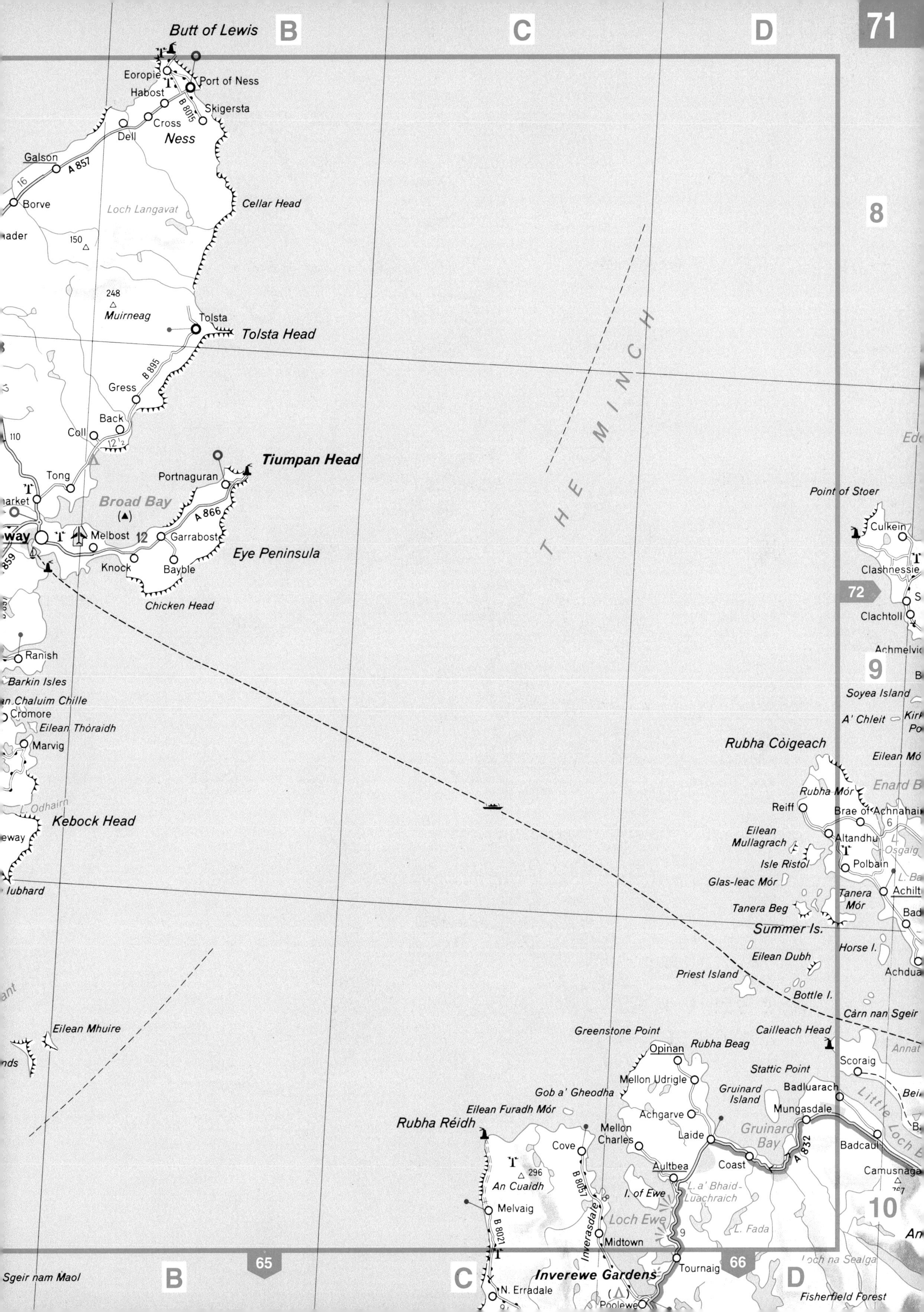
B
C
D
Butt of Lewis
Eoropie
Port of Ness
Habost
Skigersta
Cross
Dell
Ness
B 8015
Galson
A 857
Borve
Loch Langavat
Cellar Head
150
248
Muirneag
Tolsta
Tolsta Head
B 895
Gress
Back
Coll
Tong
Tiumpan Head
Portnaguran
Broad Bay
A 866
Melbost
Garrabost
Knock
Bayble
Eye Peninsula
Chicken Head
THE MINCH
Ranish
Barkin Isles
Cromore
Eilean Thòraidh
Marvig
Kebock Head
Iubhard
Eilean Mhuire
Sgeir nam Maol
Point of Stoer
Culkein
Clashnessie
72
Clachtoll
Achmelvic
Soyea Island
A' Chleit
Rubha Còigeach
Eilean Mó
Enard B
Rubha Mór
Reiff
Brae of Achnahai
Eilean Mullagrach
Altandhu
Isle Ristol
Polbain
Glas-leac Mór
Tanera Mór
Achilt
Tanera Beg
Summer Is.
Horse I.
Eilean Dubh
Priest Island
Achdua
Bottle I.
Càrn nan Sgeir
Greenstone Point
Cailleach Head
Opinan
Rubha Beag
Scoraig
Static Point
Mellon Udrigle
Gruinard Island
Badluarach
Gob a' Gheodha
Eilean Furadh Mór
Mungasdale
Little Loch B
Achgarve
Rubha Réidh
Mellon Charles
Laide
Gruinard Bay
Badcaul
Cove
A 832
Aultbea
Coast
Camusnaga
296
An Cuaidh
B 8057
L. a' Bhaid-Luachraich
I. of Ewe
Melvaig
Loch Ewe
B 8021
Inverasdale
L. Fada
Midtown
Tournaig
Inverewe Gardens
N. Erradale
Poolewe
Fisherfield Forest
8
9
10
65
66

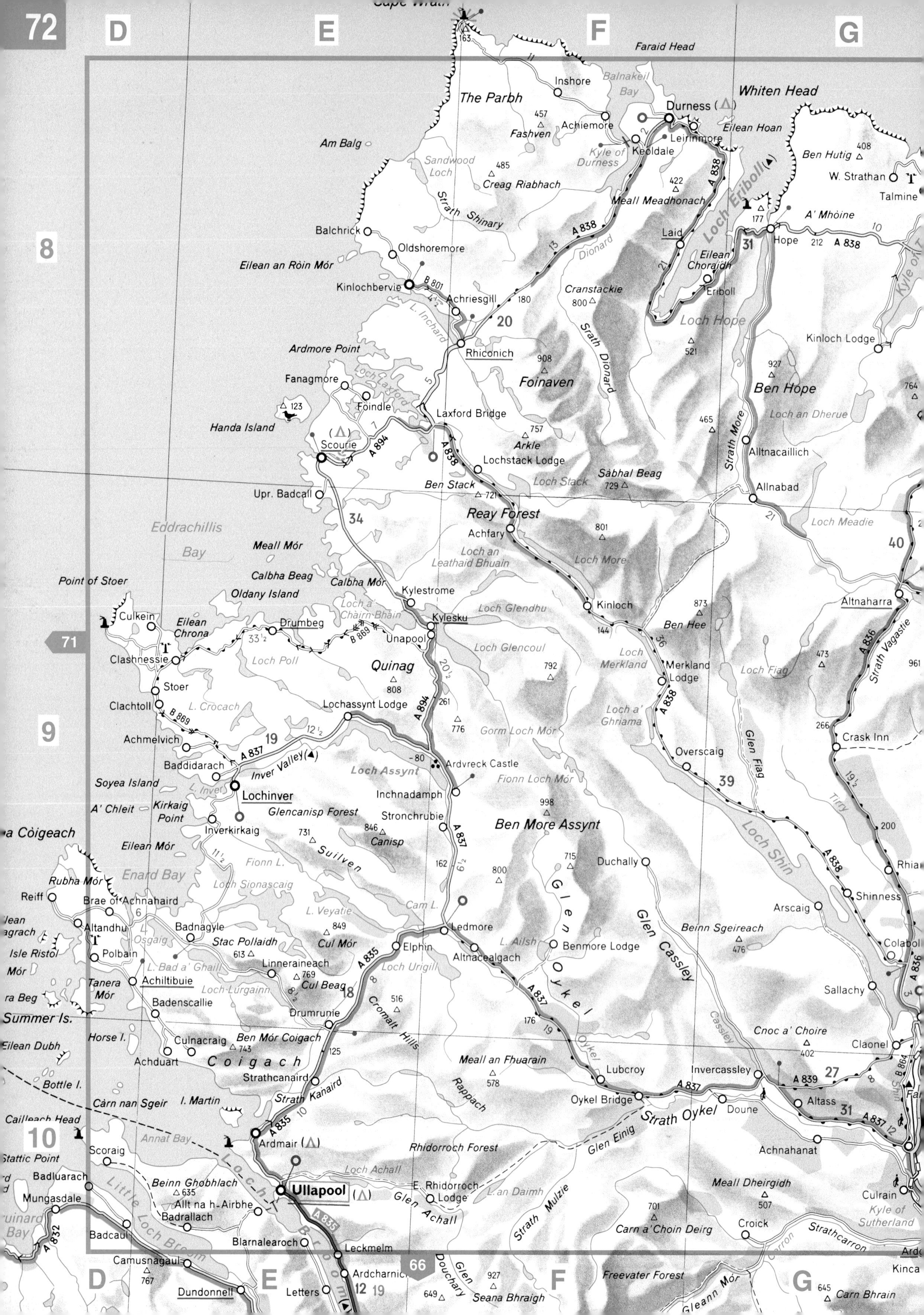
D
E
F
G
Cape Wrath
Faraid Head
Inshore
Balnakeil Bay
The Parbh
Whiten Head
Durness
Fashven
Achiemore
Eilean Hoan
Am Balg
Keoldale
Leirinmore
Kyle of Durness
Ben Hutig
W. Strathan
Talmine
Sandwood Loch
Creag Riabhach
Strath Shinary
Meall Meadhonach
Loch Eriboll
A' Mhòine
Balchrick
Oldshoremore
Laid
Hope
A 838
Dionard
Eilean Choraidh
Eilean an Ròin Mór
Kinlochbervie
B 801
Achriesgill
Eriboll
Cranstackie
L. Inchard
Loch Hope
Kinloch Lodge
Rhiconich
Ardmore Point
Strath Dionard
Fanagmore
Loch Laxford
Foinaven
Ben Hope
Foindle
Handa Island
Laxford Bridge
Loch an Dherue
Scourie
A 894
Arkle
Strath More
Alltnacaillich
Lochstack Lodge
Loch Stack
Sàbhal Beag
Ben Stack
Allnabad
Upr. Badcall
Reay Forest
Loch Meadie
Eddrachillis Bay
Achfary
Loch an Leathaid Bhuain
Loch More
Meall Mór
Calbha Beag
Point of Stoer
Calbha Mór
Oldany Island
Kylestrome
Kinloch
Altnaharra
Loch Glendhu
Culkein
Eilean Chrona
Loch a' Chàirn Bhàin
Kylesku
Ben Hee
Drumbeg
Unapool
B 869
Loch Glencoul
Loch Merkland
Merkland Lodge
Loch Fiag
Clashnessie
Loch Poll
Quinag
Strath Vagastie
A 836
Stoer
Clachtoll
L. Crocach
Lochassynt Lodge
Loch a' Ghriama
Gorm Loch Mór
Glen Fiag
Achmelvich
A 837
Crask Inn
Baddidarach
Inver Valley
Ardvreck Castle
Overscaig
Loch Assynt
Fionn Loch Mór
Soyea Island
L. Inver
Lochinver
Inchnadamph
A' Chleit
Kirkaig Point
Glencanisp Forest
Stronchrubie
Tirry
Inverkirkaig
Canisp
Ben More Assynt
Loch Shin
a Còigeach
Eilean Mór
Suilven
Fionn L.
Duchally
Enard Bay
Rubha Mór
Loch Sionascaig
Rhian
Reiff
Brae of Achnahaird
Cam L.
Glen Oykel
Glen Cassley
Shinness
L. Veyatie
Arscaig
Altandhu
Badnagyle
Ledmore
Beinn Sgeireach
L. Osgaig
Stac Pollaidh
Cul Mór
Elphin
L. Ailsh
Benmore Lodge
Colaboll
Isle Ristol
Polbain
Altnacealgach
L. Bad a' Ghaill
Linneraineach
Loch Urigill
Achiltibuie
Tanera Mór
Cul Beag
Sallachy
Loch Lurgainn
A 835
Badenscallie
Cromalt Hills
Drumrunie
Summer Is.
Cnoc a' Choire
Horse I.
Ben Mór Coigach
Claonel
Eilean Dubh
Culnacraig
Achduart
Coigach
Meall an Fhuarain
Lubcroy
Invercassley
A 839
Strathcanaird
Bottle I.
Rappach
Oykel Bridge
Altass
Strath Kanaird
Doune
Càrn nan Sgeir
I. Martin
Strath Oykel
Cailleach Head
Annat Bay
Glen Einig
Achnahanat
Ardmair
Rhidorroch Forest
Scoraig
Static Point
Loch Achall
Badluarach
Beinn Ghobhlach
E. Rhidorroch Lodge
Meall Dheirgidh
Culrain
Mungasdale
Allt na h-Airbhe
Ullapool
Glen Achall
L. an Daimh
Strath Mulzie
Kyle of Sutherland
Badrallach
Carn a' Choin Deirg
Croick
Gruinard Bay
Little Loch Broom
Loch Broom
Badcaul
Blarnalearoch
Strathcarron
Leckmelm
Camusnagaul
Ardcharnich
Glen Douchary
Freevater Forest
Dundonnell
Letters
Seana Bhraigh
Gleann Mór
Carn Bhrain
8
9
10
71
66
40
A 832
A 839
B 864

H
I
J
Strathy Point
Brims Ness
Holborn Head
Crosskirk
Scrabster
Thurso Bay
Dunnet Bay
Castletown
Thurso
A 836
A 882
B 874
Eilean nan Ròn
Rabbit Islands
Torrisdale Bay
Tongue Bay
Farr Point
Armadale
Portskerra
Melvich Bay
Lr. Dounreay
Achreamie
Reay
Shebster
Westfield
Strathy
Melvich
Farr
Kirtomy
Skerray
Bettyhill
Golval
Coldbackie
Borgie
Tongue
Strathy Forest
Bowside Lodge
Loch Calder
Calder Mains
Roadside
Halkirk
Shurrery
Loch Shurrery
Olgrinmore
Banniskirk
Spittal
Watten
Mybster
Bower
Upr. Bighouse
Skelpick
Borgie Forest
Achargary
Dalhavaig
Beinn nam Bad Mór
Loch Calaim
Westerdale
Loch Craggie
Strath Halladale
Halladale
Lochstrathy
Loch Loyal
Lettermore
Loch Strathy
Strathnaver
Altnabreac Station
Loch More
Syre
Naver
Forsinard
Loch Ruard
Grey Cairns of Camster
Loch Druim a' Chliabhain
Ben Griam Mór
Achentoul Forest
Glutt Lodge
Strathnaver
B 873
Loch Rimsdale
Loch an Ruathair
Loch nan Clàr
Knockfin Heights
Houstry
Lybster
Loch Naver
Loch Badanloch
Latheron
Forse
Ben Klibreck
Loch Truderscaig
Loch an Alltan Fhèarna
Badanloch Lodge
Kinbrace
Berriedale Wr.
Janetstown
Loch Choire Lodge
Helmsdale
Braemore
Dunbeath
Loch Choire
Morven
Borrobol Forest
Scaraben
Loch a' Bhealaich
Ben Armine
Wag
Borgue
Altanduin
Langwell Forest
Ben Armine Forest
Cnoc Tuarie
Strath Skinsdale
Kildonan Lodge
Berriedale
Strath of Kildonan
Ben Armine Lodge
Strath na Seilge
Kilphedir
A 897
Meallan Liath Mór
Beinn Dhorain
Dalnessie
Helmsdale
Black Wr.
Portgower
Brora
Lothmore
Col-Bheinn
Strath Brora
Lothbeg
Crakaig
Gordonbush
W. Langwell
Loch Brora
Rhilochan
A 839
Ben Horn
Muie
Rogart
Brora
Fleet
Pittentrail
Golspie
Dunrobin Castle
Beinn Dònuill
L. Fleet
Littleferry
Achvaich
Evelix
Embo
Bonar Bridge
Loch Migdale
Evelix
B 9168
Spinningdale
A 949
Dornoch
Clashmore
Tarbat Ness
Fearn Lodge
Innis Mhór
Wilkhaven
A 836
A 9
B 870
B 871
67
74

J
K
L
7
8
9
Dunnet Head
Langaton Point
Island of Stroma
Nethertown
Uppertown
Pentland Skerries
Brough Ness
Old Head
St. John's Point
Scarfskerry
Brough
St. John's Loch
Duncansby Head
John o' Groats
Gills
Mey
Canisbay
Barrock
Dunnet
Dunnet Bay
Holborn Head
Brims Ness
Scrabster
Thurso Bay
Thurso
Castletown
Loch Heilen
Skirza
Skirza Head
Freswick
Freswick Bay
Slickly
Achreamie
Westfield
Bower
Lyth
Sortat
Auckengill
Keiss
Loch Calder
Calder Mains
Roadside
L. Scarmclate
Myrelandhorn
Halkirk
Loch Shurrery
Olgrinmore
Banniskirk
Spittal
Loch Watten
Watten
Sinclair's Bay
Noss Head
Girnigoe and Sinclair Castles
Reiss
Staxigoe
North Head
Mybster
Westerdale
Haster
Wick
South Head
Badlipster
Tannach
Loch Hempriggs
Loch More
Thrumster
Grey Cairns of Camster
Sarclet
Loch Ruard
Ulbster
Hill o' Many Stanes
Lybster
W. Clyth
Houstry
Latheron
Forse
Janetstown
73
Braemore
Dunbeath
Scaraben
Borgue
Forest
Berriedale
Helmsdale
A 836
A 882
A 9
A 99
B 874
B 870
B 876
B 855
Sule Skerry
Stack Skerry
4°20
3°
3°20
59°
58°40
5
6
Mull Head
Bow Head
Noup Head
Papa
Pierowall
Westray
Midbea
Rapness
Westray Firth
Calfsound
Rousay
Wasbister
Egilsay
Brinyan
Wyre
Brough of Birsay
Brough Head
Birsay
Kitchener Memorial
Twatt
Georth
Gurness Broch
Gairsay
Skara Brae
Dounby
L. of Harray
Balfour
Yesnaby
Maes Howe
Finstown
Rennibister
Mainland
Ring of Brodgar
Kirkwall
Stromness
Stenness
Wideford Hill Cairn
Graemsay
Orphir
Moness
Cava
St. Mary's
Old Man of Hoy
Scapa Flow
Lamb Holm
Causeway
Rora Head
Rackwick
Fara
Burray
Lyness
Flotta
St. Margaret's
Hoy
Lerwick
Aberdeen
Tor Ness
South Walls
South Ronaldsay
Burwick
Old Head
Pentland Firth
Stroma
Pentland Skerries
Dunnet Head
Scarfskerry
Gills
Duncansby Head
Scrabster
Dunnet
John o' Groats
Thurso
Castletown

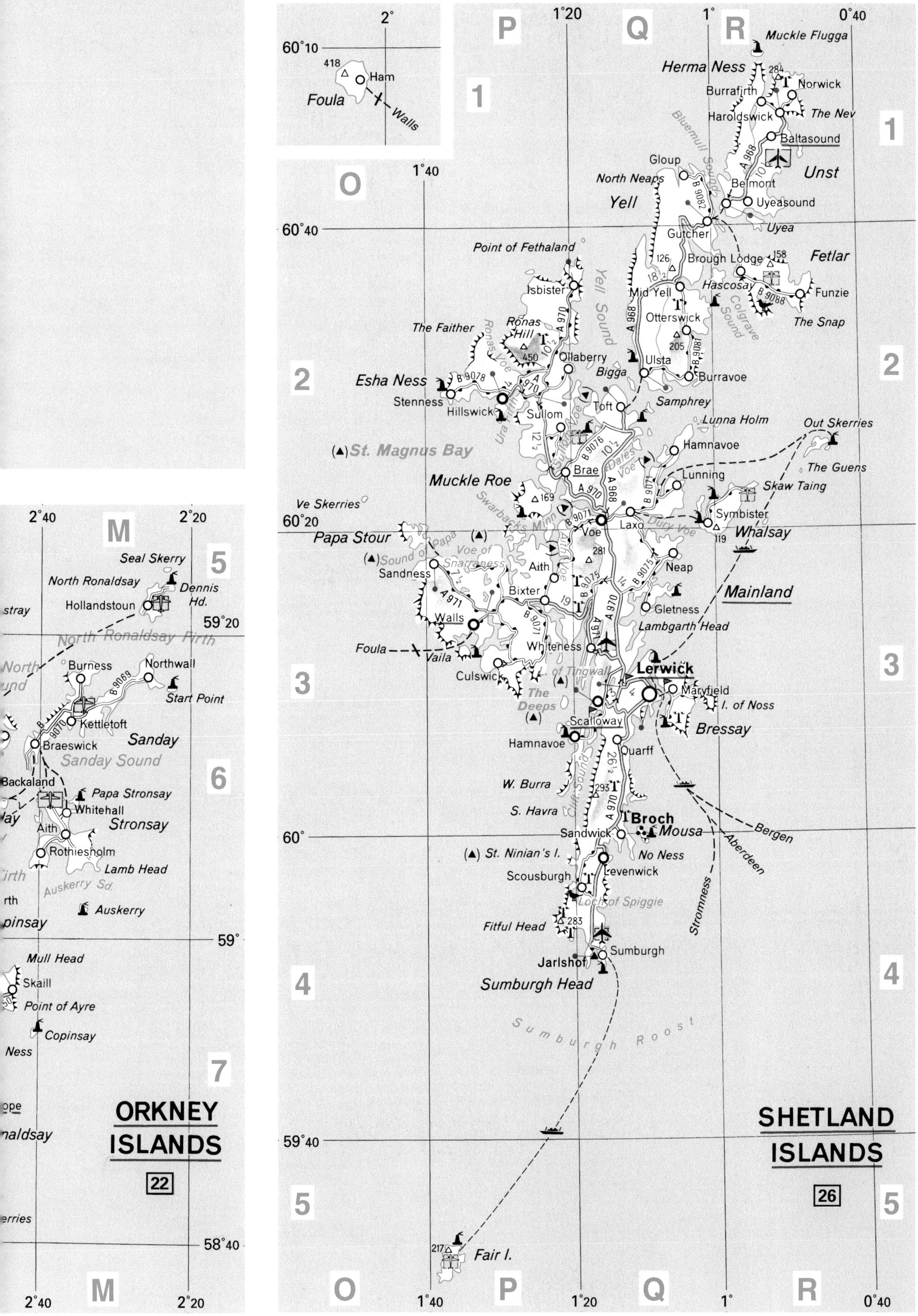
SHETLAND ISLANDS
26
ORKNEY ISLANDS
22
Foula
Ham
418
Walls
Muckle Flugga
Herma Ness
Norwick
Burrafirth
Haroldswick
The Nev
Baltasound
Unst
Bluemull Sound
Gloup
North Neaps
Belmont
Uyeasound
Uyea
Yell
Gutcher
Fetlar
Brough Lodge
Point of Fethaland
Hascosay
Funzie
Isbister
Mid Yell
Otterswick
Colgrave Sound
The Snap
Yell Sound
The Faither
Ronas Hill
450
Ollaberry
Ulsta
Burravoe
Bigga
Esha Ness
Stenness
Hillswick
Sullom
Toft
Samphrey
Lunna Holm
Out Skerries
Hamnavoe
St. Magnus Bay
Brae
Lunning
The Guens
Muckle Roe
Skaw Taing
Ve Skerries
Symbister
Whalsay
Papa Stour
Voe
Laxo
Dury Voe
Sound of Papa
Sandness
Aith
Neap
Mainland
Bixter
Gletness
Walls
Lambgarth Head
Whiteness
Foula
Vaila
Culswick
L. of Tingwall
Lerwick
Maryfield
I. of Noss
The Deeps
Scalloway
Bressay
Hamnavoe
Quarff
W. Burra
S. Havra
Cliff Sound
Broch
Sandwick
Mousa
Bergen
Aberdeen
St. Ninian's I.
No Ness
Levenwick
Scousburgh
Loch of Spiggie
Stromness
Fitful Head
283
Sumburgh
Jarlshof
Sumburgh Head
Sumburgh Roost
Fair I.
217
Seal Skerry
North Ronaldsay
Dennis Hd.
Hollandstoun
North Ronaldsay Firth
Burness
Northwall
Start Point
Kettletoft
Sanday
Braeswick
Sanday Sound
Backaland
Papa Stronsay
Whitehall
Stronsay
Aith
Rothiesholm
Lamb Head
Auskerry Sd.
Auskerry
Mull Head
Skaill
Point of Ayre
Copinsay
Ness

A
B
C
82
11
12
13
Dunmore Head
Mount Eagle
516
Beehive Huts
Blasket Island
Tearaght I.
Slea Head
R 559
Ventry Harbour
Dingle Harb.
Parkmore Pt.
Bull's Head
N 86
Doonmanagh
Castle
Minard Head
R 561
Inch
Castlemaine Harbour
Milltown
Castler
Inishnabro
Inishvickillane
Cromane
Knockaunnaglashy
Illaunstookagh
Tullig
Killorglin
Cill Orglan
L. Yganavan
Rossbeigh Creek
Caragh Br.
Caragh Lake
DINGLE BAY
R 564
Glenbeigh
493
Lough Caragh
Kilgobnet
Kells Bay
Ring of Kerry
Beenmore
668
56
35
Ballynakilly Upper
Behy
Cottoners
Finglass
Canglass Point
Knocknadobar
689
Kells
495
Shanacashel
Castlequin
Ferta
Coomasaharn Lake
Glencar
772
Bealalaw Bridge
Lough Acoose
Carrantuohill
1038
Doulus Head
Doulus Bay
Carhan House
Teeromoyle
Coomacarrea
Boheeshil
Macgillycuddy's Reeks
Beginish I.
Colly
686
Maghanlawaun
Knight's Town
Cahersiveen
Cathair Saidhbhín
Ballaghisheen Pass
Caragh
H
782
Valencia Island
R 565
Clynacantan
Chapeltown
Portmagee Channel
N 70
Kerry Way
Owroe Br.
304
Cloon Lake
G
Ballaghbeama Gap
259
Lissatinnig Br.
Bray Head
498
A
Mullaghanattin
637
Knocklomena
Portmagee
Kilpeacan Cross Roads
Inny
Killeenleagh Br.
682
R
398
Teeranearagh
Mastergeehy
Máistir Gaoithe
E
675
Knocknagantee
772
Blackwater
Ballynahow
L. Namona
Derriana Lough
V
Derreendarragh
R 566
R 567
Cloonaghlin Lough
Tullakeel
Gearha Br.
Puffin Island
Killurly
Sallahig
Cummeragh
I
Killonecaha
674
Letterfinish
R 568
413
Ballinskelligs
Baile an Sceilg
Caherbarnagh
Blackwater Bridge
St. Finan's Bay
Waterville
An Coireán
Lough Currane
Ballybrack
Sneem
Graiques
Tahilla
Kerry
410
Little Skellig
Ballinskelligs Bay
Staigue Stone Fort
63
39
Parknasilla
Coornagillagh
Great Skellig
Abbey
543
Rossmore I.
Ardea
Bolus Head
499
Eagles Hill
Garinish I.
Rossdohan Island
Hog's Head
Coomakesta Pass
309
208
Caherdaniel
Sherky I.
R 573
R 571
Sheehan's Point
Westcove
Castlecove
Bunaw
Derrynane
KENMARE RIVER
Kilmakilloge Harbour
Derreen Gardens
Lauragh
Scariff Island
Deenish I.
Lamb's Head
Ardgroom Harb.
30
Kilcatherine Point
Gortgarriff
R 571
Ardgroom
599
Glanmore Lake
Knockowen
659
Inishfarnard
Ballycrovane Harbour
Glenbeg Lough
CAHA MOUNTAINS
Coulagh Bay
Eyeries
621
B
330
Healy Pass
Beara
Cod's Head
R 575
Travara Br.
684
Adrigole
Slieve Miskish Mountains
Hungry Hill
29
Derreeny
Ballydonegan Bay
Allihies
R 572
Curryglass
Ballydonegan
489
Castletownbere
Shot Head
Garnish Point
Bere Haven
Lonehort Point
Ballynacallagh
Gable Car
Ballynakilla
Dursey Island
Firkeel
R 575
Rerrin
The Bull
Kilmichael
R 572
Cahermore
15
Fair Head
Bere Island
BANTRY
Dursey Head
Crow Head
Black Ball Head
Gouladoo
345
Ahakista
Kilcrohane
Ballyroon
Muntervary or Sheep's Head
Dunmanus Bay
Dunmanus
Toormore
314
R 591
Goleen
Three Castle Head
Toormore Bay
Dough
Streek Head
R 591
Crookhaven
Mizen Head
Barley Cove
Brow Head
Fastnet Rock

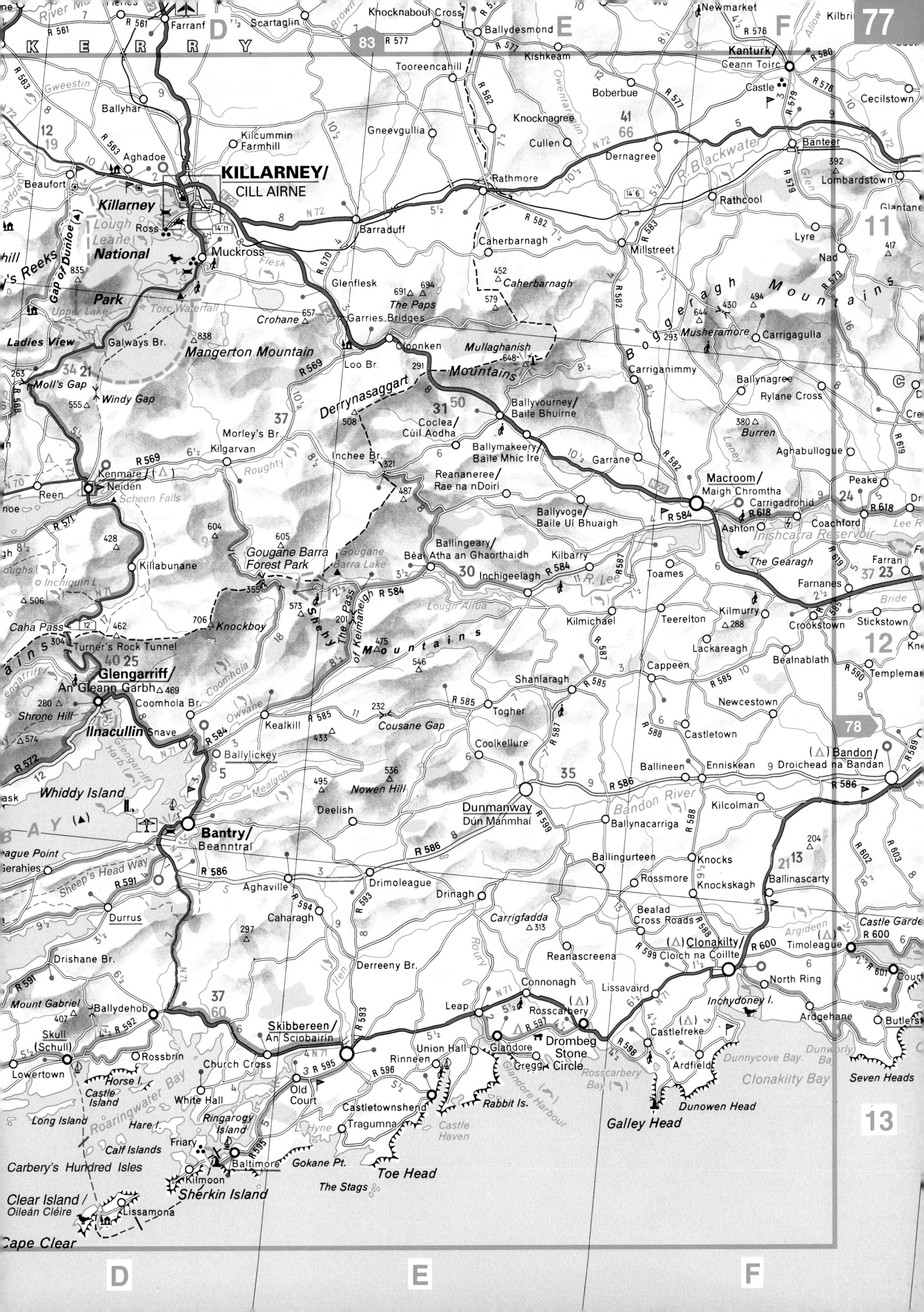
KERRY
KILLARNEY/
CILL AIRNE
Killarney
National
Park
Lough Leane
Ross
Muckross
Aghadoe
Beaufort
Ballyhar
Kilcummin
Farmhill
Farranf
Scartaglin
Knocknaboul Cross
Ballydesmond
Tooreencahill
Kishkeam
Newmarket
Kanturk/
Ceann Toirc
Castle
Boberbue
Knocknagree
Cullen
Gneevgullia
Dernagree
Banteer
Cecilstown
Lombardstown
R. Blackwater
Rathmore
Barraduff
Rathcool
Caherbarnagh
Millstreet
Lyre
Nad
Glenflesk
The Paps
Crohane
Garries Bridges
Loo Br.
Cloonken
Mullaghanish
Mountains
Musheramore
Carrigagulla
Boggeragh Mountains
Carriganimmy
Ballynagree
Rylane Cross
Burren
Aghabullogue
Peake
Gap of Dunloe
Upper Lake
Torc Waterfall
Ladies View
Galways Br.
Mangerton Mountain
Moll's Gap
Windy Gap
Derrynasaggart
Ballyvourney/
Baile Bhuirne
Coclea/
Cúil Aodha
Ballymakeery/
Baile Mhic Ire
Garrane
Morley's Br.
Kilgarvan
Inchee Br.
Roughty
Kenmare
Neidín
Reen
Scheen Falls
Reananeree/
Rae na nDoirí
Macroom/
Maigh Chromtha
Carrigadrohid
Ashton
Coachford
Inishcarra Reservoir
The Gearagh
Farran
Farnanes
Ballyvoge/
Baile Uí Bhuaigh
Ballingeary/
Béal Átha an Ghaorthaidh
Kilbarry
Inchigeelagh
R. Lee
Toames
Gougane Barra
Forest Park
Gougane Barra Lake
Killabunane
Inchiquin L.
Lough Allua
Kilmichael
Teerelton
Kilmurry
Crookstown
Stickstown
Knockboy
Caha Pass
Turner's Rock Tunnel
Shehy
The Pass of Keimaneigh
Mountains
Lackareagh
Bealnablath
Templemar
Glengarriff/
An Gleann Garbh
Coomhola
Coomhola Br.
Shrone Hill
Ilnacullin
Snave
Kealkill
Cousane Gap
Shanlaragh
Togher
Cappeen
Newcestown
Castletown
Ballylickey
Owvane
Coolkellure
Ballineen
Enniskean
Bandon/
Droichead na Bandan
Whiddy Island
Mealagh
Nowen Hill
Deelish
Dunmanway
Dún Mánmhaí
Bandon River
Ballynacarriga
Kilcolman
Bantry/
Beanntraí
BAY
Sheep's Head Way
Aghaville
Drimoleague
Drinagh
Ballingurteen
Knocks
Rossmore
Knockskagh
Ballinascarty
Durrus
Caharagh
Carrigfadda
Bealad Cross Roads
Clonakilty/
Cloich na Coillte
Timoleague
Argideen
Drishane Br.
Derreeny Br.
Reanascreena
Lissavaird
North Ring
Connonagh
Rosscarbery
Leap
Inchydoney I.
Ardgehane
Butlerstown
Mount Gabriel
Ballydehob
Skull
(Schull)
Rossbrin
Skibbereen/
An Sciobairín
Glandore
Drombeg Stone Circle
Castlefreke
Union Hall
Rinneen
Cregg
Ardfield
Lowertown
Church Cross
Horse I.
Castle Island
Roaringwater Bay
White Hall
Old Court
Castletownshend
Rabbit Is.
Glandore Harbour
Rosscarbery Bay
Dunnycove Bay
Clonakilty Bay
Seven Heads
Long Island
Hare I.
Ringarogy Island
Tragumna
Castle Haven
Galley Head
Dunowen Head
Calf Islands
Friary
Baltimore
Gokane Pt.
Toe Head
Carbery's Hundred Isles
Kilmoon
Sherkin Island
The Stags
Clear Island/
Oileán Cléire
Lissamona
Cape Clear
D
E
F

Dromina
Ardpatrick
Ballyhaght
Cullane
Anglesborough
Newtown
Ballyorgan
Boolakennedy
Freemount
Ballyhoura Mountains
Burncourt
Liscarroll
Castle
Churchtown
Knockanevin
Kilbeheny
Mitchelstown Caves
Inchnamuck
Bawn Cross Roads
Killaclug
Funshion
Buttevant
Friary
Farahy
Kildorrery
Mitchelstown/
Baile Mhistéala
Ballyporeen
Kilbrin
Allow
Castlecor
Doneraile
Awbeg
Rockmills
Kilworth Mountains
Knockmealdown
Knockshanahullion
Kilworth Camp
Shanballymore
Old Twopoldouse
New Twopoldouse Village
Annes Grove Gardens
Araglin
Castle
Ballyclough
Cecilstown
Glanworth
Castletownroche
Carrig
Labbacallee
Kilworth
Mallow
Mala
Banteer
Killavullen
Ballyhooley
Lyrenaglogh
Lombardstown
Clondulane
Ballyduff
Glantane
Drommahane
Nagles Mountains
Beennaskehy
Fermoy/
Mainistir Fhear Maí
Coole Abbey
Lyre
Ballynamona
Nad
Knockmourne
Knuttery
Knockaunalour
Castlelyons
Tallowbridge
Mountains
Bweeng
Burnfort
Bottlehill
Rathcormack
Bridebridge
Conna
Curraglass
Carrigagulla
Glenville
Bride
Britway
Ballynoe
Grenagh
Rylane Cross
C O R K
Donoughmore
Kilmona
Watergrasshill
Ardglass
Crean's Cross Roads
Carrignavar
Whitechurch
Ballincurrig
Clonmult
Martin
Aghabullogue
Matehy
Leamlara
Walshtown
Mount Uniacke
Blarney
Lisgoold
Peake
Berrings
White's Cross
Sallybrook
Knockraha
Owennacurra
Dungourney
Dangan
Carrigadrohid
Tower
Dripsey
Cloghroe
Coachford
Inishcarra
Riverstown
Inishcarra Reservoir
Lee Resr.
CORK
CORCAIGH
Glanmire
Glounthaune
Carrigtohill
Midleton/
Mainistir na Corann
Killeagh
Farran Forest Park
Mogeely
The Gearagh
Farran
Ovens
Ballincollig
Carrigrohane
Blackrock
L. Mahon
Island
Fota I.
Castlemartyr
Farnanes
Bride
Belvelly
Ballynacorra
Ladysbridge
Crookstown
Stickstown
Aherla
Waterfall
Douglas
Passage West
Great Island
Cobh/
An Cóbh
Glenbrook
East Ferry
Kilcredan
Knocknahilan
Monkstown
Cork Harbour
Saleen
Cloyne
Garryvoe
Bealnablath
Templemartin
Airport
Ballygarvan
Rostellan
Shanagarry
Cross Barry
Ballinhassig
Owenboy
Fivemilebridge
Shanbally
Ringaskiddy
Aghada
Whitegate
Churchtown
Ballycotton
Carrigaline
Crosshaven
Kilpatrick
Bandon/
Droichead na Bandan
Inishannon
Ballymartle
Roche's Point
Gyleen
Inch
Riverstick
Tracton
Ballinluska
Ringabella Bay
Power Head
Minane Bridge
Ballyfeard
Roscoff
Dunderrow
Belgooly
Kinsale/
Cionn tSáile
Nohaval
Robert's Head
Ballinadee
Ballinclashet
Flat Head
Ballinascarty
Summercove
Kilbrittain
Oysterhaven
Swansea
Ballinspittle
Castle Gardens
Kinsale Harbour
Frower Point
Argideen
Timoleague
Old Head
Courtmacsherry
North Ring
Lispatrick
Barry's Point
Ardgehane
Holeopen Bay West
Old Head of Kinsale
Butlerstown
Courtmacsherry Bay
Dunworly Bay
Clonakilty Bay
Seven Heads
F
G
H

Newchapel
Swiss Cottage
Rathkeevin
Kilcommon
Garnavilla
Knocklofty
Kilsheelan
Kilkieran
Ballyneill
Owning
Mullenbeg
Lukeswell
Ballyfasy
The Sweep
Dowling
Mullinavat
Clonmel
Cluain Meala
Tubbrid
Ardfinnan
Ballybeg
Laghtnafrankee
Glendalough
Clogheen
R. Suir
Tar
Comeragh Mountains
Rathgormuck
Knockanaffrin
Carrick-on-Suir
Carraig na Siúire
Carrickbeg
Piltown
Fiddown
Killinaspick
Farnoge
Dangan
Clogga
Mothel
Curraghmore
Mooncoin
Kilmacow
Dunkitt
Slieveroe
Granny
Newcastle
Mountains
The Gap
Knockmealdown
Ballymacarbry
Nier
Monavullagh Mountains
Coumfea
Clonea
Portlaw
R. Suir
City Walls
Kilmeadan
Licketstown
WATERFORD
PORT LÁIRGE
Knockboy
Mt. Melleray Monastery
Ballynamult
Ballynaguilkee
Feagarrid
Knockboy
Seefin
Mahon
Mahon Bridge
Kilmacthomas
Fews
Newtown
W A T E R F O R D
Kilbrien
Boolattin
Faha
Buttlerstown
Cappoquin
Ceapach Choinn
Millstreet
Colligan
Lismore
Lios Mór
Modelligo
Lemybrien
Ballylaneen
Kill
Dunhill
Fennor
Tramore
Trá Mhór
Clohernagh
Ballinaspick
River Bride
Kilgobnet
The Pike
Stradbally
Bunmahon
Annestown
Ballymacaw
Villierstown
Keereen
Dungarvan
Dún Garbhán
Ballyvoyle Head
Clonea Bay
Dunabrattin Head
Gt. Newtown Head
Tramore Bay
Brownstown
Brownstown Head
Ballynacourty
Dungarvan Harbour
Aglish
Drum Hills
The Pike
River Blackwater
Ballynagaul
Helvick Head
Ringville
An Rinn
Muggort's Bay
Boola
Cross
Licky
Clashmore
Loskeran
Grange
Kinsalebeg
Mine Head
Youghal
Eochaill
Moord
Curragh
Ardmore
Aird Mhór
Ram Head
Whiting Bay
Ballymadog
Youghal Bay
Ballymacoda
Knockadoon Head
Ballymakeagh
I
J
K
10
11
12

Kilkenny/
Cill Chainnigh
WATERFORD/
PORT LÁIRGE
New Ross/
Ros Mhic Thriúin
Carrick-on-Suir/
Carraig na Siúire
Castlecomer/
Caisleán an Chomair
Thomastown/
Baile Mhic Andáin
Graiguenamanagh/
Graig na Manach
Callan/
Callainn
Bagenalstown
(Muine Bheag)
Tramore/
Trá Mhór
Dunmore East
C A R L O
K I L K E N N Y
W E
E R F O R D
Slieveardagh Hills
Slievenamon
Comeragh Mountains
Mahon Bridge
Blackstairs Mountains
Scullogue Gap
Mount Leinster
Caher Roe's Den
Brandon Hill
Dunmore Cave
Curraghmore
Jerpoint
Duiske Abbey
J. F. Kennedy Park
River Barrow
R. Nore
R. Suir
Kings R.
Waterford Harbour
Tramore Bay
Bannow Bay
Ballyteige Bay
Dungarvan Harbour
Clonea Bay
Muggort's Bay
Helvick Head
Ballyvoyle Head
Dunabrattin Head
Gt. Newtown Head
Brownstown Head
Hook Head
Baginbun Head
Ballyragget
Freshford
Johnstown
Urlingford
Gowran
Goresbridge
Bennettsbridge
Inistioge
Mullinavat
Kilmacthomas
Piltown
Fiddown
Portlaw
Passage East
Duncannon
Fethard
Arthurstown
Ballyhack
Cheekpoint
Borris
Leighlinbridge
Myshall
Fennagh
Kells
Knocktopher
Ballyhale
Stoneyford
Windgap
Mullinahone
Kilsheelan
Stradbally
Bunmahon
Annestown
Dunhill
Kill
Lemybrien
Ballynacourty
Ballynagaul
J
K
L
79
85
86

M
N
O
9
10
11
87
Arklow/An tinbhear Mór (▲)
Gorey/Guaire
Enniscorthy/Inis Córthaidh
Wexford/Loch Garman
Rosslare Harbour/Calafort Ros Láir
Rosslare/Ros Láir
Mizen Head
Ardanairy
Johnstown
Ferrybank
Clogga
Kilmichael Point
Castletown
Courtown
Riverchapel
Roney Point
Ballygarrett
Cahore Point
Clonevin
Kilmuckridge
Killincooly
Blackwater
Blackwater Harbour
Curracloe
Wexford Bay
The Raven Point
Wexford Harbour
Rosslare Point
Rosslare Bay
Fishguard
Pembroke
Roscoff
Cherbourg
Greenore Point
Tuskar Rock
Carnsore Point
Forlorn Point
Saltee Islands
Croghan Mountain
Avoca
Woodenbridge
Aughrim
Craffield
Tinahely
Shillelagh
Carnew
Ferns
Camolin
Oulart
Castlebridge
Ferrycarrig
Drinagh
Murntown
Piercetown
Killinick
Tagoat
Kilrane
Broadway
Tacumshane
Tacumshin Lake
Lady's Island Lake
Carne
Churchtown
Kilmore Quay
Bridgetown
Mayglass
Taghmon
Irish Agricultural Museum
Heritage Park
Crossabeg
Killurin
Oilgate
Redgate
Screen
Ballylucas
Castleellis
Clondaw
Kilnamanagh
Ballyemund
The Harrow
Milltown
Ballycarney
Marshalstown
Milehouse
The Leap
Clohamon
Kilmyshall
Strahart
Tombrack
Ballyduff
Clogh
Craanford
Askamore
Bridgeswell
Knockbrandon
Monaseed
Hollyfort
Killinierin
Inch
Ballylacy
Scarnagh
Coolgreany
Ballyfad
Crosspatrick
Coolattin
Coolboy
Kilquiggin
Rathgall
Clonmore
Bridgeland
Ballard
Aghowle
Clonegall
Watch Ho. Village
Graigue More
Ballyroebuck
Balloughter
Ballycanew
Killenagh
Kilcotty
Darby's Gap
Ballaghkeen
Ballynastraw
Bree
Ballyhoge
Galbally
Waddingtown
Cleristown
Walshestown
Kilmore
Killag
Newtown
Millroad
Tomhaggard
Burrow
Wexford Coastal Path
R. Slaney
R. Bann
Owenavorragh

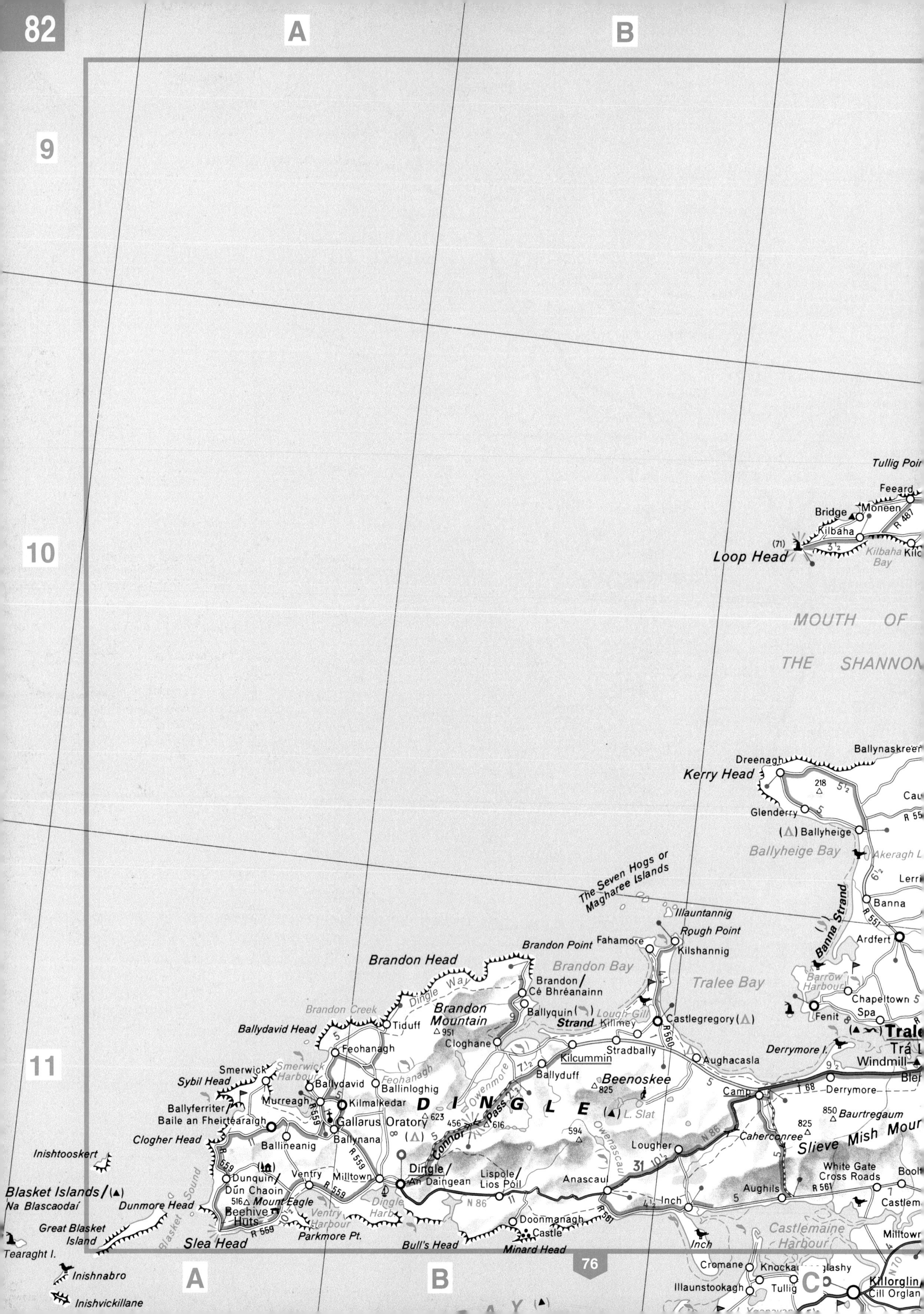
A
B
9
10
11
Tullig Poir
Feeard
Bridge
Moneen
R 487
Kilbaha
Loop Head
(71)
Kilbaha Bay
MOUTH OF
THE SHANNON
Ballynaskreen
Dreenagh
Kerry Head
218
Glenderry
(△) Ballyheige
Ballyheige Bay
Akeragh L
Lerri
Banna Strand
Banna
R 551
Ardfert
The Seven Hogs or Magharee Islands
Illauntannig
Rough Point
Brandon Point
Fahamore
Kilshannig
Brandon Head
Brandon Bay
Brandon/
Cé Bhréanainn
Tralee Bay
Barrow Harbour
Chapeltown
Fenit
Spa
Tralee
Trá L
Brandon Creek
Dingle Way
Brandon Mountain
△951
Ballyquin
Strand
Lough Gill
Killmey
Castlegregory (△)
R 560
Ballydavid Head
Tiduff
Cloghane
Stradbally
Kilcummin
Aughacasla
Derrymore I.
Windmill
Feohanagh
Smerwick
Smerwick Harbour
Sybil Head
Ballydavid
Ballinloghig
Owenmore
Ballyduff
Beenoskee
825
Camp
Derrymore
Murreagh
Kilmalkedar
DINGLE
Connor Pass
(▲) L. Slat
850 △ Baurtregaum
Ballyferriter/
Baile an Fheirtéaraigh
Gallarus Oratory
(△)
623
456
616
594
825
Caherconree
Slieve Mish Moun
Clogher Head
Ballineanig
Ballynana
R 559
Owenascaul
N 86
Lougher
Inishtooskert
Dingle/
An Daingean
Lispole/
Lios Póil
Anascaul
White Gate
Cross Roads
R 561
Dunquin/
Dún Chaoin
Ventry
Milltown
Aughils
Blasket Islands/(▲)
Na Blascaodaí
516△ Mount Eagle
N 86
Inch
Castlem
Dunmore Head
Beehive Huts
Ventry Harbour
Dingle Harb
Doonmanagh
Castle
Great Blasket Island
Blasket Sound
R 559
Parkmore Pt.
Castlemaine Harbour
Milltown
Slea Head
Bull's Head
Minard Head
Inch
Tearaght I.
76
Cromane
Knockai
Killorglin
Cill Orglan
Inishnabro
Illaunstookagh
Tullig
C
Inishvickillane

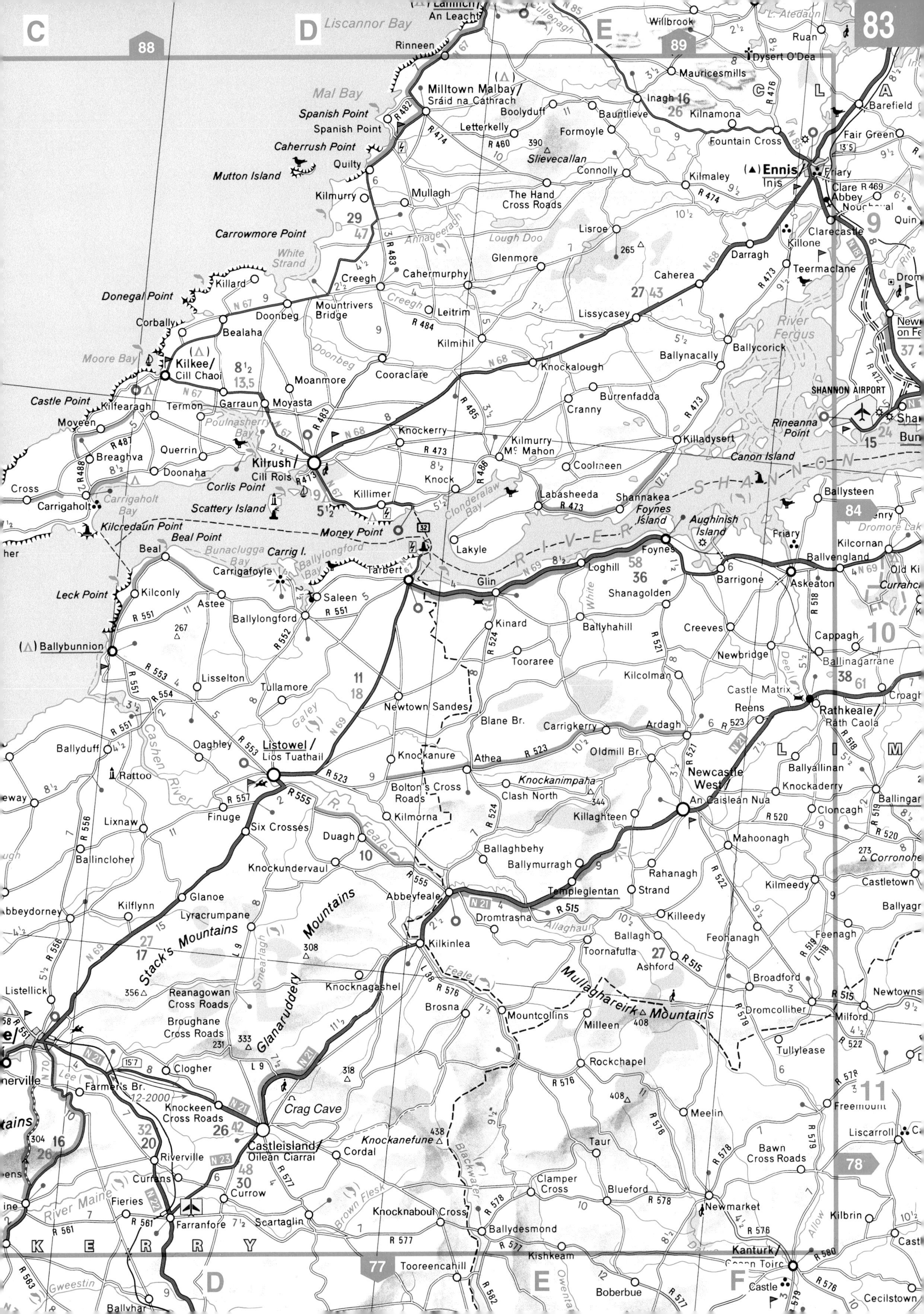

C
D
E
88
89
Liscannor Bay
An Leacht
Rinneen
Willbrook
Ruan
Dysert O'Dea
Mauricesmills
Mal Bay
Milltown Malbay/
Sráid na Cathrach
Spanish Point
Caherrush Point
Mutton Island
Quilty
Boolyduff
Letterkelly
Formoyle
Bauntlieve
Inagh
Kilnamona
Fountain Cross
Barefield
Fair Green
Slievecallan
Connolly
Ennis/
Inis
Kilmaley
Friary
Clare Abbey
Kilmurry
Mullagh
The Hand Cross Roads
Carrowmore Point
White Strand
Annageeragh
Lough Doo
Lisroe
Clarecastle
Killone
Darragh
Teermaclane
Quin
Glenmore
Cahermurphy
Creegh
Killard
Caherea
Donegal Point
Doonbeg
Mountrivers Bridge
Leitrim
Lissycasey
Corbally
Bealaha
Kilmihil
River Fergus
Ballycorick
Ballynacally
Moore Bay
Kilkee/
Cill Chaoi
Moanmore
Cooraclare
Knockalough
Burrenfadda
Cranny
Castle Point
Kilfearagh
Termon
Garraun
Moyasta
Poulnasherry Bay
SHANNON AIRPORT
Rineanna Point
Moveen
Knockerry
Killadysert
Breaghva
Querrin
Kilrush/
Cill Rois
Kilmurry Mc Mahon
Canon Island
Doonaha
Corlis Point
Knock
Coolmeen
Cross
Carrigaholt
Carrigaholt Bay
Scattery Island
Killimer
Clonderalaw Bay
Labasheeda
Shannakea
Foynes Island
SHANNON
Ballysteen
Kilcredaun Point
Money Point
Aughinish Island
Friary
84
Beal Point
Beal
Bunaclugga Bay
Carrig I.
Ballylongford Bay
Lakyle
RIVER
Foynes
Kilcornan
Ballvengland
Carrigafoyle
Tarbert
Loghill
Barrigone
Askeaton
Leck Point
Kilconly
Astee
Saleen
Glin
Shanagolden
Ballylongford
Kinard
Ballyhahill
Creeves
Cappagh
Ballybunnion
Tooraree
Newbridge
Ballinagarrane
Kilcolman
Castle Matrix
Lisselton
Tullamore
Newtown Sandes
Reens
Rathkeale/
Ráth Caola
Blane Br.
Carrigkerry
Ardagh
Ballyduff
Oaghley
Listowel/
Lios Tuathail
Knockanure
Athea
Oldmill Br.
Newcastle West/
An Caisleán Nua
Ballyallinan
Knockaderry
Rattoo
Cashen River
Bolton's Cross Roads
Knockanimpaha
Clash North
Finuge
Kilmorna
Killaghteen
Cloncagh
Lixnaw
Six Crosses
Duagh
R. Feale
Mahoonagh
Ballincloher
Knockundervaul
Ballaghbehy
Ballymurragh
Rahanagh
Kilmeedy
Corronoher
Castletown
Glanoe
Abbeyfeale
Templeglentan
Strand
Abbeydorney
Kilflynn
Lyracrumpane
Stack's Mountains
Mountains
Dromtrasna
Allaghaun
Killeedy
Ballagh
Feohanagh
Feenagh
Kilkinlea
Toornafulla
Ashford
Listellick
Reanagowan Cross Roads
Knocknagashel
Glanaruddery
Smearlagh
Feale
Mullaghareirk Mountains
Broadford
Newtown
Brosna
Mountcollins
Milleen
Dromcollihe
Milford
Broughane Cross Roads
Tullylease
Clogher
Rockchapel
Farmer's Br.
Lee
Knockeen Cross Roads
Crag Cave
Freemount
Meelin
Castleisland/
Oileán Ciarraí
Cordal
Knockanefune
Taur
Liscarroll
Riverville
Bawn Cross Roads
78
Currans
Currow
Clamper Cross
Blueford
River Maine
Fieries
Brown Flesk
Knocknaboul Cross
Newmarket
Kilbrin
Farranfore
Scartaglin
Ballydesmond
Blackwater
Allow
K E R R Y
Kishkeam
Kanturk/
Ceann Toirc
77
Tooreencahill
Owenta
Boberbue
Gweestin
Castle
Cecilstown
Ballyhar
F
9
10
11

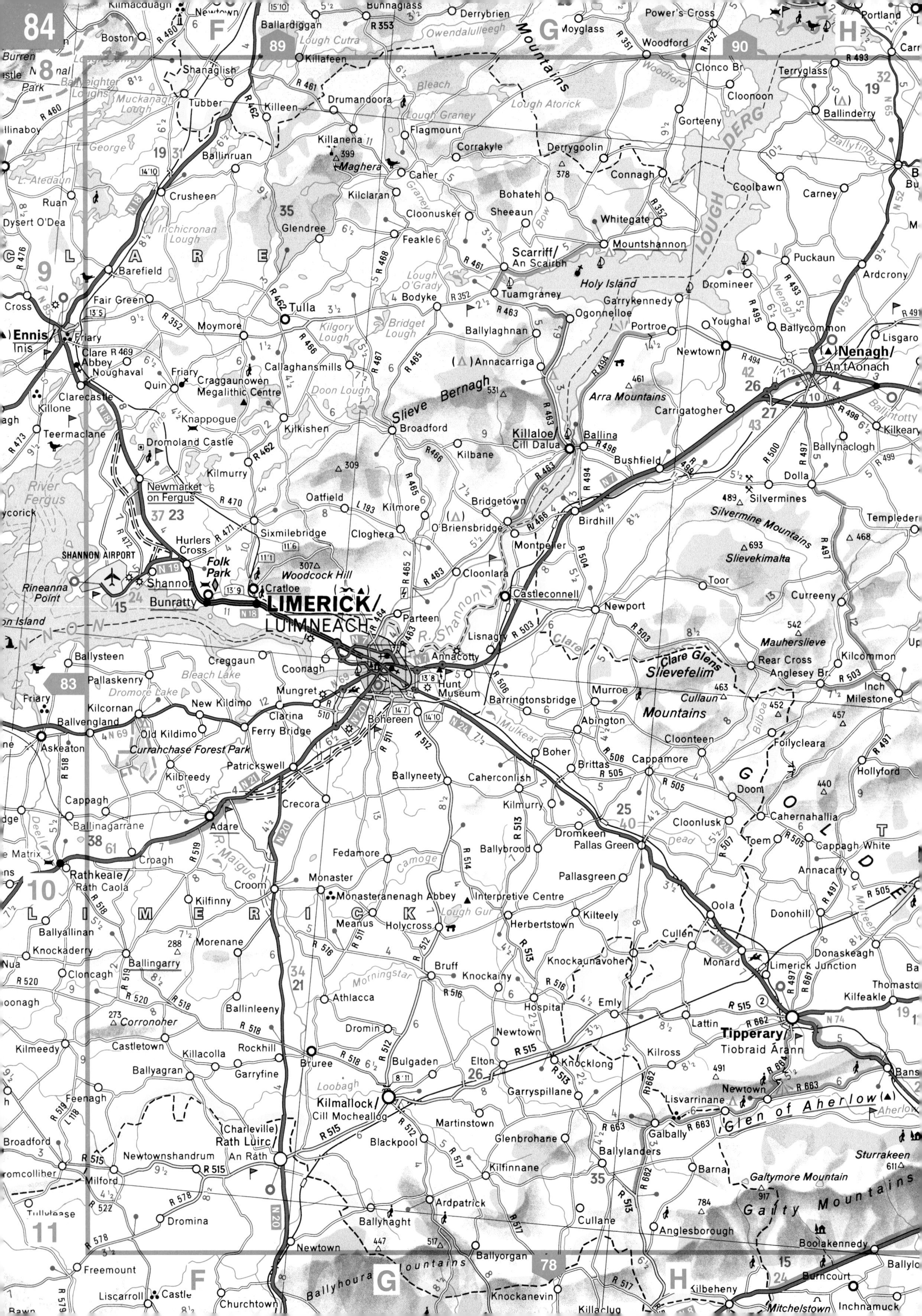
89
90
83
78
F
G
H
Kilmacduagh
Newtown
Ballardiggan
Bunnaglass
Derrybrien
Power's Cross
Portland
Boston
Lough Cutra
Owendalulleegh
Mountains
Moyglass
Woodford
Burren
Killafeen
Clonco Br.
Terryglass
Shanaglish
Ballyeighter Loughs
Bleach
Cloonoon
Ballinderry
Park
Muckanagh Lough
Tubber
Killeen
Drumandoora
Lough Atorick
Gorteeny
Lough Graney
Flagmount
DERG
Illinaboy
Killanena
Corrakyle
Derrygoolin
L. George
Ballinruan
Maghera
Caher
Connagh
Coolbawn
Carney
L. Atedaun
Ruan
Crusheen
Kilclaran
Bohateh
Dysert O'Dea
Glendree
Cloonusker
Sheeaun
LOUGH
Whitegate
Inchicronan Lough
Feakle
Mountshannon
C L A R E
Scarriff/
An Scairbh
Puckaun
Barefield
Lough O'Grady
Holy Island
Dromineer
Ardcrony
Tuamgraney
Fair Green
Bodyke
Garrykennedy
Cross
Tulla
Ogonnelloe
Portroe
Youghal
Ballycommon
Lisgaro
Ennis
Inis
Friary
Moymore
Kilgory Lough
Bridget Lough
Ballylaghnan
Newtown
Nenagh/
An t-Aonach
Clare Abbey
Noughaval
Callaghansmills
Annacarriga
Quin
Friary
Craggaunowen Megalithic Centre
Doon Lough
Slieve Bernagh
Arra Mountains
Clarecastle
Killone
Knappogue
Kilkishen
Broadford
Carrigatogher
Ballintotty
Kilkeary
Teermaclane
Dromoland Castle
Killaloe/
Cill Dalua
Ballina
Ballynaclogh
Kilbane
Bushfield
River Fergus
Kilmurry
Dolla
Newmarket on Fergus
Silvermines
Oatfield
Kilmore
Bridgetown
Silvermine Mountains
Templeder
Birdhill
Cloghera
O'Briensbridge
Hurlers Cross
Sixmilebridge
Montpelier
Slievekimalta
SHANNON AIRPORT
Folk Park
Woodcock Hill
Cloonlara
Toor
Rineanna Point
Shannon
Cratloe
Castleconnell
Curreeny
Bunratty
LIMERICK/
LUIMNEACH
Newport
Parteen
Mauherslieve
R. Shannon
Lisnagry
Clare
Kilcommon
Annacotty
Clare Glens
Rear Cross
Ballysteen
Creggaun
Slievefelim
Anglesey Br.
Coonagh
Hunt Museum
Inch
Pallaskenry
Bleach Lake
Murroe
Milestone
Mungret
Barringtonsbridge
Cullaun
Friary
Dromore Lake
Mountains
Kilcornan
New Kildimo
Clarina
Bohereen
Mulkear
Abington
Ballvengland
Old Kildimo
Ferry Bridge
Cloonteen
Foilycleara
Askeaton
Currahchase Forest Park
Boher
Brittas
Cappamore
Hollyford
Kilbreedy
Patrickswell
Ballyneety
Caherconlish
Doon
Cappagh
Kilmurry
Cahernahallia
Ballinagarrane
Crecora
Adare
Dromkeen
Cloonlusk
Pallas Green
Dead
Toem
Cappagh White
Croagh
Ballybrood
R. Maigue
Fedamore
Camoge
Rathkeale/
Rath Caola
Monaster
Pallasgreen
Annacarty
Croom
Kilfinny
Monasteranenagh Abbey
Interpretive Centre
Oola
Donohill
L I M E R I C K
Meanus
Holycross
Lough Gur
Herbertstown
Kilteely
Ballyallinan
Morenane
Cullen
Knockaderry
Bruff
Knockaunavoher
Monard
Donaskeagh
Ballingarry
Morningstar
Knockainy
Limerick Junction
Cloncagh
Athlacca
Hospital
Emly
Thomastown
Kilfeakle
Ballinleeny
Corronoher
Dromin
Lattin
Tipperary/
Tiobraid Árann
Castletown
Rockhill
Newtown
Kilmeedy
Killacolla
Bruree
Elton
Knocklong
Kilross
Ballyagran
Garryfine
Bulgaden
Loobagh
Garryspillane
Newtown
Feenagh
Kilmallock/
Cill Mocheallog
Lisvarrinane
Glen of Aherlow
(Charleville)
Rath Luirc
An Ráth
Martinstown
Glenbrohane
Galbally
Broadford
Blackpool
Ballylanders
Sturrakeen
Newtownshandrum
Kilfinnane
Barna
Galtymore Mountain
Dromcolliher
Milford
Galty Mountains
Dromina
Ardpatrick
Ballyhaght
Cullane
Anglesborough
Boolakennedy
Newtown
Ballyorgan
Freemount
Ballyhoura Mountains
Burncourt
Kilbeheny
Liscarroll
Castle
Churchtown
Knockanevin
Killaclug
Mitchelstown
Inchnamuck

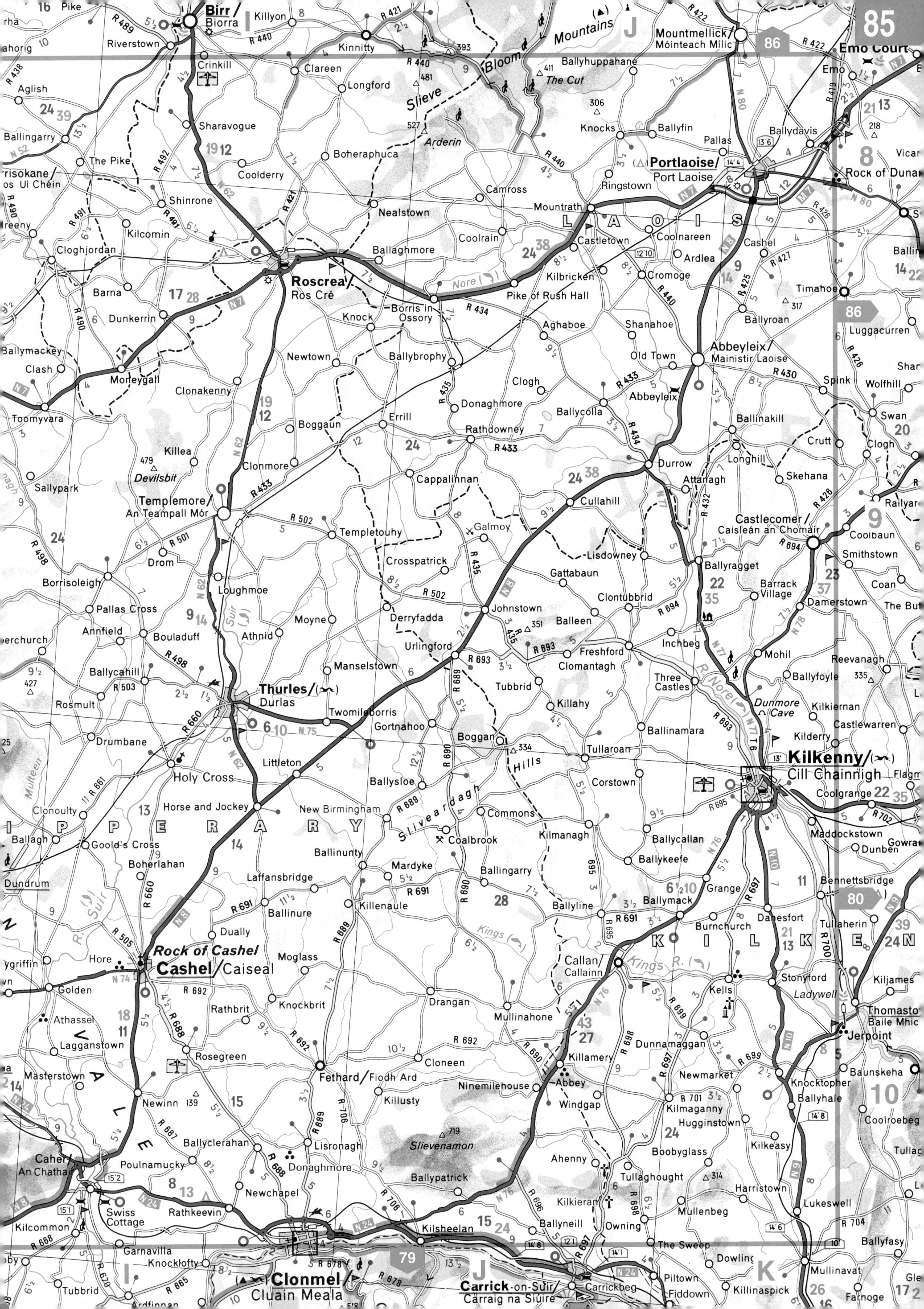

Birr / Biorra
Killyon
Kinnitty
Slieve Bloom Mountains
Mountmellick / Móinteach Mílic
Emo Court
Emo
Riverstown
Crinkill
Clareen
Longford
Ballyhuppahane
The Cut
Aglish
Arderin
Knocks
Ballyfin
Ballydavis
Ballingarry
Sharavogue
Boheraphuca
Pallas
Portlaoise / Port Laoise
Rock of Dunamase
The Pike
Coolderry
Camross
Ringstown
Shinrone
Nealstown
Mountrath
Kilcomin
Castletown
Coolnareen
Cashel
Cloghjordan
Ballaghmore
Coolrain
Ardlea
Roscrea / Ros Cré
Kilbricken
Cromoge
Timahoe
Barna
Nore
Pike of Rush Hall
Borris in Ossory
Dunkerrin
Knock
Aghaboe
Shanahoe
Ballyroan
Luggacurren
Ballymackey
Clash
Moneygall
Newtown
Ballybrophy
Old Town
Abbeyleix / Mainistir Laoise
Clonakenny
Clogh
Donaghmore
Abbeyleix
Spink
Wolfhill
Toomyvara
Ballycolla
Swan
Boggaun
Errill
Ballinakill
Rathdowney
Crutt
Clogh
Killea
Devilsbit
Clonmore
Longhill
Durrow
Skehana
Cappalinnan
Attanagh
Sallypark
Cullahill
Railyard
Templemore / An Teampall Mór
Templetouhy
Castlecomer / Caisleán an Chomair
Galmoy
Coolbaun
Drom
Lisdowney
Smithstown
Crosspatrick
Gattabaun
Ballyragget
Borrisoleigh
Barrack Village
Coan
Loughmoe
Clontubbrid
Pallas Cross
Johnstown
Damerstown
The Butts
Derryfadda
Balleen
Annfield
Moyne
Bouladuff
Athnid
Urlingford
Freshford
Inchbeg
Mohil
Clomantagh
Reevanagh
Manselstown
Ballyfoyle
Ballycahill
Tubbrid
Three Castles
Dunmore Cave
Kilkiernan
Thurles / Durlas
Rosmult
Killahy
Twomileborris
Castlewarren
Gortnahoo
Ballinamara
Kilderry
Drumbane
Boggan
Tullaroan
Littleton
Hills
Kilkenny / Cill Chainnigh
Holy Cross
Corstown
Ballysloe
Multeen
Clonoulty
Horse and Jockey
Coolgrange
New Birmingham
Slieveardagh
Commons
TIPPERARY
Maddockstown
Ballagh
Coalbrook
Kilmanagh
Goold's Cross
Ballycallan
Gowran
Dunbell
Boherlahan
Ballinunty
Ballykeefe
Mardyke
Ballingarry
Dundrum
Laffansbridge
Bennettsbridge
Grange
Killenaule
Ballyline
Ballymack
Ballinure
Danesfort
Tullaherin
Burnchurch
Dually
Kings
KILKENNY
Rock of Cashel
Cashel / Caiseal
Moglass
Hore
Callan / Callainn
Kings R.
Kells
Stonyford
Kiljames
Golden
Ladywell
Rathbrit
Drangan
Knockbrit
Mullinahone
Thomastown / Baile Mhic Andáin
Athassel
Jerpoint
Lagganstown
Rosegreen
Cloneen
Killamery
Dunnamaggan
Baunskeha
Fethard / Fiodh Ard
Masterstown
Abbey
Ninemilehouse
Newmarket
Knocktopher
VALE
Killusty
Ballyhale
Newinn
Windgap
Kilmaganny
Hugginstown
Coolroebeg
Slievenamon
Ballyclerahan
Lisronagh
Cahir / An Chathair
Poulnamucky
Kilkeasy
Ahenny
Booby glass
Tullagher
Donaghmore
Ballypatrick
Tullaghought
Newchapel
Harristown
Swiss Cottage
Rathkeevin
Kilkieran
Lukeswell
Kilcommon
Mullenbeg
Owning
Ballyneill
Kilsheelan
Ballyfasy
Garnavilla
The Sweep
Knocklofty
Dowling
Clonmel / Cluain Meala
Carrick-on-Suir / Carraig na Siúire
Carrickbeg
Piltown
Mullinavat
Tubbrid
Killinaspick
Fiddown
Farnoge
Ardfinnan
LAOIS
R. Nore
R. Suir
Suir
86
80
79

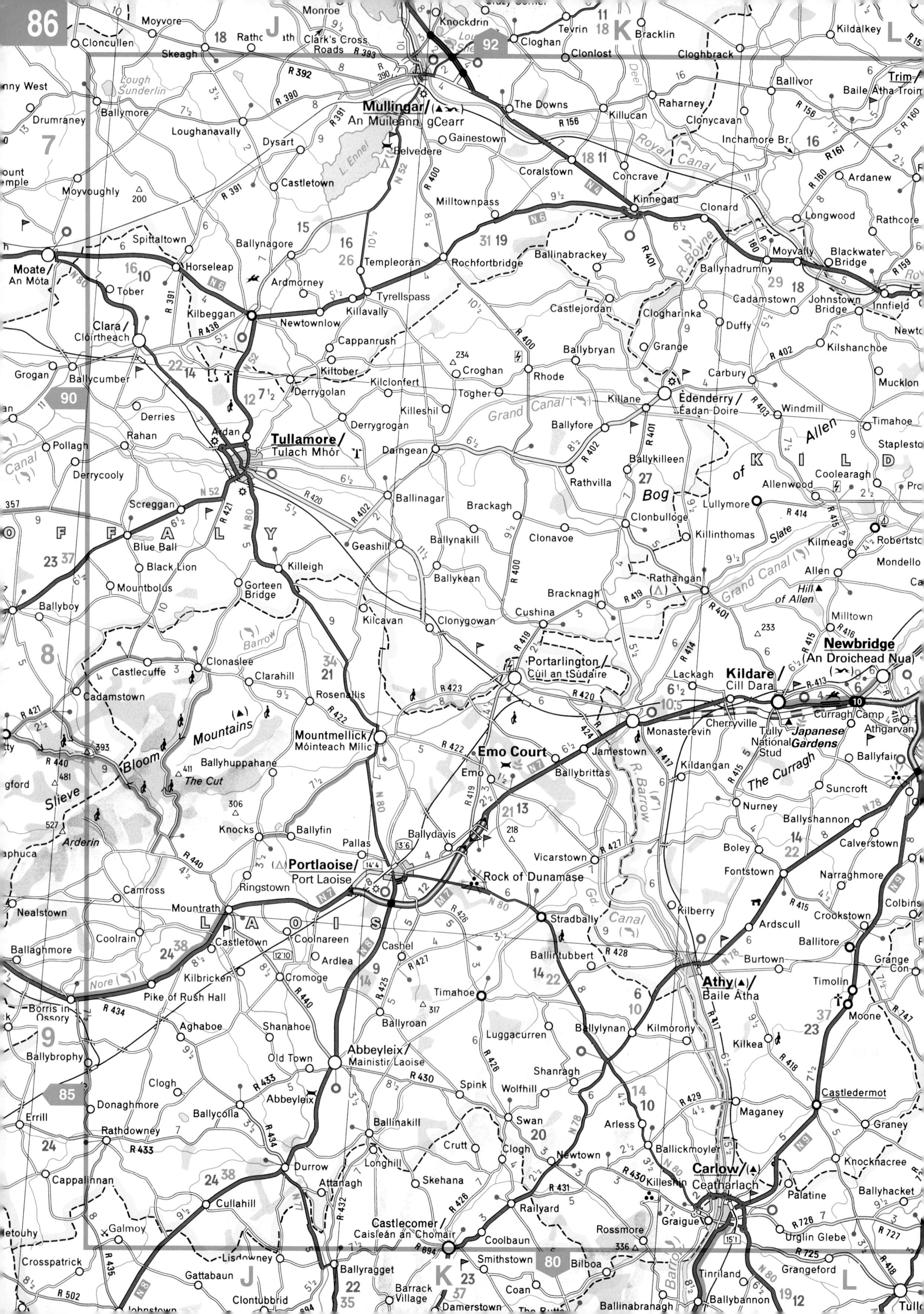
Mullingar / An Muileann gCearr
Tullamore / Tulach Mhór
Portlaoise / Port Laoise
Kildare / Cill Dara
Newbridge (An Droichead Nua)
Edenderry / Éadan Doire
Portarlington / Cúil an tSúdaire
Mountmellick / Móinteach Mílic
Abbeyleix / Mainistir Laoise
Carlow / Ceatharlach
Castlecomer / Caisleán an Chomair
Athy / Baile Átha
Moate / An Móta
Clara / Clóirtheach
Slieve Bloom Mountains
Bog of Allen
The Curragh
O F F A L Y
L A O I S
K I L D A R E
Emo Court
Rock of Dunamase
Japanese Gardens
Grand Canal
Royal Canal
R. Barrow
R. Boyne

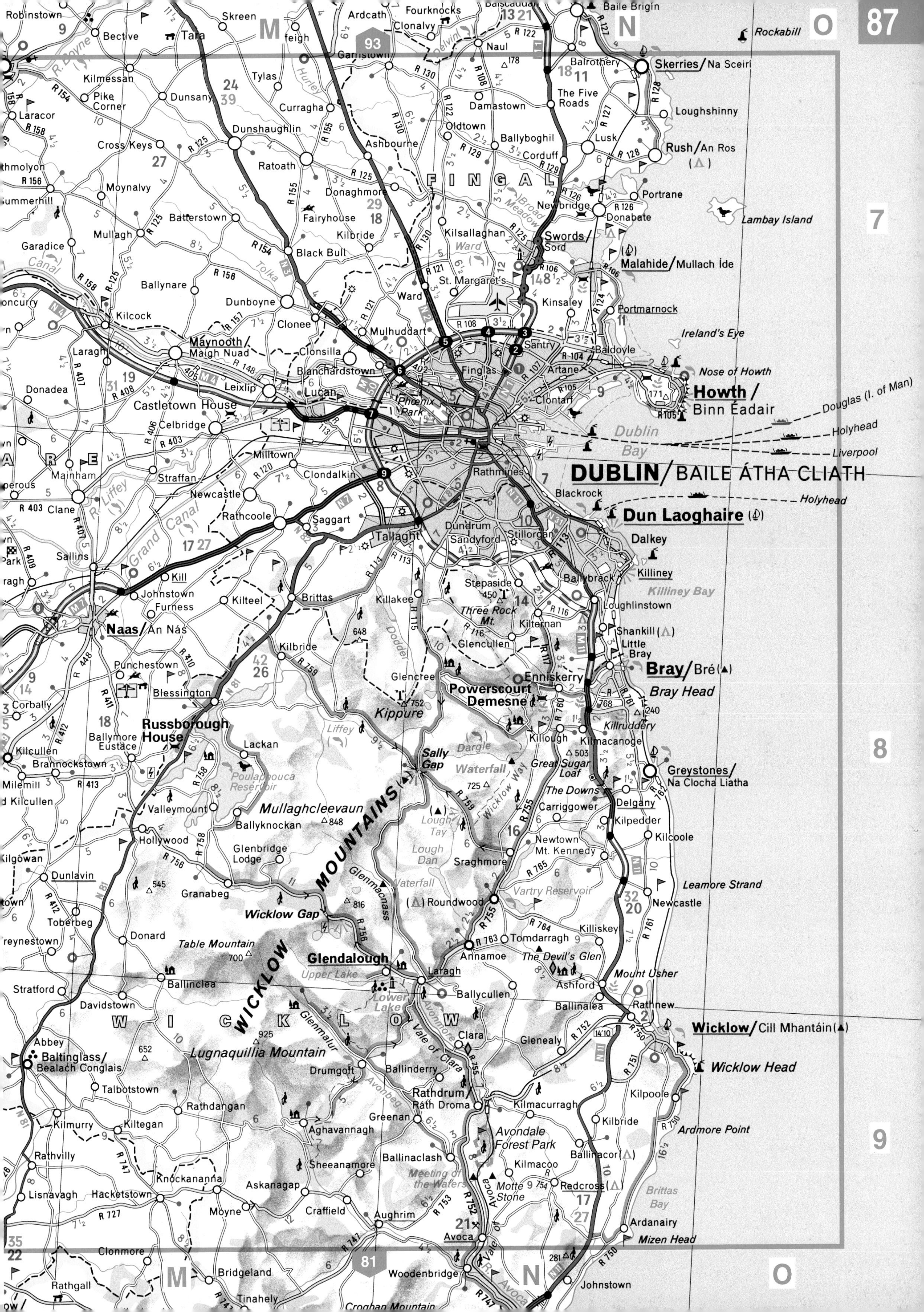
DUBLIN/BAILE ÁTHA CLIATH
Dun Laoghaire
Howth/Binn Éadair
Skerries/Na Sceirí
Rush/An Ros
Malahide/Mullach Íde
Swords/Sord
Maynooth/Maigh Nuad
Naas/An Nás
Bray/Bré
Greystones/Na Clocha Liatha
Wicklow/Cill Mhantáin
Baltinglass/Bealach Conglais
Rathdrum/Ráth Droma
FINGAL
WICKLOW
WICKLOW MOUNTAINS
Dublin Bay
Killiney Bay
Lambay Island
Ireland's Eye
Rockabill
Nose of Howth
Bray Head
Wicklow Head
Ardmore Point
Mizen Head
Brittas Bay
Leamore Strand
Douglas (I. of Man)
Holyhead
Liverpool
Powerscourt Demesne
Russborough House
Castletown House
Glendalough
Upper Lake
Lower Lake
Kippure
Mullaghcleevaun
Lugnaquillia Mountain
Table Mountain
Sally Gap
Wicklow Gap
Three Rock Mt.
Great Sugar Loaf
Vartry Reservoir
Poulaphouca Reservoir
Lough Tay
Lough Dan
Avondale Forest Park
Meeting of the Waters
Vale of Clara
Vale of Avoca
Motte Stone
Mount Usher
The Devil's Glen
Grand Canal
Royal Canal
Phoenix Park
Robinstown
Bective
Tara
Skreen
Ardcath
Fourknocks
Clonalvy
Naul
Balrothery
Baile Brigín
Garristown
Kilmessan
Pike Corner
Laracor
Dunsany
Tylas
Curragha
Dunshaughlin
Cross Keys
Ratoath
Ashbourne
Oldtown
Ballyboghil
Corduff
Damastown
The Five Roads
Lusk
Loughshinny
Portrane
Donabate
Newbridge
Moynalvy
Batterstown
Fairyhouse
Donaghmore
Kilbride
Black Bull
Mullagh
Garadice
Kilsallaghan
Ballynare
Dunboyne
Ward
St. Margaret's
Kinsaley
Portmarnock
Kilcock
Clonee
Mulhuddart
Santry
Baldoyle
Artane
Clontarf
Finglas
Clonsilla
Blanchardstown
Laragh
Leixlip
Lucan
Donadea
Celbridge
Milltown
Clondalkin
Rathmines
Blackrock
Dalkey
Mainham
Straffan
Newcastle
Clane
Rathcoole
Saggart
Tallaght
Dundrum
Sandyford
Stillorgan
Sallins
Kill
Johnstown
Furness
Kilteel
Brittas
Killakee
Stepaside
Ballybrack
Killiney
Loughlinstown
Shankill
Little Bray
Kilternan
Glencullen
Enniskerry
Punchestown
Blessington
Glencree
Corbally
Ballymore Eustace
Kilcullen
Brannockstown
Lackan
Killough
Kilmacanoge
Killruddery
Valleymount
Ballyknockan
Hollywood
Glenbridge Lodge
The Downs
Carriggower
Delgany
Kilpedder
Kilcoole
Newtown Mt. Kennedy
Sraghmore
Dunlavin
Granabeg
Roundwood
Newcastle
Toberbeg
Donard
Tomdarragh
Annamoe
Killiskey
Ashford
Laragh
Ballycullen
Ballinalea
Rathnew
Stratford
Ballinclea
Davidstown
Clara
Glenealy
Abbey
Drumgoff
Ballinderry
Talbotstown
Rathdangan
Kilmacurragh
Kilmurry
Kiltegan
Aghavannagh
Greenan
Kilbride
Kilpoole
Ballinacor
Rathvilly
Sheeanamore
Ballinaclash
Kilmacoo
Knockananna
Askanagap
Redcross
Lisnavagh
Hacketstown
Moyne
Craffield
Aughrim
Ardanairy
Avoca
Clonmore
Bridgeland
Woodenbridge
Johnstown
Rathgall
Tinahely
Croghan Mountain
M
N
O
7
8
9
93
81

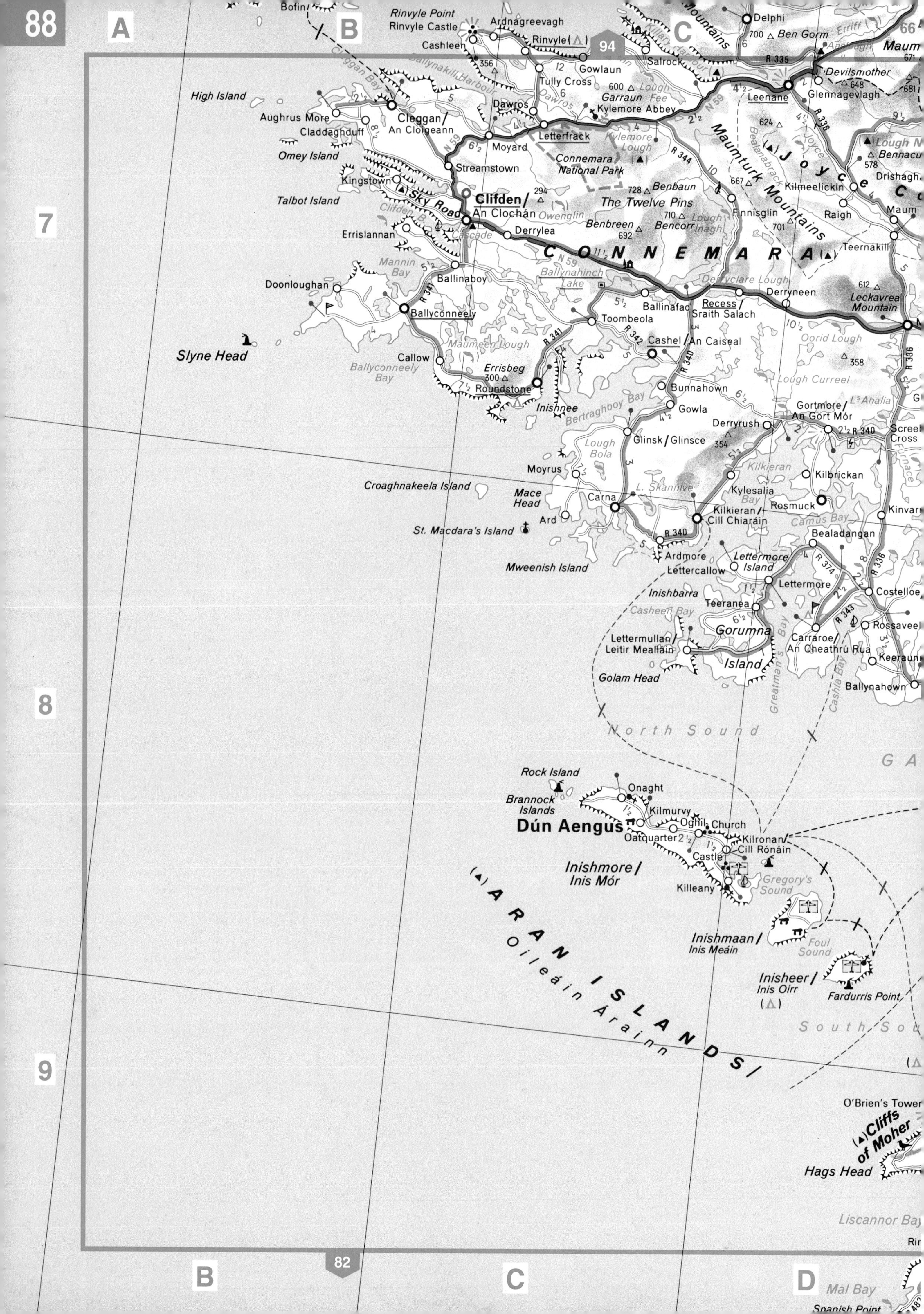
A
B
C
D
7
8
9
94
82
Bofin
Rinvyle Point
Rinvyle Castle
Cashleen
Ardnagreevagh
Rinvyle
Gowlaun
Tully Cross
Salrock
Delphi
Ben Gorm
Mountains
Maum
Devilsmother
Glennagevlagh
Leenane
Cleggan Bay
Ballynakill Harbour
High Island
Aughrus More
Claddaghduff
Cleggan/
An Cloigeann
Omey Island
Dawros
Garraun
Lough Fee
Kylemore Abbey
Letterfrack
Moyard
Kylemore Lough
Connemara
National Park
Streamstown
Kingstown
Sky Road
Talbot Island
Clifden/
An Clochán
Benbaun
The Twelve Pins
Maumturk Mountains
Joyce
Bealanabrack
Kilmeelickin
Finnisglin
Raigh
Maum
Drishagh
Bennacu
Teernakill
Errislannan
Derrylea
Owenglin
Benbreen
Bencorr
Lough Inagh
CONNEMARA
Cascade
Mannin Bay
Ballinaboy
Ballynahinch Lake
Derryclare Lough
Doonloughan
Ballyconneely
Ballinafad
Recess/
Sraith Salach
Derryneen
Leckavrea Mountain
Toombeola
Cashel/An Caiseal
Oorid Lough
Slyne Head
Callow
Maumeen Lough
Ballyconneely Bay
Errisbeg
Roundstone
Inishnee
Bunnahown
Lough Curreel
Bertraghboy Bay
Gowla
Gortmore/
An Gort Mór
Ls Ahalia
Derryrush
Screeb Cross
Lough Bola
Glinsk/Glinsce
Moyrus
Kilkieran
Kilbrickan
Croaghnakeela Island
Mace Head
L. Skannive
Carna
Kylesalia Bay
Rosmuck
Ard
Kilkieran/
Cill Chiaráin
Camus Bay
Kinvarr
St. Macdara's Island
Ardmore
Bealadangan
Mweenish Island
Lettermore Island
Lettercallow
Inishbarra
Lettermore
Costelloe
Teeranea
Casheen Bay
Gorumna Island
Rossaveel
Lettermullan/
Leitir Meallain
Carraroe/
An Cheathrú Rua
Keeraun
Golam Head
Greatman's Bay
Cashla Bay
Ballynahown
North Sound
GA
Rock Island
Onaght
Brannock Islands
Kilmurvy
Dún Aengus
Oghil
Church
Oatquarter
Kilronan/
Cill Rónáin
Castle
Inishmore/
Inis Mór
Killeany
Gregory's Sound
ARAN ISLANDS/
Oileáin Árainn
Inishmaan/
Inis Meáin
Foul Sound
Inisheer/
Inis Oírr
Fardurris Point
South Sou
O'Brien's Tower
Cliffs of Moher
Hags Head
Liscannor Bay
Mal Bay
Spanish Point
N 59
R 335
R 336
R 344
R 341
R 342
R 340
R 374
R 343

D
E
F
G
95
90
83
84
7
8
9
LOUGH MASK
LOUGH CORRIB
GALWAY BAY
Partry Mountains
Tourmakeady/ Tuar Mhic Éadaigh
Crossboyne
Ballindine
Cloonfad
Kilvin
Hollymount
Irishtown
Kilnalag
Trean
Cappanacreha
Roundfort
Ballinrobe/ Baile an Róba
Caher
Castleville
Curragh West
Maumtrasna
Inishmaine Island
Milltown
Ardcloon
Gortaleam
Finny/ Fionnaithe
Kilmaine
Foxhall
Dunmore/ Dún Mór
Cashel
Neale
Ballagh
Cloghbrack
Cong/ Conga
Kilconly
Carrowntanlis
Clonbur/ An Fhairche
Crumlin
Ashford
Cross
Tobernadarry
Ballyhear
Kilbennan
Beagh
Clonbern
Cornamona
Bunnafollistran
Shrule
Claddagh
Kilkerrin
Caggan
Inishdoorus
Inishmicatreer
Curraun
Mounthenry
Caherlistrane
Belclare
Tuam/ Tuaim
Levally
Maam Cross/ An Teach Dóite
Inchagoill
Ross
Ower
Headford/ Áth Cinn
Barnaderg
Inchiquin
Greenfield
Cloverhill
Moneen
Moylough
Oughterard/ Uachtar Ard
Ballyhale
Knockmoy Abbey
Derryerglinna
Aughnanure
Shannawona
Killarone
Knockferry
Corrofin
Killoscobe
Lettermore
Carrowmoreknock
Lettercraffroe Lough
Rosscahill
Annaghdown
Corrandulla
Ardnasodan
Skehanagh
Menlough
Aucloggeen
Cloonboo
Cloghaun
Turloughmore
Ryehill
Colmanstown
Tullokyne
Ross Lake
Lough Formoyle
Glenicmurrin Lough
Moycullen/ Maigh Cuilinn
Ballycuirke Lough
Carnoneen
Monivea
Gurteen
Claregalway/ Baile Chláir
Keeagh
Casla
Loughanillaunmore
Kilroghter
Newcastle
Cashla
Menlough
Lough Ugga Beg
Boliska Lough
Tonabrocky
Castlegar
Carnmore
Attymon
Glennascaul
Athenry/ Baile Átha an Rí
Spiddal/ An Spidéal
Inverán/ Indreabhán
Furbogh
Barna/ Bearna
Salthill
GALWAY/ GAILLIMH
Oranmore
Esker
Caheradrine
Rinville
Coldwood
Kiltullagh
Kilcaimin
Turoe Stone
Clarinbridge
Bullaun
Tawin
Tawin Island
Carrowmore
Killeeneenmore
Craughwell
Dunbulcaun Bay
Kilcolgan
Killilan Bridge
Eddy I.
Killeenaran
Loughrea/ Baile Locha Riach
Ballinderreen
Black Head
Aughinish
Newtownlynch
Parkmore
Kinvarra B.
Finavarra
Ballyclery
Kilchreest
Lough Rea
Murroogh
Cregg
Owenbristy
Ardrahan
Fanore
Burren
Crossooha
Dunguaire
Grannagh
Corcomroe Abbey
Kinvarra
Laban
Ballyvaughan
Bealaclugga
Formoyle
Funshin More
Derreen
Cahermore
Peterswell
Slieve Elva
Aillwee Cave
Cappaghmore
Francis Gap
Slieve Aught Mountains
Gregans Castle
Turlough
Killinny
Thoor Ballylee
Corkscrew Hill
The Burren
Ballaba
Drumkeary
Poulnabrone
Tulla
Tirneevin
Gort/ An Gort
Toomaghera
Kilbeacanty
Lisdoonvarna/ Lios Dúin Bhearna
Caherconnell
Carran
Kilmacduagh
Newtown
Bunnaglass
Derrybrien
Roadford
Ballardiggan
Owendalulleegh
Doolin
Noughaval
Castletown
Boston
Lough Cutra
Burren Centre Kilfenora
Burren National Park
Lough Bunny
Killafeen
Kilfenora
Leamaneh Castle
Shanaglish
Kilshanny
Crosses
Ballyeighter Loughs
Bleach
Cliffs of Moher Visitor Centre
Muckanagh Lough
Tubber
Drumandoora
Lough Atorick
Killeen
Derreen
Fergus
Killinaboy
Lough Graney
Flagmount
Liscannor
Inchiquin Lough
Killanena
Corrakyle
Lahinch/ An Leacht
Ennistimon/ Inis Díomáin
L. George
Ballinruan
Maghera
Caher
Corrofin
Kilclaran
Bohatem
Cullenagh
Willbrook
L. Atedaun
Crusheen
Cloonusker
Sheeaun
Ruan
Dysert O'Dea
Glendree
Inchicronan Lough
Feakle
Milltown Malbay/ Sráid na Cathrach
Mauricesmills
Scarriff/ An Scairbh
Boolyduff
Bauntlieve
Kilnamona
Barefield
CLARE
GALWAY

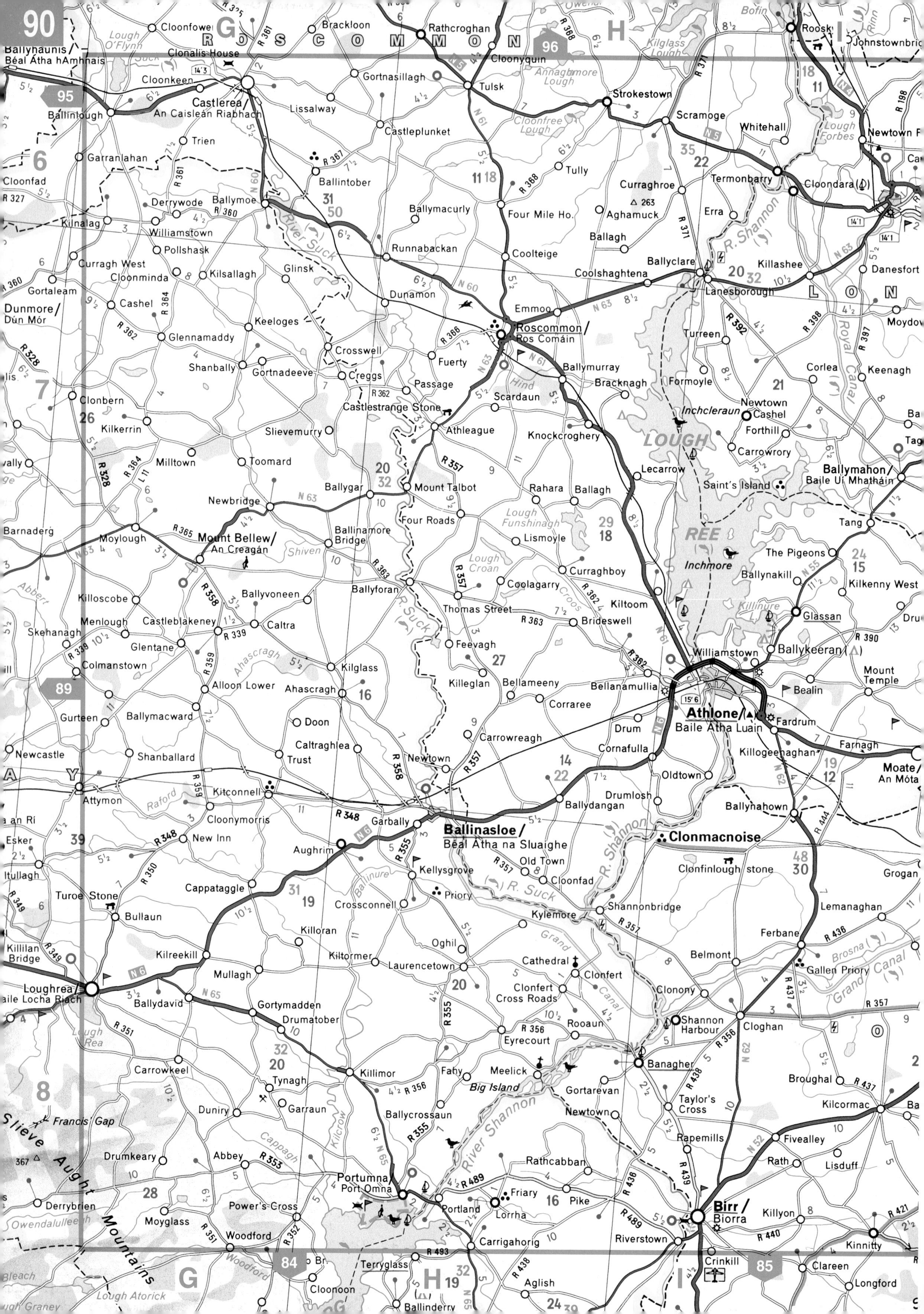

R O S C O M M O N
L O N
G A L W A Y
G
H
I
96
95
89
84
85
6
7
8
Ballyhaunis / Béal Átha hAmhnais
Cloonfower
Lough O'Flynn
Brackloon
Rathcroghan
Clonalis House
Cloonkeen
Castlerea / An Caisleán Riabhach
Ballinlough
Lissalway
Gortnasillagh
Tulsk
Cloonyquin
Annaghmore Lough
Kilglass Lough
Bofin
Rooskey
Johnstownbridge
Strokestown
Scramoge
Whitehall
Lough Forbes
Newtown Forbes
Castleplunket
Cloonfree Lough
Trien
Garranlahan
Cloonfad
Ballintober
Tully
Curraghroe
Termonbarry
Cloondara
Derrywode
Ballymoe
Kilnalag
Williamstown
Pollshask
River Suck
Ballymacurly
Four Mile Ho.
Aghamuck
Erra
Ballagh
R. Shannon
Runnabackan
Coolteige
Ballyclare
Lanesborough
Killashee
Danesfort
Curragh West
Cloonminda
Kilsallagh
Glinsk
Coolshaghtena
Gortaleam
Dunmore / Dún Mór
Cashel
Dunamon
Emmoo
Keeloges
Glennamaddy
Roscommon / Ros Comáin
Turreen
Royal Canal
Moydow
Crosswell
Fuerty
Ballymurray
Bracknagh
Formoyle
Corlea
Keenagh
Shanbally
Gortnadeeve
Creggs
Passage
Hind
Scardaun
Clonbern
Castlestrange Stone
Inchcleraun
Newtown Cashel
Forthill
Kilkerrin
Slievemurry
Athleague
Knockcroghery
LOUGH REE
Carrowrory
Milltown
Toomard
Lecarrow
Ballymahon / Baile Uí Mhatháin
Saint's Island
Ballygar
Mount Talbot
Rahara
Newbridge
Four Roads
Lough Funshinagh
Tang
Barnaderg
Moylough
Mount Bellew / An Creagán
Ballinamore Bridge
Shiven
Lismoyle
Inchmore
The Pigeons
Lough Croan
Curraghboy
Ballynakill
Kilkenny West
Abbert
Killoscobe
Ballyvoneen
Ballyforan
Coolagarry
Croos
Kiltoom
Killinure L.
Glassan
Menlough
Castleblakeney
Caltra
Thomas Street
Brideswell
Skehanagh
Glentane
Feevagh
Ahascragh
Ballykeeran
Williamstown
Colmanstown
Kilglass
Killeglan
Bellameeny
Bellanamullia
Mount Temple
Bealin
Alloon Lower
Corraree
Athlone / Baile Átha Luain
Fardrum
Gurteen
Ballymacward
Doon
Drum
Carrowreagh
Farnagh
Caltraghlea
Trust
Newtown
Cornafulla
Killogeenaghan
Moate / An Móta
Newcastle
Shanballard
Oldtown
Attymon
Raford
Kitconnell
Drumlosh
Ballydangan
Ballynahown
Cloonymorris
Garbally
Ballinasloe / Béal Átha na Sluaighe
Clonmacnoise
Esker
New Inn
Aughrim
Old Town
Clonfinlough stone
Kellysgrove
Cloonfad
Grogan
Turoe Stone
Cappataggle
Ballinure
R. Suck
Priory
Crossconnell
Shannonbridge
Lemanaghan
Bullaun
Kylemore
Killoran
Grand Canal
Ferbane
Oghil
Killilan Bridge
Kilreekill
Kiltormer
Laurencetown
Cathedral
Clonfert
Belmont
Brosna
Gallen Priory
Loughrea / Baile Locha Riach
Mullagh
Clonony
Ballydavid
Gortymadden
Clonfert Cross Roads
Drumatobber
Rooaun
Shannon Harbour
Cloghan
Lough Rea
Eyrecourt
Banagher
Carrowkeel
Killimor
Fahy
Meelick
Big Island
Tynagh
Gortarevan
Broughal
Kilcormac
Duniry
Garraun
Ballycrossaun
Taylor's Cross
Newtown
Francis' Gap
River Shannon
Kilcrow
Cappagh
Rapemills
Fivealley
Slieve Aughty Mountains
Drumkeary
Abbey
Rathcabban
Rath
Lisduff
Portumna / Port Omna
Friary
Pike
Derrybrien
Owendalulleegh
Moyglass
Power's Cross
Portland
Lorrha
Birr / Biorra
Killyon
Woodford
Carrigahorig
Riverstown
Kinnitty
Bleach
Terryglass
Crinkill
Clareen
Cloonoon
Aglish
Longford
Lough Atorick
Ballinderry
N5
N60
N61
N63
N6
N62
N65
N52
N55
R 361
R 368
R 367
R 360
R 364
R 362
R 328
R 366
R 357
R 365
R 358
R 339
R 359
R 363
R 348
R 355
R 350
R 349
R 351
R 356
R 353
R 352
R 489
R 438
R 439
R 436
R 437
R 440
R 421
R 493
R 444
R 390
R 392
R 398
R 397
R 371
R 198
263
367

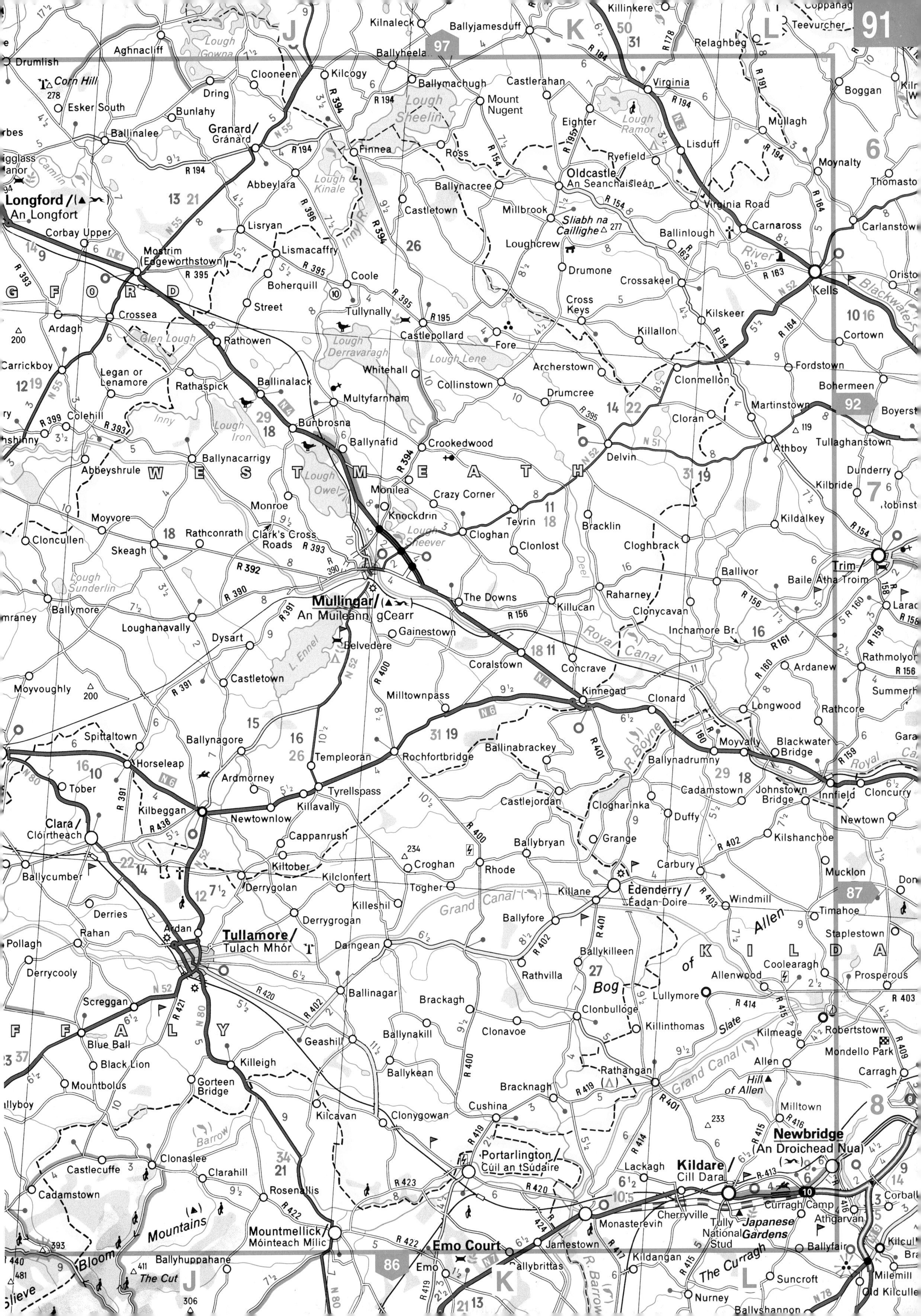

Drumlish
Corn Hill
Esker South
Aghnacliff
Lough Gowna
Clooneen
Dring
Bunlahy
Ballinalee
Granard / Gránard
Kilcogy
Kilnaleck
Ballyjamesduff
Ballyheelan
Ballymachugh
Lough Sheelin
Castlerahan
Mount Nugent
Killinkere
Virginia
Lough Ramor
Eighter
Lisduff
Mullagh
Boggan
Teevurcher
Relaghbeg
Coppanagh
Finnea
Ross
Ryefield
Oldcastle / An Seanchaisleán
Moynalty
Thomastown
Longford / An Longfort
Abbeylara
Lough Kinale
Ballynacree
Castletown
Millbrook
Sliabh na Cailligh
Virginia Road
Carnaross
Carlanstown
Corbay Upper
Lisryan
Mostrim (Edgeworthstown)
Lismacaffry
Inny R.
Loughcrew
Ballinlough
River
Kells
Boherquill
Coole
Drumone
Crossakeel
Oristown
Blackwater
LONGFORD
Street
Tullynally
Cross Keys
Kilskeer
Ardagh
Crossea
Castlepollard
Fore
Killallon
Cortown
Glen Lough
Rathowen
Lough Derravaragh
Lough Lene
Fordstown
Carrickboy
Legan or Lenamore
Whitehall
Archerstown
Clonmellon
Bohermeen
Rathaspick
Ballinalack
Collinstown
Drumcree
Martinstown
Boyerstown
Colehill
Multyfarnham
Cloran
Lough Iron
Inny
Bunbrosna
Ballynafid
Crookedwood
Delvin
Athboy
Tullaghanstown
Abbeyshrule
Ballynacarrigy
WESTMEATH
Lough Owel
Monilea
Dunderry
Kilbride
Robinstown
Crazy Corner
Monroe
Knockdrin
Tevrin
Bracklin
Kildalkey
Moyvore
Clark's Cross Roads
Rathconrath
Lough Sheever
Cloghan
Clonlost
Cloghbrack
Cloncullen
Skeagh
Trim / Baile Átha Troim
Lough Sunderlin
Ballivor
Deel
Raharney
Ballymore
Mullingar / An Muileann gCearr
The Downs
Killucan
Clonycavan
Laracor
Loughanavally
Gainestown
Inchamore Br.
Dysart
L. Ennel
Belvedere
Coralstown
Royal Canal
Rathmolyon
Ardanew
Castletown
Concrave
Moyvoughly
Milltownpass
Kinnegad
Clonard
Summerhill
Longwood
Rathcore
Spittaltown
Ballynagore
Templeoran
Rochfortbridge
Ballinabrackey
R. Boyne
Moyvally
Blackwater Bridge
Horseleap
Tober
Ardmorney
Ballynadrumny
Cadamstown
Johnstown Bridge
Innfield
Cloncurry
Tyrellspass
Clara / Clóirtheach
Kilbeggan
Newtownlow
Killavally
Castlejordan
Clogharinka
Duffy
Newtown
Cappanrush
Croghan
Ballybryan
Grange
Kilshanchoe
Ballycumber
Kiltober
Rhode
Carbury
Mucklon
Kilclonfert
Togher
Derrygolan
Killane
Edenderry / Éadan Doire
Derries
Killeshil
Grand Canal
Windmill
Timahoe
Derrygrogan
Ballyfore
Bog of Allen
Staplestown
Ardan
Rahan
Pollagh
Tullamore / Tulach Mhór
Daingean
Ballykilleen
KILDARE
Derrycooly
Rathvilla
Coolearagh
Allenwood
Prosperous
Ballinagar
Lullymore
Screggan
Brackagh
Clonbullogue
Killinthomas
Robertstown
Slate
OFFALY
Geashill
Clonavoe
Kilmeage
Blue Ball
Ballynakill
Mondello Park
Black Lion
Killeigh
Allen
Carragh
Mountbolus
Gorteen Bridge
Ballykean
Rathangan
Hill of Allen
Bracknagh
Cushina
Milltown
Kilcavan
Clonygowan
Barrow
Newbridge / An Droichead Nua
Castlecuffe
Clonaslee
Clarahill
Portarlington / Cúil an tSúdaire
Lackagh
Kildare / Cill Dara
Cadamstown
Rosenallis
Monasterevin
Cherryville
Curragh Camp
Athgarvan
Tully
Japanese Gardens
National Stud
Mountmellick / Móinteach Mílic
Emo Court
Jamestown
Ballyfair
Kilcullen
Slieve Bloom Mountains
Ballyhuppahane
The Cut
Emo
Ballybrittas
R. Barrow
Kildangan
The Curragh
Suncroft
Milemill
Old Kilcullen
Nurney
Ballyshannon

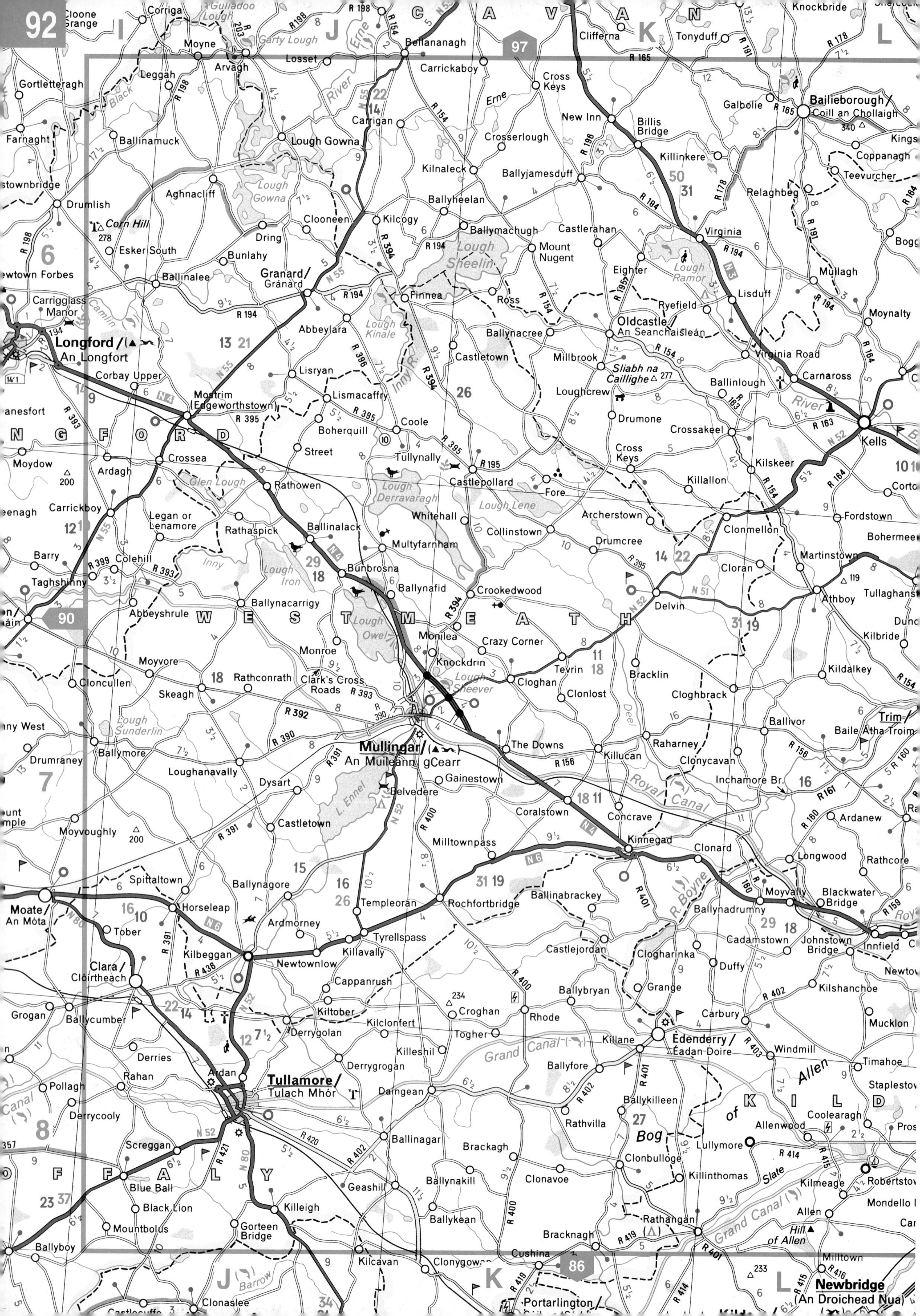
Cloone Grange
Corriga
Gulladoo Lough
Garty Lough
Moyne
Arvagh
Losset
Bellananagh
CAVAN
Clifferna
Tonyduff
Knockbride
97
Carrickaboy
Cross Keys
Leggah
Gortletteragh
Black
River
Erne
Carrigan
New Inn
Billis Bridge
Galbolie
Bailieborough/ Coill an Chollaigh
Farnaght
Ballinamuck
Lough Gowna
Crosserlough
Killinkere
Coppanagh
Kilnaleck
Ballyjamesduff
Teevurcher
Lough Gowna
Aghnacliff
Drumlish
Relaghbeg
Ballyheelan
Corn Hill
Clooneen
Kilcogy
Ballymachugh
Castlerahan
Virginia
Dring
Mount Nugent
Lough Sheelin
Esker South
Bunlahy
Eighter
Lough Ramor
Mullagh
Granard/ Gránard
Ballinalee
Finnea
Ross
Lisduff
Newtown Forbes
Carrigglass Manor
Camlin
Abbeylara
Lough Kinale
Ryefield
Oldcastle/ An Seanchaisleán
Moynalty
Ballynacree
Longford/ An Longford
Castletown
Millbrook
Virginia Road
Sliabh na Caillighe
Carnaross
Lisryan
Inny R.
Ballinlough
Corbay Upper
Mostrim (Edgeworthstown)
Lismacaffry
Loughcrew
Kells
Boherquill
Coole
Drumone
Crossakeel
Street
Tullynally
Cross Keys
LONGFORD
Moydow
Ardagh
Crossea
Castlepollard
Kilskeer
Killallon
Glen Lough
Rathowen
Lough Derravaragh
Fore
Lough Lene
Carrickboy
Whitehall
Archerstown
Fordstown
Legan or Lenamore
Collinstown
Clonmellon
Rathaspick
Ballinalack
Multyfarnham
Drumcree
Bohermeen
Barry
Colehill
Martinstown
Taghshinny
Inny
Lough Iron
Bunbrosna
Cloran
Ballynafid
Crookedwood
Delvin
Athboy
Tullaghanstown
90
Abbeyshrule
Ballynacarrigy
WESTMEATH
Lough Owel
Monilea
Crazy Corner
Kilbride
Monroe
Knockdrin
Tevrin
Bracklin
Kildalkey
Moyvore
Lough Sheever
Cloghan
Clonlost
Cloghbrack
Cloncullen
Rathconrath
Clark's Cross Roads
Skeagh
Deel
Ballivor
Trim/ Baile Átha Troim
Lough Sunderlin
The Downs
Raharney
Ballymore
Mullingar/ An Muileann gCearr
Killucan
Clonycavan
Drumraney
Gainestown
Royal Canal
Inchamore Br.
Loughanavally
Dysart
L. Ennel
Belvedere
Coralstown
Concrave
Ardanew
Castletown
Moyvoughly
Milltownpass
Kinnegad
Clonard
Longwood
Rathcore
Spittaltown
Ballynagore
Templeoran
Rochfortbridge
Ballinabrackey
R. Boyne
Moyvally
Blackwater Bridge
Moate/ An Móta
Horseleap
Ballynadrumny
Tober
Ardmorney
Tyrellspass
Cadamstown
Johnstown Bridge
Innfield
Kilbeggan
Killavally
Castlejordan
Clogharinka
Duffy
Clara/ Clóirtheach
Newtownlow
Newtown
Cappanrush
Grange
Kilshanchoe
Croghan
Ballybryan
Grogan
Ballycumber
Kiltober
Rhode
Carbury
Mucklon
Kilclonfert
Derrygolan
Togher
Killane
Edenderry/ Éadan Doire
Windmill
Derries
Killeshil
Grand Canal
Timahoe
Allen
Rahan
Ardan
Derrygrogan
Ballyfore
Pollagh
Tullamore/ Tulach Mhór
Daingean
Ballykilleen
Staplestown
Canal
Derrycooly
Bog of Allen
Coolearagh
Rathvilla
KILDARE
Allenwood
Screggan
Ballinagar
Brackagh
Lullymore
Clonbulloge
OFFALY
Blue Ball
Clonavoe
Killinthomas
Kilmeage
Robertstown
Geashill
Ballynakill
Slate
Black Lion
Killeigh
Mondello
Allen
Mountbolus
Gorteen Bridge
Ballykean
Rathangan
Bracknagh
Hill of Allen
Ballyboy
Kilcavan
Clonygowan
Cushina
86
Milltown
Barrow
Newbridge (An Droichead Nua)
Clonaslee
Portarlington
Castlecuffe

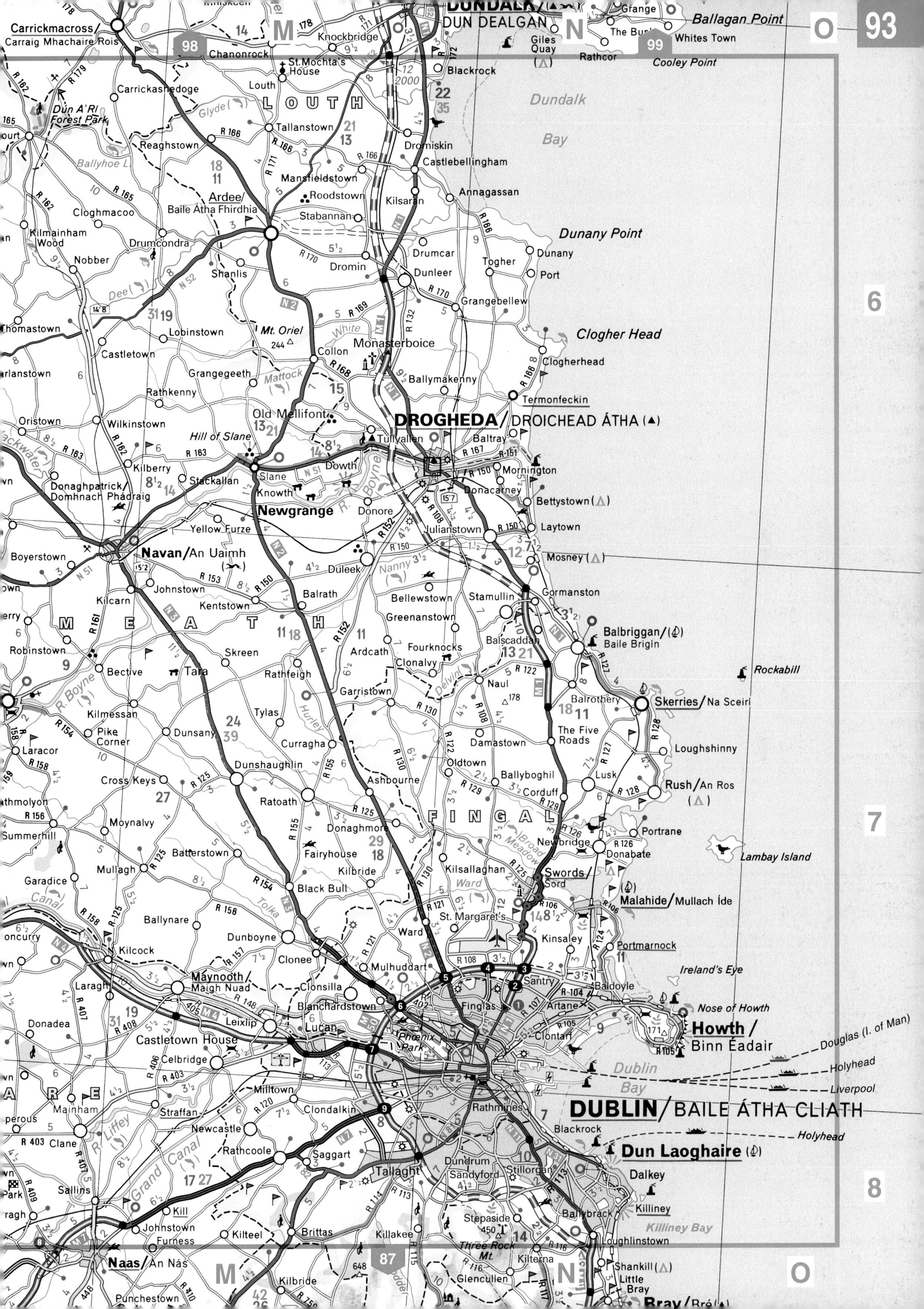
DUNDALK/DUN DEALGAN
Carrickmacross/Carraig Mhachaire Rois
Chanonrock
Knockbridge
Grange
The Bush
Ballagan Point
Whites Town
Giles Quay
Rathcor
Cooley Point
Blackrock
St.Mochta's House
Louth
LOUTH
Carrickashedoge
Dún A'Rí Forest Park
Glyde
Tallanstown
Reaghstown
Ballyhoe L.
Dundalk Bay
Dromiskin
Castlebellingham
Mansfieldstown
Roodstown
Kilsaran
Annagassan
Ardee/Baile Átha Fhirdhia
Stabannan
Cloghmacoo
Kilmainham Wood
Drumcondra
Nobber
Shanlis
Dunany Point
Dunany
Port
Drumcar
Dromin
Togher
Dunleer
Grangebellew
Dee
Chomastown
Lobinstown
Mt. Oriel
White
Monasterboice
Clogher Head
Castletown
Collon
Clogherhead
Grangegeeth
Mattock
Ballymakenny
Rathkenny
Termonfeckin
Oristown
Wilkinstown
Old Mellifont
DROGHEDA/DROICHEAD ÁTHA
Hill of Slane
Tullyallen
Baltray
Kilberry
Slane
Dowth
Mornington
Donaghpatrick/Domhnach Phádraig
Stackallan
Knowth
Boyne
Donacarney
Newgrange
Donore
Bettystown
Yellow Furze
Julianstown
Laytown
Boyerstown
Navan/An Uaimh
Duleek
Nanny
Mosney
Johnstown
Kentstown
Balrath
Bellewstown
Stamullin
Gormanston
Kilcarn
MEATH
Greenanstown
Balbriggan/Baile Brigín
Robinstown
Skreen
Ardcath
Fourknocks
Balscaddan
Bective
Tara
Rathfeigh
Clonalvy
Naul
Rockabill
Garristown
Delvin
Balrothery
Skerries/Na Sceirí
Kilmessan
Tylas
Pike Corner
Dunsany
Curragha
Hurley
The Five Roads
Damastown
Loughshinny
Laracor
Dunshaughlin
Oldtown
Ballyboghil
Lusk
Rush/An Ros
Cross Keys
Ashbourne
Corduff
Rathmolyon
Ratoath
FINGAL
Moynalvy
Donaghmore
Portrane
Summerhill
Broad Meadow
Newbridge
Donabate
Fairyhouse
Lambay Island
Batterstown
Kilsallaghan
Garadice
Mullagh
Kilbride
Swords/Sord
Black Bull
Ward
Malahide/Mullach Íde
Canal
Tolka
St. Margaret's
Ballynare
Kinsaley
Portmarnock
Dunboyne
Kilcock
Clonee
Ireland's Eye
Mulhuddart
Maynooth/Maigh Nuad
Laragh
Clonsilla
Sántry
Baldoyle
Blanchardstown
Artane
Nose of Howth
Finglas
Leixlip
Donadea
Lucan
Phoenix Park
Clontarf
Howth/Binn Éadair
Castletown House
Douglas (I. of Man)
Celbridge
Dublin Bay
Holyhead
Liverpool
Milltown
Mainham
Straffan
Clondalkin
Rathmines
DUBLIN/BAILE ÁTHA CLIATH
Newcastle
Blackrock
Clane
R. Liffey
Rathcoole
Saggart
Dun Laoghaire
Grand Canal
Tallaght
Dundrum
Stillorgan
Dalkey
Sallins
Sandyford
Kill
Killiney
Johnstown
Furness
Kilteel
Brittas
Stepaside
Ballybrack
Killiney Bay
Killakee
Three Rock Mt.
Loughlinstown
Naas/An Nás
Kilternan
Kilbride
Glencullen
Shankill
Little Bray
Punchestown
Bray/Bré

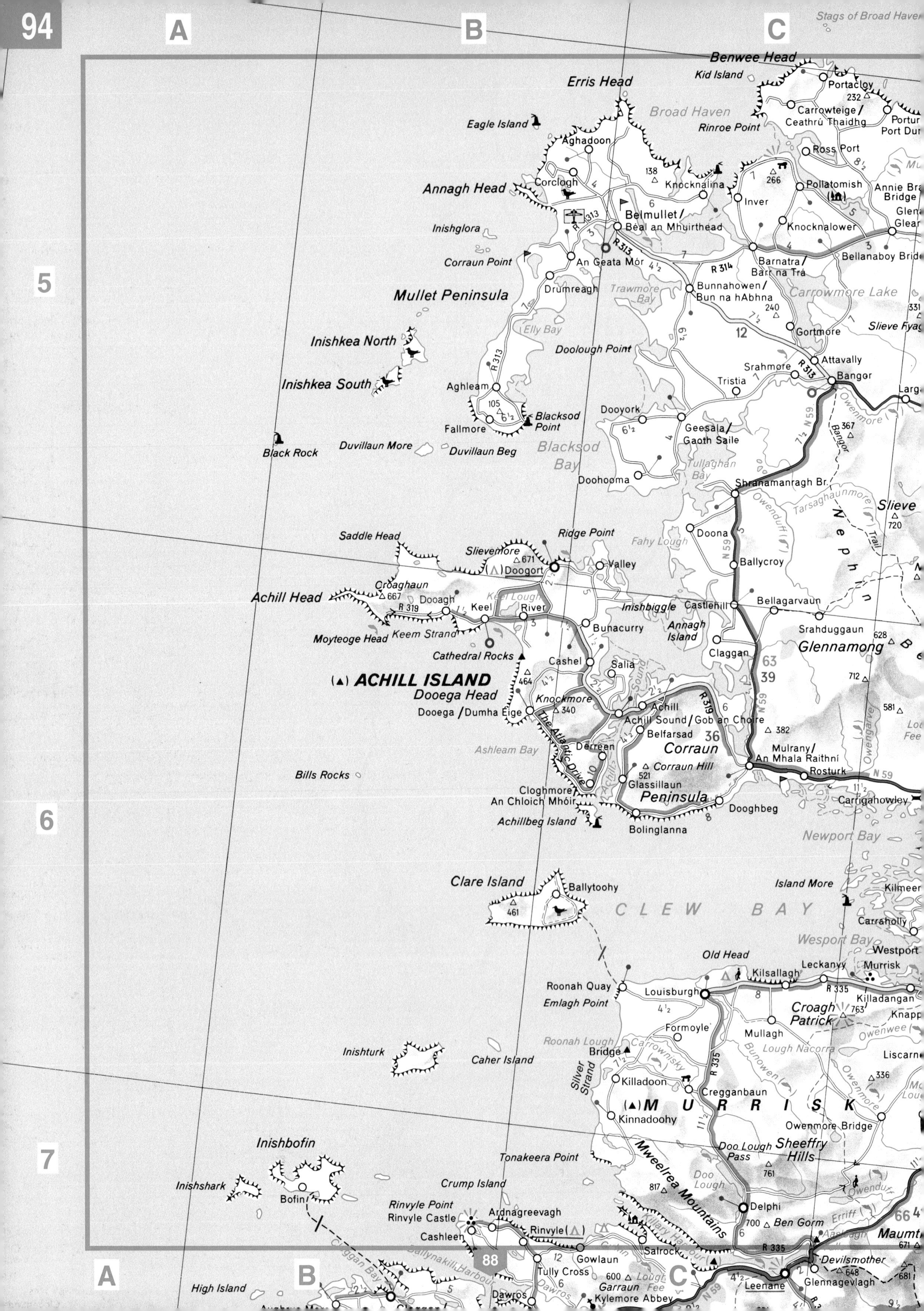
A
B
C
5
6
7
Stags of Broad Haven
Benwee Head
Kid Island
Erris Head
Portacloy
232
Carrowteige /
Ceathrú Thaidhg
Portur
Port Dur
Broad Haven
Rinroe Point
Eagle Island
Aghadoon
Ross Port
138
Knocknalina
266
Pollatomish
Annie Bra
Bridge
Annagh Head
Corclogh
Inver
Belmullet /
Béal an Mhuirthead
Knocknalower
R 313
Inishglora
Corraun Point
An Geata Mór
R 314
Barnatra /
Barr na Trá
Bellanaboy Brid
Mullet Peninsula
Drumreagh
Trawmore Bay
Bunnahowen /
Bun na hAbhna
Carrowmore Lake
240
331
Gortmore
Slieve Fyag
Elly Bay
Inishkea North
Doolough Point
12
Attavally
Srahmore
Bangor
Tristia
Inishkea South
Aghleam
105
Blacksod Point
Larg
Dooyork
Geesala /
Gaoth Saile
367
Owenmore
Fallmore
Duvillaun More
Duvillaun Beg
Black Rock
Blacksod Bay
Tullaghan Bay
Doohooma
Shranamanragh Br.
Tarsaghaunmore
Slieve
720
Nephin
Owenduff
Doona
Saddle Head
Ridge Point
Fahy Lough
Slievemore
671
Doogort
Valley
Ballycroy
N 59
Croaghaun
667
Achill Head
Dooagh
Keel Lough
Keel
River
R 319
Inishbiggle
Castlehill
Bellagarvaun
Moyteoge Head
Keem Strand
Bunacurry
Annagh Island
Srahduggaun
628
Cathedral Rocks
Claggan
Glennamong
Cashel
Salia
63
39
ACHILL ISLAND
464
712
Dooega Head
Knockmore
Achill
Dooega / Dumha Eige
340
Achill Sound / Gob an Choire
581
The Atlantic Drive
Belfarsad
36
382
Ashleam Bay
Derreen
Corraun
Mulrany /
An Mhala Raithní
Owengarve
Bills Rocks
Corraun Hill
521
Rosturk
Glassillaun
Cloghmore /
An Chloich Mhóir
Peninsula
Carrigahowley
Achillbeg Island
Dooghbeg
Bolinglanna
Newport Bay
Clare Island
Ballytoohy
Island More
Kilmeen
461
CLEW BAY
Carrowholly
Wesport Bay
Westport
Old Head
Leckanvy
Murrisk
Kilsallagh
Roonah Quay
Louisburgh
R 335
Killadangan
Emlagh Point
Croagh Patrick
763
Knapp
Formoyle
Mullagh
Owenwee
Roonah Lough
Lough Nacorra
Inishturk
Bridge
Caher Island
Carrownisky
Bunowen
Liscarn
Silver Strand
336
Killadoon
Owenmore
Cregganbaun
MURRISK
Kinnadoohy
Owenmore Bridge
Inishbofin
Doo Lough Pass
Sheeffry Hills
Tonakeera Point
761
Doo Lough
817
Mweelrea Mountains
Inishshark
Crump Island
Bofin
Rinvyle Point
Rinvyle Castle
Ardnagreevagh
Delphi
700
Ben Gorm
Erriff
66
Rinvyle
Killary Harbour
Maumt
Cashleen
671
Salrock
Aasleagh
Cleggan Bay
Ballynakill Harbour
88
Gowlaun
Devilsmother
648
681
Tully Cross
600
Lough Fee
High Island
Garraun
Leenane
Glennagevlagh
Dawros
Kylemore Abbey

D
E
F
4
5
6
Downpatrick Head
Creevagh Head
Lenadoon Point
Roskeeragh Point
Sligo Bay
Killala Bay
Aughris Head
Belderg Harbour
Glinsk
Belderrig / Béal Deirg
Ceide Fields
Maumakeogh
Benmore
Ballycastle
Gortmore
Rathlackan
Lackan Bay
Kilcummin
Killogeary
Carrowmore
Rathfran
Creevagh
Killala
Kilcon
Sheskin
Corvoley
Moyne
Rathoma
Rosserk
Doobehy
Belville
Castleconor
Inishcrone
Kilglass
Rathlee
Easky
Drinaghan
Owenbeg
Culleens
Dromore West
Templeboy
Aughris
Carrowreagh
Skreen
Corbally
Knockalongy
Ox Mountains
Slieve Gamph
Easky Lough
Bellacorick
Lough Dahybaun
Eskeragh
Crossmolina / Crois Mhaoilíona
Knockanillaun
Ballina / Béal an Átha
Crockets Town
Bunnyconnellan
Carrowneden
Carrowmore
Lavagh
Deel Bridge
Garrycloonagh
Carrowntrella
Rake Street
Lough Conn
Largan
Masshill
Cloonacool
Tobercurry / Tobar an Choire
Nephin Beg
Keenagh
Castlehill
Newtown Cloghans
Corroy
Errew
Mount Falcon
Lough Talt
Bellanagraugh Br.
Mullany's Cross
Arinagh
Toorlestraun
Attymass
Kilmacteige
Aclare
Banada
Bunaveela Lough
Lahardaun
Brackwanshagh
Cuilkillew
Nephin
Knockmore
River Moy
Corlee
Moylough
Derreen
Birreencorragh
Ballynagoraher
Glen Nephin
Nephin Range
Church Village
Cullin
Carrowmore
Owengarve
Curryghbonaun
Curry
Doocastle
Roosky
Srahmore
Bofeenaun
Levally Lough
Pontoon
Lough Cullin
Foxford
Killasser
Callow
Cloonfinish
Bellahy
Cloonmore
Charlestown
Cloondaff
Beltra
Beltra Lough
Windy Gap
Kilmore
Fisherhill
Swinford / Béal Átha na Muice
Cuilmore
Carracastle
Furnace Lough
Croaghmoyle
Burrishoole
Ross West
Strade
Gweestion River
Moy
Barnacahoge
Newport / Baile Uí Fhiacháin
Burren
Park
Bellavary
Castlebar / Caisleán an Bharraigh
Turlough
Bohola
Midfield
Tawnyinah
Connaught Airport
Kilmovee
Ballyglass
Clogher
Breaghwy
Killkelly
Aghadiffin
Urlaur
Lisacul
Westport House
Quay
Westport / Cathair na Mart
Cloonkeen
Manulla
Kiltimagh
Cloonfallagh
Derryvohy
Aghamore
Urlaur Lough
Cloonagh L.
Mannin Lake
Errit L.
Ballyhean
Belcarra
Balla
Knock
Coogue
Mace
Aghagower
Killavally
Mayo
Plains of Mayo
Ballyfarnagh
Brackloon
Carrowbehy
Island Lake
Lough O'Flynn
Suck
Ballintubber
Clogher
Ballynastangford
Ballyhaunis / Béal Átha hAmhnais
Cordarragh
Ballyglass
Barnycarroll
Bekan
Bohaun
Carrowkennedy
Carrowncaon
Curry
Claremorris / Clár Chlainne Mhuiris
Partry
Cornanagh
Ballinlough
Croaghrimbeg
Srah / An tSraith
Partry Mountains
Carrowmore
Brickeens
Lough Carra
Ballygarries
Tulrohaun
Garranlahan
Tourmakeady / Tuar Mhic Éadaigh
Crossboyne
Ballindine
Cloonfad
Robe
Dalgan
Hollymount
Scardaun
Kilvine
Trean
Lough Mask
Irishtown
Kilnalag
Cappanacreha
Caher
Ballinrobe / Baile an Róba
Roundfort
Castleville
Curragh West
Cloonminda
Western Way
Glenamoy
Oweninny
Cloonaghmore
Muing
Deel
Clydagh
Manulla
Castlebar
89
90
96
M A Y O

DONEGAL BAY
Sligo Bay
Sligo / Sligeach
Bundoran / Bun Dobhráin
Ballyshannon / Béal Átha Seanaidh
Manorhamilton / Cluainín
Ballymote / Baile an Mhóta
Boyle / Mainistir na Búille
Carrick-on-Shannon / Cora Droma Rúisc
Ballaghaderreen / Bealach an Doirín
Tobercurry / Tobar an Choire
Ballyhaunis / Béal Átha hAmhnais
Castlerea / An Caisleán Riabhach
Mohill / Maothail
Inishmurray
Mullaghmore Head
Dartry Mts.
Lough Gill
Lough Allen
Lough Arrow
Lough Key Forest Park
Lough Gara
Lough Melvin
Iron Mountains
Slieve Anierin
Curlew Mountains
Bricklieve Mountains
Marble Arch Caves
S L I G O
L E I T R I M
R O S C O M M O N

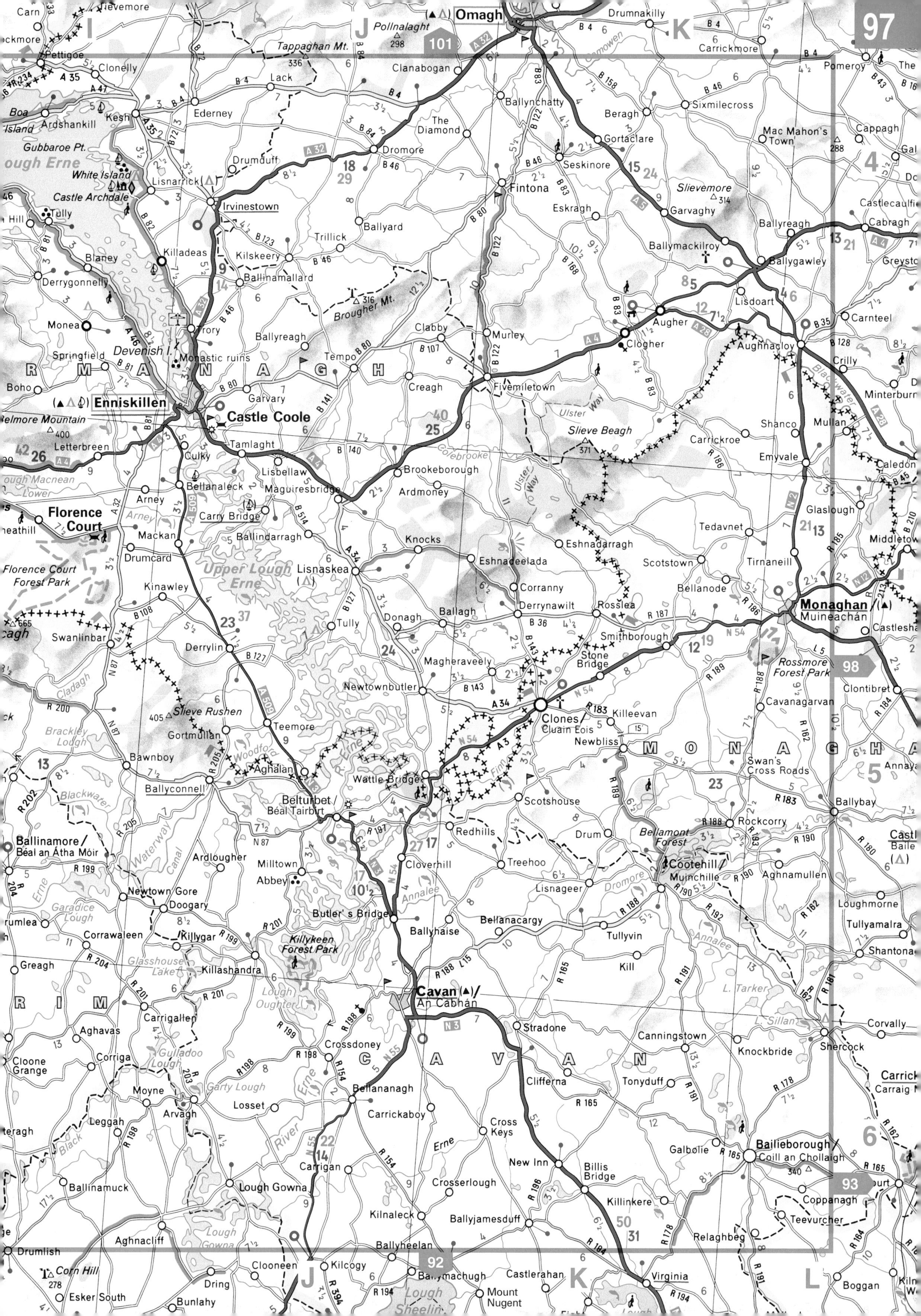
Omagh
Pollnalaght
Tappaghan Mt.
Drumnakilly
Carrickmore
Pettigoe
Clonelly
Lack
Clanabogan
Pomeroy
Ballynchatty
Beragh
Sixmilecross
Boa Island
Ardshankill
Kesh
Ederney
The Diamond
Gortaclare
Mac Mahon's Town
Cappagh
Gubbaroe Pt.
Lough Erne
White Island
Drumduff
Dromore
Seskinore
Castle Archdale
Lisnarrick
Irvinestown
Fintona
Slievemore
Garvaghy
Tully
Ballyard
Eskragh
Castlecaulfield
Ballyreagh
Cabragh
Trillick
Ballymackilroy
Killadeas
Kilskeery
Blaney
Ballygawley
Derrygonnelly
Ballinamallard
Brougher Mt.
Lisdoart
Augher
Carnteel
Monea
Trory
Clabby
Murley
Clogher
Aughnacloy
Crilly
Devenish I.
Springfield
Monastic ruins
Ballyreagh
Tempo
Boho
Creagh
Fivemiletown
Minterburn
Enniskillen
Garvary
Ulster Way
Belmore Mountain
Castle Coole
Slieve Beagh
Shanco
Mullan
Letterbreen
Tamlaght
Carrickroe
Colebrooke
Emyvale
Caledon
Lough Macnean Lower
Culky
Lisbellaw
Brookeborough
Bellanaleck
Maguiresbridge
Ardmoney
Arney
Florence Court
Carry Bridge
Glaslough
Tedavnet
Mackan
Ballindarragh
Knocks
Eshnadarragh
Middletown
Drumcard
Scotstown
Tirnaneill
Eshnadeelada
Florence Court Forest Park
Upper Lough Erne
Lisnaskea
Corranny
Bellanode
Kinawley
Derrynawilt
Rosslea
Monaghan
Muineachán
Donagh
Ballagh
Swanlinbar
Tully
Smithborough
Castleshane
Derrylin
Stone Bridge
Rossmore Forest Park
Magheraveely
Clontibret
Cladagh
Newtownbutler
Cavanagarvan
Slieve Rushen
Clones
Cluain Eois
Killeevan
Brackley Lough
Gortmullan
Teemore
Newbliss
Bawnboy
Aghalan
Wattle Bridge
Swan's Cross Roads
Annayalla
Ballyconnell
Blackwater
Scotshouse
Ballybay
Belturbet
Béal Tairbirt
Rockcorry
Bellamont Forest
Ballinamore
Béal an Átha Móir
Redhills
Drum
Ardlougher
Milltown
Treehoo
Cootehill
Muinchille
Aghnamullen
Abbey
Cloverhill
Newtown Gore
Lisnageer
Doogary
Dromore
Garadice Lough
Butler's Bridge
Loughmorne
Drumlea
Bellanacargy
Ballyhaise
Tullyvin
Tullyamalra
Corrawaleen
Killygar
Killykeen Forest Park
Shantonagh
Greagh
Glasshouse Lake
Killashandra
Kill
L. Tarker
Lough Oughter
Cavan
An Cabhán
Carrigallen
Stradone
L. Sillan
Corvally
Aghavas
Crossdoney
Canningstown
Knockbride
Shercock
Cloone Grange
Corriga
Gulladoo Lough
Clifferna
Tonyduff
Carrick
Carraig
Garty Lough
Moyne
Bellananagh
Arvagh
Losset
Carrickaboy
Leggah
Cross Keys
Galbolie
Bailieborough
Coill an Chollaigh
River Erne
Carrigan
New Inn
Billis Bridge
Ballinamuck
Lough Gowna
Crosserlough
Killinkere
Coppanagh
Kilnaleck
Ballyjamesduff
Teevurcher
Aghnacliff
Relaghbeg
Drumlish
Ballyheelan
Corn Hill
Clooneen
Kilcogy
Ballymachugh
Castlerahan
Virginia
Dring
Mount Nugent
Lough Sheelin
Esker South
Bunlahy
Boggan
FERMANAGH
MONAGHAN
CAVAN
LEITRIM

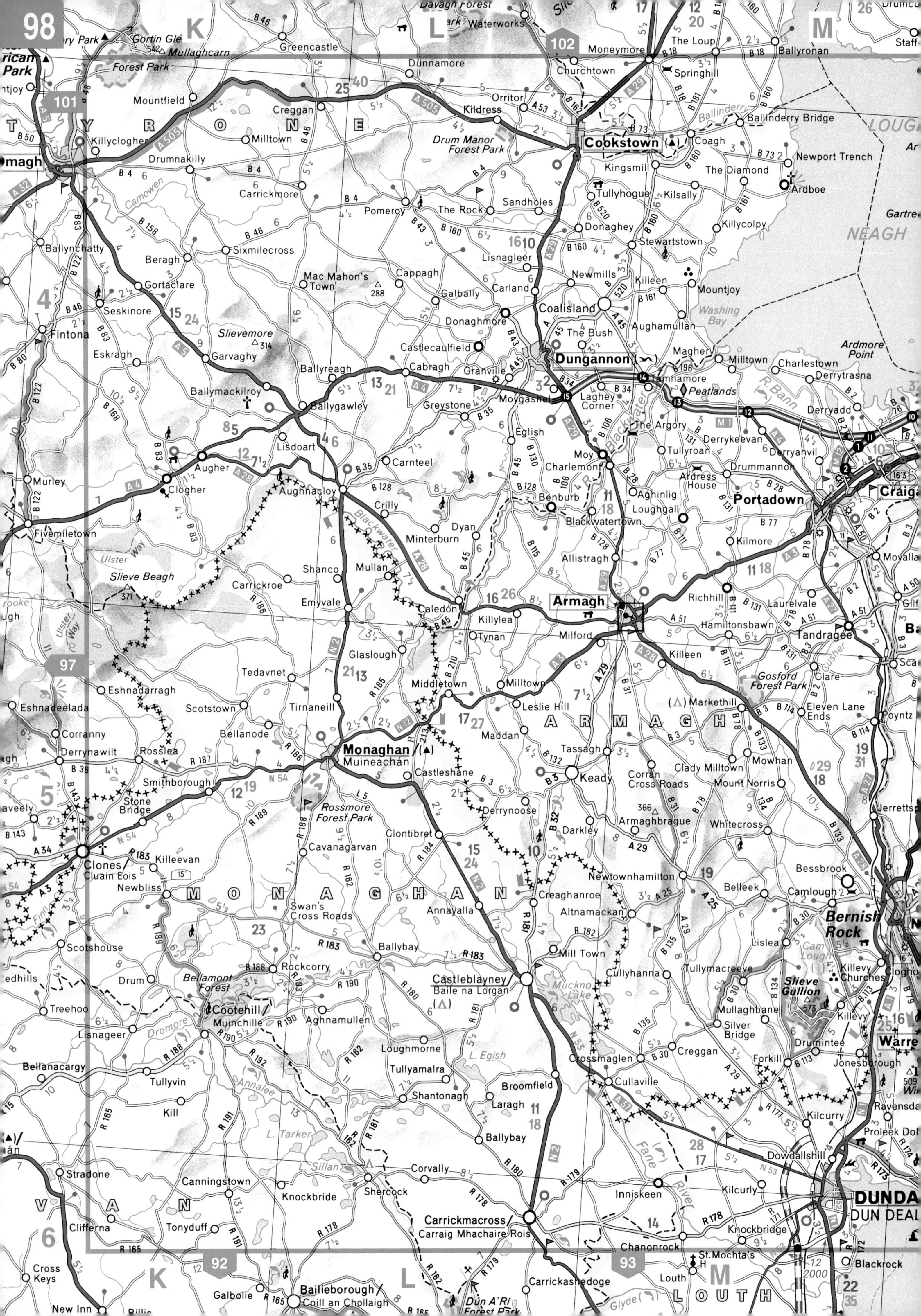
K
L
M
102
101
97
92
93
Greencastle
Gortin Gle
Mullaghcarn
Forest Park
Dunnamore
Waterworks
Moneymore
The Loup
Ballyronan
Churchtown
Springhill
Mountfield
Creggan
Orritor
Kildress
Ballinderry Bridge
TYRONE
Killyclogher
Milltown
Drum Manor Forest Park
Cookstown
Coagh
Newport Trench
Drumnakilly
Kingsmill
The Diamond
Carrickmore
Pomeroy
The Rock
Sandholes
Tullyhogue
Kilsally
Ardboe
Camowen
Donaghey
Killycolpy
Ballynchatty
Sixmilecross
Lisnagleer
Stewartstown
NEAGH
Beragh
Mac Mahon's Town
Cappagh
Newmills
Gortaclare
Galbally
Carland
Killeen
Mountjoy
Seskinore
Slievemore
Donaghmore
Coalisland
Washing Bay
Aughamullan
Fintona
Castlecaulfield
The Bush
Eskragh
Garvaghy
Dungannon
Maghery
Milltown
Charlestown
Ardmore Point
Ballyreagh
Cabragh
Granville
Tamnamore
Derrytrasna
Ballymackilroy
Ballygawley
Greystone
Moygashel
Laghey Corner
Peatlands
R. Bann
Eglish
The Argory
Derryadd
Lisdoart
Carnteel
Moy
Tullyroan
Derrykeevan
Derryanvil
Augher
Charlemont
Ardress House
Drummannon
Murley
Clogher
Aughnacloy
Crilly
Benburb
Aghinlig
Loughgall
Portadown
Craig
Fivemiletown
Blackwatertown
Kilmore
Dyan
Minterburn
Allistragh
Ulster Way
Slieve Beagh
Shanco
Mullan
Carrickroe
Emyvale
Caledon
Armagh
Richhill
Laurelvale
Killylea
Tynan
Milford
Hamiltonsbawn
Tandragee
Glaslough
Killeen
Tedavnet
Gosford Forest Park
Clare
Eshnadarragh
Middletown
Milltown
Eshnadeelada
Scotstown
Tirnaneill
Leslie Hill
Markethill
Eleven Lane Ends
Poyntz
Corranny
ARMAGH
Derrynawilt
Rosslea
Bellanode
Maddan
Monaghan
Muineachán
Tassagh
Clady Milltown
Mowhan
Castleshane
Keady
Corran Cross Roads
Mount Norris
Smithborough
Stone Bridge
Rossmore Forest Park
Derrynoose
Armaghbrague
Whitecross
Jerretts
Clontibret
Darkley
Cavanagarvan
Clones
Cluain Eois
Killeevan
Newtownhamilton
Bessbrook
Newbliss
MONAGHAN
Creaghanroe
Belleek
Camlough
Bernish Rock
Swan's Cross Roads
Annayalla
Altnamackan
Scotshouse
Ballybay
Mill Town
Lislea
Cam Lough
Killevy Churches
Bellamont Forest
Rockcorry
Castleblayney
Baile na Lorgan
Cullyhanna
Tullymacreeve
Slieve Gullion
Drum
Muckno Lake
Treehoo
Cootehill
Muinchille
Aghnamullen
Mullaghbane
Silver Bridge
Killevy
Lisnageer
Dromore
Drumintee
Loughmorne
L. Egish
Crossmaglen
Creggan
Forkill
Jonesborough
Bellanacargy
Tullyamalra
Tullyvin
Annalee
Broomfield
Cullaville
Shantonagh
Laragh
Kill
Kilcurry
Ravensdale
Ballybay
L. Tarker
Proleek Dol
Fane
Dowdallshill
L. Sillan
Corvally
Stradone
Canningstown
Knockbride
Shercock
Inniskeen
Kilcurly
River
DUNDA
DUN DEAL
Carrickmacross
Carraig Mhachaire Rois
Knockbridge
Clifferna
Tonyduff
Chanonrock
St. Mochta's
Cross Keys
Blackrock
Louth
LOUTH
Carrickashedoge
Bailieborough
Coill an Chollaigh
Galbolie
New Inn
Dún A'Rí Forest Park
Glyde

Antrim
Shanes
Templepatrick
Muckamore
Dunadry
Patterson's Spade Mill
Killealy
Lyle
Hyde Park
Loanends
Aldergrove
BELFAST AIRPORT
The Diamond
Nutt's Corner
Crumlin
Squires Hill
Clady
Legoniel
Dundrod
Divis
Glenavy
Rams Island
BELFAST
Hannahstown
Stonyford
Ballymacrevan
Lough Beg
Lower Ballinderry
Upper Ballinderry
Aghalee
Lisburn
Maghaberry
Soldierstown
Magheragall
Moira
R. Lagan
Mazetown
Dunmurry
Lambeg
Drumbeg
Lagan Valley
Ballylesson
Drumbo
Magheralin
Dollingstown
Lurgan
Taughblane
Hillsborough
Waringstown
Kilntown
Donaghcloney
Wells Cross
Clare
Dromore
Blackskull
Lawrencetown
Waringsford
Seapatrick
Banbridge
Corbet Milltown
Loughbrickland
Kilkinamurry
Annaclone
Katesbridge
Ballynaskeagh
Milltown
Moneyslane
Ballyward
Ballyroney
Rathfriland
Barnmeen
Hilltown
Mayobridge
Newry
Narrow Water Castle
Donaghaguy
Warrenpoint
Rostrevor
Omeath
Killowen
Carlingford Mt.
Carlingford
Carlingford Lough
Greencastle
Greenore
Grange
Cranfield Point
Ballagan Point
Giles Quay
The Bush
Whites Town
Rathcor
Cooley Point
Dundalk
Mourne Mountains
Spelga Dam
Shannagh
Slieve Donard
Silent Valley
Ulster Way
Attical
Lisnacree
Ballygowan
Castle
Kilkeel
Ballymartin
Annalong
Mullartown
Glasdrumman
Dunmore
Newcastle
Tollymore Forest Park
Bryansford
Kilcoo
Castlewellan
Castlewellan Forest Park
Annsborough
Lough Island Reavy
Drumena
Cashel
Maghera
Dundrum
Dundrum Bay
Ballykinler
Tyrella
Minerstown
Rossglass
Killough
Ardglass
St. John's Point
Ringfad Point
Lecale Peninsula
Chapeltown
Ballyhornan
Killard Point
Bishops Court
Church Ballee
Kilclief
Ballyquintin Point
Struell Wells
Ballynoe
Clough
Seaforde
Downpatrick
Annadorn
Loughinisland
Legananny Dolmen
Slieve Croob
Massford
Dromara
The Spa
Ballynahinch
Ballykeel
Leitrim
Drumaness
Annacloy
Inch Abbey
Quoile Countryside Centre
Saul
Ballyalton
Castle Ward
Strangford
Portaferry
Audley's Castle
Kearney
Kearney Point
Killyleagh
Delamont
Crossgar
Kilmore
Listooder
Derryboye
Raffrey
Islandmore
Strangford Lough
Killinchy
Balloo Cross Roads
Saintfield
Rowallane Gardens
Baileysmill
Boardmills
The Temple
Annahilt
Carryduff
Ballygowan
Moneyreagh
Newtownbreda
Comber
Lisbane
Ardmillan
Nendrum Monastery
Mahee Island
Castle
Wildfowl and Wetlands Trust
Grey Abbey
Mount Stewart Gardens
Temple of the Winds
Ards Peninsula
Kircubbin
Rubane
Kirkistown
Ardkeen
Ringboy
Cloghy
Cloghy Bay
Portavogie
Glastry
Ballyhalbert
Burr Point
Nuns Quarter
Balligan
Ballywalter
Cardy
Cunningburn
Carrowdore
Ballyferis Point
Newtownards
Scrabo Hill
Dundonald
Stormont Parliament House
Craigantlet
Conlig
Six Road Ends
Ballycopeland
Ballyvester
Millisle
Donaghadee
Copeland Island
Mew Island
Light House Island
Groomsport
Bangor
Crawfordsburn
Helen's Bay
Grey Point
Cultra
Holywood
Craigavad
Belfast Lough
Whitehouse
Whiteabbey
Newtownabbey
Glengormley
Mossley
Monkstown
Greenisland
Carrickfergus
Woodburn
Eden
Milebush
Whitehead
Straid
Doagh
Parkgate
Liverpool
Douglas (I. of Man)
N
O
P
3
4
5

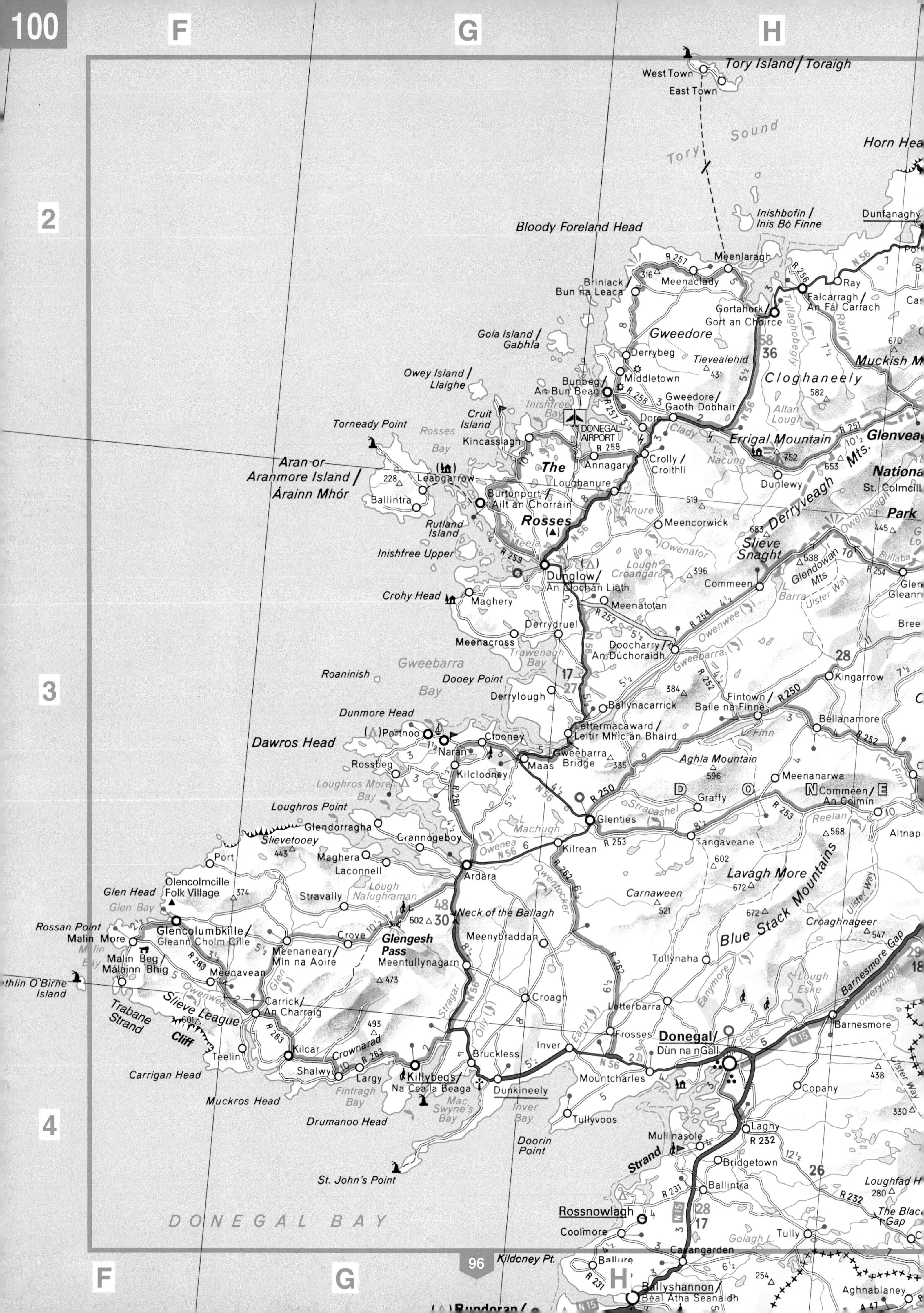
F
G
H
2
3
4
Tory Island / Toraigh
West Town
East Town
Tory Sound
Horn Head
Inishbofin / Inis Bó Finne
Dunfanaghy
Bloody Foreland Head
Meenlaragh
R 257
316
Meenaclady
Brinlack / Bun na Leaca
Ray
Falcarragh / An Fál Carrach
Gortahork / Gort an Choirce
Tullaghobegly
Gweedore
Gola Island / Gabhla
Derrybeg
Tievealehid
431
Middletown
Owey Island / Uaighe
Bunbeg / An Bun Beag
R 258
Gweedore / Gaoth Dobhair
Cloghaneely
582
670
Muckish Mt
Altan Lough
Cruit Island
Inishfree Bay
Torneady Point
Rosses Bay
Kincasslagh
DONEGAL AIRPORT
R 259
Dore
Clady
Crolly / Croithlí
L. Nacung
Errigal Mountain
752
R 251
Glenveagh
Derryveagh Mts.
653
National Park
St. Colmcille
Aran or Aranmore Island / Árainn Mhór
228
Leabgarrow
Ballintra
The Rosses
Annagary
Loughanure
Burtonport / Ailt an Chorráin
Dunlewy
519
Anure
Meencorwick
Rutland Island
Inishfree Upper
Meela
N 56
683
Slieve Snaght
Owenator
445
Lough Croangar
396
538
Glendowan Mts
R 254
Dunglow / An Clochán Liath
Commeen
Barra
Ulster Way
Crohy Head
Maghery
Meenatotan
R 252
Derrydruel
Owenwee
Meenacross
Trawenagh Bay
Doocharry / An Dúchoraidh
Gweebarra
Gweebarra Bay
Roaninish
Dooey Point
17
27
Derrylough
384
28
Kingarrow
Fintown / Baile na Finne
R 250
Ballynacarrick
Dunmore Head
Portnoo
Lettermacaward / Leitir Mhic an Bhaird
Finn
Bellanamore
Dawros Head
Naran
Clooney
Gweebarra Bridge
335
Aghla Mountain
596
Rossbeg
Maas
Kilclooney
Loughros More Bay
R 261
Meenanarwa
Graffy
DONEGAL
Commeen / An Coimín
Loughros Point
Glendorragha
Glenties
Stracashel
R 253
Reelan
568
Altnapaste
Slievetooey
443
Crannogeboy
L. Machugh
Owenea
Kilrean
Tangaveane
Port
Maghera
Laconnell
Ardara
602
Lavagh More
672
Blue Stack Mountains
Glen Head
Olencolmcille Folk Village
374
Glen Bay
Stravally
Lough Nalughraman
R 262
Owentocker
Carnaween
521
Croaghnageer
547
Rossan Point
Malin More
Malin Bay
Glencolumbkille / Gleann Cholm Cille
Crove
Glengesh Pass
502
30
48
Neck of the Ballagh
Meenybraddan
Barnesmore Gap
Malin Beg / Málainn Bhig
R 263
Meenaneary / Mín na Aoire
Meentullynagarn
Tullynaha
Lough Eske
Rathlin O'Birne Island
Meenavean
Glen
473
Stragar
Croagh
Letterbarra
Trabane Strand
Slieve League Cliff
601
Carrick / An Charraig
Owenwee
Eanymore
Barnesmore
Lowerymore
493
Frosses
Donegal / Dún na nGall
Eske
N 15
Teelin
Kilcar
Crownarad
Bruckless
Inver
Eany
Carrigan Head
Shalwy
Largy
Killybegs / Na Cealla Beaga
Dunkineely
Mountcharles
438
Copany
Muckros Head
Fintragh Bay
Mac Swyne's Bay
Inver Bay
Tullyvoos
330
Drumanoo Head
Doorin Point
Mullinasole
Laghy
R 232
Strand
Bridgetown
26
St. John's Point
Ballintra
R 231
Loughfad Hill
280
Rossnowlagh
The Black Gap
DONEGAL BAY
Coolmore
Tully
Golagh L.
96
Kildoney Pt.
Ballure
Cavangarden
254
Ballyshannon / Béal Átha Seanaidh
Aghnablaney
Bundoran

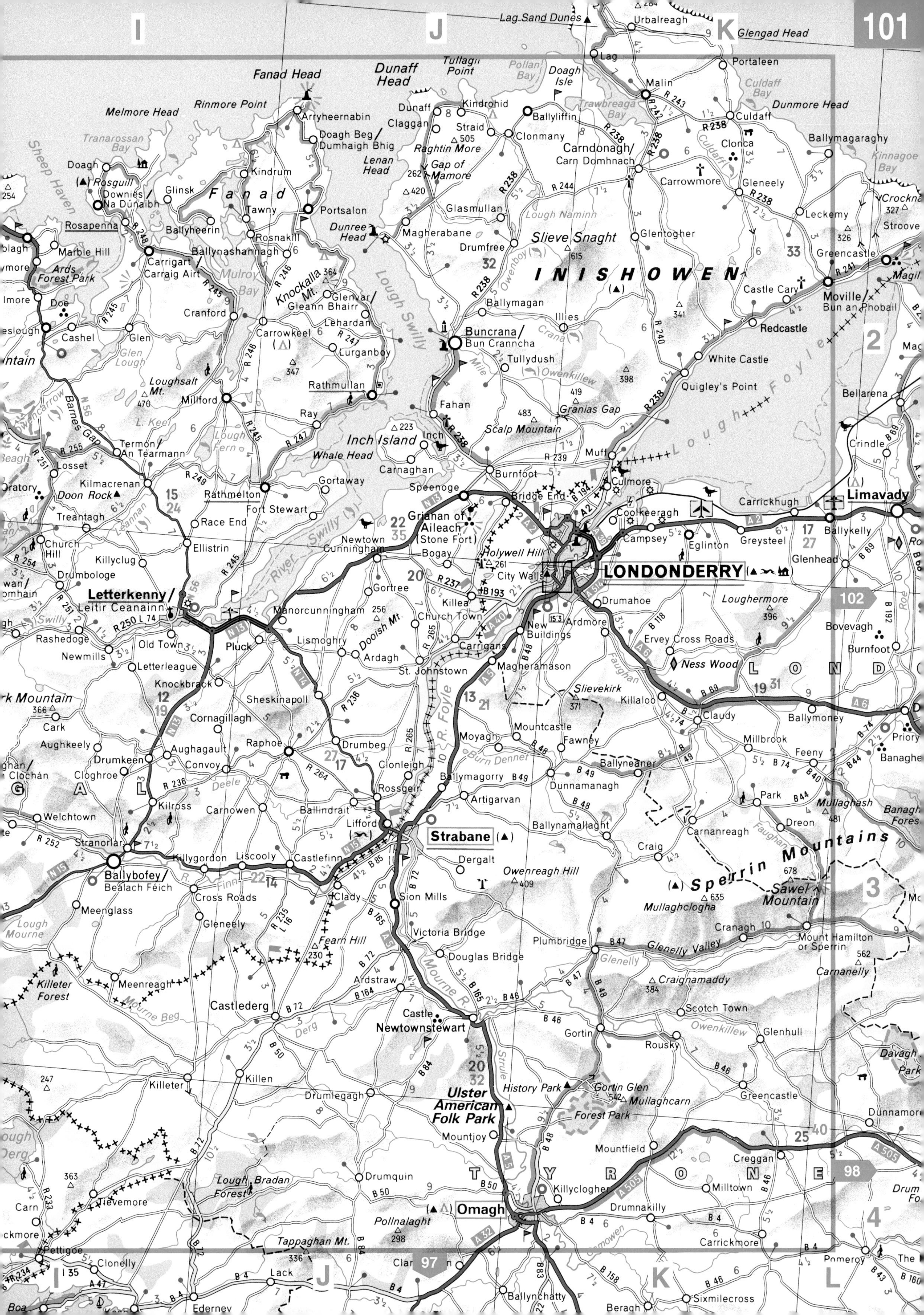

I
J
K
L
2
3
4
102
98
97
Lag Sand Dunes
Urbalreagh
Glengad Head
Lag
Portaleen
Malin
Culdaff Bay
Dunmore Head
Culdaff
Pollan Bay
Doagh Isle
Trawbreaga Bay
Tullagh Point
Dunaff Head
Fanad Head
Melmore Head
Rinmore Point
Arryheernabin
Dunaff
Kindrohid
Claggan
Straid
Ballyliffin
Clonmany
Carndonagh/
Carn Domhnach
Clonca
Ballymagaraghy
Kinnagoe Bay
Tranarossan Bay
Sheep Haven
Doagh
Rosguill
Downies/
Na Dúnaibh
Glinsk
Fanad
Doagh Beg/
Dumhaigh Bhig
Lenan Head
Raghtin More
Gap of Mamore
Carrowmore
Gleneely
Crockna
Leckemy
Stroove
Kindrum
Tawny
Portsalon
Glasmullan
Lough Naminn
Rosapenna
Ballyheerin
Rosnakill
Dunree Head
Magherabane
Slieve Snaght
Glentogher
Greencastle
Ballynashannagh
Drumfree
Marble Hill
Carrigart/
Carraig Airt
Mulroy Bay
Knockalla Mt.
INISHOWEN
Moville/
Bun an Phobail
Ards Forest Park
Glenvar/
Gleann Bhairr
Ballymagan
Illies
Castle Cary
Doe
Cranford
Lehardan
Redcastle
Cashel
Glen
Carrowkeel
Buncrana/
Bun Cranncha
Crana
Glen Lough
Lurganboy
White Castle
Tullydush
Owenkillew
Rathmullan
Quigley's Point
Loughsalt Mt.
Lough Swilly
Fahan
Granias Gap
Lough Foyle
Bellarena
Millford
L. Keel
Lough Fern
Ray
Scalp Mountain
Inch Island
Inch
Barnes Gap
Termon/
An Tearmann
Whale Head
Crindle
Losset
Muff
Carnaghan
Burnfoot
Gortaway
Culmore
Kilmacrenan
Doon Rock
Rathmelton
Speenoge
Bridge End
Limavady
Carrickhugh
Fort Stewart
Coolkeeragh
Treantagh
Race End
Grianan of Aileach
(Stone Fort)
Campsey
Eglinton
Greysteel
Ballykelly
Church Hill
Newtown Cunningham
Ellistrin
Killyclug
River Swilly
Bogay
Holywell Hill
Glenhead
Drumbologe
City Walls
LONDONDERRY
Letterkenny/
Leitir Ceanainn
Gortree
Killea
Drumahoe
Loughermore
Manorcunningham
Church Town
Ardmore
Bovevagh
Rashedoge
Old Town
Pluck
Lismoghry
Dooish Mt.
New Buildings
Erney Cross Roads
Burnfoot
Newmills
Ardagh
Carrigans
Letterleague
St. Johnstown
Magheramason
Ness Wood
LONDONDERRY
Knockbrack
Slievekirk
Killaloo
Mountain
Sheskinapoll
Faughan
Claudy
Ballymoney
Cark
Cornagillagh
Mountcastle
Fawney
Aughkeely
Drumbeg
Millbrook
Priory
Aughagault
Raphoe
Moyagh
Feeny
Banagher
Drumkeen
Convoy
Clonleigh
Burn Dennet
Ballyneaner
Cloghroe
R. Foyle
Ballymagorry
Dunnamanagh
Park
Deele
Rossgeir
Artigarvan
Mullaghash
Welchtown
Kilross
Carnowen
Ballindrait
Banagher Forest
Ballynamallaght
Carnanreagh
Dreon
Lifford
Strabane
Sperrin Mountains
Stranorlar
Craig
Killygordon
Liscooly
Castlefinn
Dergalt
Ballybofey/
Bealach Féich
Finn
Owenreagh Hill
Sperrin
Sawel Mountain
Clady
Sion Mills
Mullaghclogha
Meenglass
Cross Roads
Lough Mourne
Gleneely
Cranagh
Mount Hamilton
or Sperrin
Victoria Bridge
Fearn Hill
Plumbridge
Glenelly Valley
Douglas Bridge
Glenelly
Carnanelly
Killeter Forest
Meenreagh
Ardstraw
Craignamaddy
Mourne Beg
Castlederg
Mourne R.
Scotch Town
Castle
Newtownstewart
Derg
Gortin
Owenkillew
Glenhull
Rousky
Davagh Park
Strule
Killen
Killeter
History Park
Gortin Glen
Ulster American Folk Park
Mullaghcarn
Greencastle
Drumlegagh
Forest Park
Dunnamore
Lough Derg
Mountjoy
Mountfield
Creggan
Lough Bradan Forest
Drumquin
TYRONE
Tievemore
Killyclogher
Milltown
Carn
Omagh
Drumnakilly
Pollnalaght
Camowen
Carrickmore
Tappaghan Mt.
Pettigoe
Clonelly
Pomeroy
Lack
Ballynchatty
Sixmilecross
Beragh
Edernev
Boa

J
K
L
M
1
2
3
Inishtrahull
Inishtrahull Sound
Malin Head
Ballyhillin
Ballygorman
Lag Sand Dunes
Urbalreagh
Glengad Head
Lag
Portaleen
Pollan Bay
Doagh Isle
Malin
Culdaff Bay
Dunmore Head
Trawbreaga Bay
Kindrohid
Ballyliffin
Culdaff
Clonmany
Clonca
Ballymagaraghy
Carndonagh/
Carn Domhnach
Kinnagoe Bay
Carrowmore
Gleneely
Crocknasmug
Inishowen Head
Leckemy
Stroove
Dunagree Pt.
Lough Naminn
Slieve Snaght
Glentogher
Greencastle
Drumfree
I N I S H O W E N
Castle Cary
Moville
Bun an Phobail
Magilligan Pt.
Magilligan Strand
Ballymagan
Illies
Redcastle
Buncrana/
Bun Cranncha
Tullydush
White Castle
Owenkillew
Quigley's Point
Granias Gap
Scalp Mountain
Lough Foyle
Bellarena
Muff
Burnfoot
Culmore
Bridge End
Coolkeeragh
Campsey
Eglinton
Greysteel
Carrickhugh
Limavady
Ballykelly
Glenhead
Roe Valley
Holywell Hill
City Walls
LONDONDERRY
Drumahoe
Loughermore
New Buildings
Ardmore
Ervey Cross Roads
Ness Wood
Carrigans
Magheramason
Slievekirk
Killaloo
Claudy
L O N D O N D E R R Y
Mountcastle
Moyagh
Fawney
Burn Dennet
Ballyneaner
Dunnamanagh
Artigarvan
Ballynamallaght
Carnanreagh
Craig
Dergalt
Owenreagh Hill
Sperrin Mountains
Sawel Mountain
Mullaghclogha
Cranagh
Plumbridge
Glenelly Valley
Mount Hamilton or Sperrin
Carnanelly
Craignamaddy
Scotch Town
Gortin
Rousky
Owenkillew
Glenhull
History Park
Gortin Glen
Mullaghcarn
Forest Park
Greencastle
Dunnamore
Mountfield
Creggan
Kildress
Orritor
Davagh Forest Park
Waterworks
L. Fea
Ballymoney
Millbrook
Feeny
Priory
Banagher
Park
Dreon
Mullaghash
Banagher Forest
Dungiven
Boviel
Glenshane Pass
Carntogher
Mullaghmore
Moneyneany
Ulster Way
Bovevagh
Burnfoot
Drumsurn
Keady Mountain
Cam Forest
Springwell Forest
Stradreagh
Bolea
Crindle
Binevenagh
Magilligan
Downhill
Mussenden Temple
Castlerock
Articlave
Portstewart
Portrush
Ramore Head
The Skerries
Giant's Causeway
Causeway Head
Port Ballintrae
Dunluce Castle
Bushmills
A N T R I M   C O A
Benba
Curryshes
Castle
Lisnagunogu
Coleraine
Macosquin
Castleroe
Cloyfin
Ballyrashane
Liscolman
Ballyloughbe
Derrykeighan
Ballybogy
Dervock
Damhead
Kirkhills
Ballymoney
Crossgare
Ballylintagh
Ringsend
Mullan
Agivey
Balnamore
Milltown
Dunaghy
Bendooragh
Ardreagh
Aghadowey
Boleran
Garryduff
Finvoy
Vow
Garvagh
Moneydig
Mac Laughlins Corner
Rasharkin
Kilrea
Glenvale
Swatragh
Lislea
Aughnacleagh
Tamlaght
Upperlands
Culnady
Clady
Portglenone
Maghera
Lisnamuck
Gulladuff
Tobermore
Knockcloghrim
Draperstown
Curran
Bellaghy
Lough Beg
Newferry
Chesney's Corner
Castledawson
Desertmartin
The Six Towns
Slieve Gallion
Magherafelt
The Creagh
Toome
The Loup
Moneymore
Ballyronan
Churchtown
Springhill
101
98

N
O
P
53
Skeroblingarry
Kilchenzie
Peninver
Machrihanish Bay
Machrihanish
Campbeltown
Island Davaar
Drumlemble
Stewarton
Knocknaha
Beinn Ghuilean
Cnoc Moy
Rubha Dùin Bhàin
Feochaig
Johnston's Point
Conie Glen
S. Carrine
Macharioch
Southend
Mull of Kintyre
Sanda Sound
Sheep Island
Sanda Island
Rathlin Island
Bull Point
Church Quarter
Rathlin Sound
Rue Point
Carrick-a-rede Rope Bridge
White Park Bay
Ballintoy
Benmore or Fair Head
Murlough Bay
Ballycastle Bay
Lagavara
Carnduff
Straid
Ballycastle
Ballinlea
Ballyvoy
Torr Head
Moyarget
Carneatly
Glentaisie
Glenshesk
Ballypatrick Forest
Knocklayd
Runabay Head
Armoy
Crockaneel
Stranocum
Cushendun
Knocknacarry
Glendun
Moyle Way
Ballyhoe Bridge
Glenaan
Ossian's Grave
Cushendall
Red Bay
Kilraghts
Slieveanorra
Loughguile
Glens of Antrim
Glenballyemon
Glenariff or Waterfoot
Garron Point
Trostan
Corkey
Killagan Bridge
Glenariff Forest Park
Waterfalls
Big Trosk
Clogh Mills
Cargan
Newtown-Crommelin
Dungonnell Dam
Collin Top
Carnlough
Carnlough Bay
Clogh
Martinstown
Glenarm
Glencloy
Mac Gregor's Corner
Carnageer
The Sheddings
Feystown
Graigs
Quarrytown
Carnalbanagh Sheddings
Buckna
Broughshane
Slemish Mountain
Ballygalley Head
Carncastle
Ballygalley
Drains Bay
Galgorm
Ballymena
Larne
Gracehill
Agnew's Hill
Millbrook
Isle of Muck
Portmuck
Moorfields
Shoptown
Kilwaughter
Mullaghboy
Kildrum
Kells
Connor
Glynn
Larne Lough
Millbay
Island Magee
Whitesides Corner
Ballyboley Forest
Magheramorne
Waterfall
Glenoe
The Gobbins
Caddy
Gransha
Tardree Forest
Five Corners
Ballyeaston
Ballynure
Ballycarry
Black Head
Ballyclare
Lough Mourne
Antrim
Doagh
Straid
Whitehead
Shanes
Parkgate
Milebush
Templepatrick
Eden
Woodburn
Muckamore
Dunadry
Carrickfergus
Patterson's Spade Mill
Mossley
Monk
Greenisland
Belfast Lough
Light House
Liverpool
Douglas (I. of Man)
Churchtown Pt.
ANTRIM MOUNTAINS
ANTRIM COAST
NORTH CHANNEL
ANTRIM
99

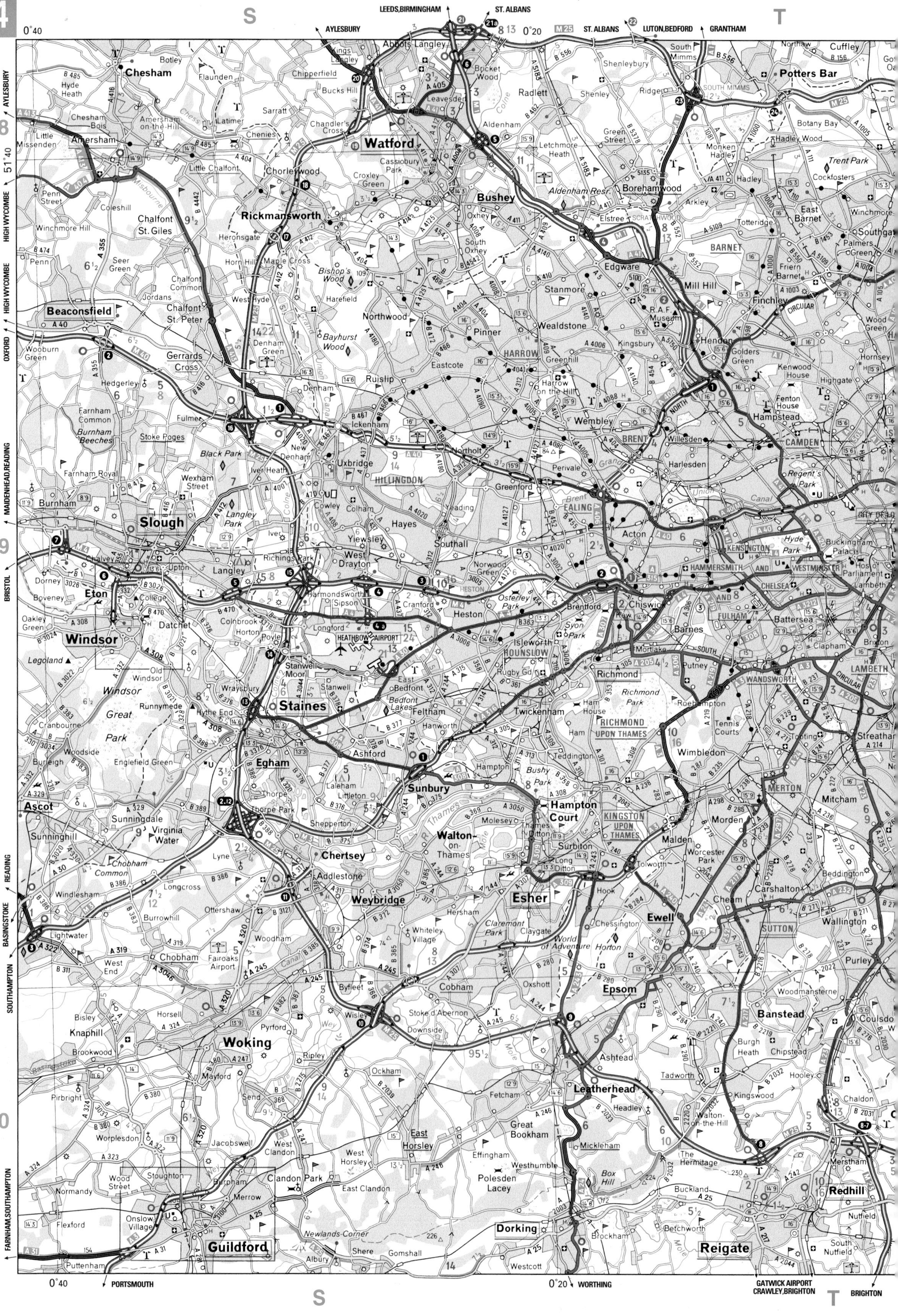
S
T
LEEDS,BIRMINGHAM
ST. ALBANS
AYLESBURY
LUTON,BEDFORD
GRANTHAM
PORTSMOUTH
WORTHING
GATWICK AIRPORT
CRAWLEY,BRIGHTON
BRIGHTON
OXFORD
HIGH WYCOMBE
MAIDENHEAD,READING
BRISTOL
READING
BASINGSTOKE
SOUTHAMPTON
FARNHAM,SOUTHAMPTON
28
29
30
0°40
0°20
51°40
Chesham
Amersham
Beaconsfield
Chalfont St. Giles
Chalfont St. Peter
Gerrards Cross
Rickmansworth
Chorleywood
Watford
Abbots Langley
Kings Langley
Bushey
Radlett
Shenley
South Mimms
Potters Bar
Borehamwood
Edgware
Stanmore
Barnet
East Barnet
Mill Hill
Finchley
Hendon
Harrow
Pinner
Northwood
Ruislip
Eastcote
Wembley
Uxbridge
Hillingdon
Denham
Slough
Eton
Windsor
Datchet
Langley
Iver
West Drayton
Hayes
Southall
Northolt
Greenford
Ealing
Acton
Brent
Camden
Hampstead
Willesden
Harlesden
Kensington
Hammersmith
Chiswick
Fulham
Chelsea
Westminster
Battersea
Barnes
Putney
Wandsworth
Lambeth
Clapham
Brixton
Streatham
Tooting
Wimbledon
Merton
Mitcham
Morden
Richmond
Richmond Park
Twickenham
Hounslow
Isleworth
Brentford
Heston
Heathrow Airport
Staines
Egham
Ashford
Feltham
Sunbury
Hampton Court
Kingston upon Thames
Surbiton
Malden
Walton-on-Thames
Weybridge
Chertsey
Esher
Ewell
Epsom
Sutton
Carshalton
Wallington
Purley
Banstead
Cobham
Leatherhead
Ashtead
Woking
Chobham
Ascot
Sunningdale
Virginia Water
Windsor Great Park
Legoland
Runnymede
Guildford
Dorking
Reigate
Redhill
Burnham
Farnham Common
Burnham Beeches
Stoke Poges
Black Park
Wraysbury
Bayhurst Wood
Bishop's Wood
Aldenham Resr.
Regent's Park
Hyde Park
Buckingham Palace
Houses of Parliament
Osterley Park
Syon Park
Bushy Park
Claremont Park
World of Adventure
Box Hill
Polesden Lacey
Great Bookham
Effingham
East Horsley
West Horsley
West Clandon
East Clandon
Ripley
Ockham
Send
Mayford
Knaphill
Pirbright
Worplesdon
Jacobswell
Merrow
Shere
Gomshall
Albury
Newlands Corner
Puttenham
Flexford
Normandy
Westcott
Brockham
Betchworth
Buckland
Merstham
Kingswood
Tadworth
Walton-on-the-Hill
Chipstead
Nutfield
Mickleham
Headley
Fetcham
Oxshott
Claygate
Chessington
Hook
Byfleet
Wisley
Pyrford
Addlestone
Ottershaw
Lyne
Thorpe
Laleham
Shepperton
Hersham
Whiteley Village
Fairoaks Airport
Bisley
Horsell
Brookwood
West End
Lightwater
Windlesham
Chobham Common
Longcross
Englefield Green
Old Windsor
Sunninghill
Woodside
Cranbourne
Dorney
Boveney
Oakley Green
Colnbrook
Poyle
Harmondsworth
Sipson
Cranford
Longford
Stanwell
Stanwell Moor
East Bedfont
Bedfont Lakes
Hanworth
Hampton
Teddington
Ham
Ham House
Roehampton
Mortlake
Kew
Worcester Park
Tolworth
Long Ditton
Thames Ditton
Molesey
Ickenham
Cowley
Yiewsley
Yeading
Perivale
Norwood Green
Kingsbury
Wealdstone
Greenhill
Harrow on the Hill
R.A.F. Museum
Golders Green
Kenwood House
Fenton House
Highgate
Hornsey
Wood Green
Southgate
Palmers Green
Winchmore Hill
Cockfosters
Hadley Wood
Hadley
Monken Hadley
Arkley
Elstree
Aldenham
Letchmore Heath
Shenleybury
Ridge
Botany Bay
Trent Park
Cuffley
Northaw
Cassiobury Park
Croxley Green
Leavesden
Bricket Wood
Oxhey
South Oxhey
Harefield
Heronsgate
Maple Cross
Sarratt
Chenies
Latimer
Flaunden
Botley
Hyde Heath
Chesham Bois
Little Missenden
Penn Street
Penn
Coleshill
Seer Green
Jordans
Chalfont Common
Little Chalfont
Wooburn Green
Hedgerley
Fulmer
Wexham Street
Farnham Royal
Iver Heath
New Denham
Denham Green
Chandler's Cross
Bucks Hill
Chipperfield
Upton
Chalvey
Thames
M25
M4
M40
M3
M1
A1
A40
A41
A3
A30
A316
A308
A23
A24
A25

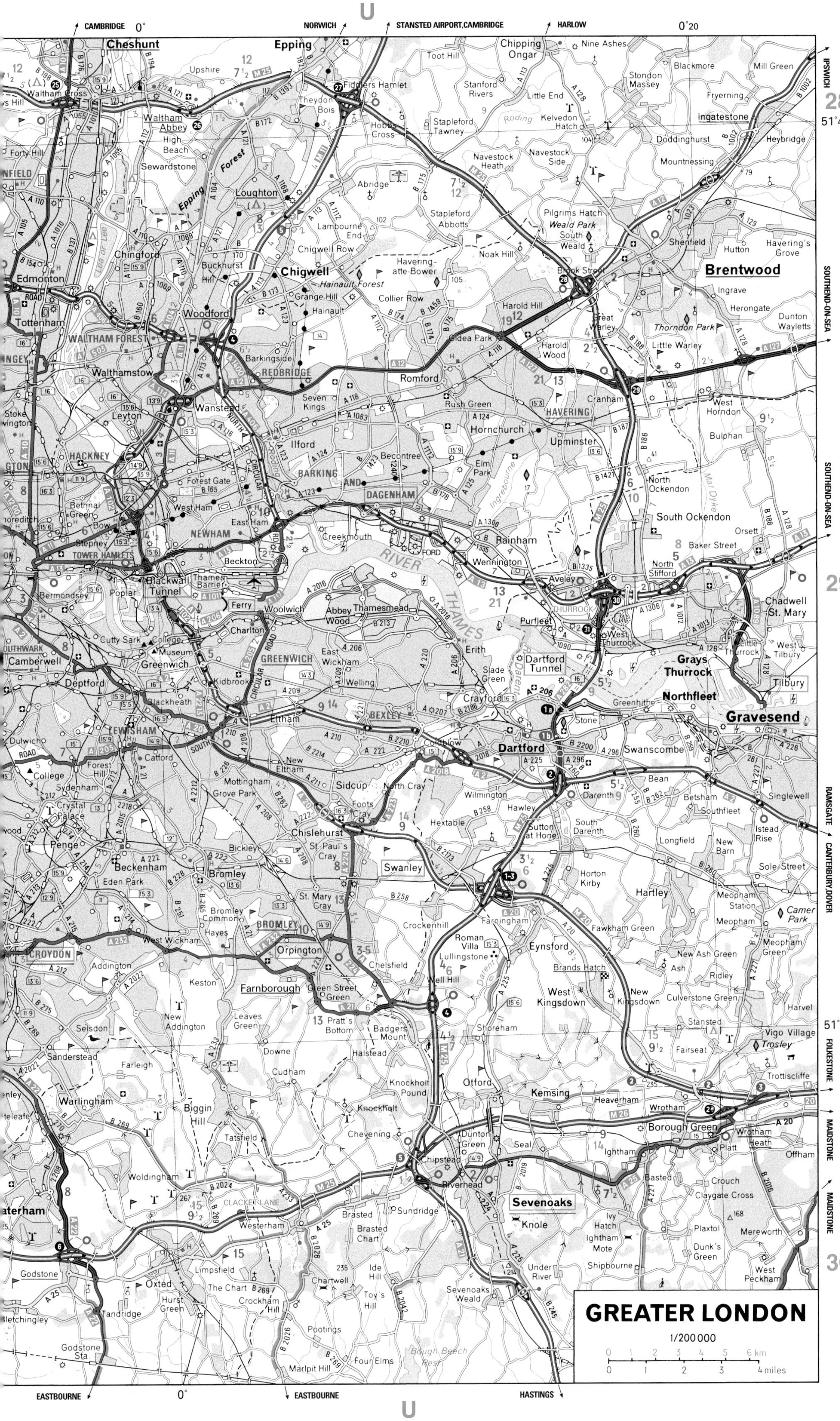

LAMBETH Borough

Underground station

Greater London Boroughs

Barking and Dagenham	105	U 29
Barnet	104	T 29
Bexley	105	U 29
Brent	104	T 29
Bromley	105	U 29
Camden	104	T 29
City of London	104	T 29
Croydon	104	T 29
Ealing	104	T 29
Enfield	104	T 29
Greenwich	105	U 29
Hackney	105	T 29
Hammersmith and Fulham	104	T 29
Haringey	104	T 29
Harrow	104	S 29
Havering	105	U 29
Hillingdon	104	S 29
Hounslow	104	S 29
Islington	104	T 29
Kensington and Chelsea	104	T 29
Kingston-upon-Thames	104	T 29
Lambeth	104	T 29
Lewisham	105	T 29
Merton	104	T 29
Newham	105	U 29
Redbridge	105	U 29
Richmond-upon-Thames	104	T 29
Southwark	104	T 29
Sutton	104	T 29
Tower Hamlets	105	T 29
Waltham Forest	105	T 29
Wandsworth	104	T 29
Westminster	104	T 29

Eochair — Allwedd

Eochair	Allwedd
Bóithre	**Ffyrdd**
Mótarbhealach agus ionaid seirbhíse	Traffordd a mannau gwasanaethu
Acomhail mótarbhealaigh : iomlán -teoranta	Cyfnewidfeyd : wedi'i chwblhau - cyfyngedig
Vimhreacha ceangail	Rhifau'r cyffyrdd
Carrbhealach dúbailte le saintréithe mótarbhealaigh	Ffordd ddeuol â nodweddion traffordd
Mórbhóthar :	Prif ffordd gysylltu :
carrshlí dhéach	ffordd ddeuol
4 lána - 2 leathanlána	4 lôn - 2 lôn lydan
2 lána - 2 chungléna	2 lôn - 2 lôn gul
Líonra réigiúnach bóithre :	Rhydwaith ffyrdd rhanbarthol :
carrshlí dhéach - 2 leathanlána	ffordd ddeuol - 2 lôn lydan
2 lána - 2 chungléna	2 lôn - 2 lôn gul
Bóithre eile : réidh - gan réitiú	Ffyrdd eraill : â wyneb - heb wyneb
Mótarbhealach, bóthar á dhéanamh (an dáta oscailte sceidealta, mas eol)	Traffordd, ffordd yn cael ei hadeiladu (Os cyfodi yr achos : dyddiad agor disgwyliedig)
Cosán - Cosán fadsli	Llwybr troed - Llwybr hir neu lwybr ceffyl
Timpeall - Bearnas is a airde (i méadair)	Cylchfan - Bwlch a'i uchder (mewn metrau)
Faid ar mhótarshlíte, ar bóithre : i mílte - i méadair	Pellter ar ffyrdd a thraffyrdd mewn miltiroedd - mewn kilometrau
Aicmiú oifigiúil bóithre	**Dosbarthiad ffyrdd swyddogol**
Mótarshlí	Traffordd
GB: Priomhbhealach	GB: Prif ffordd
IRL: Priomhbhóithre agus fobhóithre náisiúnta	IRL: Prif ffordd genedlaethol a ffordd eilradd
Bóithre eile	Ffyrdd eraill
Ceann scríbe ar ghréasán bóithre priomha	Cyrchfan ar rwydwaith y prif ffrydd
Constaicí	**Rhwystrau**
Bóthar cúng le hionaid phasála (in Albain)	Yn yr Alban : ffordd gul â mannau pasio
Bóthar : toirmeasctha - faoi theorannú	Ffordd : gwaharddedig - cyfyngiadau arni
Bacainn dola - Bóthar aonsli	Rhwystr Toll - Unffordd
IRL: Bealach deacair nó baolach	IRL: Darn anodd neu beryglus o ffordd
Ar phríomhbhóithre agus ar bhóithre réigiúnacha :	Ar brif ffyrdd a ffyrdd rhanbarthol :
Teorainneacha airde (faoi 15'6" IRL, faoi 16'6" GB)	Terfyn uchder (llai na 15'6" IRL, 16'6" GB)
Teorann Mheáchain (faoi 16 t)	Terfyn pwysau (llai na 16t)
Grádán (suas treo an gha)	Graddiant (esgyn gyda'r saeth)
Iompar	**Cludiant**
Leithead caighdeánach - Staisiún paisinéirí	Lled safonol - Gorsaf deithwyr
Larnród thraein ghaile - Ráille tionsclaíoch	Rheilffordd ager - Trac diwydiannol
Crosaire comhréidh, iarnród ag dul	Croesfan rheilffordd :
faoi bhóthar, os cionn bóthair	rheilffordd yn croesi ffordd, o dan ffordd
Cáblashlí thionsclaíoch - Cathaoir cábla	Lein gêbl ddiwydiannol - Cadair esgyn
Longsheirbhísí (seirbhísí séasúracha : dearg)	Llongau ceir (Gwasanaethau tymhorol : mewn coch)
Bád - Árthach foluaineach	llong -llong hofran
Fartha (uas-ulach : tonnaí méadracha)	Fferi (llwyth uchaf : mewn tunelli metrig)
Coisithe agus lucht rothar	Teithwyr ar droed neu feic yn unig
Aerfort - Aerpháirc	Maes awyr - Maes glanio
Bailte - Riarachán	**Trefi - Gweinyddiaeth**
Áiteanna a bhfuil plean diobh in Eolaí Michelin	Tref sydd â chynllun yn y Guide Michelin
Eolaí Dearg óstaíochta	Coch - Gwestai a Thai Bwyta
Eolaí Uaine turasóirachta	Gwyrrd - I Dwristiaid
Ionaid óstáiochta roghnaithe d'Eolaí Dearg Michelin	Tref sydd â chyfeiriadou yn y Michelin Red Guide
Teorainn Rialtais Áitúil	Llywodraeth Leol
Teorainn na hAlban agus teorainn na Breataine Bige	Ffin Cymru, ffin yr Alban
Teorainn idirnáisiúnta - Custam	Ffin ryngwladol - Tollau
Comharthaí Eile	**Symbolau eraill**
Crann teileachumarsáide - Teach Solais	Mast telathrebu - Goleudy
Stáisiún Giniúna - Cairéal - Mianach	Gorsaf bŵer - Chwarel - Mwyngloddio
Monarcha - Scaglann	Ffatri - Purfa
Ráschúrsa - Láthair champa, láthair charbhán	Rasio Ceffylau - Leoedd i wersylla
Timpeall rásaíochta - Cuan bád aeraíochta	Rasio Cerbydau - Harbwr cychod pleser
Machaire Gaiff - Páirc Fhoraoise Náisiúnta, Páirc Náisiúnta	Cwrs golf - Parc Coedwig Cenedlaethol, Parc Cenedlaethol
IRL: Iascaireacht - Brú chumann na hóige - Ráschúrsa con	IRL: Pysgota - Hostel ieuenctid - Maes rasio milgwn
Siúlóid fhoraoise - Páirc thuaithe - Aill	Llwybr coedwig - Parc gwledig - Clogwyn
Amhairc : *féach Eolaithe Michelin*	**Golygfeydd** : *gweler Llyfr Michelin*
Bailte nó áiteanna inspéise, baill lóistín	Trefi new fannau o ddiddordeb, mannau i aros
Foirgneamh Eaglasta - Fothrach	Adeilag eglwysig - Adfeilion
Caisleán, teach stairiúil	Castell, tŷ hanesyddol
Leacht meigiliteach - Pluais	Heneb fegalithig - Ogof
IRL: Dunfort - Cros Cheilteach - Cloigtheach	IRL: Caer - Croes Geltaidd - Tŵr crwn
Zú - Caomhnú nádúir, tearmannéan mara	Parc saffari, sŵ - Gwarchodfa natur
Gáirdíní - Amhairc éagsúla	Gerddi, parc - Golygfeydd amrywiol
Lánléargas - Cothrom Radhairc	Panorama - Golygfan
Bealach Aoibhinn	Ffordd dygfeydd

Comnarthaí ar phleanna bailte

Bóithre

- Mótarbhealach, carrbhealach dúbailte le saintréithe mótarbhealaigh
- Priomh-thrébhealach
- Bóthar aonslí - Sráid : coisithe
- Sráid : neamhoiriúnach do thrácht, ach í stáit speisialta
- Piccadilly — Sráid siopadóireacha - Carrchlós
- Bád fartha feithiclí - Droichead starrmhaidi

Ionaid inspéise
(Féach Eolaí Dearg Michelin)

- Ionad inspéise agus an príomhbhealach isteach
- Ionad inspéise adhartha
- B — Ionad inspéise curtha in iúl le litir thagartha

Comharthaí Éagsúla

- Ionad eolais turasóireachta - Ospidéal
- Ardeaglais - Eaglais - Reilig
- Gairdín, páirc, coill - Staidiam
- Galfchúrsa
- Galfchúrsa (sainrialacha do chuairteoiri)
- Foirgneamh poiblí curtha in iúl le litir thagartha :
- C, H — Oifigí rialtais áitiúil - Halla baile
- POL, M — Póitíní (ceanncheathrú) - Músaem
- T, U — Amharclann - Ollscoil, Coláiste
- Príomhoifig phoist le poste restante, teileafón
- Stáisiún traenach faoi thalamh

Londain

- BRENT, SOHO — Buirg - Limistéar
- Teorainn bhuirge - Teorainn limistéir

Symbolau ar gynlluniau'r trefi

Ffyrdd

- Traffordd, ffordd ddeuol
- Prif ffordd drwodd
- Unffordd - Stryd : Cerddwr
- Stryd : Anaddas i draffig, cyfyngedig
- Piccadilly — Stryd siopa - Parc ceir
- Fferi geir - Pont liferi

Golygfeydd
(Gweler Llyfr Coch Michelin)

- Man diddorol a'r brif fynedfa iddo
- Lle diddorol o addoliad
- B — Llythyren gyfeirio sy'n dynodi golygfa

Arwyddion amrywiol

- Canolfan croeso - Ysbyty
- Eglwys Gadeiriol - Eglwys - Mynwent
- Gardd, parc, coedwig - Stadiwm
- Cwrs golff
- Cwrs golff (â chyfyngiadau i ymwelwyr)
- Adeilad cyhoeddus a ddynodir gan lythyren :
- C, H — Swyddfeydd llywodraeth leol - Neuadd y Dref
- POL, M — Yr Heddlu (pencadlys) - Amgueddfa
- T, U — Theatr - Prifysgol, Coleg
- Prif swyddfa bost gyda poste restante, ffôn
- Gorsaf danddaearol

Llundain

- BRENT, SOHO — Bwrdeistref - Ardal
- Ffin Bwrdeistref - Ffin yr Ardal

TOWN PLANS

Roads

Motorway - Dual carriageway with motorway characteristics
Main traffic artery
One - way street
Unsuitable for traffic, access subject to restrictions
Pedestrian street
Piccadilly Shopping street - Car park
Lever bridge - Car ferry

Sights

(See Michelin Red Guide)
Place of interest and its main entrance
Interesting place of worship
B Reference letter locating a sight

Various signs

Tourist Information Centre - Hospital
Cathedral - Church - Cemetery
Garden, park, wood - Stadium
Golf course
Golf course (with restrictions for visitors)
Public buildings located by letter :
C H County Council Offices - Town Hall
M T U Museum - Theatre - University, College
POL. Police (in large towns police headquarters)
Main post office with poste restante, telephone
Underground station

London

BRENT Borough
WEMBLEY Area
Borough boundary - Area boundary

LES PLANS

Voirie

Autoroute - Route à chaussées séparées de type autoroutier
Grand axe de circulation
Sens unique
Rue impraticable, réglementée
Rue piétonne
Piccadilly Rue commerçante - Parking
Pont mobile - Bac pour autos

Curiosités

(voir le Guide Rouge Michelin)
Bâtiment intéressant et entrée principale
Édifice religieux intéressant
B Lettre identifiant une curiosité

Signes divers

Information touristique - Hôpital
Cathédrale - Église - Cimetière
Jardin, parc, bois - Stade
Golf
Golf (réservé)
Bâtiment public repéré par une lettre :
C H Bureau de l'Administration du Comté - Hôtel de ville
M T U Musée - Théâtre - Université, grande école
POL. Police (commissariat central)
Bureau principal de poste restante, téléphone
Station de métro

Londres

BRENT Nom: d'arrondissement (borough)
WEMBLEY de quartier (area)
Limite de " borough" - d'" area "

STADTPLÄNE

Straßen

Autobahn - Schnellstraße mit getrennten Fahrbahnen
Hauptverkehrsstraße
Einbahnstraße
Gesperrte Straße, mit Verkehrsbeschränkungen
Fußgängerzone
Piccadilly Einkaufsstraße - Parkplatz
Bewegliche Brücke - Autofähre

Sehenswürdigkeiten

(siehe Roter Michelin - Hotelführer)
Sehenswertes Gebäude mit Haupteingang
Sehenswerter Sakralbau
B Referenzbuchstabe für eine Sehenswürdigkeit

Sonstige Zeichen

Informationsstelle - Krankenhaus
Kathedrale - Kirche - Friedhof
Garten, Park, Wäldchen - Stadion
Golfplatz
Golfplatz (Zutritt bedingt erlaubt)
Öffentliches Gebäude, durch einen Buchstaben gekennzeichnet :
C H Sitz der Grafschaftsverwaltung - Rathaus
M T U Museum - Theater - Universität, Hochschule
POL. Polizei (in größeren Städten Polizeipräsidium)
Hauptpostamt (potlagernde Sendungen), Telefon
U-Bahnstation

London

BRENT Name: des Verwaltungsbezirks (borough)
WEMBLEY des Stadtteils (area)
Grenze des "borough" - des "area"

PLATTEGRONDEN

Wegen

Autosnelweg - Weg met gescheiden rijbanen van het type autosnelweg
Hoofdverkeersweg
Eenrichtingsverkeer
Onbegaanbare straat, beperkt toegankelijk
Voetgangersgebied
Piccadilly Winkelstraat - Parkeerplaats
Beweegbare brug - Auto-veerpont

Bezienswaardigheden

(Zie die Rode Michelingids)
Interessant gebouw met hoofdingang
Interessant kerkelijk gebouw
B Letter die een bezienswaardigheid aangeeft

Overige tekens

Informatie voor toeristen - Ziekenhuis
Kathedraal,kerk - Begraafplaats
Tuin, park, bos - Stadion
Golfterrein
Golfterrein (beperkt toegankelijk voor bezoekers)
Openbaar gebouw, aangegeven met een letter :
C H Administratiekantoor van het graafschap - Stadhuis
M T U Museum - Schouwburg - Universiteit, hogeschool
POL. Politie (in grote steden, hoofdbureau)
Hoofdkantoor voor poste-restante, Telefoon
Metrostation

Londen

BRENT Naam: van het arrondissement (borough)
WEMBLEY van de wijk (area)
Grens van de "borough" - van de "area"

LE PIANTE

Viabilità

Autostrada - Strada a carriagate separate di tipo autostradale
Asse principale di circolazione
Senso unico
Via impraticabile, a circolazione regolamentata
Via pedonale
Piccadilly Via commerciale - Parcheggio
Ponte mobile - Traghetto per auto

Curiosità

(Vedere la Guida Rossa Michelin)
Edificio interessante ed entrata principale
Costruzione religiosa interessante
B Lettera identificante una meta o luogo d'interesse

Simboli vari

Ufficio informazioni turistiche
Cattedrale - Chiesa - Cimitero
Giardino, parco, bosco - Stadio
Golf
Golf riservato
Edificio pubblico indicato con lettera :
C H Sede dell'Amministrazione di Contea - Municipio
M T U Museo - Teatro - Università, grande scuola
POL. Polizia (Questura, nelle grandi città)
Ufficio centrale di fermo posta, telefono
Stazione della Metropolitana

Londra

BRENT Nome: del distretto amministrativo (borough)
WEMBLEY del quatiere (area)
Limite del "borough" - di "area"

PLÀNOS

Vías de circulación

Autopista - Autovía
Vía importante de circulacíon
Sentido único
Calle impraticable, de uso restringido
Calle peatonal
Piccadilly Calle comercial - Aparcamiento
Puente móvil - Barcaza para coches

Curiosidades

(Ver Guía Roja Michelin)
Edificio interesante y entrada principal
Edificio religioso interesante
B Letra que identifica una curiosidad

Signos diversos

Oficina de información de Turismo - Hospital
Catedral - Iglesia - Cementerio
Jardín, parque, bosque - Estadio
Golf
Golf (sólo para socios)
Edificio público localizado con letra :
C H Oficina de Administración del Condado - Ayuntamiento
M T U Museo - Teatro - Universidad, Escuela Superior
POL. Policía (en las grandes ciudades : Jefatura)
Oficina central de lista de correos - Teléfonos
Boca de metro

Londres

BRENT Nombre: del distrito (borough)
WEMBLEY del barrio (area)
Limite del "borough" - del "area"

Great Britain

A

Abbas Combe 8 M 30
Abberley 26 M 27
Abbey 13 X 30
Abbey Dore 17 L 28
Abbey Town 44 K 19
Abbeydale 35 P 23
Abbeystead 38 L 22
Abbots Bromley 35 O 25
Abbots Langley 20 S 28
Abbotsbury 8 M 32
Abbotsford House 50 L 17
Abbotskerswell 4 J 32
Aberaeron 24 H 27
Aberaman 16 J 28
Aberangell 25 I 25
Abercarn 16 K 29
Aberchirder 69 M 11
Abercynon 16 J 29
Aberdare / Aberdâr 16 J 28
Aberdaron 32 F 25
Aberdaugleddau / Milford Haven 14 E 28
Aberdeen 69 N 12
Aberdour 56 K 15
Aberdour Bay 69 N 10
Aberdovey / Aberdyfi 24 H 26
Abereiddy 14 E 28
Aberfeldy 61 I 14
Aberffraw 32 G 24
Aberford 40 P 22
Aberfoyle 55 G 15
Abergavenny / Y-Fenni 16 K 28
Abergele 33 J 24
Abergwaun / Fishguard 14 F 28
Abergwesyn 25 I 27
Abergwyngregyn 32 H 24
Abergynolwyn 25 I 26
Aberhonddu / Brecon 16 J 28
Aberlady 56 L 15
Aberlemno 63 L 13
Aberlour 68 K 11
Abermaw / Barmouth 24 H 25
Abernethy 56 K 15
Aberpennar / Mountain Ash 16 J 28
Aberporth 24 G 27
Abersoch 32 G 25
Abersychan 16 K 28
Abertawe / Swansea 15 I 29
Aberteifi / Cardigan 24 G 27
Abertillery 16 K 28
Aberuthven 56 J 15
Aberystwyth 24 H 26
Abingdon 19 Q 28
Abinger Common 11 S 30
Abington (South Lanarkshire) 49 I 17
Abington (Cambs.) 22 U 27
Aboyne 63 L 12
Abridge 20 U 29
Accrington 39 M 22
Achallader 60 F 14
Achanalt 66 F 11
Achaphubuil 60 E 13
Acharn 61 H 14
Achiltibuie 72 D 9
Achmelvich 72 E 9
Achmore 66 D 11
Achnasheen 66 E 11
Achnashellach Forest 66 E 11
Achray (Loch) 55 G 15
Achriesgill 72 F 8
Acklington 51 P 18
Ackworth 40 P 23
Acle 31 Y 26
Acomb 51 N 19
Acrise Place 13 X 30
Acton Turville 17 N 29
Adderbury 19 Q 27
Addingham 39 O 22
Addlestone 19 S 29
Adlington 38 M 23
Adlington Hall 35 N 24
Advie 68 J 11
Adwick-le-Street 40 Q 23
Ae (Forest of) 49 J 18
Affric (Glen) 66 F 12
Afon Dyfrdwy / Dee (River) 33 K 24
Ailort (Loch) 59 C 13
Ailsa Craig 42 E 18
Ainort (Loch) 65 B 12
Ainsdale 38 K 23
Ainwick 51 O 17
Aird (The) 67 G 11
Airdrie 55 I 16
Airigh na h-Airde (Loch) 70 Z 9
Airth 55 I 15
A La Ronde 4 J 32
Albourne 11 T 31
Albrighton 26 N 26
Albyn or Mor (Glen) 61 F 12
Alcester 27 O 27
Alconbury 29 T 26
Aldbourne 18 P 29
Aldbrough 41 T 22
Aldbury 19 S 28
Alde (River) 23 Y 27
Aldeburgh 23 Y 27
Aldenham 20 S 28
Alderley Edge 34 N 24
Alderney (Channel I.) 5
Aldershot 10 R 30
Aldridge 27 O 26
Aldringham 23 Y 27
Aldwick 10 R 31
Alexandria 55 G 16
Alfold Crossways 10 S 30
Alford (Aberdeenshire) 69 L 12
Alford (Lincs.) 37 U 24
Alfreton 35 P 24
Alfrick 26 M 27
Alfriston 11 U 31
Aline (Loch) 59 C 14
Alkborough 41 S 22
Alkham 13 X 30
Allendale Town 45 N 19
Allerston 41 S 21
Alligin Shuas 66 D 11
Alloa 55 I 15
Alloway 48 G 17
All Stretton 26 L 26
Alltan Fhèarna (Loch an) 73 H 9
Almond (Glen) 61 I 14
Almondbank 62 J 14
Almondsbury 17 M 29
Alness 67 H 10
Alnmouth 51 P 17
Alnwick 51 O 17
Alpheton 22 W 27
Alphington 7 J 31
Alpraham 34 M 24
Alrewas 27 O 25
Alsager 34 N 24
Alsh (Loch) 66 D 12
Alston 45 M 19
Alswear 7 I 31
Altarnun 3 G 32
Altnacealgach 72 F 9
Altnaharra 72 G 9
Alton (Hants.) 10 R 30
Alton (Staffs.) 35 O 25
Alton Towers 35 O 25
Altrincham 34 M 23
Alum Bay 9 P 31
Alva 55 I 15
Alvechurch 27 O 26
Alvediston 9 N 30
Alves 68 J 11
Alvie 67 I 12
Alyth 62 K 14
Amberley 10 S 31
Amble 51 P 18
Amblecote 27 N 26
Ambleside 44 L 20
Amersham 19 S 29
Amesbury 9 O 30
Amlwch 32 G 23
Ammanford / Rhydaman 15 I 28
Ampleforth 40 Q 21
Ampthill 28 S 27
Amroth 14 G 28
An Riabhachan 66 E 11
An Socach 62 J 13
An Teallach 66 E 10
Ancroft 51 O 16
Andover 9 P 30
Andoversford 18 O 28
Andreas 42 G 20
Angle 14 E 28
Anglesey (Isle of) 32 F 24
Anglesey Abbey 22 U 27
Angmering 11 S 31
Annan 49 K 19
Annan (River) 49 J 17
Annat 66 D 11
Annat Bay 72 E 10
Annbank Station 48 G 17
Anne Hathaway's Cottage 27 O 27
Annfield Plain 46 O 19
Anstey 28 Q 25
Anston 36 Q 23
Anstruther 57 L 15
Antony House 3 H 32
Appin 60 E 14
Appleby 45 M 20
Appleby Magna 27 P 25
Appledore (Devon) 6 H 30
Appledore (Kent) 12 W 30
Appleford 19 Q 29
Aran Fawddwy 33 I 25
Arber Low 35 O 24
Arberth / Narberth 14 F 28
Arbirlot 63 M 14
Arbroath 63 M 14
Arbury Hall 27 P 26
Archiestown 68 K 11
Ard (Loch) 55 G 15
Ardarroch 66 D 11
Ardcharnich 66 E 10
Ardechive 60 E 13
Ardeonaig 61 H 14
Ardersier 67 H 11
Ardfern 54 D 15
Ardgay 73 G 10
Ardgour 60 D 13
Ardingly 11 T 30
Ardivachar 64 X 11
Ardleigh 22 W 28
Ardlui 54 F 15
Ardlussa 52 C 15
Ardmore Point 65 A 11
Ardnamurchan 59 B 13
Ardnave Point 52 B 16
Ardrishaig 54 D 15
Ardrossan 48 F 17
Ardvasar 65 C 12
Ardverikie Forest 61 G 13
Argyll 54 D 15
Argyll Forest Park 54 F 15
Arienas (Loch) 59 C 14
Arinagour 59 A 14
Arisaig 59 C 13
Arivruaich 70 Z 9
Arkaig (Loch) 60 E 13
Arkengarthdale 46 O 20
Arklet (Loch) 55 G 15
Arlingham 17 M 28
Arlington Court 6 I 30
Armadale (West Lothian) 56 I 16
Armadale Bay 65 C 12
Armadale (Highland) 73 H 8
Armitage 27 O 25
Armthorpe 40 Q 23
Arncliffe 39 N 21
Arncott 19 Q 28
Arnesby 28 Q 26
Arnisdale 66 D 12
Arnol 70 A 8
Arnold 36 Q 25
Arnside 38 L 21
Aros 59 B 14
Arran (Isle of) 53 E 17
Arreton 10 Q 31
Arrochar 54 F 15
Arundel 10 S 31
Ascot 19 R 29
Ascott House 19 R 28
Ascrib Islands 65 A 11
Asfordby 36 R 25
Ash (Kent) 13 X 30
Ash (Surrey) 10 R 30
Ash Mill 7 I 31
Ashbourne 35 O 24
Ashburton 4 I 32
Ashbury 18 P 29
Ashby de la Zouch 27 P 25
Ashcott 8 L 30
Ashford (Derbs.) 35 O 24
Ashford (Kent) 12 W 30
Ashford (Surrey) 20 S 29
Ashie (Loch) 67 H 11
Ashingdon 21 W 29
Ashington (Northumb.) 51 P 18
Ashington (West Sussex) 11 S 31
Ashover 35 P 24
Ashperton 26 M 27
Ashtead 20 T 30
Ashton-in-Makerfield 34 M 23
Ashton Keynes 18 O 29
Ashton-under-Lyne 39 N 23
Ashton-upon-Mersey 34 M 23
Ashwell 29 T 27
Askam in Furness 38 K 21
Askern 40 Q 23
Askernish 64 X 12
Askerswell 8 L 31
Askham 45 L 20
Askrigg 45 N 21
Aspatria 44 K 19
Aspley Guise 28 S 27
Assynt (Loch) 72 E 9
Aston 35 Q 23
Aston Clinton 19 R 28
Aston Rowant 19 R 28
Aston Tirrold 19 Q 29
Astwood Bank 27 O 27
Atcham 26 L 25
Athelhampton Hall 9 N 31
Athelney 8 L 30
Atherington 6 H 31
Atherstone 27 P 26
Atherton 39 M 23
Atholl (Forest of) 61 H 13
Attleborough 30 X 26
Auchenblae 63 M 13
Auchencairn 43 I 19
Auchinleck 48 H 17
Auchleven 69 M 12
Auchnagatt 69 N 11
Auchterarder 56 I 15
Auchterderran 56 K 15
Auchterhouse 62 K 14
Auchtermuchty 56 K 15
Auchtertyre 66 D 12
Auckengill 74 K 8
Audenshaw 35 N 23
Audlem 34 M 25
Audley 34 N 24
Audley End 22 U 27
Aughton (Lancs.) 38 L 23
Auldearn 67 I 11
Auldhouse 55 H 16
Aultbea 71 D 10
Aust 17 M 29
Austwick 39 M 21
Avebury 18 O 29
Aveley 20 U 29
Avening 18 N 28
Aveton Gifford 4 I 33
Aviemore 67 I 12
Avoch 67 H 11
Avon (Glen) 68 J 12
Avon (River) 9 O 31
Avon (River) (Wilts.) 9 O 31
Avon (River) (R. Severn) 28 Q 26
Avonbridge 55 I 16
Avonmouth 17 L 29
Awe (Loch) 54 E 15
Awliscombe 7 K 31
Awre 17 M 28
Axbridge 8 L 30
Axminster 8 L 31
Axmouth 7 K 31
Aylesbury 19 R 28
Aylesford 12 V 30
Aylesham 13 X 30
Aylsham 31 X 25
Aymestrey 26 L 27
Aynho 19 Q 28
Ayr 48 G 17
Aysgarth 46 O 21
Ayton 47 S 21

B

Bà (Loch) 59 C 14
Babbacombe Bay 4 J 32
Backaland 74 L 6
Backwater Reservoir 62 K 13
Baconsthorpe 31 X 25
Bacton 31 Y 25
Bacup 39 N 22
Bad a' Ghaill (Loch) 72 E 9
Bad an Sgalaig (Loch) 66 D 10
Badachro 65 C 10
Badanloch (Loch) 73 H 9
Badcaul 72 D 10
Baddidarach 72 E 9
Badenoch 61 H 13
Badluarach 72 D 10
Badminton 17 N 29
Badrallach 72 E 10
Bae Colwyn / Colwyn Bay 33 I 24
Bagh nam Faoileann 64 Y 11
Bagillt 33 K 24
Bagshot 19 R 29
Baile Mòr 59 A 15
Bainbridge 45 N 21
Bainton 41 S 22
Bakewell 35 O 24
Bala 33 J 25
Balallan 70 A 9
Balbeggie 62 J 14
Balblair 67 H 10
Balcary Point 43 I 19
Balchrick 72 E 8
Balcombe 11 T 30
Balderton 36 R 24
Baldock 20 T 28
Balemartine 58 Z 14
Balephetrish Bay 58 Z 14
Balephuil Bay 58 Z 14
Baleshare 64 X 11
Balfour 74 L 6
Balfron 55 H 15
Balintore 73 I 10
Balivanich 64 X 11
Ballabeg 42 F 21
Ballachulish 60 E 13
Ballantrae 48 E 18
Ballasalla 42 G 21
Ballater 62 K 12
Ballaugh 42 G 21
Ballingry 56 K 15
Balmaha 55 G 15
Balmedie 69 N 12
Balmoral Castle 62 K 12
Balmullo 56 L 14
Balnakeil Bay 72 F 8
Balvicar 54 D 15

ABERDEEN

Bon Accord Centre Y
Broad Street Y 6
Castle Street Y 7
College Street Z 9
Craigie Loanings Y 12
Denburn Road Y 14
East North Street Y 16
George Street Y
Great Southern Road Z 18
Guild Street Z 19
Justice Street Y 21
Millburn Street Z 23
Rosemount Terrace Y 25
Rosemount Viaduct Y 26
St. Andrew Street Y 28
St Nicholas Centre Y 29
St Nicholas Street YZ 30
School Hill YZ 32
South Esplanade West Z 33
South Mount Street Y 34
Springbank Terrace Z 35
Spring Garden Y 36
Trinity Centre Z
Trinity Quay Z 37
Union Street Z
Union Terrace Z 39
Upperkirkgate Y 40
Victoria Street Z 42
Waverley Place Z 43
Wellington Place Z 45
Wellington Road Z 47
Woolmanhill Y 48

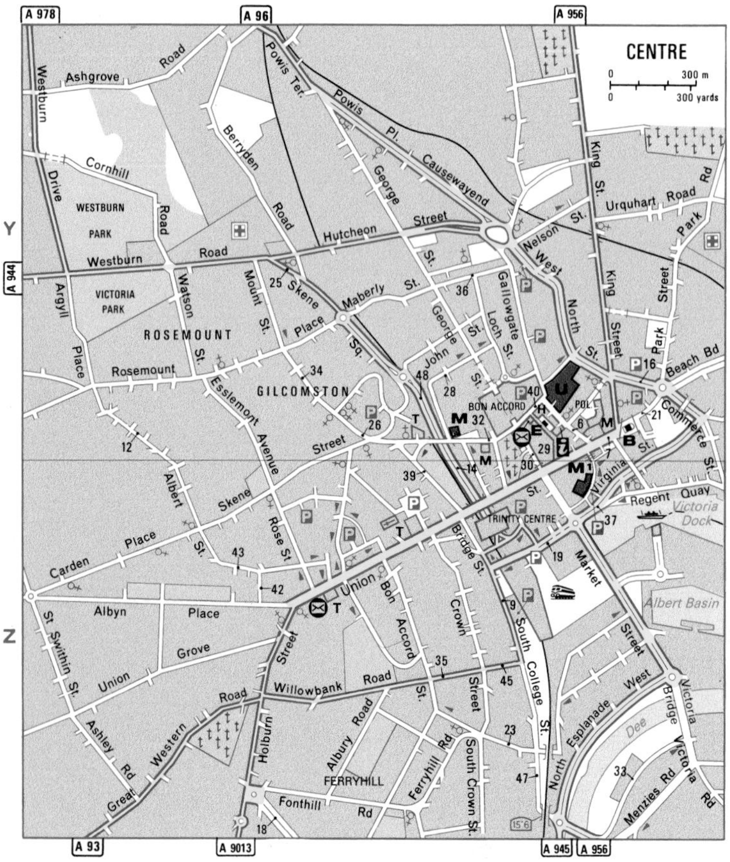

BATH CENTRE

Ambury . . . . . BX 2
Argyle Street . . . . . BV 3
Bennett Street . . . . . AV 4
Bridge Street . . . . . BVX 6
Broad Quay . . . . . BX 7
Chapel Row . . . . . AVX 9
Charles Street . . . . . AX 10
Charlotte Street . . . . . AV 12
Cheap Street . . . . . BX 13
Churchill Bridge . . . . . BX 14
Circus Place . . . . . AV 16
Gay Street . . . . . AV
Grand Parade . . . . . BX 17
Great Stanhope Street . . . . . AV 18
Green Street . . . . . BV 21
Guinea Lane . . . . . BV 23
Henry Street . . . . . BX 24
Lower Borough Walls . . . . . BX 26
Milsom Street . . . . . BV
Monmouth Place . . . . . AVX 28
Monmouth Street . . . . . AX 30
New Bond Street . . . . . BV 31
New Orchard Street . . . . . BX 32
Nile Street . . . . . AV 34
Northgate Street . . . . . BVX 35
Old Bond Street . . . . . BX 36
Orange Grove . . . . . BX 38
Pierrepont Street . . . . . BX 39
Quiet Street . . . . . BV 41
Russell Street . . . . . AV 42
Southgate Street . . . . . BX 43
Stanley Road . . . . . BX 45
Terrace Walk . . . . . BX 46
Upper Borough Walls . . . . . BX 48
Westgate Buildings . . . . . AX 49
Westgate Street . . . . . ABX 50
Wood Street . . . . . AV 52
York Street . . . . . BX 53

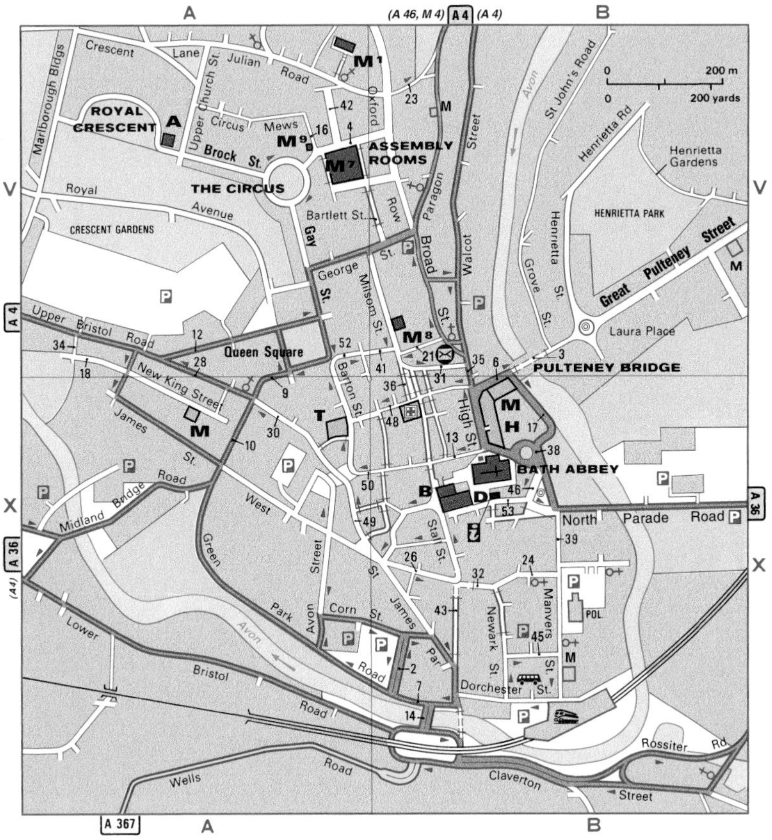

Bamburgh Castle	51	O 17
Bampton (Cumbria)	45	L 20
Bampton (Devon)	7	J 31
Bampton (Oxon.)	18	P 28
Banavie	60	E 13
Banbury	27	P 27
Banchory	69	M 12
Banff	69	M 10
Bangor	32	H 24
Bankfoot	62	J 14
Bankhead	69	N 12
Banks	38	L 22
Bannockburn	55	I 15
Banstead	20	T 30
Banwell	17	L 30
Bapchild	12	W 30
Bar Hill	29	U 27
Barbaraville	67	H 10
Barbon	45	M 21
Barcombe Cross	11	U 31
Bardney	37	T 24
Bardsea	38	K 21
Bardsey Island	32	F 25
Barfreston	13	X 30
Bargoed	16	K 28
Barham	13	X 30
Barking and Dagenham (London Borough)	20	U 29
Barkston	36	S 25
Barkway	20	U 28
Barkwith	37	T 24
Barlaston	35	N 25
Barlborough	36	Q 24
Barley	29	U 27
Barmouth / Abermaw	24	H 25
Barmouth Bay	24	H 25
Barmston	41	T 21
Barnard Castle	46	O 20
Barnby Moor (East Riding of Yorks.)	40	R 22
Barnby Dun	40	Q 23
Barnby Moor (Notts.)	36	Q 23
Barnet (London Borough)	20	T 29
Barnetby-le-Wold	41	S 23
Barnhill	68	J 11
Barnoldswick	39	N 22
Barnsley	40	P 23
Barnstaple	6	H 30
Barr	48	F 18
Barra	58	X 13
Barra (Sound of)	64	X 12
Barra Head	58	X 13
Barrhead	55	G 16
Barrhill	48	F 18
Barri / Barry	16	K 29
Barrington Court	8	L 31
Barrisdale Bay	60	D 12
Barrow	22	V 27
Barrow-in-Furness	38	K 21
Barrow-upon-Humber	41	S 22
Barrow-upon-Soar	28	Q 25
Barrowby	36	R 25
Barrowford	39	N 22
Barry (Angus)	63	L 14
Barry / Barri (Vale of Glamorgan)	16	K 29
Bartestree	26	M 27
Barton (Lancs.)	38	L 22
Barton (Staffs.)	27	O 25
Barton in the Clay	20	S 28
Barton Mills	30	V 26
Barton-on-Sea	9	P 31
Barton-upon-Humber	41	S 22
Barvas	70	A 8
Barwell	27	P 26
Barwick-in-Elmet	40	P 22
Baschurch	34	L 25
Basildon (Berks.)	19	Q 29
Basildon (Essex)	21	V 29
Basingstoke	10	Q 30
Baslow	35	P 24
Bass Rock	57	M 15
Bassenthwaite	44	K 19
Bassingham	36	S 24
Bath	17	M 29
Bathgate	56	J 16
Batley	39	P 22
Battle	12	V 31
Baumber	37	T 24
Bawdeswell	30	X 25
Bawdsey	23	Y 27
Bawtry	36	Q 23
Bayble	71	B 9
Bayhead	64	X 11
Beachy Head	11	U 31
Beacon (The)	2	E 33
Beaconsfield	19	S 29
Beadnell Bay	51	P 17
Beaford	6	H 31
Beaminster	8	L 31
Beamish Hall	46	P 19
Bearsden	55	G 16
Bearsted	12	V 30
Beattock	49	J 18
Beauchief	35	P 24
Beaulieu	9	P 31
Beauly	67	G 11
Beauly Firth	67	G 11
Beaumaris	32	H 24
Beaupré Castle	16	J 29
Bebington	34	L 23
Beccles	31	Y 26
Beckingham	36	R 23
Beckington	8	N 30
Beckton	20	U 29
Bedale	46	P 21
Beddgelert	32	H 24
Beddingham	11	U 31
Bedford	28	S 27
Bedford Levels	29	T 26
Bedfordshire (County)	28	S 27
Bedgebury Pinetum	12	V 30
Bedlington	51	P 18
Bedwas	16	K 29
Bedworth	27	P 26
Bee (Loch)	64	X 11
Beer	7	K 31
Beeston	36	Q 25
Beeswing	49	I 18
Beinn a' Ghlò	62	I 13
Beinn a' Mheadhoin (Loch)	66	F 12
Beinn Dearg (Perthshire and Kinross)	61	I 13
Beinn Dearg (Highland)	66	F 10
Beinn Heasgarnich	61	G 14
Beinn Ime	54	F 15
Beith	55	G 16
Belbroughton	27	N 26
Belford	51	O 17
Bellingham	50	N 18
Bellshill	55	H 16
Belmont	75	R 1
Belnahua	52	C 15
Belper	35	P 24
Belsay	51	O 18
Belton (North Lincs.)	40	R 23
Belton House (Lincs.)	36	S 25
Belton (Norfolk)	31	Y 26
Belvoir	36	R 25
Bembridge	10	Q 31
Bempton	41	T 21
Ben Alder	61	G 13
Ben Armine Forest	73	H 9
Ben Chonzie	61	I 14
Ben Cruachan	60	E 14
Ben-damph Forest	66	D 11
Ben Hope	72	G 8
Ben Klibreck	72	G 9
Ben Lawers	61	H 14
Ben Ledi	55	H 15
Ben Lomond	55	G 15
Ben Loyal	73	G 8
Ben Macdui	62	I 12
Ben More (Argyll and Bute)	59	C 14
Ben More (Stirling)	55	G 14
Ben More Assynt	72	F 9
Ben Nevis	60	E 13
Ben Starav	60	E 14
Ben Vorlich	55	H 14
Ben Wyvis	67	G 10
Benbecula	64	X 11
Benderloch	60	E 14
Benenden	12	V 30
Benfleet	21	V 29
Benigton	37	U 25
Benllech	32	H 24
Benmore Lodge	72	F 9
Benson	19	Q 29
Bentley	40	Q 23
Benwick	29	T 26
Beoraid (Loch)	60	D 13
Bere Alston	3	H 32
Bere Regis	8	N 31
Berkeley	17	M 28
Berkhamsted	19	S 28
Berneray (near Barra)	58	X 13
Berneray (near North Uist)	64	Y 10
Bernisdale	65	B 11
Berriew	25	K 26
Berrington Hall	26	L 27
Berrow	8	K 30
Berry Head	4	J 32
Berry Hill	17	M 28
Berrynarbor	6	H 30
Bervie Bay	63	N 13
Berwick-upon-Tweed	57	O 16
Berwyn	33	J 25
Bethersden	12	W 30
Bethesda	32	H 24
Bettyhill	73	H 8
Betws-y-Coed	33	I 24
Beverley	41	S 22
Bewcastle	50	L 18
Bewdley	26	N 26
Bexhill	12	V 31
Bexley (London Borough)	20	U 29
Beyton	22	W 27
Bhaid-Luachraich (Loch)	71	D 10
Bhealaich (Loch a')	72	G 9
Bhraoin (Loch a')	66	E 10
Bhrollum (Loch)	70	A 10
Bibury	18	O 28
Bicester	19	Q 28
Bickington	4	I 32
Bickleigh	7	J 31
Bicton gardens	7	K 31
Biddenden	12	V 30
Biddestone	17	N 29
Biddulph	35	N 24
Bidean nam Bian	60	E 14
Bideford	6	H 30
Bidford	27	O 27
Bieldside	69	N 12
Bierton	19	R 28
Bigbury	4	I 33
Bigbury-on-Sea	4	I 33
Biggar	49	J 17
Biggleswade	29	T 27

BIRMINGHAM CENTRE

Albert St. . . . . . KZ 2
Bull Ring Centre . . . . . KZ
Bull St. . . . . . KY 13
Corporation Street . . . . . KYZ
Dale End . . . . . KZ 21
Hall St. . . . . . JY 29
Holloway Circus . . . . . JZ 32
James Watt Queensway . . . . . KY 35
Jennen's Rd. . . . . . KY 36
Lancaster Circus . . . . . KY 39
Lancaster St. . . . . . KY 41
Masshouse Circus . . . . . KY 43
Moor St. Queensway . . . . . KZ 46
Navigation St. . . . . . JZ 49
New St. . . . . . JKZ
Newton St. . . . . . KY 52
Paradise Circus . . . . . JZ 56
Paradise Forum Shopping Centre . . . . . JZ
Priory Queensway . . . . . KY 57
St Chads Circus . . . . . JKY 62
St Chads Ringway . . . . . KY 63
St Martin's Circus . . . . . KZ 64
Shadwell St. . . . . . KY 70
Smallbrook Queensway . . . . . KZ 71
Snow Hill Queensway . . . . . KY 73
Summer Row . . . . . JY 77
Temple Row . . . . . KZ 80
Waterloo St. . . . . . JZ 84

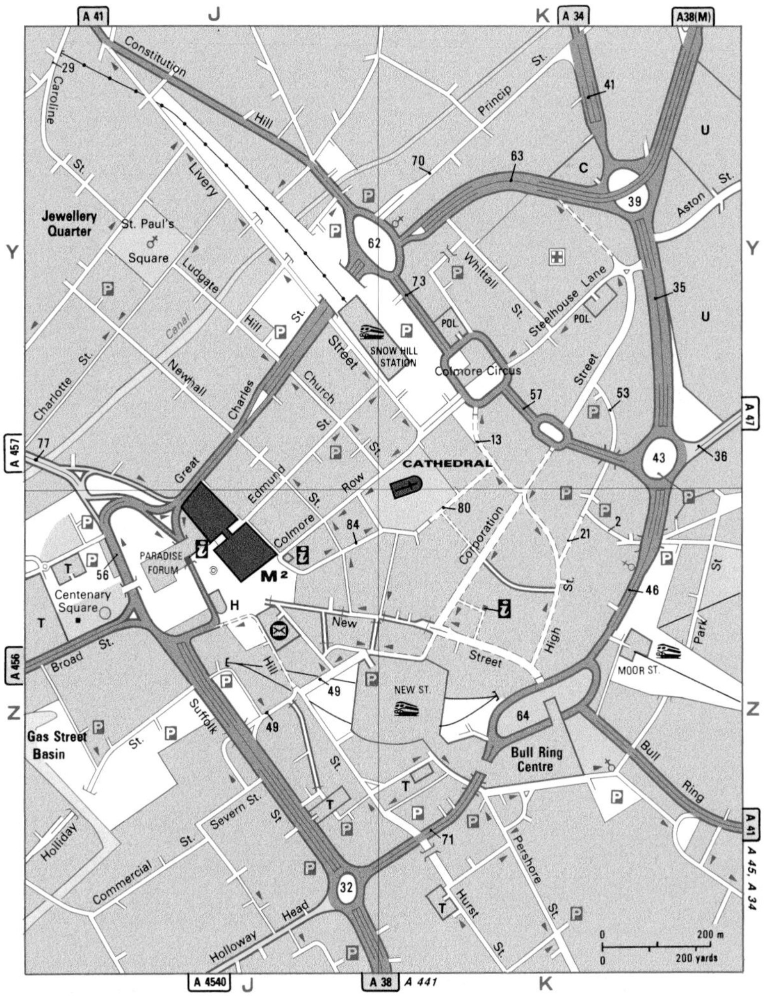

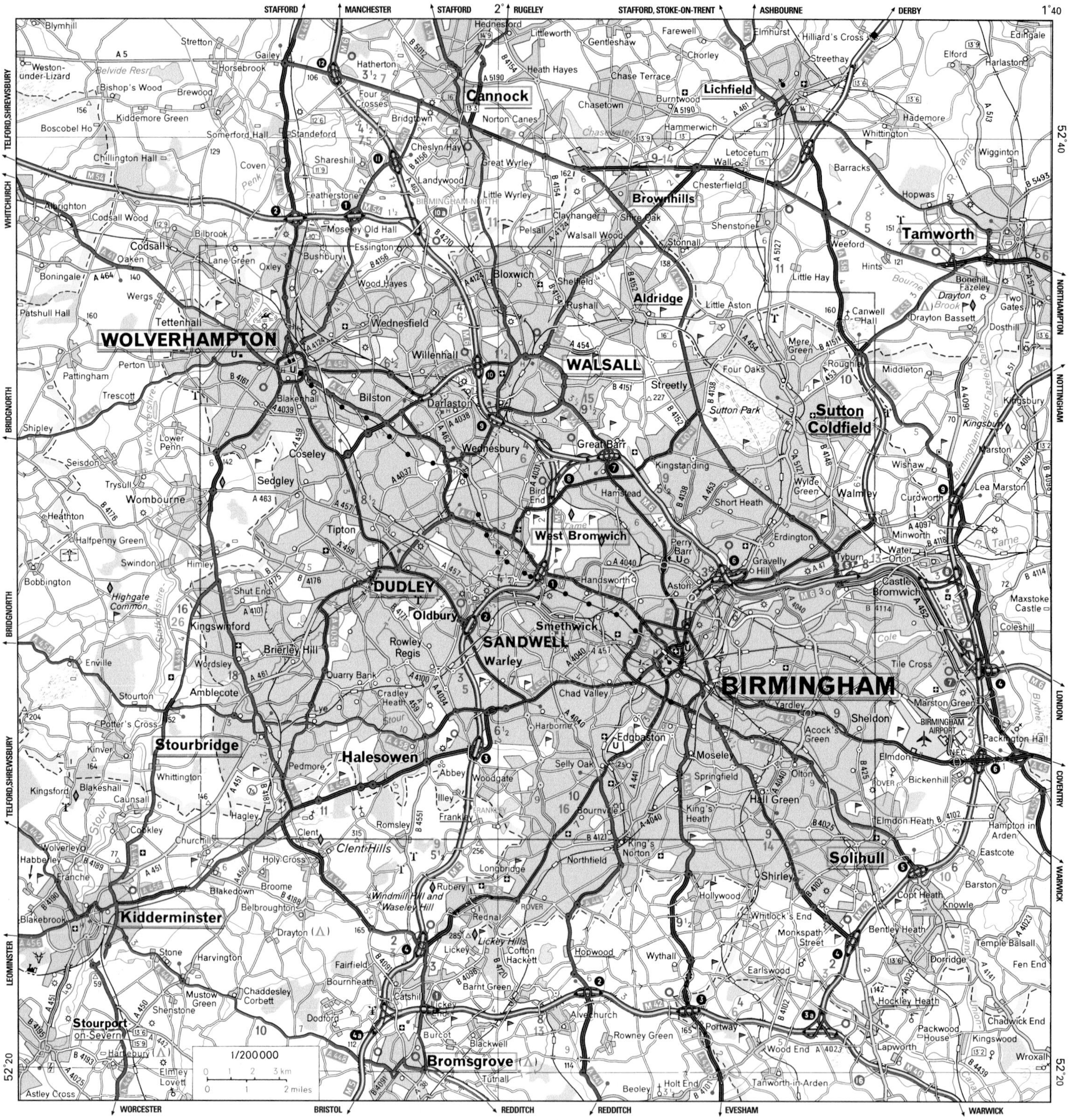
STAFFORD
MANCHESTER
STAFFORD
RUGELEY
STAFFORD, STOKE-ON-TRENT
ASHBOURNE
DERBY
TELFORD, SHREWSBURY
WHITCHURCH
BRIDGNORTH
BRIDGNORTH
TELFORD, SHREWSBURY
LEOMINSTER
NORTHAMPTON
NOTTINGHAM
LONDON
COVENTRY
WARWICK
WORCESTER
BRISTOL
REDDITCH
REDDITCH
EVESHAM
WARWICK
Cannock
Lichfield
Tamworth
Brownhills
Aldridge
WOLVERHAMPTON
WALSALL
Sutton Coldfield
Wednesbury
West Bromwich
DUDLEY
Oldbury
SANDWELL
Smethwick
Warley
BIRMINGHAM
Stourbridge
Halesowen
Solihull
Kidderminster
Stourport-on-Severn
Bromsgrove
1/200000
0 1 2 3 km
0 1 2 miles

Bildeston 22 W 27
Bill of Portland 5 M 32
Billericay 21 V 29
Billesdon 28 R 26
Billingborough 37 S 25
Billinge 34 L 23
Billingham 46 Q 20
Billinghay 37 T 24
Billingshurst 11 S 30
Bilsington 12 W 30
Bilsthorpe 36 Q 24
Bilston 27 N 26
Binfield 19 R 29
Bingham 36 R 25
Bingley 39 O 22
Binham 30 W 25
Binns (The) 56 J 16
Birchington 13 X 29
Birdham 10 R 31
Birdworld 10 R 30
Birkenhead 33 K 23
Birling Gap 11 U 31
Birmingham 27 O 26
Birnam 62 J 14
Birsay 74 K 6
Birsemore 68 L 12
Birstall 28 Q 25
Birtley 46 P 19
Birtsmorton Court 17 N 27
Bishop Auckland 46 P 20
Bishop Monkton 40 P 21
Bishop's Castle 26 L 26
Bishop's Caundle 8 M 31
Bishop's Cleeve 17 N 28
Bishop's Nympton 7 I 31
Bishop's Palace (near St. David's) 14 E 28
Bishop's Palace (near Tenby) 14 F 28
Bishop's Stortford 20 U 28
Bishop's Tawton 6 H 30
Bishop's Waltham 10 Q 31
Bishops Lydeard 7 K 30
Bishopsteignton 4 J 32
Bishopstocke 10 Q 31
Bishopston 15 I 28
Bishopstone 18 P 29
Bishopthorpe 40 Q 22
Bishopton 55 G 16
Bix 19 R 29
Blaby 28 Q 26
Black Bay 53 D 17
Black Down Hills 7 K 31
Black Isle 67 G 11
Black Mount 60 F 14
Black Mountain 15 I 28
Black Mountains 16 K 28
Black Water Valley 67 F 11
Blackburn (Aberdeenshire) 69 N 12
Blackburn (West Lothian) 56 J 16
Blackburn (Lancs.) 38 M 22
Blackfield 9 P 31
Blackford (Perthshire and Kinross) 55 I 15
Blackford (Cumbria) 45 L 19
Blacklunans 62 J 13
Blackmoor Gate 7 I 30
Blackness Castle 56 J 15
Blackpool 38 K 22
Blackridge 55 I 16
Blackthorn 19 Q 28
Blackwater (River) 22 W 28
Blackwater Reservoir 60 F 13
Blackwaterfoot 53 D 17
Blackwood 16 K 29
Bladnoch 42 G 19
Bladon 18 P 28
Blaenau Ffestiniog 33 I 25
Blaenavon 16 K 28
Blaengarw 16 J 29
Blagdon 17 L 30
Blaich 60 E 13
Blaina 16 K 28
Blair Atholl 61 I 13
Blair Castle 61 I 13
Blairgowrie 62 J 14
Blakeney (Glos.) 17 M 28
Blakeney (Norfolk) 30 X 25
Blakesley 28 Q 27
Blandford Forum 9 N 31
Blarnalearoch 72 E 10
Blawith 44 K 21
Blaydon 46 O 19
Bleaklow Hill 35 O 23
Blean 13 X 30
Blenheim Palace 18 P 28
Bletchley 19 R 27
Blewbury 19 Q 29
Blickling Hall 31 X 25
Blidworth 36 Q 24
Blindley Heath 11 T 30
Blisland 3 F 32
Blisworth 28 R 27
Blithe 35 O 25
Blithfield Hall 35 O 25
Blithfield Reservoir 35 O 25
Blockley 18 O 27
Blofield 31 Y 26
Bloxham 18 P 27
Blue John Cavern 35 O 23
Bluemull Sound 75 Q 1
Blyth (Northumb.) 51 P 18
Blyth (Notts.) 36 Q 23
Blythburgh 31 Y 27
Blyton 36 R 23
Bo' Ness 56 J 15
Boarhills 57 L 15
Boat of Garten 67 I 12
Bocking 22 V 28
Boddam 69 O 11
Bodenham 26 L 27
Bodiam Castle 12 V 30
Bodmin 3 F 32
Bodmin Moor 3 G 32
Bodnant Garden 33 I 24
Bognor Regis 10 R 31
Boisdale (Loch) 64 Y 12
Boldon 46 P 19
Bollin (River) 34 N 23
Bollington 35 N 24
Bolney 11 T 31
Bolsover 36 Q 24
Boltby 46 Q 21
Bolton 39 M 23
Bolton Abbey 39 O 22
Bolton-le-Sands 38 L 21
Bolton-upon-Dearne 40 Q 23
Bonar Bridge 73 G 10
Bonawe Quarries 60 E 14
Boncath 24 G 27
Bonhill 55 G 16
Bonnybridge 55 I 16
Bonnyrigg 56 K 16
Bont-faen / Cowbridge 16 J 29
Boosbeck 47 R 20
Bootle (Cumbria) 44 J 21
Bootle (Merseyside) 34 K 23
Border Forest Park (The) 50 M 18
Boreham 22 V 28
Boreham Street 12 V 31
Borehamwood 20 T 29
Borgue 43 H 19
Borness 43 H 19

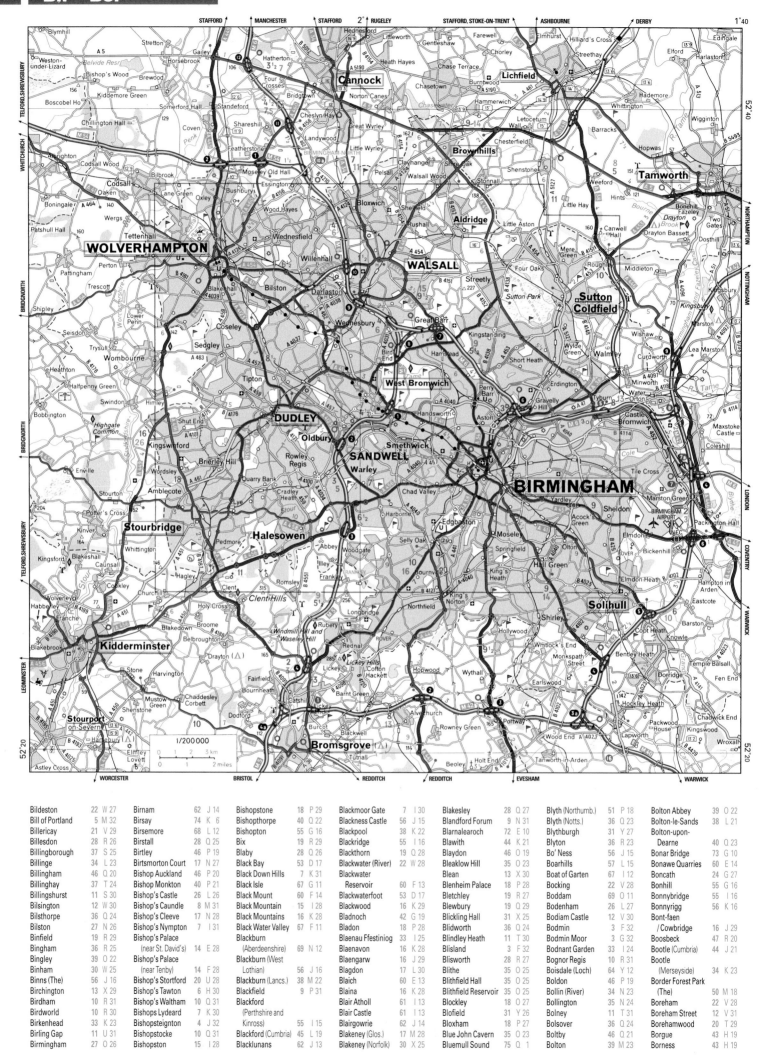

BLACKPOOL CENTRE

Abingdon Street AY 2
Adelaide Street AY 3
Caunce Street AY 7
Church Street
Clifton Street AY 12
Cookson Street AY 14
Deansgate AY 15
George Street AY 17
Grosvenor Street AY 21
High Street AY 22
King Street AY 23
Lark Hill Street AY 24
New Bonny Street AY 25
Pleasant Street AY 27
South King St AY 35
Talbot Square AY 39
Topping Street AY 40

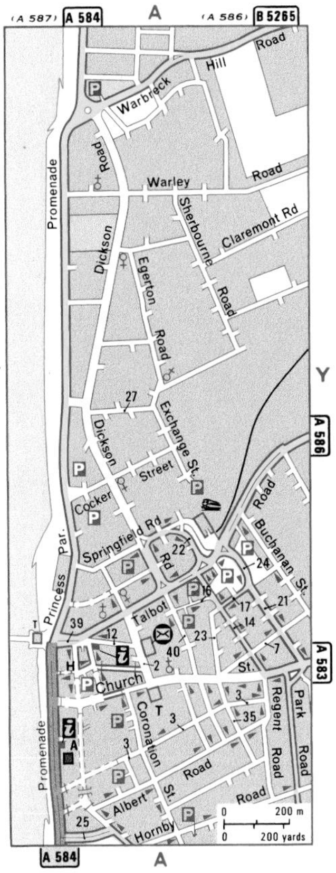

A 584
B 5265
Promenade
Warbreck Hill Road
Warley Road
Dickson Road
Sherbourne Road
Claremont Rd
Egerton Road
Exchange St.
Cocker Street
Springfield Rd
Buchanan St.
Princess Par.
Talbot Rd
Church St
Coronation St.
Regent Road
Park Road
Albert Road
Hornby Road
A 586
A 583
200 m
200 yards

Borough Green 20 U 30
Boroughbridge 40 P 21
Borrobol Forest 73 H 9
Borrowash 35 P 25
Borth 24 H 26
Borve (Barra Isle) 58 X 13
Borve (Isle of Lewis) 71 A 8
Bosbury 26 M 27
Boscastle 6 F 31
Boscombe 9 O 31
Bosham 10 R 31
Bosherston 14 F 29
Boston 37 T 25
Boston Spa 40 P 22
Botesdale 30 W 26
Bothel 44 K 19
Bothwell 55 H 16
Botley 10 Q 31
Bottesford 36 R 25
Bottisham 22 U 27
Boughton 36 Q 24
Boughton House 28 R 26
Boughton Street 12 W 30
Boultham 36 S 24
Bourne 37 S 25
Bournemouth 9 O 31
Bourton 8 N 30
Bourton-on-the-Water 18 O 28
Bovey Tracey 4 I 32
Bovingdon 19 S 28
Bowerchalke 9 O 30
Bowes 46 N 20
Bowhill 50 L 17
Bowland (Forest of) 38 M 22
Bowmore 52 B 16
Bowness-on-Windermere 45 L 20
Bowness-on-Solway 44 K 19
Bowood House 18 N 29
Box 17 N 29
Box Hill 11 T 30
Boxford 22 W 27
Boxworth 29 T 27
Brabourne Lees 13 W 30
Bracadale (Loch) 65 A 12
Bracebridge Heath 36 S 24
Brackley 28 Q 27
Bracknell 19 R 29
Braco 55 I 15
Bradan Resr (Loch) 48 G 18
Bradfield 19 Q 29
Bradford 39 O 22
Bradford Abbas 8 M 31
Bradford-on-Avon 17 N 29
Brading 10 Q 31
Bradwell 35 O 24
Bradwell-on-Sea 22 W 28
Bradworthy 6 G 31
Brae 75 P 2
Brae Roy Lodge 61 F 13
Braemar 62 J 12
Braeriach 62 I 12
Braich y Pwll 32 F 25
Bràigh Mór 70 Y 9
Brailes 27 P 27
Brailsford 35 P 25
Braintree 22 V 28
Braishfield 9 P 30
Braithwell 36 Q 23
Bramcote 36 Q 25
Bramfield 31 Y 27
Bramford 23 X 27
Bramhall 35 N 23
Bramham 40 P 22
Bramhope 39 P 22
Bramley (South Yorks.) 36 Q 23
Bramley (Surrey) 10 S 30
Brampton (Cambs.) 29 T 27
Brampton (Cumbria) 45 L 19
Brampton (Rotherham.) 40 P 23
Brampton (Suffolk) 31 Y 26
Brancaster 30 V 25
Branderburgh 68 K 10
Brandesburton 41 T 22
Brandon (Durham) 46 P 19
Brandon (Suffolk) 30 V 26
Branscombe 7 K 31
Bransgore 9 O 31
Branston 36 S 24
Bratton Fleming 6 I 30
Braughing 20 U 28
Braunston 28 R 26
Braunstone 28 Q 27
Braunton 6 H 30
Bray-on-Thames 19 R 29
Bray Shop 3 G 32
Brayton 40 Q 22
Breadalbane 61 G 14
Bream 17 M 28
Breamore House 9 O 31
Breasclete 70 Z 9
Breaston 35 Q 25
Brechin 63 M 13
Breckland 30 V 26
Brecon / Aberhonddu 16 J 28
Brecon Beacons National Park 16 J 28
Bredbury 35 N 23
Brede 12 V 31
Bredenbury 26 M 27
Bredon 27 N 27
Bredwardine 26 L 27
Brenchley 12 V 30
Brendon Hills 7 J 30
Brenig Reservoir 33 J 24
Brent (London Borough) 20 T 29
Brent Knoll 8 L 30
Brent Pelham 20 U 28
Brentwood 20 U 29
Brenzett 12 W 30

BOURNEMOUTH CENTRE

Branksome Wood Road CY 9
Commercial Road CY 13
Durley Road CZ 17
Exeter Road CDZ 20
Fir Vale Road DY 23
Gervis Place DY 24
Hinton Road DZ 27
Lansdowne (The) DY 28
Lansdowne Road DY 30
Madeira Road DY 34
Manor Road EY 35
Meyrick Road EYZ 36
Old Christchurch Road DY
Post Office Road CY 43
Priory Road CZ 45
Richmond Hill CY 47
Russell Cotes Road DZ 49
St. Michael's Road CZ 51
St. Paul's Road EY 52
St. Peter's Road DY 53
St. Stephen's Road CY 55
St. Swithuns Road South EY 56
Square (The) CY 63
Suffolk Road CY 64
Triangle (The) CY 67
Upper Hinton Road DZ 68
West Cliff Promenade CZ 71
Westover Road DZ 75

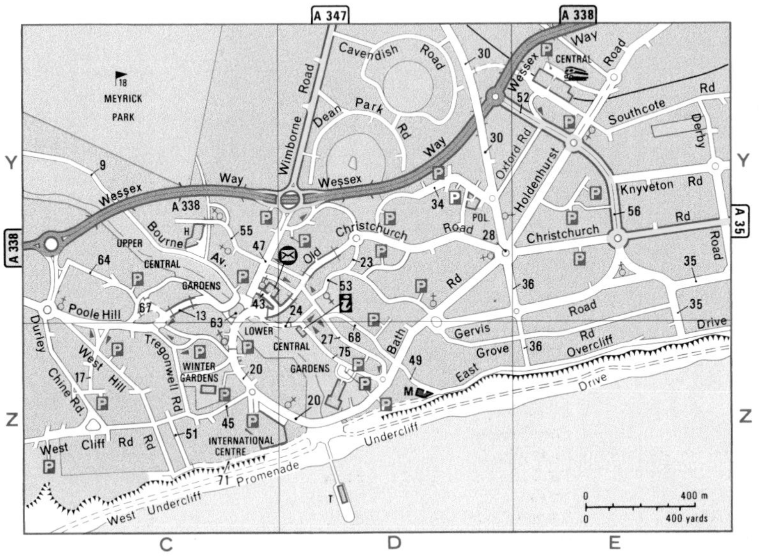

A 347
A 338
MEYRICK PARK
Cavendish Road
Wimborne Road
Dean Park Rd
Wessex Way
Southcote Rd
Derby Rd
Oxford Rd
Holdenhurst Road
Knyveton Rd
Christchurch Road
UPPER CENTRAL GARDENS
Poole Hill
Durley Chine Rd.
West Hill
Tregonwell Rd
WINTER GARDENS
LOWER CENTRAL GARDENS
Bath Rd
Gervis Rd
East Overcliff Drive
Grove Road
West Cliff Rd
INTERNATIONAL CENTRE
Promenade
West Undercliff
Undercliff Drive
A 35
400 m
400 yards

BRADFORD CENTRE

Bank Street AZ 4
Broadway BZ 8
Canal Road BZ 10
Charles Street BZ 13
Cheapside BZ 14
Darley Street AZ 18
Drewton Road AZ 19
East Parade BZ 22
Harris Street BZ 23
Ivegate AZ 25
Kirkgate Centre AZ 26
Market Street BZ 28
Otley Road BZ 31
Peckover Street BZ 32
Prince's Way AZ 33
Stott Hill BZ 39

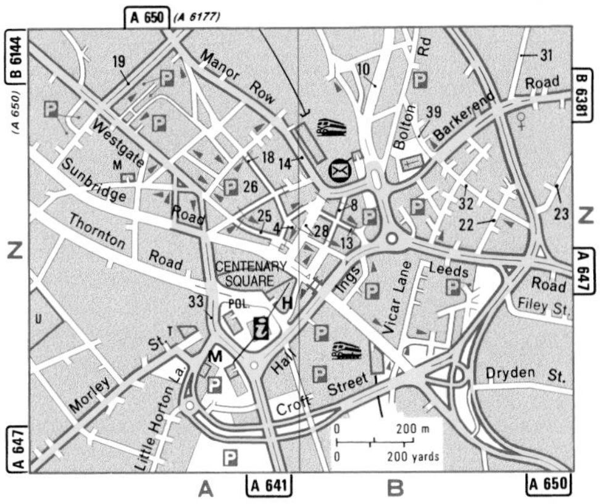

A 650
B 6144
Manor Row
Westgate
Sunbridge Road
Thornton Road
CENTENARY SQUARE
Bolton Rd
Barkerend Road
Leeds Road
Vicar Lane
Filey St.
Dryden St.
Morley St.
Little Horton La.
Croft Street
Hall Ings
B 6381
A 647
A 641
200 m
200 yards

Bressay 75 Q 3
Bretherton 38 L 22
Brewlands Bridge 62 K 13
Brewood 27 N 25
Bride 42 G 20
Bridestowe 6 H 31
Bridge 13 X 30
Bridge of Allan 55 I 15
Bridge of Avon 68 J 11
Bridge of Craigisla 62 K 13
Bridge of Don 69 N 12
Bridge of Earn 56 J 14
Bridge of Gairn 68 K 12
Bridge of Orchy 60 F 14
Bridgemary 10 Q 31
Bridgend / Pen-y-bont (Bridgend) 16 J 29
Bridgend (Perthshire and Kinross) 56 J 14
Bridgend (Islay) 52 B 16
Bridgend of Lintrathen 62 K 13
Bridgnorth 26 M 26
Bridgwater 8 L 30
Bridlington 41 T 21
Bridport 8 L 31
Brierfield 39 N 22
Brierley Hill 27 N 26
Brigg 41 S 23
Brighouse 39 O 22
Brighstone 9 P 32
Brightlingsea 21 X 28
Brighton 11 T 31
Brightwell 19 Q 29
Brigstock 28 S 26
Brill 19 Q 28
Brimfield 26 L 27
Brimham Rocks 39 O 21
Brimington 35 P 24
Brinkburn Priory 51 O 18
Brinklow 27 P 26
Brinkworth 18 O 29
Brinyan 74 L 6
Brisley 30 W 25
Bristol 17 M 29
Briston 30 X 25
Briton Ferry 15 I 29
Brittle (Loch) 65 B 12
Brittwell Salome 19 Q 29
Brixham 4 J 32
Brixworth 28 R 27
Brize Norton 18 P 28
Broad Bay 71 B 9
Broad Blunsdon 18 O 29
Broad Chalke 9 O 30
Broad Law 49 J 17
Broadclyst 7 J 31
Broadford 65 C 12
Broadlands 9 P 31
Broadmayne 8 M 31
Broadstairs 13 Y 29
Broadstone 9 O 31
Broadwas 26 M 27
Broadway 27 O 27
Broadwey 8 M 32
Broadwindsor 8 L 31
Broch of Gurness 49 J 17
Brockenhurst 9 P 31
Brockley 17 L 29
Brockworth 18 N 28
Brodick 53 E 17
Brodick Castle 53 E 17
Brodick Bay 53 E 17
Brodie Castle 67 I 11
Brolass 59 B 14
Bromborough 34 L 24
Brome 31 X 26
Bromfield 26 L 26
Bromham 18 N 29
Bromley (London Borough) 20 U 29
Brompton (near Northallerton) 46 P 20
Brompton-by-Sawdon 41 S 21
Brompton (Kent) 21 V 29
Brompton on Swale 46 O 20
Brompton Regis 7 J 30
Bromsgrove 27 N 26
Bromyard 26 M 27
Bronllys 16 K 27
Brooke 31 Y 26
Brookmans Park 20 T 28
Broom (Loch) 72 E 10
Broomfield 7 K 30
Broomhaugh 46 O 19
Brora 73 H 9
Brotherton 40 Q 22
Brotton 47 R 20
Brough 45 N 20
Brough Head 74 J 6
Brough Lodge 75 R 2
Brough of Birsay 74 J 6
Broughton (Cumbria) 44 J 19
Broughton (North Lincs.) 41 S 23
Broughton (Hants.) 9 P 30
Broughton (Lancs.) 38 L 22
Broughton (Northants.) 28 R 26
Broughton (Oxon.) 27 P 27
Broughton-in-Furness 44 K 21
Broughty Ferry 62 L 14
Brownhills 27 O 26
Brownsea Island 9 O 31
Broxbourne 20 T 28
Broxburn 56 J 16
Bruichladdich 52 A 16
Brundall 31 Y 26
Brushford 7 J 30
Bruton 8 M 30
Brymbo 34 K 24
Brympton d'Evercy 8 L 31
Brynamman 15 I 28
Brynbuga / Usk 17 L 28
Bryncethin 16 J 29
Bryn-Henllan 14 F 27
Brynmawr 16 K 28
Bubwith 40 R 22
Buchlyvie 55 H 15
Buckden (Cambs.) 29 T 27
Buckden (North Yorks.) 39 N 21
Buckfast Abbey 4 I 32
Buckfastleigh 4 I 32
Buckhaven 56 K 15
Buckie 68 L 10
Buckingham 28 R 27
Buckinghamshire (County) 19 R 28
Buckland (Herts.) 20 T 28
Buckland (Oxon.) 18 P 28
Buckland Abbey 3 H 32
Buckland Newton 8 M 31
Buckland St. Mary 7 K 31
Bucklers Hard 9 P 31
Buckley / Bwcle 34 K 24
Buckminster 36 R 25
Bucknell 26 L 26
Bucksburn 69 N 12
Bude 6 G 31
Budleigh Salterton 4 K 32
Bugle 3 F 32
Bugthorpe 40 R 21
Buildwas Abbey 26 M 26
Builth Wells / Llanfair-ym-Muallt 25 J 27
Bulford 9 O 30
Bulkington 27 P 26
Bulwell 36 Q 24
Bunarkaig 60 F 13
Bunessan 59 B 15
Bungay 31 Y 26
Buntingford 20 T 28
Burbage (Leics.) 27 P 26
Burbage (Wilts.) 18 O 29
Bures 22 W 28
Burford 18 P 28
Burgess Hill 11 T 31
Burgh-by-Sands 44 K 19
Burgh-le-Marsh 37 U 24
Burghead 68 J 10
Burghley House 29 S 26
Burley 9 O 31
Burley-in-Wharfedale 39 O 22
Burneside 45 L 20
Burnham 19 S 29
Burnham Market 30 W 25
Burnham-on-Crouch 21 W 29
Burnham-on-Sea 8 L 30
Burnhaven 69 O 11
Burniston 47 S 21
Burnley 39 N 22
Burntisland 56 K 15
Burravoe 75 Q 2
Burray 74 L 7
Burrelton 62 K 14

BRIGHTON AND HOVE

Adelaide Crescent . . . . . AY 2
Brunswick Place . . . . . AY 3
Brunswick Square . . . . . AYZ 4
Chatham Place . . . . . BX 6
Churchill Square Shopping Centre . . . . . BYZ
Denmark Road . . . . . BY 7
East Street . . . . . CZ 8
Gladstone Terrace . . . . . CX 12
Gloucester Place . . . . . CY 13
Gloucester Road . . . . . CY 14
Goldsmid Road . . . . . BX 15
Grand Junction Road . . . . . CZ 16
London Road CX
Market Place . . . . . CX 20
Marlborough Place . . . . . CY 21
Montpelier Place . . . . . BY 22
North Street . . . . . CZ
Old Steine . . . . . CZ 23
Pavilion Parade . . . . . CZ 26
Richmond Place . . . . . CY 27
Richmond Terrace . . . . . CX 28
St. George's Place . . . . . CY 30
St. Peter's Place . . . . . CX 31
Terminus Road . . . . . BCX 32
Upper Lewes Road . . . . . CX 33
Waterloo Place . . . . . CX 39
Western Road . . . . . ABY
York Place . . . . . CY 42

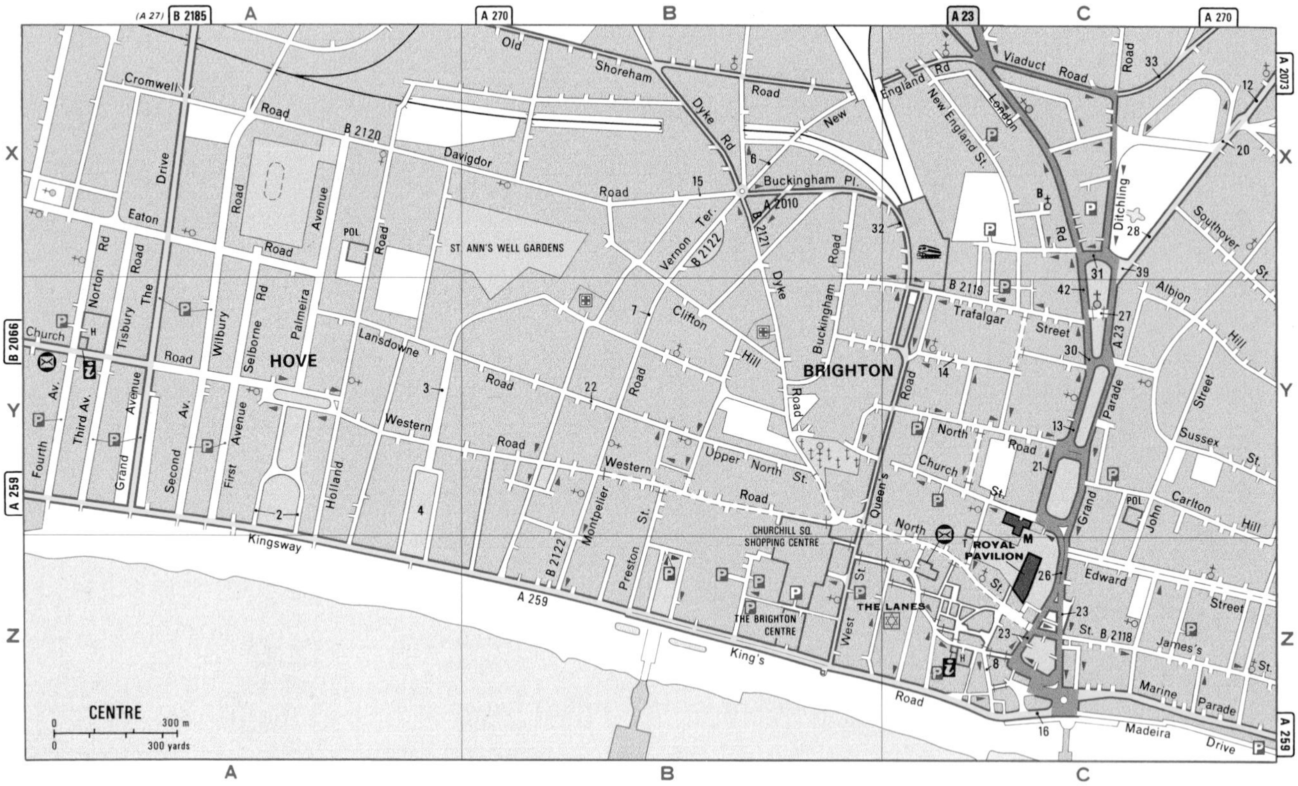

BRISTOL CENTRE

Bedminster Parade . . . . . CZ 5
Bridgehead . . . . . CZ 9
Broad Quay . . . . . CYZ 13
Broad St. . . . . . CY 14
Broadmead . . . . . DY
College Green . . . . . CZ 30
College St. . . . . . CYZ 32
Colston Avenue . . . . . CY 33
Fairfax St. . . . . . CDY 35
Frog Lane . . . . . CY 37
Galleries' Shopping Centre (The) . . . . . DY
Haymarket . . . . . DY 38
High St. . . . . . CDY 39
Horse Fair (The) . . . . . DY
Lower Castle St. . . . . . DY 43
Marlborough St. . . . . . CDY 46
Merchant St. . . . . . DY 47
Narrow Plain . . . . . DY 50
Nelson St. . . . . . CY 51
North St. . . . . . DY 52
Old Market St. . . . . . DY 54
Park St. . . . . . CY
Passage St. . . . . . DY 55
Quay St. . . . . . CY 58
Queen Charlotte St. . . . . . CZ 60
Redcliffe Mead Lane . . . . . DZ 61
Rupert St. . . . . . CY 65
St. Augustine's Parade . . . . . CY 66
Temple Gate . . . . . DZ 75
Trenchard St. . . . . . CY 77
Wine St. . . . . . DY 80

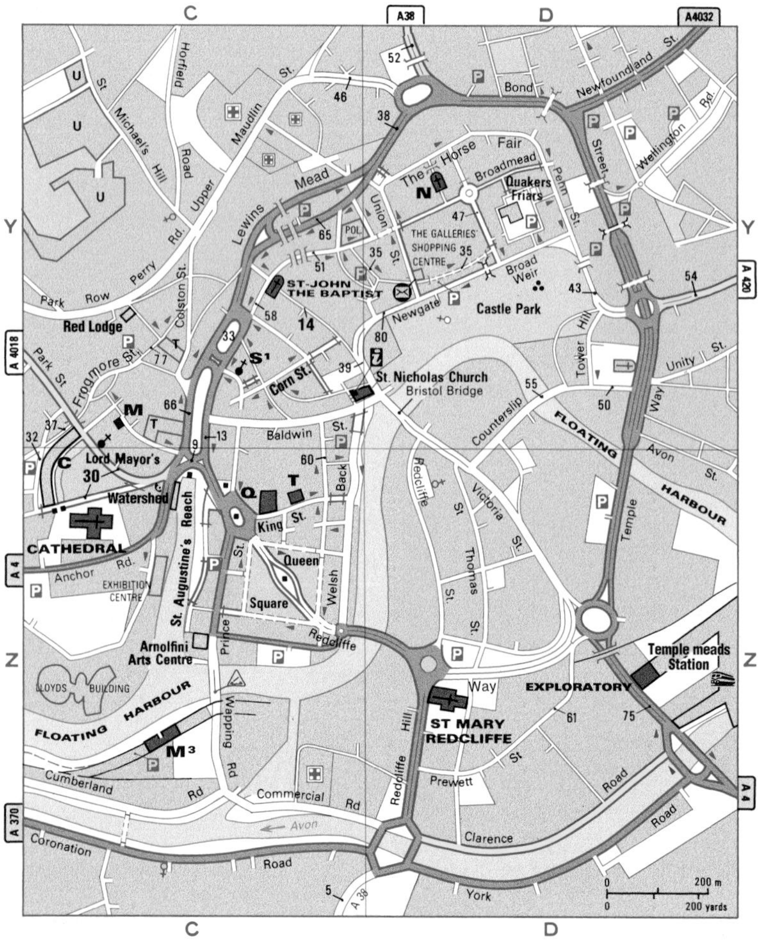

Burrington 6 I 31
Burrow Head 42 G 19
Burry Port / Porth Tywyn 15 H 28
Burscough 38 L 23
Burscough Bridge 34 L 23
Bursledon 10 Q 31
Burslem 35 N 24
Burton 38 L 21
Burton Agnes 41 T 21
Burton Bradstock 8 L 31
Burton Constable Hall 41 T 22
Burton in Lonsdale 38 M 21
Burton Joyce 36 Q 25
Burton Latimer 28 R 26
Burton Leonard 40 P 21
Burton Pidsea 41 T 22
Burton-upon-Stather 40 R 23
Burton-upon-Trent 35 O 25
Burwarton 26 M 26
Burwell (Cambs.) 22 U 27
Burwell (Lincs.) 37 U 24
Bury 39 N 23
Bury St. Edmunds 22 W 27
Busby 55 H 16
Buscot 18 P 28
Bushey 20 S 29
Bute (Kyles of) 54 E 16
Bute (Island of) 54 E 16
Bute (Sound of) 54 E 16
Butt of Lewis 71 B 8
Buttermere 44 K 20
Buxted 11 U 31
Buxton (Derbs.) 35 O 24
Buxton (Norfolk) 31 X 25
Bwcle / Buckley 34 K 24
Bwlch 16 K 28
Bwlch Oerddrws 25 I 25
Bwlch-y-Groes 15 I 28
Bwlch-y-Sarnau 25 J 26
Byfield 28 Q 27
Byfleet 19 S 30
Byland Abbey 40 Q 21

C

Cabrach 68 K 12
Cadair Idris 25 I 25
Cadhay 7 K 31
Cadishead 34 M 23
Cadnam 9 P 31
Caerdydd / Cardiff 16 K 29
Caerffili / Caerphilly 16 K 29
Caerfyrddin / Carmarthen 15 H 28
Caergwrle 34 K 24
Caergybi / Holyhead 32 G 24
Caerlaverock Castle 49 J 19
Caerleon 17 L 29
Caernarfon 32 H 24
Caernarfon Bay 32 G 24
Caerphilly / Caerffili 16 K 29
Caersws 25 J 26
Caerwent 17 L 29
Cailliness Point 42 F 19
Cairn Edward Forest 48 H 18
Cairn Gorm 62 J 12
Cairn Table 49 H 17
Cairn Toul 62 I 12
Cairnborrow 68 L 11
Cairndow 54 F 15
Cairnpapple Hill 56 J 16
Cairnryan 42 E 19
Cairnsmore of Carsphairn 48 H 18
Cairnsmore of Fleet 42 G 19
Cairraig Fhada 52 B 17
Caister-on-Sea 31 Z 26
Caistor 41 T 23
Calbourne 9 P 31
Caldbeck 44 K 19
Caldecott 28 R 26
Calder (Loch) 73 J 8
Calder Bridge 44 J 20
Caldercruix 55 I 16
Calderdale 39 N 22
Caldey Island 14 F 29
Calf of Man 42 F 21
Calfsound 74 L 6
Calgary Bay 59 B 14
Caliach Point 59 B 14
Calke Abbey 35 P 25
Callander 55 H 15
Callater (Glen) 62 J 13
Callington 3 H 32
Calne 18 N 29
Calow 35 P 24
Calstock 3 H 32
Calvay 64 Y 12
Calvine 61 I 13
Cam 22 U 27
Cam Loch 72 E 9
Camas Chil Mhalieu 60 D 14
Camber 12 W 31
Camberley 19 R 30
Camborne 2 E 33
Cambrian Mountains 25 I 27
Cambridge 29 U 27
Cambridgeshire (County) 29 T 26
Cambusbarron 55 I 15
Camden (London Borough) 20 T 29
Camelford 3 F 32
Cammachmore 63 N 12
Campbeltown 53 D 17
Campsie Fells 55 H 15
Canewdon 21 W 29
Canisbay 74 K 8
Canna 65 A 12
Cannich 66 F 11
Cannich (Glen) 66 F 11
Cannington 7 K 30
Cannock 27 N 25
Canonbie 50 L 18
Canterbury 13 X 30
Canvey Island 21 V 29
Caol 60 E 13
Caolas a' Mhòrain 64 Y 10
Caolis 58 X 13
Caolisport (Loch) 53 D 16
Cape Cornwall 2 C 33
Cape Wrath 72 E 8
Capel 11 T 30
Capel Curig 33 I 24
Capel Garmon 33 I 24
Capel Le Ferne 13 X 30
Capel St. Mary 23 X 27
Capesthorne Hall 34 N 24
Caputh 62 J 14

CAMBRIDGE CENTRE

Bridge Street........ Y 2
Corn Exchange Street Z 6
Downing Street...... Z 7
Free School Lane .... Z 12
Grafton Centre ...... Y
Hobson Street....... Y 14
King's Parade........ Z 15
Lion Yard Centre..... Z
Madingley Rd .... Y 16
Magdalene St........ Y 17
Market Hill .... Z 18
Market Street .... Y 19
Milton Road......... Y 20
Newmarket Road .... Y 21
Northampton Street............ Y 22
Parker Street........ Z 23
Peas Hill............ Z 25
Pembroke Street .... Z 26
Petty Cury .... Z 27
Rose Crescent ...... Y 28
St. Andrew's St...... Z 30
St John's Street..... Y 31
Short Street .... Y 32
Sidney Street .... Y 34
Trinity Street....... Y 36
Trumpington Road ... Z 37
Wheeler Street...... Z 39

COLLEGES

CHRIST'S .... Y A
CLARE............. Z B
CORPUS CHRISTI.......... Z G
DARWIN............ Z D
DOWNING .... Z E
EMMANUEL......... Z F
GONVILLE AND CAIUS ...... Y G
HUGUES HALL ..... Z J
JESUS............. Y K
KING'S............ Z
LUCY CAVENDISH...... Y O
MAGDALENE .... Y N
PEMBROKE......... Z N
PETERHOUSE ...... Z O
QUEENS' .... Z
ST CATHARINE'S ... Z R
ST EDMUNDS HOUSE.......... Y U
ST JOHN'S .... Y
SIDNEY SUSSEX......... Y P
TRINITY .... Y
TRINITY HALL...... Y V

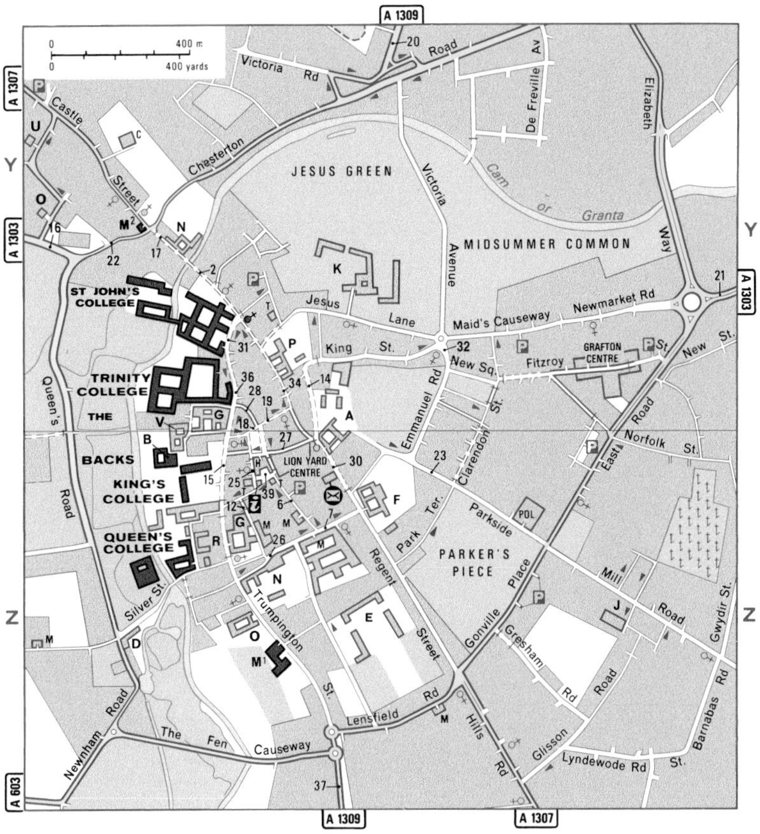

CARDIFF/ CAERDYDD

Capitol Centre................ BZ
Castle Street.................. BZ 9
Cathays Terrace .... BY 10
Central Square .... BZ 12
Church Street .... BZ 14
City Hall Road................. BY 15
College Road.................. BY 20
Corbett Road .... BY 21
Customhouse Street........... BZ 23
David Street .... BZ 25
Duke Street.................... BZ 26
Dumfries Place................. BY 28
Greyfriars Road .... BY 29
Guilford Street .... BZ 30
Hayes (The).................... BZ 32
High Street .... BZ
King Edward VII Avenue ...... BY 36
Mary Ann Street .... BZ 39
Moira Terrace .... BZ 42
Nantes (Boulevard de)........ BY 44
Penarth Road.................. BZ 49
Queen Street .... BZ
Queens Arcade Shopping Centre............ BZ 54
St. Andrews Place .... BY 56
St. David's Centre............. BZ
St. John Street .... BZ 58
St. Mary Street .... BZ
Station Terrace................ BZ 61
Stuttgarter Strasse............ BY 62
Working Street .... BZ 67

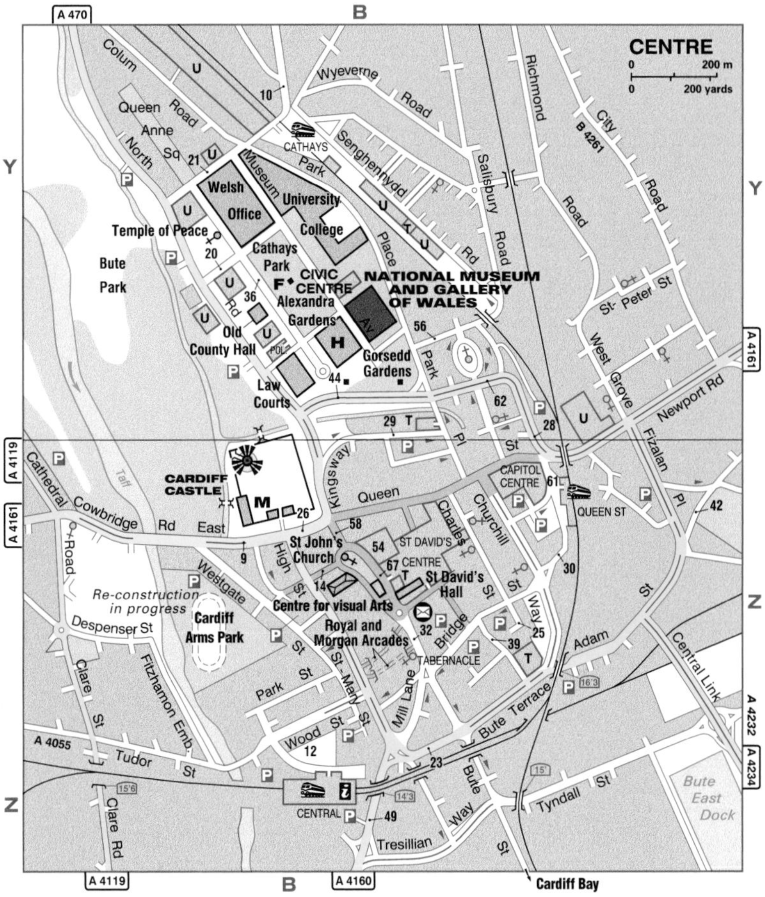

CANTERBURY

Beercart Lane................... YZ 2
Borough (The)................... Y 4
Burgate .... Y
Butchery Lane................... Y 5
Guildhall Street .... Y 6
High Street .... Y 8
Lower Bridge Street .... Z 9
Lower Chantry Lane .... Z 10
Mercery Lane................. Y 12
Palace Street .... Y
Rhodaus Town .... Z 13
Rosemary Lane .... Z 14
St. George's Place............ Z 16
St. George's Street............ Z 17
St. Margaret's Street.......... YZ 18
St. Mary's Street............... Z 19
St. Peter's Street .... Y 20
St. Radigund's Street............................ Y 21
Upper Bridge Street .... Z 23
Watling Street .... Z 25

Cara Island	53	C 17	Cardinham	3	G 32	Cark	38	L 21
Carbis Bay	2	D 33	Cardross	55	G 16	Carlisle	44	L 19
Carbost	65	A 12	Carew	14	F 28	Carloway	70	Z 9
Cardiff / Caerdydd	16	K 29	Carhampton	7	J 30	Carlton (Notts.)	36	Q 25
Cardigan / Aberteifi	24	G 27	Carinish	64	Y 11	Carlton (South. Yorks.)	40	Q 22
Cardigan Bay	24	G 26	Carisbrooke	10	Q 31			

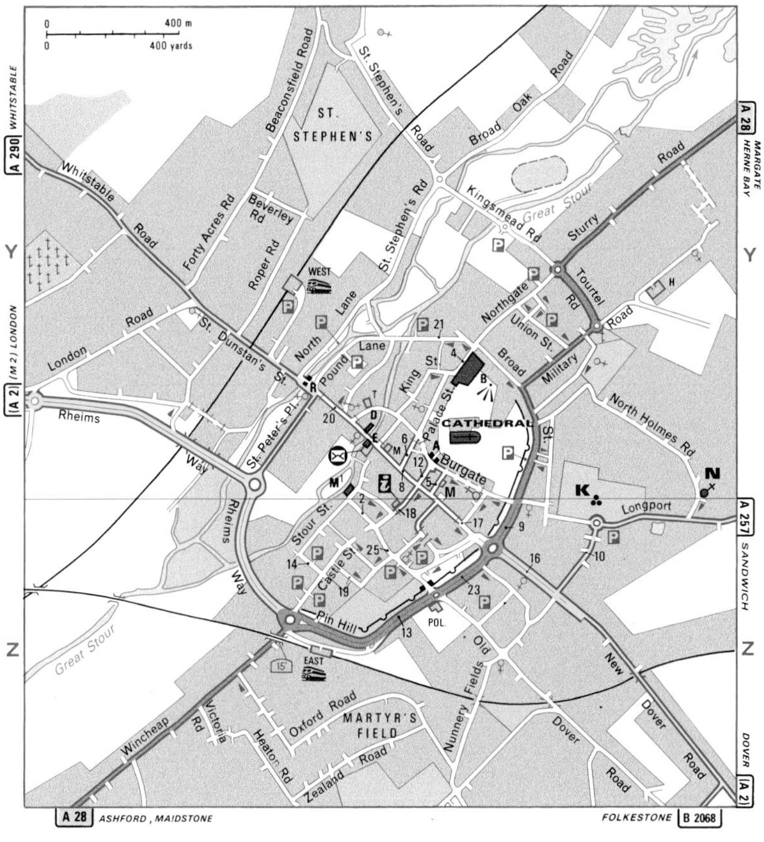

CARLISLE

Annetwell Street............ AY 2
Botchergate .... BZ
Bridge Street................ AY 3
Brunswick Street .... BZ 4
Castle Street .... BY 6
Cecil Street .... BZ 5
Charlotte Street............. AZ 7
Chiswick Street.............. BY 8
Church Street .... AY 10
Eden Bridge.................. BY 12
English Street .... BY 13
Lonsdale Street.............. BY 14
Lowther Street .... BY 15
Port Road .... AY 16
St. Marys Gate .... BY 17
Scotch Street................. BY 19
Spencer Street .... BY 20
Tait Street.................... BZ 21
The Lanes Shopping Centre............ BY
Victoria Viaduct.............. ABZ 24
West Tower Street............ BY 26
West Walls .... ABY 27
Wigton Road .... AZ 29

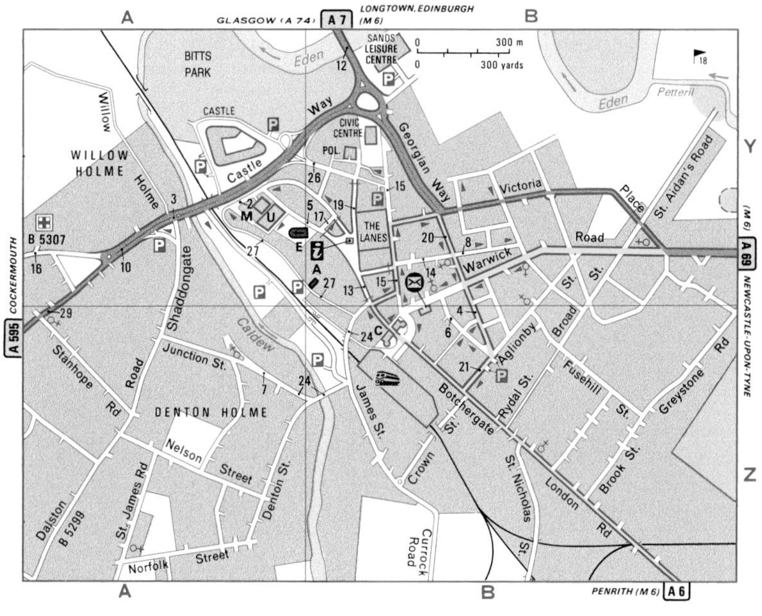

CHESTER

Boughton	2
Bridge Street	3
Eastgate Street	5
Frodsham Street	6
Grosvenor Park Road	7
Grosvenor Street	8
Handbridge	10
Little St. John Street	12
Liverpool Road	13
Lower Bridge Street	15
Nicholas Street	17
Northgate Street	18
Parkgate Road	20
Pepper Street	21
St. John Street	23
St. Martins Way	24
Vicar's Lane	25
Watergate Street	

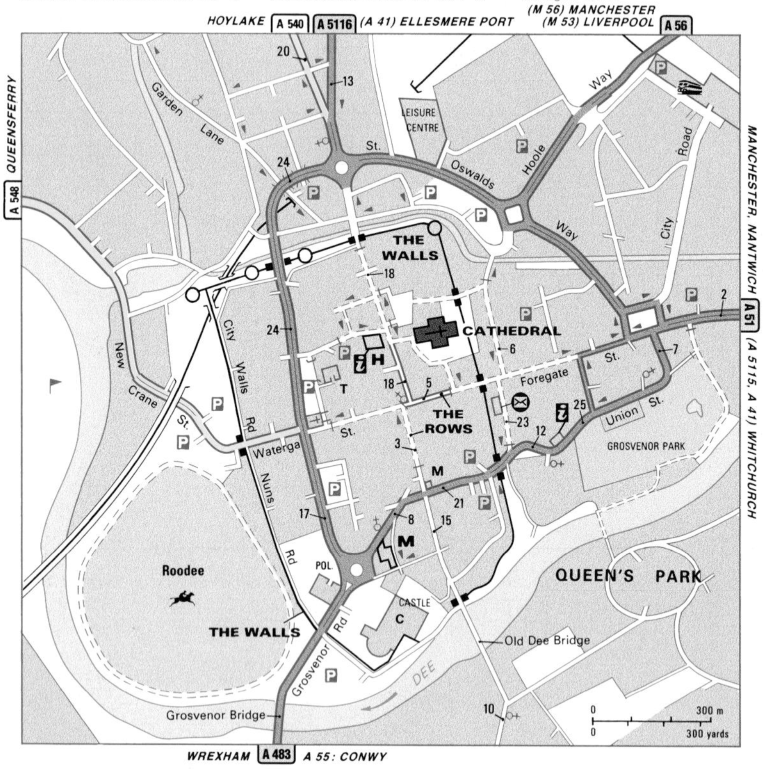

Carlton Colville 31 Z 26
Carlton in Lindrick 36 Q 23
Carlton-on-Trent 36 R 24
Carluke 55 I 16
Carmarthen / Caerfyrddin 15 H 28
Carmel Head 32 G 23
Carmunnock 55 H 16
Carn Ban 61 H 12
Carn Coire na h-Easgainn 67 H 12
Carn Eige 66 E 12
Carn Glas-choire 67 I 11
Carn Mairg 61 H 14
Carnedd Llewelyn 33 I 24
Carnforth 38 L 21
Carnoustie 63 L 14
Carnwath 56 J 16
Carradale 53 D 17
Carradale Bay 53 D 17
Carrbridge 67 I 12
Carrick 54 F 15
Carrick Roads 2 E 33
Carron (Loch) 65 C 11
Carse of Gowrie 56 K 14
Carsluith 42 G 19
Carsphairn 48 H 18
Carstairs 56 I 16
Carterton 18 P 28
Carterway Heads 46 O 19
Cartmel 38 L 21
Cas-Gwent / Chepstow 17 M 29
Casnewydd / Newport 17 L 29
Cassley (Glen) 72 F 9
Castell-Nedd / Neath 15 I 29
Castell Newydd Emlyn / Newcastle Emlyn 24 G 27
Castle Acre 30 W 25
Castle Ashby 28 R 27
Castle Bolton 46 O 21
Castle Campbell 56 I 15
Castle Cary 8 M 30
Castle Combe 17 N 29
Castle Donington 35 P 25
Castle Douglas 43 I 19
Castle Drogo 4 I 31
Castle Fraser 69 M 12
Castle Hedingham 22 V 28
Castle Howard 40 R 21
Castle Kennedy 42 F 19
Castle Lachlan 54 E 15
Castle Loch 42 F 19
Castle Rising 30 V 25
Castlebay 58 X 13
Castleford 40 P 22
Castlemartin 14 E 29
Castlerigg 44 K 20
Castleton (North Yorks.) 47 R 20
Castleton (Derbs.) 35 O 23
Castletown 42 G 21
Castletown 74 J 8
Catacol Bay 53 D 16
Caterham 11 T 30
Catfield 31 Y 25
Catlodge 61 H 12
Caton 38 L 21
Catrine 48 H 17
Catteral 38 L 22
Catterick 46 P 20
Catterick Garrison 46 O 20
Catworth 29 S 26
Cauldcleuch Head 50 L 18
Cava 74 K 7
Cavendish 22 V 27
Cawdor 67 I 11
Cawood 40 Q 22
Caythorpe 36 S 24
Ceall (Loch nan) 59 C 13
Cefn-Coed-y-cymmer 16 J 28
Cefn Bryn 15 H 29
Cefn-mawr 34 K 25
Ceinewydd / New Quay 24 G 27
Ceiriog (Vale of) 33 K 25
Cemaes 32 G 23
Cemaes Head 14 F 27
Cemmaes 25 I 26
Cenarth 24 G 27
Cerne Abbas 8 M 31
Cerrigydrudion 33 J 24
Chadderton 39 N 23
Chaddesden 35 P 25
Chadlington 18 P 28
Chadwell St. Mary 20 V 29
Chagford 4 I 31
Chàirn Bhain (Loch a') 72 E 9
Chalfont St. Giles 19 S 29
Chalfont St. Peter 19 S 29
Chalford 18 N 28
Chalgrove 19 Q 29
Challock 12 W 30
Chambercombe Manor 6 H 30
Chandler's Ford 9 P 31
Channel Islands 5
Chapel-en-le-Frith 35 O 24
Chapel St. Leonards 37 V 24
Chapelhall 55 I 16
Chapeltown 35 P 23
Chapmanslade 8 N 30
Chard 8 L 31
Chardstock 8 L 31
Charing 12 W 30
Charlbury 18 P 28
Charlecote Park 27 P 27
Charleston Manor 11 U 31
Charlestown 3 F 33
Charlton Kings 18 N 28
Charlton Marshall 9 N 31
Charlwood 11 T 30
Charminster 8 M 31
Charmouth 8 L 31
Charsfield 23 X 27
Chartham 13 X 30
Chartwell 11 U 30
Chastleton 18 P 28
Chatburn 39 M 22
Chatham 21 V 29
Chatsworth House 35 P 24
Chatteris 29 U 26
Chatton 51 O 17
Chawleigh 7 I 31
Cheadle (Gtr. Mches.) 35 N 23
Cheadle (Staffs.) 35 O 25
Cheddar Gorge 8 L 30
Cheddington 19 S 28
Cheddleton 35 N 24
Chedington 8 L 31
Chedworth 18 O 28
Chelford 34 N 24
Chellaston 35 P 25
Chelmsford 22 V 28
Cheltenham 18 N 28
Chelveston 28 S 27
Chepstow / Cas-Gwent 17 L 29
Cheriton Bishop 4 I 31
Chertsey 19 S 29
Cherwell (River) 19 Q 28
Cheselbourne 8 M 31
Chesham 19 S 28
Chesham Bois 19 S 28
Cheshire (County) 34 M 24
Cheshunt 20 T 28
Chesil Beach 8 M 32
Cheslyn Hay 27 N 26
Chester 34 L 24
Chester-le-Street 46 P 19
Chesterfield 35 P 24
Chesters Fort 51 N 18
Chesterton 19 Q 28
Cheviot (The) 51 N 17
Cheviot Hills (The) 50 M 17
Chew Magna 17 M 29
Chewton Mendip 8 M 30
Chichester 10 R 31
Chickerell 8 M 32
Chicklade 9 N 30
Chiddingfold 10 S 30
Chiddingstone 11 U 30
Chideock 8 L 31
Chigwell 20 U 29
Chilcompton 8 M 30
Chilham 12 W 30
Chillingham 51 O 17
Chilmark 9 N 30
Chiltern Hills 19 R 29
Chilton 19 Q 29
Chippenham 18 N 29
Chipping 38 M 22
Chipping Campden 27 O 27
Chipping Norton 18 P 28
Chipping Ongar 20 U 28
Chipping Sodbury 17 M 29
Chipping Warden 28 Q 27
Chirbury 25 K 26
Chirk 34 K 25
Chirk Castle 33 K 25
Chirnside 57 N 16
Chiseldon 18 O 29
Chislet 13 X 30
Chitterne 9 N 30
Chittlehamholt 6 I 31
Chittlehampton 6 I 30
Chobham 19 S 29
Choire (Loch) 73 H 9
Cholesbury 19 S 28
Cholsey 19 Q 29
Chon (Loch) 55 G 15
Chopwell 46 O 19
Chorley 38 M 23
Chorleywood 19 S 29
Christchurch 9 O 31
Chroisg (Loch a') 66 E 11
Chudleigh 4 J 32
Chulmleigh 7 I 31
Church 39 M 22
Church Eaton 26 N 25
Church Fenton 40 Q 22
Church Stoke 26 K 26
Church Stretton 26 L 26
Churchill (North Somerset) 17 L 29
Churchill (Oxon.) 18 P 28
Churnet 34 N 24
Churt 10 R 30
Cilcain 33 K 24
Cilgerran 24 G 27
Cilmery 25 J 27
Cinderford 17 M 28
Cirencester 18 O 28
City of London (London Borough) 20 T 29
Clachan 53 D 16
Clachan Mór 58 Z 14
Clachan of Glendaruel 54 E 15
Clackavoid 62 J 13
Clackmannan 55 I 15
Clacton-on-Sea 21 X 28
Claggain Bay 52 B 16
Claidh (Loch) 70 A 10
Clandon Park 10 S 30
Clapham (Beds.) 28 S 27
Clapham (North Yorks.) 39 M 21
Clàr (Loch nan) 73 H 9
Clare 22 V 27
Clashmore 67 H 10
Clashnessie 72 E 9
Clatteringshaws (Loch) 48 H 18
Clauchlands Point 53 E 17
Clavering 20 U 28
Claverley 26 N 26
Claverton Manor 17 N 29
Clawdd-newydd 33 J 24
Clawton 6 G 31
Claxton 40 R 21
Clay Cross 35 P 24
Claydon 23 X 27
Claydon House 19 R 28
Clayton 11 T 31
Clayton-le-Moors 39 M 22
Clayton West 39 P 23
Cleadale 59 B 13
Cleadon 46 P 19
Cleator Moor 44 J 20
Cleckheaton 39 O 22
Cleehill 26 M 26
Cleethorpes 41 T 23
Cleeve Abbey 7 J 30
Clehonger 26 L 27
Cleigh 59 D 14
Clent 27 N 26
Cleobury Mortimer 26 M 26
Cleobury North 26 M 26
Clephanton 67 I 11
Clevedon 17 L 29
Cleveland Hills 46 Q 20
Cleveleys 38 K 22
Cley Next the Sea 30 X 25
Cliffe 21 V 29
Clifton Hampden 19 Q 29
Clisham 70 Z 10
Clitheroe 39 M 22
Cliveden House 19 R 29
Clocaenog Forest 33 J 24
Clola 69 O 11
Clophill 29 S 27
Clouds Hill 8 N 31
Cloughton 47 S 20
Clova (Glen) 62 K 13
Clovelly 6 G 31
Clovulin 60 E 13
Clowne 36 Q 24
Cluanie Loch 66 E 12
Clumber Park 36 Q 24
Clun 26 K 26
Clunbury 26 L 26
Clunes Forest 60 F 13
Clunie 62 J 14
Clutton 17 M 30
Clwydian Range 33 K 24
Clydach 15 I 28
Clyde (Firth of) 48 F 17
Clyde (River) 49 I 16
Clydebank 55 G 16
Clydesdale 49 I 16
Clywedog Resr. 25 J 26
Coalville 27 P 25
Coatbridge 55 H 16
Cobham 20 S 30
Cock Bridge 68 K 12
Cockburnspath 57 M 16
Cockenzie and Port Seton 56 L 16
Cockermouth 44 J 20
Cocking 10 R 31
Codford St. Mary 9 N 30
Codicote 20 T 28
Codnor 35 P 24
Codsall 27 N 26
Coe (Glen) 60 F 14
Coed y Brenin Forest 33 I 25
Coedpoeth 34 K 24
Coggeshall 22 W 28
Coigach 72 E 10
Coignafearn Forest 67 H 12
Colby 42 F 21
Colchester 22 W 28
Cold Fell 45 M 19
Coldbackie 73 G 8
Colden Common 10 Q 31
Coldingham 57 N 16
Coldstream 50 N 17
Coleford (Glos.) 17 M 28
Coleford (Somerset) 8 M 30
Coleshill 27 O 26
Colgrave Sound 75 R 2
Coll 59 A 14
Collieston 69 O 11
Collin 49 J 18
Collingham (Notts.) 36 R 24
Collingham (West Yorks.) 40 P 22
Collyweston 28 S 26
Colmonell 48 F 18
Coln (River) 18 O 28
Colnabaichin 68 K 12
Colne 39 N 22
Colne (River) 21 X 28
Colonsay 52 B 15
Colpy 69 M 11
Colquhon Castle 69 N 11
Colsterworth 36 S 25
Coltishall 31 Y 25
Colwall Stone 26 M 27
Colwyn Bay / Bae Colwyn 33 I 24
Colyton 7 K 31
Combe Florey 7 K 30
Combe Martin 6 H 30
Combwich 7 K 30
Compton (Berks.) 19 Q 29
Compton (West Sussex) 10 R 31
Compton Castle 4 J 32
Compton Wynyates 27 P 27
Comrie 55 I 14
Cona Glen 60 D 13
Condover 26 L 26
Congleton 34 N 24
Congresbury 17 L 29
Coningsby 37 T 24
Conisbrough 36 Q 23
Coniston 44 K 20
Connah's Quay 34 K 24
Connel 60 D 14
Conon Bridge 67 G 11
Consett 46 O 19
Constantine Bay 2 E 32
Contin 67 G 11
Convinth (Glen) 67 G 11
Conway Falls 33 I 24

COVENTRY

Bayley Lane	3
Bishop Street	5
Broadgate	6
Burges	7
Corporation Street	
Earl Street	10
Fairfax Street	12
Far Gosford Street	13
Gosford Street	15
Greyfriars Lane	16
Hales Street	17
High Street	22
Ironmonger Road	23
Jordan Well	26
Leicester Row	29
Light Lane	30
Little Park Street	31
Primrose Hill Street	34
Queen Victoria Road	35
St. Johns (Ringway)	38
St. Nicholas (Ringway)	39
Shopping Precincts	
Swanswell (Ringway)	40
Trinity Street	41
Upper Well Street	43
Vecqueray Street	45
Victoria Street	46
Warwick Road	49
White Street	51
Windsor Street	52
White Friars (Ringway)	54

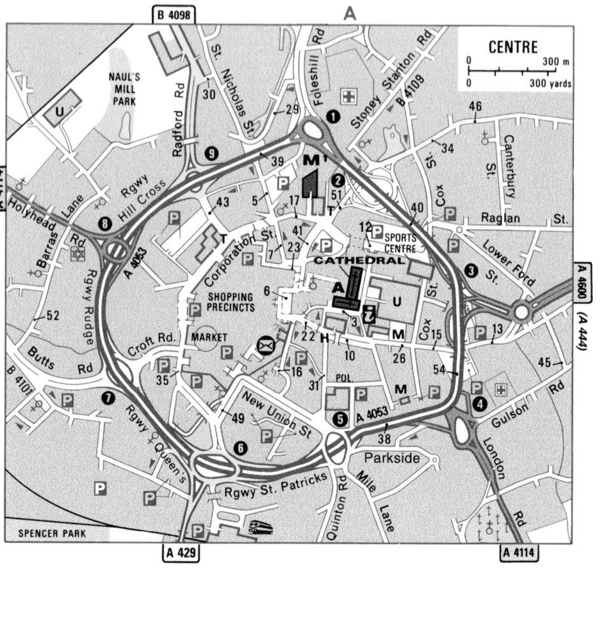

Conwy 33 I 24
Conwy (River) 33 I 24
Conwy (Vale of) 33 I 24
Cooden Beach 12 V 31
Cookham 19 R 29
Coolham 11 S 31
Coombe Bissett 9 O 30
Copdock 23 X 27
Copmanthorpe 40 Q 22
Copplestone 4 I 31
Copthorne 11 T 30
Coquet (River) 51 N 17
Corbridge 45 N 19
Corby 28 R 26
Corby Glen 36 S 25
Corfe Castle 9 N 32
Corhampton 10 Q 31
Cornhill 69 L 11
Cornhill-on-Tweed 50 N 17
Cornwall (County) 3 G 32
Cornwood 4 I 32
Corpach 60 E 13
Corpusty 31 X 25
Corran 60 E 13
Corrie 53 E 17
Corrimony 66 F 11
Corringham 21 V 29
Corryvreckan (Gulf of) 52 C 15
Corscombe 8 L 31
Corsham 18 N 29
Corsham Court 18 N 29
Corstopitum 51 N 19
Corwen 33 J 25
Cosby 28 Q 26
Cosham 10 Q 31
Costessey 31 X 26
Cotherstone 46 O 20
Cothi (River) 15 H 28
Cotswold Wildlife Park 18 O 28
Cottenham 29 U 27
Cottered 20 T 28
Cottingham (East Riding of Yorks.) 41 S 22
Cottingham (Northants.) 28 R 26
Countesthorpe 28 Q 26
Coupar Angus 62 K 14
Cove Bay 69 N 12
Coventry 27 P 26
Coverack 2 E 33
Cowal 54 E 15
Cowan Bridge 38 M 21
Cowbridge / Bont-faen 16 J 29
Cowdenbeath 56 K 15
Cowdray House 10 R 31
Cowes 10 Q 31
Cowfold 11 T 31
Cowplain 10 Q 31
Coxheath 12 V 30
Coylton 48 G 17
Crackington Haven 6 G 31
Cragside Gardens 51 O 18
Craig 66 E 11
Craig-y-nos 15 I 28
Craigellachie 68 K 11
Craighead 57 M 15
Craighouse 52 C 16
Craigievar Castle 68 L 12
Craignish (Loch) 54 D 15
Craignure 59 C 14
Craigrothie 56 L 15
Craik 50 K 17
Crail 57 M 15
Cramlington 51 P 18
Cramond 56 K 16
Cranborne 9 O 31
Cranbrook 12 V 30
Cranleigh 11 S 30
Crathes Castle 69 M 12
Crathie 62 K 12
Crathorne 46 Q 20
Craven Arms 26 L 26
Crawford 49 J 17
Crawley (Hants.) 9 P 30
Crawley (West Sussex) 11 T 30
Crawley Down 11 T 30
Creag Meagaidh 61 G 13
Creagorry 64 Y 11
Crediton 7 J 31
Creetown 42 G 19
Creran (Loch) 60 D 14
Cressage 26 M 26
Creswell 36 Q 24
Crewe 34 M 24
Crewkerne 8 L 31
Crianlarich 55 G 14
Criccieth 32 H 25
Crich 35 P 24
Crichton 56 L 16
Crick 28 Q 26
Cricket St. Thomas 8 L 31
Crickhowell 16 K 28
Cricklade 18 O 29
Crickley Hill 18 N 28
Crieff 55 I 14
Crimond 69 O 11
Crinan 54 D 15
Crinan (Loch) 54 D 15
Cringleford 31 X 26
Crocketford 49 I 18
Crockham Hill 11 U 30
Croft 26 L 27
Croft-on-Tees 46 P 20
Croggan 59 C 14
Cromalt Hills 72 E 9
Cromar 68 L 12
Cromarty 67 H 10
Cromarty Firth 67 H 11
Cromdale 68 J 11
Cromdale (Hills of) 68 J 12
Cromer 31 X 25
Cromford 35 P 24
Crondall 10 R 30
Crook 46 O 19
Crook of Devon 56 J 15
Crookham Village 10 R 30
Cropwell Bishop 36 R 25
Crosby 34 K 23
Crosby Ravensworth 45 M 20
Croscombe 8 M 30
Cross 71 B 8
Cross Fell 45 M 19
Cross Hands 15 H 28
Cross Inn 24 H 27
Crossapoll 58 Z 14
Crosshill (South Ayrshire) 48 G 18
Crosshill (Fife) 56 K 15
Crosshouse 48 G 17
Crosskeys 16 K 29
Crosskirk 73 J 8
Crossmichael 43 I 19
Crouch (River) 21 W 29
Crowborough 11 U 30
Crowcombe 7 K 30
Crow Hill 17 M 28
Crowhurst 12 V 31
Crowland 29 T 25
Crowle 40 R 23
Crowlin Island 65 C 11
Crowthorne 19 R 29
Croxley Green 20 S 29
Croy 67 H 11
Croyde 6 H 30
Croydon (London Borough) 20 T 29
Cruden Bay 69 O 11
Crudgington 26 M 25
Crudwell 18 N 29
Crug-y-bar 24 I 27
Crulivig 70 Z 9
Crymmych 14 G 28
Crynant 15 I 28
Cuckfield 11 T 30
Cuckney 36 Q 24
Cuddington 34 M 24
Cudworth 40 P 23
Cuffley 20 T 28
Cuillin Sound 65 B 12
Cuillins (The) 65 B 12
Culdrose 2 E 33
Cullen 68 L 10
Cullen Bay 68 L 10
Cullipool 54 D 15
Cullompton 7 J 31
Culmington 26 L 26
Culmstock 7 K 31
Culrain 72 G 10
Culross 56 J 15
Culter Fell 49 J 17
Cults 69 N 12
Culzean Castle 48 F 17
Cumbernauld 55 I 16
Cumbria (County) 44 K 19
Cumbrian Moutains 44 K 20
Cuminestown 69 N 11
Cummersdale 44 L 19
Cummertrees 49 J 19
Cumnock 48 H 17
Cumnor 18 P 28
Cunninghame 48 G 17
Cunninghamhead 48 G 17
Cupar 56 K 15
Curdridge 10 Q 31
Currie 56 K 16
Curry Rivel 8 L 30
Cwm 16 K 28
Cwm Bychan 32 H 25
Cwm Taf 16 J 28
Cwmbrân 17 L 29
Cwmllynfell 15 I 28
Cwmystwyth 25 I 26
Cydweli / Kidwelly 15 H 28
Cymmer 16 J 29
Cymyran Bay 32 G 24

D

Dailly 48 F 18
Daimh (Loch an) 61 G 14
Dairsie or Osnaburgh 56 L 14
Dalavich 54 E 15
Dalbeattie 43 I 19
Dalby 42 F 21
Dale 14 E 28
Daliburgh 64 X 12
Dalkeith 56 K 16
Dallas 68 J 11
Dallington 12 V 31
Dalmally 54 F 14
Dalmellington 48 G 18
Dalmeny 56 J 16
Dalnabreck 59 C 13
Dalry (North Ayrshire) 54 F 16
Dalry (Dumfries and Galloway) 48 H 18
Dalrymple 48 G 17
Dalston 44 L 19
Dalton (Dumfries and Galloway) 49 J 18
Dalton (North Yorks.) 40 P 21
Dalton in Furness 38 K 21
Damh (Loch) 66 D 11
Dan-yr-Ogof 15 I 28
Danbury 22 V 28
Dane 34 N 24
Darenth 20 U 29
Darfield 40 P 23
Darlington 46 P 20
Darowen 25 I 26
Dartford 20 U 29
Dartford Tunnel 20 U 29
Dartington 4 I 32
Dartmeet 4 I 32
Dartmoor National Park 4 I 32
Dartmouth 4 J 32
Darton 40 P 23
Darvel 48 H 17
Darwen 39 M 22
Datchet 19 S 29
Dava 68 J 11
Daventry 28 Q 27
Davidstow 3 G 32
Daviot 67 H 11
Dawley 26 M 26
Dawlish 4 J 32
Deal 13 Y 30
Dean Forest Park 17 M 28
Deanich Lodge 66 F 10
Deanston 55 H 15
Dearham 44 J 19
Deben (River) 23 X 27
Debenham 23 X 27
Deddington 19 Q 28
Dedham 21 W 28
Dee (River) (Scotland) 69 N 12
Dee / Afon Dyfrdwy (River) (Wales) 33 K 24
Deene 28 S 26
Deeping St. Nicholas 29 T 25
Deeps (The) 75 P 3
Defford 27 N 27
Delabole 3 F 32
Delamere Forest 34 L 24
Delph 39 N 23
Denbigh / Dinbych 33 J 24
Denby Dale 39 P 23
Denham 19 S 29
Denholm 50 L 17
Denmead 10 Q 31
Dennington 23 Y 27
Denny 55 I 15
Dent 45 M 21
Denton 35 N 23
Derby 35 P 25
Derbyshire (County) 35 O 24
Dersingham 30 V 25
Dervaig 59 B 14
Derwent (River) (R. Ouse) 40 R 22
Derwent (River) (R. Trent) 35 P 24
Derwent (River) (R. Tyne) 46 O 19
Derwent Dale 35 O 23
Derwent Reservoir (Derbs.) 35 O 23
Derwent Reservoir (Northumb.) 45 N 19
Derwent Water 44 K 20
Desborough 28 R 26
Desford 28 Q 26
Detling 12 V 30
Deveron (River) 69 M 11
Devil's Beef Tub 49 J 17
Devil's Bridge / Pontarfynach 25 I 26
Devil's Elbow 62 J 13
Devil's Punch Bowl 10 R 30
Devizes 18 O 29
Devon (County) 4 J 31
Devonport 3 H 32
Dewsbury 39 P 22
Dherue (Loch an) 72 G 8
Didcot 19 Q 29
Diddlebury 26 L 26
Dilwyn 26 L 27
Dinas Dinlle 32 G 24
Dinas Head 14 F 27
Dinbych / Denbigh 33 J 24
Dinbych-y-pysgod / Tenby 14 F 28
Dingwall 67 G 11
Dinnet 68 L 12
Dinnington 36 Q 23
Dinton 9 O 30
Dirleton 57 L 15
Dishforth 40 P 21
Diss 31 X 26
Distington 44 J 20
Ditcheat 8 M 30
Ditchley Park 18 P 28
Ditchling 11 T 31
Ditton Priors 26 M 26
Doc Penfro / Pembroke Dock 14 F 28
Docherty (Glen) 66 E 11
Dochgarroch 67 H 11
Docking 30 V 25
Doddington (Cambs.) 29 U 26
Doddington (Kent) 12 W 30
Doddington (Lincs.) 36 S 24
Doddington (Northumb.) 51 O 17
Dodman Point 3 F 33
Dodworth 40 P 23
Dolfor 25 K 26
Dolgellau 25 I 25
Dolgoch Falls 24 I 26
Dollar 56 I 15
Dolton 6 H 31
Don (River) 40 Q 23
Don (River) 68 K 12
Doncaster 40 Q 23
Donington 37 T 25
Donington Park Circuit 35 P 25
Donington-on-Bain 37 T 24
Donisthorpe 27 P 25
Donnington (Berks.) 19 Q 29
Donnington (Salop) 26 M 25
Donyatt 8 L 31
Doon (Loch) 48 G 18
Dorchester (Dorset) 8 M 31

DERBY

Albert Street Z 2
Babington Lane Z 3
Bold Lane Y 4
Bradshaw Way Z 5
Cathedral Road Y 7
Charnwood Street Z 9
Corn Market Z 13
Corporation Street YZ 14
Duffield Road Y 17
Eagle Shopping Centre Z
East Street Z 18
Full Street Y 19
Iron Gate Y 22
Jury Street Y 23
King Street Y 25
Liversage St. Z 26
Market Place YZ 27
Midland Road Z 28
Mount Street Z 29
Normanton Road Z 31
Queen Street Y 32
St. Mary's Gate Y 33
St. Peter's Street Z 34
Sacheveral Street Z 36
Stafford Street Z 37
Victoria Street Z 41
Wardwick Z 43

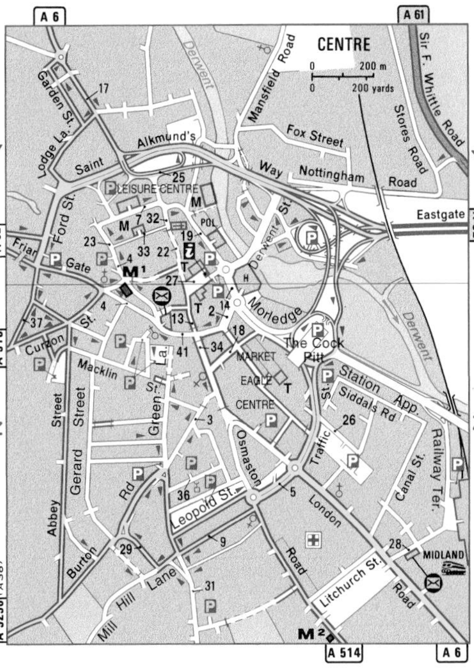

A 6
A 61
CENTRE
200 m
200 yards
Mansfield Road
Garden St.
Alkmund's
Fox Street
Sir F. Whittle Road
Stores Road
Saint
Way
Nottingham
Road
Lodge La.
Ford St.
LEISURE CENTRE
Eastgate
A 52
Friar Gate
Morledge
Derwent
A 516
Curzon St.
Macklin
MARKET
EAGLE CENTRE
The Cock Pitt
Station App.
Siddals Rd
Green La.
Osmaston
Traffic St.
Railway Ter.
Canal St.
Street
Street
Gerard
Abbey
Rd
Leopold St.
London
Road
Burton
Mill Hill Lane
Litchurch St.
Road
MIDLAND
A 5250
A 514

Dorchester (Oxon.) 19 Q 29
Dordon 27 P 26
Dorking 11 T 30
Dormans Land 11 U 30
Dormanstown 47 Q 20
Dornie 66 D 12
Dornoch 67 H 10
Dornoch Firth 67 H 10
Dorrington 26 L 26
Dorset (County) 8 M 31
Dorstone 26 K 27
Douchary (Glen) 66 F 10
Douglas (South Lanarkshire) 49 I 17
Douglas (Isle of Man) 42 G 21
Douglastown 62 L 14
Dounby 74 K 6
Doune 55 H 15
Dove (River) 35 O 24
Dove Cottage 44 K 20
Dovedale 35 O 24
Dover 13 X 30
Doveridge 35 O 25
Dovey / Dyfi (River) 24 I 26
Downderry 3 G 32
Downham 29 U 26
Downham Market 30 V 26
Downies 63 N 12
Downton 9 O 31
Draycott 35 P 25
Draycott-in-the-Moors 35 N 25
Drayton (Norfolk) 31 X 25
Drayton (Oxon.) 19 Q 29
Dreghorn 48 G 17
Drenewydd / Newtown 25 K 26
Dreswick Point 42 G 21
Drigg 44 J 20
Drimnin 59 C 14
Droitwich 27 N 27
Dronfield 35 P 24
Drongan 48 G 17
Druidibeg (Loch) 64 Y 12
Druim a' Chliabhain (Loch) 73 H 8

DOVER

Bench Street 3
Biggin Street 4
Cannon Street 5
Castle Street 6
Charlton Green 7
High Street
King Street 13
Ladywell, Park Street 15
London Road 17
Pencester Road
Priory Road 18
Priory Street 19
Queen St. 20
Worthington Street 25

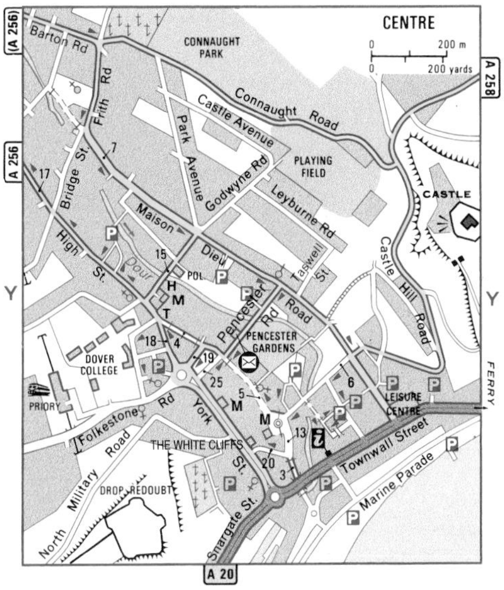

A 256
CENTRE
200 m
200 yards
A 258
Barton Rd
CONNAUGHT PARK
Frith Rd
Connaught Road
Castle Avenue
Park Avenue
Godwyne Rd
PLAYING FIELD
Leyburn Rd
CASTLE
Bridge St.
Maison Dieu
High St.
Castle Hill Road
Taswell St.
Pencester Rd
PENCESTER GARDENS
DOVER COLLEGE
PRIORY
LEISURE CENTRE
Folkestone Road
York St.
THE WHITE CLIFFS
Townwall Street
Marine Parade
Military
North
DROP REDOUBT
Snargate St.
FERRY
A 20

DUNDEE

Bell Street 6
City Square 7
Commercial Street 8
East Marketgait 15
High Street 17
Meadowside 23
Murraygate 25
Nethergate 26
Overgate Centre
Reform Street 35
St. Andrews Street 36
South Union Street 39
Trades Lane 41
Ward Road 42
Wellgate Centre
West Bell Street 43
West Marketgait 44

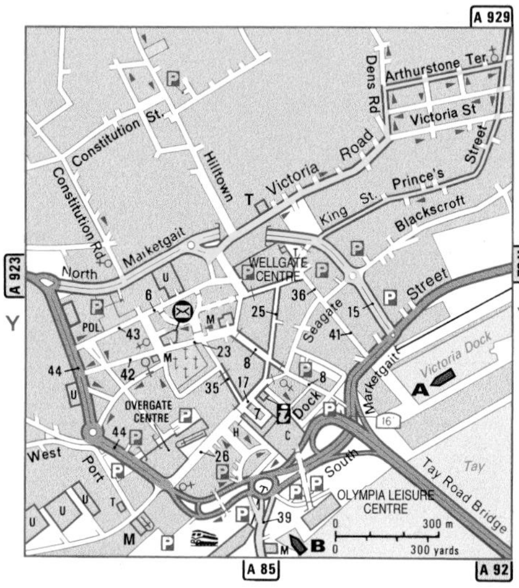

DURHAM

Alexander Crescent A 2
Castle Chare A 3
Court Lane B 5
Elvet Bridge B 6
Elvet Crescent B 7
Flass Street A 8
Framwelgate Bridge B 10
Framwelgate Waterside B 12
Gilesgate B 14
Grove Street A 15
High Street B 16
Market Place B 17
Millburngate A 19
Neville Street A 20
Potters Bank A 21
Providence Row B 21
Saddler Street B
Silver Street B 24
Sutton Street A 25

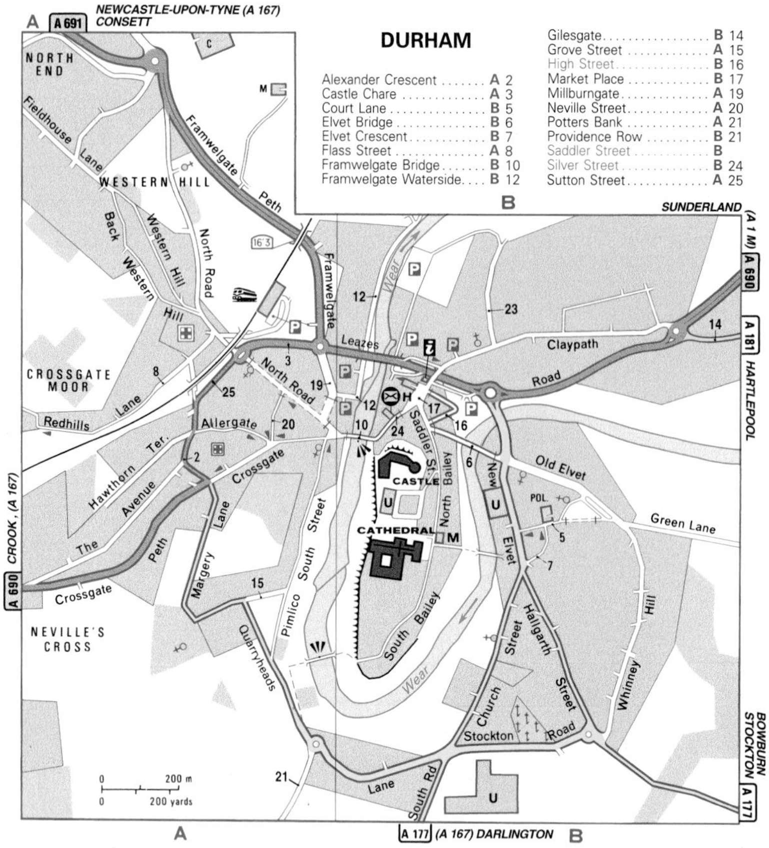

Drum Castle 69 M 12
Drumbeg 72 E 9
Drumclog 48 H 17
Drumlanrig Castle 49 I 18
Drumlithie 63 M 13
Drummond Castle 55 I 14
Drummore 42 F 19
Drummossie Muir 67 H 11
Drumnadrochit 67 G 11
Drumtochty Forest 63 M 13
Druridge Bay 51 P 18
Drybrook 17 M 28
Dryburgh Abbey 50 M 17
Drygarn Fawr 25 J 27
Drymen 55 G 15
Ducklington 18 P 28
Duddington 28 S 26
Dudley 27 N 26
Duff House 69 M 11
Duffield 35 P 25
Dufftown 68 K 11
Duffus 68 J 10
Duich (Loch) 66 D 12
Duirinish 65 C 12
Duke's Pass 55 G 15
Dukinfield 35 N 23
Dulnain Bridge 68 J 12
Duloe 3 G 32
Dulverton 7 J 30
Dumbarton 55 G 16
Dumfries 49 J 18
Dun Carloway Broch 70 Z 9
Dunbar 57 M 15
Dunbeath 74 J 9
Dunblane 55 I 15
Duncansby Head 74 K 8
Dunchurch 28 Q 26
Duncton 10 S 31
Dundee 62 K 14
Dundonald 48 G 17
Dundrennan 43 I 19
Dunecht 69 M 12
Dunfermline 56 J 15
Dungeness 13 W 31
Dunholme 36 S 24
Dunkeld 62 J 14
Dunkery Beacon 7 J 30
Dunlop 55 G 16
Dunnet 74 J 8
Dunnet Bay 74 J 8
Dunnet Head 74 J 7
Dunning 56 J 15
Dunnottar Castle 63 N 13
Dunoon 54 F 16
Dunrobin Castle 67 I 10
Duns 57 M 16
Dunscore 49 I 18
Dunsfold 10 S 30
Dunsford 4 I 31
Dunsop Bridge 38 M 22
Dunstable 19 S 28
Dunstaffnage Castel 60 D 14
Dunstanburgh Castle 51 P 17
Dunster 7 J 30
Duntelchaig (Loch) 67 H 11
Dunure 48 F 17
Dunvegan 65 A 11
Dunvegan (Loch) 65 A 11
Dunvegan Castle 65 A 11
Dunvegan Head 64 Z 11
Dunwich 31 Y 27
Durdle Door 8 N 32
Durham 46 P 19
Durham (County) 45 N 19
Durlston Head 9 O 32
Durness 72 F 8
Durrington 9 O 30
Dursley 17 M 28
Dury Voe 75 Q 2
Duston 28 R 27
Duxford 29 U 27
Dyce 69 N 12
Dyfi / Dovey (River) 24 I 26
Dykehead 62 K 13
Dykends 62 K 13
Dymchurch 13 W 30
Dymock 17 M 28
Dyrham 17 M 29
Dyrham Park 17 M 29
Dyserth 33 J 24

E

Eaglescliffe 46 P 20
Eaglesham 55 H 16
Eakring 36 R 24
Ealing (London Borough) 20 T 29
Earba (Lochan na h-) 61 G 13
Earby 39 N 22
Eardisley 26 K 27
Earl Shilton 27 Q 26
Earl Soham 23 X 27
Earl Stonham 23 X 27
Earley Winnersh 19 R 29
Earls Barton 28 R 27
Earl's Colne 22 W 28
Earls Colne 22 W 28
Earlsferry 56 L 15
Earlston 50 L 17
Earn (Loch) 55 H 14
Earn (River) 61 H 14
Earn (River) 56 J 14
Easdale 54 D 15
Easebourne 10 R 31
Easington 46 P 19
Easington Lane 46 P 19
Easingwold 40 Q 21
East Aberthaw 16 J 29
East Barkwith 37 T 24
East Bergholt 21 X 28
East Brent 8 L 30
East Budleigh 4 K 32
East Cowes 10 Q 31
East Dereham 30 W 25
East Glen (River) 36 S 25
East Grinstead 11 T 30
East Hagbourne 19 Q 29
East Hanney 18 P 29
East Harling 30 W 26
East Hendred 18 P 29
East Hoathly 11 U 31
East Horsley 11 S 30
East Huntspill 8 L 30
East Ilsley 19 Q 29
East Kilbride 55 H 16
East Knoyle 9 N 30
East Lambrook 8 L 31
East Leake 36 Q 25
East Linton 57 M 16
East Loch Roag 70 Z 9
East Loch Tarbet 70 Z 10
East Looe 3 G 32
East Lulworth 8 N 32
East Markham 36 R 24
East Meon 10 Q 31
East Midlands Airport 36 Q 25
East Moor 35 P 24
East Rhidorroch Lodge 72 F 10
East Sussex (County) 11 U 30
East Wemyss 56 K 15
East Wittering 10 R 31
East Witton 46 O 21
Eastbourne 11 U 31
Eastchurch 21 W 29
Eastdean 11 U 31
Easter Ross 67 G 10
Eastergate 10 S 31
Eastham 34 L 24
Eastington 17 N 28
Eastleigh 9 P 31
Easton (Dorset) 5 M 32
Easton (Norfolk) 31 X 26
Easton-in-Gordano 17 L 29
Eastriggs 49 K 19
Eastry 13 X 30
Eastville 37 U 24
Eastwood 36 Q 24
Ebbw Vale / Glyn Ebwy 16 K 28
Ebchester 46 O 19
Ecclefechan 49 K 18
Eccles 34 M 23
Eccleshall 34 N 25
Echt 69 M 12
Eckington (Worc.) 27 N 27
Eckington (Derbs.) 35 P 24
Edale 35 O 23
Eday 74 L 6
Edderton 67 H 10
Eddrachillis Bay 72 E 9
Edenbridge 11 U 30

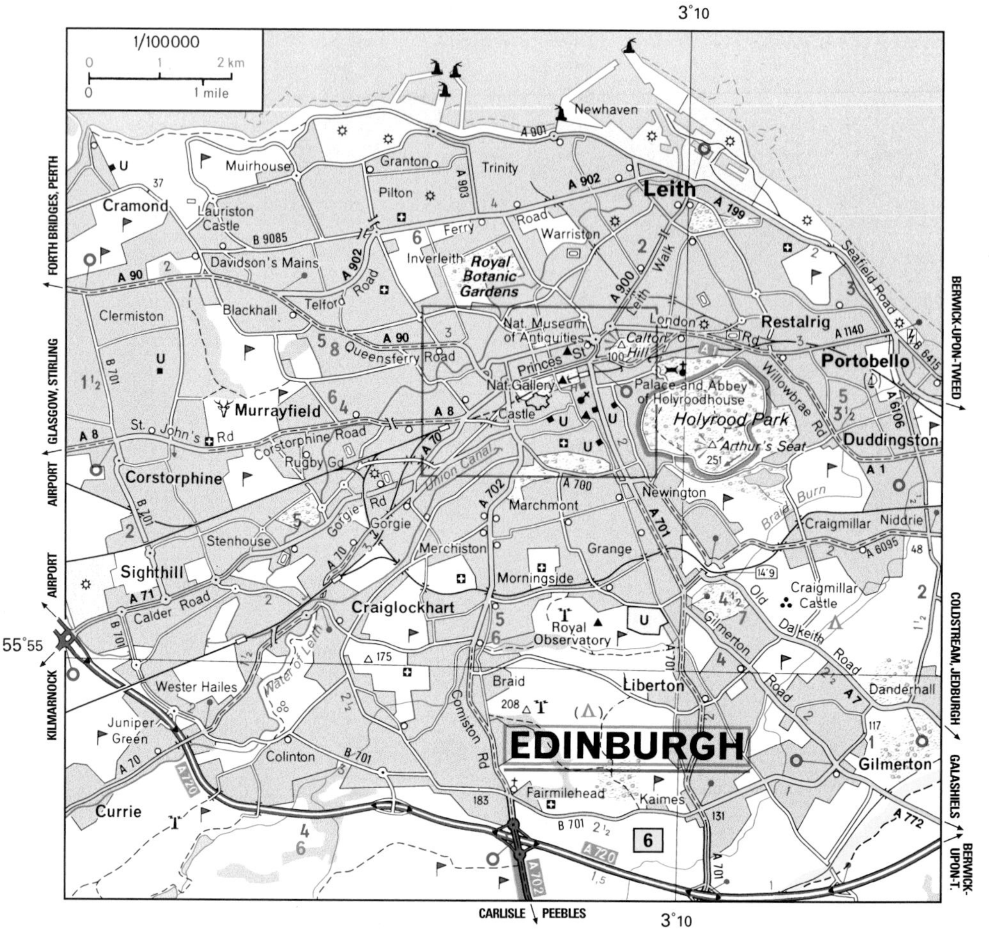

EDINBURGH CENTRE

Bernard Terrace	EZ	3
Bread Street	DZ	6
Bristo Place	EZ	7
Candlemaker Row	EZ	9
Castle Street	DY	
Castlehill	DZ	10
Chambers Street	EZ	12
Chapel Street	EZ	13
Charlotte Square	CY	14
Deanhaugh Street	CY	23
Douglas Gardens	CY	25
Drummond Street	EZ	27
Forrest Road	EZ	31
Frederick Street	DY	
Gardner's Crescent	CZ	32
George IV Bridge	EZ	33
George Street	DY	
Grassmarket	DZ	35
Hanover Street	DY	
High Street	EYZ	37
Home Street	DZ	38
Hope Street	CY	39
Johnston Terrace	DZ	42
King's Bridge	DZ	44
King's Stables Road	DZ	45
Lawnmarket	EYZ	46
Leith Street	EY	47
Leven Street	DZ	48
Lothian Street	EZ	51
Mound (The)	DY	55
North Bridge	EY	61
North St. Andrew Street	EY	66
Princes Street	DY	
Raeburn Place	CY	69
Randolph Crescent	CY	71
St. Andrew Square	EY	73
St. James Centre	EY	
St. Mary's Street	EY	75
Shandwick Place	CYZ	77
South Charlotte Street	DY	78
South St. David Street	DEY	79
Spittal Street	DZ	83
Victoria Street	EZ	84
Waterloo Place	EY	87
Waverley Bridge	EY	89
Waverley Market	EY	
West Maitland Street	CZ	92

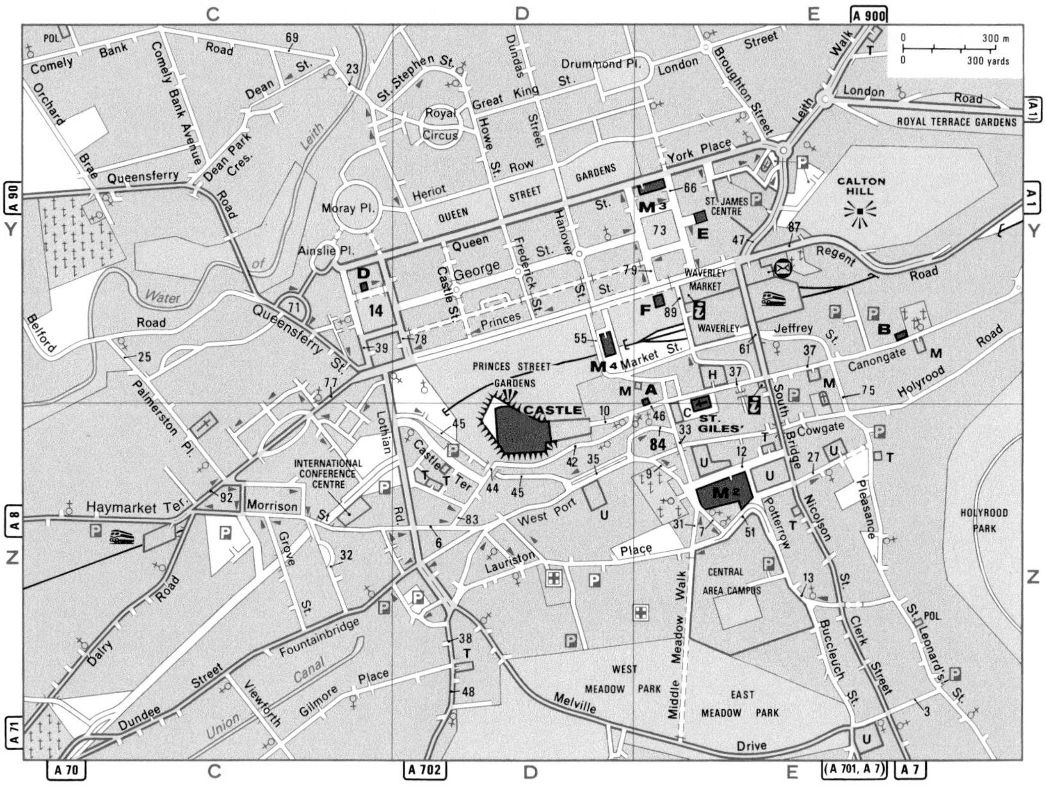

Eden (River)	44	K 19
Edgmond	34	M 25
Edinburgh	56	K 16
Edington	9	N 30
Edith Weston	28	S 26
Edlesborough	19	S 28
Edwinstowe	36	Q 24
Edzell	63	M 13
Eggerness Point	42	G 19
Eggleston	46	N 20
Egham	19	S 29
Egilsay	74	L 6
Eglingham	51	O 17
Egremont	44	J 20
Egton	47	R 20
Eigg	59	B 13
Eigheach (Loch)	61	G 13
Eight Ash Green	22	W 28
Eil (Loch)	60	E 13
Eilde Mór (Loch)	60	F 13
Eilean a' Chalmain	52	A 15
Eilean Beag	65	C 11
Eilean Chathastail	59	B 13
Eilean Donan Castle	66	D 12
Eilean Flodigarry	65	B 10
Eilean Mullagrach	72	D 9
Eilean nan Each	59	B 13
Eilean Trodday	65	B 10
Eilt (Loch)	60	D 13
Eishort (Loch)	65	C 12
Elan Valley	25	J 27
Elan Village	25	J 27
Elgin	68	K 11
Elgol	65	B 12
Elham	13	X 30
Elie	56	L 15
Elkesley	36	R 24
Elkstone	18	N 28
Elland	39	O 22
Ellastone	35	O 25
Ellesmere	34	L 25
Ellesmere Port	34	L 24
Ellon	69	N 11
Elmdon	29	U 27
Elmswell	22	W 27
Elphin	72	E 9
Elsenham	20	U 28
Elstead	10	R 30
Elstree	20	T 29
Elswick	38	L 22
Eltisley	29	T 27
Elton	29	S 26
Elvington	40	R 22
Ely	29	U 26
Emberton	28	R 27
Embleton	51	P 17
Embo	73	I 10
Embsay	39	O 22
Emneth	29	U 26
Empingham	28	S 26
Emsworth	10	R 31
Enard Bay	72	D 9
Enderby	28	Q 26
Endon	35	N 24
Enfield (London Borough)	20	T 29
Enford	9	O 30
Englefield Green	19	S 29
Enham Alamein	9	P 30
Enmore	7	K 30
Ensay	59	B 14
Enstone	18	P 28
Enville	26	N 26
Eoropie	71	B 8
Eorsa	59	B 14
Eport (Loch)	64	Y 11
Epping	20	U 28
Epping Forest	20	U 29
Epsom	20	T 30
Epworth	40	R 23
Eredine Forest	54	D 15
Eriboll (Loch)	72	F 8
Ericht (Loch)	61	G 13
Eriska	60	D 14
Eriskay	64	Y 12
Erisort (Loch)	70	A 9
Ermington	4	I 32
Erpingham	31	X 25
Erraid	52	A 15
Errochty (Loch)	61	H 13
Errol	56	K 14
Ersary	58	X 13
Erskine Bridge	55	G 16
Esha Ness	75	P 2
Esher	20	S 29
Esk (Glen)	62	L 13
Esk (River)	50	K 19
Eskdale	50	K 18
Eskdalemuir	49	K 18
Essendon	20	T 28
Essex (County)	22	V 28
Essich	67	H 11
Eston	46	Q 20
Etchingham	12	V 30
Etherow (River)	35	N 23
Etherow Park	35	N 23
Etive (Glen)	60	F 14
Etive (Loch)	60	E 14
Eton	19	S 29
Ettington	27	P 27
Ettrick	50	K 17
Ettrick Forest	50	K 17
Ettrick Pen	49	K 17
Euxton	38	L 22
Evanton	67	G 11
Evercreech	8	M 30
Everleigh	9	O 30
Evershot	8	M 31
Everton	36	R 23
Evesham	27	O 27
Evesham (Vale of)	27	O 27
Ewe (Isle of)	71	D 10
Ewell	20	T 29
Ewelme	19	Q 29
Ewhurst	11	S 30
Exbourne	4	I 31
Exe (River)	7	J 31
Exebridge	7	J 30
Exeter	7	J 31
Exford	7	J 30
Exminster	7	J 31
Exmoor National Park	7	I 30
Exmouth	4	J 32
Exton	7	J 30
Eyam	35	O 24
Eye (Cambs.)	29	T 26
Eye (Suffolk)	31	X 27
Eye Peninsula	71	B 9
Eyemouth	57	N 16
Eynort (Loch) (Highland)	65	A 12
Eynort (Loch) (Western Isles)	64	Y 12
Eynsford	20	U 29
Eynsham	18	P 28
Eyre Point	65	B 12
Eythorne	13	X 30

EXETER CENTRE

Alphington Rd	Z	2
Barnfield Rd	Z	3
Bedford St.	Y	6
Castle St.	Y	7
Cathedral Close Walk	YZ	13
Cowick St.	Z	15
Edmund St.	Z	18
Fore St.	Z	
Guildhall Shopping Centre	Y	
High St.	Y	
King St.	Z	22
Mary Arches St.	Z	26
Mint (The)	Z	28
New Bridge St.	Z	31
Palace Gate	Z	36
Paul St.	Y	37
Preston St.	Z	40
Princesshay	Y	44
Quay Hill	Z	45
Queen's Terrace	Y	46
St. Martin's Lane	Y	49
Stepcote Hill	Z	50

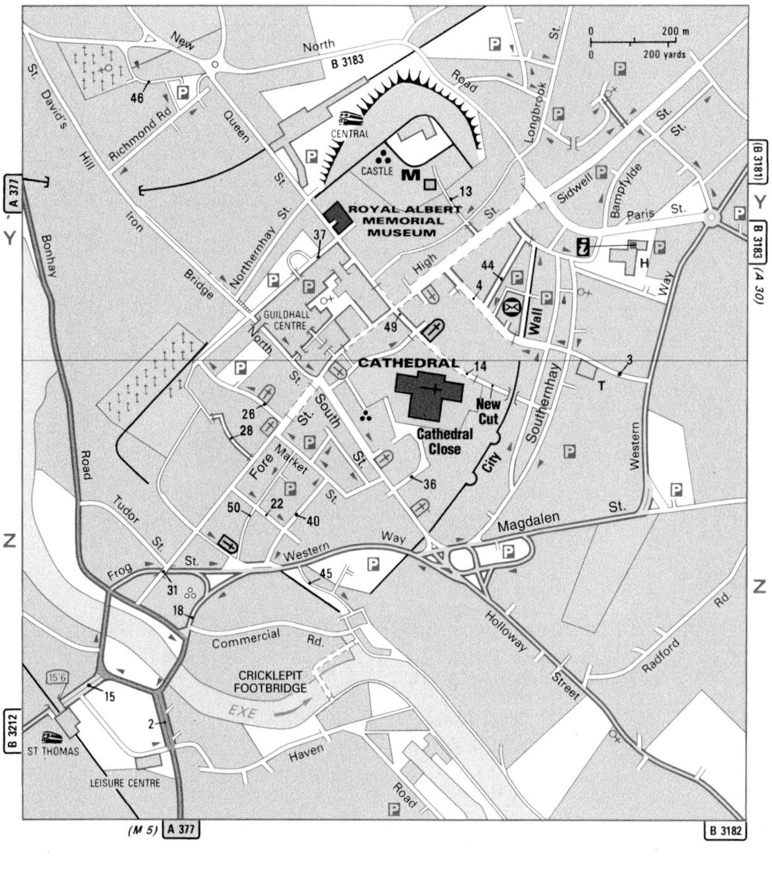

F

Fada (Loch) 64 Y 11
Fair Isle 75 P 5
Fair Oak 10 Q 31
Fairbourne 24 H 25
Fairford 18 O 28
Fairlie 54 F 16
Fairlight 12 V 31
Fakenham 30 W 25
Falfield 17 M 29
Falkirk 55 I 16
Falkland 56 K 15
Fallin 55 I 15
Falmouth 2 E 33
Fanagmore 72 E 8
Fannich (Loch) 66 E 11
Fara 74 K 7
Fareham 10 Q 31
Faringdon 18 P 29
Farleigh-Hungerford 17 N 30
Farley Mount 9 P 30
Farmborough 17 M 29
Farmtown 68 L 11
Farnborough (Hants.) 10 R 30
Farnborough (Warw.) 27 P 27
Farndon 36 R 24
Farne Islands 51 P 17
Farnham (Dorset) 9 N 31
Farnham (Surrey) 10 R 30
Farnham Royal 19 S 29
Farningham 20 U 29
Farnsfield 36 Q 24
Farnworth 39 M 23
Farrington Gurney 8 M 30
Farway 7 K 31
Fasnakyle Forest 66 F 11
Fasque 63 M 13
Fauldhouse 56 I 16
Faversham 12 W 30
Fawley 9 P 31
Fazeley 27 O 26
Fearnan 61 H 14
Fearnmore 65 C 11
Featherstone (Staffs.) 27 N 26
Featherstone (West Yorks.) 40 P 22
Feering 22 W 28
Felindre 25 K 26
Felinheli 32 H 24
Felixstowe 23 Y 28
Felling 46 P 19
Felpham 10 S 31
Felsted 22 V 28
Feltham 20 S 29
Felton 51 O 18
Feltwell 30 V 26
Fenstanton 29 T 27
Fenwick 51 O 17
Feochan (Loch) 54 D 14
Feolin Ferry 52 B 16
Ferndown 9 O 31
Ferness 67 I 11
Fernhurst 10 R 30
Ferryden 63 M 13
Ferryhill 46 P 19
Feshie (Glen) 61 I 12
Fetcham 11 S 30
Fetlar 75 R 2
Fetterangus 69 N 11
Fettercairn 63 M 13
Ffestiniog 33 I 25
Ffestiniog (Vale of) 32 H 25
Fflint / Flint 34 K 24
Fforest Fawr 16 J 28
Fiaray 64 X 12
Filey 41 T 21
Filton 17 M 29
Finchampstead 19 R 29
Finchingfield 22 V 28
Findhorn 68 J 11
Findhorn (River) 67 H 12
Findhorn Bay 68 J 11
Findochty 68 L 10
Findon 11 S 31
Finedon 28 S 26
Fingest 19 R 29
Finningley 36 R 23
Finsbay 70 Z 10
Finstock 18 P 28
Finstown 74 K 6
Fintry 55 H 15
Fionn Loch 66 D 10
Fionn Loch Mór 72 F 9
Fionnphort 59 A 15
Fishbourne 10 Q 31
Fisherfield Forest 66 D 10
Fishguard / Abergwaun 14 F 28
Fittleworth 10 S 31
Flackwell Heath 19 R 29
Fladbury 27 N 27
Fladda-Chùain 65 A 10
Flamborough 41 T 21
Flamborough Head 41 T 21
Flamingo Park 40 R 21
Flamstead 20 S 28
Flash 35 O 24
Flatford Mill 21 X 28
Fleckney 28 Q 26
Fleet 10 R 30
Fleet (Islands of) 43 H 19
Fleet (Loch) 73 H 10
Fleetwood 38 K 22
Flimby 44 J 19
Flint / Fflint 34 K 24
Flitton 20 S 27
Flitwick 19 S 27
Flodday (near Hellisay) 58 X 13
Flodday (near Sandray) 58 X 13
Flodden Field 51 N 17
Flodigarry 65 B 11
Floors Castle 50 M 17
Flotta 74 K 7
Flowerdale Forest 66 D 11
Fochabers 68 K 11
Foinaven 72 F 8
Folkestone 13 X 30
Folkingham 36 S 25
Fontmell Magna 8 N 31
Ford 54 D 15
Forde Abbey 8 L 31
Fordham 30 V 27
Fordingbridge 9 O 31
Fordoun 63 M 13
Fordyce 68 L 11
Foreland 10 Q 31
Foreland Point 7 I 30
Foremark Reservoir 35 P 25
Forest Row 11 U 30
Forfar 62 L 14
Formby 38 K 23
Formby Point 38 K 23
Fornham All Saints 22 W 27
Forres 68 J 11
Forsinard 73 I 8
Fort Augustus 66 F 12
Fort George 67 H 11
Fort Victoria 9 P 31
Fort William 60 E 13
Forter 62 K 13
Forth 56 I 16
Forth (Firth of) 56 K 15
Forth (River) 55 G 15
Forth Bridges 56 J 15
Fortingall 61 H 14
Forton 34 M 25
Fortrose 67 H 11
Fortuneswell 5 M 32
Fosdyke 37 T 25
Fotheringhay 29 S 26
Foulness Point 21 W 29
Foulridge 39 N 22
Foulsham 30 X 25
Fountains Abbey 39 P 21
Four Crosses 25 K 25
Four Elms 11 U 30
Four Marks 10 Q 30
Foveran 69 N 12
Fowey 3 G 32
Fowlmere 29 U 27
Fownhope 17 M 27
Foxdale 42 G 21
Foxholes 41 S 21
Foyers 67 G 12
Fraddon 2 F 32
Framfield 11 U 31
Framlingham 23 Y 27
Frampton-on-Severn 17 M 28
Framwellgate Moor 46 P 19
Frant 11 U 30
Fraserburgh 69 O 10
Fraserburgh Bay 69 O 10
Freckenham 30 V 27
Freckleton 38 L 22
Freethorpe 31 Y 26
Freevater Forest 66 F 10
Fremington 6 H 30
Frensham 10 R 30
Freshwater 9 P 31
Freshwater Bay 9 P 31
Freshwater East 14 F 29
Freshwater West 14 E 29
Fressingfield 31 X 26
Freuchie (Loch) 61 I 14
Friday Bridge 29 U 26
Fridaythorpe 41 S 21
Frimley 19 R 30
Frinton-on-Sea 23 X 28
Friockheim 63 M 14
Frisa (Loch) 59 B 14
Friskney 37 U 24
Frittenden 12 V 30
Frizington 44 J 20
Frodsham 34 L 24
Froggatt 35 P 24
Frome 8 N 30
Fuday 64 X 12
Fuiay 58 X 13
Fulbourn 22 U 27
Fulwood 38 M 22

Folkestone Terminal

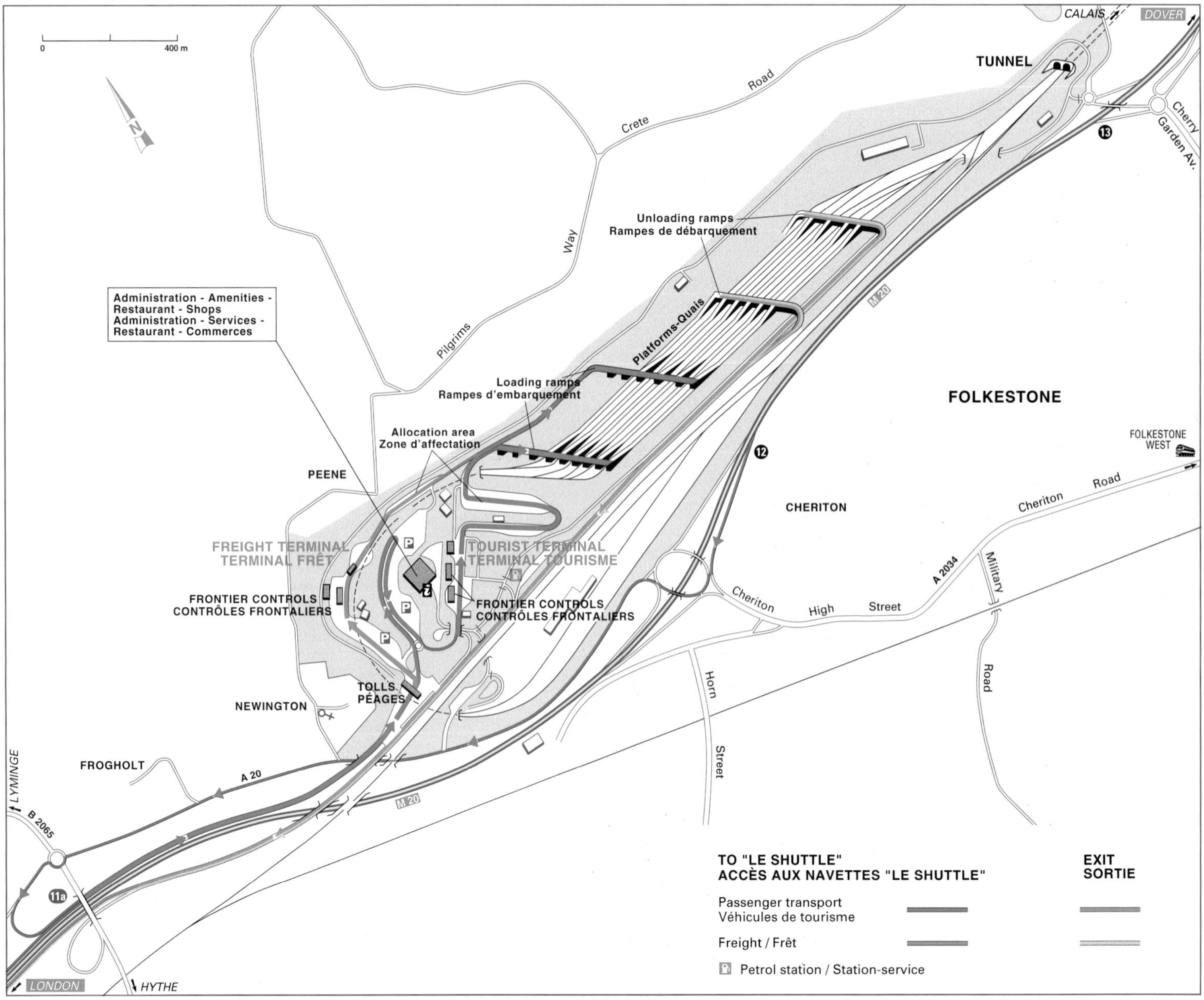

0
400 m
N
CALAIS
DOVER
TUNNEL
Crete Road
Cherry Garden Av.
Unloading ramps
Rampes de débarquement
Way
Pilgrims
Administration - Amenities - Restaurant - Shops
Administration - Services - Restaurant - Commerces
Platforms-Quais
M 20
Loading ramps
Rampes d'embarquement
Allocation area
Zone d'affectation
FOLKESTONE
FOLKESTONE WEST
PEENE
CHERITON
Cheriton Road
FREIGHT TERMINAL
TERMINAL FRÊT
TOURIST TERMINAL
TERMINAL TOURISME
A 2034
Military Road
FRONTIER CONTROLS
CONTRÔLES FRONTALIERS
Cheriton High Street
Horn Street
TOLLS
PÉAGES
NEWINGTON
FROGHOLT
A 20
LYMINGE
B 2065
LONDON
HYTHE
TO "LE SHUTTLE"
ACCÈS AUX NAVETTES "LE SHUTTLE"
EXIT
SORTIE
Passenger transport
Véhicules de tourisme
Freight / Frêt
Petrol station / Station-service

Terminal de Calais

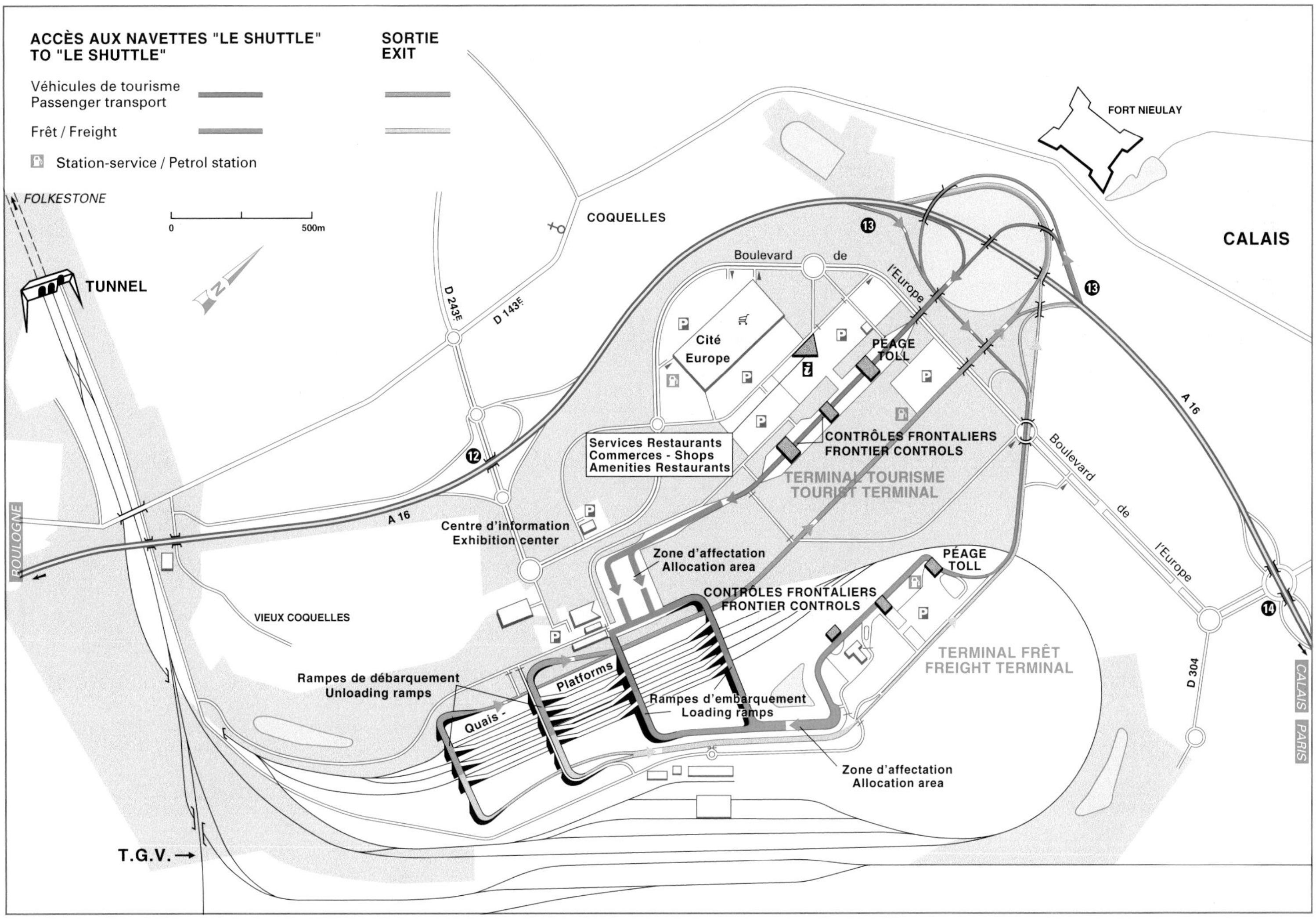
ACCÈS AUX NAVETTES "LE SHUTTLE"
TO "LE SHUTTLE"
SORTIE
EXIT
Véhicules de tourisme
Passenger transport
Frêt / Freight
Station-service / Petrol station
FOLKESTONE
0
500m
TUNNEL
COQUELLES
FORT NIEULAY
CALAIS
Boulevard de l'Europe
D 243E
D 143E
Cité Europe
PÉAGE TOLL
CONTRÔLES FRONTALIERS
FRONTIER CONTROLS
Services Restaurants
Commerces - Shops
Amenities Restaurants
TERMINAL TOURISME
TOURIST TERMINAL
A 16
Centre d'information
Exhibition center
Zone d'affectation
Allocation area
BOULOGNE
VIEUX COQUELLES
Rampes de débarquement
Unloading ramps
Quais - Platforms
Rampes d'embarquement
Loading ramps
TERMINAL FRÊT
FREIGHT TERMINAL
D 304
CALAIS
PARIS
T.G.V.

Funzie 75 R 2
Furness Abbey 38 K 21
Furness Fells 44 K 20
Fyfield (Essex) 20 U 28
Fyvie 69 M 11

G

Gainford 46 O 20
Gainsborough 36 R 23
Gairloch 66 C 10
Gairlochy 60 F 13
Gairsay 74 L 6
Galashiels 50 L 17
Galgate 38 L 22
Gallan Head 70 Y 9
Galloway Forest Park 48 G 18
Galmisdale 59 B 13
Galmpton 4 J 32
Galson 71 A 8
Galston 48 G 17
Galtrigill 64 Z 11
Gamlingay 29 T 27
Gamston 36 R 24
Ganton 41 S 21
Garboldisham 30 W 26
Gardenstown 69 N 10
Garelochhead 54 F 15
Garenin 70 Z 9
Garforth 40 P 22
Gargrave 39 N 22
Gargunnock 55 H 15
Garioch 69 M 12
Garlieston 42 G 19
Garmouth 68 K 11
Garrabost 71 B 9
Garrisdale Point 65 A 12
Garry (Glen) (Perthshire and Kinross) 61 H 13
Garry (Glen) (Highland) 60 E 12
Garry (Loch) 60 F 12
Garsington 19 Q 28
Garten (Loch) 67 I 12
Garth 25 J 27
Gartmore 55 G 15
Garton-on-The-Wolds 41 S 21
Garve 67 F 11
Garvellachs 52 C 15
Garvock 54 F 16
Garynahine 70 Z 9
Gatehouse of Fleet 43 H 19
Gateshead 46 P 19
Gateside 56 K 15
Gatley 34 N 23
Gatwick Airport 11 T 30
Gaulden Manor 7 K 30
Gayton 30 V 25
Geddington 28 R 26
Gedney Drove End 37 U 25
Gedney Hill 29 T 25
Georgeham 6 H 30
Georth 74 K 6
Gerrards Cross 19 S 29
Gifford 57 L 16
Gigha (Sound of) 53 C 17
Gigha Island 52 C 16
Gighay 64 Y 12
Gildersome 39 P 22
Gillingham (Dorset) 8 N 30
Gillingham (Kent) 21 V 29
Gilmerton 55 I 14
Girvan 48 F 18
Gisburn 39 N 22
Gittisham 7 K 31
Glaisdale 47 R 20
Glamis 62 K 14
Glamis Castle 62 L 14
Glanaman 15 I 28
Glas Maol 62 J 13
Glasbury 25 K 27
Glascarnoch (Loch) 66 F 10
Glasgow 55 H 16
Glass (Loch) 67 G 10
Glasson 38 L 22
Glastonbury 8 L 30
Gleann Beag 66 F 10
Gleann Mór 67 G 10
Glemsford 22 V 27
Glen Brittle Forest 65 B 12
Glen Finglas Reservoir 55 G 15
Glen More Forest Park 62 I 12
Glen Shee 62 J 13
Glenbarr 53 C 17
Glenborrodale 59 C 13
Glenbuck 49 I 17
Glencarse 56 K 14
Glencoe 60 E 13
Glencoul (Loch) 72 F 9
Glendurgan Garden 2 E 33
Glenelg 66 D 12
Glenelg Bay 66 D 12
Glenfarg 56 J 15
Glenfield 28 Q 26
Glenfinnan 60 D 13
Glenforsa Airport 59 C 14
Glengorm 59 B 14
Glengrasco 65 B 11
Glenkens (The) 48 H 18
Glenlivet 68 J 11
Glenluce 42 F 19
Glenmore 59 C 13
Glenrothes 56 K 15
Glentham 36 S 23
Glentress 50 K 17
Glentworth 36 S 23
Glinton 29 T 26
Glossop 35 O 23
Gloucester 17 N 28
Gloucestershire (County) 18 N 28
Glusburn 39 O 22
Glyn Ceiriog 33 K 25
Glyn-Ebwy /Ebbw Vale 16 K 28
Glyn-neath 16 J 28
Glyncorrwg 16 J 28
Glynde 11 U 31
Gnosall 34 N 25
Goat Fell 53 E 17
Goathland 47 R 20
Gobowen 34 K 25
Godalming 10 S 30
Godmanchester 29 T 27
Godmanstone 8 M 31
Godshill 10 Q 32
Godstone 11 T 30
Goil (Loch) 54 F 15
Golborne 34 M 23
Goldthorpe 40 Q 23
Golspie 73 I 10
Gomersal 39 O 22
Gometra 59 B 14
Gomshall 11 S 30
Goodrich 17 M 28
Goodrington 4 J 32
Goodwick 14 F 27
Goodwood House 10 R 31
Goole 40 R 22
Gordon 50 M 16
Gorebridge 56 K 16
Goring 19 Q 29
Gorm Loch Mór 72 F 9
Gorran Haven 3 F 33
Gorseinon 15 H 29
Gorsleston-on-Sea 31 Z 26
Gosberton 37 T 25
Gosforth (Cumbria) 44 J 20
Gosforth (Newcastle upon Tyne) 51 P 18
Gosport 10 Q 31
Gotham 36 Q 25
Gott Bay 58 Z 14
Goudhurst 12 V 30
Gourdon 63 N 13
Gourock 54 F 16
Gowerton 15 H 29
Goxhill 41 T 22
Graemsay 74 K 7
Grain 21 W 29
Grandtully 61 I 14
Grange-over-Sands 38 L 21
Grangemouth 56 I 15
Grantham 36 S 25
Grantown-on-Spey 62 J 12
Grantshouse 57 N 16
Grasmere 44 K 20
Grassington 39 O 21
Gravesend 21 V 29
Grayrigg 45 M 20
Grays Thurrock 20 V 29
Grayshott 10 R 30
Grayswood 10 R 30
Great Ayton 46 Q 20
Great Baddow 22 V 28
Great Bardfield 22 V 28
Great Barford 29 S 27
Great Barr 27 O 26
Great Bedwyn 18 P 29
Great Bentley 21 X 28
Great Bernera 70 Z 9
Great Bircham 30 V 25
Great Bookham 11 S 30
Great Bridon 46 P 20
Great Broughton 46 Q 20
Great Chesterford 22 U 27
Great Chishill 29 U 27
Great Clifton 44 J 20
Great Coates 41 T 23
Great Cumbrae Island 54 F 16
Great Driffield 41 S 21
Great Dunmow 22 V 28
Great Easton (Essex) 20 U 28
Great Easton (Leics.) 28 R 26
Great Eccleston 38 L 22
Great Ellingham 30 W 26
Great Gonerby 36 S 25
Great Grimsby 41 T 23
Great Harwood 39 M 22
Great Hockham 30 W 26
Great Horwood 19 R 28
Great Houghton 40 P 23
Great Livermere 30 W 27
Great Malvern 26 N 27
Great Massingham 30 W 25
Great Milton 19 Q 28
Great Missenden 19 R 28
Great Musgrave 45 M 20
Great Oakley 21 X 28
Great Ormes Head 33 I 23
Great Ouse (River) 30 V 25
Great Ouseburn 40 Q 21
Great Ponton 36 S 25
Great Ryburgh 30 W 25
Great Sampford 22 V 28
Great Shefford 18 P 29
Great Shelford 29 U 27
Great Somerford 18 N 29
Great Torrington 6 H 31
Great Wakering 21 W 29
Great Waltham 22 V 28
Great Whernside 39 O 21
Great Witley 26 M 27
Great Wolford 18 P 27
Great Wyrley 27 N 26
Great Yarmouth 31 Z 26
Great Yeldham 22 V 27
Greater Manchester (Metropolitan County) 34 N 23
Greatham (Cleveland) 46 Q 20
Greatham (Hants.) 10 R 30
Greatstone-on-Sea 13 W 31
Greenhead 50 M 19
Greenholm 48 H 17
Greenlaw 57 M 16
Greenock 54 F 16
Greenodd 38 K 21
Greens Norton 28 Q 27
Greenwich (London Borough) 20 U 29
Grendon Underwood 19 Q 28
Gresford 34 L 24
Greshornish (Loch) 65 A 11
Gretna 50 K 19
Gretton 28 R 26
Greys Court 19 R 29
Greystoke 45 L 19
Grimoldby 37 U 23
Grimsay 64 Y 11
Groby 28 Q 26
Groombridge 11 U 30
Grosmont 47 R 20
Grove 18 P 29
Gruinard Bay 71 D 10
Gruinard Island 71 D 10

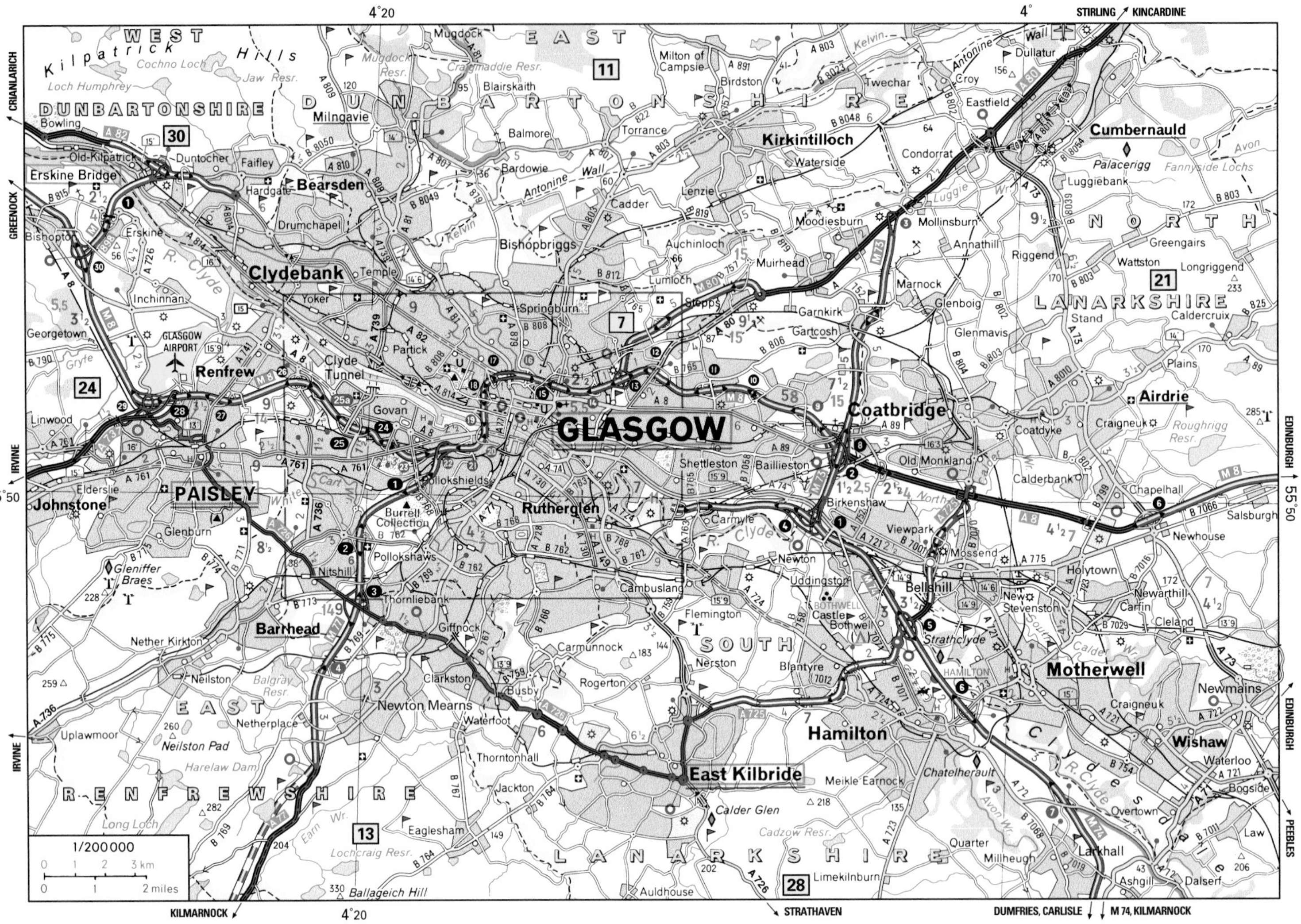
GLASGOW
Clydebank
Paisley
Johnstone
Renfrew
Bearsden
Milngavie
Kirkintilloch
Cumbernauld
Coatbridge
Airdrie
Bellshill
Motherwell
Wishaw
Hamilton
East Kilbride
Rutherglen
Barrhead
Erskine Bridge
Bishopbriggs
WEST DUNBARTONSHIRE
EAST DUNBARTONSHIRE
NORTH LANARKSHIRE
SOUTH LANARKSHIRE
EAST RENFREWSHIRE
GLASGOW AIRPORT
Clyde Tunnel
1/200000
STIRLING
KINCARDINE
CRIANLARICH
GREENOCK
IRVINE
KILMARNOCK
STRATHAVEN
DUMFRIES, CARLISLE
M 74, KILMARNOCK
EDINBURGH
PEEBLES
4°20
4°
55°50

Gruinart (Loch) 52 B 16
Grunavat (Loch) 70 Z 9
Grundisburgh 23 X 27
Guardbridge 56 L 14
Guernsey (Channel I.) 5
Guildtown 62 J 14
Guildford 10 S 30
Guisborough 47 Q 20
Guiseley 39 O 22
Guist 30 W 25
Gullane 56 L 15
Gunna 58 Z 14
Gunnislake 3 H 32
Gunthorpe 36 R 25
Gurnard 10 Q 31
Gutcher 75 Q 1
Guyhirn 29 U 26
Gwalchmai 32 G 24
Gwaun-Cae-Gurwen 15 I 28
Gwbert-on-Sea 14 F 27
Gweek 2 E 33
Gwyddgrug 15 H 28
Gwydir Castle 33 I 24

H

Habost 71 B 8
Hackney (London Borough) 20 T 29
Haddenham (Bucks.) 19 R 28
Haddenham (Cambs.) 29 U 26
Haddington 56 L 16
Haddiscoe 31 Y 26
Haddo House 69 N 11
Haddon Hall 35 P 24
Hadleigh (Essex) 21 V 29
Hadleigh (Suffolk) 22 W 27
Hadlow 12 V 30
Hadnall 34 L 25
Hadrian's Wall 50 M 18
Hagley 27 N 26
Hagworthingham 37 U 24
Hailsham 11 U 31
Hainton 37 T 23
Halberton 7 J 31
Hale 34 M 23
Halesowen 27 N 26
Halesworth 31 Y 26
Halford 27 P 27
Halifax 39 O 22
Halkirk 74 J 8
Hall 55 G 16
Halland 11 U 31
Halling 21 V 29
Hallow 26 N 27
Halstead 22 V 28
Haltham 37 T 24
Haltwhistle 50 M 19
Halwell 4 I 32
Halwill Junction 6 H 31
Hamble 10 Q 31
Hambleden 19 R 29
Hambledon (Hants.) 10 Q 31
Hambledon (Surrey) 10 S 30
Hambleton (Lancs.) 38 L 22
Hambleton (North Yorks.) 40 Q 22
Hambleton Hills (The) 46 Q 21
Hambridge 8 L 31
Hamilton 55 H 16
Hammersmith and Fulham (London Borough) 20 T 29
Hamnavoe 75 P 3
Hampshire (County) 9 P 30
Hampstead Norris 19 Q 29
Hampton 27 O 26
Hampton Court 20 S 29
Hamstead Marshall 18 P 29
Hamsterley 46 O 19
Hamstreet 12 W 30
Hamworthy 9 N 31
Handa Island 72 E 8
Handcross 11 T 30
Handforth 39 N 23
Handsworth 35 P 23
Hanley 35 N 24
Hanley Swan 26 N 27
Hanslope 28 R 27
Happisburgh 31 Y 25
Hapton 39 N 22
Harbertonford 4 I 32
Harbottle 51 N 17
Harbury 27 P 27
Harby 36 R 25
Hardham 10 S 31
Hardwick Hall 35 Q 24
Hardy Monument 8 M 31
Hare Street 20 U 28
Harewood House 40 P 22
Hargrave Green 22 V 27
Haringey (London Borough) 20 T 29
Harlech 32 H 25
Harleston 31 X 26
Harley 26 M 26
Harlington 19 S 28
Harlow 20 U 28
Harmston 36 S 24
Haroldswick 75 R 1
Harpenden 20 S 28
Harpley 30 V 25
Harport (Loch) 65 A 12
Harray (Loch of) 74 K 6
Harringworth 28 S 26
Harris (Highland) 59 A 13
Harris (Western Isles) 70 Y 10
Harris (Sound of) 64 Y 10
Harrogate 39 P 22
Harrow (London Borough) 19 S 29
Harston 29 U 27
Hartest 22 W 27
Hartfield 11 U 30
Harthill 55 I 16
Harting 10 R 31
Hartington 35 O 24
Hartland 6 G 31
Hartlebury 26 N 26
Hartlepool 46 Q 19
Hartley 20 U 29
Hartley Wintney 19 R 30
Hartpury 17 N 28
Hartshill 27 P 26
Hartwell 19 R 28
Harvington 27 O 27
Harwell 19 Q 29
Harwich 23 X 28
Harworth 36 Q 23
Hascosay 75 R 2
Haselbury Plucknett 8 L 31
Hasland 35 P 24
Haslemere 10 R 30
Haslingden 39 N 22
Haslingfield 29 U 27
Hastings 12 V 31
Hatch Court 8 L 31
Hatfield (Herts.) 20 T 28
Hatfield (South Yorks.) 40 Q 23
Hatfield Broad Oak 20 U 28
Hatfield Heath 20 U 28
Hatfield Peverel 22 V 28
Hatherleigh 6 H 31
Hathern 36 Q 25
Hathersage 35 P 24
Hatton (Aberdeenshire) 69 O 11
Hatton (Derbs.) 35 O 25
Haugh of Urr 43 I 19
Haughton 34 N 25
Havant 10 R 31
Havenstreet 10 Q 31
Haverfordwest / Hwlffordd 14 F 28
Haverhill 22 V 27
Haverigg 38 K 21
Havering (London Borough) 20 U 29
Haverthwaite 44 K 21
Hawarden 34 K 24
Hawes 45 N 21
Hawick 50 L 17
Hawkedon 22 V 27
Hawkhurst 12 V 30
Hawkridge 7 J 30
Hawkshead 44 L 20
Hawkwell 21 V 29
Hawley 19 R 30
Haworth 39 O 22
Haxby 40 Q 21
Haxey 36 R 23
Hay-on-Wye 25 K 27
Haydock 34 M 23
Haydon Bridge 50 N 19
Hayfield 35 O 23
Hayle 2 D 33
Hayling Island 10 R 31
Haywards Heath 11 T 31
Hazelbank 49 I 16
Hazel Grove 35 N 23
Hazlemere 19 R 29
Heacham 30 V 25
Headcorn 12 V 30
Headington 19 Q 28
Headless Cross 27 O 27
Headley 10 R 30
Heads of Ayr 48 F 17
Heanor 35 P 24
Heath End 19 Q 29
Heath Hayes 27 O 25
Heathfield 11 U 31
Heathrow Airport 20 S 29
Hebburn 46 P 19
Hebden Bridge 39 N 22
Hebrides (Sea of the) 64 Z 12
Heckfield 19 R 29
Heckington 37 T 25
Hednesford 27 O 25
Hedon 41 T 22
Heighington (Durham) 46 P 20
Heighington (Lincs.) 36 S 24
Helensburgh 54 F 15
Helford 2 E 33
Hell's Mouth or Porth Neigwl 32 G 25
Hellifield 39 N 22
Hellisay 64 X 12
Helmdon 28 Q 27
Helmsdale 73 J 9
Helmsley 47 Q 21
Helperby 40 Q 21
Helpringham 37 T 25
Helsby 34 L 24
Helston 2 E 33
Helton 45 L 20
Helvellyn 44 K 20
Hemel Hempstead 20 S 28
Hemingbrough 40 R 22
Hempnall 31 X 26
Hemsby 31 Z 25
Hemsworth 35 P 23
Hemyock 7 K 31
Hendy 15 H 28
Henfield 11 T 31
Hengoed 16 K 29
Henham 20 U 28
Henley 27 O 27
Henley-on-Thames 19 R 29
Henlow 29 T 27
Hennock 4 J 32
Henstridge 8 M 31
Heptonstall 39 N 22
Hereford 26 L 27
Herefordshire 26 M 27
Herm (Channel I.) 5
Herma Ness 75 R 1
Hermitage 19 Q 29
Hermitage Castle 50 L 18
Herne Bay 13 X 29
Herstmonceux 11 U 31
Hertford 20 T 28
Hertfordshire (County) 20 T 28
Hessle 41 S 22
Hest Bank 38 L 21
Heswall 33 K 24
Hetton-le-Hole 46 P 19
Heveningham 31 Y 27
Hever 11 U 30
Heversham 45 L 21
Hevingham 31 X 25
Hexham 45 N 19
Heybridge 22 W 28
Heysham 38 L 21
Heyshott 10 R 31
Heytesbury 9 N 30
Heywood 39 N 23
Hibaldstow 41 S 23
Hidcote Manor Garden 27 O 27
High Bentham 38 M 21
High Bickington 6 I 31
High Easter 22 V 28
High Ercall 26 M 25
High Force (The) 45 N 20
High Halden 12 W 30
High Halstow 21 V 29
High Ham 8 L 30
High Ongar 20 U 28
High Peak 35 O 23
High Willhays 4 I 31
High Wycombe 19 R 29
Higham (Kent) 21 V 29
Higham (Lancs.) 39 N 22
Higham (Suffolk) 22 V 27
Higham Ferrers 28 S 27
Highbridge 8 L 30
Highclere 18 P 29
Highcliffe 9 O 31
Higher Penwortham 38 L 22
Highland Wildlife Park 61 I 12
Highley 26 M 26
Highnam 17 N 28
Hightae 49 J 18
Hightown 38 K 23
Highworth 18 O 29
Hildenborough 11 U 30
Hilderstone 35 N 25
Hilgay 30 V 26
Hill 17 M 29
Hill of Fearn 67 I 10
Hill of Tarvit 56 L 15
Hillside 63 M 13
Hillswick 75 P 2
Hilperton 18 N 30
Hilpsford Point 38 K 21

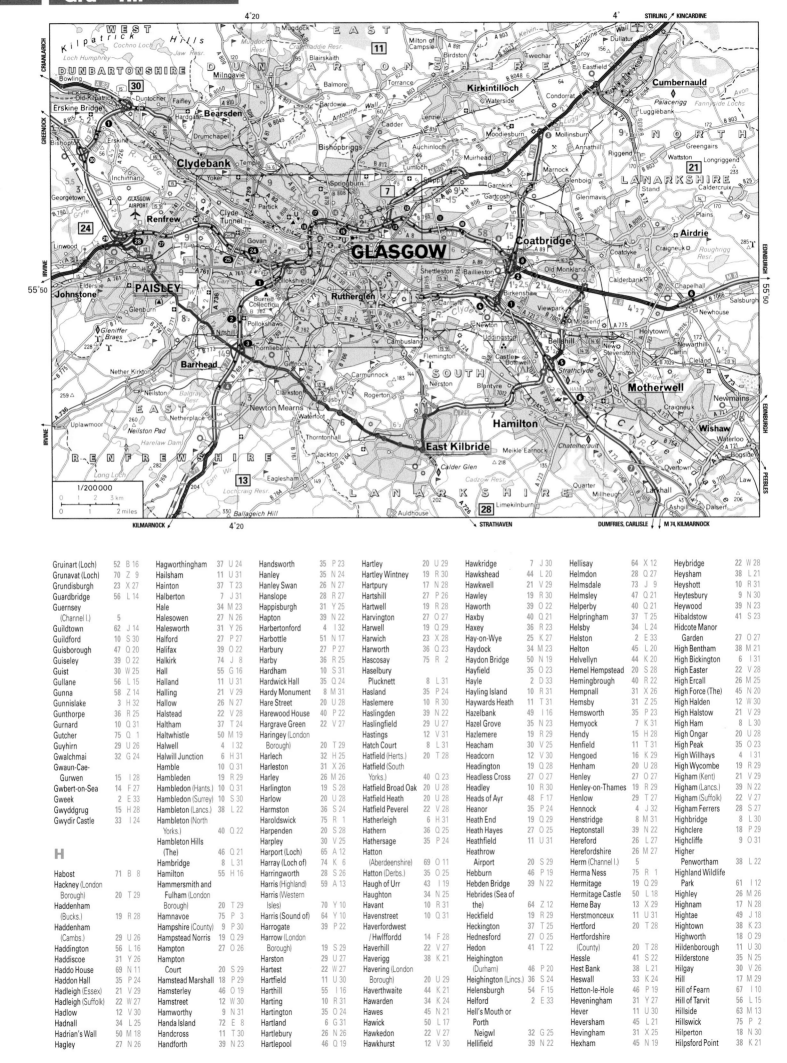

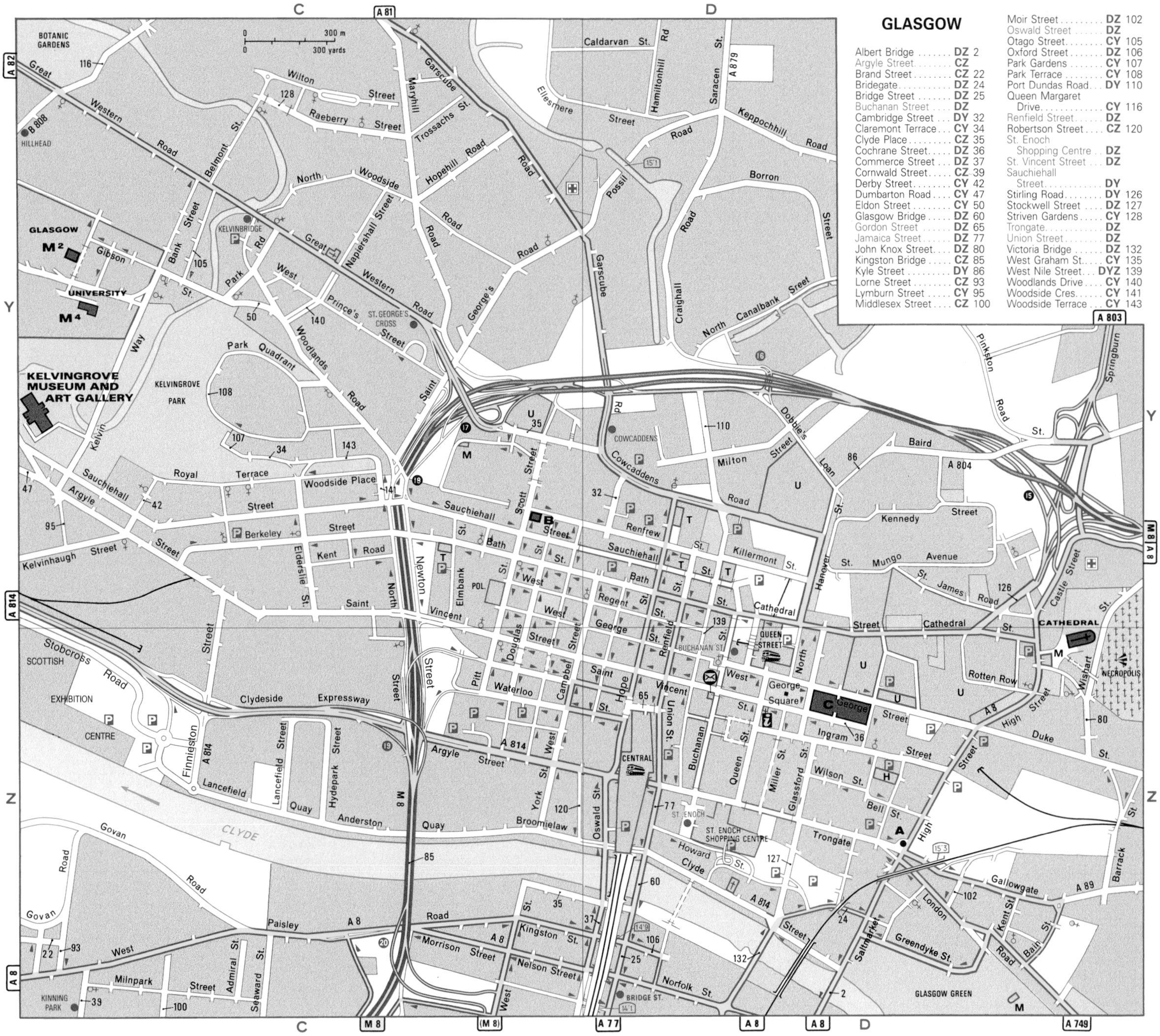

GLASGOW

Albert Bridge .... DZ 2
Argyle Street .... CZ
Brand Street .... CZ 22
Bridegate .... DZ 24
Bridge Street .... DZ 25
Buchanan Street ..... DZ
Cambridge Street .... DY 32
Claremont Terrace ... CY 34
Clyde Place .... CZ 35
Cochrane Street ..... DZ 36
Commerce Street ..... DZ 37
Cornwald Street ..... CZ 39
Derby Street .... CY 42
Dumbarton Road ...... CY 47
Eldon Street .... CY 50
Glasgow Bridge ...... DZ 60
Gordon Street .... DZ 65
Jamaica Street ...... DZ 77
John Knox Street .... DZ 80
Kingston Bridge ..... CZ 85
Kyle Street .... DY 86
Lorne Street .... CZ 93
Lymburn Street ...... CY 95
Middlesex Street .... CZ 100
Moir Street .... DZ 102
Oswald Street .... DZ
Otago Street .... CY 105
Oxford Street .... DZ 106
Park Gardens .... CY 107
Park Terrace .... CY 108
Port Dundas Road .... DY 110
Queen Margaret Drive .... CY 116
Renfield Street ..... DZ
Robertson Street .... CZ 120
St. Enoch Shopping Centre .. DZ
St. Vincent Street .. DZ
Sauchiehall Street .... DY
Stirling Road .... DY 126
Stockwell Street .... DZ 127
Striven Gardens ..... CY 128
Trongate .... DZ
Union Street .... DZ
Victoria Bridge ..... DZ 132
West Graham St. ..... CY 135
West Nile Street .... DYZ 139
Woodlands Drive ..... CY 140
Woodside Cres. ...... CY 141
Woodside Terrace .... CY 143

Hilton	35	P 25
Hinchingbrooke House	29	T 27
Hinckley	27	P 26
Hinderwell	47	R 20
Hindhead	10	R 30
Hindley	38	M 23
Hindon	9	N 30
Hingham	30	W 26
Hinstock	34	M 25
Hintlesham	23	X 27
Hirwaun	16	J 28
Histon	29	U 27
Hitcham	22	W 27
Hitchin	20	T 28
Hockering	30	X 25
Hockley	21	V 29
Hockley Heath	27	O 26
Hockliffe	19	S 28
Hoddesdon	20	T 28
Hodnet	34	M 25
Hogsthorpe	37	U 24
Holbeach	37	U 25
Holbrook	21	X 28
Holbury	9	P 31
Holcombe	8	M 30
Holdenby	28	R 27
Holford	7	K 30
Holkam Hall	30	W 25
Hollesley Bay	23	Y 27
Hollingworth	35	O 23
Hollybush	48	G 17
Holme	38	L 21
Holme upon Spalding-Moor	40	R 22
Holmes Chapel	34	M 24
Holmesfield	35	P 24
Holmhead	48	H 17
Holsworthy	6	G 31
Holt (Wrexham)	34	L 24
Holt (Dorset)	9	O 31
Holt (Norfolk)	31	X 25
Holt (Wilts.)	18	N 29
Holton (Lincs.)	37	T 24
Holton (Norfolk)	31	Y 26
Holy Island (Anglesey)	32	F 24
Holy Island (North Ayrshire)	53	E 17
Holy Island (Northumb.)	51	O 16
Holybourne	10	R 30
Holyhead / Caergybi	32	G 24
Holystone	51	N 18
Holywell / Treffynnon	33	K 24
Holywell Bay	2	E 32
Honiton	7	K 31
Hoo St. Werburgh	21	V 29
Hook	10	R 30
Hooke	8	M 31
Hook Norton	18	P 28
Hope (Flintshire)	34	K 24
Hope (Derbs.)	35	O 23
Hope (Loch)	72	G 8
Hope under Dinmore	26	L 27
Hopeman	68	J 10
Hopetoun House	56	J 16
Hopton	31	Z 26
Horam	11	U 31
Horbury	40	P 23
Horden	46	Q 19
Horeb	24	G 27
Horley	11	T 30
Hornby	38	M 21
Horncastle	37	T 24
Horning	31	Y 25
Horninglow	35	P 25
Horn's Cross	6	H 31
Hornsea	41	T 22
Horrabridge	3	H 32
Horseheath	22	V 27
Horsell	19	S 30
Horsforth	39	P 22
Horsham	11	T 30
Horsham St. Faith	31	X 25
Horsmonden	12	V 30
Horsted Keynes	11	T 30
Horton	9	O 31
Horton Court	17	M 29
Horton-in-Ribblesdale	39	N 21
Horwich	38	M 23
Houghton Hall	30	V 25
Houghton House	28	S 27
Houghton-le-Spring	46	P 19
Hourn (Loch)	66	D 12
House of The Binns (The)	56	J 16
Housesteads Fort	50	N 18
Hove	11	T 31
Hoveton	31	Y 25
Hovingham	40	R 21
How Caple	17	M 28
Howden	40	R 22
Howe of the Mearns	63	M 13
Howmore	64	X 12
Hoxa (Sound of)	74	K 7
Hoy	74	J 7
Hoylake	33	K 23
Hoyland Nether	35	P 23
Hucknall	36	Q 24
Huddersfield	39	O 23
Hugh Town (I. of Scilly)	2	
Hughenden	19	R 29
Huish Episcopi	8	L 30
Hull (River)	41	S 22
Hullbridge	21	V 29
Humber (River)	41	T 23
Humber Bridge	41	S 22
Humberston	41	T 23

GLOUCESTER CENTRE

Black Dog Way .... Y 5
Commercial Road .... Y 6
Eastgate Shopping Centre .... Y
Eastgate Street .... Y 10
Great Western Road ...... Y 12
Heathville Road .... Y 13
Lower Westgate Street .... Y 15
Northgate Street .... Y 16
Parliament Street .... Y 18
Pitt Street .... Y 19
Quay Street .... Y 20
Royal Oak Road .... Y 21
St. Aldate Street .... Y 22
St. Johns Lane .... Y 23
Southgate Street .... Y
Spa Road .... Y 26
Worcester Street .... Y 31

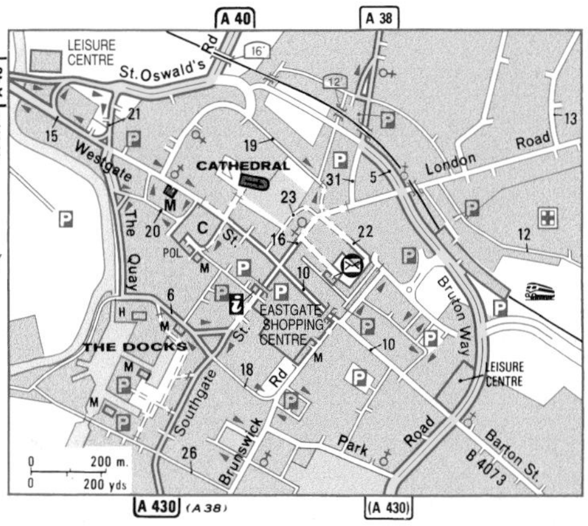

IPSWICH

Argyle Street 2
Bond Street 6
Buttermarket Centre 9
Carr Street 10
College Street 15
Corn Hill 16
Dogs Head Street 18
Falcon Street 21
Franciscan Way 24
Friars Street 25
Grey Friars Road 26
Handford Road 30
Lloyds Avenue 31
Lower Orwell Street 32
Northgate Street 33
Orwell Place 34
Queen Street 37
St. Helen's Street 39
St. Margarets Street 40
St. Nicholas Street 41
St. Peter's Street 42
Salthouse Street 43
Silent Street 46
Tavern Street
Tower Ramparts Centre 47
Upper Orwell Street 49
Waterworks Street 51
Westgate Street 52

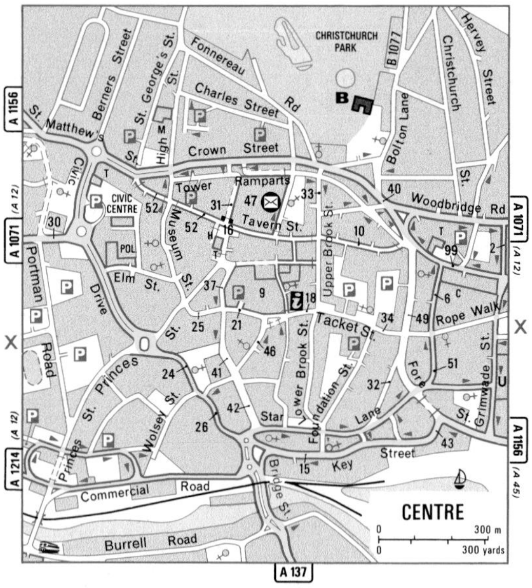

LEEDS

Aire Street FZ 2
Albion Street GZ 3
Bond Street GZ 8
Bridge Street GY 10
Briggate GZ
City Square GZ 15
Commercial Street GZ 18
Cookridge Street GY 19
County Arcade GZ 20
Cross Stamford St GY 21
Crown Point Road GZ 22
Duncan Street GZ 25
East Parade FGZ 27
Eastgate GZ 31
Hanover Way FY 39
Headrow (The) GY
Infirmary Street GZ 44
King Street FZ 46
Kirkgate GZ 48
Lands Lane GZ 49
Marsh Lane GZ 51
Meadow Lane GZ 52
Merrion Centre GY
Merrion Street GY 53
Merrion Way GY 55
New Briggate GY 57
New York Road GY 60
Park Lane FY 64
Portland Crescent GY 65
Queen Street FZ 68
St. John's Centre GY
St. Paul's Street FZ 72
St. Peter's Street GZ 73
Sheepscar St. South GY 75
Skinner Lane GY 76
South Parade FGZ 78
Trinity St. Shopping Centre GZ
Victoria Road GZ 81
Wade Lane GY 82
Wellington Road FZ 83
West Street FZ 84
Westgate FZ 85

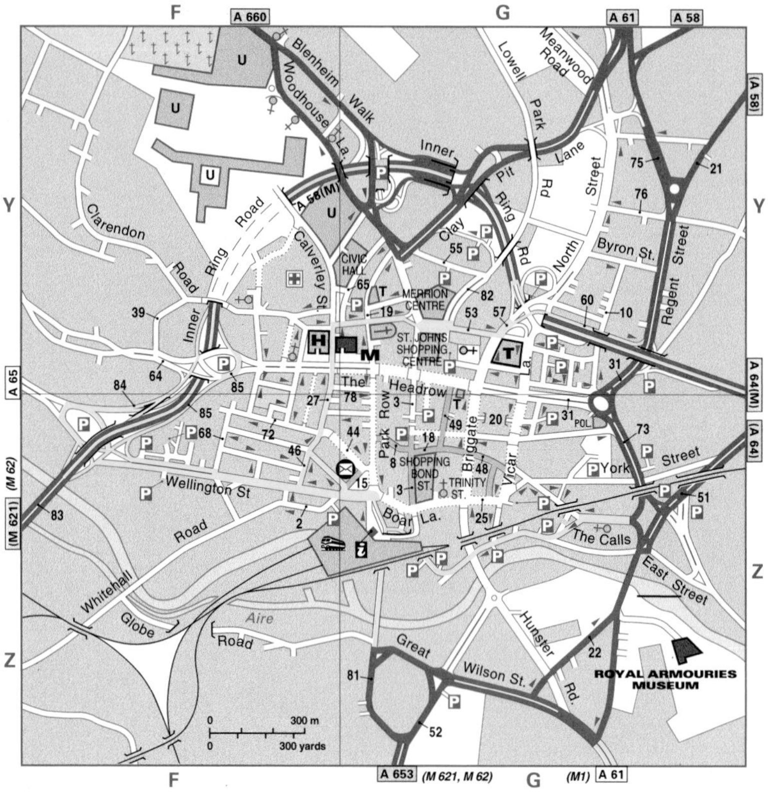

Hungerford	18 P 29	Hurlford	48 G 17
Hunmanby	41 T 21	Hursley	9 P 30

Hungerford 18 P 29
Hunmanby 41 T 21
Hunstanton 30 V 25
Huntingdon 29 T 26
Huntingtower Castle 56 J 14
Huntly 68 L 11
Huntspill 8 L 30
Hurlford 48 G 17
Hursley 9 P 30
Hurst Green 12 V 30
Hurstbourne Priors 9 P 30
Hurstbourne Tarrant 9 P 30
Hurstpierpoint 11 T 31
Hurworth-on-Tees 46 P 20
Husbands Bosworth 28 Q 26
Huthwaite 36 Q 24
Huttoft 37 U 24
Hutton Cranswick 41 S 22
Hutton Rudby 46 Q 20
Huyton 34 L 23

KINGSTON-UPON-HULL

Bond Street X 3
Carr Lane Y
Commercial Road Y 8
Dock Office Row X 10
Dock Street X 12
Ferensway XY 14
George Street X
Grimston Street X 15
Humber Dock Street Y 16
Jameson Street Y 17
Jarratt Street X 18
King Edward Street Y 19
Lowgate Y 23
Market Place Y 24
Paragon Street Y 29
Prince's Dock Street Y 32
Princes Quay Shopping Centre Y
Prospect Shopping Centre X
Prospect Street X
Queen Street Y 35
Queen's Dock Avenue X 36
Reform Street X 37
Sculcoates Bridge X 42
Waterhouse Lane Y 47
Whitefriargate Y 49
Wilberforce Drive X 50
Worship Street X 52

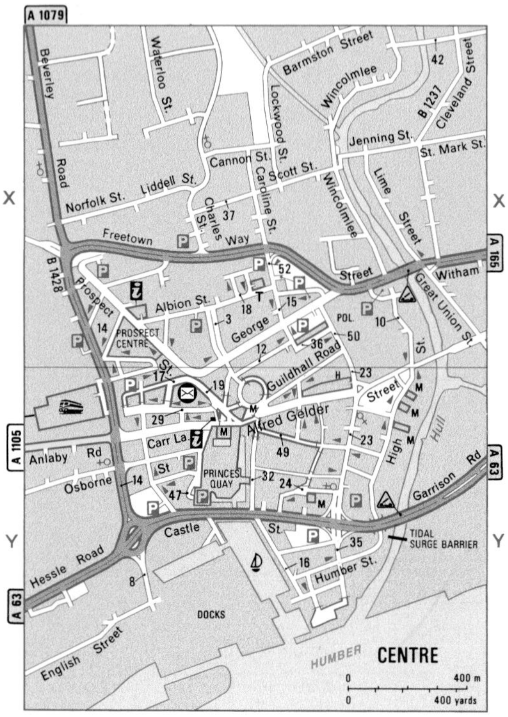

Hwlfford / Haverfordwest 14 F 28
Hyde 35 N 23
Hynish Bay 58 Z 14
Hythe (Hants.) 9 P 31
Hythe (Kent) 13 X 30

I

Ibstock 27 P 25
Ickleford 20 T 28
Icklingham 30 V 27
Ickworth House 22 V 27
Iden 12 W 31
Iden Green 12 V 30
Idrigill Point 65 A 12
Ightham 20 U 30
Ightham Mote 11 U 30
Ilchester 8 L 30
Ilderton 51 O 17
Ilfracombe 6 H 30
Ilkeston 35 Q 25
Ilkley 39 O 22
Illogan 2 E 33
Ilmington 27 O 27
Ilminster 8 L 31
Ilsington 4 I 32
Ilsley 19 Q 29
Immingham 41 T 23
Immingham Dock 41 T 23
Ince-in-Makerfield 38 M 23
Inch Kenneth 59 B 14
Inchard (Loch) 72 E 8
Inchkeith 56 K 15
Inchlaggan 60 E 12
Inchmarnock 54 E 16
Inchnadamph 72 F 9
Inchture 62 K 14
Indaal (Loch) 52 A 16
Ingatestone 22 V 28
Ingham 30 W 27
Ingleton (Durham) 46 O 20
Ingleton (North Yorks.) 39 M 21
Inglewood Forest 45 L 19
Ingliston 56 J 16
Ingoldmells 37 V 24
Ingoldsby 36 S 25
Ings 45 L 20
Innellan 54 F 16
Inner Hebrides 58 Y 14
Inner Sound 65 C 11
Innerleithen 50 K 17
Insch 69 M 11
Instow 6 H 30
Inver (Loch) 72 E 9
Inver Bay 67 I 10
Inver Valley 72 E 9
Inverallochy 69 O 10
Inveraray 54 E 15
Inverbeg 55 G 15
Inverbervie 63 N 13
Invercreran 60 E 14
Inverewe Gardens 66 C 10
Inverey 62 J 13
Invergarry 60 F 12
Invergordon 67 H 10
Invergowrie 62 K 14
Inverkeithing 56 J 15
Inverkeithny 69 M 11
Inverkip 54 F 16
Inverkirkaig 72 E 9
Inverliever Forest 54 D 15
Invermoriston 67 G 12
Inverness 67 H 11
Inversanda 60 D 13
Inverurie 69 M 12
Iona 59 A 15
Ipplepen 4 J 32
Ipstones 35 O 24
Ipswich 23 X 27
Ireby 44 K 19
Irlam 34 M 23
Iron Acton 17 M 29
Iron-Bridge 26 M 26
Irthlingborough 28 S 27
Irvine 48 F 17
Isla (Glen) 62 K 13
Islay (Sound of) 52 B 16
Isleham 30 V 26
Isle of Whithorn 42 G 19
Isleornsay 65 C 12
Islington (London Borough) 20 T 29
Islip 19 Q 28
Ithon (River) 25 K 27
Iver 19 S 29
Iver Heath 19 S 29
Ivinghoe 19 S 28
Ivybridge 4 I 32
Ivychurch 12 W 30
Iwerne Minster 8 N 31
Ixworth 30 W 27

J

Jacobstowe 6 H 31
Janetstown 74 J 9
Jarrow 51 P 19
Jaywick 21 X 28
Jedburgh 50 M 17
Jedburgh Abbey 50 M 17
Jersey (Channel I.) 5
Jevington 11 U 31
John o' Groats 74 K 8
Johnshaven 63 N 13
Johnston 14 F 28
Johnstone 55 G 16
Jura (Isle of) 52 B 16
Jura (Sound of) 52 C 16
Jura Forest 52 B 16
Jurby West 42 G 20

K

Kames 54 E 16
Katrine (Loch) 55 G 15
Keal 37 U 24
Keal (Loch na) 59 B 14
Kearsley 39 M 23
Kebock Head 71 A 9
Kedleston Hall 35 P 25
Kegworth 36 Q 25
Keighley 39 O 22
Keinton Mandeville 8 M 30
Keir Mill 49 I 18
Keiss 74 K 8
Keith 68 L 11
Kellas 62 L 14
Kellie Castle 57 L 15
Kelly Bray 3 H 32
Kelsall 34 L 24
Kelso 50 M 17
Keltneyburn 61 H 14
Kelty 56 J 15
Kelvedon 22 W 28
Kelvedon Hatch 20 U 29
Kemble 18 N 28
Kemnay 69 M 12
Kempsey 26 N 27
Kempston 28 S 27
Kemsing 20 U 30
Kendal 45 L 21
Kenilworth 27 P 26
Kenmore (Perthshire and Kinross) 61 I 14
Kenmore (Highland) 65 C 11
Kennet (River) 18 O 29
Kennethmont 68 L 11
Kenninghall 31 X 26
Kennington (Kent) 12 W 30
Kennington (Oxon.) 19 Q 28
Kennoway 56 K 15
Kenovay 58 Z 14
Kensaleyre 65 B 11
Kensington and Chelsea (London Borough) 20 T 29
Kent (County) 12 V 30
Kentallen 60 E 13
Kentford 22 V 27
Kentisbeare 7 K 31
Kenton 4 J 32
Keoldale 72 F 8
Kerrera 60 D 14
Kerry 25 K 26
Kershader 70 A 9
Kesgrave 23 X 27
Kessingland 31 Z 26

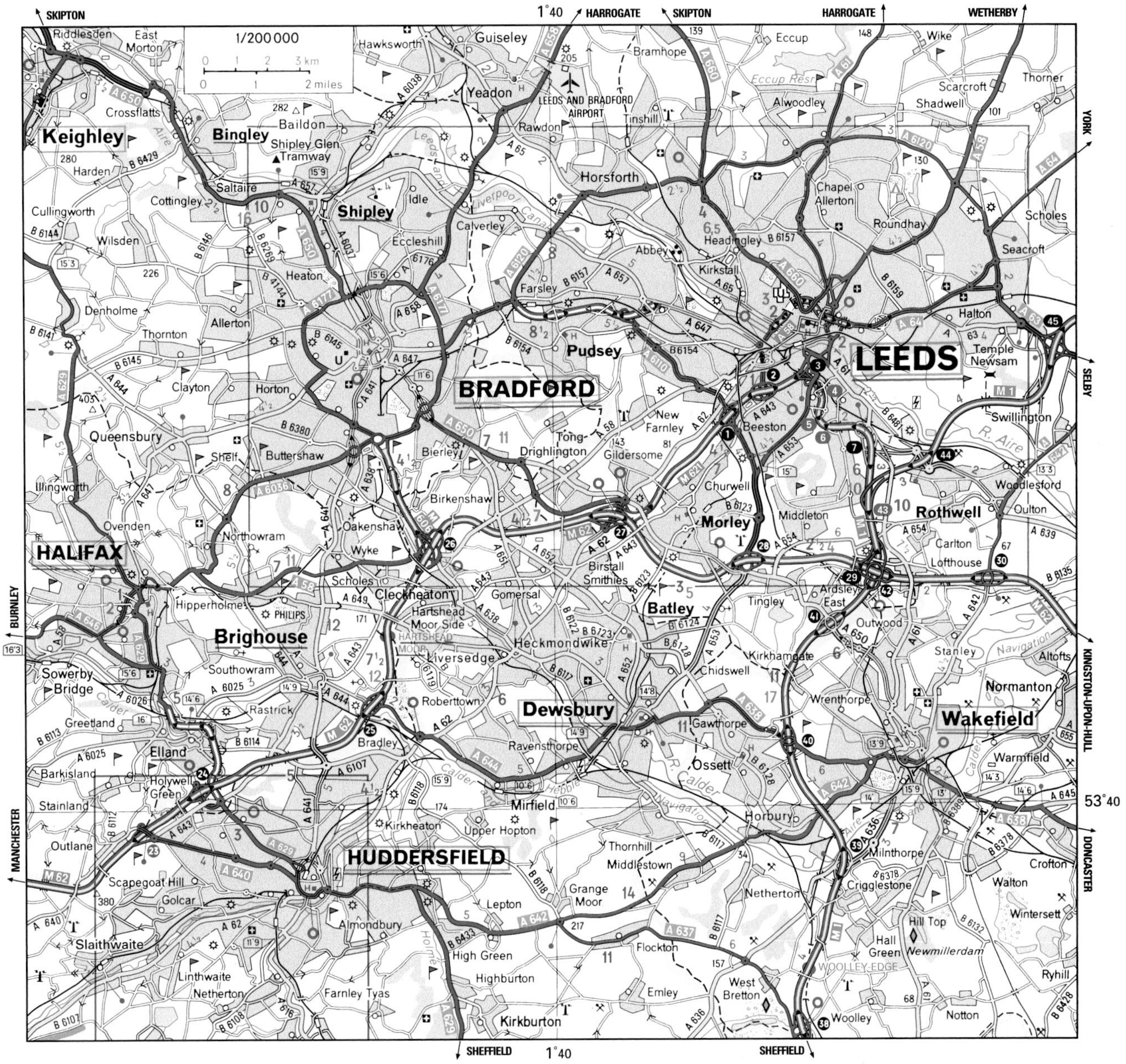
SKIPTON
1°40
HARROGATE
SKIPTON
HARROGATE
WETHERBY
1/200 000
3 km
2 miles
Keighley
Bingley
Shipley
BRADFORD
LEEDS
Pudsey
Horsforth
Guiseley
Yeadon
LEEDS AND BRADFORD AIRPORT
Morley
Rothwell
Batley
Dewsbury
HALIFAX
Brighouse
Heckmondwike
Cleckheaton
Wakefield
Normanton
Ossett
Mirfield
HUDDERSFIELD
Elland
Sowerby Bridge
Slaithwaite
Kirkburton
Horbury
YORK
SELBY
BURNLEY
MANCHESTER
KINGSTON-UPON-HULL
DONCASTER
53°40
SHEFFIELD
1°40
SHEFFIELD

Keswick 44 K 20
Kettering 28 R 26
Kettleshulme 35 N 24
Kettletoft 74 M 6
Kettlewell 39 N 21
Ketton 28 S 26
Kew 20 T 29
Kexby 36 R 23
Keyingham 41 T 22
Keymer 11 T 31
Keynsham 17 M 29
Keyworth 36 Q 25
Kibworth Harcourt 28 R 26
Kidderminster 26 N 26
Kidlington 19 Q 28
Kidsgrove 34 N 24
Kidwelly / Cydweli 15 H 28
Kielder 50 M 18
Kielder Forest 50 M 18
Kielder Reservoir 50 M 18
Kilbarchan 55 G 16
Kilbirnie 54 F 16
Kilbrannan Sound 53 D 17
Kilbride 54 D 14
Kilcadzow 55 I 16
Kilchattan 54 E 16
Kilchenzie 53 C 17
Kilchoan 59 B 13
Kilchrenan 54 E 14
Kilconquhar 56 L 15
Kilcreggan 54 F 16
Kildonan 53 E 17
Kildrummy 68 L 12
Kildrummy Castle 68 L 12
Kilham 41 S 21
Kilkhampton 6 G 31
Killearn 55 G 15
Killerton 7 J 31
Killichronan 59 C 14
Killin 61 H 14
Killinghall 40 P 21
Kilmacolm 55 G 16
Kilmaluag 65 B 10
Kilmany 56 L 14
Kilmarnock 48 G 17
Kilmartin 54 D 15
Kilmaurs 48 G 17
Kilmelford 54 D 15
Kilmorack 67 G 11
Kilmun 54 F 16
Kilninver 54 D 14
Kilnsey 39 N 21
Kiloran 52 B 15
Kilpeck 17 L 28
Kilrenny 57 L 15
Kilsyth 55 H 16
Kilt Rock 65 B 11
Kilwinning 48 F 17
Kimberley 30 X 26
Kimble 19 R 28
Kimbolton 29 S 27
Kimmeridge 9 N 32
Kimpton 20 T 28
Kinbrace 73 I 9
Kincardine 56 I 15
Kincardine O'Neil 69 L 12
Kinclaven 62 J 14
Kincraig 61 I 12
Kinfauns 56 J 14
King's Bromley 27 O 25
King's Cliffe 28 S 26
King's Lynn 30 V 25
King's Somborne 9 P 30
King's Sutton 19 Q 27
Kingairloch 60 D 14
Kingarth 54 E 16
Kinghorn 56 K 15
Kinglassie 56 K 15
Kings Langley 20 S 28
Kings Worthy 10 Q 30
Kingsbarns 57 M 15
Kingsbridge 4 I 33
Kingsclere 19 Q 30
Kingsdown 13 Y 30
Kingskerswell 4 J 32
Kingskettle 56 K 15
Kingsland 26 L 27
Kingsley 35 O 24
Kingsmuir 62 L 14
Kingsnorth 12 W 30
Kingsteignton 4 J 32
Kingston (Moray) 68 K 10
Kingston (Devon) 4 I 33
Kingston Bagpuize 18 P 28
Kingston Lacy 9 N 31
Kingston-upon-Hull 41 S 22
Kingston-upon-Thames (London Borough) 20 T 29
Kingstone 17 L 27
Kingswear 4 J 32
Kingswinford 27 N 26
Kingswood (South Glos.) 17 M 29
Kingswood (Glos.) 17 M 29
Kington 26 K 27
Kington Langley 18 N 29
Kingussie 61 H 12
Kinloch 59 B 12
Kinloch Rannoch 61 H 13
Kinlochard 55 G 15
Kinlochbervie 72 E 8
Kinlocheil 60 E 13
Kinlochewe 66 E 11
Kinlochleven 60 F 13
Kinlochmoidart 59 C 13
Kinloss 68 J 11
Kinneff 63 N 13
Kinnersley 26 L 27
Kinross 56 J 15
Kintbury 18 P 29
Kintore 69 M 12
Kintyre (Peninsula) 53 D 17
Kinver 26 N 26
Kippax 40 P 22
Kippen 55 H 15
Kippford 43 I 19
Kirby Cross 21 X 28
Kirby Hall 28 S 26
Kirby Muxloe 28 Q 26
Kirdford 10 S 30
Kirk Ella 41 S 22
Kirk Ireton 35 P 24
Kirk Michael 42 G 21
Kirkbean 44 J 19
Kirkbride 44 K 19
Kirkburton 39 O 23
Kirkby 34 L 23
Kirkby Fleetham 46 P 20
Kirkby-in-Ashfield 36 Q 24
Kirkby Lonsdale 38 M 21
Kirkby Malham 39 N 21
Kirkby Malzeard 39 P 21
Kirkby Stephen 45 M 20
Kirkby Thore 45 M 20
Kirkbymoorside 47 R 21
Kirkcaldy 56 K 15
Kirkcolm 42 E 19
Kirkconnel 49 I 17
Kirkcowan 42 G 19
Kirkcudbright 43 H 19
Kirkcudbright Bay 43 H 19
Kirkfieldbank 49 I 16
Kirkham 38 L 22
Kirkhill 67 G 11
Kirkinner 42 G 19
Kirkintilloch 55 H 16
Kirklees 39 O 23
Kirklevington 46 P 20
Kirklington 36 R 24
Kirkmichael (Perthshire and Kinross) 62 J 13
Kirkmichael (South Ayrshire) 48 G 17
Kirkmuirhill 49 I 17
Kirknewton 56 J 16
Kirkoswald 48 F 18
Kirkpatrick Durham 49 I 18
Kirkpatrick-Fleming 50 K 18
Kirkstone Pass 45 L 20
Kirkton of Culsalmond 69 M 11
Kirkton of Durris 69 M 12
Kirkton of Glenisla 62 K 13
Kirkton of Kingoldrum 62 K 13
Kirkton of Largo 56 L 15
Kirkton of Skene 69 N 12
Kirkton of Strathmartine 62 K 14
Kirktown of Auchterless 69 M 11
Kirkwall 74 L 7
Kirkwhelpington 51 N 18
Kirriemuir 62 K 13
Kirtlebridge 49 K 18
Kirtlington 19 Q 28
Kirtomy 73 H 8
Kirton 37 T 25
Kirton-in-Lindsey 36 S 23
Kishorn (Loch) 66 D 11
Kitchener Memorial 74 J 6
Knaresborough 40 P 21
Knarsdale 45 M 19
Knebworth 20 T 28
Kneesworth 29 T 27
Knighton / Trefyclawdd 26 K 26
Knightshayes Court 7 J 31
Kniveton 35 O 24
Knock (Moray) 68 L 11
Knock (Western Isles) 71 B 9
Knockie Lodge 67 G 12
Knockin 34 L 25
Knole 11 U 30
Knossington 36 R 25
Knottingley 40 Q 22
Knowle 27 O 26
Knowsley 34 L 23
Knoydart 60 D 12
Knutsford 34 M 24
Kyle Forest 48 G 17
Kyle of Durness 72 F 8
Kyle of Lochalsh 65 C 12
Kyle of Sutherland 72 G 10
Kyle of Tongue 72 G 8
Kyleakin 65 C 12
Kylerhea 65 C 12
Kyles Scalpay 70 Z 10
Kylestrome 72 E 9
Kynance Cove 2 E 34

L

Laceby 41 T 23
Lacey Green 19 R 28
Lacock 18 N 29
Ladder Hills 68 K 12
Ladock 2 F 33
Ladybank 56 K 15
Ladybower Reservoir 35 O 23
Lagg 52 C 16
Laggan (near Invergarry) 60 F 12
Laggan (near Newtonmore) 61 H 12
Laggan (Loch) 61 G 13
Laggan Point 52 B 16
Laide 71 D 10
Lair 66 E 11
Lairg 72 G 9
Lake District National Park 44 K 20
Lakenheath 30 V 26
Lamberhurst 12 V 30
Lambeth (London Borough) 20 T 29
Lambourn 18 P 29
Lamerton 3 H 32
Lamlash 53 E 17
Lamlash Bay 53 E 17
Lammermuir Hills 56 L 16

LONDON

Abingdon Rd .... EY 2
Allsop Pl. .... HU 4
Appold Street .... PU 5
Atterbury St. .... LZ 9
Battersea Park Rd. .... JZ 19
Belvedere Rd. .... MX 23
Bernard St. .... LT 25
Bessborough St. .... KZ 30
Bethnal Green Rd. .... PT 32
Bevis Marks .... PU 34
Bishopsgate .... PU 36
Blackfriars Bridge .... NV 38
Bloomsbury St. .... LU 39
Bowling Green Lane .... NT 43
Bridgefoot .... LZ 49
Broad Sanctuary .... LY 52
Brompton Rd. .... HY
Byward St. .... PV 62
Calthorpe St. .... MT 65
Camden Passage .... NS 70
Camomile St. .... PU 71
Carriage Drive North .... IZ 75
Chapel Market .... NS 78
Charlbert St. .... HT 79
Charterhouse Sq. .... OU 81
Charterhouse St. .... NU 83
Cornwall Rd. .... MX 108
Corporation Row .... NT 110
Cowcross St. .... NU 113
Crawford Pl. .... HU 116
Cromwell Cres .... EZ 119
Crucifix Lane .... PX 125
Curtain Rd. .... PT 126
Dante Rd. .... NZ 129
Dufferin St. .... OT 141
Duke's Pl. .... PV 145
Durham St. .... MZ 150
Eardley Cres. .... EZ 151
Eastcheap .... PV 154
Ebury Bridge .... IZ 156
Edwardes Sq. .... EY 158
Elephant Rd. .... OZ 163
Fann St. .... OU 166
Farringdon St. .... NU 168
Fetter Lane .... NU 169
Garden Row .... NY 173
Giltspur St. .... OU 178
Goodge St. .... KU 184
Gracechurch St. .... PV 187
Great Eastern St. .... PT 192
Great George St. .... LY 193
Great Smith St. .... LY 196
Great Tower St. .... PV 197
Greycoat Pl. .... KY 200
Gunter Grove .... FZ 202
Harleyford St. .... MZ 211
Herbrand St. .... LT 218
Hercules Rd. .... MY 219
Holland Walk .... EY 225
Horseguards Av. .... LX 228
Hornton St. .... FY 229
Howland St. .... KU 232
Hunter St. .... LT 233
Hyde Rd. .... PS 235
Kensington High St. .... EY
Kenway Rd. .... FZ 245
Knightsbridge .... HY
King's Rd. .... GHZ
King Edward St. .... OU 247
King William St. .... PV 250
Leadenhall St. .... PV 260
Little Britain .... OU 264
Lloyd Baker St. .... MT 265
Lombard St. .... PV 268
Long Lane CITY .... OU 270
Lothbury .... PU 273
Lower Marsh .... MY 277
Lower Thames St. .... PV 278
Mansell St. .... PV 282
Middlesex St. .... PU
Miles St. .... LZ 290
Montague St. .... OU 291
Moreland St. .... OT 293
Myddelton St. .... NT 296
Nevern Place .... EZ 298
Nevern Sq. .... EZ 299
New Bridge St. .... NV 301
New Change .... OV 304
Newington Butts .... OZ 306
Newington Causeway .... OY 307
Northumberland Av. .... LX 317
Old Bailey .... NV 318
Old Broad St. .... PU 319
Old Marylebone Rd. .... HU 324
Oxford St. .... KU
Paddington St. .... IU 333
Park Cres. .... IU 337
Parliament St. .... LY 340
Parry St. .... LZ 341
Pembroke Gdns .... EY 342
Penn St. .... PS 343
Penton Rise .... MT 344
Penton St. .... MT 345
Penywern Rd. .... FZ 347
Philbeach Gdns .... EZ 348
Piccadilly .... JX
Pilgrimage St. .... PY 349
Poole St. .... PS 350
Porchester Rd. .... FU 351
Portobello Rd. .... EV
Poultry .... OV 352
Princes St. .... PV 357
Queen's Circus .... IZ 361
Queen St. .... OV 365
Regent St. .... KV
Rossmore Rd. .... HT 369
St. Andrews St. .... NU 372
St. Bride St. .... NV 376
St. John's Wood High St. .... GT 378
St. John's Wood Park .... GS 379
St. Martin's-le-Grand .... OU 380
Shoreditch High St. .... PT 384
Sidmouth St. .... LT 385
Sloane St. .... HY
Snows Fields .... PX 386
Southampton Row .... LU 387
South Pl. .... PU 391
Southwark Bridge .... OV 395
Spencer St. .... NT 398
Spital Sq. .... PU 399
Storeys Gate .... LY 402
Tabard St. .... OY 408
Tavistock Sq. .... LT 409
Templeton Pl. .... EZ 410
Threadneedle St. .... PV 417
Throgmorton St. .... PU 418
Tower Hill .... PV 425
Trebovir Rd. .... FZ 426
Upper Ground .... NX 428
Upper Thames St. .... OV 431
Upper Woburn Pl. .... LT 432
Vincent St. .... LZ 436
Warwick Av. .... FU 441
Westbourne Park Villas .... FU 449
Westbourne Ter. Rd. .... FU 452
West Smithfield .... NU 454
Wharfdale Rd. .... LS 455
Whitechapel High St. .... PU 456
Whitehall Court .... LX 460
Whitehall Pl. .... LX 462
Whitmore Rd. .... PS 464
Wormwood St. .... PU 472

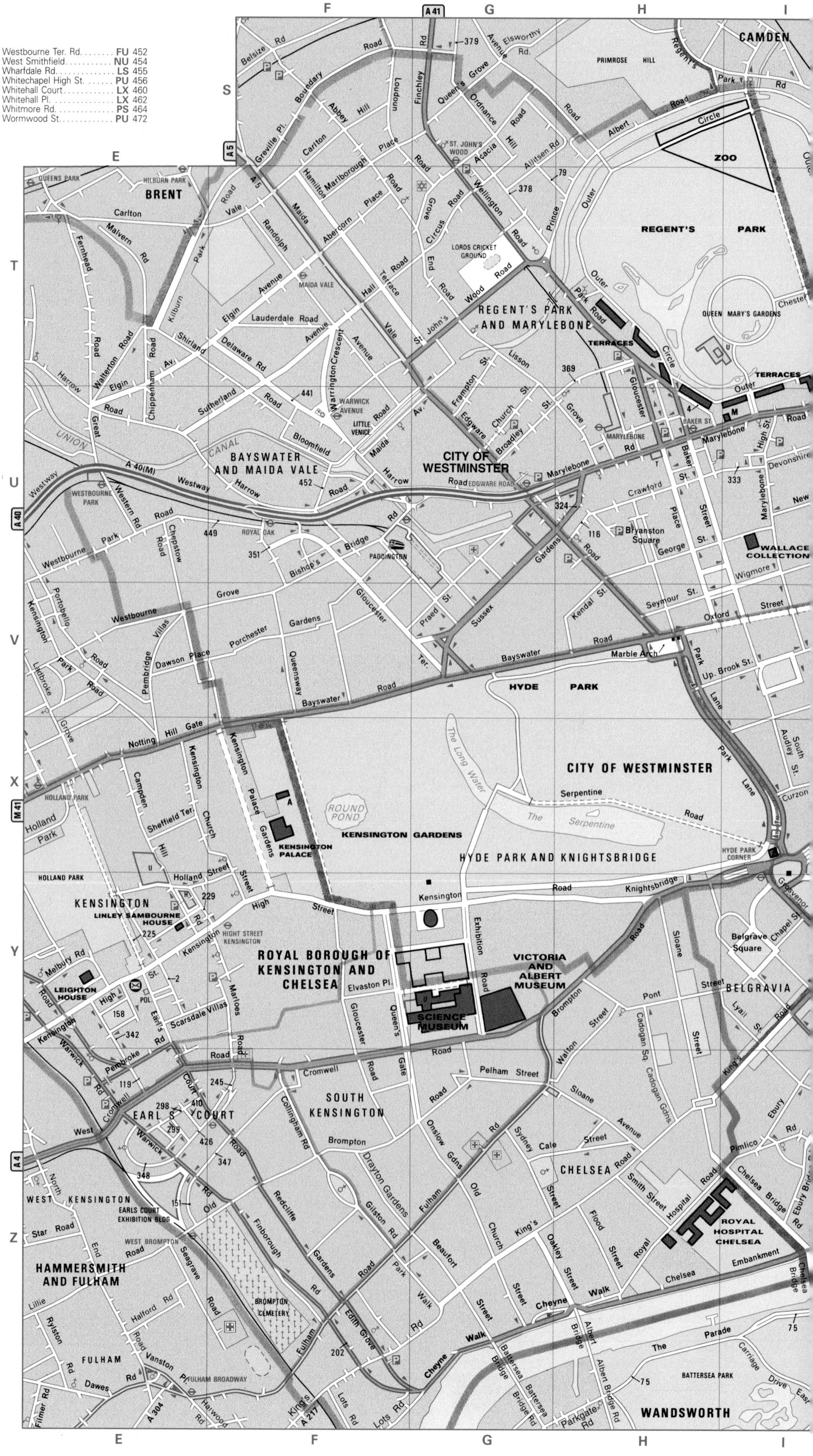

CAMDEN
PRIMROSE HILL
ZOO
REGENT'S PARK
QUEEN MARY'S GARDENS
BRENT
LORDS CRICKET GROUND
REGENT'S PARK AND MARYLEBONE
TERRACES
BAYSWATER AND MAIDA VALE
CITY OF WESTMINSTER
WALLACE COLLECTION
HYDE PARK
ROUND POND
KENSINGTON GARDENS
KENSINGTON PALACE
HYDE PARK AND KNIGHTSBRIDGE
HOLLAND PARK
KENSINGTON
LINLEY SAMBOURNE HOUSE
LEIGHTON HOUSE
ROYAL BOROUGH OF KENSINGTON AND CHELSEA
VICTORIA AND ALBERT MUSEUM
SCIENCE MUSEUM
BELGRAVIA
SOUTH KENSINGTON
EARL'S COURT
WEST KENSINGTON
EARLS COURT EXHIBITION BLDG
CHELSEA
ROYAL HOSPITAL CHELSEA
HAMMERSMITH AND FULHAM
BROMPTON CEMETERY
FULHAM
FULHAM BROADWAY
BATTERSEA PARK
WANDSWORTH

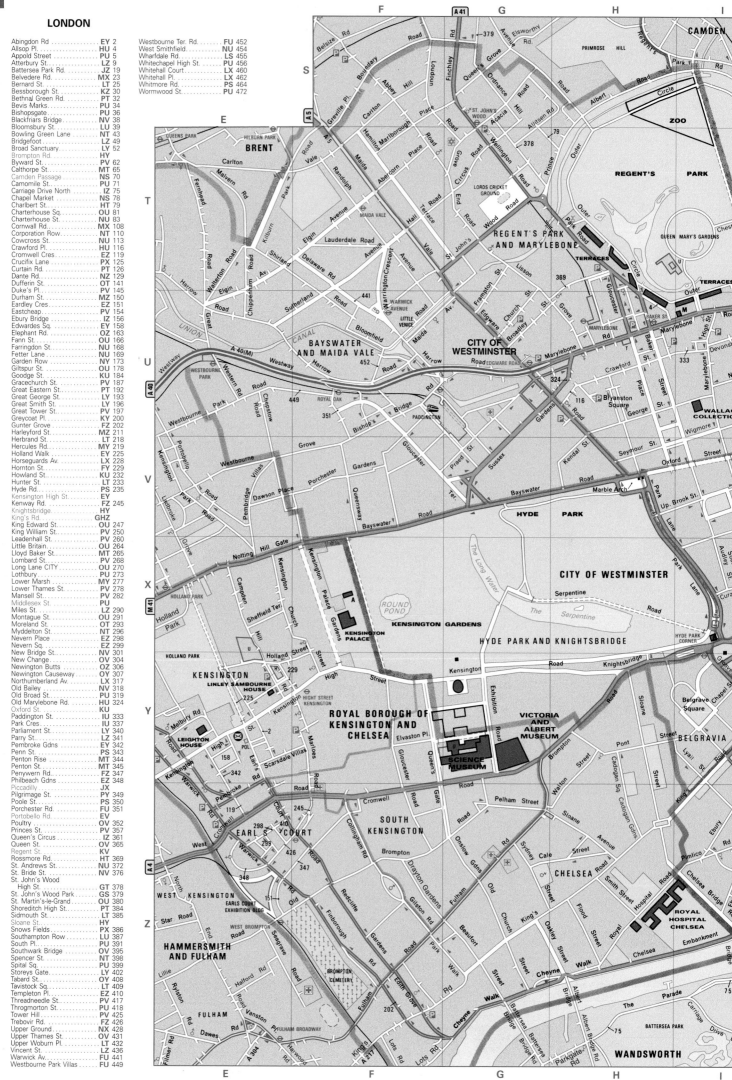

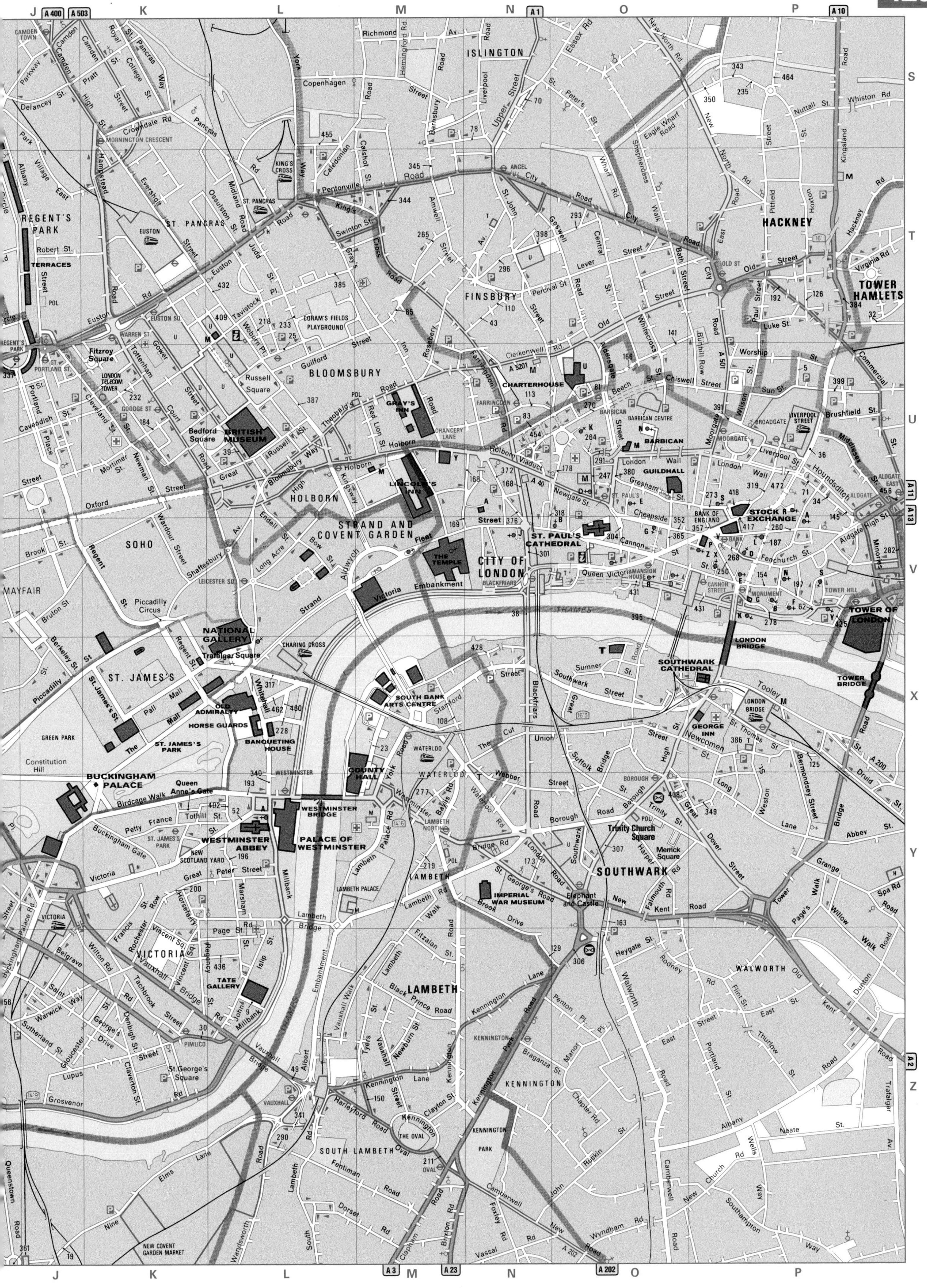
ISLINGTON
REGENT'S PARK
ST. PANCRAS
KING'S CROSS
EUSTON
BLOOMSBURY
FINSBURY
HACKNEY
TOWER HAMLETS
SOHO
MAYFAIR
HOLBORN
STRAND AND COVENT GARDEN
CITY OF LONDON
ST. PAUL'S CATHEDRAL
BRITISH MUSEUM
BARBICAN
GUILDHALL
STOCK EXCHANGE
BANK OF ENGLAND
THE TEMPLE
LINCOLN'S INN
GRAY'S INN
CHARTERHOUSE
NATIONAL GALLERY
Trafalgar Square
ST. JAMES'S
ST. JAMES'S PARK
GREEN PARK
BUCKINGHAM PALACE
HORSE GUARDS
BANQUETING HOUSE
OLD ADMIRALTY
WESTMINSTER ABBEY
PALACE OF WESTMINSTER
WESTMINSTER BRIDGE
COUNTY HALL
SOUTH BANK ARTS CENTRE
WATERLOO
LAMBETH
LAMBETH PALACE
IMPERIAL WAR MUSEUM
Elephant and Castle
SOUTHWARK
SOUTHWARK CATHEDRAL
LONDON BRIDGE
TOWER OF LONDON
TOWER BRIDGE
THAMES
VICTORIA
TATE GALLERY
PIMLICO
KENNINGTON
THE OVAL
SOUTH LAMBETH
WALWORTH
NEW COVENT GARDEN MARKET
Trinity Church Square
J K L M N O P
S T U V X Y Z
A 400 A 503 A 1 A 10 A 11 A 13 A 2 A 3 A 23 A 202

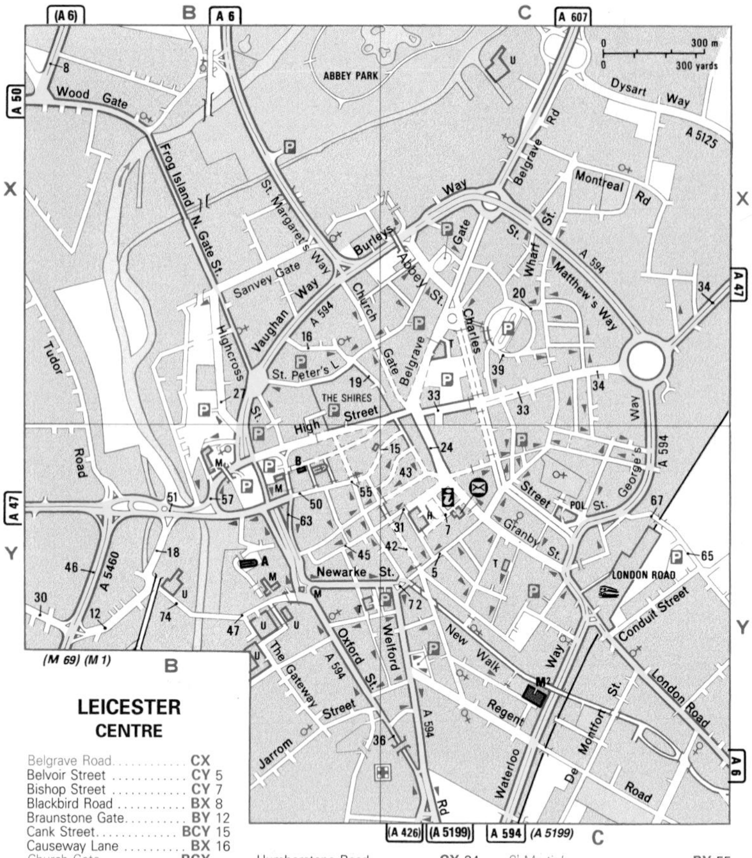

LEICESTER CENTRE

Belgrave Road	CX	
Belvoir Street	CY	5
Bishop Street	CY	7
Blackbird Road	BX	8
Braunstone Gate	BY	12
Cank Street	BCY	15
Causeway Lane	BX	16
Church Gate	BCX	
Duns Lane	BY	19
East Bond Street	BCX	20
Fleet Street	CX	21
Gallowtree Gate	CY	24
Great Central Street	BX	27
Hinckley Road	BY	30
High Street	BXY	
Horsefair Street	CY	31
Humberstone Gate	CX	33
Humberstone Road	CX	34
Infirmary Road	BCY	36
Lee Street	CX	39
Market Street	CY	42
Market (The)	CY	43
Millstone Lane	BY	45
Narborough Road North	BY	46
Newarke (The)	BY	47
Peacock Lane	BY	50
St. Augustine Road	BY	51
St Martin's	BY	55
St. Nicholas Circle	BY	57
Shires (The) Shopping Centre	BX	
Southgate Street	BY	63
Sparkenhoe Street	CY	65
Swain Street	CY	67
Welford Place	CY	72
Western Boulevard	BY	74

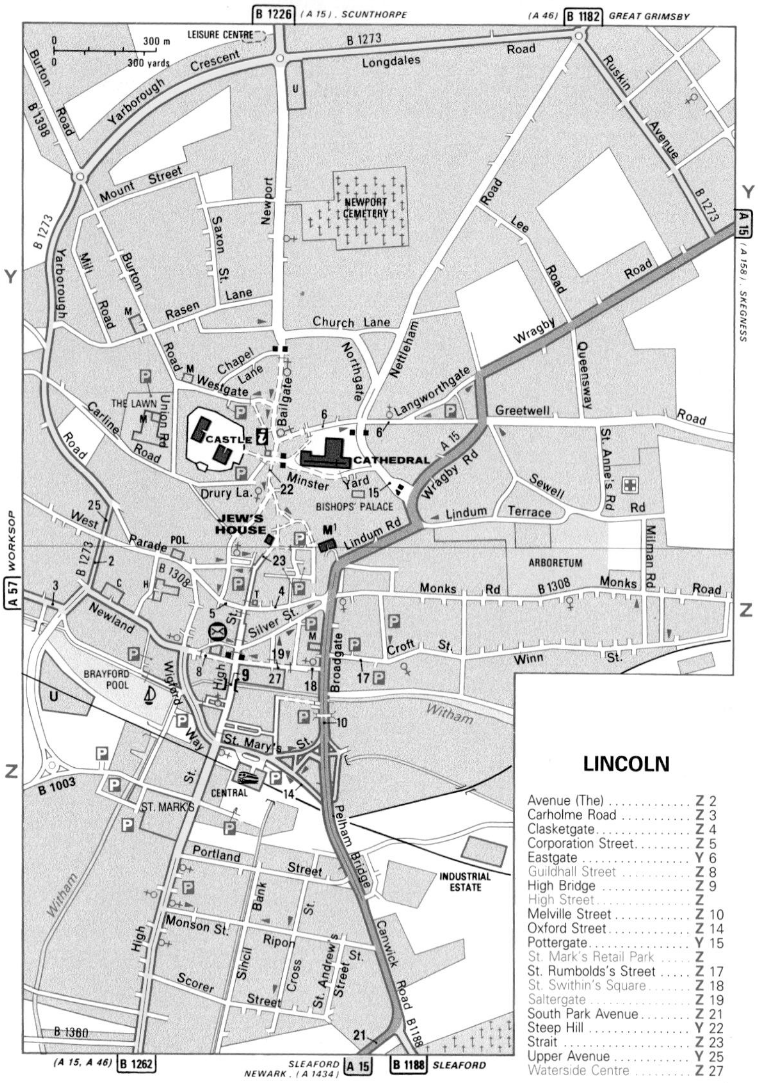

LINCOLN

Avenue (The)	Z	2
Carholme Road	Z	3
Clasketgate	Z	4
Corporation Street	Z	5
Eastgate	Y	6
Guildhall Street	Z	8
High Bridge	Z	9
High Street	Z	
Melville Street	Z	10
Oxford Street	Z	14
Pottergate	Y	15
St. Mark's Retail Park	Z	
St. Rumbolds's Street	Z	17
St. Swithin's Square	Z	18
Saltergate	Z	19
South Park Avenue	Z	21
Steep Hill	Y	22
Strait	Z	23
Upper Avenue	Y	25
Waterside Centre	Z	27

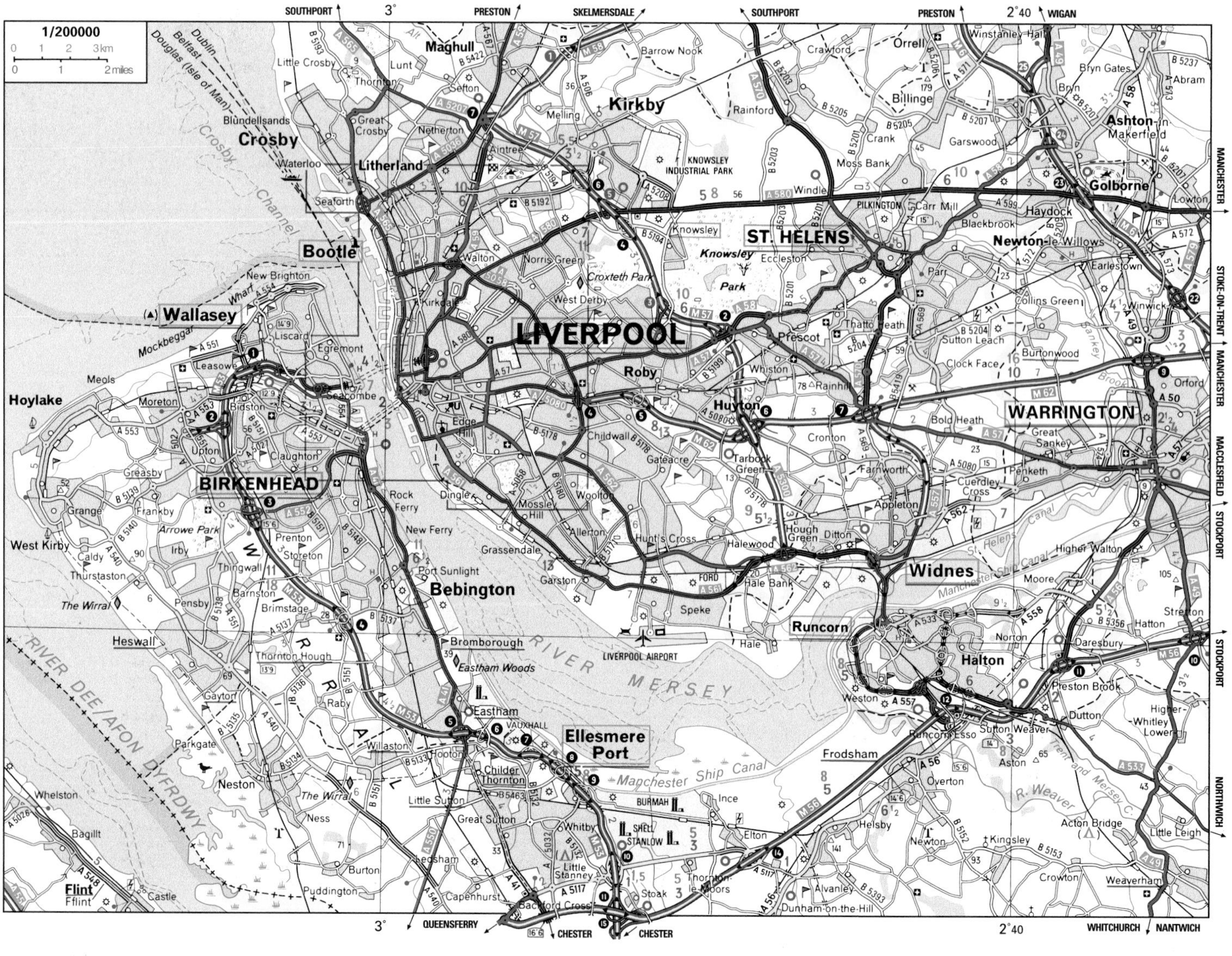

LIVERPOOL CENTRE

Argyle St. .... DZ 6
Blackburne Place .... EZ 11
Bold St. .... DZ
Brunswick Road .... EY 19
Canada Boulevard .... CYZ 22
Canning Place .... CZ 23
Church St. .... DY
Churchill Way .... DY 25
Clarence St. .... EYZ 26
College Lane .... DZ 28
Commutation Row .... DY 30
Cook St. .... CY 32
Crosshall St. .... DY 36
Daulby St. .... EY 40
Erskine St. .... EY 45
Fontenoy St. .... DY 48
Forrest St. .... DZ 49
George's Dock Gate ...... CY 51
Grafton St. .... DZ 53
Great Charlotte St. .... DY 54
Great Howard St. .... CY 56
Hatton Garden .... DY 57
Haymarket .... DY 58
Hood St. .... DY 62
Houghton St. .... DY 65
Huskisson St. .... EZ 66
James St. .... CY 68
King Edward St. .... CY 69
Knight St. .... EZ 72
Leece St. .... EZ 73
Lime St. .... DY
Liver St. .... CZ 76
London Road .... DEY
Lord St. .... CDY
Mansfield St. .... DEY 80
Mathew St. .... CDY 81
Moss St. .... EY 86
Mount St. .... EZ 88
Myrtle St. .... EZ 89
Newington .... DZ 92
New Quay .... CY 93
North John St. .... CY 96
Norton St. .... EY 97
Parker St. .... DY 103
Prescot St. .... EY 105
Prince's Road .... EZ 107
Ranelagh St. .... DY 108
Renshaw St. .... DEZ
Richmond St. .... DY 109
Roe St. .... DY 114
St. James Place .... EZ 117
St. Johns Centre .... DY
St. John's Lane .... DY 118
School Lane .... DYZ 122
Scotland Place .... DY 123
Sefton St. .... DZ 129
Seymour St. .... EY 130
Skelhorne St. .... DY 133
Stanley St. .... CDY 135
Suffolk St. .... DZ 137
Tarleton St. .... DY 139
Victoria St. .... DY 143
Water St. .... CY 150
William Brown St. .... DY 156
York St. .... DZ 157

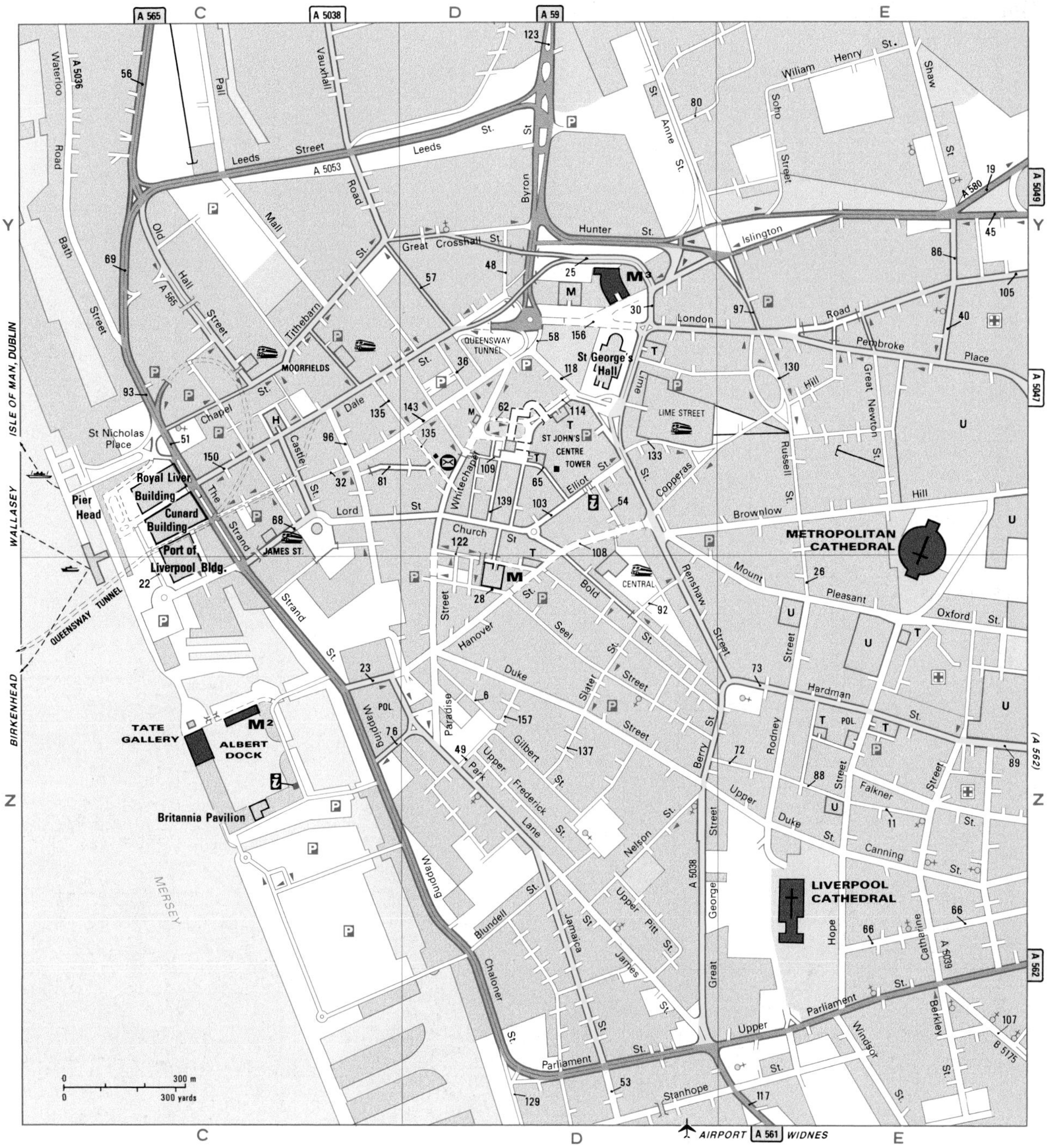

Lampeter / Llanbe dr Pont Steffan 24 H 27
Lanark 49 I 16
Lancashire (County) 38 M 22
Lancaster 38 L 21
Lanchester 46 O 19
Land's End 2 C 33
Landrake 3 H 32
Lanercost 50 L 19
Langavat (Loch) (Lewis) 70 Z 9
Langavat (Loch) (South Harris) 70 Z 10
Langbank 55 G 16
Langdale Valley 44 K 20
Langenhoe 22 W 28
Langford 29 T 27
Langholm 50 L 18
Langley 19 S 29
Langold 36 Q 23
Langport 8 L 30
Langsett 35 O 23
Langstrothdale Chase 39 N 21
Langtoft 41 S 21
Langton Matravers 9 O 32
Langwathby 45 L 19
Lanhydrock 3 F 32
Lanivet 3 F 32
Lanreath 3 G 32
Lansallos 3 G 32
Lapford 7 I 31
Larbert 55 I 15
Largs 54 F 16
Larkhall 55 I 16
Larkhill 9 O 30
Lasswade 56 K 16
Lastingham 47 R 21
Latchingdon 22 W 28
Lauder 57 L 16
Lauderdale 57 L 16
Laugharne 15 G 28
Laughton 11 U 31
Launceston 3 G 32
Laurencekirk 63 M 13
Lauriston Castle 56 K 16
Lavant 10 R 31
Lavenham 22 W 27
Laverstoke 9 P 30
Lawford 21 X 28
Laxey 42 G 21
Laxey Bay 42 G 21
Laxfield 31 Y 27
Laxford (Loch) 72 E 8
Laxford Bridge 72 E 8
Laxo 75 Q 2
Layer-de-la-Haye 22 W 28
Layer Marney 22 W 28
Lazonby 45 L 19
Leaden Roding 20 U 28
Leadenham 36 S 24
Leadgate 45 M 19
Leadhills 49 I 17
Lealholm 47 R 20
Leasingham 37 S 24
Leathaid Bhuain (Loch an) 72 F 9
Leatherhead 20 T 30
Leathley 39 P 22
Lecale Peninsula 99 O 5
Lechlade 18 O 28
Lecht Road 68 K 12
Ledbury 26 M 27
Ledmore 72 F 9
Lee 6 H 30
Lee-on-the-Solent 10 Q 31
Leebotwood 26 L 26
Leeds (Kent) 12 V 30
Leeds (West Yorks.) 40 P 22
Leedstown 2 D 33
Leek 35 N 24
Leeming Bar 46 P 21
Leicester 28 Q 26
Leicestershire (County) 27 P 26
Leigh 38 M 23
Leigh-on-Sea 21 V 29
Leighton Buzzard 19 S 28
Leintwardine 26 L 26
Leiston 23 Y 27
Leith 56 K 16
Lemreway 70 A 9
Lenham 12 W 30
Lennoxtown 55 H 16
Leominster 26 L 27
Lerwick 75 Q 3
Lesbury 51 P 17
Leslie 56 K 15
Lesmahagow 49 I 17
Leswalt 42 E 19
Letchworth 20 T 28
Letham (Angus) 63 L 14
Letham (Fife) 56 K 15
Letheringsett 30 X 25
Letterewe Forest 66 D 10
Letterston 14 F 28
Leuchars 56 L 14
Leven (East Riding of Yorks.) 41 T 22
Leven (River) (Highland) 60 F 13
Leven (Fife) 56 K 15
Leven (Loch) 60 E 13
Levens 45 L 21
Levens Hall 45 L 21
Levenwick 75 Q 4
Leverington 29 U 25
Leverton with Habblesthorpe 36 R 24
Lewdown 3 H 32
Lewes 11 U 31
Lewis and Harris (Isle of) 70 Z 8
Lewisham (London Borough) 20 T 29
Leyburn 46 O 21
Leyland 38 L 22
Leysdown-on-Sea 21 W 29
Lezant 3 G 32
Lhanbryde 68 K 11
Liathach 66 D 11
Lichfield 27 O 25
Liddesdale 50 L 18
Lidgate 22 V 27
Lifton 3 H 32
Ligger or Perran Bay 2 E 32
Lilleshall 26 M 25
Limpsfield 11 U 30
Lincoln 36 S 24
Lincolnshire (County) 37 T 24
Lincolnshire Wolds 37 T 23
Lindfield 11 T 30
Lindores 56 K 14
Lingay (near Eriskay) 64 X 12
Lingay (near Pabbay) 58 X 13
Lingfield 11 T 30
Liniclate 64 X 11
Linlithgow 56 J 16
Linn of Dee 62 J 13
Linn of Tummel 61 I 13
Linney Head 14 E 29
Linnhe (Loch) 60 D 14
Linslade 19 R 28
Lintmill 68 L 10
Linton 22 U 27
Linton-on-Ouse 40 Q 21
Lintrathen (Loch of) 62 K 13
Linwood 55 G 16
Liphook 10 R 30
Liskeard 3 G 32
Lismore 60 D 14
Liss 10 R 30
Litcham 30 W 25
Litherland 34 L 23
Little Berkhamsted 20 T 28
Little Budworth 34 M 24
Little Bytham 28 S 25
Little Chalfont 19 S 28
Little Clacton 21 X 28
Little Colonsay 59 B 14
Little Cumbrae Island 54 F 16
Little Glenshee 62 J 14
Little Hadham 20 U 28
Little Hallingbury 20 U 28
Little Loch Broom 72 D 10
Little Loch Roag 70 Z 9
Little Minch (The) 64 Z 11
Little Moreton Hall 34 N 24
Little Ouse (River) 30 V 26
Little Ouseburn 40 Q 21
Little Snoring 30 W 25
Little Walsingham 30 W 25
Little Waltham 22 V 28
Littleborough 39 N 23
Littlebourne 13 X 30
Littlebury 22 U 27
Littlecote House 18 P 29
Littlehampton 10 S 31
Littleport 29 U 26
Littlestone-on-Sea 13 W 31
Liverpool 34 L 23
Liverton 47 R 20
Livet (Glen) 68 K 12
Livingston 56 J 16
Lizard 2 E 34
Lizard Peninsula 2 E 33
Llanarth 24 H 27
Llanbadarn Fawr 24 H 26
Llanbedr 32 H 25
Llanbedr Pont Steffan / Lampeter 24 H 27
Llanbedrog 32 G 25
Llanberis 32 H 24
Llanbister 25 K 26
Llanbrynmair 25 J 26
Llanddewi Brefi 24 I 27
Llandegla 33 K 24
Llandeilo 15 I 28
Llandenny 17 L 28
Llandissilio 14 F 28
Llandovery / Llanymddyfri 15 I 28
Llandrindod Wells 25 J 27
Llandrinio 26 K 25
Llandudno 33 I 24
Llandudno Junction 33 I 24
Llandybie 15 H 28

Llandygai 32 H 24
Llandysul 24 H 27
Llanegryn 24 H 26
Llanelli 15 H 28
Llanelltyd 33 I 25
Llanengan 32 G 25
Llanerchymedd 32 G 24
Llanfair 32 H 25
Llanfair-Caereinion 25 K 26
Llanfair-Pwllgwyngyll 32 H 24
Llanfair-ym-Muallt / Builth 25 J 27
Llanfairfechan 33 I 24
Llanfyllin 33 K 25
Llangadog 15 I 28
Llangammarch Wells 25 J 27
Llangefni 32 H 24
Llangeinor 16 J 29
Llangeitho 24 H 27
Llangollen 33 K 25
Llangorse 16 K 28
Llangrannog 24 G 27
Llangunllo 25 K 27
Llangurig 25 J 26
Llangwn 17 L 28
Llangwnnadl 32 F 25
Llangwyryfon 24 H 27
Llangybi 24 H 27
Llangynidr 16 K 28
Llangynog 33 J 25
Llanhilleth 16 K 28
Llanidloes 25 J 26
Llanilar 24 H 26
Llanmadoc 15 H 29
Llannefydd 33 J 24
Llanrhaeadr-ym-Mochnant 33 K 25
Llanrhidian 15 H 29
Llanrhystud 24 H 27
Llanrwst 33 I 24
Llansanffraid Glan Conwy 33 I 24
Llansantffraid 24 H 27
Llansantffraid-ym-Mechain 33 K 25
Llansawel 15 H 27
Llansilin 33 K 25
Llansoy 17 L 28
Llanthony 17 K 28
Llantwit Major 16 J 29
Llanuwchllyn 33 I 25
Llanwddyn 33 J 25
Llanwenog 24 H 27
Llanwrda 15 I 28
Llanwrtyd Wells 25 J 27
Llanybydder 24 H 27
Llanymddyfri / Llandovery 15 I 28
Llanymynech 33 K 25
Llanystumdwy 32 H 25
Lledrod 24 I 27
Lleyn Peninsula 32 G 25
Llwyngwril 24 H 25
Llwynmawr 33 K 25
Llyfnant Valley 25 I 26
Llyn Brianne 25 I 27
Llyn Celyn 33 I 25
Llyn Tegid or Bala Lake 33 J 25
Llyswen 25 K 27
Loanhead 56 K 16
Lochaber 66 D 12
Lochailort 60 D 13
Lochaline 59 C 14
Lochans 42 E 19
Locharbriggs 49 J 18
Lochawe 60 E 14
Lochay (Glen) 61 G 14
Lochboisdale 64 Y 12
Lochbuie 59 C 14
Lochcarron 66 D 11
Lochearnhead 55 H 14
Locheport 64 Y 11
Lochgarthside 67 G 12
Lochgelly 56 K 15
Lochgilphead 54 D 15
Lochgoilhead 54 F 15
Lochinver 72 E 9
Lochluichart 66 F 11
Lochmaben 49 J 18
Lochmaddy 64 Y 11
Lochore 56 K 15
Lochranza 54 E 16
Lochsie (Glen) 62 J 13
Lochton 63 M 12
Lochwinnoch 55 G 16
Lochy (Loch) 60 F 13
Lockerbie 49 J 18
Locking 17 L 30
Loddon 31 Y 26
Lode 22 U 27
Lodsworth 10 R 31
Loftus 47 R 20
Logan Gardens 42 F 19
Logie Coldstone 68 L 12
Logiealmond 62 I 14
Lomond (Loch) 55 G 15
London 20 T 29
London Colney 20 T 28
Merton (London Borough) 20 T 29
Long Bennington 36 R 25
Long Buckby 28 Q 27
Long Crendon 19 R 28
Long Eaton 36 Q 25
Long Hanborough 18 P 28
Long (Loch) (Angus) 62 K 14
Long (Loch) (Argyll and Bute) 54 F 15
Long Man (The) 11 U 31
Long Marston 40 Q 22
Long Melford 22 W 27
Long Mountain 26 K 26
Long Mynd (The) 26 L 26
Long Preston 39 N 21
Long Stratton 31 X 26
Long Sutton (Lincs.) 37 U 25
Long Sutton (Somerset) 8 L 30
Longay 65 C 12
Longbenton 51 P 18
Longbridge Deverill 9 N 30
Longburton 8 M 31
Longfield 20 U 29
Longforgan 62 K 14
Longhope 74 K 7
Longhorsley 51 O 18
Longhoughton 51 P 17
Longleat House 8 N 30
Longniddry 56 L 16
Longnor 35 O 24
Longridge 38 M 22
Longside 69 O 11
Longton 35 N 25
Longtown 50 L 18
Lonmore 65 A 11
Looe 3 G 32
Lorn 60 E 14
Lorn (Firth of) 60 D 14
Lossiemouth 68 K 10
Lostwithiel 3 G 32
Loudwater 19 R 29
Loughborough 36 Q 25
Loughor (River) 15 H 29
Loughton 20 U 29
Louth 37 U 23
Low Street 31 Y 25
Lowca 44 J 20
Lowdham 36 Q 24
Lower Bentham 38 M 21
Lower Cam 17 M 28
Lower Diabaig 66 C 11
Lowestoft 31 Z 26
Lowick 51 O 17
Lowick Bridge 44 K 21
Lowther 49 I 17
Lowther Hills 49 J 18
Loxwood 10 S 30
Loyal (Loch) 73 G 8
Loyne (Loch) 60 E 12
Lùb Score 65 A 10
Lubenham 28 R 26
Lubnaig (Loch) 55 H 15
Luccombe 7 J 30
Luce Bay 42 F 19
Ludgershall (Bucks.) 19 Q 28
Ludgershall (Wilts.) 9 P 30
Ludgvan 2 D 33
Ludham 31 Y 25
Ludlow 26 L 26
Lugton 55 G 16
Luichart (Loch) 66 F 11
Luing 54 D 15
Lulworth Cove 8 N 32
Lumphanan 69 L 12
Lunanhead 62 L 14
Lundie (Loch) 66 C 11
Lundin Links 56 L 15
Lundy 6 G 30
Lurgainn (Loch) 72 E 9
Luss 55 G 15
Luthrie 56 K 14
Luton 20 S 28
Luton Hoo 20 S 28
Lutterworth 28 Q 26
Luxborough 7 J 30
Lybster 74 K 9
Lydbury North 26 L 26
Lydd 12 W 31
Lydd-on-Sea 13 W 31
Lydford 3 H 32
Lydham 26 L 26
Lydiard Park 18 O 29
Lydney 17 M 28
Lyme Bay 5 L 32
Lyme Park 35 N 23
Lyme Regis 8 L 31
Lyminge 13 X 30
Lymington 9 P 31
Lymm 34 M 23
Lympne 13 X 30
Lympstone 4 J 32
Lyndhurst 9 P 31
Lyneham 18 O 29
Lyness 74 K 7
Lynmouth 7 I 30
Lynton 7 I 30
Lyon (Glen) 61 H 14
Lyonshall 26 L 27
Lytchett Minster 9 N 31
Lytes Cary 8 L 30
Lytham 38 L 22
Lytham St. Anne's 38 K 22

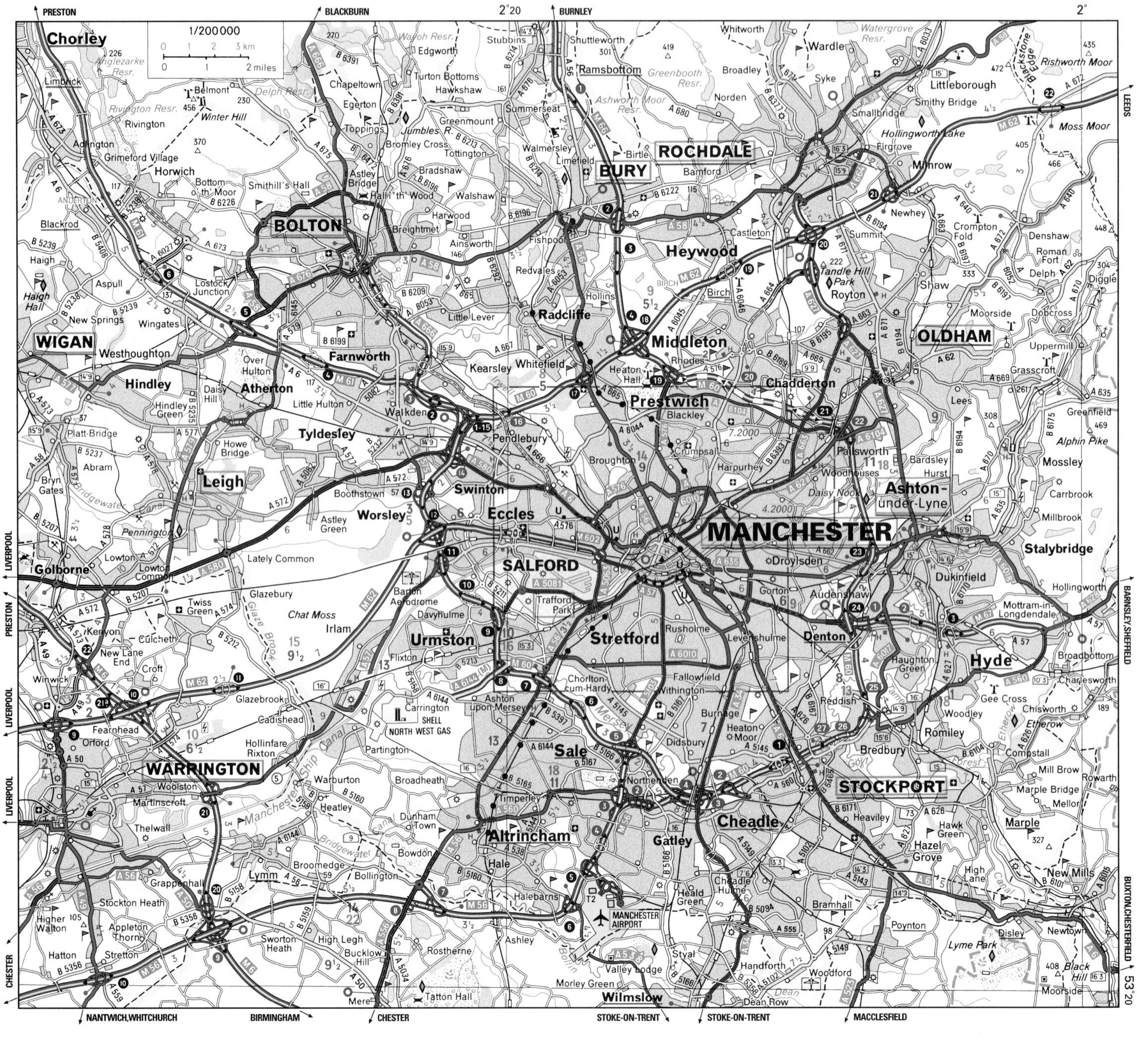
PRESTON
BLACKBURN
BURNLEY
LEEDS
1/200 000
0 1 2 3 km
0 1 2 miles
Chorley
Rochdale
Bury
Bolton
Heywood
Middleton
Radcliffe
Oldham
Wigan
Hindley
Atherton
Farnworth
Prestwich
Chadderton
Tyldesley
Leigh
Swinton
Eccles
Worsley
Salford
MANCHESTER
Ashton-under-Lyne
Stalybridge
Droylsden
Dukinfield
Golborne
Urmston
Stretford
Denton
Hyde
Sale
Warrington
Stockport
Cheadle
Altrincham
Gatley
Hale
Marple
Wilmslow
MANCHESTER AIRPORT
Chat Moss
Manchester Ship Canal
Tatton Hall
Lyme Park
LIVERPOOL
CHESTER
NANTWICH,WHITCHURCH
BIRMINGHAM
STOKE-ON-TRENT
MACCLESFIELD
BUXTON,CHESTERFIELD
BARNSLEY,SHEFFIELD
2°20
2°
53°20

MANCHESTER
CENTRE

Addington Street . . . . CY 2
Albert Square . . . . CZ 6
Aytoun Street . . . . CZ 10
Blackfriars Road . . . . CY 15
Blackfriars Street . . . . CY 17
Brazennose Street . . . . CZ 18
Charlotte Street . . . . CZ 25
Cheetham Hill Road . . . . CY 27
Chepstow Street . . . . CZ 28
Chorlton Street . . . . CZ 29
Church Street . . . . CY 31
Corn Exchange . . . . CY 34
Dale Street . . . . CZ 38
Deansgate . . . . CYZ
Ducie Street . . . . CZ 45
Fairfield Street . . . . CZ 49
Fennel Street . . . . CY 50
Great Bridgewater Street . . . . CZ 53
Great Ducie Street . . . . CY 57
High Street . . . . CY 62
John Dalton Street . . . . CZ 63
King Street . . . . CZ 64
Liverpool Road . . . . CZ 68
Lloyd Street . . . . CZ 69
Lower Byrom St. . . . . CZ 70
Lower Mosley Street . . . . CZ 71
Mosley Street . . . . CZ
Nicholas Street . . . . CZ 84
Parker Street . . . . CZ 91
Peter Street . . . . CZ 92
Princess Street . . . . CZ
St. Ann's Street . . . . CY 101
St. Peter's Square . . . . CZ 104
Spring Gardens . . . . CZ 106
Viaduct Street . . . . CY 109
Whitworth Street West . . . . . CZ 112
Withy Grove . . . . CY 113
York Street . . . . CZ 115

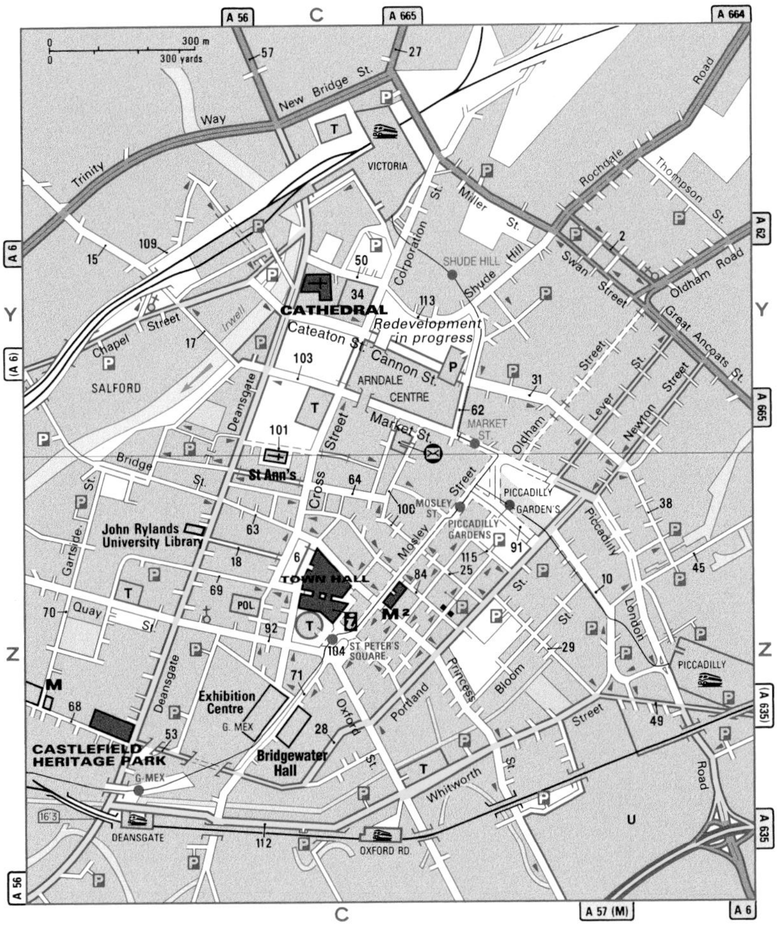
A 56
C
A 665
A 664
300 m
300 yards
New Bridge St.
Trinity
Way
VICTORIA
Corporation St.
Miller St.
Rochdale
Thompson St.
Road
SHUDE HILL
Shude Hill
Swan Street
Oldham Road
Great Ancoats St.
CATHEDRAL
Redevelopment in progress
Cateaton St.
Cannon St.
ARNDALE CENTRE
Chapel Street
SALFORD
Irwell
Deansgate
MARKET ST.
Market St.
Oldham
Lever St.
Newton Street
Bridge St.
St Ann's
Cross Street
PICCADILLY GARDEN'S
Piccadilly
John Rylands University Library
MOSLEY ST.
Mosley
PICCADILLY GARDENS
Gartside St.
TOWN HALL
Quay St.
POL
ST. PETER'S SQUARE
Princess
Bloom
London
PICCADILLY
Exhibition Centre
G. MEX
Portland
Oxford
Street
CASTLEFIELD HERITAGE PARK
G-MEX
Bridgewater Hall
Whitworth
DEANSGATE
OXFORD RD.
Road
U
A 57 (M)
A 6
A 62
A 665
A 635
Y
Z

M

Maaruig 70 Z 10
Mablethorpe 37 U 23
Mc Arthur's Head 52 B 16
Macaskin (Island) 54 D 15
Macclesfield 35 N 24
Macduff 69 M 10
Machars (The) 42 G 19
Machir Bay 52 A 16
Machrihanish 53 C 17
Machrihanish Bay 53 C 17
Machynlleth 25 I 26
Madderty 56 I 14
Maddy (Loch) 64 Y 11
Madeley (Salop) 26 M 26
Madeley (Staffs.) 34 M 24
Madingley 29 U 27
Madron 2 D 33
Maenclochog 14 F 28
Maentwrog 32 I 25
Maerdy 16 J 28
Maes Howe 74 K 7
Maesteg 16 J 29
Maghull 38 L 23
Magor 17 L 29
Maiden Bradley 8 N 30
Maiden Castle 8 M 31
Maiden Newton 8 M 31
Maidenhead 19 R 29
Maidens 48 F 17
Maidford 28 Q 27
Maidstone 12 V 30
Mainland (Orkney Islands) 74 J 6
Mainland (Shetland Islands) 75 R 3
Maisemore 17 N 28
Malborough 4 I 33
Malden Bradley 8 N 30
Maldon 22 W 28
Malham 39 N 21
Mallaig 59 C 12
Mallory Park Circuit 27 P 26
Mallwyd 25 I 25
Malmesbury 18 N 29
Malpas 34 L 24
Maltby 36 Q 23
Maltby-le-Marsh 37 U 24
Malton 40 R 21
Malvern Wells 26 N 27
Mamble 26 M 26
Mamore Forest 60 F 13
Man (Isle of) 42 G 21
Manaton 4 I 32
Manchester 35 N 23
Manea 29 U 26
Mangotsfield 17 M 29
Manningtree 21 X 28
Manorbier 14 F 29
Mansfield 36 Q 24
Mansfield Woodhouse 36 Q 24
Manton 28 R 26
Manuden 20 U 28
Mapledurham 19 Q 29
Mar (Forest of) 68 J 12
Marazion 2 D 33
March 29 U 26
Marcham 18 P 29
Marchwood 9 P 31
Marden 12 V 30
Maree (Loch) 66 D 10
Mareham-le-Fen 37 T 24
Maresfield 11 U 31
Margam 15 I 29
Margaretting 22 V 28
Margate 13 Y 29
Margnaheglish 53 E 17
Market Bosworth 27 P 26
Market Deeping 37 T 25
Market Drayton 34 M 25
Market Harborough 28 R 26
Market Lavington 9 O 30
Market Rasen 37 T 23
Market Weighton 41 S 22
Markfield 28 Q 25
Markinch 56 K 15
Marks Tey 22 W 28
Markyate 20 S 28
Marlborough 18 O 29
Marldon 4 J 32
Marlow 19 R 29
Marnhull 8 N 31
Marple 35 N 23
Marsden 39 O 23
Marsham 31 X 25
Marshchapel 37 U 23
Marshfield 17 N 29
Marske-by-the-Sea 47 Q 20
Marston Magna 8 M 31
Marston Moretaine 28 S 27
Martham 31 Y 25
Martin 9 O 31
Martin (Isle) 72 E 10
Martley 26 M 27
Martock 8 L 31
Marwell Zoological Park 10 Q 31
Mary Arden's House 27 O 27
Mary Tavy 3 H 32
Maryburgh 67 G 11
Maryculter 69 N 12
Marykirk 63 M 13
Marypark 68 J 11
Maryport 44 J 19
Marywell 63 M 14
Masham 39 P 21
Matlock 35 P 24
Matlock Bath 35 P 24
Mattishall 30 X 26
Mauchline 48 G 17
Maud 69 N 11
Maughold Head 42 H 21
Mawbray 44 J 19
Maybole 48 F 17
Mayfield (East Sussex) 11 U 30
Mayfield (Staffs.) 35 O 24
Meadie (Loch) 72 G 9
Mealsgate 44 K 19
Meare 8 L 30
Measach (Falls of) 66 E 10
Measham 27 P 25
Medbourne 28 R 26
Medmenham 19 R 29
Medway (River) 21 W 29
Meidrim 15 G 28
Meigle 62 K 14
Melbost 71 B 9
Melbourn 29 U 27
Melbourne 35 P 25
Melfort 54 D 15
Melksham 18 N 29
Mellerstain 50 M 17
Melling 38 M 21
Mellon Udrigle 71 D 10
Melmerby 45 M 19
Melrose 50 L 17
Meltham 39 O 23
Melton Mowbray 36 R 25
Melvaig 71 C 10
Melvich 73 I 8
Menai Bridge / Porthaethwy 32 H 24
Menai Strait 32 H 24
Mendip Hills 17 L 30
Menston 39 O 22
Menteith Hills 55 H 15
Mentmore 19 R 28
Meonstoke 10 Q 31
Meopham 20 V 29
Mere (Cheshire) 34 M 24
Mere (Wilts.) 8 N 30
Mereworth 12 V 30
Meriden 27 P 26
Merrick 48 G 18
Merriott 8 L 31
Mersey (River) 34 M 23
Merseyside (Metropolitan County-Liverpool) 34 L 23
Merthyr Tydfil 16 J 28
Merton (Devon) 6 H 31
Meshaw 7 I 31
Messingham 41 S 23
Metheringham 37 S 24
Methil 56 K 15
Methlick 69 N 11
Methven 56 J 14
Methwold 30 V 26
Mevagissey 3 F 33
Mexborough 40 Q 23
Mhór (Loch) 67 G 12
Miavaig 70 Z 9
Michelham Priory 11 U 31
Mickleover 35 P 25
Mickleton 27 O 27
Mid Ardlaw 69 N 10
Mid Calder 56 J 16
Mid Sannox 53 E 17
Mid Yell 75 Q 2
Midbea 74 L 6
Middle Wallop 9 P 30
Middleham 46 O 21
Middle Rasen 37 S 23
Middlesbrough 46 Q 20
Middlestown 39 P 23
Middleton (Argyll and Bute) 58 Z 14
Middleton (Gtr. Mches.) 39 N 23
Middleton Cheney 28 Q 27
Middleton-in-Teesdale 45 N 20
Middleton-on-Sea 10 S 31
Middleton St George 46 P 20
Middletown 26 K 25
Middlewich 34 M 24
Midhurst 10 R 31
Midlem 50 L 17
Midsomer Norton 8 M 30
Migdale (Loch) 73 H 10
Milborne Port 8 M 31
Milborne St. Andrew 8 N 31
Mildenhall 30 V 26
Mile End 22 W 28
Milford 10 S 30
Milford Haven / Aberdaugleddau 14 E 28
Milford-on-Sea 9 P 31
Millom 38 K 21
Millport 54 F 16
Milltown (Moray) 68 L 11
Milltown (Highland) 66 F 11
Milnathort 56 J 15
Milngavie 55 H 16
Milnrow 39 N 23
Milnthorpe 38 L 21
Milovaig 64 Z 11
Milton (Cambs.) 29 U 27
Milton (Dumfries and Galloway) 42 F 19
Milton Abbas 8 N 31
Milton Abbot 3 H 32
Milton Bryan 19 S 28
Milton Ernest 28 S 27
Milton Keynes 28 R 27
Milton Libourne 18 O 29
Milton of Campsie 55 H 16
Milverton 7 K 30
Milwich 35 N 25
Minard 54 E 15
Minch (The) 71 C 9
Minehead 7 J 30
Minety 18 O 29
Mingary 64 X 12
Minginish 65 B 12
Mingulay 58 X 13
Minnigaff 42 G 19
Minster (near Ramsgate) 13 X 29
Minster (near) 21 W 29
Minsterley 26 L 26
Minsterworth 17 N 28
Minterne Magna 8 M 31
Mintlaw 69 O 11
Minto 50 L 17
Mirfield 39 O 22
Misterton (Notts.) 36 R 23
Misterton (Somerset) 8 L 31
Mistley 21 X 28
Mitcheldean 17 M 28
Mitchell 2 E 32
Modbury 4 I 32
Moelfre 32 H 23
Moffat 49 J 17
Moidart 60 C 13
Moira 27 P 25
Mold / Yr Wyddgrug 33 K 24
Monadhliath Mountains 67 H 12
Monar (Loch) 66 E 11
Monaughty Forest 68 J 11
Moneydie 62 J 14
Moniaive 49 I 18
Monifieth 62 L 14
Monikie 62 L 14
Monk Fryston 40 Q 22
Monkokehampton 6 H 31
Monks Eleigh 22 W 27
Monksilver 7 K 30
Monmouth / Trefynwy 17 L 28
Monreith 42 G 19
Montacute 8 L 31
Montgarrie 68 L 12
Montgomery / Trefaldwyn 25 K 26
Montrose 63 M 13
Monymusk 69 M 12
Moonen Bay 64 Z 11
Moorfoot Hills 56 K 16
Moors (The) 42 F 19
Morar 59 C 13
Moray Firth 67 H 11
Morchard Bishop 7 I 31
Mordiford 26 M 27
More (Glen) 59 C 14
More (Loch) (near Kinloch) 72 F 9
More (Loch) (near Westerdale) 73 J 8
Morebath 7 J 30
Morecambe 38 L 21
Morecambe Bay 38 L 21
Moreton-in-the-Marsh 18 O 28
Moreton-in-the-Marsh 20 U 28
Moreton-hampstead 4 I 32
Morfa Nefyn 32 G 25
Moricambe Bay 44 K 19
Morie (Loch) 67 G 10
Moriston (Glen) 66 F 12
Morley 39 P 22
Morlich (Loch) 67 I 12
Morpeth 51 O 18
Morte Bay 6 H 30
Mortehoe 6 H 30
Mortimer 19 Q 29
Morton (near Bourne) 37 S 25
Morton (near Gainsborough) 36 R 23
Morven 74 I 9
Morvern 59 C 14
Morville 26 M 26
Morwelham 3 H 32
Morwenstow 6 G 31
Moss Bank 34 L 23
Mossend 55 H 16
Mossley 39 N 23
Mosstodloch 68 K 11
Motherwell 55 I 16
Moulton (Lincs.) 37 T 25
Moulton (Northants.) 28 R 27
Moulton Chapel 29 T 25
Mountain Ash / Aberpennar 16 J 28
Mount's Bay 2 D 33
Mountsorrel 28 Q 25
Mousa 75 Q 4
Mousehole 2 D 33
Mouswald 49 J 18
Mow Cop 34 N 24
Moy 67 H 11
Much Hoole 38 L 22
Much Wenlock 26 M 26
Muchalls 63 N 12
Muck 59 B 13
Muckle Roe 75 P 2
Mudford 8 M 31
Muick (Loch) 62 K 13
Muir of Fowlis 68 L 12
Muir of Ord 67 G 11
Muirdrum 63 L 14
Muirhead 55 H 16
Muirkirk 49 H 17
Muirshearlich 60 E 13
Muker 45 N 20
Muldoanich 58 X 13
Mull (Isle of) 59 B 14
Mull (Sound of) 59 C 14
Mull of Oa 52 A 17
Mull of Galloway 42 F 20
Mullardoch (Loch) 66 E 12
Mullion 2 E 33
Mumbles (The) 15 I 29
Mundesley 31 Y 25
Mundford 30 V 26
Munlochy 67 H 11
Munlochy Bay 67 H 11
Munslow 26 L 26
Murrayfield 56 K 16
Murton 46 P 19
Musselburgh 56 K 16
Muthill 55 I 15
Mwnt 24 G 27
Mybster 74 J 8
Mynach Falls 25 I 26
Mynydd Eppynt 25 J 27
Mynydd Preseli 14 F 28

N

Na Cùiltean	52	C 16
Nafferton	41	S 21
Nailsworth	17	N 28
Nairn	67	I 11
Nant (Loch)	54	E 14
Nant-y-Moch Reservoir	25	I 26
Nantgwynant Valley	32	H 24
Nantwich	34	M 24
Nantyglo	16	K 28
Napton	28	Q 27
Narberth / Arberth	14	F 28
Narborough	30	V 25
Nash Point	16	J 29
Nateby	45	M 20
National Exhibition Centre (N.E.C.)	27	O 26
National Motor Museum	9	P 31
Navenby	36	S 24
Naver (Loch)	72	G 9
Nayland	22	W 28
Naze (The)	23	X 28
Neath (River)	15	I 28
Neath / Castell-nedd	15	I 29
Needham Market	23	X 27
Needles (The)	9	P 32
Nefyn	32	G 25
Neidpath Castle	49	K 17
Neilston	55	G 16
Neist Point	64	Z 11
Nelson	39	N 22
Nene (River)	29	T 26
Ness	71	B 8
Ness (Loch)	67	G 12
Neston	34	K 24
Nether Broughton	36	R 25
Nether Langwith	36	Q 24
Nether Stowey	7	K 30
Netheravon	9	O 30
Netherhampton	9	O 30
Nethertown	74	K 7
Nethy Bridge	68	J 12
Netley	9	P 31
Nettlebed	19	R 29
Nettleham	36	S 24
Nevern	14	F 27
Nevis (Glen)	60	E 13
Nevis (Loch)	60	C 12
New Abbey	49	J 19
New Aberdour	69	N 11
New Alresford	10	Q 30
New Buckenham	31	X 26
New Byth	69	N 11
New Cumnock	48	H 17
New Deer	69	N 11
New Forest	9	P 31
New Forest Forest Park	9	P 31
New Galloway	48	H 18
New Holland	41	S 22
New Hythe	12	V 30
New Leeds	69	N 11
New Mills	35	O 23
New Milton	9	P 31
New Pitsligo	69	N 11
New Quay / Ceinewydd	24	G 27
New Romney	12	W 31
New Rossington	36	Q 23
New Sauchie	55	I 15
New Scone	56	J 14
New Tredegar	16	K 28
Newark-on-Trent	36	R 24
Newbiggin-by-the-Sea	51	P 18
Newbigging	62	L 14
Newbold Verdon	27	P 26
Newborough	32	G 24
Newbridge-on-Wye	25	J 27
Newburgh ((Lancashire))	38	L 23
Newburgh (Aberdeenshire)	69	N 12
Newburgh (Fife)	56	K 14

NEWPORT

Allt-yr-yn Avenue	AY 2
Blewitt Street	AX 7
Bellevue Lane	BX 5
Caerau Crescent	AXY 9
Cambrian Centre	AX
Capel Street	AY 10
Clarence Place	AX 12
Clyffard Crescent	AX 13
Clytha Park Road	AX 14
Commercial Street	AXY 15
Dewsland Park Road	AY 17
Dock Street	AX 19
Godfrey Road	AX 21
Hereford Street	AX 24
High Street	AX 26
John Frost Square	AX 27
Kensington Place	AX 30
Keynsham Avenue	AY 32
Kingsway Centre	AX
Lower Dock Street	AXY 35
Malpas Road	AX 37
Newport Bridge	AX 39
Oakfield Road	AX 42
Queensway	AX 44
Summerhill Avenue	AX 47
Waterloo Road	AY 50

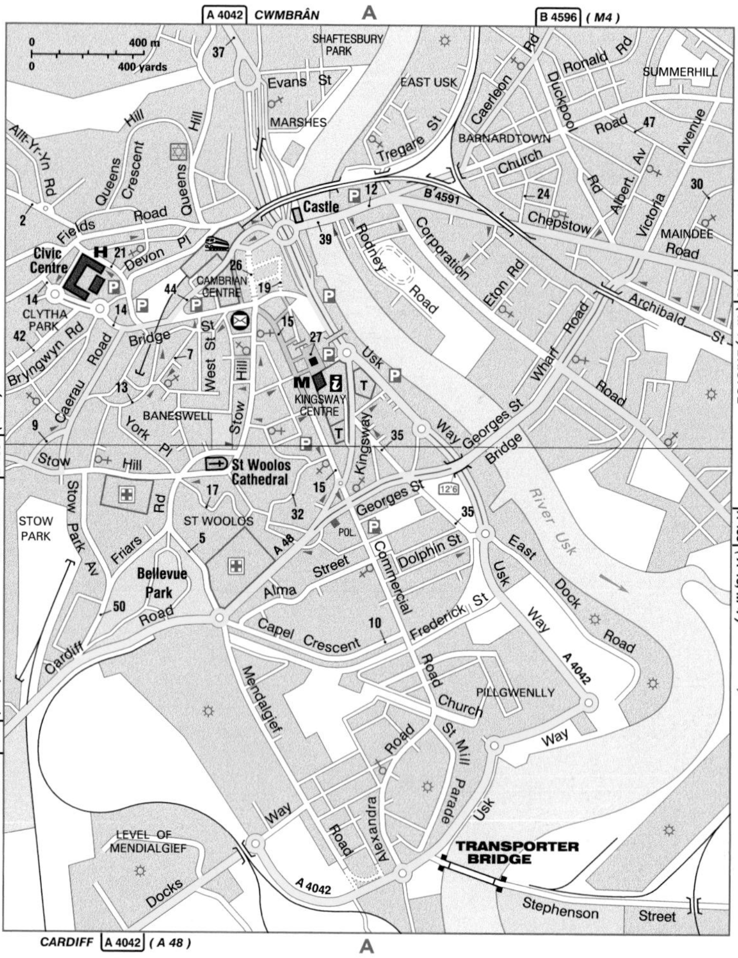

A 4042 CWMBRÂN
B 4596 (M4)
SHAFTESBURY PARK
EAST USK
SUMMERHILL
MARSHES
BARNARDTOWN
Castle
Civic Centre
CAMBRIAN CENTRE
CLYTHA PARK
KINGSWAY CENTRE
BANESWELL
St Woolos Cathedral
ST WOOLOS
STOW PARK
Bellevue Park
PILLGWENLLY
River Usk
LEVEL OF MENDIALGIEF
TRANSPORTER BRIDGE
A 48 (M4) BRISTOL
A 455 (A 48, M 4)
CAERPHILLY B 4591 (M4)
CARDIFF A 48 (M4)
CARDIFF A 4042 (A 48)

NEWCASTLE UPON TYNE

Blackett Street	CY
Bridge Street	CZ 10
Broad Chare	CZ 12
Collingwood Street	CZ 25
Eldon Square Shopping Centre	CYZ
Forth Street	CZ 30
George Street	CZ 32
Great North Road	CY 33
Grey Street	CZ
Jesmond Road	CY 40
John Dobson Street	CY 41
Leazes Park Road	CY 43
Low Friar Street	CZ 46
Market Street	CZ 47
Mosley Street	CZ 50
Neville Street	CZ 52
New Bridge St. West	CY 53
Newgate Street	CZ
Northumberland Street	CY 56
Pilgrim Street	CZ 57
Railway Street	CZ 60
St. Mary's Place	CY 65
St. Nicholas Street	CZ 66
Scotswood Road	CZ 70
Thornton Street	CZ 80
Wellington Street	CY 84
Westmorland Rd	CZ 88

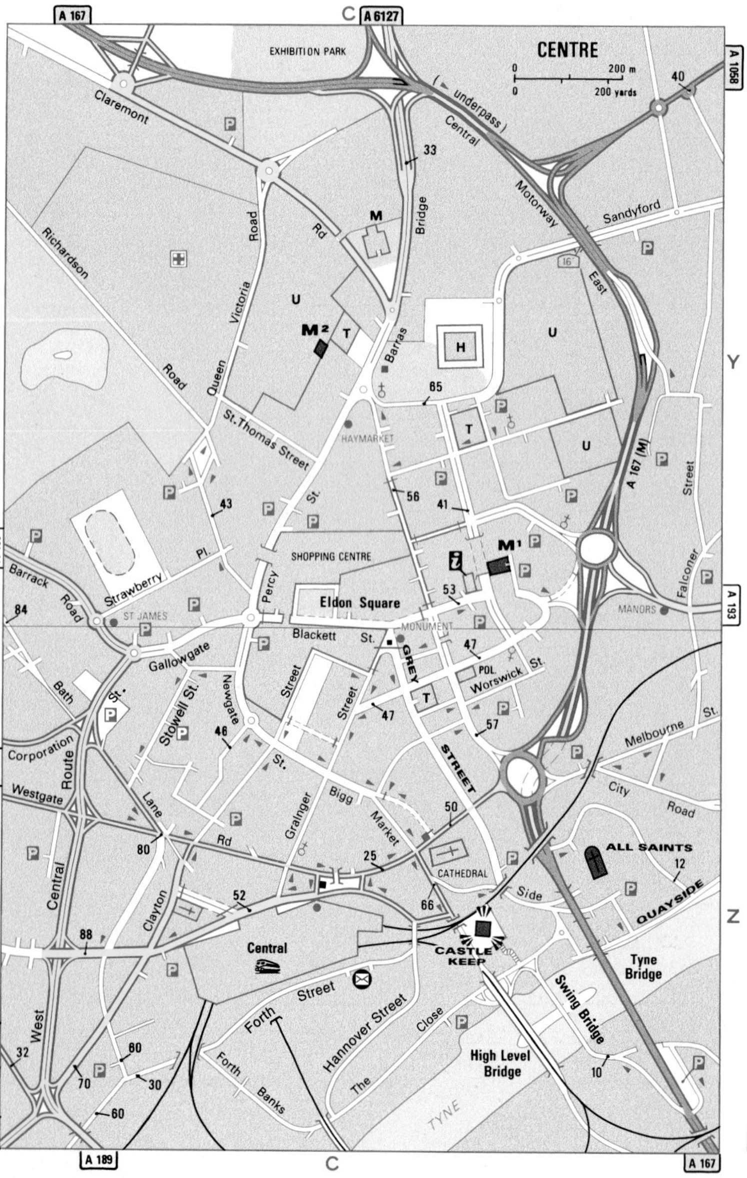

CENTRE
EXHIBITION PARK
HAYMARKET
SHOPPING CENTRE
Eldon Square
MONUMENT
ST JAMES
MANORS
CATHEDRAL
ALL SAINTS
QUAYSIDE
Central
CASTLE KEEP
Tyne Bridge
Swing Bridge
High Level Bridge
TYNE

NORWICH CENTRE

Bank Plain	Y 2
Bethel Street	Z 4
Castle Mall Shopping Centre	Z
Castle Meadow	Z 6
Cattle Market Street	Z 7
Chapel Field North	Z 9
Charing Cross	Y 10
Colegate	Y 14
Elm Hill	Y
Exchange Street	YZ 15
Gentleman's Walk	Z 17
Grapes Hill	Y 19
London Street	YZ 26
Market Avenue	Z 28
Rampant Horse Street	Z 32
Red Lion Street	Z 33
St. Andrew's Street	Y 36
St. George's Street	Y 38
St. Stephen's Street	Z
Thorn Lane	Z 42
Timber Hill	Z 43
Tombland	Y 45
Upper King Street	Y 46
Wensum Street	Y 49
Westlegate	Z 50
Whitefriars	Y 51

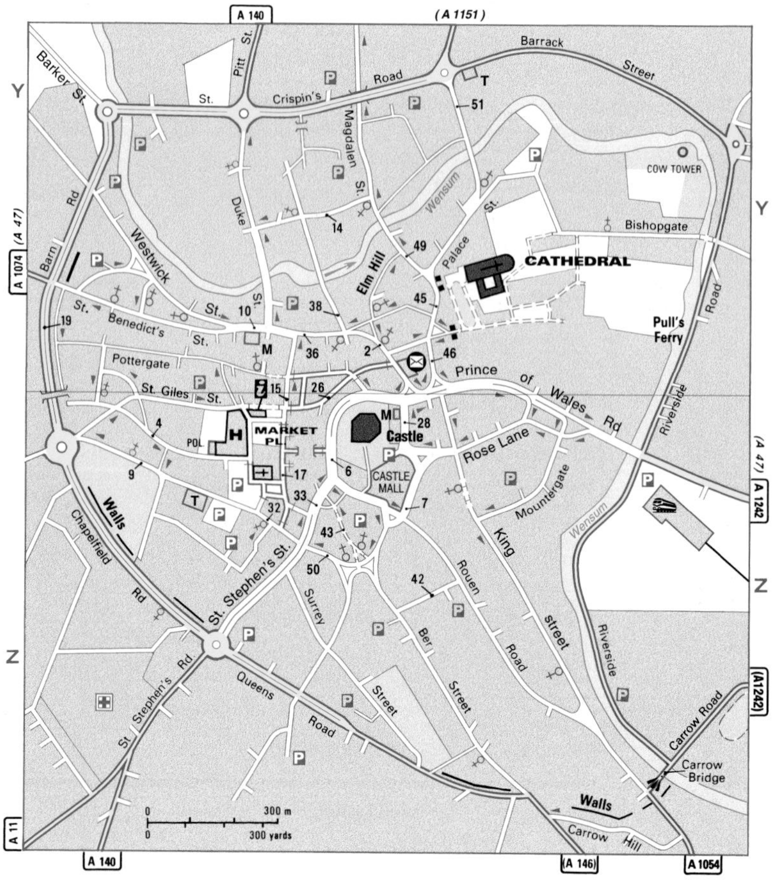

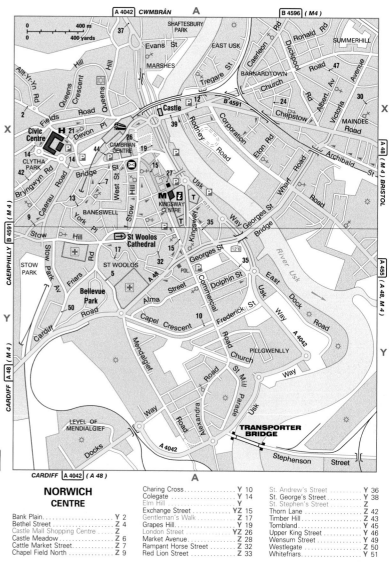

COW TOWER
CATHEDRAL
Pull's Ferry
Castle
CASTLE MALL
MARKET PL.
Wensum
Carrow Bridge
Walls

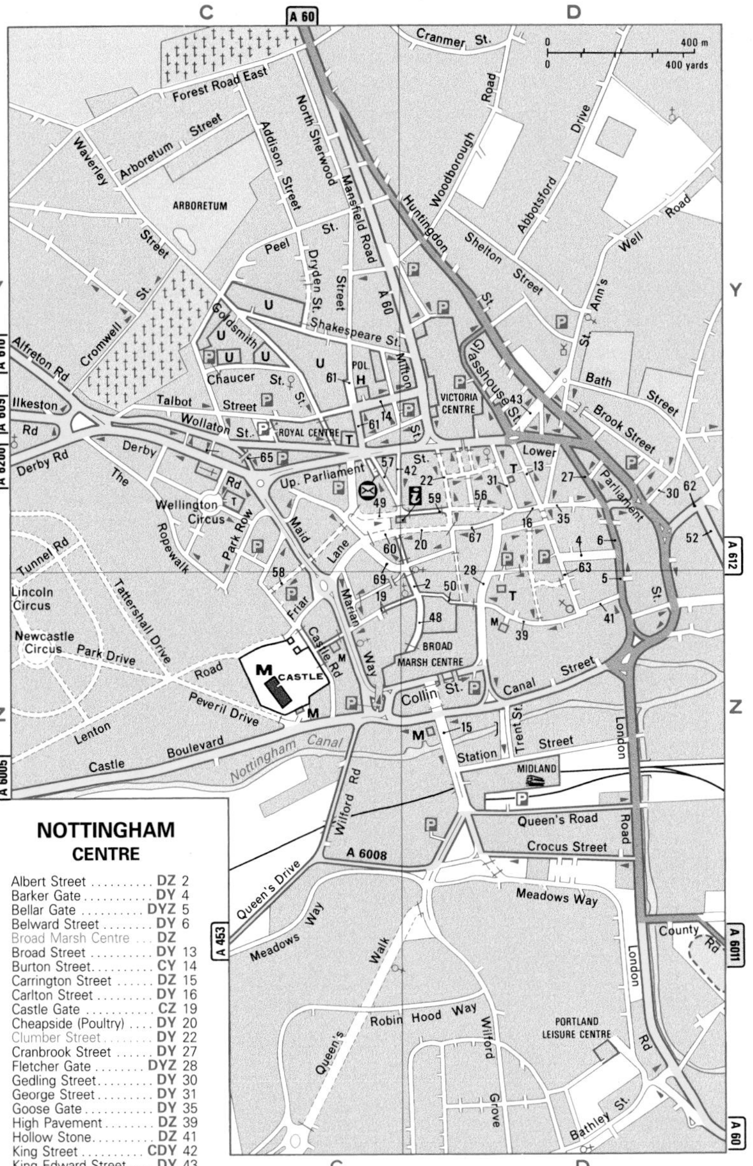
C
D
A 60
Cranmer St.
400 m
400 yards
Forest Road East
Waverley
Arboretum Street
ARBORETUM
Addison Street
North Sherwood St.
Mansfield Road
Woodborough Road
Huntingdon
Abbotsford
Drive
Well Road
Shelton
Street
St. Ann's
Peel St.
Dryden St.
Goldsmith St.
Shakespeare St.
Cromwell St.
Alfreton Rd
Chaucer St.
Talbot Street
Ilkeston Rd
Derby Rd
Wollaton St.
ROYAL CENTRE
Milton St.
VICTORIA CENTRE
Glasshouse St.
Bath Street
Brook Street
Up. Parliament St.
Lower Parliament
The Wellington Circus
Ropewalk
Park Row
Maid Marian Way
Tunnel Rd
Tattershall Drive
Lincoln Circus
Newcastle Circus
Park Drive
Friar Lane
Castle Rd
CASTLE
Peveril Drive
Road
BROAD MARSH CENTRE
Collin St.
Canal Street
Lenton
Castle Boulevard
Nottingham Canal
Wilford Rd
Trent St.
Station
Street
MIDLAND
London Road
Queen's Road
Crocus Street
A 6008
Queen's Drive
Meadows Way
County Rd
A 6011
A 453
Walk
Robin Hood Way
Queen's
Wilford Grove
PORTLAND LEISURE CENTRE
Bathley St.
A 60
A 612
Y
Z

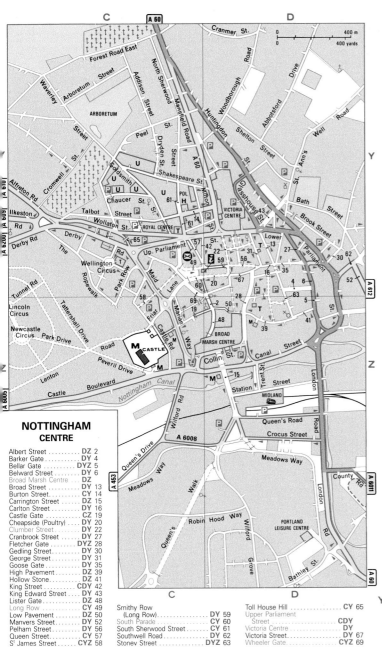

NOTTINGHAM CENTRE

Albert Street DZ 2
Barker Gate DY 4
Bellar Gate DYZ 5
Belward Street DY 6
Broad Marsh Centre DZ
Broad Street DY 13
Burton Street CY 14
Carrington Street DZ 15
Carlton Street DY 16
Castle Gate CZ 19
Cheapside (Poultry) DY 20
Clumber Street DY 22
Cranbrook Street DY 27
Fletcher Gate DYZ 28
Gedling Street DY 30
George Street DY 31
Goose Gate DY 35
High Pavement DZ 39
Hollow Stone DZ 41
King Street CDY 42
King Edward Street DY 43
Lister Gate DZ 48
Long Row CY 49
Low Pavement DZ 50
Manvers Street DY 52
Pelham Street DY 56
Queen Street CY 57
S' James Street CYZ 58
Smithy Row (Long Row) DY 59
South Parade CY 60
South Sherwood Street CY 61
Southwell Road DY 62
Stoney Street DYZ 63
Toll House Hill CY 65
Upper Parliament Street CDY
Victoria Centre DY
Victoria Street DY 67
Wheeler Gate CYZ 69

Newburn 51 O 19
Newbury 19 Q 29
Newby Bridge 38 L 21
Newby Hall 40 P 21
Newcastle Emlyn / Castell Newydd E mlyn 24 G 27
Newcastle-under-Lyme 34 N 24
Newcastle-upon-Tyne Airport 51 O 18
Newcastle-upon-Tyne 51 P 19
Newcastleton 50 L 18
Newchurch 12 W 30
Newdigate 11 T 30
Newent 17 M 28
Newgale 14 E 28
Newhall 34 M 24
Newham (London Borough) 20 U 29
Newhaven 11 U 31
Newick 11 U 31
Newington 21 V 29
Newland 17 M 28
Newlyn 2 D 33
Newmachar 69 N 12
Newmains 55 I 16
Newmarket (Isle of Lewis) 71 A 9
Newmarket (Suffolk) 22 V 27
Newmill 68 L 11
Newmilns 48 G 17
Newnham (Glos.) 17 M 28
Newnham (Kent) 12 W 30
Newnham Bridge 26 M 27
Newport / Casnewydd (Newport) 17 L 29
Newport (Pembrokes) 14 F 27
Newport (Essex) 20 U 28
Newport (I.O.W.) 10 Q 31
Newport (Salop) 34 M 25
Newport-on-Tay 62 L 14
Newport Pagnell 28 R 27
Newquay 2 E 32
Newstead 36 Q 24
Newstead Abbey 36 Q 24
Newton 39 M 22
Newton Abbot 4 J 32
Newton-Aycliffe 46 P 20
Newton Ferrers 4 H 33
Newton-le-Willows 34 M 23
Newton Longville 19 R 28
Newton Mearns 55 H 16
Newton Poppleford 7 K 31
Newton St. Cyres 7 J 31
Newton Stewart 42 G 19
Newton Wamphray 49 J 18
Newtongrange 56 K 16
Newtonmore 61 H 12
Newtown (Cheshire) 35 N 23
Newtown (Heref.) 26 M 27
Newtown / Drenewydd (Powys) 25 K 26
Newtown St. Boswells 50 L 17
Newtyle 62 K 14
Neyland 14 F 28
Nigg Bay 67 H 10
Nine Ladies 35 P 34
Ninfield 12 V 31
Nith (River) 44 J 19
Niths 49 I 18
Niton 10 Q 32
Norfolk (County) 30 W 25
Norfolk Broads 31 Y 25
Norham 57 N 16
Normandy 10 S 30
Normanton 40 P 22
North Ashton 34 L 23
North Baddesley 9 P 31
North Ballachulish 60 E 13
North Berwick 57 L 15
North Bovey 4 I 32
North Bradley 8 N 30
North Cadbury 8 M 30
North Cave 41 S 22
North Channel 53 D 18
North Creake 30 W 25
North Curry 8 L 30
North Erradale 65 C 10
North Esk (Riv.) 63 L 13
North Foreland 13 Y 29
North Grimston 40 R 21
North Harris 64 Z 10
North Hinksey 19 Q 28
North Holmwood 11 T 30
North Kelsey 41 S 23
North Kessock 67 H 11
North Leigh 18 P 28
North Morar 60 C 13
North Newbald 41 S 22
North Nibley 17 M 29
North Petherton 8 K 30
North Petherwin 6 G 31
North Ronaldsay 74 M 5
North Shields 51 P 18
North Somercotes 37 U 23
North Sound (The) 74 L 6
North Sunderland 51 P 17
North Thoresby 37 T 23
North Tidworth 9 P 30
North Uist 64 X 11
North Walsham 31 Y 25
North Warnborough 10 R 30
North Weald Bassett 20 U 28
North York Moors National Park 47 R 20
Northallerton 46 P 20
Northam 6 H 30
Northampton 28 R 27
Northamptonshire (County) 28 R 26
Northchapel 10 S 30
Northchurch 19 S 28
Northfleet 20 V 29
Northiam 12 V 31
Northleach 18 O 28
Northop 33 K 24
Northton 70 Y 10
Northumberland (County) 50 M 18
Northumberland National Park 51 N 18
Northwich 34 M 24
Northwold 30 V 26
Norton 40 R 21
Norton Fitzwarren 7 K 30
Norton St. Philip 8 N 30
Norwich 31 X 26
Noss Head 74 K 8
Noss (Isle of) 75 Q 3
Nottingham 36 Q 25
Nottinghamshire (County) 36 Q 24
Nuneaton 27 P 26
Nunney 8 M 30
Nunthorpe 46 Q 20
Nunton 64 X 11
Nutley 11 U 30

O

Oa (The) 52 B 17
Oadby 28 Q 26
Oakengates 26 M 25
Oakham 36 R 25
Oakhill 8 M 30
Oare 12 W 30
Oathlaw 62 L 13
Oban 60 D 14
Ochil Hills 56 I 15
Ochiltree 48 G 17
Ockley 10 S 30
Odiham 10 R 30
Ogbourne St. George 18 O 29
Ogmore Vale 16 J 29
Ogmore-by-Sea 16 J 29
Oich (Loch) 61 F 12
Oidhche (Loch na h-) 66 D 11
Oigh-Sgeir 59 Z 13
Okeford Fitzpaine 8 N 31
Okehampton 6 H 31
Old Alresford 10 Q 30
Old Bolingbroke 37 U 24
Old Deer 69 N 11
Old Fletton 29 T 26
Old Harry Rocks 9 O 32
Old Head 74 L 7
Old Kilpatrick 55 G 16
Old Knebworth 20 T 28
Old Leake 37 U 24
Old Man of Hoy 74 J 7
Old Man of Storr 65 B 11
Old Radnor 25 K 27
Old Rayne 69 M 11
Old' Sarum 9 O 30
Old Sodbury 17 M 29
Old Warden 29 S 27
Old Windsor 19 S 29
Oldany Island 72 E 9

OXFORD

Blue Boar Street BY 2
Broad Street BZ 3
Castle Street BZ 5
Clarendon Shopping Centre BZ
Cornmarket Street BZ 6
George Street BZ 9
High Street BZ
Hythe Bridge Street BZ 12
Little Clarendon Street BY 13
Logic Lane BZ 14
Magdalen Street BYZ 16
Magpie Lane BZ 17
New Inn Hall Street BZ 20
Norfolk Street BZ 21
Old Greyfriars Street BZ 23
Oriel Square BZ 24
Park End Street BZ 30
Pembroke Street BZ 31
Queen's Lane BZ 33
Queen Street BZ 34
Radcliffe Square BZ 35
St. Michael Street BZ 40
Turl Street BZ 41
Walton Crescent BY 42
Westgate Shopping Centre BZ
Worcester Street BZ 47

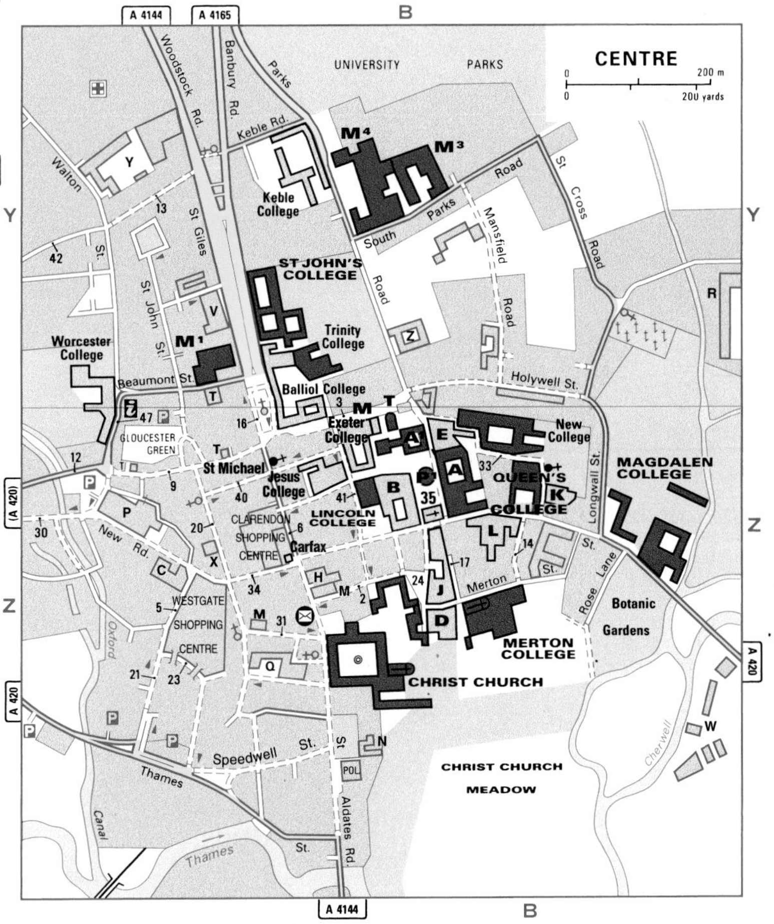
A 4144
A 4165
B
UNIVERSITY PARKS
CENTRE
200 m
200 yards
Woodstock Rd.
Banbury Rd.
Parks Rd.
Keble Rd.
Walton St.
Keble College
St Giles
South Parks Road
Mansfield Road
St. Cross Road
ST JOHN'S COLLEGE
Trinity College
Worcester College
St. John St.
Beaumont St.
Balliol College
Holywell St.
Exeter College
New College
GLOUCESTER GREEN
St Michael
Jesus College
LINCOLN COLLEGE
QUEEN'S COLLEGE
MAGDALEN COLLEGE
Longwall St.
CLARENDON SHOPPING CENTRE
Carfax
New Rd.
Merton St.
Rose Lane
Botanic Gardens
WESTGATE SHOPPING CENTRE
MERTON COLLEGE
CHRIST CHURCH
Oxford
Speedwell St.
Thames St.
Aldates Rd
St.
CHRIST CHURCH MEADOW
Cherwell
Canal
Thames
A 420
A 4144
Y
Z

COLLEGES

ALL SOULS BZ E
BALLIOL BY
BRASENOSE BZ D
CHRIST CHURCH BZ
CORPUS CHRISTI BZ K
EXETER BZ
HERTFORD BZ P
JESUS BZ
KEBLE BY
LINACRE BZ A
LINCOLN BZ
MAGDALEN BZ
MERTON BZ
NEW BZ
NUFFIELD BZ B
ORIEL BZ J
PEMBROKE BZ Q
QUEEN'S BZ
ST CATHERINE'S BY V
ST CROSS BY W
ST EDMUND'S BZ N
ST HILDA'S BZ Z
ST JOHN'S BY
ST PETER'S BZ U
SOMERVILLE BY R
TRINITY BY
UNIVERSITY BZ L
WADHAM BY X
WORCESTER BY

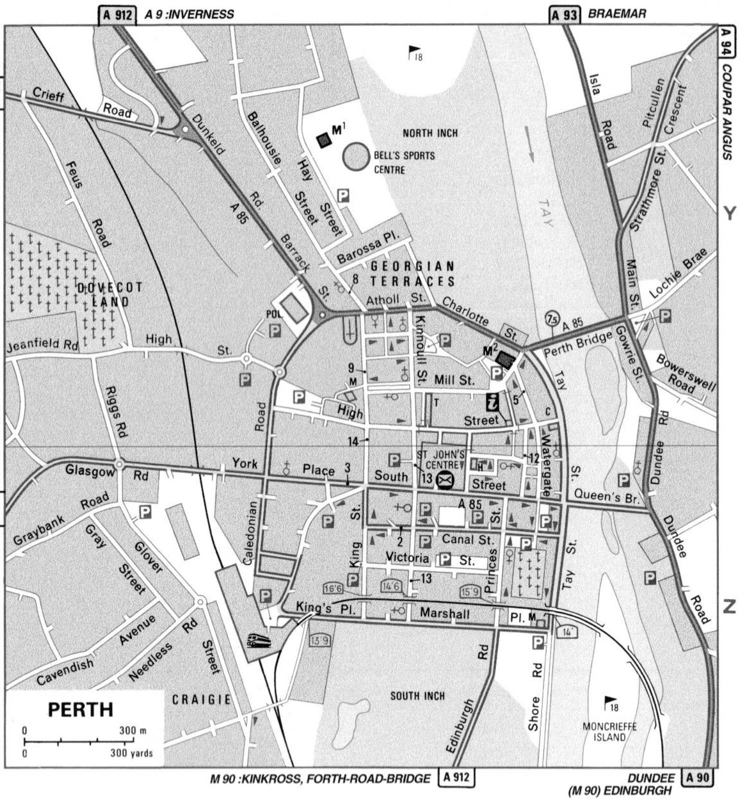

A 912 A 9 :INVERNESS
A 93 BRAEMAR
A 94 COUPAR ANGUS
A 85 CRIANLARICH
A 93 A 9 :STIRLING
Y
Z
PERTH
300 m
300 yards
NORTH INCH
BELL'S SPORTS CENTRE
GEORGIAN TERRACES
DOVECOT LAND
SOUTH INCH
CRAIGIE
MONCRIEFFE ISLAND
TAY
Crieff Road
Dunkeld Rd
Bathousie St.
Hay Street
Barrack St.
Barossa Pl.
Atholl St.
Charlotte St.
Perth Bridge
Kinnoull St.
Mill St.
High Street
South Street
York Place
Glasgow Rd
Graybank Road
Gray Street
Glover Street
Avenue
Needless Rd
Cavendish
Jeanfield Rd
High St.
Feus Road
Riggs Rd
Caledonian Rd
King St.
Canal St.
Victoria St.
King's Pl.
Marshall Pl.
Edinburgh Rd
Shore Rd
Tay St.
Watergate
Princes St.
Queen's Br.
Dundee Road
Dundee Rd
Isla Road
Pitcullen Crescent
Strathmore St.
Main St.
Lochie Brae
Gowrie St.
Bowerswell Road
ST JOHN'S CENTRE
M 90 :KINKROSS, FORTH-ROAD-BRIDGE A 912
DUNDEE A 90 (M 90) EDINBURGH

Oldbury 27 N 26
Oldcotes 36 Q 23
Oldham 39 N 23
Oldmeldrum 69 N 11
Ollaberry 75 P 2
Ollay (Loch) 64 X 12
Ollerton 36 Q 24
Olney 28 R 27
Olveston 17 M 29
Ombersley 26 N 27
Onchan 42 G 21
Onich 60 E 13
Orchy (Glen) 60 F 14
Ord 65 C 12
Orford 23 Y 27
Orford Ness 23 Y 27
Ormesby 46 Q 20
Ormesby St. Margaret 31 Z 25
Ormskirk 38 L 23
Oronsay 52 B 15
Orosay (near Fuday) 64 X 12
Orosay (near Lochboisdale) 64 X 12
Orphir 74 K 7
Orrin (Glen) 66 F 11
Orrin Reservoir 66 F 11
Orsay 52 A 16
Orsett 20 V 29
Orton 45 M 20
Orwell 29 T 27
Orwell (River) 21 X 28
Osborne House 10 Q 31
Osdale 65 A 11
Osgaig (Loch) 72 E 9
Osmington 8 M 32
Ossett 39 P 22
Oswaldtwistle 39 M 22
Oswestry 34 K 25
Otford 20 U 30
Othery 8 L 30
Otley (Suffolk) 23 X 27
Otley (West Yorks.) 39 O 22
Otterbourne 9 P 30
Otterburn 51 N 18
Otterswick 75 Q 2
Otterton 4 K 32
Ottery St. Mary 7 K 31
Oulton Park Circuit 34 M 24
Oulton Broad 31 Z 26
Oundle 28 S 26
Ouse (River) (English Channel) 11 T 30
Ouse (River) (North Sea) 40 Q 21
Out Skerries 75 R 2
Outer Hebrides 70 W 10
Outwell 29 U 26
Overseal 27 P 25
Overstrand 31 Y 25
Overton (Wrexham) 34 L 25
Overton (Hants.) 10 Q 30
Overton (Lancs.) 38 L 21
Overtown 55 I 16
Ower 9 P 31
Owermoigne 8 N 32
Owslebury 10 Q 30
Oxburgh Hall 30 V 26
Oxford 19 Q 28
Oxfordshire (County) 18 P 28
Oxted 11 T 30
Oxwich Bay 15 H 29
Oykel (Glen) 72 F 9
Oykel Bridge 72 F 10
Oyne 69 M 12

P

Pabay 65 C 12
Pabbay (near Harris) 70 Y 10
Pabbay (near Mingulay) 58 X 13
Pabbay (Sound of) 70 Y 10
Padbury 19 R 28
Paddock Wood 12 V 30
Padiham 39 N 22
Padstow 2 F 32
Pagham 10 R 31
Paignton 4 J 32
Painscastle 25 K 27
Painswick 17 N 28
Paisley 55 G 16
Palnackie 43 I 19
Pangbourne 19 Q 29
Papa Stour 75 O 3
Papa Westray 74 L 5
Paps of Jura 52 B 16
Parbh (The) 72 F 8
Parbold 38 L 23
Parc Cefn Onn 16 K 29
Parham House 11 S 31
Park Gate 10 Q 31
Park of Pairc 70 A 9
Parkeston 21 X 28
Parkhurst 10 Q 31
Parnham House 8 L 31
Parrett (River) 8 K 30
Partney 37 U 24
Parton 44 J 20
Partridge Green 11 T 31
Pass of LLanberis 32 H 24
Patchway 17 M 29
Pateley Bridge 39 O 21
Path of Condie 56 J 15
Pathhead 56 L 16
Patna 48 G 17
Patrington 41 T 22
Patrixbourne 13 X 30
Patterdale 45 L 20
Pattingham 26 N 26
Paulerspury 28 R 27
Paull 41 T 22
Paulton 17 M 30
Peacehaven 11 T 31
Peak District National Park 35 O 23
Peasedown St. John 17 M 30
Peasenhall 23 Y 27
Peasmarsh 12 W 31
Peat Inn 56 L 15
Peatknowe 69 M 11
Peebles 49 K 17
Peel 42 F 21
Peel Fell 50 M 18
Pegwell Bay 13 Y 30
Peldon 22 W 28
Pelynt 3 G 32
Pembridge 26 L 27
Pembroke Dock / Doc Penfro 14 F 28
Pembroke / Penfro 14 F 28
Pembrokeshire Coast National Park 14 F 29
Pembury 12 V 30
Pen-y-bont / Bridgend 16 J 29
Pen-y-groes 32 H 24
Penalun 14 F 29
Penarth 16 K 29
Pencarrow 3 F 32
Pendine 14 G 28
Pendine Sands 15 G 28
Pendlebury 39 N 23
Penfro / Pembroke 14 F 28
Penicuik 56 K 16
Penifiler 65 B 11
Penistone 39 P 23
Penketh 34 L 23
Penkridge 27 N 25
Penmaenmawr 33 I 24
Pennines (The) 45 N 19
Pennyghael 59 B 14
Penpont 49 I 18
Penrhyn Bay 33 I 24
Penrhyndeudraeth 32 H 25
Penrith 45 L 19
Penryn 2 E 33
Penshaw 46 P 19
Penshurst 11 U 30
Pentire Point 2 F 32
Pentland Firth 74 K 7
Pentland Hills 56 J 16
Pentland Skerries 74 L 7
Penwith 2 D 33
Penybont 25 K 27
Penzance 2 D 33
Perranporth 2 E 32
Pershore 27 N 27
Perth 56 J 14
Peterborough 29 T 26
Peterculter 69 N 12
Peterhead 69 O 11
Peterlee 46 P 19
Petersfield 10 R 30
Peterstow 17 M 28
Petham 13 X 30
Pett 12 V 31
Pettaugh 23 X 27
Petworth 10 S 31
Pevensey Bay 12 V 31
Pewsey 18 O 29
Pickering 47 R 21
Picton Castle 14 F 28
Piddletrenthide 8 M 31
Piercebridge 46 O 20
Pierowall 74 L 6
Pilgrims Hatch 20 U 29
Pilling 38 L 22
Pilning 17 M 29
Pilton 8 M 30
Pinchbeck 37 T 25
Pinhoe 7 J 31
Pirbright 10 S 30
Pirton 20 T 28
Pitcaple 69 M 12
Pitlochry 62 I 13
Pitmedden 69 N 11
Pittenween 57 L 15
Pladda 53 E 17
Plaistow 10 S 30
Plas Newydd (Anglesey) 32 H 24
Plas Newydd (Denbighshire) 33 K 25
Pleasley 36 Q 24
Plockton 66 D 11
Pluckley 12 W 30
Plumbland 44 K 19
Plymouth 3 H 32
Plympton 4 H 32
Plymstock 3 H 32
Plynlimon (Pumlumon Fawr) 25 I 26
Pocklington 40 R 22
Point of Ayr (Flintshire) 33 K 23
Point Lynas 32 H 23
Point of Ayre (Isle of Man) 42 G 20
Polbain 72 D 9
Polegate 11 U 31
Polesden Lacey 11 S 30
Polesworth 27 P 26
Polkerris 3 F 32
Pollock House 55 H 16
Polmont 56 I 16
Polperro 3 G 33
Polruan 3 G 33
Pondersbridge 29 T 26
Pontardawe 15 I 28
Pontarddulais 15 H 28
Pontarfynach / Devil's Bridge 25 I 26
Pontefract 40 Q 22
Ponteland 51 O 18
Ponterwyd 25 I 26
Pontesbury 26 L 26
Pontlottyn 16 K 28
Pontrhydygroes 25 I 26
Pontrilas 17 L 28
Pontsticill 16 J 28
Pontyclun 16 J 29
Pontycymer 16 J 29
Pontypool / Pontypwl 17 K 28
Pontypridd 16 J 29
Pontypwl / Pontypool 17 K 28
Poole 9 O 31
Poole Bay 9 O 31
Poolewe 66 D 10
Pooley Bridge 45 L 20
Pooltiel (Loch) 64 Z 11
Porlock 7 J 30
Port Appin 60 D 14
Port Askaig 52 B 16
Port Bannatyne 54 E 16
Port Charlotte 52 A 16
Port Ellen 52 B 17
Port Erin 42 F 21
Port-Eynon 15 H 29
Port-Eynon Point 15 H 29
Port Glasgow 54 F 16
Port Henderson 65 C 10
Port Isaac 3 F 32
Port Lamont 54 E 16
Port Logan 42 F 19
Port Mór 59 B 13
Port of Menteith 55 H 15
Port of Ness 71 B 8
Port St. Mary 42 F 21
Port Talbot 15 I 29
Port William 42 G 19
Portchester 10 Q 31
Portesham 8 M 31
Portgordon 68 K 11
Porth 16 J 29
Porth Neigwl or Hell's Mouth 32 G 25
Porth Tywyn / Burry Port 15 H 28
Porthaethwy / Menai Bridge 32 H 24
Porthcawl 15 I 29
Porthcurno 2 D 33
Porthgwarra 2 C 33
Porthleven 2 E 33
Porthmadog 32 H 25
Porthyrhyd 15 H 28
Portinnisherrich 54 E 15
Portishead 17 L 29
Portknockie 68 L 10
Portland (Isle of) 5 M 32
Portlethen 69 N 12
Portmahomack 67 I 10
Portnacroish 60 D 14
Portnaguran 71 B 9
Portnahaven 52 A 16
Portobello 56 K 16
Portreath 2 E 33
Portree 65 B 11
Portscatho 2 F 33
Portskerra 73 I 8
Portskewett 17 L 29
Portslade 11 T 31
Portsmouth 10 Q 31
Portsoy 69 L 10
Portuairk 59 B 13
Postbridge 4 I 32
Potter Heigham 31 Y 25
Potter Street 20 U 28
Potterne 18 N 30
Potters Bar 20 T 28
Potterspury 28 R 27
Potton 29 T 27
Poughill 6 G 31
Poulton-le-Fylde 38 L 22
Poundstock 6 G 31
Powburn 51 O 17
Powerstock 8 L 31
Powick 26 N 27
Powis 25 K 26
Powmill 56 J 15
Powys (County) 25 J 26
Poynings 11 T 31
Poynton 35 N 23
Praa Sands 2 D 33
Praze-an-Beeble 2 E 33
Prees 34 M 25
Preesall 38 L 22
Prescot 34 L 23
Prestatyn 33 J 23
Prestbury 35 N 24
Presteigne 26 K 27
Preston (East Riding of Yorks.) 41 T 22
Preston (Kent) 13 X 30
Preston (Lancs.) 38 L 22
Preston (West Sussex) 11 S 31
Preston Candover 10 Q 30
Prestonpans 56 L 16
Prestwich 39 N 23
Prestwick 48 G 17
Prestwood 19 R 28
Priest Island 71 D 10
Princes Risborough 19 R 28
Princethorne 27 P 26
Princetown 4 I 32
Priors Marston 28 Q 27
Probus 2 F 33
Prosen (Glen) 62 K 13
Prudhoe 46 O 19
Puckeridge 20 U 28
Puddletown 8 M 31
Pudsey 39 P 22
Pulborough 10 S 31
Pulham Market 31 X 26
Purbeck (Isle of) 9 N 32
Purbrook 10 Q 31
Purley 19 Q 29
Purse Caundle Manor 8 M 31
Purston Jaglin 40 P 22
Purton 18 O 29
Putsborough 6 H 30
Pwllheli 32 G 25
Pyecombe 11 T 31
Pyle 15 I 29

Q

Quainton 19 R 28
Quantock Hills 7 K 30
Quarr 10 Q 31
Quedgeley 17 N 28
Queen Camel 8 M 30
Queen Elizabeth Forest Park 55 G 15
Queenborough 21 W 29
Queensbury 39 O 22
Queensferry 34 K 24
Quinag 72 E 9
Quinish Point 59 B 14
Quiraing 65 B 11
Quoich (Loch) 60 E 12
Quorndon 28 Q 25
Quothquan 49 J 17

R

Raasay (Island of) 65 B 11
Raasay (Sound of) 65 B 11
Rackwick 74 J 7
Radcliffe 39 N 23
Radcliffe-on-Trent 36 Q 25
Radlett 20 T 29
Radnor Forest 25 K 27
Radstock 8 M 30
Radyr 16 K 29
Rafford 68 J 11
Raglan 17 L 28
Ragley Hall 27 O 27
Rainford 38 L 23
Rainham 21 V 29
Rainworth 36 Q 24
Ramsbottom 39 N 23
Ramsbury 18 P 29
Ramsey (Cambs.) 29 T 26
Ramsey (Isle of Man) 42 G 21
Ramsey Bay 42 G 21
Ramsey Island 14 D 28
Ramsey St. Mary's 29 T 26
Ramsgate 13 Y 29
Ramsgill 39 O 21
Ranfurly 55 G 16
Rannoch (Loch) 61 H 13
Rannoch Moor 61 F 14
Ranskill 36 Q 23
Ranworth 31 Y 25
Rapness 74 L 6
Rappach 72 F 10
Ratby 28 Q 26
Rathen 69 O 11
Rattray 62 K 14
Rattray Head 69 O 11
Raunds 28 S 26
Ravenglass 44 J 20
Ravenstonedale 45 M 20
Rawcliffe 40 R 22
Rawmarsh 35 P 23
Rawtenstall 39 N 22
Rayleigh 21 V 29
Read 39 M 22
Reading 19 R 29
Reay 73 I 8
Reay Forest 72 F 9
Reculver 13 X 29
Red Wharf Bay 32 H 24
Redbourn 20 S 28
Redbourne 36 S 23
Redbridge (London Borough) 20 U 29
Redcar 47 Q 20
Redcliff Bay 17 L 29
Redditch 27 O 27
Redford 63 L 14
Redhill 11 T 30
Redpoint 65 C 11
Redruth 2 E 33
Redwick 17 L 29
Reedham 31 Y 26
Reekie Linn 62 K 13
Reeth 46 O 20
Reigate 11 T 30
Reighton 41 T 21
Reiss 74 K 8
Rempstone 36 Q 25
Rendham 23 Y 27
Renfrew 55 G 16
Renish Point 70 Z 10
Renishaw 35 P 24
Renton 55 G 16
Resort (Loch) 70 Z 9

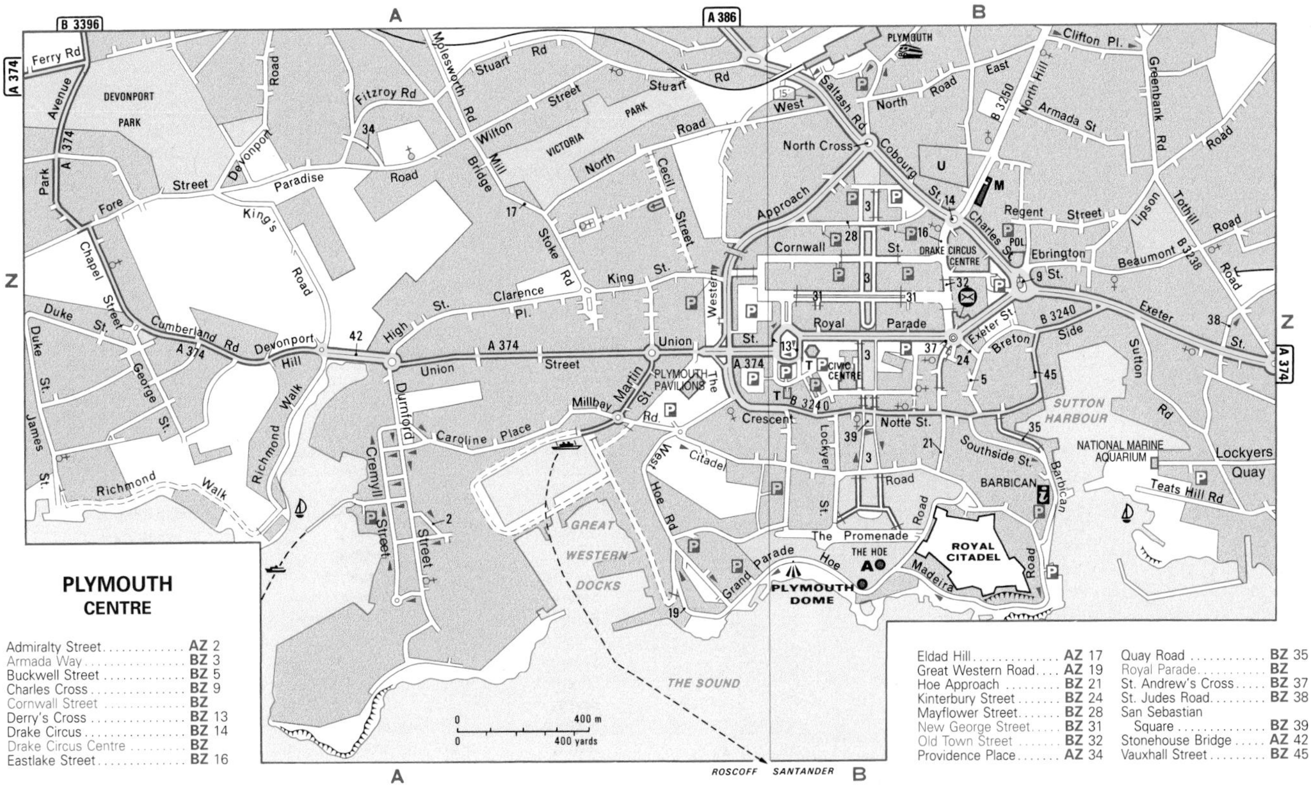

PLYMOUTH
CENTRE

Admiralty Street	AZ 2
Armada Way	BZ 3
Buckwell Street	BZ 5
Charles Cross	BZ 9
Cornwall Street	BZ
Derry's Cross	BZ 13
Drake Circus	BZ 14
Drake Circus Centre	BZ
Eastlake Street	BZ 16
Eldad Hill	AZ 17
Great Western Road	AZ 19
Hoe Approach	BZ 21
Kinterbury Street	BZ 24
Mayflower Street	BZ 28
New George Street	BZ 31
Old Town Street	BZ 32
Providence Place	AZ 34
Quay Road	BZ 35
Royal Parade	BZ
St. Andrew's Cross	BZ 37
St. Judes Road	BZ 38
San Sebastian Square	BZ 39
Stonehouse Bridge	AZ 42
Vauxhall Street	BZ 45

PORTSMOUTH
AND SOUTHSEA

Alec Rose Lane	CY 2
Arundel St.	CY 5
Bellevue Terrace	CZ 6
Cascade Centre	CY
Charlotte St.	CY 7
Commercial Rd	CY
Eldon St.	CY 10
Great Southsea St.	CZ 15
Guildhall Walk	CY 17
Hampshire Terrace	CY 18
Hard (The)	BY 20
High St.	BYZ 21
Isambard Brunel Rd	CY 22
Landport Terrace	CY 25
Lombard St.	BYZ 29
Main Rd.	BY 31
Norfolk St.	CYZ 32
Ordnance Row	BY 34
Palmerston Rd	CZ
Paradise St.	CY 35
Penny St.	BZ 36
St. George's Square	BY 39
St. Michael's Rd	CY 41
Southsea Terrace	CZ 43
Spring St.	CY 45
Stanhope Rd	CY 48
Unicorn Rd	CY 49
Warblington St.	BY 53
White Hart Rd	BYZ 57
Wiltshire St.	CY 59

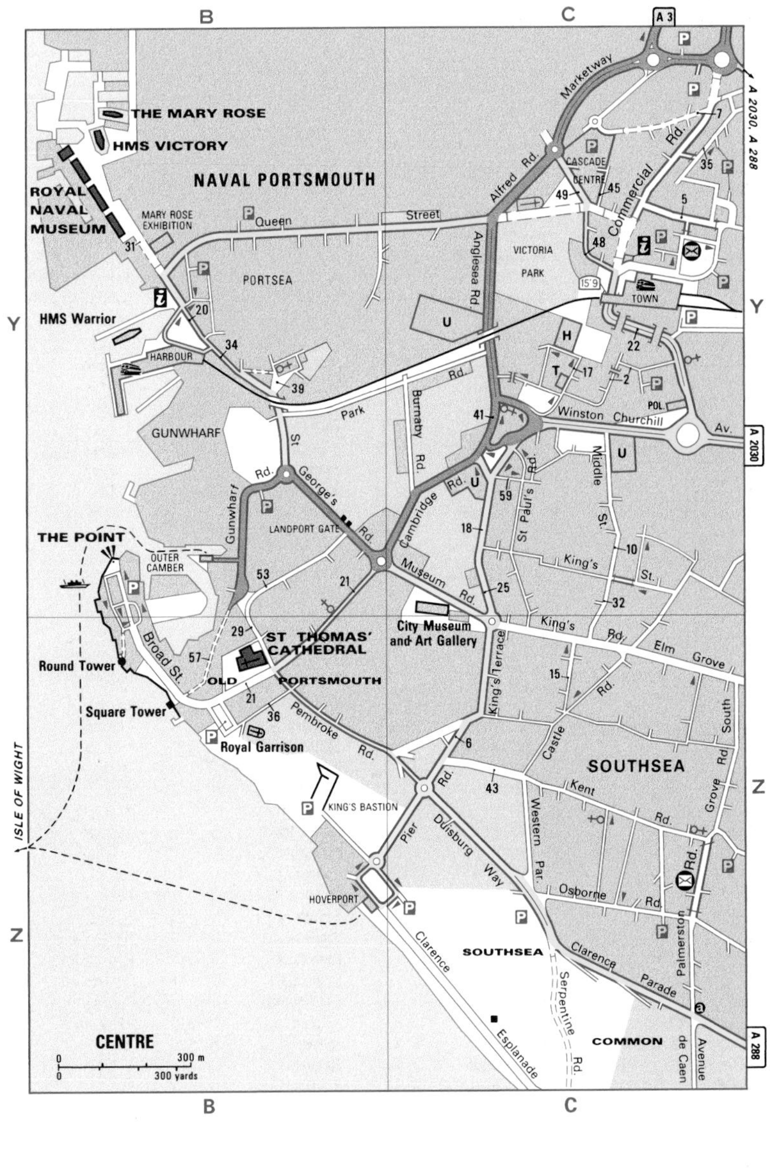

Restalrig	56	K 16
Restormel Castle	3	G 32
Retford	36	R 24
Rhaeadr / Rhayader	25	J 27
Rhaeadr Ddu	33	I 25
Rhayader / Rhaeadr	25	J 27
Rheidol (Vale of)	25	I 26
Rhiconich	72	F 8
Rhinns of Galloway (The)	42	E 19
Rhinns of Kells	48	G 18
Rhondda	16	J 29
Rhoose	16	J 29
Rhoscolyn	32	G 24
Rhoscrowther	14	E 28
Rhosllanerchrugog	34	K 24
Rhosneigr	32	G 24
Rhossili	15	H 29
Rhu	54	F 15
Rhuddlan	33	J 24
Rhum	59	A 13
Rhuthun / Ruthin	33	K 24
Rhyd-Ddu	32	H 24
Rhydaman / Ammanford	15	I 28
Rhydcymerau	24	H 27
Rhydd	26	N 27
Rhyddhywel	25	J 26
Rhydowen	24	H 27
Rhyl	33	J 24
Rhymney / Rhymmi	16	K 28
Rhynie	68	L 12
Ribble (River)	39	N 22
Ribblesdale	39	N 21
Ribchester	38	M 22
Riccall	40	Q 22
Riccarton	48	G 17
Richborough	13	X 30
Richmond	46	O 20
Richmond-upon-Thames (London Borough)	20	T 29
Rickmansworth	19	S 29
Ridgeway Path (The)	18	P 29
Rievaulx Abbey	46	Q 21
Rigside	49	I 17
Rillington	40	R 21
Rimsdale (Loch)	73	H 9
Ringford	43	H 19
Ringmer	11	U 31
Ringstead	28	S 26
Ringwood	9	O 31
Ringwould	13	Y 30
Rinnes (Glen)	68	K 11
Rinns of Islay	52	A 16
Rinns Point	52	A 16
Ripe	11	U 31
Ripley (Derbs.)	35	P 24
Ripley (North Yorks.)	40	P 21
Ripley (Surrey)	19	S 30
Ripon	40	P 21
Rippingale	37	S 25
Ripponden	39	O 22
Risca	16	K 29
Rishton	39	M 22
Ristol (Isle)	72	D 9
Roag (Loch)	70	Z 9
Roberton	50	L 17
Robertsbridge	12	V 31
Robin Hood's Bay	47	S 20
Roby	34	L 23
Rocester	35	O 25
Rochdale	39	N 23
Roche	3	F 32
Rochester	21	V 29
Rochford	21	W 29
Rock	3	F 32
Rockcliffe (Cumbria)	44	K 19
Rockcliffe (Dumfries and Galloway)	43	I 19
Rode	8	N 30
Rodel	64	Z 10
Rogart	73	H 9
Rogerstone	16	K 29
Rolleston-on-Dove (Staffs.)	35	P 25
Rolleston (Notts.)	36	R 24
Rolvenden	12	V 30
Roman Villa	10	S 31
Romiley	35	N 23
Romney Marsh	12	W 30
Romsey	9	P 31
Romsley	27	N 26
Rona (Island of)	65	C 11
Ronaldsway	42	G 21
Ronas Voe	75	P 2
Ronay	64	Y 11
Roos	41	T 22
Rootpark	56	I 16
Ropsley	36	S 25
Rora Head	74	J 7
Rosedale Abbey	47	R 20
Rosehearty	69	N 10
Rosemarket	14	F 28
Rosemarkie	67	H 11
Roshven	59	C 13
Roslin	56	K 16
Ross of Mull	52	B 15
Ross-on-Wye	17	M 28
Rossall Point	38	K 22
Rossett	34	L 24
Rothbury	51	O 18
Rothbury Forest	51	O 18
Rotherfield	11	U 30
Rotherham	35	P 23
Rothes	68	K 11
Rothesay	54	E 16
Rothienorman	69	M 11
Rothiesholm	74	M 6
Rothwell (Leeds.)	40	P 22
Rothwell (Northants.)	28	R 26
Rottingdean	11	T 31
Roughton	31	X 25
Rousay	74	K 6
Rowland's Castle	10	R 31
Rowland's Gill	46	O 19
Rownhams	9	P 31
Rowsley	35	P 24
Roxwell	22	V 28
Roy (Glen)	60	F 13
Royal Greenwich Observatory	12	V 31
Royal Leamington Spa	27	P 27
Royal Military Academy	19	R 29
Royal Tunbridge Wells	11	U 30
Roybridge	60	F 13
Roydon (Essex)	20	U 28
Roydon (Norfolk)	31	X 26
Royston (Herts.)	29	T 27
Royston (South Yorks.)	40	P 23
Royton	39	N 23
Ruabon	34	K 25
Ruan High Lanes	2	F 33
Ruan Minor	2	E 34
Ruardean	17	M 28
Rubbha na Faing	52	A 16
Rubh'an Dùnain	65	A 12
Rubha a' Mhail	52	B 16
Rubha Còigeach	72	D 9
Rubha Dubh	58	Z 14
Rubha Hunish	65	A 10
Rubha na h-Easgainne	65	B 12
Rubha Réidh	71	C 10
Rubha Suisnish	65	B 12
Rudbaxton	14	F 28
Ruddington	36	Q 25
Rudgeway	17	M 29
Rudgwick	11	S 30
Rudston	41	T 21
Rufford Old Hall	38	L 23
Rugby	28	Q 26

READING

Blagrave Street .... Y 3
Bridge Street .... Z 4
Broad Street .... Y
Broad Street Mall
Shopping Centre .... Z
Castle Street .... Z 6
Chain Street .... Z 7
Church Street .... X 12
Duke Street .... Z 15
Greyfriars Road .... Y 17
Gun Street .... Z 18
King Street .... Z 20
Mill Lane .... Z 21
Minster Street .... Z 22
Mount Pleasant .... Z 23
Queen Victoria Street ..... Y 28
St. Mary's Butts .... Z 29
Station Hill .... Y 30
Station Road .... Y 31
Tilehurst Road .... Z 33
Tudor Road .... Y 34
Valpy Street .... Y 37
Watlington Street .... Z 40
West Street .... Y 41

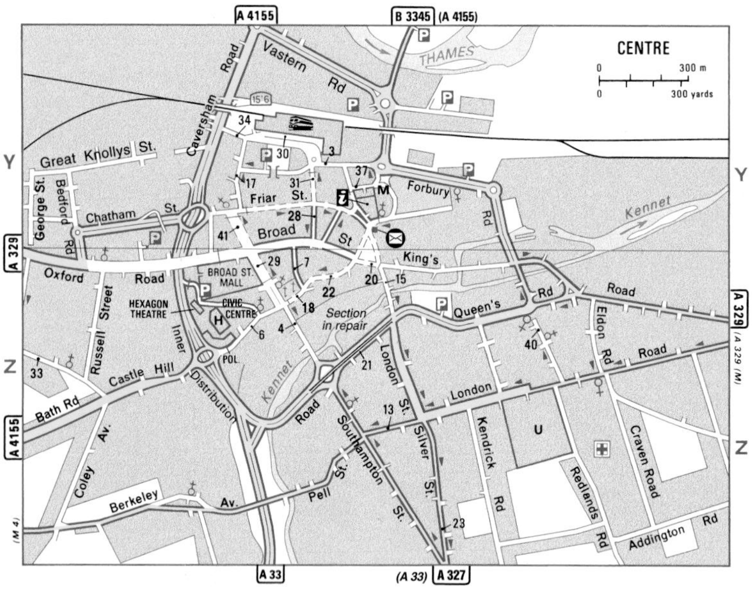

Rugeley 27 O 25
Rumney 16 K 29
Runcorn 34 L 23
Runwell 21 V 29
Rushden 28 S 27
Ruskington 37 S 24
Rusper 11 T 30
Rustington 10 S 31
Ruswarp 47 S 20
Rutherglen 55 H 16
Ruthin / Rhuthun 33 K 24
Ruthven 62 K 14
Ruthven (Loch) 67 H 12
Ruthwell 49 J 19
Rutland Water 28 S 26
Ruyton of the Eleven Towns 34 L 25
Ryan (Loch) 42 E 19
Rycote 19 Q 28
Rydal 44 L 20
Ryde 10 Q 31
Rye 12 W 31
Ryhall 28 S 25
Ryhill 40 P 23
Ryhope 46 P 19
Ryton 51 O 19

S

Sadberge 46 P 20
Saddell Bay 53 D 17
Saffron Walden 22 U 27
St. Abb's Head 57 N 16
St. Agnes 2 E 33
St. Albans 20 T 28
St. Aldhelm's Head 9 N 32
St. Andrews 57 L 14
St. Ann's Head 14 E 28
St. Arvans 17 L 29
St. Asaph 33 J 24
St. Athan 16 J 29
St. Austell 3 F 32
St. Bees 44 J 20
St. Bees Head 44 J 20
St. Blazey 3 F 32
St. Breock 3 F 32
St. Briavels 17 M 28
St. Brides Major 16 J 29
St. Brides -Super-Ely 16 K 29
St. Buryan 2 D 33
St. Catherine's Point 10 Q 32
St. Clears / Sanclêr 15 G 28
St. Cleer 3 G 32
St. Columb Major 2 F 32
St. Combs 69 O 11
St. Cyrus 63 M 13
St. David's Head 14 D 28
St. David's / Tyddewi 14 E 28
St. Day 2 E 33
St. Dennis 3 F 32
St. Dogmaels 14 F 27
St. Donats 16 J 29
St. Ewe 3 F 33
St. Fagans 16 K 29
St. Fergus 69 O 11
St. Gennys 6 G 31
St. Germans 3 H 32
St. Govan's Head 14 F 29
St. Helens (I.O.W.) 10 Q 31
St. Helens (Merseyside) 34 L 23
St. Ishmael's 14 E 28
St. Issey 3 F 32
St. Ive 3 G 32
St. Ives (Cambs.) 29 T 27
St. Ives (Cornwall) 2 D 33
St. John's 42 G 21
St. John's Loch 74 J 8
St. John's Chapel 45 N 19
St. Just 2 C 33
St. Just in Roseland 2 E 33
St. Keverne 2 E 33
St. Kew 3 F 32
St. Leonards (Dorset) 9 O 31
St. Leonards (East Sussex) 12 V 31
St. Mabyn 3 F 32
St. Magnus Bay 75 P 2
St. Margaret's at Cliffe 13 Y 30
St. Margaret's Bay 13 Y 30
St. Margaret's Hope 74 L 7
St. Martin's 33 K 25
St. Mary in the Marsh 12 W 30
St. Mary's 74 L 7
St. Mary's Loch 50 K 17
St. Mawes 2 E 33
St. Mawgan 3 F 32
St. Mellion 3 H 32
St. Merryn 2 F 32
St. Michael's Mount 2 D 33
St. Michaels-on-Wyre 38 L 22
St. Monans 57 L 15
St. Neot 3 G 32
St. Neots 29 T 27
St. Nicholas-at-Wade 13 X 29
St. Ninian's Isle 75 P 4
St. Osyth 21 X 28
St. Patrick's Isle 42 F 21
St. Paul's Walden 20 T 28
St. Peter Port (Channel I.) 5
St. Peter's 13 Y 29
St. Stephen 3 F 32
St. Teath 3 F 32
St. Tudwal's Islands 32 G 25
St. Tudy 3 F 32
St. Vigeans 63 M 14
Salcombe 4 I 33
Sale 34 N 23
Salen (Argyll and Bute) 59 C 14
Salen (Highland) 59 C 13
Salfleet 37 U 23
Salford 34 N 23
Salfords 11 T 30
Saline 56 J 15
Salisbury 9 O 30
Salisbury Plain 9 O 30
Saltash 3 H 32
Saltburn 67 H 10
Saltburn-by-the-Sea 47 R 20
Saltcoats 48 F 17
Saltford 17 M 29
Samala 64 X 11
Samlesbury Old Hall 38 M 22
Sampford Courtenay 4 I 31
Sampford Peverell 7 J 31
Sancreed 2 D 33
Sand Side 38 K 21
Sanda Island 53 D 18
Sanday (Highland) 65 A 12
Sanday (Orkney Islands) 74 M 6
Sandbach 34 M 24
Sandbank 54 F 16
Sandbanks 9 O 31
Sandend 68 L 10
Sandford 7 J 31
Sandford Orcas 8 M 31
Sandgate 13 X 30
Sandgreen 43 H 19
Sandhaven 69 N 10
Sandhurst (Berks.) 19 R 29
Sandhurst (Kent) 12 V 30
Sandleigh 19 Q 28
Sandlins 23 Y 27
Sandness 75 P 3
Sandon 35 N 25
Sandown 10 Q 32
Sandray 58 X 13
Sandridge 20 T 28
Sandringham House 30 V 25
Sandwell 27 O 26
Sandwich 13 Y 30
Sandwood Loch 72 E 8
Sandy 29 T 27
Sandygate 42 G 20
Sandyhills 43 I 19
Sanquhar 49 I 17
Santon Head 42 G 21
Sarisbury 10 Q 31
Sark (Channel I.) 5
Sarre 13 X 29
Satterthwaite 44 K 21
Saundersfoot 14 F 28
Saunderton 19 R 28
Sawbridgeworth 20 U 28
Sawrey 44 L 20
Sawston 22 U 27
Sawtry 29 T 26
Saxilby 36 S 24
Saxlingham Nethergate 31 X 26
Saxmundham 23 Y 27
Saxtead Green 23 X 27
Scadavay (Loch) 64 Y 11
Scaddle (Glen) 60 D 13
Scafell Pikes 44 K 20
Scalasaig 52 B 15
Scalby 47 S 21
Scalloway 75 Q 3
Scalpay (Highland) 65 C 12
Scalpay (Western Isles) 70 A 10
Scampton 36 S 24
Scapa Flow 74 K 7
Scarba 52 C 15
Scarborough 47 S 21
Scarcliffe 36 Q 24
Scarisbrick 34 L 23
Scarista 70 Y 10
Scarp 70 Y 9
Scavaig (Loch) 65 B 12
Schiehallion 61 H 13
Scilly (Isles of) 2 B 34
Scone Palace 56 J 14
Scopwick 37 S 24
Scorton 46 P 20
Scotch-Corner 46 P 20
Scothern 36 S 24
Scotlandwell 56 K 15
Scotney 12 V 30
Scotter 41 S 23
Scourie 72 E 8
Scousburgh 75 Q 4
Scrabster 74 J 8
Scridain (Loch) 59 B 14
Scunthorpe 41 S 23
Sea Palling 31 Y 25
Seaford 11 U 31
Seaforth (Loch) 70 Z 10
Seaham 46 P 19
Seale 10 R 30
Sealga (Loch na) 66 D 10
Seasalter 13 X 29
Seascale 44 J 20
Seaton 7 K 31
Seaton Carew 46 Q 20
Seaton Delaval 51 P 18
Seaton Delaval Hall 51 P 18
Seaview 10 Q 31
Sebergham 44 L 19
Sedbergh 45 M 21
Sedgebrook 36 R 25
Sedgley 27 N 26
Sedlescombe 12 V 31
Seend 18 N 29
Seething 31 Y 26
Seil (Isle of) 54 D 15
Seilich (Loch an t-) 61 H 13
Selborne 10 R 30
Selby 40 Q 22
Selker Bay 44 J 21
Selkirk 50 L 17
Sellindge 13 W 30
Selmeston 11 U 31
Selsey 10 R 31
Selworthy 7 J 30
Semley 9 N 30
Senghenydd 16 K 29
Sennen 2 C 33
Sennybridge 16 J 28
Settle 39 N 21
Seven Sisters (Neath and Port Talbot) 15 I 28
Seven Sisters (East Sussex) 11 U 31
Sevenoaks 11 U 30
Severn (River) 17 M 28
Severn Bridge 17 M 29
Sgibacleit (Loch) 70 A 9
Sgiwen 15 I 29
Sgurr Mór 66 E 10
Shaftesbury 8 N 30
Shalbourne 18 P 29
Shaldon 4 J 32
Shalford 10 S 30
Shandon 54 F 15
Shanklin 10 Q 32
Shap 45 L 20
Shapinsay 74 L 6
Sharnbrook 28 S 27

SHEFFIELD
CENTRE

Angel Street .... DY 3
Blonk Street .... DY 6
Castle Gate .... DY 13
Charter Row .... CZ 14
Church Street .... CZ 15
Commercial Street .... DZ 16
Cumberland
Street .... CZ 17
Fargate .... CZ
Fitzwilliam Gate .... CZ 19
Flat Street .... DZ 20
Furnival Gate .... CZ 21
Furnival Street .... CZ 22
Haymarket .... DY 25
High Street .... DZ
Leopold Street .... CZ 31
Moorfields .... CY 35
Pinstone Street .... CZ 37
Queen Street .... CY 38
St. Mary's Gate .... CZ 40
Shalesmoor .... CY 41
Snig Hill .... DY 42
Waingate .... DY 44
West Bar Green .... CY 45
West Street .... CZ

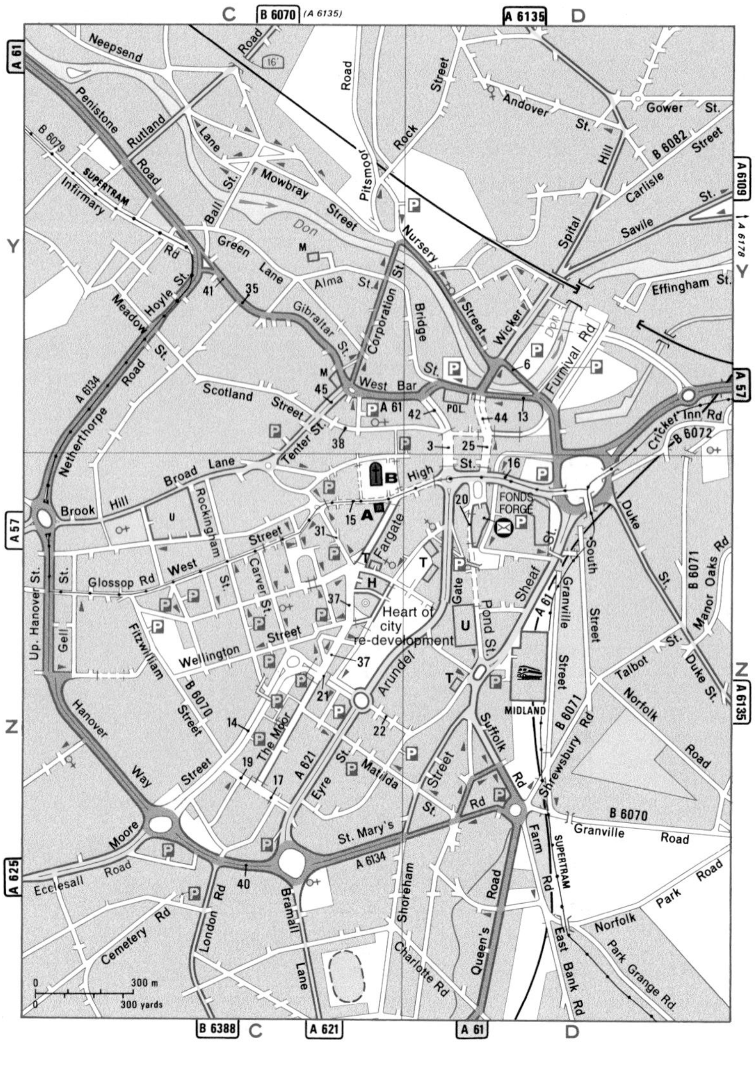

Sharpness 17 M 28
Shaw (Gtr. Mches.) 39 N 23
Shaw (Wilts.) 18 N 29
Shawbost 70 Z 9
Shawbury 34 M 25
Shawford 10 Q 30
Shebbear 6 H 31
Shebster 73 I 8
Sheepwash 6 H 31
Sheering 20 U 28
Sheerness 21 W 29
Sheffield 35 P 23
Sheffield Park 11 T 31
Shefford 29 S 27
Sheldon 18 N 29
Sheldon Manor 18 N 29
Sheldwich 12 W 30
Shell or Sealg (Loch) 70 A 9
Shelley 39 O 23
Shenstone 27 O 26
Shenval 68 K 11
Shepley 39 O 23
Sheppey (Isle of) 21 W 29
Shepreth 29 U 27
Shepshed 36 Q 25
Shepton Mallet 8 M 30
Sherborne 8 M 31
Sherborne St. John 19 Q 30
Sherburn 41 S 21
Sherburn-in-Elmet 40 Q 22
Shere 11 S 30
Sheriff Hutton 40 Q 21
Sheriffhales 26 M 25
Sheringham 31 X 25
Sherston 17 N 29
Sherwood Forest 36 Q 24
Shiant (Sound of) 71 A 10
Shiel (Glen) 66 D 12
Shiel (Loch) 60 D 13
Shieldaig 66 D 11
Shieldaig (Loch) 66 C 11
Shifnal 26 M 25
Shilbottle 51 O 17
Shildon 46 P 20
Shillingford 7 J 30
Shillington 20 S 28
Shimpling 31 X 26
Shin (Loch) 72 G 9
Shinfield 19 R 29
Shipdham 30 W 26
Shipley (Salop) 26 N 26
Shipley (West Yorks.) 39 O 22
Shipston-on-Stour 27 P 27
Shipton 26 M 26
Shipton-under-Wychwood 18 P 28
Shira (Lochan) 54 F 14
Shirebrook 36 Q 24
Shirley 27 O 26
Shobdon 26 L 27
Shoeburyness 21 W 29
Shoreham 11 T 31
Shorne 21 V 29
Shorwell 9 P 32
Shotley Bridge 46 O 19
Shotley Gate 23 X 28
Shottermill 10 R 30
Shotton Colliery Thornley 46 P 19
Shotts 55 I 16
Shrewsbury 26 L 25
Shrewton 9 O 30
Shrivenham 18 P 29
Shropshire (County) 26 M 26
Shuna Sound 54 D 15
Shurdington 18 N 28
Sible Hedingham 22 V 28
Sibsey 37 U 24
Sidbury 7 K 31
Siddlington 34 N 24
Sidford 7 K 31
Sidlaw Hills 62 K 14
Sidlesham 10 R 31
Sidmouth 7 K 31
Sighthill 56 K 16
Sileby 28 Q 25
Silecroft 38 K 21
Silkstone 40 P 23
Silloth 44 J 19
Silsden 39 O 22
Silver End 22 V 28
Silverdale 38 L 21
Silverstone Circuit 28 Q 27
Silverton 7 J 31
Simonsbath 7 I 30
Sinclair's Bay 74 K 8
Sionascaig (Loch) 72 E 9
Sissinghurst 12 V 30
Sittingbourne 21 W 29
Skara Brae 74 J 6
Skares 48 H 17
Skeabost 65 B 11
Skegness 37 V 24
Skellingthorpe 36 S 24
Skelmanthorpe 39 P 23
Skelmersdale 38 L 23
Skelmorlie 54 F 16
Skelton (Cleveland) 47 R 20
Skelton (Cumbria) 45 L 19
Skelwith Bridge 44 K 20
Skenfrith 17 L 28
Skerray 73 H 8
Skervuile Lighthouse 52 C 16
Skiddaw 44 K 20
Skilgate 7 J 30
Skipness 53 D 16
Skipport (Loch) 64 Y 12
Skipsea 41 T 22
Skipton 39 N 22
Skirza 74 K 8
Skokholm Island 14 E 28
Skomer Island 14 E 28
Skye (Isle of) 65 B 12
Slaidburn 39 M 22
Slaithwaite 39 O 23
Slamannan 55 I 16
Slapin (Loch) 65 B 12
Slapton 4 J 33
Sleaford 37 S 25
Sleat (Sound of) 59 C 12
Sledmere 41 S 21
Sleekburn 51 P 18
Sleights 47 S 20
Sligachan 65 B 12
Sligachan (Loch) 65 B 12
Slimbridge 17 M 28
Slindon 10 S 31
Slockavullin 54 D 15
Slough 19 S 29
Sloy (Loch) 54 F 15
Small Hythe 12 W 30
Smallfield 11 T 30
Smarden 12 W 30
Smedmore 9 N 32
Snaefell 42 G 21
Snainton 47 S 21
Snaith 40 Q 22
Snape 23 Y 27
Snetterton Circuit 30 W 26
Snettisham 30 V 25
Snizort (Loch) 65 A 11
Snodland 12 V 30
Snowdon / Yr Wyddfa 32 H 24
Snowdonia National Park 33 I 24
Snowshill 18 O 27
Soa 58 Z 14
Soa Island 52 A 15
Soar (River) 36 Q 25
Soay 65 B 12
Soay Sound 65 B 12
Soham 30 V 26
Solent (The) 10 Q 31
Solihull 27 O 26
Sollas 64 X 11
Solva 14 E 28
Solway Firth 44 J 19
Somercotes 35 P 24
Somerset (County) 8 M 29
Somersham 29 U 26
Somerton (Norfolk) 31 Y 25
Somerton (Oxon.) 19 Q 28
Somerton (Somerset) 8 L 30
Sompting 11 S 31
Sonning Caversham 19 R 29
Sonning Common 19 R 29
Sopley 9 O 31
Sorbie 42 G 19
Sorn 48 H 17
Sound (The) 3 H 32
South Brent 4 I 32
South Cave 41 S 22
South Cerney 18 O 28
South Downs 10 R 31
South Elmsall 40 Q 23
South Esk (River) 63 L 13
South Foreland 13 Y 30
South Hanningfield 21 V 29
South Harris 70 Z 10
South Harris Forest 70 Z 10
South Hayling 10 R 31
South Kelsey 36 S 23
South Kirkby 40 Q 23
South Lancing 11 T 31
South Leverton 36 R 24
South Lopham 30 X 26
South Mimms 20 T 28
South Molton 7 I 30
South Morar 60 C 13
South Normanton 35 P 24
South Ockendon 20 U 29
South Oxhey 20 S 29
South Petherton 8 L 31
South Petherwin 3 G 32
South Queensferry 56 J 16
South Ronaldsay 74 L 7
South Shields 51 P 19
South Stack 32 F 24
South Tawton 4 I 31
South Uist 64 X 12
South Walls 74 K 7
South Warnborough 10 R 30
South Woodham Ferrers 21 V 29
South Zeal 4 I 31
Southam 27 P 27
Southampton 9 P 31
Southborough 11 U 30
Southbourne (Dorset) 9 O 31
Southbourne (West Sussex) 10 R 31
Southend 53 D 18
Southend-on-Sea 21 W 29
Southery 30 V 26
Southminster 21 W 29
Southport 38 K 23
Southsea 10 Q 31
Southwark (London Borough) 20 T 29
Southwater 11 S 30
Southwell 36 R 24
Southwick (West Sussex) 11 T 31
Southwick (Wilts.) 8 N 30
Southwick Widley 10 Q 31
Southwold 31 Z 27
Sowerby Bridge 39 O 22
Spalding 37 T 25
Spaldwick 29 S 26
Spanish Head 42 F 21
Sparkford 8 M 30
Spean (Glen) 61 F 13
Spean Bridge 60 F 13
Spelve (Loch) 59 C 14
Spennymoor 46 P 19
Spey (River) 61 G 12
Spey Bay 68 K 10
Speymouth Forest 68 K 11
Spilsby 37 U 24
Spinningdale 73 H 10
Spithead 10 Q 31
Spittal (Highland) 74 J 8
Spittal (Northumb.) 57 O 16
Spittal of Glenshee 62 J 13
Spofforth 40 P 22
Spondon 35 P 25
Spreyton 4 I 31
Springfield 56 K 15
Sprotbrough 40 Q 23
Spurn Head 41 U 23
St. Bride's Bay 14 E 28
St. Nicholas (Pembrokes) 14 E 28
St. Nicholas (Vale of Glamorgan) 16 K 29
Stack (Loch) 72 F 8
Stack Island 64 Y 12
Stack Rocks 14 E 29
Staffa 59 A 14
Staffin Bay 65 B 11
Stafford 35 N 25
Staffordshire (County) 35 N 25
Staindrop 46 O 20
Staines 19 S 29
Stainforth (North Yorks.) 39 N 21
Stainforth (South Yorks.) 40 Q 23
Staithes 47 R 20
Stalbridge 8 M 31
Stalham 31 Y 25
Stalmine 38 L 22
Stalybridge 35 N 23
Stamford 28 S 26
Stanbridge 19 S 28
Standing Stones 70 Z 9
Standlake 18 P 28
Standon 20 U 28
Standford-in-the-Vale 18 P 29
Stanford-le-Hope 21 V 29
Stanford-on-Avon 28 Q 26
Stanhope 46 N 19
Stanley (Perthshire and Kinross) 62 J 14
Stanley (Durham) 46 O 19
Stanley (Wakefield.) 40 P 22
Stanmer Park 11 T 31
Stanstead Abbotts 20 U 28
Stansted Mountfitched 20 U 28
Stanton 30 W 27
Stanton Harcourt 18 P 28
Stanwell 20 S 29
Stapleford (Notts.) 36 Q 25
Stapleford (Wilts.) 9 O 30
Staplehurst 12 V 30
Start Point 4 J 33
Startforth 46 O 20
Stathern 36 R 25
Staughton Highway 29 S 27
Staunton 17 N 28
Staveley (Cumbria) 45 L 20
Staveley (Derbs.) 35 P 24
Staxigoe 74 K 8
Staxton 41 S 21
Staylittle 25 J 26
Stedham 10 R 31
Steeple 22 W 28
Steeple Ashton 18 N 30
Steeple Aston 19 Q 28
Steeple Bumpstead 22 V 27
Steeple Claydon 19 R 28
Steeple Morden 29 T 27
Stenhousemuir 55 I 15
Stenness (Orkney Islands) 74 K 7
Stenness (Shetland Islands) 75 P 2
Stevenage 20 T 28
Stevenston 48 F 17
Steventon 19 Q 29
Stewartby 28 S 27
Stewarton 55 G 16
Stewkley 19 R 28
Steyning 11 T 31
Sticklepath 4 I 31
Stilligarry 64 X 12
Stillington 40 Q 21
Stilton 29 T 26
Stirling 55 I 15
Stithians 2 E 33
Stob Choire Claurigh 60 F 13
Stock 21 V 29
Stockbridge 9 P 30
Stockland 7 K 31
Stockport 35 N 23
Stocksbridge 35 P 23
Stockton Heath 34 M 23
Stockton-on-Tees 46 P 20
Stockton-on-Teme 26 M 27
Stoer 72 D 9
Stogumber 7 K 30
Stogursey 7 K 30
Stoke Albany 28 R 26
Stoke-by-Nayland 22 W 28
Stoke Climsland 3 H 32
Stoke Fleming 4 J 33
Stoke Gabriel 4 J 32
Stoke Lacy 26 M 27
Stoke Mandeville 19 R 28
Stoke-on-Trent 35 N 24
Stoke Poges 19 S 29
Stoke sub Hamdon 8 L 31
Stokenchurch 19 R 29
Stokenham 4 I 33
Stokesay 26 L 26
Stokesley 46 Q 20
Stone (Bucks.) 19 R 28
Stone (Staffs.) 35 N 25
Stonehaven 63 N 13
Stonehenge 9 O 30
Stonehouse (South Lanarkshire) 55 I 16
Stonehouse (Devon) 3 H 32
Stonehouse (Glos.) 17 N 28
Stonesfield 18 P 28
Stoneybridge 64 X 12
Stoneykirk 42 F 19
Stoneywood 69 N 12
Stony Stratford 28 R 27
Stornoway 71 A 9
Storr (The) 65 B 11
Storrington 11 S 31
Stort (River) 20 U 28
Stotfold 20 T 27
Stottesdon 26 M 26
Stour (River) (English Channel) 9 N 31
Stour (River) (North Sea) 22 V 27
Stour (River) (R. Severn) 26 N 26
Stourbridge 27 N 26
Stourhead House 8 N 30
Stourport-on Severn 26 N 26
Stow 50 L 16
Stow-on-the-Wold 18 O 28
Stowe School 28 Q 27
Stowmarket 22 W 27
Strachan 63 M 12
Strachur 54 E 15
Stradbroke 31 X 27
Stradishall 22 V 27
Stradsett 30 V 26
Straiton 48 G 18
Straloch 62 J 13
Stranraer 42 E 19
Strata Florida Abbey 25 I 27
Stratfield Saye 19 Q 29
Stratford St. Mary 22 W 28
Stratford-upon-Avon 27 O 27
Strath Brora 73 H 9
Strath Dearn 67 I 11
Strath Halladale 73 I 8
Strath Isla 68 K 11
Strath More 66 E 10
Strath Mulzie 72 F 10
Strath of Kildonan 73 I 9
Strath Oykel 72 F 10
Strath Skinsdale 73 H 9
Strath Tay 62 J 14
Strathallan 55 I 15
Strathardle 62 J 13
Strathaven 49 H 16
Strathbeg (Loch of) 69 O 11
Strathblane 55 H 16
Strathbogie 68 L 11
Strathbraan 62 I 14
Strathcarron 66 D 11
Strathconon 66 F 11
Strathconon Forest 66 F 11
Strathearn 55 I 14
Stratherrick 67 G 12
Strathkinness 56 L 14
Strathmiglo 56 K 15
Strathmore 62 K 14
Strathnairn 67 H 11
Strathnaver 73 H 8
Strathpeffer 67 G 11
Strathspey 68 J 11
Strathvaich Lodge 66 F 10
Strathy 73 I 8
Strathy Point 73 H 8
Strathyre 55 H 15
Stratton (Cornwall) 6 G 31
Stratton (Glos.) 18 O 28
Stratton-on-the-Fosse 8 M 30
Stratton-St. Margaret 18 O 29
Streatley 19 Q 29
Street 8 L 30
Strensall 40 Q 21
Stretford 34 N 23
Stretham 29 U 26
Stretton (Cheshire) 34 M 23
Stretton (Staffs.) 27 N 25
Strichen 69 N 11
Striven (Loch) 54 E 16
Stroma (Island of) 74 K 7
Stromeferry 66 D 11
Stromemore 66 D 11
Stromness 74 K 7
Stronachlachar 55 G 15
Stronchreggan 60 E 13
Stronsay 74 M 6
Stronsay Firth 74 L 6
Strontian 60 D 13
Stroud 17 N 28
Strumble Head 14 E 27
Stuart Castel 67 H 11
Stuartfield 69 N 11

SOUTHAMPTON CENTRE

Above Bar Street
Avenue (The) 3
Bargate Street 4
Brunswick Place 6
Central Bridge 7
Central Station Bridge 8
Civic Centre Road 13
Cumberland Place 14
Hanover Buildings 17
High Street
Houndwell Place 20
Inner Avenue 22
Marlands Shopping Centre 25
Marsh Lane 26
Mountbatten Way 27
Orchard Place 32
Oxford Avenue 33
Portland Street 34
Pound Tree Road 35
Queen's Terrace 38
Queen's Way 39
Radcliffe Road 41
St. Andrew's Road 43
South Front 48
Terminus Terrace 52
Threefield Lane 56
Town Quay 57

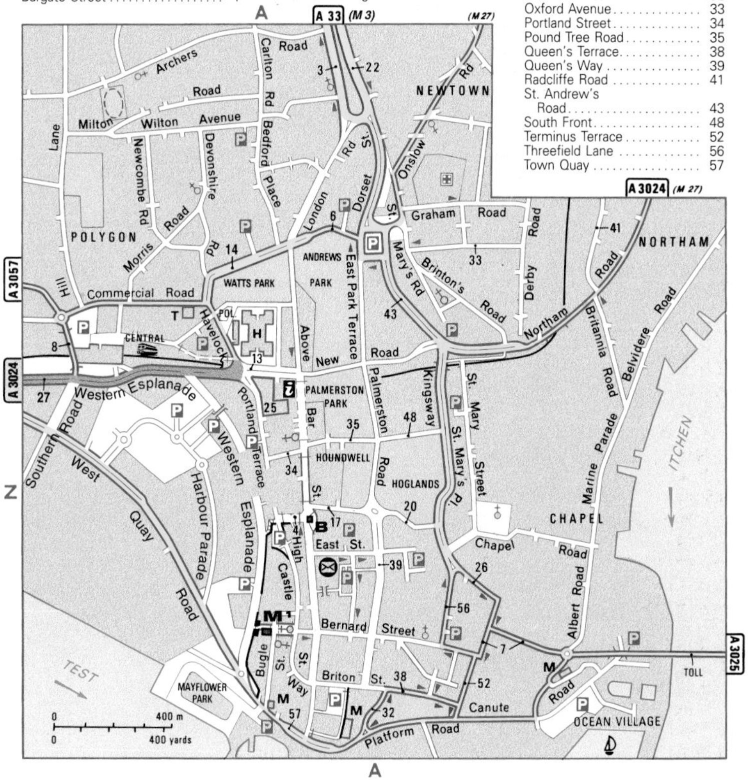
A 33 (M 3)
NEWTOWN
POLYGON
NORTHAM
CENTRAL
PALMERSTON PARK
HOUNDWELL
HOGLANDS
CHAPEL
ITCHEN
TEST
MAYFLOWER PARK
OCEAN VILLAGE
TOLL
A 3024
A 3057
A 3025
Western Esplanade
Commercial Road
400 m
400 yards

STIRLING CENTRE

Barnton Street .... B 2
Causewayhead Road .... B 4
Corn Exchange Road .... B 5
Drummond Place .... B 9
Dumbarton Road .... B 10
Goosecroft Road .... B 12
King Street .... B 13
Leisure Centre .... B
Murray Place .... B 15
Port Street .... B
Queen Street .... B 20
St. John Street .... B 23
St. Mary's Wynd .... B 24
Seaforth Place .... B 25
Spittal Street .... B 27
Thistle Centre .... B
Union Street .... B 28
Upper Craigs .... B 29

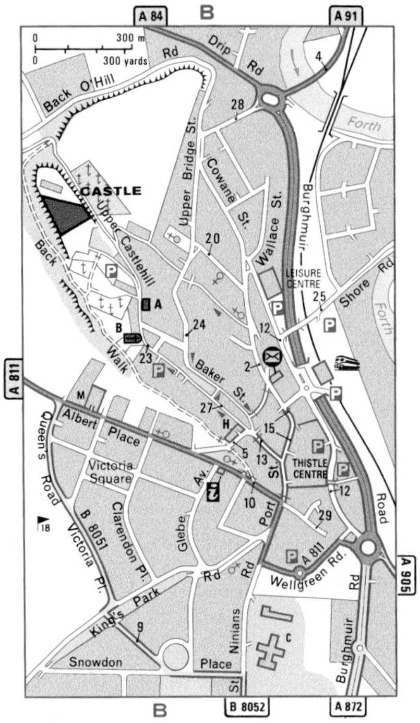

A 84
B
A 91
300 m
300 yards
Drip Rd
Back O'Hill
CASTLE
Upper Castlehill
Upper Bridge St.
Cowane St.
Wallace St.
Burghmuir
LEISURE CENTRE
Shore Rd
Forth
Baker St.
Albert Place
Queen's Road
Victoria Square
Clarendon Pl.
Victoria Pl.
Glebe Av.
Port St.
THISTLE CENTRE
Wellgreen Rd.
King's Park
Snowdon Place
St. Ninians Rd
A 811
A 905
B 8051
B 8052
A 872

STOKE

Campbell Place 14
Church Street
Elenora Street 26
Fleming Road 28
Hartshill Road 33
London Road 42
Shelton Old Road .. 62
Station Road 66
Vale Street 72

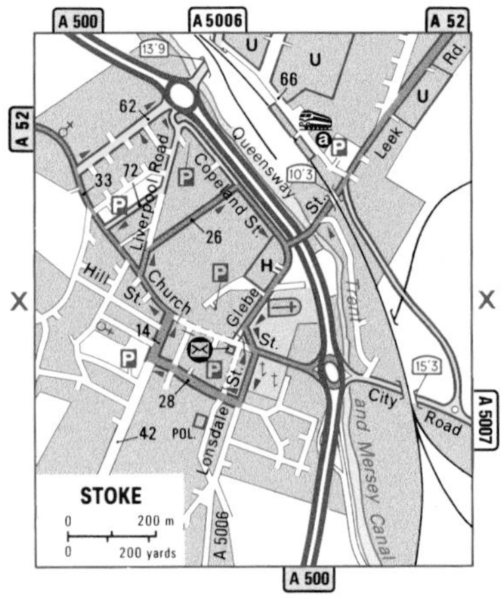

A 500
A 5006
A 52
Queensway
Liverpool Road
Copeland St.
Leek
Hill St.
Church St.
Glebe St.
Lonsdale St.
City Road
Trent and Mersey Canal
A 5007
STOKE
200 m
200 yards

Stubbington 10 O 31
Studland 9 O 32
Studley (Warw.) 27 O 27
Studley (Wilts.) 18 N 29
Studley Royal Gardens 39 P 21
Stuley 64 Y 12
Sturminster Marshall 9 N 31
Sturminster Newton 8 N 31
Sturry 13 X 30
Sturton-le-Steeple 36 R 23
Suainaval (Loch) 70 Z 9
Sudbury (Derbs.) 35 O 25
Sudbury (Suffolk) 22 W 27
Sudbury Hall 35 O 25
Sudeley Castle 18 O 28
Suffolk (County) 23 X 27
Sùil Ghorm 59 A 13
Sulby 42 G 21
Sulgrave 28 Q 27
Sullom Voe 75 P 2
Sumburgh 75 Q 4
Sumburgh Roost 75 P 4
Summer Bridge 39 O 21
Summer Island 72 D 9
Summercourt 2 F 32
Sunart 60 D 13
Sunart (Loch) 59 C 13
Sunbury 20 S 29
Sunderland 46 P 19
Sunningdale 19 S 29
Sunninghill 19 S 29
Surfleet 37 T 25
Surrey (County) 10 S 30
Sutterton 37 T 25
Sutton (Cambs.) 29 U 26

STOKE-ON-TRENT NEWCASTLE-UNDER-LYME BUILT UP AREA

Alexandra Road .... U 3
Bedford Road .... U 4
Brownhills Road .... U 12
Church Lane .... U 19
Cobridge Road .... U 21
Davenport Street .... U 23
Elder Road .... U 24
Etruria Vale Road .... U 27
Grove Road .... V 30
Hanley Road .... U 31
Heron Street .... V 34
High Street .... U 35
Higherland .... V 37
Manor Street .... V 44
Mayne Street .... V 45
Moorland Road .... U 48
Porthill Road .... U 59
Snow Hill .... U 63
Stoke Road .... U 68
Strand (The) .... V 69
Victoria Park Road .... U 75
Victoria Place Link .... V 76
Watlands View .... U 77
Williamson Street .... U 78

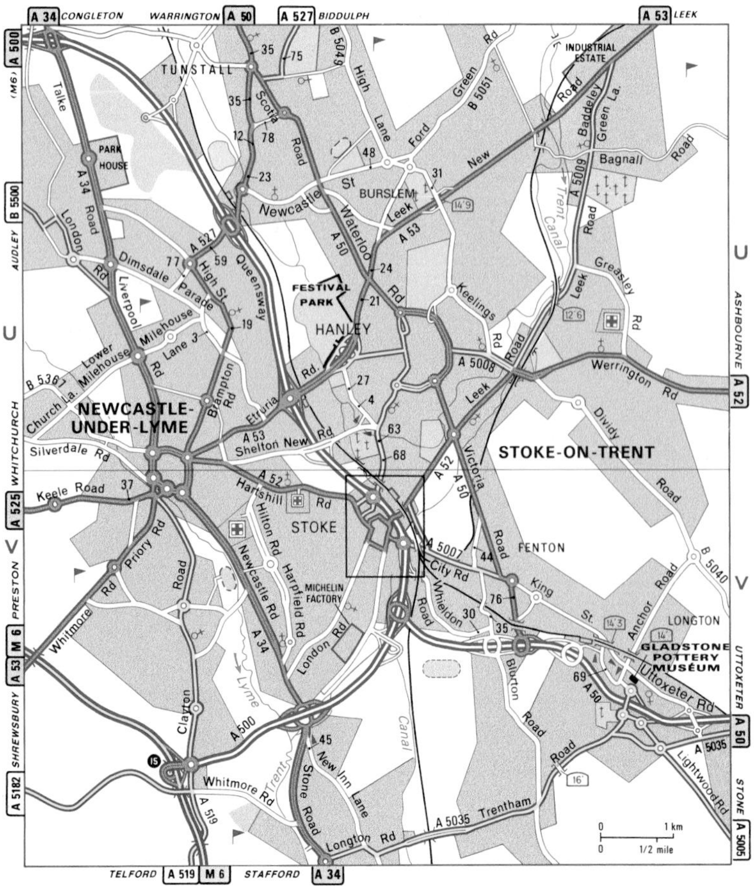

A 34 CONGLETON
WARRINGTON A 50
A 527 BIDDULPH
A 53 LEEK
TUNSTALL
INDUSTRIAL ESTATE
PARK HOUSE
BURSLEM
Bagnall
FESTIVAL PARK
HANLEY
NEWCASTLE-UNDER-LYME
STOKE-ON-TRENT
STOKE
MICHELIN FACTORY
FENTON
LONGTON
GLADSTONE POTTERY MUSEUM
AUDLEY B 5500
WHITCHURCH
PRESTON M 6
SHREWSBURY A 53
A 5182
ASHBOURNE A 52
UTTOXETER A 50
STONE A 5005
TELFORD A 519 M 6 STAFFORD A 34
1 km
1/2 mile

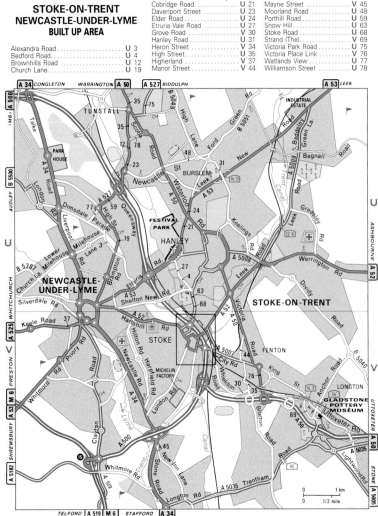

Sutton (London Borough) 20 T 29
Sutton-on-the-Forest 40 Q 21
Sutton (Salop) 34 M 25
Sutton Bank 46 Q 21
Sutton Benger 18 N 29
Sutton Bridge 37 U 25
Sutton Coldfield 27 O 26
Sutton Courtenay 19 Q 29
Sutton-in-Ashfield 36 Q 24
Sutton-on-Hull 41 T 22
Sutton-on-Sea 37 U 24
Sutton-on-Trent 36 R 24
Sutton Scotney 10 P 30
Sutton Valence 12 V 30
Swadlincote 35 P 25
Swaffham 30 W 26
Swaffham Bulbeck 22 U 27
Swale (River) 40 P 21
Swale (The) 21 W 29
Swale Dale 46 O 20
Swallow 41 T 23
Swallow Falls 33 I 24
Swanage 9 O 32
Swanland 41 S 22
Swanley 20 U 29
Swanscombe 20 U 29
Swansea / Abertawe 15 I 29
Swarbacks Minn 75 P 2
Sway 9 P 31
Swaythling 9 P 31
Swimbridge 6 I 30
Swinbrook 18 P 28
Swindon 18 O 29
Swineshead 37 T 25
Swinton (Scottish Borders) 57 N 16
Swinton (Rotherham.) 35 Q 23
Swynnerton 34 N 25
Symbister 75 Q 2
Symonds Yat 17 M 28
Symonds Yat Rock 17 M 28
Symondsbury 8 L 31
Syresham 28 Q 27
Syston 28 Q 25

T

Tadcaster 40 Q 22
Tadley 19 Q 29
Tadmarton 27 P 27
Tadworth 20 T 30
Taff (River) 16 K 29
Taibach 15 I 29
Tain 67 H 10
Takeley 20 U 28
Tal-y-bont (Dyfed) 24 I 26
Tal-y-Llyn Lake 25 I 25
Talgarth 16 K 28
Talke 34 N 24
Talladale 66 D 10
Talley 15 I 28
Talsarnau 32 H 25
Talybont-on-Usk (Powys) 16 K 28
Tamanavay (Loch) 70 Y 9
Tamar (River) 6 G 31
Tamworth 27 O 26
Tan Hill 45 N 20
Tanera Beg 72 D 9
Tanera Mòr 72 D 9
Tannadice 62 L 13
Tantallon Castle 57 M 15
Taransay 70 Y 10
Taransay (Sound of) 70 Z 10
Tarbat Ness 67 I 10
Tarbert (Argyll and Bute) 53 D 16
Tarbert (Western Isles) 70 Z 10
Tarbert (Loch) 52 C 16
Tarbet 54 F 15
Tarbolton 48 G 17
Tardy Gate 38 L 22
Tarland 68 L 12
Tarleton 38 L 22
Tarn (The) 45 L 20
Tarporley 34 M 24
Tarrant Hinton 9 N 31
Tarrant Keyneston 9 N 31
Tarrington 26 M 27
Tarskavaig Point 65 B 12
Tarves 69 N 11
Tarvin 34 L 24
Tattershall 37 T 24
Tatton Hall 34 M 24
Taunton 7 K 30
Taunton Deane 7 K 30
Taverham 31 X 25
Tavistock 3 H 32
Taw (River) 6 I 31
Tay (Firth of) 56 K 14
Tay (Loch) 61 H 14
Tay Road Bridge 62 L 14
Taynuilt 60 E 14
Tayport 62 L 14
Tayvallich 54 D 15
Teacuis (Loch) 59 C 14
Tebay 45 M 20
Tedburn St. Mary 4 I 31
Tees (River) 46 P 20
Teesdale 45 N 20
Teifi (River) 24 G 27
Teignmouth 4 J 32
Telford 26 M 25
Teme (River) 26 M 27
Temple Ewell 13 X 30
Temple Sowerby 45 M 20
Templeton 14 F 28
Tempsford 29 T 27
Tenbury Wells 26 M 27
Tenby / Dinbych-y-pysgod 14 F 28
Tendring 21 X 28
Tenterden 12 W 30
Terling 22 V 28
Tern Hill 34 M 25
Terrington St. Clement 37 U 25
Tetbury 18 N 29
Tetford 37 T 24
Tetney 41 T 23
Tettenhall 26 N 26
Teviotdale 50 L 17
Tewin 20 T 28
Tewkesbury 18 N 28
Texa 52 B 17
Teynham 12 W 30
Thakeham 11 S 31
Thame 19 R 28
Thame (River) 19 R 28
Thames (River) 19 Q 29
Thanet (Isle of) 13 Y 29
Thatcham 19 Q 29
Thaxted 22 V 28
Theale (Berks.) 19 Q 29
Theale (Somerset) 8 L 30
Theddlethorpe St. Helen 37 U 23
Thetford 30 W 26
Theydon Bois 20 U 28
Thirsk 46 P 21
Thoralby 46 N 21
Thornaby-on-Tees 46 Q 20
Thornaganby 40 R 22
Thornbury (South Glos.) 17 M 29
Thornbury (Heref.) 26 M 27
Thornby 28 Q 26
Thorne 40 R 23
Thorner 40 P 22
Thorney 29 T 26
Thornham 30 V 25
Thornhill (Stirling) 55 H 15
Thornhill (Dumfries and Galloway) 49 I 18
Thornton (Fife) 56 K 15
Thornton (Lancs.) 38 K 22
Thornton Curtis 41 S 23
Thornton Dale 47 R 21
Thornton-in-Craven 39 N 22
Thornyhive Bay 63 N 13
Thorpe (Derbs.) 35 O 24
Thorpe (Essex) 21 W 29
Thorpe-le-Soken 21 X 28
Thorpe-on-the-Hill 36 S 24
Thorpeness 23 Y 27
Thorrington 21 X 28
Thorverton 7 J 31
Thrapston 28 S 26
Three Cocks 25 K 27
Threlkeld 44 K 20
Throckley 51 O 19
Throwleigh 4 I 31
Thruxton Circuit 9 P 30
Thundersley 21 V 29
Thurcroft 36 Q 23
Thurlby 29 S 25
Thurlestone 4 I 33
Thurlow 22 V 27
Thurmaston 28 Q 25
Thursby 44 K 19
Thurso 74 J 8
Thwaite 45 N 20
Tibberton (Glos.) 17 M 28
Tibberton (Salop) 34 M 25
Tibshelf 35 P 24
Ticehurst 12 V 30
Tickhill 36 Q 23
Ticknall 35 P 25
Tideswell 35 O 24
Tigerton 63 L 13
Tigharry 64 X 11
Tighnabruaich 54 E 16
Tilbury 20 V 29
Tillicoultry 55 I 15
Tillington 10 S 31
Tilshead 9 O 30
Tilt (Glen) 63 I 13
Tilton-on-the-Hill 28 R 26
Timberscombe 7 J 30
Timsbury 17 M 30
Tingwall (Loch) 75 P 3
Tintagel 3 F 32
Tintern Abbey 17 L 28
Tintinhull 8 L 31
Tipton 27 N 26
Tiptree 22 W 28
Tiree 58 Z 14

STRATFORD-UPON-AVON

Banbury Road B 2
Benson Road B 3
Bridge Foot B 6
Bridge Street B 8
Chapel Lane A 13
Chapel Street A 14
Church Street A 16
Clopton Bridge B 18
College Lane A 19
Ely Street A 22
Evesham Place A 24
Great William Street A 25
Greenhill Street A 27
Guild Street A 28
Henley Street A 29
High Street A 31
Rother Street A 32
Scholars Lane A 33
Sheep Street AB 35
Tiddington Road B 38
Trinity Street A 40
Warwick Road B 42
Waterside B 43
Windsor Street A 45
Wood Street A 47

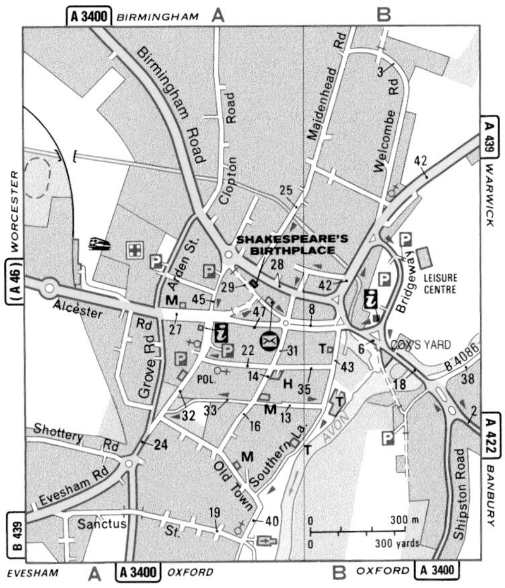

Tirga Mór 70 Z 10
Tiroran 59 B 14
Tisbury 9 N 30
Titchfield 10 Q 31
Tiumpan Head 71 B 9
Tiverton 7 J 31
Tobermory 59 B 14
Toberonochy 54 D 15
Tobson 70 Z 9
Toddington 19 S 28
Todmorden 39 N 22
Toe Head 70 Y 10
Toll of Birness 69 O 11
Tollerton 40 Q 21
Tollesbury 22 W 28
Tolleshunt d'Arcy 22 W 28
Tolpuddle 8 N 31
Tolsta 71 B 8
Tolsta Chaolais 70 Z 9
Tolsta Head 71 B 8
Tomatin 67 I 11
Tombreck 67 H 11
Tomintoul 68 J 12
Tonbridge 11 U 30
Tongland 43 H 19
Tongue 73 G 8
Tonna 15 I 28
Tonypandy 16 J 29
Tonyrefail 16 J 29
Topcliffe 40 P 21
Topsham 7 J 31
Tor Ness 74 K 7
Torbay 4 J 32
Torcross 4 J 33
Torksey 36 R 24
Torlundy 60 E 13
Torphichen 56 J 16
Torphins 69 M 12
Torpoint 3 H 32
Torquay 4 J 32
Torridon (Loch) 65 C 11
Torrisdale Bay 73 H 8
Torthorwald 49 J 18
Torver 44 K 20
Totland 9 P 31
Totnes 4 I 32
Totton 9 P 31
Tow Law 46 O 19
Towcester 28 R 27
Tower Hamlets (London Borough) 20 T 29
Town Yetholm 50 N 17
Towneley Hall 39 N 22
Traboth 48 G 17
Trallwng / Welshpool 25 K 26
Tranent 56 L 16
Traquair House 50 K 17
Trawden 39 N 22
Trawsfynydd 33 I 25
Trealaval (Loch) 70 A 9
Trearddur Bay 32 G 24
Trecastle 16 J 28
Trefaldwyn / Montgomery 25 K 26
Treffynnon / Holywell 33 K 24
Trefnant 33 J 24
Trefyclawdd / Knighton 26 K 26
Trefynwy / Monmouth 17 L 28
Tregaron 25 I 27
Tregony 3 F 33
Treharris 16 K 29
Treherbert 16 J 28
Treig (Loch) 60 F 13
Trelech 15 G 28
Trelissick Gardens 2 E 33
Trelleck 17 L 28
Tremadog 32 H 25
Tremadog Bay 32 H 25
Trengwainton Garden 2 D 33
Trent (River) 35 N 25
Trentham 35 N 25
Treorchy 16 J 29
Trerice 2 E 32
Treshnish Isles 59 A 14
Treshnish Point 59 A 14
Tretower 16 K 28
Trevone 2 F 32
Trevor 32 G 25
Trevose Head 2 E 32
Trewithen 3 F 33
Trimdon 46 P 19
Trimley Heath 23 X 28
Trimsaran 15 H 28
Tring 19 R 28
Trispen 2 E 33
Trochry 62 J 14
Troedyrhiw 16 J 28
Trollamarig (Loch) 70 Z 10
Tromie (Glen) 61 H 12
Troon 48 G 17
Trossachs (The) 55 G 15
Trotternish 65 B 11
Troutbeck 44 L 20
Trowbridge 8 N 30
Truim (Glen) 61 H 13
Trull 7 K 31
Trumpington 29 U 27
Truro 2 E 33
Trwyn Cilan 32 G 25
Tuath (Loch) 59 B 14
Tuddenham 30 V 27
Tudweiliog 32 G 25
Tugford 26 M 26
Tulla (Loch) 60 F 14
Tullibody 55 I 15
Tumble 15 H 28
Tummel (Loch) 61 I 13
Tunstall (Staffs.) 35 N 24
Tunstall (Suffolk) 31 Y 25
Turnberry 48 F 18
Turnditch 35 P 24
Turret (Loch and Reservoir) 61 I 14
Turriff 69 M 11
Turvey 28 S 27
Tusker Rock 15 I 29
Tutbury 35 O 25
Tuxford 36 R 24
Twatt 74 K 6
Tweed (River) 49 J 17
Tweeddale 49 J 17
Tweedmouth 57 N 16
Tweedsmuir Hills 49 J 17
Twickenham 20 S 29
Twyford (Berks.) 19 R 29
Twyford (Hants.) 10 Q 30
Twyford (Leics.) 36 R 25
Twynholm 43 H 19
Tyddewi / St. David's 14 E 28
Tyldesley 39 M 23
Tyne (River) 46 P 19
Tynemouth 51 P 18
Tynewydd 16 J 28
Tytherington 17 M 29
Tywardreath 3 F 32
Tywi (River) 25 I 27
Tywyn 24 H 26

U

Uckfield 11 U 31
Uddingston 55 H 16
Uffculme 7 K 31
Ufford 23 Y 27
Ugadale Bay 53 D 17
Ugborough 4 I 32
Uig (Highland) 65 A 11
Uig (Western Isles) 70 Y 9
Uisg (Loch) 59 C 14
Uiskevagh (Loch) 64 Y 11
Uley 17 N 28
Ullapool 72 E 10
Ulleskelf 40 Q 22
Ullesthorpe 28 Q 26
Ullswater 45 L 20
Ulpha 44 K 21
Ulsta 75 Q 2
Ulva 59 B 14
Ulverston 38 K 21
Unapool 72 E 9
Unst 75 R 1
Upavon 9 O 30
Uphall 56 J 16
Uphill 17 L 30
Uplyme 8 L 31
Upottery 7 K 31
Upper Badcall 72 E 9
Upper Beeding 11 T 31
Upper Chapel 25 J 27
Upper Dicker 11 U 31
Upper Knockando 68 J 11
Upper Loch Torridon 66 D 11
Upper Poppleton 40 Q 22
Upper Tean 35 O 25

SUNDERLAND

Albion Place 2
Bedford Street 4
Borough Road 5
Bridge Street 6
Chester Road 10
Crowtree Road 11
Derwent Street 12
Fawcett Street
High Street West 15
Holmeside
John Street 16
Livingstone Road 18
New Durham Road 19
Park Lane 23
St. Mary's Way 27
Southwick Road 30
The Bridges
Vine Place 36

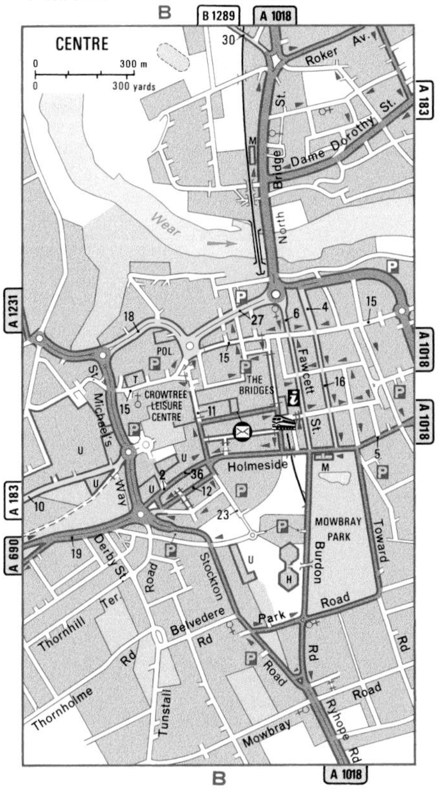

SWANSEA/ ABERTAWE

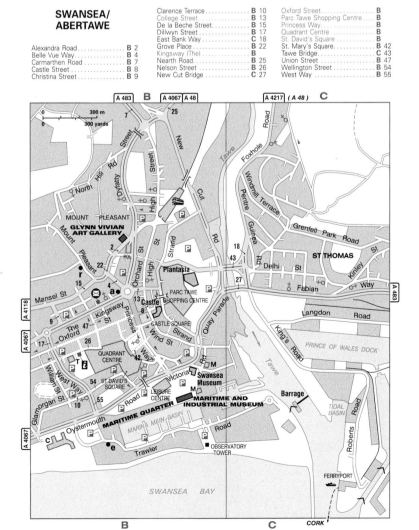

Alexandra Road B 2
Belle Vue Way B 4
Carmarthen Road B 7
Castle Street B 8
Christina Street B 9
Clarence Terrace B 10
College Street B 13
De la Beche Street B 15
Dillwyn Street B 17
East Bank Way C 18
Grove Place B 22
Kingsway (The) B
Nearth Road B 25
Nelson Street B 26
New Cut Bridge C 27
Oxford Street B
Parc Tawe Shopping Centre B
Princess Way B
Quadrant Centre B
St. David's Square B
St. Mary's Square B 42
Tawe Bridge C 43
Union Street B 47
Wellington Street B 54
West Way B 55

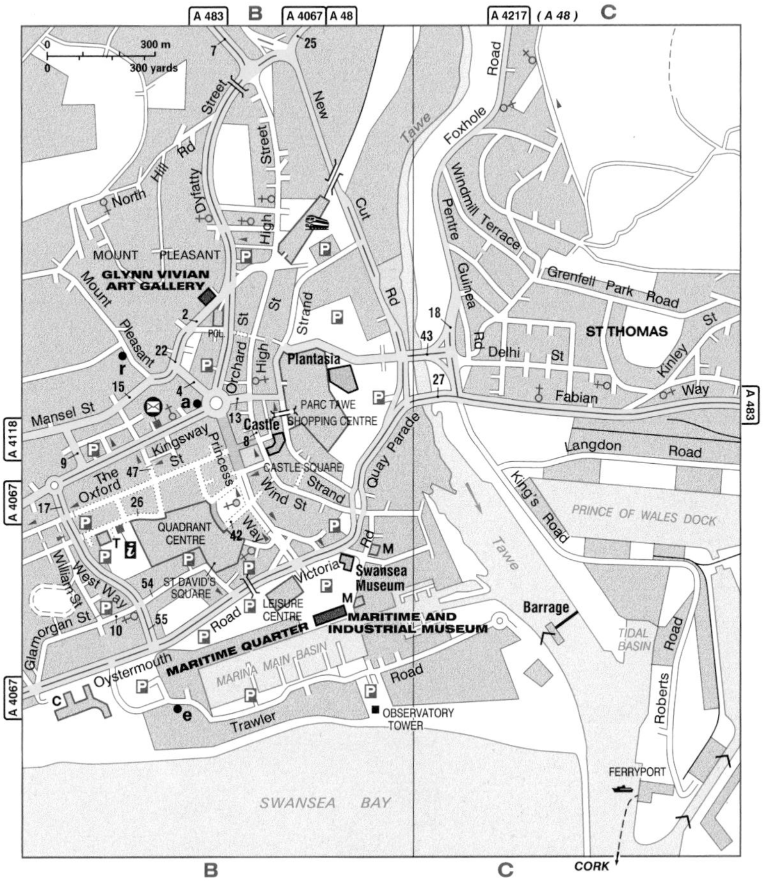

SWINDON

Beckhampton Street . . . . Y 3
Bridge Street . . . . Y 7
Brunel Shopping Centre . . . YZ
Canal Walk . . . . Y 9
Cricklade Street . . . . Z 13
Cross Street . . . . Z 15
Deacon Street . . . . Z 16
Dryden Street . . . . Z 19
Edmund Street . . . . Z 21
Faringdon Road . . . . Y 22
Farnsby Street . . . . YZ 24
High Street . . . . Z 27
Islington Street . . . . Y 29
London Street . . . . Y 31
Milton Road . . . . YZ 33
North Star Avenue . . . . Y 37
North Street . . . . Z 39
Ocotal Way . . . . Y 40
Prospect Hill . . . . Z 45
Regent Street . . . . YZ 46
Sheppard Street . . . . Y 49
South Street . . . . Z 52
Southampton Street . . . . Y 54
Spring Gardens . . . . Y 55
The Parade . . . . Y 58
Upham Road . . . . Z 60
Warwick Road . . . . Z 63
Wood Street . . . . Z 67

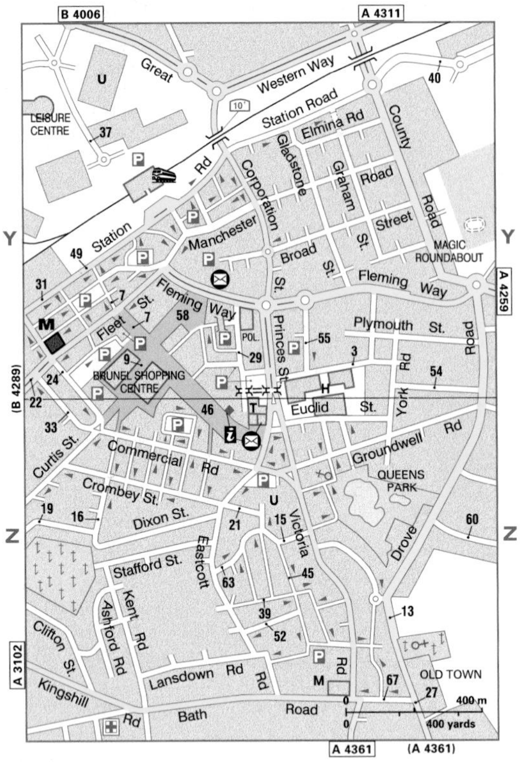

WINCHESTER

Andover Road 3
Bridge Street 6
Broadway (The) 7
Brooks Shopping Centre 8
City Road 10
Clifton Terrace 12
East Hill 15
Eastgate Street 16
Friarsgate 19
High Street
Magdalen Hill 23
Middle Brook Street 24
St. George's Street 32
St. Paul's Hill 33
St. Peter's Street 34
Southgate Street 35
Stockbridge Road 37
Sussex Street 38
Union Street 39
Upper High Street 40

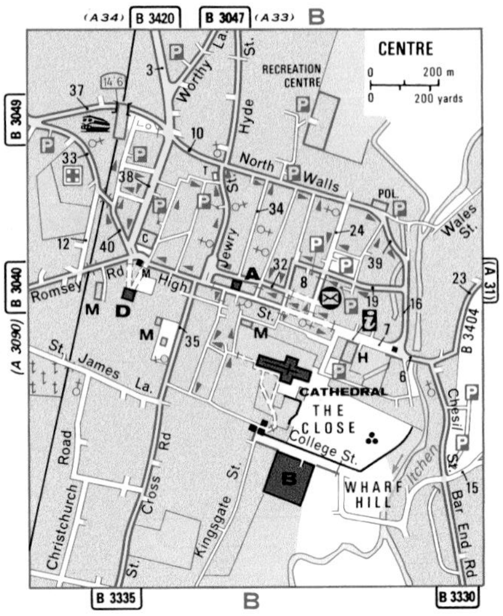

Uppertown 74 K 7
Uppingham 28 R 26
Upton (Dorset) 9 N 31
Upton (Notts.) 36 R 24
Upton Grey 10 Q 30
Upton House 27 P 27
Upton Magna 26 M 25
Upton-upon-Severn 26 N 27
Upwell 29 U 26
Urchfont 18 O 30
Ure (River) 40 Q 21
Urigill (Loch) 72 F 9
Urmston 34 M 23
Urquhart Castle 67 G 12
Urquhart (Glen) 67 G 11
Urrahag (Loch) 70 A 8
Urswick 38 K 21
Usk (River) 16 J 28
Usk / Brynbuga 17 L 28
Uttoxeter 35 O 25
Uyea 75 R 2
Uyeasound 75 R 1

V

Vallay Strand 64 X 11
Valle Crucis 33 K 25
Valley 32 G 24
Valtos 70 Z 9
Vatersay 58 X 13
Ve Skerries 75 O 2
Venachar (Loch) 55 H 15
Ventnor 10 Q 32
Verwood 9 O 31
Veryan 2 F 33
Veyatie (Loch) 72 E 9
Vindolanda 50 M 19
Voe 75 Q 2
Voil (Loch) 55 G 14
Vowchurch 17 L 27
Vyrnwy (Lake) 33 J 25

W

Waddesdon 19 R 28
Waddington (Lancs.) 39 M 22
Waddington (Lincs.) 36 S 24
Wadebridge 3 F 32
Wadhurst 11 U 30
Wainfleet All Saints 37 U 24
Wakefield 40 P 22
Wakes Colne 22 W 28
Walberswick 31 Y 27
Walderslade 21 V 29
Walkden 39 M 23
Walkeringham 36 R 23
Walkern 20 T 28
Wall 27 O 26
Wallace Monument 55 I 15
Wallasey 33 K 23
Wallingford 19 Q 29
Wallington House 51 O 18
Walls 75 P 3
Wallsend 51 P 18
Walney (Isle of) 38 K 21
Walpole St. Andrew 30 U 25
Walpole St. Peter 30 U 25
Walsall 27 O 26
Waltham (North East Lincs.) 41 T 23
Waltham (Kent) 13 X 30
Waltham Abbey 20 U 28
Waltham Forest (London Borough) 20 T 29
Waltham-on-the-Wolds 36 R 25
Walton-le-Dale 38 M 22
Walton-on-Thames 20 S 29
Walton-on-the-Naze 23 X 28
Wanborough 18 O 29
Wandsworth (London Borough) 20 T 29
Wanlockhead 49 I 17
Wansford 29 S 26
Wanstrow 8 M 30
Wantage 18 P 29
Wappenham 28 Q 27
Warboys 29 T 26
Wardington 28 Q 27
Wardour Castle 9 N 30
Ware 20 T 28
Wareham 9 N 31
Wargrave 19 R 29
Wark 50 N 17
Wark Forest 50 M 18
Warkworth 51 P 17
Warley 27 O 26
Warlingham 20 T 30
Warmington 27 P 27
Warminster 9 N 30
Warmsworth 40 Q 23
Warren (The) 13 X 30
Warrington 34 M 23
Warsash 10 Q 31
Warsop 36 Q 24
Warton (near Morecambe) 38 L 21
Warton (near Preston) 38 L 22
Warwickshire (County) 27 P 27
Warwickshire (County) 27 P 27
Wasbister 74 K 6
Wasdale Head 44 K 20
Wash (The) 37 U 25
Washington (Tyne and Wear) 46 P 19
Washington (West Sussex) 11 S 31
Wast Water 44 K 20
Watchet 7 K 30
Watchfield 18 P 29
Watchgate 45 L 20
Water Orton 27 O 26
Waterbeach 22 U 27
Watergate Bay 2 E 32
Waterhouses 35 O 24
Wateringbury 12 V 30
Waterlooville 10 Q 31
Waternish Point 65 A 11
Waters Upton 34 M 25
Waterside 48 G 17
Watford 20 S 29
Wath-upon-Dearne 35 P 23
Watlington 19 Q 29
Watten 74 K 8
Watton 30 W 26
Watton at Stone 20 T 28
Waunfawr 32 H 24
Waveney (River) 31 Y 26
Wear (River) 46 O 20
Weardale 45 N 19
Weaver (River) 34 M 24
Weaverthorpe 41 S 21
Wedmore 8 L 30
Wednesbury 27 N 26
Wednesfield 27 N 26
Weedon-Bec 28 Q 27
Week St. Mary 6 G 31
Weeley 21 X 28
Weem 61 I 14
Welcombe 6 G 31
Welham Green 20 T 28
Welland 26 N 27
Welland (River) 37 T 25
Wellesbourne 27 P 27
Wellingborough 28 R 27
Wellington (Salop) 26 M 25
Wellington (Somerset) 7 K 31
Wells 8 M 30
Wells-next-the-Sea 30 W 25
Welshpool / Trallwng 25 K 26
Welton 36 S 24
Welwyn 20 T 28
Welwyn Garden City 20 T 28
Wem 34 L 25
Wembdon 8 K 30
Wembley 20 T 29
Wembury 4 H 33
Wembworthy 6 I 31
Wemyss Bay 54 F 16
Wendens Ambo 20 U 27
Wendover 19 R 28
Wendron 2 E 33
Wenlock Edge 26 L 26
Wennington 38 M 21
Wensley 46 O 21
Wensleydale 46 O 21
Wentbridge 40 Q 23
Weobley (Hereford and Worcester) 26 L 27
Wereham 30 V 26
West Alvington 4 I 33
West Auckland 46 O 20
West Bay 5 M 32
West Bergholt 22 W 28
West Bridgford 36 Q 25
West Bromwich 27 O 26
West Calder 56 J 16
West Camel 8 M 30
West Charleton 4 I 33
West Chiltington 11 S 31
West Coker 8 L 31
West Dean 9 P 30
West Down 6 H 30
West End 10 Q 31
West Farleigh 12 V 30
West Geirinish 64 X 11
West Harptree 17 M 30
West Hoathly 11 T 30
West Kilbride 54 F 16
West Kingsdown 20 U 29
West Kirby 33 K 23
West Linton 56 J 16
West Loch Roag 70 Z 9
West Loch Tarbert (Argyll and Bute) 53 D 16
West Loch Tarbert (Western Isles) 70 Z 10
West Looe 3 G 32
West Lulworth 8 N 32
West Malling 12 V 30
West Malvern 26 M 27
West Meon 10 Q 30
West Mersea 22 W 28
West Midlands (Metropolitan County Birmingham) 27 O 26
West Moors 9 O 31
West Runton 31 X 25
West Sussex (County) 10 S 30
West Tanfield 39 P 21
West Thorney 10 R 31
West Walton 29 U 25
West Wellow 9 P 31
West Wittering 10 R 31
West Witton 46 O 21
West Wycombe 19 R 29
Westbourne 10 R 31
Westbury (Cheshire) 26 L 25
Westbury (Wilts.) 9 N 30
Westbury-on-Severn 17 M 28
Westcliff 21 W 29
Westcott 11 S 30
Wester Ross 66 D 11
Westerham 11 U 30
Western Cleddau 14 E 28
Westfield 12 V 31
Westgate-on-Sea 13 Y 29
Westham 11 U 31
Westhoughton 38 M 23
Westleton 23 Y 27
Westmill 20 T 28
Westminster (London Borough) 20 T 29
Westnewton 44 J 19
Weston (Devon) 7 K 31
Weston (Staffs.) 35 N 25
Westonbirt 17 N 29
Weston-on-the-Green 19 Q 28
Weston-on-Trent 35 P 25
Weston-super-Mare 17 L 29
Weston Turville 19 R 28
Weston-under-Lizard 26 N 25
Weston-under-Penyard 17 M 28
Westonzoyland 8 L 30
Westray 74 K 6
Westruther 57 M 16
Westward Ho 6 H 30
Westwood 17 N 30
Wetheral 45 L 19
Wetherby 40 P 22
Wethersfield 22 V 28
Wetwang 41 S 21
Wey (River) 10 R 30
Weybourne 31 X 25
Weybridge 20 S 29
Weyhill 9 P 30
Weymouth 8 M 32
Whaley Bridge 35 O 24
Whalley 39 M 22
Whalsay 75 R 2
Whaplode 29 T 25
Wharfe (River) 40 O 22
Wharfedale 39 O 22
Whauphill 42 G 19

WARWICK

Bowling Green Street . . . . Y 9
Brook Street . . . . Y 12
Butts (The) . . . . Y 13
Castle Hill . . . . Y 15
Church Street . . . . Y 17
High Street . . . . Y 23
Jury Street . . . . Y
Lakin Road . . . . Y 25
Linen Street . . . . Y 26
Market Place . . . . Y 29
North Rock . . . . Y 32
Old Square . . . . Y 35
St. John's Road . . . . Y 42
St. Nicholas Church Street . . . . Y 43
Smith Street . . . . Y
Swan Street . . . . Y 46
Theatre Street . . . . Y 48
West Street . . . . Y 50

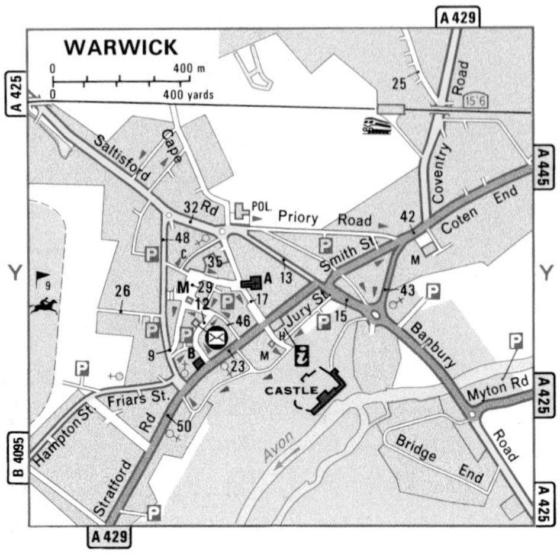

WINDSOR

Bexley Street .... Z 2
Castle Hill .... Z 4
Claremont Road .... Z 6
Clarence Crescent .... Z 7
Clewer Crescent Road .... Z 8
Datchet Rd .... Z 9
Goswell Road .... Z 10
Grove Road .... Z 12
High Street .... Z 14
Keats Lane .... Z 17
King Edward Court Centre .... Z
Peascod Street .... Z 18
Peascod Street .... Z
River Street .... Z 22
Stovell Road .... Z 23
Thames Avenue .... Z 24
Thames Street .... Z 25
Trinity Place .... Z 27
Windsor Bridge .... Z 28

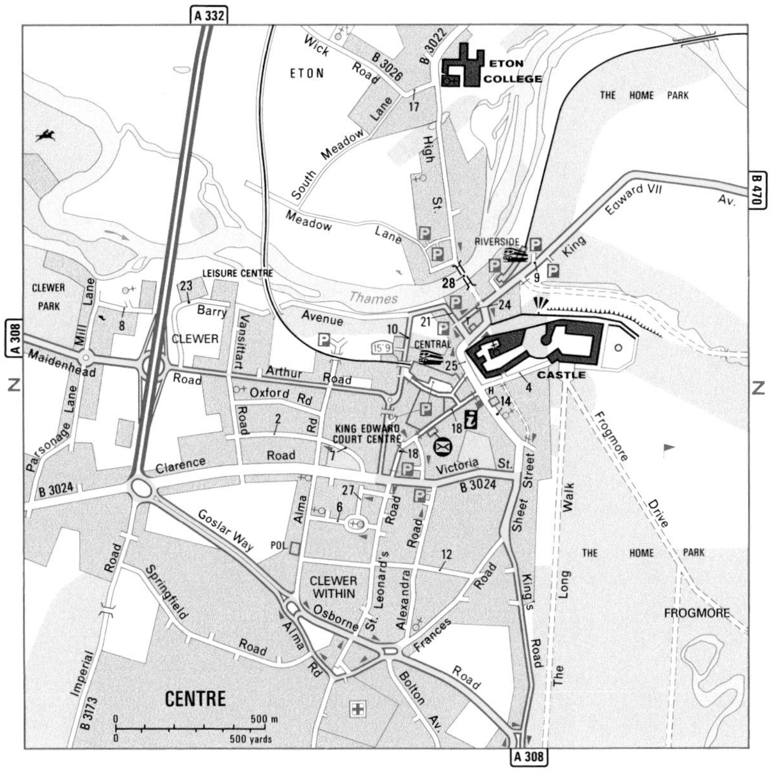

WOLVERHAMPTON

Cleveland Street 7
Darlington Street
Garrick Street 8
Lichfield Street 12
Mander Centre
Market Street 14
Princess Street 15
Queen Square 17
Railway Drive 20
Salop Street 22
Victoria Street 24
Wulfrun Centre

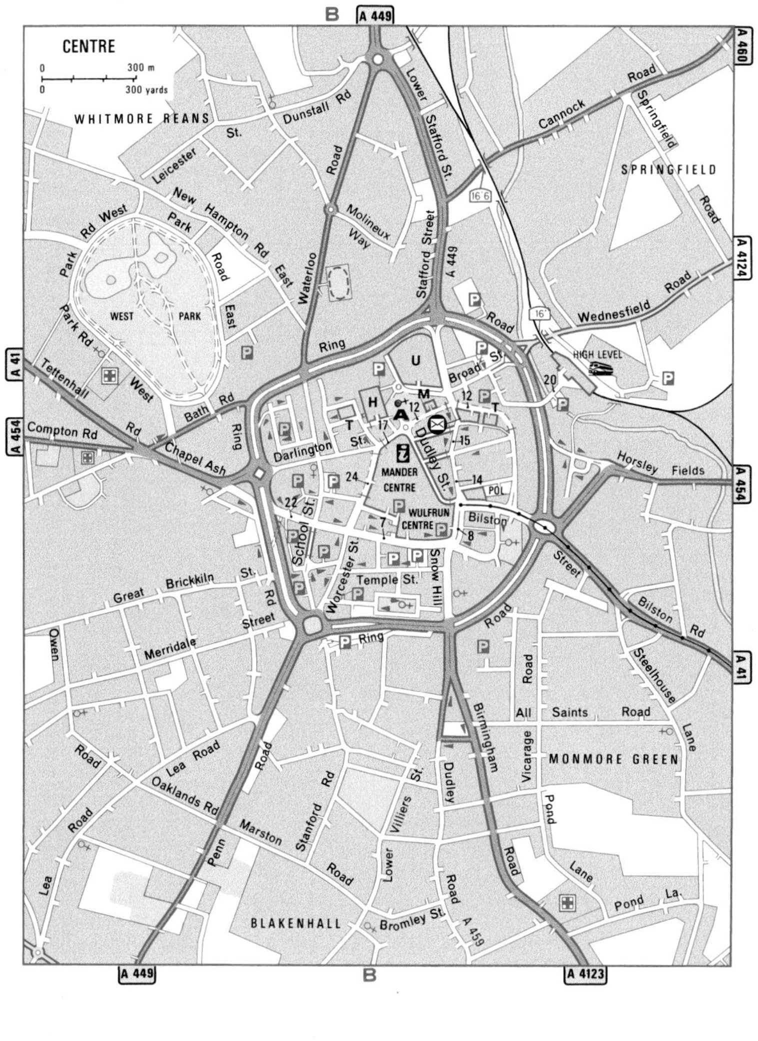

YORK CENTRE

Bishopgate Street .... CZ 3
Bishophill Senior .... CZ 4
Blake Street .... CY 5
Church Street .... DY 8
Clifford Street .... DY 10
Colliergate .... DY 12
Coney Street .... CY 13
Cromwell Road .... CZ 15
Davygate .... CY 16
Deangate .... DY 18
Duncombe Place .... CY 20
Fawcett Street .... DZ 21
Fetter Lane .... CY 22
Goodramgate .... DY 25
High Ousegate .... DY 26
High Petergate .... CY 28
Leeman Road .... CY 30
Lendal .... CY 32
Lord Mayor's Walk .... DX 33
Low Petergate .... DY 35
Museum Street .... CY 39
Parliament Street .... DY 42
Pavement .... DY 43
Peasholme Green .... DY 45
Penley's Grove Street .... DX 46
Queen Street .... CZ 49
St. Leonard's Place .... CY 52
St. Maurice's Road .... DXY 53
Shambles (The) .... DY 54
Station Road .... CY 55
Stonebow (The) .... DY 56
Stonegate .... CY 58
Tower Street .... DZ 59

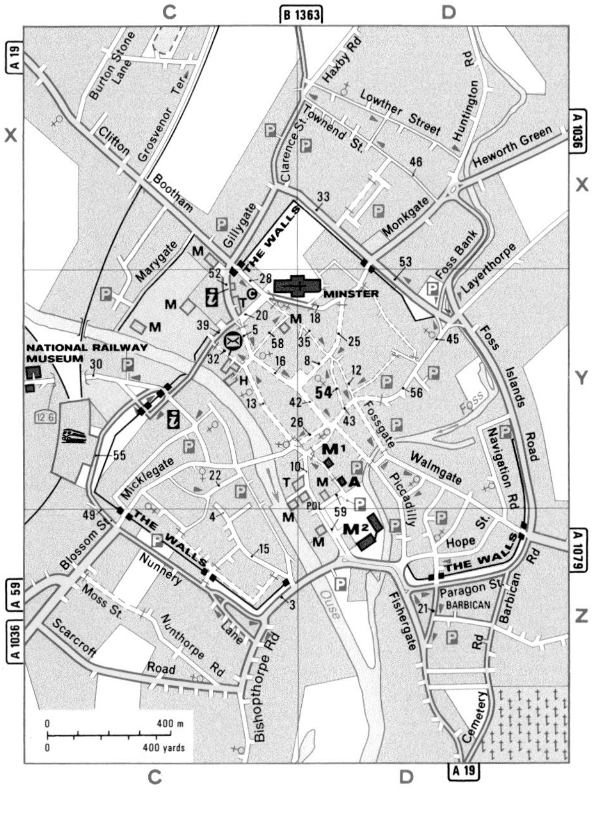

Whauphill 42 G 21
Wheathampstead 20 T 28
Wheatley (Notts.) 36 R 23
Wheatley (Oxon.) 19 Q 28
Wheatley Hill 46 P 19
Wheaton Aston 26 N 25
Wheldrake 40 R 22
Whernside 39 M 21
Wherwell 9 P 30
Whickham 46 O 19
Whimple 7 J 31
Whipsnade 19 S 28
Whissendine 36 R 25
Whitburn (West Lothian) 56 I 16
Whitburn (South Tyneside) 46 P 19
Whitby 47 S 20
Whitchurch (Bath and N.E. Somerset) 17 M 29
Whitchurch (Bucks.) 19 R 28
Whitchurch (Devon) 3 H 32
Whitchurch (Heref. and Worc.) 17 M 28
Whitchurch (Oxon.) 19 Q 29
Whitchurch (Salop) 34 L 25
White Coomb 49 K 17
White Horse Hill 18 P 29
White Scarcaves 38 M 21
White Waltham 19 R 29
Whitebridge 67 G 12
Whitefield 39 N 23
Whitehaven 44 J 20
Whitehill 10 R 30
Whitehills 69 M 10
Whitehouse 53 D 16
Whiten Head 72 G 8
Whiteness Sands 67 I 10
Whiteparish 9 P 30
Whiterashes 69 N 12
Whitesand Bay (Pembrokes) 14 E 28
Whitesand Bay (Cornwall) 2 C 33
Whitewell 38 M 22
Whitfield 13 X 30
Whithorn 42 G 19
Whiting Bay 53 E 17
Whitland 14 G 28
Whitley 19 R 29
Whitley Bay 51 P 18
Whitsand Bay 3 H 32
Whitstable 13 X 29
Whitstone 6 G 31
Whittingham 51 O 17
Whittington (Derbs.) 35 P 24
Whittington (Lancs.) 38 L 21
Whittington (Salop) 34 L 25
Whittle le Woods 38 M 22
Whittlebury 28 R 27
Whittlesey 29 T 26
Whitton (Powys) 25 K 27
Whitton (Suffolk) 23 X 27
Whittonstall 46 O 19
Whitwell (Derbs.) 36 Q 24
Whitwell (I.O.W.) 10 Q 32
Whitwell-on-the-Hill 40 R 21
Whitwick 27 P 25
Whitworth 39 N 23
Wiay (Highland) 65 A 11
Wiay (Western Isles) 64 Y 11
Wick (South Glos.) 17 M 29
Wick (Highland) 74 K 8
Wicken (Cambs.) 28 R 27
Wicken (Northants.) 30 U 27
Wickenby 37 S 24
Wickford 21 V 29
Wickham 10 Q 31
Wickhambrook 22 V 27
Wickham Market 23 Y 27
Wickwar 17 M 29
Widecombe-in-the-Moor 4 I 32
Wideford Hill Cairn 74 K 7
Widford 20 U 28
Widnes 34 L 23
Wigan 34 M 23
Wiggenhall St. Mary Magdalen 30 V 25
Wight (Isle of) (County) 9 P 32
Wigmore 21 V 29
Wigston 28 Q 26
Wigton 44 K 19
Wigtown 42 G 19
Wigtown Bay 43 H 19
Wilberfoss 40 R 22
Wilcot 18 O 29
Wild Animal Kingdom 19 S 28
Willand 7 J 31

Willenhall	27	N 26
Willerby	41	S 22
Willersey	27	O 27
Willingdon	11	U 31
Willingham	29	U 27
Willingham Forest	37	T 23
Willington (Beds.)	29	S 27
Willington (Derbs.)	35	P 25
Willington (Durham)	46	O 19
Williton	7	K 30
Wilmcote	27	O 27
Wilmington (East Essex)	11	U 31
Wilmington (Kent)	20	U 29
Wilmslow	34	N 24
Wilton	9	O 30
Wiltshire (County)	9	O 30
Wimbledon	20	T 29
Wimblington	29	U 26
Wimborne Minster	9	O 31
Wimborne St. Giles	9	O 31
Wincanton	8	M 30
Winchcombe	18	O 28
Winchelsea	12	W 31
Winchester	10	P 30
Windermere	45	L 20
Windlesham	19	S 29
Windrush	18	O 28
Windrush (River)	18	O 28
Windsor	19	S 29
Windsor Great Park	19	S 29
Windygates	56	K 15
Winfarthing	31	X 26
Winforton	25	K 27
Winfrith Newburgh	8	N 32
Wing	19	R 28
Wingate	46	P 19
Wingfield	35	P 24
Wingham	13	X 30
Wingrave	19	R 28
Winkfield	19	R 29
Winkleigh	6	I 31
Winnersh	19	R 29
Winscombe	17	L 30
Winsford (Cheshire)	34	M 24
Winsford (Somerset)	7	J 30
Winshill	35	P 25
Winslow	19	R 28
Winster	35	P 24
Winterborne Kingston	8	N 31
Winterborne Stickland	8	N 31
Winterborne Whitechurch	8	N 31
Winterbourne	17	M 29
Winterbourne Abbas	8	M 31
Winterbourne Stoke	9	O 30
Winteringham	41	S 22
Winterton	41	S 23
Winterton-on-Sea	31	Z 25
Winton	45	N 20
Winwick	29	S 26
Wirksworth	35	P 24
Wirral	34	K 24
Wisbech	29	U 25
Wisborough Green	10	S 30
Wishaw	55	I 16
Wisley	20	S 30
Wissey (River)	30	V 26
Witchford	29	U 26
Witham	22	V 28
Witham (River)	37	T 24
Witheridge	7	I 31
Withernsea	41	U 22
Withington	18	O 28
Withycombe	4	J 32
Withypool	7	J 30
Witley	10	S 30
Witney	18	P 28
Wittering	28	S 26
Wittersham	12	W 30
Wiveliscombe	7	K 30
Wivenhoe	22	W 28
Woburn	19	S 28
Woburn Abbey	19	S 28
Woburn Sands	19	S 27
Woking	19	S 30
Wokingham	19	R 29
Woldingham	20	T 30
Wollaston	28	S 27
Wollaton Hall	36	Q 25
Wolsingham	46	O 19
Wolvercote	19	Q 28
Wolverhampton	27	N 26
Wolverton	28	R 27
Wolviston	46	Q 20
Wombourn	27	N 26
Wombwell	40	P 23
Womersley	40	Q 22
Wonersh	10	S 30
Wood Dalling	31	X 25
Woodbridge	23	X 27
Woodbury	7	J 31
Woodchurch	12	W 30
Woodcote	19	Q 29
Woodford Halse	28	Q 27
Woodhall Spa	37	T 24
Woodham Ferrers	21	V 29
Woodingdean	11	T 31
Woodnesborough	13	X 30
Woodseaves	34	N 25
Woodstock	18	P 28
Woodton	31	Y 26
Woody Bay	6	I 30
Wookey Hole	8	L 30
Wool	8	N 31
Woolacombe	6	H 30
Wooler	51	N 17
Woolfardisworthy	6	G 31
Woolpit	23	X 27
Woolsthorpe	36	R 25
Woore	34	M 25
Wootton Bassett	18	O 29
Wootton Courtenay	7	J 30
Wootton-Wawen	27	O 27
Worcester	26	N 27
Worcester (County)	26	N 27
Workington	44	J 20
Worksop	36	Q 24
Worle	17	L 29
Wormit	56	L 14
Worms Head	15	H 29
Worplesdon	10	S 30
Worsbrough	40	P 23
Worsley	34	M 23
Worthen	26	L 26
Worthing	11	S 31
Wortwell	31	Y 26
Wotton-under-Edge	17	M 29
Wragby	37	T 24
Wrangle	37	U 24
Wrawby	41	S 23
Wray	38	M 21
Wrea Green	38	L 22
Wrecsam / Wrexham	34	L 24
Wremtham	31	Z 26
Wrexham / Wrecsam	34	L 24
Wrington	17	L 29
Writtle	22	V 28
Wrotham	20	U 30
Wroughton	18	O 29
Wroxham	31	Y 25
Wroxton	27	P 27
Wyche	26	M 27
Wye	12	W 30
Wye (River)	17	M 28
Wylam	51	O 19
Wylye	9	O 30
Wymondham (Leics.)	36	R 25
Wymondham (Norfolk)	31	X 26
Wyre	74	L 6
Y		
Y-Fenni / Abergavenny	17	L 28
Y Ffor	32	G 25
Y Llethr	32	I 25
Yafforth	46	P 20
Yalding	12	V 30
Yapton	10	S 31
Yardley Hastings	28	R 27
Yare (River)	30	W 26
Yarm	46	P 20
Yarmouth	9	P 31
Yate	17	M 29
Yateley	19	R 29
Yatton	17	L 29
Yaxham	30	W 26
Yaxley	29	T 26
Yeadon	39	O 22
Yealmpton	4	I 32
Yedingham	41	S 21
Yell	75	Q 1
Yelverton	4	H 32
Yeolmbridge	3	G 32
Yeovil	8	M 31
Yesnaby	74	J 6
Yetminster	8	M 31
Yetts o' Muckhart	56	J 15
Ynys / Lochtyn	24	G 27
York	40	Q 22
Yorkletts	13	X 30
Yorkley	17	M 28
Yorkshire Dales National Park	45	N 21
Yorkshire Wolds	41	S 21
Youlgreave	35	O 24
Yoxall	35	O 25
Yoxford	23	Y 27
Yr Wyddgrug / Mold	33	K 24
Ysbyty Ifan	33	I 24
Ystalyfera	15	I 28
Ystrad-Aeron	24	H 27
Ystradgynlais	15	I 28
Ystwyth (River)	24	H 26

Ireland

A

Abbeydorney 83 C 10
Abbeyfeale 83 E 10
Abbeylara 92 J 6
Abbeyleix / Mainistir Laoise 85 J 9
Achill Head 94 B 6
Achill Island 94 B 6
Achill Sound / Gob an Choire 94 C 6
Achillbeg Island 94 C 6
Aclare 95 F 5
Acoose (Lough) 76 C 11
Adamstown 80 L 10
Adare 84 F 10
Adrigole 76 C 12
Aghaboe 85 J 9
Aghabullogue 78 F 12
Aghada 78 H 12
Aghalee 99 N 4
Aghavannagh 87 M 9
Aghaville 77 D 13
Aghla Mountain 100 H 3
Aglish 79 I 11
Ahakista 77 D 13
Ahalia (Loughs) 88 D 7
Ahascragh 90 G 7
Ahenny 85 J 10
Aherlow (Glen of) 84 H 10
Ahoghill 102 M 3
Aillwee Cave 89 E 8
Ailt an Chorráin / Burtonport 100 G 3
Aird Mhór / Ardmore 79 I 12
Allen (Bog of) 86 K 8
Allen (Lough) 96 H 5
Allenwood 86 L 8
Allihies 76 B 13
Allua (Lough) 77 E 12
Altan Lough 100 H 2
An Blascaod Mór / Blasket Islands 82 A 11
An Bun Beag / Bunbeg 100 H 2
An Cabhán / Cavan 97 J 6
An Caiseal / Cashel (Galway) 88 C 7
An Caisleán Nua / Newcastle West 83 E 10
An Caisleán Riabhach / Castlerea 96 G 6
An Charraig / Carrick 100 G 4
An Chathair / Caher 85 I 10
An Cheathrú Rua / Carraroe 88 D 8
An Chloich Mhóir / Cloghmore 94 C 6
An Clochán / Clifden 88 B 7
An Clochán / Cloghan (Donegal) 100 I 3
An Clochán Liath / Dunglow 100 G 3
An Cloigeann / Cleegan 88 B 7
An Cóbh / Cobh 78 H 12
An Coimín / Commeen 100 I 3
An Coireán / Waterville 76 B 12
An Corrán / Currane 94 C 6
An Creagán / Mount Bellew 90 G 7
An Daingean / Dingle 82 B 11
An Droichead Nua / Newbridge 86 L 8
An Dúchoraidh / Doocharry 100 H 3
An Fál Carrach / Falcarragh 100 H 2
An Fhairche / Clonbur 89 D 7
An Geata Mór 94 B 5
An Gleann Garbh / Glengarriff 77 D 12
An Gort / Gort 89 F 8
An Gort Mór / Gortmore 88 D 7
An Leacht / Lahinch 89 D 9
An Longfort / Longford 90 I 6
An Mám / Maam Cross 88 D 7
An Mhala Raithní / Mulrany 94 C 6
An Móta / Moate 90 I 7
An Muileann gCearr / Mullingar 92 J 7
An Nás / Naas 87 M 8
An Ráth / Charleville 84 F 10
An Ráth / Rath Luirc (Charleville) 84 F 10
An Ros / Rush 93 N 7
An Scairbh / Scarriff 84 G 9
An Sciobairín / Skibbereen 77 E 13
An Seanchaisleán / Oldcastle 92 K 6
An Spidéal / Spiddal 89 E 8
An tAonach / Nenagh 84 H 9
An Teampall Mór / Templemore 85 I 9
An Tearmann / Termon 101 I 2
An tInbhear Mór / Arklow 81 N 9
An tSraith / Srah 95 E 6
An Tulach / Tullow 80 L 9
An Uaimh / Navan 93 L 7
Anascaul 82 B 11
Annacarriga 84 G 9
Annacotty 84 G 9
Annagary 100 H 2
Annagassan 93 M 6
Annageeragh (River) 83 D 9
Annagh Head 94 B 5
Annaghdown 89 E 7
Annaghmore Lough 90 H 6
Annalee 97 J 5
Annalong 99 O 5
Annamoe 87 N 8
Annestown 80 K 11
Antrim 103 N 3
Antrim (County) 102 M 3
Antrim Coast 75 O 2
Antrim (Glens of) 103 N 2
Antrim Mountains 103 N 2
Anure (Lough) 100 H 3
Araglin 78 H 11
Árainn Mhór / Aran or Aranmore Island 100 G 2
Árainn (Oiléáin) / Aran Islands 88 C 8
Aran Islands / Oileáin Árainn 88 C 8
Aran or Aranmore Island / Árainn Mhór 100 G 2
Archdale (Castle) 97 I 4
Ardagh 83 E 10
Ardara 100 G 3
Ardboe 98 M 4
Ardcath 93 M 7
Ardcrony 84 H 9
Ardea 76 C 12
Ardee / Baile Átha Fhirdhia 93 M 6
Ardfert 82 C 11
Ardfinnan 79 I 11
Ardglass 75 P 5
Ardgroom 76 C 12
Ardkeen 75 P 4
Ardmore / Aird Mhór 79 I 12
Ardrahan 89 F 8
Ardress House 98 M 4
Ards Forest Park 101 I 2
Ards Peninsula 75 P 4
Argideen 77 F 13
Argory (The) 98 M 4
Arigna 96 H 5
Arklow / An tInbhear Mór 81 N 9
Armagh 98 M 4
Armagh (County) 74 L 5
Armoy 103 N 2
Arney 97 I 5
Arrow (Lough) 96 H 5
Arthurstown 80 L 11
Arvagh 97 J 6
Ashbourne 93 M 7
Ashford 87 N 8
Ashford Castle 89 E 7
Askeaton 83 F 10
Astee 83 D 10
Áth Cinn / Headford 89 E 7
Athassel Abbey 85 I 10
Athboy 92 L 7
Athea 83 E 10
Athenry / Baile Átha an Rí 89 F 8
Athleague 90 H 7
Athlone / Baile Átha Luain 90 I 7
Athy / Baile Átha Í 86 L 9
Attymon 89 G 8
Audley's Castle 75 P 4
Augher 97 K 4
Aughils 82 C 11
Aughnacloy 98 L 4
Aughnanure Castle 89 E 7
Aughrim (Galway) 90 H 8
Aughrim (Wicklow) 87 N 9
Aughris Head 95 F 5
Avoca 87 N 9
Avoca (River) 81 N 9
Avoca (Valle of) 87 N 9
Avonbeg 87 M 9
Avondale Forest Park 87 N 9

B

Bagenalstown / Muine Bheag 80 L 9
Baile an Fheirtéaraigh / Ballyferriter 82 A 11
Baile an Mhóta / Ballymote 96 G 5
Baile an Róba / Ballinrobe 89 E 7
Baile an Sceilg / Ballinskelligs 76 B 12
Baile Átha an Rí / Athenry 89 F 8
Baile Átha Cliath / Dublin 87 N 8
Baile Átha Fhirdhia / Ardee 93 M 6
Baile Átha Í / Athy 86 L 9
Baile Átha Luain / Athlone 90 I 7
Baile Átha Troim / Trim 93 L 7
Baile Bhuirne / Ballyvourney 77 E 12
Baile Brigín / Balbriggan 93 N 7
Baile Chláir / Claregalway 89 F 7
Baile Locha Riach / Loughrea 90 G 8
Baile Mhic Andáin / Thomastown 80 K 10
Baile Mhic Íre / Ballymakeery 77 E 12
Baile Mhistéala / Mitchelstown 78 H 11
Baile na Finne / Fintown 100 H 3
Baile na Lorgan / Castleblayney 98 L 5
Baile Uí Fhiacháin / Newport 95 D 6
Baile Uí Mhatháin / Ballymahon 90 I 7
Bailieborough / Coill an Chollaigh 92 L 6
Balbriggan / Baile Brigín 93 N 7
Baldoyle 93 N 7
Balla 95 E 6
Ballagan Point 99 N 5
Ballaghaderreen / Bealach an Doirín 96 G 6
Ballaghbeama Gap 76 C 12
Ballaghisheen Pass 76 C 12
Ballina / Béal an Átha 95 E 5
Ballina (Tipperary) 84 G 9
Ballinaboy 88 B 7
Ballinadee 78 G 12
Ballinafad 96 G 5
Ballinagar 86 J 8

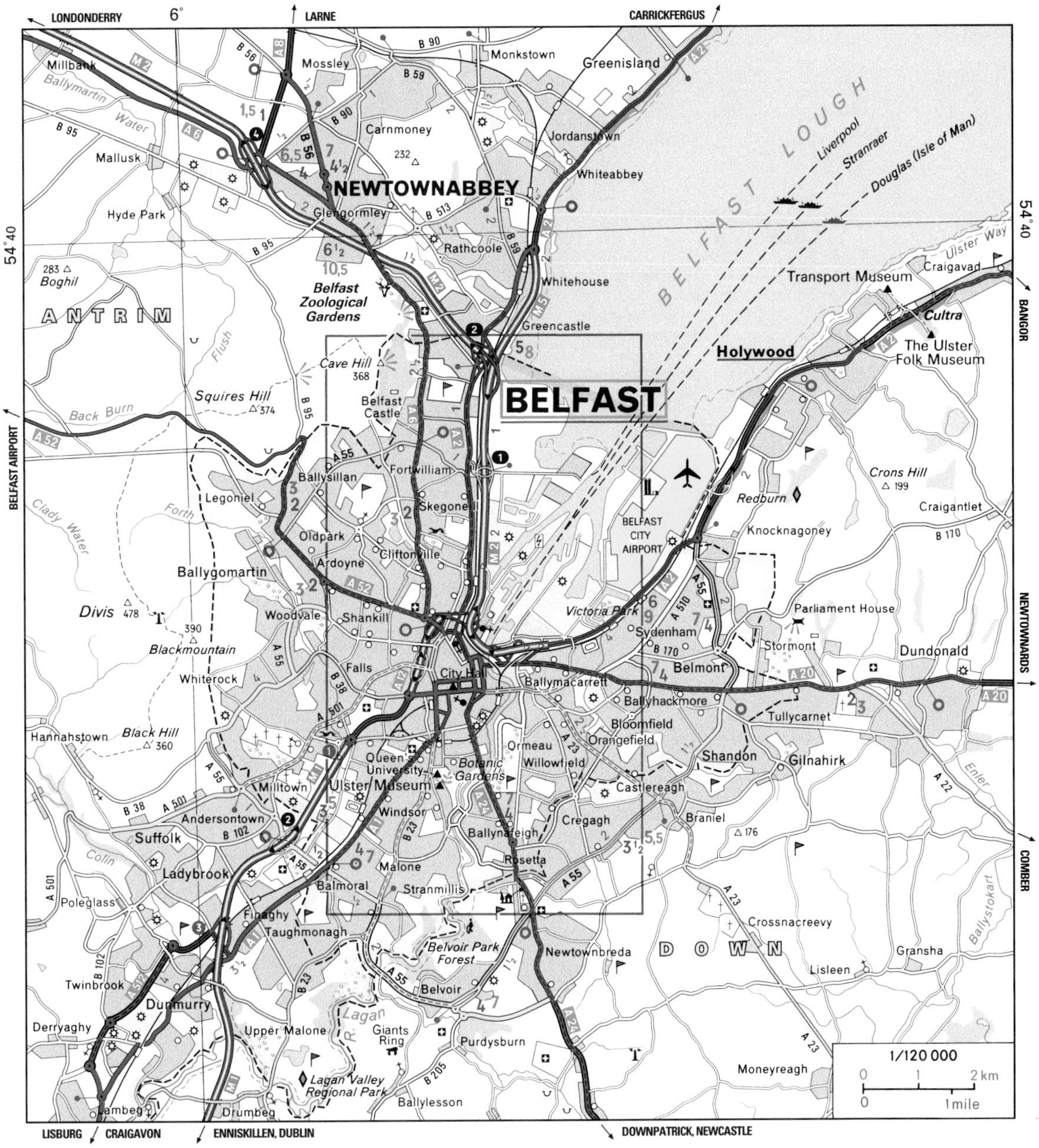
LONDONDERRY
LARNE
CARRICKFERGUS
BANGOR
NEWTOWNARDS
COMBER
DOWNPATRICK, NEWCASTLE
ENNISKILLEN, DUBLIN
LISBURG / CRAIGAVON
BELFAST AIRPORT
BELFAST
NEWTOWNABBEY
BELFAST LOUGH
ANTRIM
DOWN
Holywood
Greenisland
Monkstown
Carnmoney
Jordanstown
Whiteabbey
Glengormley
Rathcoole
Whitehouse
Greencastle
Mossley
Millbank
Mallusk
Hyde Park
Belfast Zoological Gardens
Cave Hill
Belfast Castle
Squires Hill
Ballysillan
Legoniel
Fortwilliam
Skegoneill
Oldpark
Cliftonville
Ardoyne
Ballygomartin
Divis
Black Mountain
Woodvale
Shankill
Whiterock
Falls
City Hall
Ballymacarrett
Ballyhackmore
Bloomfield
Orangefield
Ormeau
Willowfield
Queen's University
Botanic Gardens
Ulster Museum
Milltown
Andersonstown
Suffolk
Ladybrook
Windsor
Ballynafeigh
Cregagh
Castlereagh
Braniel
Malone
Stranmillis
Rosetta
Balmoral
Finaghy
Taughmonagh
Belvoir Park Forest
Newtownbreda
Belvoir
Purdysburn
Upper Malone
Giants Ring
Lagan Valley Regional Park
Ballylesson
Drumbeg
Lambeg
Derryaghy
Twinbrook
Dunmurry
Poleglass
Hannahstown
Black Hill
Victoria Park
Sydenham
Belmont
Stormont
Parliament House
Dundonald
Tullycarnet
Shandon
Gilnahirk
Knocknagoney
Redburn
Crons Hill
Craigantlet
Crossnacreevy
Gransha
Lisleen
Moneyreagh
Transport Museum
Craigavad
Cultra
The Ulster Folk Museum
BELFAST CITY AIRPORT
Liverpool
Stranraer
Douglas (Isle of Man)
1/120 000
2 km
1 mile

BELFAST

Albert Square . . . . . BY 3
Ann Street . . . . . BZ 5
Bridge Street . . . . . BZ 12
Castlecourt Shopping Centre BYZ
Castle Place . . . . . BZ
Clifton Street . . . . . BY 15
Corporation Square . . . . . BY 16
Donegal Place . . . . . BZ
Donegall Quay . . . . . BYZ 19
Donegall Square . . . . . BZ 20
Great Victoria Street . . . . . BZ 26
High Street . . . . . BYZ 28
Howard Street . . . . . BZ 29
Lagan Bridge . . . . . BY 32
Queen Elizabeth Bridge . . . . . BZ 40
Queen's Bridge . . . . . BZ 41
Queen's Square . . . . . BYZ 42
Rosemary Street . . . . . BZ 44
Royal Avenue . . . . . BYZ
Waring Street . . . . . BY 54
Wellington Place . . . . . BZ 55

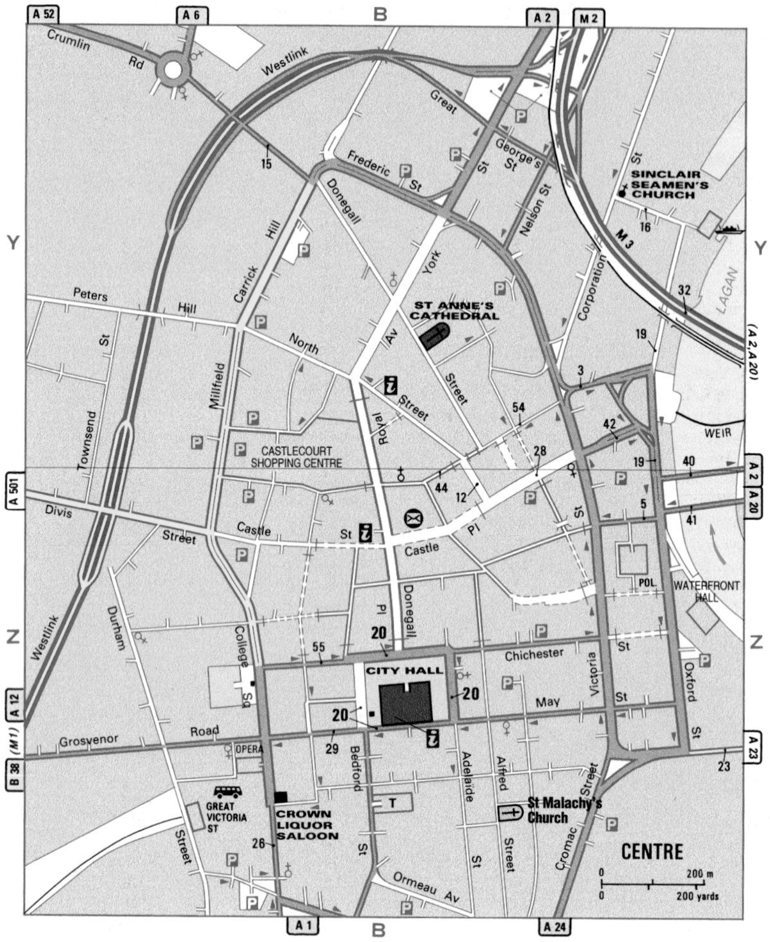

Ballinakill 86 K 9
Ballinalack 92 J 7
Ballinalea 87 N 8
Ballinalee 92 J 6
Ballinamallard 97 J 4
Ballinamore / Béal an Átha Mhóir 97 I 5
Ballinamore Bridge 90 G 7
Ballinascarty 77 F 12
Ballinasloe / Béal Átha na Sluaighe 90 H 8
Ballincollig 78 G 12
Ballincrea 80 K 11
Ballincurrig 78 H 12
Ballindarragh 74 J 5
Ballinderry 84 H 8
Ballindine 95 F 6
Ballineen 77 F 12
Ballingarry (Galway) 85 H 8
Ballingarry (Limerick) 84 F 10
Ballingarry (Tipperary) 85 J 10
Ballingeary / Béal Átha an Ghaorthaidh 77 E 12
Ballinhassig 78 G 12
Ballinlough 90 G 6
Ballinrobe / Baile an Róba 89 E 7
Ballinskelligs / Baile an Sceilg 76 B 12
Ballinskelligs Bay 76 B 12
Ballinspittle 78 G 12
Ballintober (Roscommon) 90 G 6
Ballintogher 96 G 5
Ballintoy 102 M 2
Ballintra 100 H 4
Ballinure 85 I 10
Ballitore 86 L 8
Ballivor 92 L 7
Ballon 80 L 9
Ballyagran 84 F 10
Ballybay 98 L 5
Ballybofey / Bealach Féich 101 I 3
Ballyboghil 93 N 7
Ballyboy 90 I 8
Ballybrittas 86 K 8
Ballybrophy 85 J 9
Ballybunnion 83 D 10
Ballycanew 81 N 10
Ballycarney 81 M 10
Ballycastle (Antrim) 103 N 2
Ballycastle (Mayo) 95 D 5
Ballycastle Bay 103 N 2
Ballyclare (Antrim) 103 N 3
Ballyclare (Roscommon) 90 I 6
Ballyclough 78 F 11
Ballycolla 85 J 9
Ballyconneely 88 B 7
Ballyconneely Bay 88 B 7
Ballyconnell 97 J 5
Ballycopeland 75 P 4
Ballycotton 78 H 12
Ballycotton Bay 78 H 12
Ballycroy 94 C 5
Ballydavid 82 A 11
Ballydavid Head 82 A 11
Ballydavis 86 K 8
Ballydehob 77 D 13
Ballydesmond 83 E 11
Ballydonegan 76 B 13
Ballyduff (Dingle) 82 B 11
Ballyduff (Kerry) 83 D 10
Ballyduff (Waterford) 78 H 11
Ballyeighter Loughs 89 F 9
Ballyfarnan 96 H 5
Ballyferriter / Baile an Fheirtéaraigh 82 A 11
Ballyforan 90 H 7
Ballygalley 75 O 3
Ballygalley Head 75 O 3
Ballygar 90 H 7
Ballygawley (Sligo) 96 G 5
Ballygawley (Tyrone) 97 K 4
Ballygorman 102 K 1
Ballygowan (near Belfast) 99 O 4
Ballyhack 80 L 11
Ballyhahill 83 E 10
Ballyhaise 97 K 5
Ballyhalbert 75 P 4
Ballyhale 80 K 10
Ballyhaunis / Béal Átha hAmhnais 95 F 6
Ballyhean 95 E 6
Ballyheige 82 C 10
Ballyheige Bay 82 C 10
Ballyhoe Lough 93 L 6
Ballyhooly 78 G 11
Ballyhoura Mountains 78 G 11
Ballyjamesduff 92 K 6
Ballykeeran 90 I 7
Ballykelly 102 K 2
Ballylanders 84 G 10
Ballylickey 77 D 12
Ballyliffin 101 J 2
Ballylongford 83 D 10
Ballylongford Bay 83 D 10
Ballylynan 86 K 9
Ballymacarbry 79 I 11
Ballymacoda 79 I 12
Ballymagorry 101 J 3
Ballymahon / Baile Uí Mhatháin 90 I 7
Ballymakeery / Baile Mhic Íre 77 E 12
Ballymartin 99 O 5
Ballymena 103 N 3
Ballymoe 90 G 6
Ballymoney (Antrim) 102 M 2
Ballymore 91 I 7
Ballymore Eustace 87 M 8
Ballymote / Baile an Mhóta 96 G 5
Ballymurphy 80 L 10
Ballynabola 80 L 10
Ballynacarrigy 92 J 7
Ballynacorra 78 H 12
Ballynagore 92 J 7
Ballynagree 77 F 12
Ballynahinch 99 O 4
Ballynahinch Lake 88 C 7
Ballynahown 88 D 8
Ballynakill Harbour 88 B 7
Ballyneety 84 G 10
Ballynoe 78 H 11
Ballynure 75 O 3
Ballyorgan 84 G 11
Ballypatrick 85 J 10
Ballyporeen 78 H 11
Ballyquintin Point 75 P 5
Ballyragget 85 J 9
Ballyroan 86 K 9
Ballyronan 102 M 3
Ballyroney 99 N 5
Ballysadare 96 G 5
Ballyshannon / Béal Átha Seanaidh 96 H 4
Ballysteen 83 F 10
Ballyteige Bay 80 L 11
Ballyvaughan 89 E 8
Ballyvaughan Bay 89 E 8
Ballyvourney / Baile Bhuirne 77 E 12
Ballywalter 75 P 4
Ballywilliam 80 L 10
Balrath 93 M 7
Baltimore 77 D 13
Baltinglass / Bealach Conglais 87 L 9
Baltray 93 N 6
Banagher 90 I 8
Banbridge 99 N 4
Bandon / Droichead na Bandan 78 F 12
Bandon River 77 F 12
Bangor (Down) 99 O 4
Bangor (Mayo) 94 C 5
Bann (River) (Lough Neagh) 99 N 5
Bann (River) (R. Slaney) 81 M 10
Banna Strand 82 C 11
Bannow 80 L 11
Bansha 84 H 10
Banteer 77 F 11
Bantry / Beanntrai 77 D 12
Bantry Bay 76 C 13
Barefield 84 F 9
Barley Cove 76 C 13
Barna / Bearna 89 E 8
Barnaderg 89 F 7
Barnatra / Barr na Trá 94 C 5
Barnesmore Gap 100 I 3
Baronscourt Forest 101 J 3
Barra (Lough) 100 H 3
Barraduff 77 D 11
Barr na Trá / Barnatra 94 C 5
Barrow (River) 86 J 8
Barrow Harbour 82 C 11
Barrow (River) 86 K 8
Beagh (Lough) 100 I 2
Béal an Átha / Ballina 95 E 5
Béal an Átha Mhóir / Ballinamore 97 I 5
Béal an Mhuirthead / Belmullet 94 C 5
Béal Átha an Ghaorthaidh / Ballingeary 77 E 12
Béal Átha hAmhnais / Ballyhaunis 95 F 6
Béal Átha na Muice / Swinford 95 F 6
Béal Átha na Sluaighe / Ballinasloe 90 H 8
Béal Átha Seanaidh / Ballyshannon 96 H 4
Béal Deirg / Belderrig 95 D 5
Béal Tairbirt / Belturbet 97 J 5
Bealach an Doirín / Ballaghaderreen 96 G 6
Bealach Conglais / Baltinglass 87 L 9
Bealach Féich / Ballybofey 101 I 3
Bealaclugga 89 E 8
Bealadangan 88 D 8
Bealaha 83 D 9
Beanntraí / Bantry 77 D 12
Beara 76 C 12
Bearna / Barna 89 E 8
Beaufort 77 D 11
Beehive Huts 82 A 11
Beenoskee 82 B 11
Beg (Lough) 102 M 3
Behy 76 C 11
Belcarra 95 E 6
Belclare 89 F 7
Belcoo 97 I 5
Belderrig / Béal Deirg 95 D 5
Belfast 99 O 4
Belfast Lough 75 O 3
Belgooly 78 G 12
Belhavel Lough 96 H 5
Bellacorick 95 D 5
Bellaghy 102 M 3
Bellanagare 96 G 6
Bellanaleck 74 J 5
Bellananagh 97 J 6
Bellavary 95 E 6
Belleek (Armagh) 74 M 5
Belleek (Fermanagh) 96 H 4
Belmullet / Béal an Mhuirthead 94 C 5
Beltra 95 D 6
Beltra Lough 95 D 6
Belturbet / Béal Tairbirt 97 J 5
Benbane Head 102 M 2
Benbrack 96 I 5
Benbulben 96 G 4
Benburb 98 L 4
Bencroy or Gubnaveagh 96 I 5
Benmore or Fair Head 103 N 2
Benettsbridge 80 K 10
Benwee Head 94 C 4
Beragh 97 K 4
Bere Island 76 C 13
Bernish Rock 74 M 5
Bertraghboy Bay 88 C 7
Bessbrook 74 M 5
Bettystown 93 N 6
Binevenagh 102 L 2
Binn Éadair / Howth 93 N 7
Biorra / Birr 90 I 8
Birdhill 84 G 9
Birr / Biorra 90 I 8
Black Head (Antrim) 75 O 3
Black Head (Clare) 89 E 8
Black Ball Head 76 B 13
Black Bull 93 M 7
Black Gap (The) 100 I 4
Blacklion 96 I 5
Blackrock 87 N 8
Blackrock (Louth) 93 M 6
Blacksod Bay 94 B 5
Blacksod Point 94 B 5
Blackstairs Mountains 80 L 10
Blackwater 81 M 10
Blackwater Bridge 76 C 12
Blackwater (River) (Cork) 77 F 11
Blackwater (River) (Lough Neagh) 98 L 4
Blackwater (River) (R. Boyne) 93 L 6
Blarney 78 G 12
Blasket Islands / An Blascaod Mór 82 A 11
Blennerville 83 C 11
Blessington 87 M 8
Bloody Foreland 100 H 2
Blue Ball 86 J 8
Blue Stack Mountains 100 H 3
Boderg (Lough) 96 I 6
Bodyke 84 G 9
Bofin (Lough) (Galway) 89 D 7
Bofin (Lough) (Roscommon) 96 I 6
Boggeragh Mountains 77 E 12
Boheraphuca 84 I 8
Boherbue 77 E 11
Bohermeen 93 L 7
Bola (Lough) 88 C 7
Boley 86 L 8
Boliska Lough 89 E 8
Bolus Head 76 A 12
Bonet 96 H 5
Boobyglass 80 K 10
Borris 80 L 10
Borris in Ossory 85 J 9
Borrisokane / Buiríos Uí Chéin 84 H 9
Borrisoleigh 85 I 9
Bouladuff 85 I 9
Boyle / Mainistir na Búille 96 H 6
Boyle (River) 96 H 6
Boyne (River) 92 K 7
Bracklin 92 K 7
Brandon / Cé Bhréanainn 82 B 11
Brandon Bay 82 B 11
Brandon Head 82 B 11
Brandon Hill 80 L 10
Bray / Bré 87 N 8
Bray Head (Kerry) 76 A 12
Bray Head (Wicklow) 87 N 8
Bré / Bray 87 N 8
Breenagh 101 I 3
Bride (River) 79 I 11
Bridebridge 78 H 11
Bridge End 101 J 2
Bridgeland 81 M 9
Bridget Lough 84 G 9
Bridgetown 81 M 11
Briensbridge 84 G 9
Brinlack / Bun na Leaca 100 H 2
Brittas 87 M 8
Brittas Bay 87 N 9
Broad Haven 94 C 5
Broad Meadow 93 N 7
Broadford (Clare) 84 G 9
Broadford (Limerick) 83 F 10
Broadway 81 M 11
Brookeborough 74 J 5
Brosna 83 E 11
Brosna (River) 90 I 8
Broughshane 103 N 3
Brow Head 76 C 13
Brown Flesk 83 D 11
Brownstown Head 80 K 11
Bruff 84 G 10
Bruree 84 G 10
Buckode 96 H 4
Buiríos Uí Chéin / Borrisokane 84 H 9
Bull Point 103 N 2
Bull's Head 82 B 11
Bullaun 90 G 8
Bun an Phobail / Moville 102 K 2
Bun Cranncha / Buncrana 101 J 2
Bun Dobhráin / Bundoran 96 H 4
Bun na hAbhna / Bunnahowen 94 C 5
Bun na Leaca / Brinlack 100 H 2
Bunacurry 94 C 6
Bunbeg / An Bun Beag 100 H 2
Bunclody 81 M 10
Buncrana / Bun Cranncha 101 J 2
Bundoran / Bun Dobhráin 96 H 4
Bunmahon 79 J 11
Bunnahowen / Bun na hAbhna 94 C 5
Bunnanaddan 96 G 5
Bunny (Lough) 89 F 8
Bunnyconnellan 95 E 5
Bunowen 94 C 6
Bunratty 84 F 9
Burncourt 78 H 11
Burnfort 78 G 11
Burren (The) 89 E 8
Burrishoole Abbey 95 D 6
Burtonport / Ailt an Chorráin 100 G 3
Bush 102 M 2
Bushfield 84 G 9
Bushmills 102 M 2
Butler's Bridge 97 J 5
Butlerstown 78 F 13
Buttevant 78 F 11
Bweeng 78 F 11

C

Caha Mountains 76 C 12
Caharagh 77 E 13
Caher / An Chathair 85 I 10
Caher Island 94 B 6
Caherbarnagh 77 E 11
Caherconlish 84 G 10
Caherdaniel 76 B 12
Cahersiveen / Cathair Saidhbhín 76 B 12
Cahore Point 81 N 10
Caiseal / Cashel (Tipperary) 85 I 10
Caisleán an Bharraigh / Castlebar 95 E 6
Caisleán an Chomair / Castlecomer 86 K 9
Calafort Ros Láir / Rosslare Harbour 81 M 11
Caledon 98 L 4
Callainn / Callan 85 J 10
Callan / Callainn 85 J 10

Caltra 90 G 7
Camlough 74 M 5
Camolin 81 M 10
Camp 82 C 11
Campile 80 L 11
Canglass Point 76 B 12
Canningstown 97 K 6
Cappagh White 84 H 10
Cappamore 84 G 10
Cappoquin / Ceapach Choinn 79 I 11
Car (Slieve) 94 D 5
Caragh (Lough) 76 C 11
Caragh (River) 76 C 12
Carbery's Hundred Isles 77 D 13
Carbury 92 L 7
Carhan House 76 B 12
Cark Mountain 101 I 3
Carlanstown 92 L 6
Carlingford 99 N 5
Carlingford Lough 99 N 5
Carlow / Ceatharlach 86 L 9
Carlow (County) 80 L 9
Carn Domhnach / Carndonagh 102 K 2
Carna 88 C 8
Carncastle 75 O 3
Carndonagh / Carn Domhnach 102 K 2
Carne 81 M 11
Carnew 81 M 9
Carney 96 G 4
Carnlough 75 O 3
Carnlough Bay 75 O 3
Carnsore Point 81 M 11
Carra (Lough) 95 E 6
Carraig Airt / Carrigart 101 I 2
Carraig Mhachaire Rois / Carrickmacross 98 L 6
Carraig na Siúire / Carrick-on-Suir 79 J 10
Carran 89 E 8
Carrantuohill 76 C 11
Carraroe / An Cheathrú Rua 88 D 8
Carrick-a-Rede Rope Bridge 102 M 2
Carrick / An Charraig (Donegal) 100 G 4
Carrick (Wexford) 80 L 11
Carrick-on-Shannon-Cora Droma Rúisc 96 H 6
Carrick-on-Suir / Carraig na Siúire 79 J 10
Carrickboy 91 I 7
Carrickfergus 75 O 3
Carrickmacross / Carraig Mhachaire Rois 98 L 6
Carrickmore 97 K 4
Carrigafoyle Castle 83 D 10
Carrigaholt 83 C 10
Carrigaline 78 G 12
Carrigallen 97 J 6
Carriganimmy 77 E 12
Carrigans 101 J 3
Carrigart / Carraig Airt 101 I 2
Carrigglass Manor 92 I 6
Carrigkerry 83 E 10
Carrigtohill 78 H 12
Carrowkeel 101 J 2
Carrowmore 96 G 5
Carrowmore Lake 94 C 5
Carrownisky 94 C 6
Carrowteige / Ceathrú Thaidhg 94 C 5
Carrybeg 79 J 10
Carryduff 99 O 4
Cashel / An Caiseal (Galway) 88 C 7
Cashel / Caiseal (Tipperary) 85 I 10
Cashel (Rock of) 85 I 10
Cashen River 83 D 10
Cashla Bay 88 D 8
Casla / Costelloe 88 D 8
Castle Coole 97 J 4
Castle Espie Centre 99 O 4
Castle Gardens 78 F 13
Castle Haven 77 E 13
Castle Point 83 C 10
Castlebaldwin 96 G 5
Castlebar / Caisleán an Bharraigh 95 E 6
Castlebellingham 93 M 6
Castleblakeney 90 G 7
Castleblayney / Baile na Lorgan 98 L 5
Castlebridge 81 M 10
Castlecaulfield 98 L 4
Castlecomer / Caisleán an Chomair 86 K 9
Castleconnell 84 G 9
Castlecove 76 B 12
Castledawson 102 M 3
Castlederg 101 J 3
Castledermot 86 L 9
Castlefinn 101 J 3
Castlefreke 77 F 13
Castlegal 96 G 4
Castlegregory 82 B 11
Castlehill 94 C 6
Castleisland / Oileán Ciarraí 83 D 11
Castlelyons 78 H 11
Castlemaine 83 C 11
Castlemaine Harbour 82 C 11
Castlemartyr 78 H 12
Castleplunket 90 G 6
Casltepollard 92 K 6
Castlerea / An Caisleán Riabhach 90 G 6
Castlerock 102 L 2
Castletown (Laois) 85 J 9
Castletown (Westmeath) 92 J 7
Castletown (Wexford) 81 N 9
Castletownbere 76 C 13
Castletownroche 78 G 11
Castletownshend 77 E 13
Castleward House 75 P 4
Castlewellan 99 O 5
Castlewellan Forest Park 99 O 5
Cathair na Mart / Westport 95 D 6
Cathair Saidhbhín / Cahersiveen 76 B 12
Causeway 83 C 10
Cavan / An Cabhán 97 J 6
Cavan (County) 92 J 6
Cé Bhréanainn / Brandon 82 B 11
Ceanannas / Ceanannus Mór (Kells) 92 L 6
Ceanannus Mór (Kells) / Ceanannas 92 L 6
Ceann Toirc / Kanturk 77 F 11
Ceapach Choinn / Cappoquin 79 I 11
Ceatharlach / Carlow 86 L 9
Ceathrú Thaidhg / Carrowteige 94 C 5
Cecilstown 78 F 11
Celbridge 93 M 7
Chapeltown 75 P 5
Charlestown (Armagh) 98 M 4
Charlestown (Mayo) 95 F 6
Charleville (Ráth Luirc) / An Ráth 84 F 10
Church Hill 101 I 3
Church Quarter 103 N 2
Churchtown 80 L 11
Cill Airne / Killarney 77 D 11
Cill Chainnigh / Kilkenny 80 K 10
Cill Chaoi / Kilkee 83 D 9
Cill Chiaráin / Kilkieran 88 C 8
Cill Dalua / Killaloe 84 G 9
Cill Dara / Kildare 86 L 8
Cill Mhantáin / Wicklow 87 N 9
Cill Mocheallóg / Kilmallock 84 G 10
Cill Orglan / Killorglin 76 C 11
Cill Rois / Kilrush 83 D 10
Cill Rónáin / Kilronan 88 C 8
Cionn tSáile / Kinsale 78 G 12
Clady 101 J 3
Clane 87 L 8
Clár Chlainne Mhuiris / Claremorris 95 F 6
Clara / Clóirtheach (Offaly) 92 J 7
Clara (Wicklow) 87 N 9
Clare (County) 83 F 9
Clare Island 94 B 6
Clare (River) 89 F 7
Clarecastle 83 F 9
Claregalway / Baile Chláir 89 F 7
Claremorris / Clár Chlainne Mhuiris 95 F 6
Clarinbridge 89 F 8
Clashmore 79 I 11
Claudy 102 K 3
Clear (Cape) 77 D 13
Clear Island / Cléire (Oileán) 77 D 13
Cleegan Bay 88 B 7
Cleggan / An Cloigeann 88 B 7
Cléire (Oileán) / Clear Island 77 D 13
Clew Bay 94 C 6
Clifden / An Clochán 88 B 7
Cliffony 96 G 4
Clogh (Antrim) 103 N 3
Clogh (Kilkenny) 86 K 9
Clogh (Wexford) 81 M 10
Clogh Mills 103 N 3
Cloghan / An Clochán (Donegal) 100 I 3
Cloghan (Offaly) 90 I 8
Cloghan (Westmeath) 92 K 7
Cloghane 82 B 11
Cloghaneely 100 H 2
Cloghbrack 89 D 7
Clogheen 79 I 11
Clogher 97 K 4
Clogher Head (Kerry) 82 A 11
Clogher Head 93 N 6
Clogherhead 93 N 6
Cloghjordan 85 H 9
Cloghmore / An Chloch Mhóir 94 C 6
Cloghy 75 P 4
Clohamon 81 M 10
Cloich na Coillte / Clonakilty 77 F 13
Clóirtheach / Clara 92 J 7
Clonakilty / Cloich na Coillte 77 F 13
Clonakilty Bay 77 F 13
Clonalis House 90 G 6
Clonaslee 86 J 8
Clonbern 89 G 7
Clonbulloge 86 K 8
Clonbur / An Fhairche 89 D 7
Clonco Bridge 90 G 8
Clondalkin 87 M 8
Clonea 79 J 11
Clonea Bay 79 J 11
Clonee 93 M 7
Cloneen 85 J 10
Clonegall 81 M 9
Clones / Cluain Eois 97 K 5
Clonfert 90 H 8
Clonmacnois 90 I 8
Clonmany 101 J 2
Clonmel / Cluain Meala 85 I 10
Clonmellon 92 K 7
Clonmore 81 M 9
Clonmult 78 H 12
Clonroche 80 L 10
Clontarf 93 N 7
Clontibret 98 L 5
Clonygowan 86 K 8
Cloon Lake 76 C 12
Cloonacleigha Lake 96 G 5
Cloonacool 95 F 5
Cloonaghmore 95 D 5
Cloondara 90 I 6
Cloone 97 I 6
Cloonee Loughs 76 C 12
Cloonfad 95 F 6
Cloonfree Lough 90 H 6
Cloonlara 84 G 9
Clough 99 O 5
Cloyne 78 H 12
Cluain Eois / Clones 97 K 5
Cluain Meala / Clonmel 85 I 10
Cluainín / Manorhamilton 96 H 5
Coachford 78 F 12
Coagh 98 M 4
Coalisland 98 L 4
Cobh / An Cóbh 78 H 12
Cod's Head 76 B 13
Coill an Chollaigh / Bailieborough 92 L 6
Coleraine 102 L 2
Colgah Lough 96 G 5
Colligan (River) 79 I 11
Collinstown 92 K 7
Collon 93 M 6
Collooney 96 G 5
Comber 99 O 4
Comeragh Mountains 79 J 11
Commeen / An Coimín 100 I 3
Cong / Conga 89 E 7
Conga / Cong 89 E 7
Conlig 99 O 4
Conn (Lough) 95 E 5
Conna 78 H 11
Connemara 88 C 7
Connemara National Park 88 C 7
Connor Pass 82 B 11
Convoy 101 I 3
Cookstown 98 L 4
Coola 96 G 5
Coolaney 96 G 5
Coole (Castle) 97 J 4
Coolea / Cúil Aodha 77 E 12
Coolgreany 81 N 9
Coolmore 100 H 4
Coolrain 85 J 9
Coomacarrea 76 B 12
Coomhola 77 D 12
Cooraclare 83 D 9
Cootehill / Muinchille 97 K 5
Copeland Island 75 P 3
Cora Droma Rúisc / Carrick-on-Shannon 96 H 6
Corbally 95 E 5
Corcaigh / Cork 78 G 12
Corcomroe Abbey 89 E 8
Cork / Corcaigh 78 G 12
Cork (County) 77 F 12
Cork Harbour 78 H 12
Corkscrew Hill 89 E 8
Cornamona 89 D 7
Corrandulla 89 F 7
Corraun Peninsula 94 C 6
Corrib (Lough) 89 E 7
Corrigeenroe 96 H 5
Corrofin 89 E 9
Costelloe / Casla 88 D 8
Cottoners 76 C 11
Coulagh Bay 76 B 12
Courtmacsherry 78 F 13
Courtmacsherry Bay 78 G 13
Courtown 81 N 10
Cousane Gap 77 E 12
Crag Cave 83 D 11
Craggaunowen Megalithic Centre 84 F 9
Craigavon 98 M 4
Crana 101 J 2
Cranfield Point 99 N 5
Cranford 101 I 2
Cratloe 84 F 9
Craughwell 89 F 8
Crawfordsburn 99 O 4
Creeslough 101 I 2
Creevykeel 96 G 4
Creggs 90 G 7
Croagh 84 F 10
Croagh Patrick 94 C 6
Croaghnageer 100 I 3
Croaghnakeela Island 88 C 8
Croangar (Lough) 100 H 3
Croghan 96 H 6
Crohy Head 100 G 3
Crois Mhaoilíona / Crossmolina 95 E 5
Croithlí / Crolly 100 H 2
Crolly / Croithlí 100 H 2
Cromane 76 C 11
Crookedwood 92 K 7
Crookhaven 76 C 13
Crookstown 77 F 12
Croom 84 F 10
Croos 90 H 7
Cross 89 E 7
Cross Barry 78 G 12
Cross (River) 95 D 7
Crossakeel 92 K 6
Crossdoney 97 J 6
Crossgar 99 O 4
Crosshaven 78 H 12
Crossmaglen 74 M 5
Crossmolina / Crois Mhaoilíona 95 E 5
Crow Head 76 B 13
Cruit Island 100 G 2
Crumlin 99 N 4
Crusheen 84 F 9
Cúil an tSúdaire / Portarlington 86 K 8
Cúil Aodha / Coolea 77 E 12
Cuilcagh 97 I 5
Culdaff 102 K 2
Culdaff Bay 102 K 2
Culleens 95 F 5
Cullenagh (River) 89 E 9
Cullin (Lough) 95 E 6
Cullybackey 102 M 3
Cummeragh 76 B 12
Curlew Mountains 96 G 6
Curracloe 81 M 10
Curragh (The) 86 L 8
Curraghmore Gardens 79 J 11
Curraghroe 90 H 6
Currahchase Forest Park 84 F 10
Currane / An Corran 94 C 6
Currane (Lough) 76 B 12
Currans 83 D 11
Curreel (Lough) 88 C 7
Cushendall 103 N 2
Cushendun 103 N 2
Cushina 86 K 8
Cutra (Lough) 89 F 8
Daingean 86 K 8
Dalkey 87 N 8
Dan (Lough) 87 N 8
Darragh 83 E 9
Dartry Mountains 96 G 4
Davagh Forest Park 102 L 3
Dawros Head 100 G 3
Deel 83 F 10
Deel (Mayo) 95 D 5
Delamont 99 O 4
Delgany 87 N 8
Delphi 94 C 7
Delvin 92 K 7
Delvin (River) 93 N 7
Derg 101 J 3
Derg (Lough) 84 H 9
Derg (Lough) (Donegal) 101 I 4
Dernagree 77 E 11
Derravaragh (Lough) 92 J 7
Derreeny Bridge 77 F 13
Derriana Lough 76 C 12
Derrybeg 100 H 2

CORK/ CORCAICH

Camden Place .... Y 5
Coburg Street .... Y 10
Corn Market Street ...... Y 13
Dominick Street .... Y 15
Eason's Hill .... Y 17
Emmet Place .... Y 18
Gerald Griffin St. .... Y 21
Infirmary Road .... Z 24
John Redmond Street .... Y 26
Lancaster Quay .... Z 28
Langford Row .... Z 29
Lower Glanmire Road .... Y 30
Merchant's Quay .... Y 32
Merchant's Quay Shopping Centre .... Y
Newsom's Quay .... Y 34
North Mall .... Y 35
O'Connell's Square ...... Y 36
Oliver Plunkett Street .... Z
Parnell Place .... Z 38
Pembroke Street .... Z 39
Proby's Quay .... Z 40
Roman Street .... Y 42
St Patrick's Quay .... Y 44
St Patrick's Street ...... Z
Southern Road .... Z 45
South Link .... Z 46
South Main Street .... Z 47
Summer Hill .... Y 48
Wolfe Tone Street .... Y 56

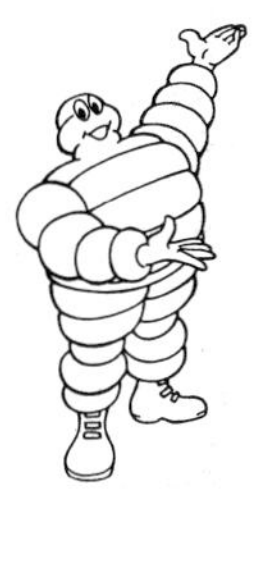

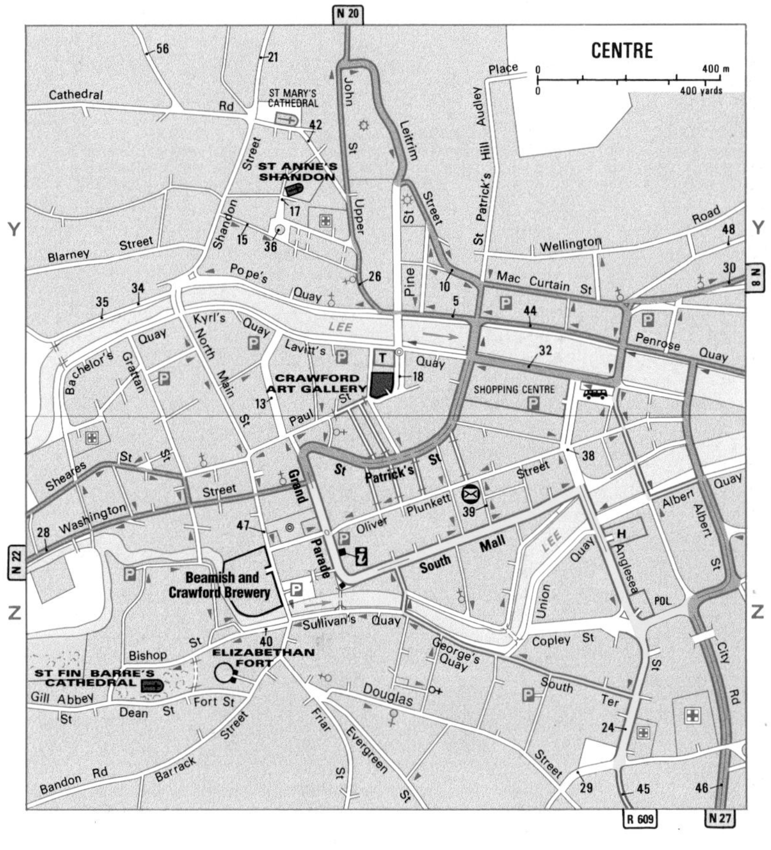

Derryclare Lough 88 C 7
Derrycraff 95 D 6
Derrygonnelly 97 I 4
Derrylin 74 J 5
Derrynane 76 B 12
Derrynane House 76 B 12
Derrynasaggart Mountains 77 E 11
Derryveagh Mountains 100 H 3
Dervock 102 M 2
Devenish Island 97 J 4
Devilsbit 85 I 9
Dingle / An Daingean 82 B 11
Dingle Bay 76 B 11
Dingle Harbour 82 B 11
Divis 99 N 4
Doagh 101 I 2
Doagh Beg / Dumhaigh Bhig 101 J 2
Doe Castle 101 I 2
Dolla 84 H 9
Domhnach Phádraig / Donaghpatrick 93 L 6
Donabate 93 N 7
Donagh 74 J 5
Donaghadee 75 P 4
Donaghmore 98 L 4
Donaghpatrick / Domhnach Phádraig 93 L 6
Donard 87 M 8
Donard (Slieve) 99 O 5
Donegal / Dún na nGall 100 H 4
Donegal (County) 100 H 3
Donegal Airport 100 G 2
Donegal Bay 96 G 5
Doneraile 78 G 11
Donoughmore 78 F 12
Doo Lough 94 C 7
Dooagh 94 B 6
Doocharry / An Dúchoraidh 100 H 3
Dooega / Dumha Éige 94 B 6
Dooega Head 94 B 6
Doogort 94 B 5
Doohooma 94 C 5
Doon Lough 84 F 9
Doonaha 83 D 10
Doonbeg 83 D 9
Douglas 78 G 12
Doulus Head 76 A 12
Down (County) 99 N 4
Downhill 102 L 2
Downings / Na Dúnaibh 101 I 2
Downpatrick 99 O 5
Downpatrick Head 95 D 5
Downs (The) 92 K 7
Dowra 96 H 5
Dowth 93 M 6
Drangan 85 J 10
Draperstown 102 L 3
Drimoleague 77 E 13
Drinagh 77 E 13
Dripsey 78 F 12
Drishane Bridge 77 D 13
Drogheda / Droichead Átha 93 M 6
Droichead Átha / Drogheda 93 M 6
Droichead na Bandan / Bandon 78 F 12
Dromahair 96 H 5
Dromara 99 N 4
Dromcolliher 83 F 10
Dromin 93 M 6
Dromina 84 F 11
Dromineer 84 H 9
Dromiskin 93 M 6
Dromod 96 I 6
Dromore (Down) 99 N 4
Dromore (Tyrone) 97 J 4
Dromore West 95 F 5
Drum 97 K 5
Drum Hills 79 I 11
Drum Manor Forest Park 98 L 4
Drumbeg 99 O 4
Drumcliff 96 G 5
Drumcondra 93 M 6
Drumena Cashel 99 O 5
Drumfin 96 G 5
Drumfree 101 J 2
Drumgoft 87 M 9
Drumkeeran 96 H 5
Drumlaheen Lough 96 I 5
Drumlish 92 I 6
Drumone 92 K 6
Drumquin 97 J 4
Drumshanbo 96 H 5
Drumsna 96 H 6
Dublin / Baile Átha Cliath 87 N 8
Dublin Bay 93 N 7
Dublin (County) 93 N 7
Duff 96 H 4
Duleek 93 M 7
Dumha Éige / Dooega 94 B 6
Dumhaigh Bhig / Doagh Beg 101 J 2
Dún A'Rí Forest Park 93 L 6
Dún Aengus 88 C 8
Dún Chaoin / Dunquin 82 A 11
Dún Dealgan / Dundalk 98 M 5
Dún Garbhán / Dungarvan 79 J 11
Dun Laoghaire 87 N 8
Dún Mánmhaí / Dunmanway 77 E 12
Dún Mór / Dunmore 89 F 7
Dún na nGall / Donegal 100 H 4
Dunaff Head 101 J 2
Dunamase (Rock of) 86 K 8
Dunany Point 93 N 6
Dunboyne 93 M 7
Dunbrody Abbey 80 L 11
Duncannon 80 L 11
Duncormick 80 M 11
Dundalk / Dún Dealgan 98 M 5
Dundalk Bay 93 N 6
Dundonald 99 O 4
Dundrum (Down) 99 O 5
Dundrum (Dublin) 87 N 8
Dundrum (Tipperary) 84 H 10
Dundrum Bay 99 O 5
Dunfanaghy 100 I 2
Dungannon 98 L 4
Dunganstown 80 L 10
Dungarvan / Dún Garbhán 79 J 11
Dungarvan Harbour 79 J 11
Dungiven 102 L 3
Dunglow / An Clochán Liath 100 G 3
Dungonnell Dam 103 N 3
Dungourney 78 H 12
Dunguaire Castle 89 F 8
Dunkerrin 85 I 9
Dunkineely 100 G 4
Dunlavin 87 L 8
Dunleer 93 M 6
Dunlewy 100 H 2
Dunloe (Gap of) 77 D 11
Dunluce Castle 102 M 2
Dunmanus Bay 76 C 13
Dunmanway / Dún Mánmhaí 77 E 12
Dunmore / Dún Mór 89 F 7
Dunmore Cave 80 K 9
Dunmore Head 82 A 11
Dunmore East 80 L 11
Dunmurry 99 N 4
Dunnamanagh 102 K 3
Dunowen Head 77 F 13
Dunquin / Dún Chaoin 82 A 11
Dunshaughlin 93 M 7
Durlas / Thurles 85 I 9
Durrow 85 J 9
Durrus 77 D 13
Dursey Head 76 B 13
Dursey Island 76 B 13
Duvillaun More 94 B 5
Dysert O'Dea 83 E 9

E

Éadan Doire / Édenderry 92 K 7
Eany 100 H 3
Eanymore 100 H 3
Easky 95 F 5
East Ferry 78 H 12
Édenderry / Éadan Doire 92 K 7
Ederny 97 J 4
Edgeworthstown 92 J 6
Egish (Lough) 98 L 5
Eglinton 102 K 2
Emly 84 G 10
Emo 86 K 8
Emyvale 98 L 4
Ennel (Lough) 92 J 7
Ennis / Inis 83 F 9
Enniscorthy / Inis Córthaidh 81 M 10
Enniskean 77 F 12
Enniskerry 87 N 8
Enniskillen 97 J 4
Ennistimon / Inis Díomáin 89 E 9
Eochaill / Youghal 79 I 12
Erne (Lower Lough) 97 I 4
Erne (River) 97 J 6
Erne (Upper Lough) 74 J 5
Errew Abbey 95 E 5
Erriff (River) 94 D 7
Errigal Mountain 100 H 2
Erris Head 94 B 5
Eske (Lough) 100 H 3
Eyeries 76 C 12

F

Fahan 101 J 2
Fairy Glen 99 N 5
Fairymount 96 G 6
Falcarragh / An Fál Carrach 100 H 2
Fanad 101 I 2
Fanad Head 101 J 2
Fane River 98 M 5
Fanore 89 E 8
Farnanes Cross Roads 78 F 12
Farran Forest Park 78 F 12
Farranfore 83 D 11
Fastnet Rock 77 D 13
Feakle 84 G 9
Feale (River) 83 D 10
Fedamore 84 G 10
Fee (Lough) 88 C 7
Feeagh (Lough) 95 D 6
Feeny 102 K 3
Fenagh 96 I 5
Fenit 82 C 11
Feohanagh (River) 82 B 11
Ferbane 90 I 8
Fergus (River) 89 E 9
Fermanagh (County) 97 I 4
Fermoy / Mainistir Fhear Maí 78 H 11
Fern (Lough) 101 I 2
Ferns 81 M 10
Ferrycarrig 81 M 10
Ferta 76 B 12
Fethard / Fiodh Ard (Tipperary) 85 I 10
Fethard (Wexford) 80 L 11
Fiddown 80 K 10

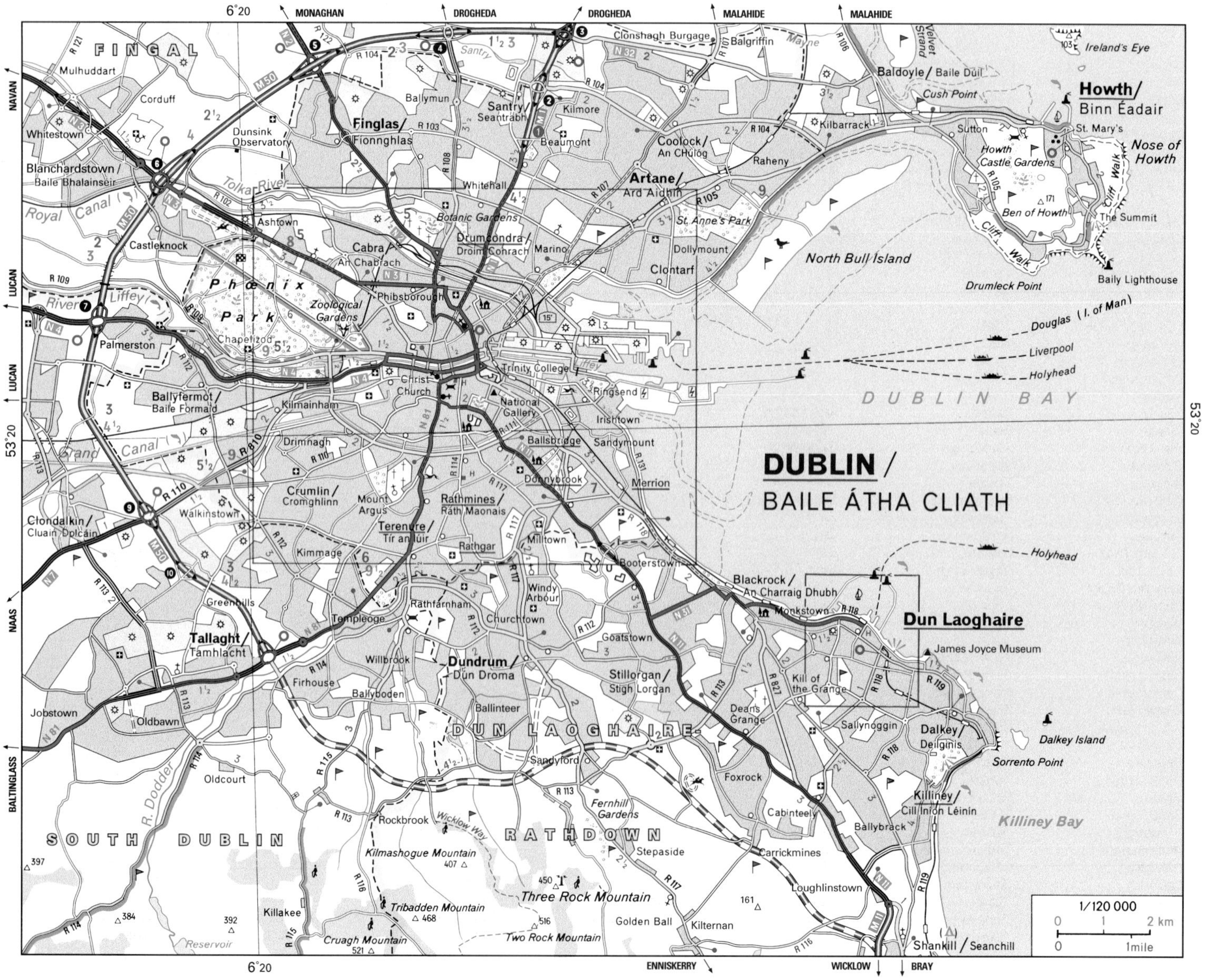

DUBLIN / BAILE ÁTHA CLIATH
MONAGHAN
DROGHEDA
MALAHIDE
NAVAN
LUCAN
NAAS
BALTINGLASS
ENNISKERRY
WICKLOW
BRAY
FINGAL
SOUTH DUBLIN
DUN LAOGHAIRE
RATHDOWN
Howth/ Binn Éadair
Dun Laoghaire
Finglas/ Fionnghlas
Blanchardstown / Baile Bhlainséir
Tallaght/ Tamhlacht
Dundrum / Dún Droma
Artane/ Ard Aidhin
Coolock/ An Chúlóg
Clondalkin / Cluain Dolcáin
Phœnix Park
North Bull Island
DUBLIN BAY
Ireland's Eye
Killiney Bay
Dalkey Island
Three Rock Mountain
Two Rock Mountain
Kilmashogue Mountain
Tribadden Mountain
Cruagh Mountain
Douglas (I. of Man)
Liverpool
Holyhead
1/120 000
0 1 2 km
0 1mile
6°20
53°20

DUBLIN/ BAILE ÁTHA CLIATH
CENTRE

Anne Street South .... JYZ 6
Brunswick Street North ..... HX 24
Buckingham Street.......... KX 25
Bull Alley .... HZ 27
Chancery Street .... HY 33
Clanbrassil Street .... HZ 40
College Green .... JY 45
College Street .... JY 46
Cornmarket .... HY 49
Dawson Street .... JYZ
D'Olier Street............... JY 51
Duke Street .... JY 58
Earlsfort Terrace............. JZ 60
Essex Quay .... HY 66
Fishamble Street .... HY 67
George's Quay .... KY 69
Golden Lane .... HZ 70
Grafton Street............. JYZ
Henrietta Street .... HX 75
Henry Street .... JX
High Street .... HY 78
Ilac Centre................. HJX
Irish Life Mall Centre ...... JKX
Kevin Street Upper.......... HZ 85
Kildare Street.............. JKZ 87
King Street South .... JZ 88
Marlborough Street .... JX 100
Merchants Quay............ HY 103
Montague Street............ JZ 106
Mount Street Upper......... KZ 112
Nicholas Street .... HY 118
North Great Georges Street.. JX 119
O'Connell Street .... JX
Parnell Square East .... JX 126
Parnell Squatre North........ JX 127
Parnell Square West .... HJX 129
St Mary's Abbey Street ..... HY 148
St Patrick Close............ HZ 150
Stephen Street............ HJY 165
Tara Street .... KY 171
Wellington Quay........... HJY 181
Werburgh Street............ HY 183
Westland Row.............. KY 186
Westmoreland Street........ JY 187
Wexford Street .... HZ 189
Winetavern Street .... HY 193
Wood Quay .... HY 196

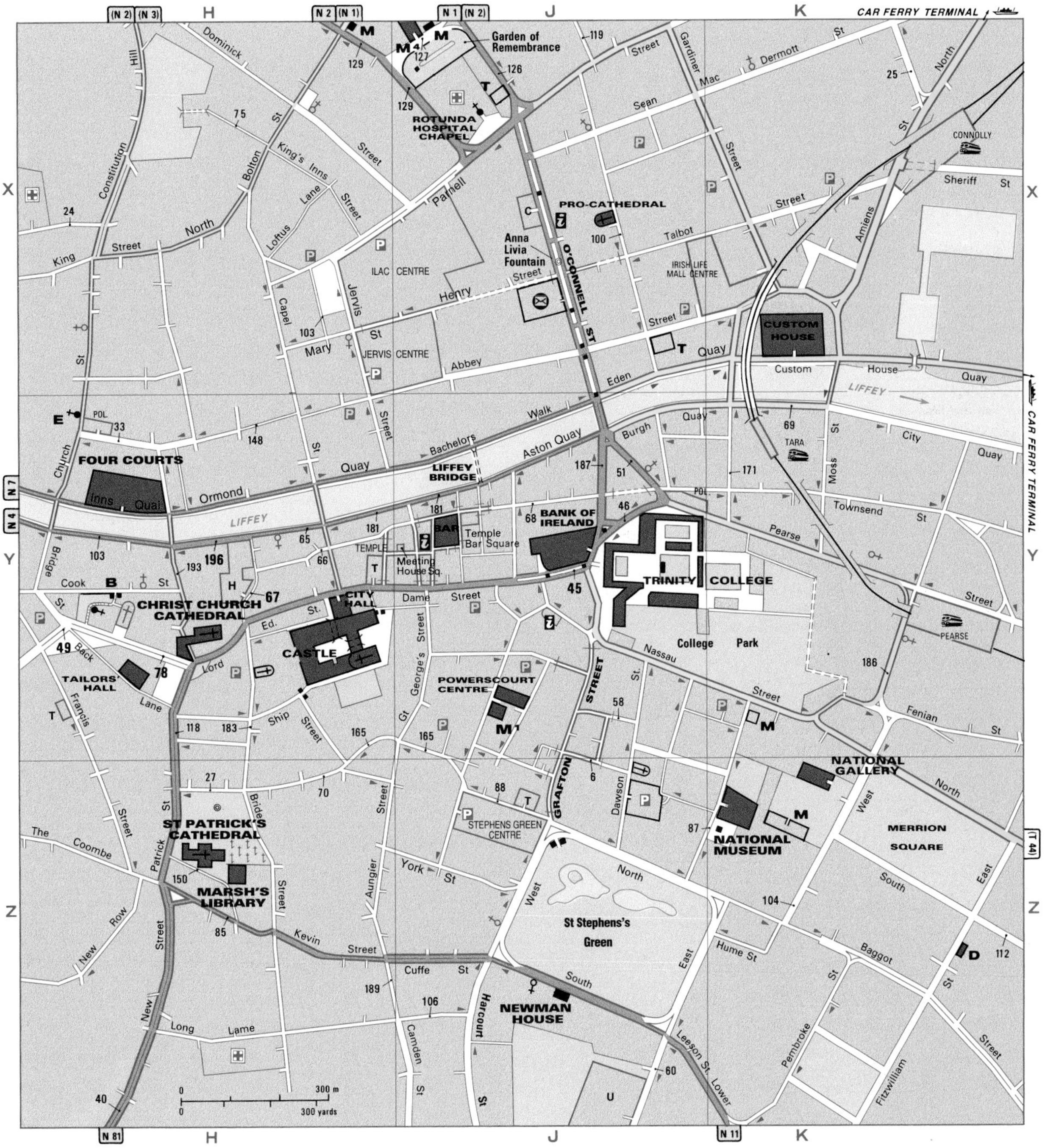

CAR FERRY TERMINAL
Garden of Remembrance
ROTUNDA HOSPITAL CHAPEL
PRO-CATHEDRAL
Anna Livia Fountain
ILAC CENTRE
JERVIS CENTRE
IRISH LIFE MALL CENTRE
CUSTOM HOUSE
LIFFEY
FOUR COURTS
LIFFEY BRIDGE
BANK OF IRELAND
Temple Bar Square
Meeting House Sq.
TRINITY COLLEGE
College Park
CHRIST CHURCH CATHEDRAL
CITY HALL
CASTLE
TAILORS' HALL
POWERSCOURT CENTRE
NATIONAL GALLERY
MERRION SQUARE
NATIONAL MUSEUM
STEPHENS GREEN CENTRE
ST PATRICK'S CATHEDRAL
MARSH'S LIBRARY
St Stephens's Green
NEWMAN HOUSE
O'CONNELL ST
GRAFTON STREET
300 m
300 yards

Finglas 93 N 7
Finglass 76 C 11
Finn (Lough) 100 H 3
Finn (River) 101 J 3
Finnea 92 J 6
Finny / Fionnaithe 89 D 7
Fintona 97 K 4
Fintown / Baile na Finne 100 H 3
Fintragh Bay 100 G 4
Fiodh Ard / Fethard 85 I 10
Fionnaithe / Finny 89 D 7
Fivealley 90 I 8
Fivemiletown 97 K 4
Flat Head 78 G 12
Flesk 77 D 11
Florence Court 97 I 5
Florence Court Forest Park 97 I 5
Foaty Island 78 H 12
Fontstown 86 L 8
Forbes (Lough) 90 I 6
Fore 92 K 6
Forkill 74 M 5
Forlorn Point 81 M 11
Formoyle (Lough) 89 D 7
Fota Island 78 H 12
Foul Sound 88 D 8
Foulksmills 80 L 11
Four Mile House 90 H 6
Fourknocks 93 N 7
Foxford 95 E 6
Foxhall 89 E 7
Foyle (Lough) 102 K 2
Foynes 83 E 10
Freemount 83 F 11
Frenchpark 96 G 6
Freshford 85 J 9
Fuerty 90 H 7
Furnace 88 D 7
Furnace Lough 95 D 6

G

Gabhla / Gola Island 100 G 2
Gabriel (Mount) 77 D 13
Gaddagh 77 C 11
Gaillimh / Galway 89 E 8
Galbally 84 H 10
Galey 83 D 10
Gallarus Oratory 82 A 11
Galley Head 77 F 13
Gallion (Slieve) 102 L 3
Galty Mountains 84 H 10
Galtymore Mountain 84 H 10
Galway / Gaillimh 89 E 8
Galway (County) 89 F 7
Galway Bay 89 D 8
Galways Bridge 77 D 12
Gaoth Dobhair / Gweedore 100 H 2
Gaoth Sáile / Geesala 94 C 5
Gara (Lough) 96 G 6
Garadice Lough 97 I 5
Garrane 77 E 12
Garrison 96 H 4
Garristown 93 M 7
Garron Point 75 O 2
Garryvoe 78 H 12
Gartan Lough 101 I 3
Garty Lough 97 J 6
Garvagh 102 L 3
Garvagh 96 I 6
Gearagh (The) 77 F 12
Geashill 86 K 8
Geesala / Gaoth Sáile 94 C 5
Geevagh 96 H 5
Gerahies 77 D 13
Giant's Causeway 102 M 2
Giles Quay 99 N 6
Gilford 98 M 4
Gill (Lough) 96 G 5
Glanaruddery Mountains 83 D 11
Glandore 77 E 13
Glandore Harbour 77 E 13
Glangevlin 96 I 5
Glanmire 78 G 12
Glantane 78 F 11
Glanworth 78 G 11
Glasdrumman 99 O 5
Glaslough 98 L 5
Glassan 90 I 7
Glasshouse Lake 97 J 5
Gleann Bhairr / Glenvar 101 J 2
Gleann na Muaidhe / Glenamoy 94 C 5
Gleann Cholm Cille / Glencolumbkille 96 F 3
Gleann Domhain / Glendowan 100 I 3
Glen 101 I 2
Glen Bay 100 F 3
Glen Head 100 F 3
Glen Lough (Donegal) 101 I 2
Glen Lough (Westmeath) 92 J 7
Glen (River) (Donegal) 100 G 3
Glenade Lough 96 H 4
Glenamoy / Gleann na Muaidhe 94 C 5
Glenamoy (River) 95 D 5
Glenariff 103 N 2
Glenariff Forest Park 103 N 2
Glenariff or Waterfoot 103 N 2
Glenarm 75 O 3
Glenavy 99 N 4
Glenbeigh 76 C 11
Glenbrook 78 G 12
Glencar 76 C 12
Glencar Lough 96 G 4
Glencolmcille Folk Village 100 F 3
Glencolumbkille / Gleann Cholm Cille 100 F 3
Glencree 87 N 8
Glendalough 87 M 8
Glendovan Mountains 100 H 3
Glendowan / Gleann Domhain 100 I 3
Glenealy 87 N 9
Gleneely 102 K 2
Glenelly Valley 102 K 3
Glenfarne 96 I 5
Glenflesk 77 D 11
Glengad Head 102 K 1
Glengarriff / An Gleann Garbh 77 D 12
Glengarriff Harbour 77 D 12
Glengarriff (River) 77 D 12
Glengesh Pass 100 G 3
Glengormley 75 O 3
Glenicmurrin Lough 89 D 8
Glenmalur 87 M 9
Glenmore (Clare) 83 E 9
Glenmore (Kilkenny) 80 K 10
Glennamaddy 90 G 7
Glenoe 75 O 3
Glenshane Pass 102 L 3
Glenties 100 H 3
Glenvar / Gleann Bhairr 101 J 2
Glenveagh National Park 100 I 2
Glenville 78 G 11
Glin 83 E 10
Glin Castle 83 E 10
Glinsce / Glinsk 88 C 7
Glinsk / Glinsce 88 C 7
Glyde (River) 93 M 6
Glynn 75 O 3
Gob an Choire / Achill Sound 94 C 6
Gobbins (The) 75 O 3
Gola Island / Gabhla 100 G 2
Golden 85 I 10
Golden Vale 84 H 10
Goleen 76 C 13
Goold's Cross 85 I 10
Goresbridge 80 K 10
Gorey / Guaire 81 N 9
Gormanston 93 N 7
Gort / An Gort 89 F 8
Gort an Choirce / Gortahork 100 H 2
Gortahork / Gort an Choirce 100 H 2
Gorteen 96 G 6
Gortin 102 K 3
Gortin Glen Forest Park 102 K 3
Gortmore / An Gort Mór 88 D 7
Gorumna Island 88 C 8
Gosford Forest Park 74 M 5
Gougane Barra Forest Park 77 D 12
Gougane Barra Lake 77 E 12
Gowla 88 C 7
Gowna (Lough) 97 J 6
Gráig na Manach / Graiguenamanagh 80 L 10
Graiguenamanagh / Graig na Manach 80 L 10
Gránard / Granard 92 J 6
Grand Canal 90 I 8
Graney 86 L 9
Grange (Kilkenny) 80 K 10
Grange (Louth) 99 N 5
Grange (Sligo) 96 G 4

GALWAY/ GAILLIMH

Claddagh Bridge AZ 2
Corrib Shopping Centre BY
Dominick Street AZ 3
Father Griffin Avenue AZ 5
Forster Street BY 6
High Street BY 7
Main Guard St. BY 8
Market Street BY 9
Mary Street BY 10
New Dock Street BZ 13
Newton Smith BY 14
O'Brien Bridge AY 15
Presentation Street AY 17
Quay Street BZ 18
St. Francis Street BY 20
St. Vincent's Avenue BY 21
Shantalia Road AY 22
Shop Street BY 24
William Street BY 25

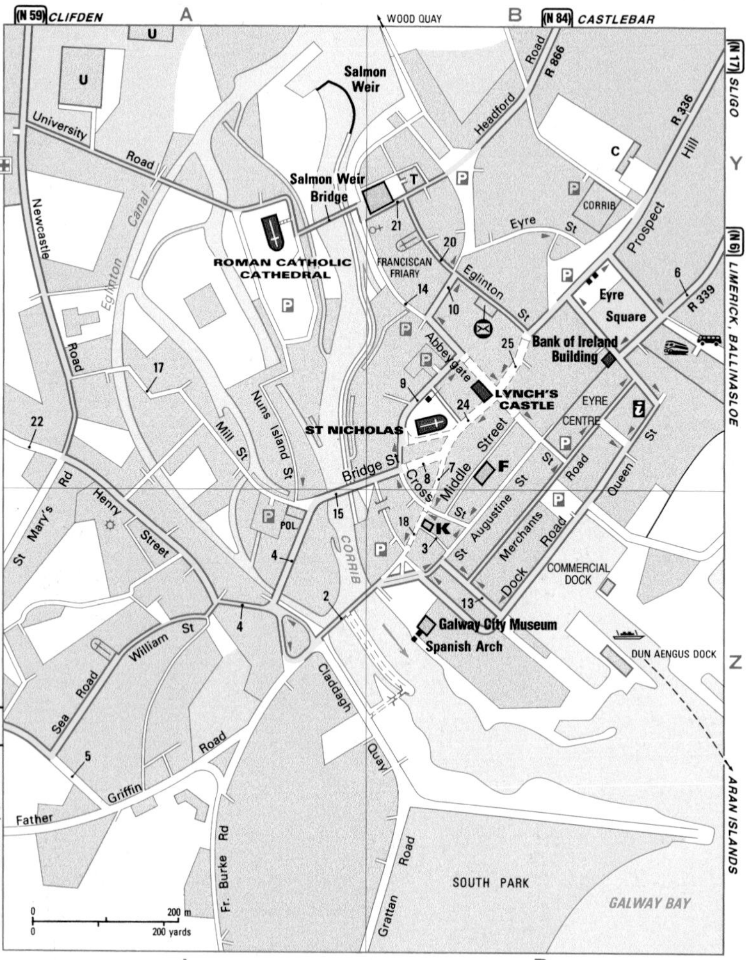

Gransha 75 O 3
Great Island 78 H 12
Great Blasket Island 82 A 11
Great Newtown Head 80 K 11
Great Skellig 76 A 12
Greenan 87 N 9
Greencastle (Donegal) 102 L 2
Greencastle (Down) 99 N 5
Greencastle (Tyrone) 102 K 3
Greenfield 89 E 7
Greenisland 75 O 3
Greenore 99 N 5
Greenore Point 81 N 11
Grey Abbey 75 P 4
Grey Point 75 O 3
Greystones / Na Clocha Liatha 87 N 8
Grianan of Aileach 101 J 2
Groomsport 75 P 3
Guaire / Gorey 81 N 9
Gulladoo Lough 97 J 6
Gullion (Slieve) 74 M 5
Gur (Lough) 84 G 10
Gurteen 90 G 7
Gwebarra Bridge 100 H 3
Gweebarra Bay 100 G 3
Gweedore / Gaoth Dobhair 100 H 2
Gweestin 77 D 11
Gyleen 78 H 12

H

Hacketstown 87 M 9
Hags Head 88 D 9
Headford / Áth Cinn 89 E 7
Healy Pass 76 C 12
Helvick Head 79 J 11
Herbertstown 84 G 10
Hillsborough 99 N 4
Hilltown 99 N 5
Hog's Head 76 B 12
Hollyford 84 H 10
Hollyfort 81 M 9
Hollymount 95 E 7
Hollywood 87 M 8
Holy Cross 85 I 10
Holy Island 84 G 9
Holycross 84 G 10
Holywood 99 O 4
Hook Head 80 L 11
Hore Abbey 85 I 10
Horn Head 100 I 2
Horseleap 92 J 7
Hospital 84 G 10
Howth / Binn Éadair 93 N 7
Hugginstown 80 K 10
Hungry Hill 76 C 12
Hurlers Cross 84 F 9
Hyne (Lough) 77 E 13

I

Ilen 77 E 13
Inagh 83 E 9
Inagh (Lough) 88 C 7
Inch 82 C 11
Inch Abbey 99 O 4
Inch Island 101 J 2
Inchigeelagh 77 E 12
Inchiquin Lough (Kerry) 77 D 12
Inchydoney Island 77 F 13
Indreabhán / Inveran 89 D 8
Inis / Ennis 83 F 9
Inis Bó Finne / Inishbofin 100 H 2
Inis Córthaidh / Enniscorthy 81 M 10
Inis Díomáin / Ennistimon 89 E 9
Inis Meáin / Inishmaan 88 D 8
Inis Mór / Inishmore 88 C 8
Inis Oírr / Inisheer 88 D 8
Inishannon 78 G 12
Inishbofin / Inis Bó Finne (Donegal) 100 H 2
Inishbofin (Galway) 94 B 7
Inishcarra Reservoir 77 F 12
Inishcrone 95 E 5
Inisheer / Inis Oírr 88 D 8
Inishfree Bay 100 G 2
Inishglora 94 B 5
Inishkea North 94 B 5
Inishkea South 94 B 5
Inishmaan / Inis Meáin 88 D 8
Inishmore / Inis Mór 88 C 8
Inishmurray 96 G 4
Inishnabro 82 A 11
Inishowen 101 J 2
Inishowen Head 102 L 2
Inishshark 94 B 7
Inishtrahull 102 K 1
Inishtrahull Sound 102 K 1
Inishturk 94 B 6
Inistioge 80 K 10
Innfield 92 L 7
Inniskeen 98 M 5
Inny (River) 92 J 6
Inver 100 H 4
Inver (Mayo) 94 C 5
Inveran / Indreabhán 89 D 8
Ireland's Eye 93 N 7
Irish Agricultural Museum 81 M 11
Irishtown 95 F 7
Iron (Lough) 92 J 7
Iron Mountains 96 I 5
Irvinestown 97 J 4
Iveragh 76 B 12

J

Jamestown 96 H 6
Japanese Gardens 86 L 8
Jerpoint Abbey 80 K 10
Johnstown 85 J 9
Jonesborough 74 M 5
Joyce 88 D 7
Julianstown 93 N 6

K

Kanturk / Ceann Toirc 77 F 11
Katesbridge 99 N 5
Keadew 96 H 5
Keady 74 L 5
Kealduff 76 C 12
Kealkill 77 D 12
Kearney 75 P 4
Keel 94 B 6
Keel Lough 94 B 6
Keem Strand 94 B 6
Keimaneigh (The pass of) 77 E 12
Kells (Antrim) 103 N 3
Kells (Kerry) 76 B 12
Kells (Ceanannus Mor) / Ceanannas (Meath) 92 L 6
Kells Bay 76 B 11
Kenmare / Neidín 77 D 12
Kenmare River 76 B 12
J. F. Kennedy Park 80 L 11
Kerry (County) 83 D 11
Kerry Head 82 C 10
Kerry (Ring of) 76 B 12
Kesh 97 I 4
Key (Lough) 96 H 5
Key (Lough) Forest Park 96 H 6
Kilbaha 82 C 10
Kilbeggan 92 J 7
Kilbeheny 78 H 11
Kilberry 93 L 6
Kilbricken 85 J 9
Kilbride (near Blessington) 87 M 8
Kilbrittain 78 F 12
Kilcar 100 G 4
Kilchreest 89 G 8
Kilclief 75 P 5
Kilcock 93 L 7
Kilcolgan 89 F 8
Kilconly (Galway) 89 F 7
Kilcoo 99 N 5
Kilcormac 90 I 8
Kilcrohane 76 C 13
Kilcullen 87 L 8
Kilcummin (Kerry) 82 B 11
Kildare / Cill Dara 86 L 8
Kildare (County) 86 L 8
Kildorrery 78 G 11
Kilfenora 89 E 9
Kilfinnane 84 G 10
Kilgarvan 77 D 12
Kilglass 95 E 5
Kilglass Lough 96 H 6
Kilgobnet 76 C 11
Kilgory Lough 84 F 9
Kilkee / Cill Chaoi 83 D 9
Kilkeel 99 N 5
Kilkeeran High Crosses 85 J 10
Kilkenny / Cill Chainnigh 80 K 10
Kilkenny (County) 85 J 10
Kilkieran / Cill Chiaráin 88 C 8
Kilkishen 84 F 9
Kill 79 J 11
Killadoon 94 C 6
Killadysert 83 E 9
Killala 95 E 5
Killala Bay 95 E 5
Killaloe / Cill Dalua 84 G 9
Killamery 85 J 10
Killann 80 L 10
Killard Point 75 P 5
Killarga 96 H 5
Killarney / Cill Airne 77 D 11
Killarney National Park 77 D 11
Killary Harbour 94 C 7
Killashandra 97 J 5
Killavally 95 D 6
Killavullen 78 G 11
Killeagh 78 H 12
Killeigh 86 J 8
Killenagh 81 N 10
Killenaule 85 I 10
Killerrig 86 L 9
Killeshin 86 K 9
Killeter 101 I 3
Killeter Forest 101 I 3
Killevy Churches 74 M 5
Killimer 83 D 10
Killimor 90 H 8
Killinaboy 89 E 9
Killiney Bay 87 N 8
Killiney (Dublin) 87 N 8
Killinick 81 M 11
Killinure Lough 90 I 7
Killkelly 95 F 6
Killmuckbridge 81 N 10

KILLARNEY/ CILL AIRNE CENTRE

Bohereen Na Goun CX 3
Bohereencael DX 4
Brewery Lane DX 6
College Square DX 7
College Street DX 9
Green Lawn CX 10
Hillard's Lane DX 12
Mangerton DX 13
Marian Terrace DX 15
Muckross Drive DXY 16
O' Connell's Terrace DX 18
O' Sullivan's Place DX 19
Plunkett Street DX 21
St. Anthony's Place DX 22

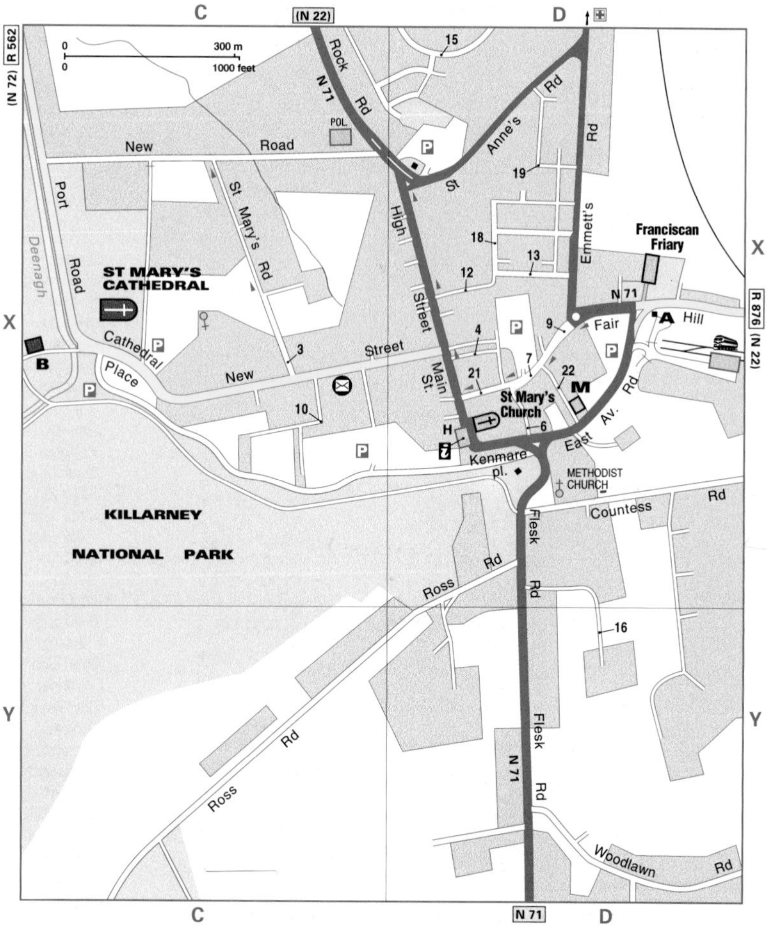

Killorglin / Cill Orglan 76 C 11
Killough 75 P 5
Killucan 92 K 7
Killurin 81 M 10
Killybegs / Na Cealla Beaga 100 G 4
Killygordon 101 I 3
Killykeen Forest Park 97 J 5
Killylea 98 L 4
Killyleagh 75 P 4
Kilmacduagh Monastery 89 F 8
Kilmacow 80 K 11
Kilmacrenan 101 I 2
Kilmacthomas 79 J 11
Kilmaganny 80 K 10
Kilmaine 89 E 7
Kilmalkedar 82 B 11
Kilmallock / Cill Mocheallóg 84 G 10
Kilmanagh 85 J 10
Kilmeage 86 L 8
Kilmeedy 83 F 10
Kilmessan 93 M 7
Kilmichael 77 E 12
Kilmichael Point 81 N 9
Kilmihil 83 E 9
Kilmore 81 M 11
Kilmore Quay 81 M 11
Kilmurry (near Kilkishen) 84 F 9
Kilmurvy 88 C 8
Kilnaleck 92 K 6
Kilrane 81 M 11
Kilrea 102 M 3
Kilreekill 90 G 8
Kilronan / Cill Rónáin 88 C 8
Kilrush / Cill Rois 83 D 10
Kilshanny 89 E 9
Kilsheelan 85 J 10
Kiltealy 80 L 10
Kiltegan 87 M 9
Kilternan 87 N 8
Kiltimagh 95 E 6
Kiltoom 90 H 7
Kiltormer 90 H 8
Kiltyclogher 96 H 4
Kilworth 78 H 11
Kilworth Mountains 78 H 11
Kinale (Lough) 92 J 6
Kincasslagh 100 G 2
Kings River 85 J 10
Kingscourt 93 L 6
Kinlough 96 H 4
Kinnegad 92 K 7
Kinnitty 90 I 8
Kinsale / Cionn tSáile 78 G 12
Kinsale (Old Head of) 78 G 13
Kinvarra 89 F 8
Kinvarra Bay 89 F 8
Kinvarra (near Screeb) 88 D 7
Kippure 87 N 8
Kircubbin 75 P 4
Kitconnell 90 G 8
Knappagh 95 D 6
Knappogue Castle 84 F 9
Knight's Town 76 B 12
Knock (Clare) 83 E 10
Knock (Mayo) 95 F 6
Knockadoon Head 79 I 12
Knockainy 84 G 10
Knockalongy 95 F 5
Knockcroghery 90 H 7
Knockferry 89 E 7
Knocklayd 103 N 2
Knocklong 84 G 10
Knockmealdown 79 I 11
Knockmealdown Mountains 78 H 11
Knockmoy Abbey 89 F 7
Knocknadobar 76 B 12
Knocknagree 77 E 11
Knockraha 78 G 12
Knocktopher 80 K 10
Knowth 93 M 6
Kylemore Abbey 88 C 7
Kylemore Lough 88 C 7

L

Labasheeda 83 E 10
Lack 97 J 4
Ladies View 77 D 12
Lady's Island Lake 81 M 11
Ladysbridge 78 H 12
Ladywell 80 K 10
Lagan (River) 99 N 4
Lagan Valley 99 O 4
Laghy 100 H 4
Lahinch / An Leacht 89 D 9
Lamb's Head 76 B 12
Lambay Island 93 N 7
Lanesborough 90 I 6
Laois (County) 85 J 9
Laragh 87 N 8
Larne 75 O 3
Larne Lough 75 O 3
Laune (River) 77 C 11
Lauragh 76 C 12
Laurencetown 90 H 8
Lavagh More 100 H 3
Lawrencetown 99 N 4
League (Slieve) 100 F 4
Leamaneh Castle 89 E 9
Leane (Lough) 77 D 11
Leannan (River) 101 I 2
Leap 77 E 13
Leap (The) 81 M 10
Lecarrow (Leitrim) 96 H 5
Lecarrow (Roscommon) 90 H 7
Leckanvy 94 C 6
Leckavrea Mountain 88 D 7
Lee 83 C 11
Lee (River) 78 G 12
Leenane 88 C 7
Leganany Dolmen 99 N 5
Leighlinbridge 80 L 9
Leinster (Mount) 80 L 10
Leitir Ceanainn / Letterkenny 101 I 3
Leitir Mealláin / Lettermullan 88 C 8
Leitir Mhic an Bhaird / Lettermacaward 100 H 3
Leitrim 96 H 6
Leitrim (County) 96 I 6
Leixlip 93 M 7
Lemybrien 79 J 11
Lene (Lough) 92 K 7
Letterfrack 88 C 7
Letterkenny / Leitir Ceanainn 101 I 3
Lettermacaward / Leitir Mhic an Bhaird 100 H 3
Lettermore 88 D 8
Lettermore Island 88 C 8
Lettermullan / Leitir Mealláin 88 C 8
Liffey (River) 87 M 8
Lifford 101 J 3
Limavady 102 L 2
Limerick / Luimneach 84 G 9
Limerick (County) 84 F 10
Limerick Junction 84 H 10
Lios Dúin Bhearna / Lisdoonvarna 89 E 8
Lios Mór / Lismore 79 I 11
Lios Póil / Lispole 82 B 11

LIMERICK/ LUIMNEACH

Arthur Quay Y 2
Arthur Quay Shopping Centre Y
Baal's Bridge Y 4
Bank Place Y 5
Barrington Street Z 6
Bridge Street Y 7
Broad Street Y 8
Castle Street Y 10
Cathedral Place Z 12
Charlotte's Quay Y 13
The Crescent Z 14
Cruises Street Z 15
Gerald Griffen St. Z 16
Grattan Street Y 17
High Street Z 18
Honan's Quay Y 19
John Square Z 20
Lock Quay Y 21
Lower Cecil Street Z 22
Lower Mallow Street Z 23
Mathew Bridge Y 24
Mount Kenneth Z 26
Newtown Mahon Z 28
North Circular Rd Z 29
O'Connell Street Z
O'Dwyer Bridge Y 30
Patrick Street YZ 32
Penniwell Road Z 33
Roches Street Z
Rutland Street Y 34
St Alphonsus St. Z 35
St Gerard St. Z 36
St Lelia Street YZ 37
Sarfield Street Y 39
Sexton Street North Y 40
Shannon Street Z 42
South Circular Rd. Z 43
Thomond Bridge Y 45
Wickham Street Z 47
William Street Z

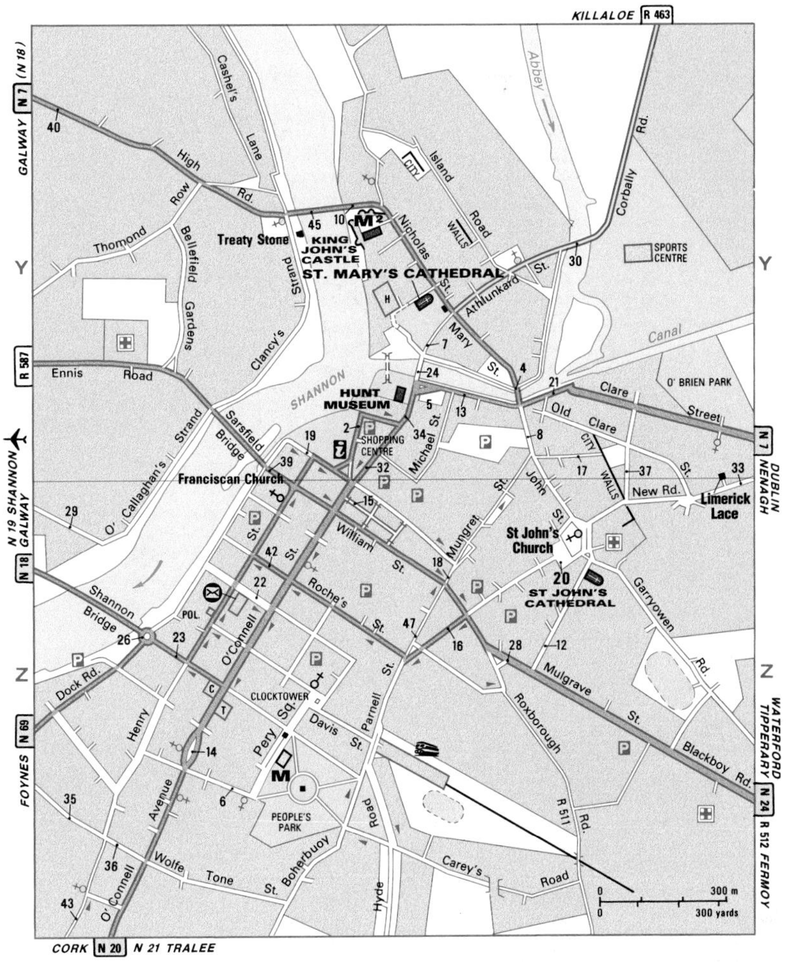
KILLALOE R 463
GALWAY N 7 (N 18)
N 19 SHANNON N 18 GALWAY
R 587
N 7 DUBLIN NENAGH
WATERFORD TIPPERARY N 24 R 512 FERMOY
FOYNES N 69
CORK N 20 N 21 TRALEE
KING JOHN'S CASTLE
ST. MARY'S CATHEDRAL
Treaty Stone
HUNT MUSEUM
Franciscan Church
St John's Church
ST JOHN'S CATHEDRAL
Limerick Lace
SPORTS CENTRE
O' BRIEN PARK
PEOPLE'S PARK
CLOCKTOWER
SHANNON
Canal
300 m
300 yards

Lios Tuathail / Listowel 83 D 10
Lisbellaw 74 J 5
Lisburn 99 N 4
Liscannor 89 D 9
Liscannor Bay 89 D 9
Liscarroll 78 F 11
Lisdoonvarna / Lios Dúin Bhearna 89 E 8
Lismacaffry 92 J 6
Lismore / Lios Mór 79 I 11
Lisnacree 99 N 5
Lisnarrick 97 I 4
Lisnaskea 74 J 5
Lispole / Lios Póil 82 B 11
Lissadell House 96 G 4
Lissatinnig Bridge 76 C 12
Lisselton 83 D 10
Lissycasey 83 E 9
Listowel / Lios Tuathail 83 D 10
Little Island 78 G 12
Little Skellig 76 A 12
Littleton 85 I 10
Lixnaw 83 D 10
Loch Garman / Wexford 81 M 10
Loghill 83 E 10
Londonderry 102 K 3
Londonderry (County) 102 K 3
Long Island 77 D 13
Longford (County) 90 I 6
Longford / An Longfort (Longford) 90 I 6
Longford (Offaly) 84 I 8
Loo Bridge 77 D 12
Loop Head 82 C 10
Lorrha 90 H 8
Lough Gowna 97 J 6
Loughgall 98 M 4
Loughbrickland 99 N 5
Loughglinn 96 G 6
Loughinisland 99 O 4
Loughrea / Baile Locha Riach 90 G 8
Loughros More Bay 100 G 3
Loughshinny 93 N 7
Louisburgh 94 C 6
Loup (The) 102 M 3
Louth 93 M 6
Louth (County) 93 M 6
Lower Lake 87 N 8
Lower Ballinderry 99 N 4
Lucan 93 M 7
Lugnaquillia Mountain 87 M 9
Luimneach / Limerick 84 G 10
Lullymore 86 L 8
Lurgan 99 N 4
Lusk 93 N 7
Lyracrumpane 83 D 10

M

Maam Cross / An Teach Dóite 88 D 7
Maas 100 G 3
Macgillycuddy's Reeks 76 C 12
Macnean Upper (Lough) 97 I 5
Macroom / Maigh Chromtha 77 F 12
Maganey 86 L 9
Magee (Island) 75 O 3
Maghera (Down) 99 O 5
Maghera (Donegal) 100 G 3
Maghera (Londonderry) 102 L 3
Magherafelt 102 M 3
Magheralin 99 N 4
Maghery 98 M 4
Magilligan 102 L 2
Magilligan Strand 102 L 2
Maguiresbridge 74 J 5
Mahee Island 75 P 4
Mahon 79 J 11
Mahoonagh 83 E 10
Maigh Chromtha / Macroom 77 F 12
Maigh Cuilinn / Moycullen 89 E 7
Maigh Nuad / Maynooth 93 M 7
Maigue (River) 84 F 10
Main 103 N 3
Maine (River) 83 C 11
Mainistir Fhear Maí / Fermoy 78 H 11
Mainistir Laoise / Abbey Leix 85 J 9
Mainistir na Búille / Boyle 96 H 6
Mainistir na Corann / Midleton 78 H 12
Máistir Gaoithe / Mastergeehy 76 B 12
Mal Bay 83 D 9
Mala / Mallow 78 G 11
Malahide / Mullach Íde 93 N 7
Málainn Bhig / Malin Beg 100 F 3
Malin 102 K 2
Malin Bay 100 F 3
Malin Beg / Málainn Bhig 100 F 3
Malin Head 102 J 1
Malin More 100 F 3
Mallow / Mala 78 G 11
Mamore (Gap of) 101 J 2
Mangerton Mountain 77 D 12
Mannin Bay 88 B 7
Mannin Lake 95 F 6
Manorcunningham 101 J 3
Manorhamilton / Cluainín 96 H 5
Mansfieldstown 93 M 6
Manulla 95 E 6
Maothail / Mohill 96 I 6
Marble Arch Caves 97 I 5
Marble Hill 101 I 2
Markethill 74 M 5
Mask (Lough) 89 D 7

LONDONDERRY

Barrack Street X 2
Clooney Terrace X 5
Creggan Street X 6
Custom House Street X 7
Dungiven Road X 8
Duke Street X 9
Foyle Road X 10
Foyle Street X 12
Francis Street X 13
Glendermott Road X 14
Harbour Square X 15
Infirmary Road X 17
John Street X 18
Lecky Road X 19
Limavady Road X 20
Little James Street X 22
Long Tower Street X 23
Sackville Street X 26
Simpsons Brae X 29
Strand Road X 30
Water Street X 32
William Street X 34

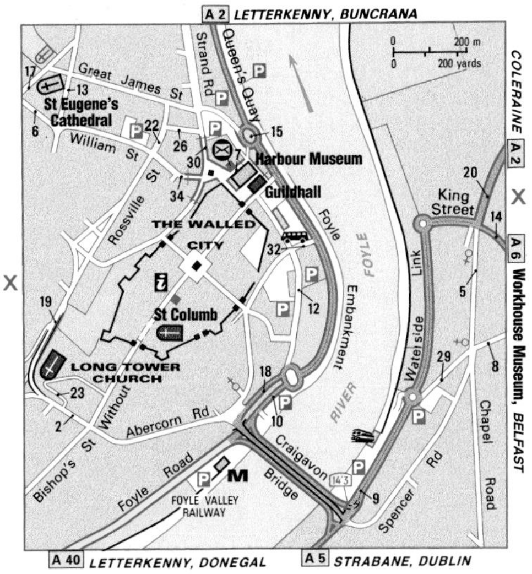
A 2 LETTERKENNY, BUNCRANA
COLERAINE A 2
A 6 Workhouse Museum, BELFAST
A 40 LETTERKENNY, DONEGAL
A 5 STRABANE, DUBLIN
St Eugene's Cathedral
Harbour Museum
Guildhall
THE WALLED CITY
St Columb
LONG TOWER CHURCH
FOYLE VALLEY RAILWAY
FOYLE
RIVER
200 m
200 yards

Mastergeehy / Máistir Gaoithe 76 B 12
Matrix (Castle) 83 F 10
Mattock (River) 93 M 6
Maum 88 D 7
Maumeen Lough 88 B 7
Maumtrasna 94 D 7
Maumturk Mountains 88 C 7
Maynooth / Maigh Nuad 93 M 7
Mayo 95 E 6
Mayo (County) 95 E 6
Mayo (Plains of) 95 E 6
Mealagh 77 D 12
Meath (County) 92 L 7
Meela (Lough) 100 G 3
Meenaneary / Mín na Aoire 100 G 3
Meenavean 100 F 3
Meeting of the Waters 87 N 9
Mellifont Abbey 93 M 6
Melmore Head 101 I 2
Melvin (Lough) 96 H 4
Menlough 90 G 7
Mew Island 75 P 3
Middletown (Armagh) 74 L 5
Middletown (Donegal) 100 H 2
Midleton / Mainistir na Corann 78 H 12
Milestone 84 H 9
Milford 84 F 10
Millford 101 I 2
Millisle 75 P 4
Millstreet 77 E 11
Milltown (Cavan) 97 J 5
Milltown (Galway) 89 F 7
Milltown (Kerry) 83 C 11
Milltown Malbay / Sráid na Cathrach 83 D 9
Mín na Aoire / Meenaneary 100 G 3
Minane Bridge 78 G 12
Minard Head 82 B 11
Mine Head 79 J 12
Mitchelstown / Baile Mhistéala 78 H 11
Mizen Head 76 C 13
Moate / An Móta 90 I 7
Moher (Cliffs of) 88 D 9
Moher Lough 95 D 6
Mohill / Maothail 96 I 6
Móinteach Mílic / Mountmellick 86 K 8
Moll's Gap 77 D 12
Monaghan / Muineachán 98 L 5
Monaghan (County) 97 K 5
Monasteraden 96 G 6
Monasteranenagh Abbey 84 G 10
Monasterboice 93 M 6
Monasterevin 86 K 8
Monavullagh Mountains 79 J 11
Mondello Park 87 L 8
Monea 97 I 4
Moneygall 85 I 9
Moneymore 102 L 3
Monivea 89 F 7
Monkstown (Antrim) 75 O 3
Monkstown (Cork) 78 G 12
Mooncoin 80 K 11
Moone 86 L 9
Moore Bay 82 C 9
Moorfields 103 N 3
Morley's Bridge 77 D 12
Mosney 93 N 7
Moss-Side 102 M 2
Mossley 75 O 3
Mostrim 92 J 6
Motte Stone 87 N 9
Mount Bellew / An Creagán 90 G 7
Mount Melleray Monastery 79 I 11
Mount Norris 74 M 5
Mount Nugent 92 K 6
Mount Stewart Gardens 75 P 4
Mount Usher Gardens 87 N 8
Mountcharles 100 H 4
Mountfield 97 K 4
Mountmellick / Móinteach Mílic 86 K 8
Mountrath 86 J 8
Mountshannon 84 G 9
Mourne (Lough) 75 O 3
Mourne Mountains 99 N 5
Mourne River 101 J 3
Moville / Bun an Phobail 102 K 2
Moy 98 L 4
Moy (River) 95 E 5
Moyard 88 B 7
Moyasta 83 D 9
Moycullen / Maigh Cuilinn 89 E 7
Moylough 90 G 7
Moynalty 92 L 6
Moyne Abbey 95 E 5
Moyvally 93 L 7
Moyvore 92 J 7
Muck (Isle of) 75 O 3
Muckamore 103 N 3
Muckanagh Lough 84 F 9
Muckish Mountain 100 H 2
Muckno Lake 98 L 5
Muckros Head 100 G 4
Muckross 77 D 11
Muff 102 K 2
Muggort's Bay 79 J 11
Muinchille / Cootehill 97 K 5
Muine Bheag / Bagenalstown 80 L 9
Muineachán / Monaghan 98 L 5
Muing 95 D 5
Muingnabo 94 C 5
Mulkear 84 G 10
Mullach de / Malahide 93 N 7
Mullagh (Cavan) 92 L 6
Mullagh (Meath) 93 M 7
Mullaghareirk Mountains 83 E 10
Mullaghcleevaun 87 M 8
Mullaghmore 96 G 4
Mullet Peninsula 94 B 5
Mullinahone 85 J 10
Mullinavat 80 K 10
Mullingar / An Muileann gCearr 92 J 7
Mulrany / An Mhala Raithní 94 C 6
Mulroy Bay 101 I 2
Multyfarnham 92 J 7
Mungret 84 F 10
Muntervary or Sheep's Head 76 C 13
Murlough Bay 103 N 2
Murntown 81 M 11
Murrisk 94 D 6
Murroe 84 G 10
Mussenden Temple 102 L 2
Mutton Island 83 D 9
Mweelrea Mountains 94 C 7
Myshall 80 L 9

N

Na Cealla Beaga / Killybegs 100 G 4
Na Clocha Liatha / Greystones 87 N 8
Na Dúnaibh / Downings 101 I 2
Na Sceirí / Skerries 93 N 7
Naas / An Nás 87 M 8
Nacung (Lough) 100 H 2
Nad 78 F 11
Nafooey (Lough) 88 D 7
Nagles Mountains 78 G 11
Naminn (Lough) 101 J 2
Namona (Lough) 76 B 12
Nanny 93 M 7
Naran 100 G 3
Narrow Water Castle 99 N 5
Naul 93 N 7
Navan / An Uaimh 93 L 7
Neagh (Lough) 98 M 4
Neale 89 E 7
Neidín / Kenmare 77 D 12
Nenagh / An tAonach 84 H 9
Nephin 95 D 5
Nephin (Glen) 95 D 6
Nephin Beg 94 D 5
Nephin Beg Range 94 C 5
New Inn (Cavan) 92 K 6
New Inn (Galway) 90 G 8
New Kildimo 84 F 10
New Ross / Ros Mhic Thriúin 80 L 10
Newbawn 80 L 10
New Birmingham 85 J 10
Newbliss 97 K 5
Newbridge / An Droichead Nua 86 L 8
Newbridge 93 N 7
Newcastle (Down) 99 O 5
Newcastle (Dublin) 87 M 8
Newcastle (Tipperary) 79 I 11
Newcastle (Wicklow) 87 N 8
Newcastle West / An Caisleán Nua 83 E 10
Newgrange 93 M 6
Newinn 85 I 10
Newmarket 83 F 11
Newmarket on Fergus 84 F 9
Newport / Baile Uí Fhiacháin (Mayo) 95 D 6
Newport (Tipperary) 84 G 9
Newport Bay 94 C 5
Newry 74 M 5
Newtown Cashel 90 I 7
Newtown-Crommelin 103 N 3
Newtown (Laois) 86 K 9
Newtown (Offaly) 90 H 8
Newtownabbey 99 O 4
Newtown Forbes 90 I 6
Newtown Gore 97 I 5
Newtown Mount Kennedy 87 N 8
Newtownards 99 O 4
Newtownbutler 74 J 5
Newtownhamilton 74 M 5
Newtownshandrum 84 F 10
Newtownstewart 101 J 3
Nier 79 J 11
Ninemilehouse 85 J 10
Nobber 93 L 6
Nohaval 78 G 12
Nore 85 J 9
Nore (River) 80 K 10
North Sound 88 C 8
North Ring 77 F 13
Nurney 86 L 8
Nurney (Carlow) 80 L 9

O

O'Brien's Tower 89 D 9
O'Grady (Lough) 84 G 9
Oileán Ciarraí / Castleisland 83 D 11
Oilgate 81 M 10
Oily 100 G 4
Old Court 77 E 13
Old Head 94 C 6
Old Kildimo 84 F 10
Oldcastle / An Seanchaisleán 92 K 6
Oldleighlin 80 K 9
Old Ross 80 L 10
Omagh 97 K 4
Omeath 99 N 5
Omey Island 88 B 7
Oola 84 H 10
Oorid Lough 88 D 7
Oranmore 89 F 8
Ossian's Grave 103 N 2
Oughterard / Uachtar Ard 89 E 7
Ougther (Lough) 97 J 6
Ovens 78 G 12
Owel (Lough) 92 J 7
Owenascaul 82 B 11
Owenator 100 H 3
Owenavorragh 81 M 10
Owenbeg (River) 96 G 5
Owenboliska 89 E 8
Owencarrow 101 I 2
Owenea 100 G 3
Owengarve 94 D 6
Owenglin 88 C 7
Oweniny 95 D 5
Owenkillew 102 K 3
Owenkillew 101 J 2
Owenriff 89 D 7
Owentocker 100 H 3
Owey Island / Uaigh 100 G 2
Owvane 77 D 12
Oysterhaven 78 G 12

P

Pallas Green 84 G 10
Pallaskenry 84 F 10
Paps (The) 77 E 11
Parke's Castle 96 H 5
Parkmore Point 82 A 11
Parknasilla 76 C 12
Partry 95 E 6
Partry Mountains 95 D 7
Passage East 80 L 11
Passage West 78 G 12
Patrickswell 84 F 10
Peake 78 F 12
Peatlands 98 M 4
Pettigoe 97 I 4
Phoenix Park 93 M 7
Piltown 80 K 10
Pluck 101 J 3
Plumbridge 102 K 3
Pomeroy 98 L 4
Pontoon 95 E 6
Port Durlainne / Porturlin 94 C 5
Port Láirge / Waterford 80 K 11
Port Laoise / Portlaoise 86 K 8
Port Omna / Portumna 90 H 8
Portacloy 94 C 5
Portadown 98 M 4
Portaferry 75 P 4
Portarlington / Cúil an tSúdaire 86 K 8
Portavogie 75 P 4
Port Ballintrae 102 M 2
Portglenone 102 M 3
Portlaoise / Port Laoise 86 K 8
Portlaw 80 K 11
Portmagee 76 A 12
Portmagee Channel 76 A 12
Portmarnock 93 N 7
Portmuck 75 O 3
Portnablagh 101 I 2
Portnoo 100 G 3
Portrane 93 N 7
Portroe 84 G 9
Portrush 102 M 2
Portsalon 101 J 2
Portstewart 102 L 2
Portumna / Port Omna 90 H 8
Porturlin / Port Durlainne 94 C 5
Poulaphouca Reservoir 87 M 8
Poulnasherry Bay 83 D 10
Powerscourt Demesne 87 N 8
Poyntz Pass 74 M 5
Prosperous 87 L 8
Puckaun 84 H 9
Puffin Island 76 A 12

Q

Quigley's Point 102 K 2
Quilty 83 D 9
Quin 84 F 9

R

Rae na nDoirí / Reananeree 77 E 12
Raghly 96 G 5
Raharney 92 K 7
Ram Head 79 I 12
Ramor (Lough) 92 K 6
Randalstown 103 N 3
Raphoe 101 J 3
Rasharkin 102 M 3
Rath 90 I 8
Ráth Caola / Rathkeale 83 F 10
Ráth Droma / Rathdrum 87 N 9
Rath Luirc (Charleville) / An Ráth 84 F 10
Rathangan 86 L 8
Rathcool 77 F 11
Rathcoole 87 M 8
Rathcormack 78 H 11
Rathcroghan 96 H 6
Rathdangan 87 M 9
Rathdowney 85 J 9
Rathdrum / Ráth Droma 87 N 9
Rathfriland 99 N 5
Rathgormuck 79 J 11
Rathkeale / Ráth Caola 83 F 10
Rathlackan 95 E 5
Rathlin Island 103 N 2
Rathlin Sound 103 N 2
Rathmelton 101 J 2
Rathmolyon 92 L 7
Rathmore 77 E 11
Rathmullan 101 J 2
Rathnew 87 N 9
Rathowen 92 J 7
Rathvilla 86 K 8
Rathvilly 87 L 9
Ratoath 93 M 7
Raven Point (The) 81 M 10
Ray 100 H 2
Rea (Lough) 90 G 8
Reananeree / Rae na nDoirí 77 E 12
Rear Cross 84 H 9
Recess / Straith Salach 88 C 7
Red Bay 103 N 2
Redcastle 102 K 2
Redcross 87 N 9
Redhills 97 K 5
Ree (Lough) 90 I 7
Reelan 100 H 3
Relaghbeg 92 L 6
Rhode 92 K 7
Richhill 98 M 4
Ringabella Bay 78 H 12
Ringsend 102 L 2
Ringville / An Rinn 79 J 11
Rinn Lough 96 I 6
Rinvyle 94 C 7
Rinvyle Castle 94 B 7
Riverstown 96 G 5
Roadford 89 D 8
Roaringwater Bay 77 D 13
Robert's Head 78 H 12
Robertstown 86 L 8
Rochestown 80 K 11
Rochfortbridge 92 K 7
Rockabill 93 N 7
Rockchapel 83 E 11
Rockcorry 97 K 5
Rockhill 84 F 10
Rockmills 78 G 11
Roe 102 L 3
Roonah Quay 94 C 6
Roosky 96 I 6
Ros an Mhil / Rossaveel 88 D 8
Ros Comáin / Roscommon 90 H 7
Ros Cré / Roscrea 85 I 9
Ros Láir / Rosslare 81 M 11
Ros Mhic Thriúin / New Ross 80 L 10
Rosapenna 101 I 2
Roscommon / Ros Comáin 90 H 7
Roscommon (County) 96 G 6
Roscrea / Ros Cré 85 I 9
Rosegreen 85 I 10
Rosenallis 86 J 8
Rosmuck 88 D 7
Rosnakill 101 I 2
Ross Abbey 89 E 7
Ross Port 94 C 5
Ross Lake 89 E 7
Rossaveel / Ros an Mhil 88 D 8
Rossbeg 100 G 3
Rossbeigh Creek 76 C 11
Rosscarbery 77 E 13
Rosscarbery Bay 77 E 13
Rosserk Abbey 95 E 5
Rosses (The) 100 G 2
Rosses Point 96 G 5
Rossinver 96 H 4
Rosslare / Ros Láir 81 M 11
Rosslare Bay 81 M 11
Rosslare Harbour / Calafort Ros Láir 81 M 11
Rosslare Point 81 M 11
Rosslea 74 K 5
Rossmore Forest Park 98 L 5
Rossnowlagh 100 H 4
Rostrevor 99 N 5
Rough Point 82 B 11
Roughty 77 D 12
Roundstone 88 C 7
Roundwood 87 N 8
Rower (The) 80 L 10
Royal Canal 90 I 7
Royaloak 80 L 9
Rue Point 103 N 2
Runabay Head 103 N 2
Rush / An Ros 93 N 7
Russborough House 87 M 8
Rylane Cross 77 F 12

S

Saggart 87 M 8
St. Fachtnan's 83 E 9
St. Finan's Bay 76 A 12
St. John's Lough 96 I 5
St. John's Point (Donegal) 100 G 4
St. John's Point (Down) 75 P 5
St. Johnstown 101 J 3
St. Macdara's Island 88 C 8
St. Mochta's House 93 M 6
Saintfield 99 O 4
Sallins 87 M 8
Sally Gap 87 N 8
Sallybrook 78 G 12
Saltee Islands 81 M 11
Salthill 89 E 8
Santry 93 N 7
Saul 99 O 4
Sawel Mountain 101 K 3
Scarriff / An Scairbh 84 G 9
Scarriff Island 76 B 12
Scartaglin 83 D 11
Scarva 74 M 5
Schull / Skull 77 D 13
Scolban (Lough) 96 H 4
Scotshouse 97 K 5
Scotstown 97 K 5
Scrabo Hill 99 O 4
Scramoge 90 H 6
Screeb Cross 88 D 7
Screen 81 M 10
Scur (Lough) 96 I 5
Seaforde 99 O 5
Seven Heads 78 F 13
Seven Hogs or Magharee Islands (The) 82 B 11
Shanagarry 78 H 12
Shanagolden 83 E 10
Shanballymore 78 G 11
Shanes Castle 103 N 3
Shankill 87 N 8
Shannagh (Lough) 99 N 5
Shannon 84 F 9
Shannon Airport 84 F 9
Shannon (River) 90 H 8
Shannonbridge 90 H 8
Shannon Harbour 90 I 8
Shantonagh 98 L 5
Sheddings (The) 103 N 3
Sheeffry Hills 94 C 6
Sheelin (Lough) 92 K 6
Sheep Haven 101 I 2
Sheever (Lough) 92 K 7
Shehy Mountains 77 D 12
Shercock 98 L 6
Sherkin Island 77 D 13
Shillelagh 81 M 9
Shinrone 85 I 9
Shrule 89 E 7
Silent Valley 99 O 5
Sillan (Lough) 98 L 5
Silver Strand 94 C 6
Silvermine Mountains 84 H 9
Silvermines 84 H 9
Sion Mills 101 J 3
Six Towns (The) 102 L 3
Sixmilebridge 84 F 9
Sixmilecross 97 K 4
Skannive (Lough) 88 C 8
Skerries / Na Sceirí 93 N 7
Skibbereen / An Sciobairín 77 E 13
Skreen 96 F 5
Skull / Schull 77 D 13
Sky Road 88 B 7
Slade 80 L 11
Slane 80 L 10
Slane (Hill of) 93 M 6
Slaney (River) 81 M 10
Slea Head 82 A 11
Slemish Mountain 103 N 3
Slieve Anierin 96 I 5
Slieve Aught Mountains 89 G 8
Slieve Bernagh 84 G 9
Slieve Bloom Mountains 86 J 8
Slieve Gamph or the Ox Mountains 95 F 5
Slieve Mish Mountains 82 C 11
Slieve Miskish Mountains 76 C 13
Slieveanorra 103 N 2
Slievefelim Mountains 84 H 9
Slievenamon 85 J 10
Slievetooey 100 G 3
Sligeach / Sligo 96 G 5
Sligo / Sligeach 96 G 5
Sligo Bay 95 F 5
Sligo (County) 95 F 5
Sliveardagh Hills 85 J 10
Slyne Head 88 B 7
Smerwick 82 A 11
Smerwick Harbour 82 A 11
Smithborough 97 K 5
Snaght (Slieve) (Derryveagh Mts.) 100 H 3
Snaght (Slieve) (Inishowen) 101 J 2
Snave 77 D 12
Sneem 76 C 12
Sord / Swords 93 N 7
South Sound 88 D 8
Spa 82 C 11
Spanish Point 83 D 9
Spelga Dam 99 N 5
Sperrin Mountains 102 K 3
Spiddal / An Spidéal 89 E 8
Spink 86 K 9
Springhill 102 M 3
Srah / An tSraith 95 E 6
Srahmore 95 D 6
Sráid na Cathrach / Milltown Malbay 83 D 9
Stack's Mountains 83 D 11
Staigue Stone Fort 76 B 12
Stamullin 93 N 7
Stewartstown 98 L 4
Stonyford 80 K 10

Strabane 101 J 3
Stracashel 100 H 3
Stradbally (Kerry) 82 B 11
Stradbally (Laois) 86 K 8
Stradbally (Waterford) 79 J 11
Strade 95 E 6
Stradone 97 K 6
Straffan 87 M 8
Straid (Antrim) 75 O 3
Straid (Donegal) 101 J 2
Straith Salach / Recess 88 C 7
Strandhill 96 G 5
Strangford 75 P 4
Strangford Lough 75 P 4
Stranorlar 101 I 3
Stratford 87 L 9
Strokestown 90 H 6
Stroove 102 L 2
Struell Wells 99 O 5
Suck 90 G 6
Suck (River) 90 G 6
Suir 85 I 9
Suir (River) 79 I 11
Summerhill 93 L 7
Sunderlin (Lough) 91 I 7
Swan 86 K 9
Swan's Cross Roads 97 K 5
Swanlinbar 97 I 5
Swatragh 102 L 3
Swilly (River) 101 I 3
Swilly (Lough) 101 J 2
Swilly (River) 101 J 2
Swinford / Béal Atha na Muice 95 F 6
Swords / Sord 93 N 7
Sybil Head 82 A 11

T

Table Mountain 87 M 8
Tacumshane 81 M 11
Tacumshin Lake 81 M 11
Taghmon 81 M 11
Tagoat 81 M 11
Tahilla 76 C 12
Tallaght 87 M 8
Tallanstown 93 M 6
Tallow 78 H 11
Tandragee 98 M 4
Tang 90 I 7
Tara (Hill of) 93 M 7
Tarbert 83 D 10
Tarker (Lough) 98 L 5
Tarsaghaunmore 94 C 5
Tay 79 J 11
Tay (Lough) 87 N 8
Teelin 100 G 4
Temple of the Winds 75 P 4
Temple (The) 99 O 4
Templeboy 95 F 5
Templeglentan 83 E 10
Templehouse Lake 96 G 5
Templemore / An Teampall Mór 85 I 9
Templenoe 76 C 12
Templepatrick 103 N 3
Templetouhy 85 I 9
Tempo 97 J 4
Terenure 87 N 8
Termon / An Tearmann 101 I 2
Termonbarry 90 I 6
Termonfeckin 93 N 6
Terryglass 84 H 8
Thomastown / Baile Mhic Andáin 80 K 10
Thoor Ballylee 89 F 8
Three Castle Head 76 C 13
Thurles / Durlas 85 I 9
Timahoe (Kildare) 86 L 8
Timoleague 78 F 13
Timolin 86 L 9
Tiobraid Árann / Tipperary 84 H 10
Tipperary / Tiobraid Árann 84 H 10
Tipperary (County) 85 H 10
Tobar an Choire / Tobercurry 95 F 5
Tobercurry / Tobar an Choire 95 F 5
Toberscanavan 96 G 5
Toe Head 77 E 13
Tollymore Forest Park 99 O 5
Tomhaggard 81 M 11
Toombeola 88 C 7
Toome 102 M 3
Toomyvara 85 H 9
Toormore 76 D 13
Toraigh / Tory Island 100 H 2
Torr Head 103 N 2
Tory Island / Toraigh 100 H 2
Tory Sound 100 H 2
Tourig (River) 78 I 11
Tourmakeady / Tuar Mhic Éadaigh 95 D 7
Tower 78 G 12
Trá Lí / Tralee 82 C 11
Trá Mhór / Tramore 80 K 11
Trabane Strand 100 F 4
Trafrask 76 D 12
Tragumna 77 E 13
Tralee / Trá Lí 82 C 11
Tralee Bay 82 C 11
Tramore / Trá Mhór 80 K 11
Tramore Bay 80 K 11
Tranarossan Bay 101 I 2
Trean 89 D 7
Trillick 97 J 4
Trim / Baile Átha Troim 93 L 7
Trostan 103 N 2
Tuaim / Tuam 89 F 7
Tuam / Tuaim 89 F 7
Tuamgraney 84 G 9
Tuar Mhic Éadaigh / Tourmakeady 95 D 7
Tulach Mhór / Tullamore 86 J 8
Tulla 84 F 9
Tullaghan 96 G 4
Tullaghobegly 100 H 2
Tullamore / Tulach Mhór 86 J 8
Tullaroan 85 J 10
Tullig Point 82 C 10
Tullow / An Tulach 80 L 9
Tully 97 I 4
Tully Cross 88 C 7
Tully National Stud 86 L 8
Tullyallen 93 M 6
Tullycanna 80 L 11
Tullyhogue 98 L 4
Tullynally Castle 92 J 6
Tulsk 90 H 6
Turlough (Mayo) 95 E 6
Turloughmore 89 F 7
Turner's Rock Tunnel 77 D 12
Tuskar Rock 81 N 11
Twelve Pins (The) 88 C 7
Tynagh 90 G 8
Tyrella 99 O 5
Tyrellspass 92 J 7
Tyrone (County) 97 J 4

U

Uachtar Ard / Oughterard 89 E 7
Uaigh / Owey Island 100 G 2
Ugga Beg (Lough) 89 D 8
Ulster American Folk Park 97 J 4
Union Hall 77 E 13
Unshin 96 G 5
Upper Ballinderry 99 N 4
Upperchurch 85 H 9
Urlingford 85 J 9

V

Valencia Island 76 A 12
Valley 94 C 5
Ventry 82 A 11
Ventry Harbour 82 A 11
Villierstown 79 I 11
Virginia 92 K 6

W

Ward 93 N 7
Waringstown 99 N 4
Warrenpoint 99 N 5
Waterfoot or Glenariff 103 N 2
Waterford / Port Láirge 80 K 11
Waterford (County) 79 J 11
Waterford Harbour 80 L 11
Watergrasshill 78 G 11
Waterville / An Coireán 76 B 12
Wellington Bridge 80 L 11
Wesport Bay 94 C 6
Westmeath (County) 92 J 7
Westport / Cathair na Mart 95 D 6
Westport House 95 D 6
Wexford / Loch Garman 81 M 10
Wexford Bay 81 N 10
Wexford (County) 80 L 10
Wexford Harbour 81 M 10
Wheathill 97 I 5
Whiddy Island 77 D 12
White Park Bay 102 M 2
Whitechurch 78 G 12
Whitegate 78 H 12
Whitehead 75 O 3
Wicklow (County) 87 M 9
Wicklow / Cill Mhantáin 87 N 9
Wicklow Gap 87 M 8
Wicklow Mountains 87 N 8
Wildfowl and Wetlands Trust 99 O 4
Wilkinstown 93 L 6
Williamstown 90 G 6
Windgap 85 J 10
Windy Gap 98 N 5
Woodenbridge 81 N 9
Woodford 74 J 5

Y

Youghal / Eochaill 79 I 12
Youghal Bay 79 I 12